Students learn best when they attend lectures and keep up with their reading and assignments... but learning shouldn't end when class is over.

MyEconLab *Picks Up Where Lectures and Office Hours Leave Off*

Instructors choose MyEconLab:

"MyEconLab offers them a way to practice every week. They receive immediate feedback and a feeling of personal attention. As a result, my teaching has become more targeted and efficient."

— **Kelly Blanchard, Purdue University**

"Students tell me that offering them MyEconLab is almost like offering them individual tutors."

— **Jefferson Edwards, Cypress Fairbanks College**

"Chapter quizzes offset student procrastination by ensuring they keep on task. If a student is having a problem, MyEconLab indicates exactly what they need to study."

— **Diana Fortier, Waubonsee Community College**

Students choose MyEconLab:

In a recent study, 87 percent of students who used MyEconLab regularly felt it improved their grade.

"It was very useful because it had EVERYTHING, from practice exams to exercises to reading. Very helpful."

— **student, Northern Illinois University**

"It was very helpful to get instant feedback. Sometimes I would get lost reading the book, and these individual problems would help me focus and see if I understood the concepts."

— **student, Temple University**

"I would recommend taking the quizzes on MyEconLab because they give you a true account of whether or not you understand the material."

— **student, Montana Tech**

myeconlab

Get Ahead of the Curve

MACROECONOMIC STRUCTURE

The organization of the macroeconomics chapters continues to reflect the authors' view that in order for students to understand aggregate demand and aggregate supply curves, they must first understand how the goods market and the money market function. The logic behind the simple demand curve is wrong when applied to the relationship between aggregate demand and the price level. Similarly, the logic behind the simple supply curve is wrong when applied to the relationship between aggregate supply and the price level.

The authors believe the best way to teach the reasoning embodied in the aggregate demand and aggregate supply curves without creating serious confusion is to build up to them carefully. The accompanying visual gives you an overview of the macroeconomic structure.

CHAPTERS 8-9 examine the market for goods and services.

CHAPTERS 10-11 examine the money market.

CHAPTER 12 brings the two markets together, explaining the links between aggregate output (Y) and the interest rate (r), and derives the aggregate demand curve.

CHAPTER 13 introduces the aggregate supply curve and determines the price level (P).

CHAPTER 14 shows how the labor market fits into this macroeconomic picture.

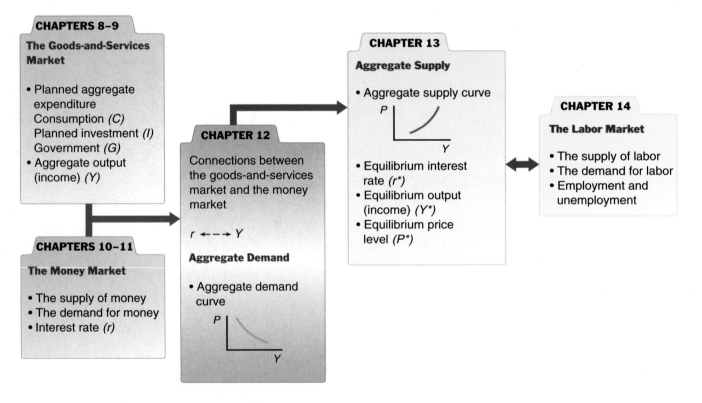

▲ **The Core of Macroeconomic Theory**

ECONOMICS IN PRACTICE FEATURE

To help pique students' interest in the economic world, the authors have created a new feature entitled *Economics in Practice*. This feature either (1) describes a personal observation or a research idea and provides an analysis using the concepts of the chapter or (2) presents a newspaper excerpt that relates to the concepts of the chapter.

NINTH EDITION

Principles of
Macroeconomics

Karl E. Case
Wellesley College

Ray C. Fair
Yale University

Sharon M. Oster
Yale University

Prentice Hall
UPPER SADDLE RIVER, NJ 07458

Library of Congress Cataloging-in-Publication Data
Case, Karl E.
 Principles of macroeconomics / Karl E. Case, Ray C. Fair, Sharon M. Oster.
   p. cm.
 Includes index.
 ISBN-13: 978-0-13-605896-0 (pbk.)
 ISBN-10: 0-13-605896-5 (pbk.)
 1. Macroeconomics. I. Fair, Ray C. II. Oster, Sharon M. III. Title.
 HB172.5.C375 2008
 339--dc22

                        2008031126

Dedicated To
Professor Richard A. Musgrave
and
Professor Robert M. Solow
and
Professor Richard Caves

VP/Publisher: Natalie E. Anderson
Acquisitions Editor, Print: Jodi Bolognese
Senior Development Editor: Lena Buonanno
Director, Product Development: Pamela Hersperger
Editorial Project Manager: Virginia Guariglia
VP/Director of Development: Steve Deitmer
Editorial Assistant: Terenia McHenry
AVP/Executive Editor, Media: Richard Keaveny
AVP/Executive Producer, Media: Lisa Strite
Advanced Media Project Manager: Dana Davis
Editorial Media Project Manager: Alana Coles
Production Media Project Manager: Lorena Cerisano
Director of Marketing: Kate Valentine
AVP/Executive Marketing Manager: Lori DeShazo
Marketing Assistant: Justin Jacob
Senior Managing Editor: Cynthia Zonneveld
Production Project Manager: Lynne Breitfeller

Manager of Rights & Permissions: Charles Morris
Senior Operations Specialist: Nick Sklitsis
Senior Art Director: Jonathan Boylan
AV Project Manager: Rhonda Aversa
Interior Design: John Christiana
Cover Design: Jonathan Boylan
Illustration (Interior): LaserWords
Director, Image Resource Center: Melinda Patelli
Manager, Rights and Permissions: Zina Arabia
Manager, Visual Research: Beth Brenzel
Image Permission Coordinator: Cynthia Vincenti
Photo Researcher: Sheila Norman
Composition: GEX Publishing Services
Full-Service Project Management: Marisa Taylor/ GEX Publishing Services
Printer/Binder: Courier
Typeface: 10/12 Minion

Credits and acknowledgments borrowed from other sources and reproduced, with permission, in this textbook appear on appropriate page within text (or on page 440).

Pearson Education Ltd., London
Pearson Education Singapore, Pte. Ltd
Pearson Education, Canada, Inc.
Pearson Education–Japan

Pearson Education North Asia Ltd., Hong Kong
Pearson Educación de Mexico, S.A. de C.V.
Pearson Education Malaysia, Pte. Ltd.
Pearson Education, Upper Saddle River, New Jersey
Pearson Education Australia PTY, Limited

10 9 8 7 6 5 4 3 2
ISBN-13: 978-0-13-605896-0
ISBN-10: 0-13-605896-5

About the Authors

Karl E. Case is the Katharine Coman and A. Barton Hepburn Professor of Economics at Wellesley College, where he has taught for over 30 years and served several tours of duty as Department Chair. For two decades, he has been a Visiting Scholar at the Federal Reserve Bank of Boston where he serves as a member of the Bank's Academic Advisory Board.

Before coming to Wellesley, he served as Head Tutor in Economics (director of undergraduate studies) at Harvard, where he won the Allyn Young Teaching Prize. He was Associate Editor of the *Journal of Economic Perspectives* and the *Journal of Economic Education* and was a member of the AEA's Committee on Economic Education. He teaches at least one section of the principles course every year.

Professor Case received his B.A. from Miami University in 1968; spent three years on active duty in the Army, including a year in Vietnam; and received his Ph.D. in Economics from Harvard University in 1976.

Professor Case's research has been in the areas of real estate, housing, and public finance. He is author or coauthor of five books, including *Principles of Economics, Economics and Tax Policy*, and *Property Taxation: The Need for Reform*, and has published numerous articles in professional journals.

He also is a founding partner in the real estate research firm of Fiserv Case Shiller Weiss, Inc., which produces the S&P Case Shiller Indexes of home prices and serves as a member of the Boards of Directors of the Mortgage Guaranty Insurance Corporation (MGIC) and the Depositors Insurance Fund of Massachusetts.

Ray C. Fair is Professor of Economics at Yale University. He is a member of the Cowles Foundation at Yale and a Fellow of the Econometric Society. He received a B.A. in Economics from Fresno State College in 1964 and a Ph.D. in economics from MIT in 1968. He taught at Princeton University from 1968 to 1974 and has been at Yale since 1974.

Professor Fair's research has primarily been in the areas of macroeconomics and econometrics, with particular emphasis on macroeconometric model building. He also has done work in the areas of finance, voting behavior, and aging in sports. His publications include *Specification, Estimation, and Analysis of Macroeconometric Models* (Harvard Press, 1984); *Testing Macroeconometric Models* (Harvard Press, 1994); and *Estimating How the Macroeconomy Works* (Harvard Press, 2004).

Professor Fair has taught introductory and intermediate macroeconomics at Yale. He has also taught graduate courses in macroeconomic theory and macroeconometrics.

Professor Fair's U.S. and multicountry models are available for use on the Internet free of charge. The address is http://fairmodel.econ.yale.edu. Many teachers have found that having students work with the U.S. model on the Internet is a useful complement to an introductory macroeconomics course.

Sharon M. Oster is Professor of Economics at Yale University. She is a new coauthor to this ninth edition. Professor Oster is the Frederic Wolfe Professor of Management and Entrepreneurship at the Yale School of Management. She has a B.A. in Economics from Hofstra University and a Ph.D. in Economics from Harvard University.

Professor Oster's research is in the area of industrial organization. She has worked on problems of diffusion of innovation in a number of different industries, on the effect of regulations on business, and on competitive strategy. She has published a number of articles in these areas and is the author of several books, including *Modern Competitive Analysis* and *The Strategic Management of Nonprofits*.

Prior to joining the School of Management at Yale, Professor Oster taught for a number of years in Yale's Department of Economics. In the department, Professor Oster taught introductory and intermediate microeconomics to undergraduates as well as several graduate courses in industrial organization. Since 1982, Professor Oster has taught primarily in the Management School, where she teaches the core microeconomics class for MBA students and a course in the area of competitive strategy. Professor Oster also consults widely for businesses and nonprofit organizations and has served on the boards of several publicly traded companies and nonprofit organizations.

Brief Contents

Contents

Preface

Our goal in the ninth edition, as it was in the first edition, is to instill in students a fascination with both the functioning of the economy and the power and breadth of economics. The first line of every edition of our book has been "The study of economics should begin with a sense of wonder." We hope that readers will come away from our book with a basic understanding of how market economies function, an appreciation for the things they do well, and a sense of the things they do poorly. We hope too that readers will learn that the proper role of government in a market economy is the subject of great debate around the world. That debate serves as the organizing principle behind this book.

For an economics text to be effective, it must address the economic issues of the time. Since the publication of our eighth edition, the economic landscape has changed substantially.

From 2003 through the end of 2007, the U.S. economy added over 8 million payroll jobs to the labor market, bringing the total to over 138 million. From a high of 6.3 percent in 2003, the unemployment rate dropped steadily to 4.4 percent by mid-2007.

The beginning of 2008 brought worries that the United States was in recession. During the first two quarters, the number of payroll jobs fell by nearly half a million and the unemployment rate jumped back up to 5.5 percent. The biggest issue facing the economy was a sharp downturn in the housing market and the resulting partial collapse of the mortgage market.

The housing downturn first hit the economy through a sharp downturn in the demand for housing and a 55 percent drop in new home construction. Prices of homes also fell nationwide for the first time in over 30 years. Falling home prices led to a decline in household wealth and a dramatic increase in mortgage defaults and foreclosures. This was made worse by the significant increase in lending to less creditworthy borrowers in what is called the subprime market.

The collapse of the usually stable mortgage market sent shock waves through the financial system worldwide. Banks, investment houses, and other financial service companies, as well as private investors lost hundreds of billions of dollars as many investors lost faith in the credit markets. To make matters worse, oil prices rose to over $147 per barrel, squeezing corporate profits, causing more layoffs, and pushing gasoline prices up.

The government reacted in several ways. Congress and the president announced a fiscal stimulus package including rebates to taxpayers of over $120 billion. The Federal Reserve dropped interest rates for the seventh consecutive time in early 2008 and took unprecedented action, directly participating in the rescue of Bear Stearns, the fifth-largest U.S. investment bank, from bankruptcy. In July, the Treasury and Federal Reserve jointly announced a plan to prevent the collapse of Fannie Mae and Freddie Mac, publicly held companies originally set up by the government to channel money into the mortgage market. Fannie and Freddie together held over $5 trillion in mortgages, about half of all the mortgages in the United States. This precipitated a national debate on the role of the Federal Reserve, which will not be easily resolved.

Internationally, the rise in oil prices was accompanied by a decline in the value of the dollar, making U.S. imports more expensive. Given this fact and a sharp increase in food and commodity prices, the possibility of serious inflation in the United States increased. The word *stagflation* came back in vogue.

On the positive side, the cheaper dollar led to a dramatic increase in U.S. net exports. Nonresidential construction continued to boom, and consumption remained surprisingly strong despite a huge drop in consumer confidence and the loss in housing wealth. While many were convinced that a recession was under way by the second quarter of 2008, others claimed that it was not yet in the numbers. All of this will influence the election of a new president in November 2008.

To understand these events requires a working knowledge of at least the basic "vocabulary" of economics.

New to this Edition

We have made every effort in this new edition to be responsive to the rapidly changing times, the recommendations of our reviewers, and our own teaching experiences. Here is a summary of the key changes:

1. Revised the organization of the aggregate demand and aggregate supply presentation
2. Streamlined the stock market chapter and merged the relevant content into Chapter 15, "Policy Timing, Deficit Targeting, and Stock Market Effects"
3. Streamlined the globalization chapter and merged the relevant content into Chapter 19, "International Trade, Comparative Advantage, and Protectionism"
4. Added a new feature, *Economics in Practice*, to help students think critically about economics in the world around them
5. Added modern topics, including behavioral economics

New Organization of Aggregate Demand and Aggregate Supply Chapters

The AD curve is now derived at the end of Chapter 12, "Aggregate Demand in the Goods and Money Markets" (rather than as before in Chapter 13). Since each point on the AD curve is an equilibrium in the goods and money markets and since Chapter 12 combines the goods and money markets, it is natural to derive the AD curve at the end of this chapter. Chapter 13, "Aggregate Supply and the Equilibrium Price Level," then presents the AS curve, which allows the equilibrium price level to be determined. We are then in a position to use the complete AS/AD framework for analysis—all but the labor market, which is discussed in Chapter 14, "The Labor Market in the Macroeconomy."

Newly Streamlined and Integrated Stock Market and Globalization Chapters

We moved the relevant material in the old stock market chapter into Chapter 15, "Policy Timing, Deficit Targeting, and Stock Market Effects." We moved the relevant material in the old globalization chapter into Chapter 19, "International Trade, Comparative Advantage, and Protectionism."

New Feature: *Economics in Practice*

To help pique students' interest in the economic world, we have created a new feature entitled *Economics in Practice*. This feature either (1) describes a personal observation or a research idea and provides an analysis using the concepts of the chapter or (2) presents a newspaper excerpt that relates to the concepts of the chapter. The *Economics in Practice* feature saves instructors time by providing a variety of real-world examples and helps keep students engaged in the chapter. Each feature includes a related end-of-chapter problem so that instructors can test students' understanding of the concepts applied in the feature. Additional *Economics in Practice* features appear in the *Instructor's Manual* so that instructors can present real-world examples in class that do not appear in the main text and in the PowerPoint® to aid in class discussion of the topics. Also, MyEconLab and the Test Item Files include questions related to the *Economics in Practice* feature for instructors who want to assess students' understanding of the examples presented.

Here (to the left) is an example of an *Economics in Practice* feature that appears in Chapter 3, "Demand, Supply, and Market Equilibrium."

For a complete list of the *Economics in Practice* features in this book, please see the detailed table of contents, which begins on page v.

CHAPTER 3 Demand, Supply, and Market Equilibrium **69**

ECONOMICS IN PRACTICE

Why Do the Prices of Newspapers Rise?

In 2006, the average price for a daily edition of a Baltimore newspaper was $0.50. In 2007, the average price had risen to $0.75. Three different analysts have three different explanations for the higher equilibrium price.

Analyst 1: The higher price for Baltimore newspapers is good news because it means the population is better informed about public issues. These data clearly show that the citizens of Baltimore have a new, increased regard for newspapers.

Analyst 2: The higher price for Baltimore newspapers is bad news for the citizens of Baltimore. The higher cost of paper, ink, and distribution reflected in these higher prices will further diminish the population's awareness of public issues.

Analyst 3: The higher price for Baltimore newspapers is an unfortunate result of newspapers trying to make money as many consumers have turned to the Internet to access news coverage for free.

As economists, we are faced with two tasks in looking at these explanations: Do they make sense based on what we know about economic principles? And if they do make sense, can we figure out which explanation applies to the case of rising newspaper prices in Baltimore?

What is Analyst 1 saying? Her observation about consumers' new increased regard for newspapers tells us something about the demand curve. Analyst 1 seems to be arguing that tastes have changed in favor of newspapers, which would mean a shift in the demand curve to the right. With upward-sloping supply, such a shift would produce a price increase. So Analyst 1's story is plausible.

Analyst 2 refers to an increased cost of newsprint. This would cause production costs of newspapers to rise, shifting the supply curve to the left. A downward-sloping demand curve also results in increased prices. So Analyst 2 also has a plausible story.

Since Analyst 1 and Analyst 2 have plausible stories based on economic principles, we can look at evidence to see who is in fact right. If you go back to the graphs in Figure 3.12 on p. 66, you will find a clue. When demand shifts to the right (as in Analyst 1's story) the price rises, but so does the quantity as shown in Figure (a) below. When supply shifts to the left (as in Analyst 2's story) the price rises, but the quantity falls as shown in Figure (b) below. So we would look at what happened to newspaper circulation during this period to see whether the price increase is from the demand side or the supply side. In fact, in most markets, including Baltimore, quantities of newspapers bought have been falling, so Analyst 2 is most likely correct.

But be careful. Both analysts may be correct. If demand shifts to the right and supply shifts to the left by a greater amount, the price will rise and the quantity sold will fall.

What about Analyst 3? Analyst 3 clearly never had an economics course! Free Internet access to news is a substitute for print media. A decrease in the price of this substitute should shift the demand for newspapers to the left. The result should be a lower price, not a price increase. The fact that the newspaper publishers are "trying to make money" faced with this new competition does not change the laws of supply and demand.

a. Demand shifts to the right

b. Supply shifts to the left

Modern Topics

We have added examples and coverage of behavioral economics and experimental economics. For example, Chapter 8, "Aggregate Expenditure and Equilibrium Output," includes material on anomalies in saving decisions: Do pension savings respond to opt-in versus opt-out requirements?

We have also updated the chapters with current events regarding fiscal policy and monetary policy and the recent housing crisis. Here are some examples of the new coverage:

- Chapter 5, "Introduction to Macroeconomics," covers the economy in 2008 and the way it affected the presidential election outcome."
- Chapter 13, "Aggregate Supply and the Equilibrium Price Level," covers Federal Reserve Board policies through 2008.
- Chapter 15, "Policy Timing, Deficit Targeting, and Stock Market Effects," covers the bursting of the housing bubble and its implications for Federal Reserve policy. The chapter also covers the 2008 fiscal stimulus package.
- Chapter 17, "Long-Run Growth," covers how firms are dealing with high health care costs by increasing the availability of wellness programs for diet, exercise, and smoking cessation, for example. Also included in this chapter is a new section on "Growth and Environmental Issues of Sustainability." This section covers the Millennium Development Goals adopted by the United Nations.

In addition to the preceding changes, we also updated all tables and graphs with the latest data.

The Foundation

Despite a new chapter, a new feature, updates, and other revisions, the themes of *Principles of Macroeconomics*, Ninth Edition, are the same themes of the first eight editions. The purposes of this book are to introduce the discipline of economics and to provide a basic understanding of how economies function. This requires a blend of economic theory, institutional material, and real-world applications. We have maintained a balance between these ingredients in every chapter. The hallmark features of our book are its:

1. Three-tiered explanations of key concepts (*stories-graphs-equations*).
2. Intuitive and accessible structure.
3. International coverage.

Three-Tiered Explanations: Stories-Graphs-Equations

Professors who teach principles of economics are faced with a classroom of students with different abilities, backgrounds, and learning styles. For some students, analytical material is difficult no matter how it is presented; for others, graphs and equations seem to come naturally. The problem facing instructors and textbook authors is how to convey the core principles of the discipline to as many students as possible without selling the better students short. Our approach to this problem is to present most core concepts in the following three ways:

First, we present each concept in the context of a simple intuitive *story* or example in words often followed by a table. Second, we use a *graph* in most cases to illustrate the story or example. And finally, in many cases where appropriate, we use an *equation* to present the concept with a mathematical formula.

Macroeconomic Structure

We remain committed to the view that it is a mistake simply to throw aggregate demand and aggregate supply curves at students in the first few chapters of a principles book. To understand the AS and AD curves, students need to know about the functioning of both the goods market and the money market. The logic behind the simple demand curve is wrong when it is applied to the relationship between aggregate demand and the price level. Similarly, the logic behind the simple supply curve is wrong when it is applied to the relationship between aggregate supply and the price level.

Part of teaching economics is teaching economic reasoning. Our discipline is built around deductive logic. Once we teach students a pattern of logic, we want and expect them to apply it to new circumstances. When they apply the logic of a simple demand curve or a simple supply curve to the aggregate demand or aggregate supply curve, the logic does not fit. We believe that the best way to teach the reasoning embodied in the aggregate demand and aggregate supply curves without creating confusion for students is to build up to those topics carefully.

In Chapter 8, "Aggregate Expenditure and Equilibrium Output," and Chapter 9, "The Government and Fiscal Policy," we examine the market for goods and services. In Chapter 10, "The Money Supply and the Federal Reserve," and Chapter 11, "Money Demand and the Equilibrium Interest Rate," we examine the money market. We bring the two markets together in Chapter 12, "Aggregate Demand in the Goods and Money Markets," which explains the links between aggregate output (Y) and the interest rate (r) and derives the AD curve. In Chapter 13, "Aggregate Supply and the Equilibrium Price Level," we introduce the AS curve and determine the equilibrium price level (P). We then explain in Chapter 14, "The Labor Market in the Macroeconomy," how the labor markets fits into this macroeconomic picture. The following figure from page 139 gives you an overview of this structure.

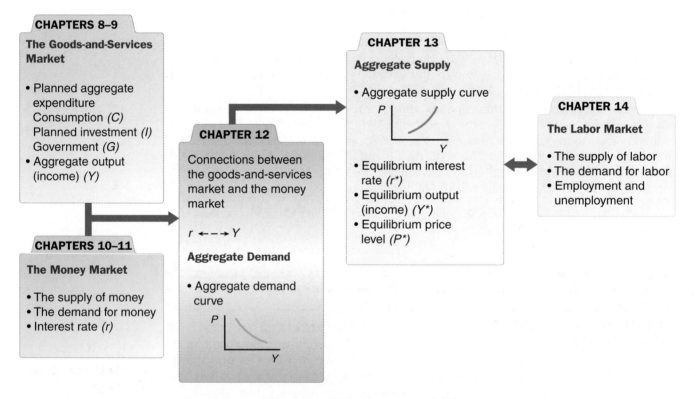

▲ FIGURE III.1 The Core of Macroeconomic Theory

One of the big issues in the organization of the macroeconomic material is whether long-run growth issues should be taught before short-run chapters on the determination of national income and countercyclical policy. In the last three editions, we moved a significant discussion of growth to Chapter 7, "Unemployment, Inflation, and Long-Run Growth," and highlighted it. However, while we wrote the major chapter on long-run growth, Chapter 17, "Long-Run Growth," so that it can be taught before or after the short-run chapters, we remain convinced that it is easier for students to understand the growth issue once they have come to grips with the logic and controversies of short-run cycles, inflation, and unemployment.

International Coverage

As in previous editions, we continue to integrate international examples and applications in many chapters. Here are examples of our coverage:

- Chapter 1, "The Scope and Method of Economics," discusses the many countries that contribute to creating the iPod.
- Chapter 6, "Measuring National Output and National Income," compares the per-capita national income for over 30 countries.
- Chapter 11, "Money Demand and the Equilibrium Interest Rate," discusses ATM use in Italy.
- Chapter 17, "Long-Run Growth," compares GDP growth rates in various countries and discusses the role of institutions in attracting capital. The chapter explains how market reforms in China affected its productivity gains in the last 20 years and its recent foreign direct investments in parts of Africa and Asia. Also included in this chapter is a discussion of industrial policy in developing countries such as Taiwan.

We also include two full chapters on the world economy: Chapter 19, "International Trade, Comparative Advantage, and Protectionism," and Chapter 21, "Economic Growth in Developing and Transitional Economies." These chapters cover the increasing economic interdependence among countries and their citizens. We focus on the causes and consequences of increased international trade of goods and services, increased cross-border movements of labor, and the outsourcing of jobs to low-wage labor markets outside the United States.

Tools for Learning

As authors and teachers, we understand the challenges of the principles of economics course. Our pedagogical features are designed to illustrate and reinforce key economic concepts through real-world examples and applications.

Economics in Practice

As described earlier, the *Economics in Practice* feature presents a real-world personal observation, current research work, or a news article that supports the key concept of the chapter and helps students think critically about how economics is a part of their daily lives. The end-of-chapter problem sets include a question specific to each *Economics in Practice* feature. Students can visit www.myeconlab.com for additional updated news articles and related exercises.

Graphs

Reading and interpreting graphs is a key part of understanding economic concepts. The Chapter 1 Appendix, "How to Read and Understand Graphs," shows readers how to interpret the 200-plus graphs featured in this book. We use red curves to illustrate the behavior of firms and blue curves to show the behavior of households. We use a different shade of red and blue to signify a shift in a curve.

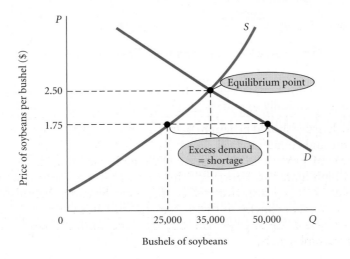

Excess Demand, or Shortage
At a price of $1.75 per bushel, quantity demanded exceeds quantity supplied. When excess *demand* exists, there is a tendency for price to rise. When quantity demanded equals quantity supplied, excess demand is eliminated and the market is in equilibrium. Here the equilibrium price is $2.50 and the equilibrium quantity is 35,000 bushels.

Problems and Solutions

Each chapter and appendix ends with a problem set that asks students to think about and apply what they've learned in the chapter. These problems are not simple memorization questions. Rather, they ask students to perform graphical analysis or to apply economics to a real-world situation or policy decision. More challenging problems are indicated by an asterisk. Additional questions specific to the Economics in Practice feature have been added. Several problems have been updated. The solutions to all of the problems are available in the *Instructor's Manual*. Instructors can provide the solutions to students so that they can check their understanding and progress. Please see the *Instructor's Manual*.

MyEcon Lab myeconlab

Both the text and supplement package provide ways for instructors and students to assess their knowledge and progress through the course. MyEconLab, the new standard in personalized online learning, is a key part of Case, Fair, and Oster's integrated learning package for the ninth edition.

For the Instructor

MyEconLab is an online course management, testing, and tutorial resource. Instructors can choose how much or how little time to spend setting up and using MyEconLab. Each chapter contains two Sample Tests, Study Plan Exercises, and Tutorial Resources. Student use of these materials requires no initial set-up by their instructor. The online Gradebook records each student's performance and time spent on the Tests and Study Plan and generates reports by student or by chapter. Instructors can assign tests, quizzes, and homework in MyEconLab using four resources:

- Preloaded Sample Test questions
- Problems similar to the end-of-chapter problems
- Test Item File questions
- Self-authored questions using Econ Exercise Builder

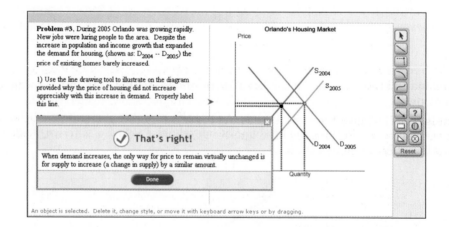

Exercises use multiple-choice, graph drawing, and free-response items, many of which are generated algorithmically so that each time a student works them, a different variation is presented. MyEconLab grades every problem, even those with graphs. When working homework exercises, students receive immediate feedback with links to additional learning tools.

Customization and Communication   MyEconLab in CourseCompass™ provides additional optional customization and communication tools. Instructors who teach distance learning courses or very large lecture sections find the CourseCompass format useful because they can upload course documents and assignments, customize the order of chapters, and use communication features such as Digital Drop Box and Discussion Board.

For the Student

MyEconLab puts students in control of their learning through a collection of tests, practice, and study tools tied to the online, interactive version of the textbook, and other media resources. Within MyEconLab's structured environment, students practice what they learn, test their understanding, and pursue a personalized Study Plan generated from their performance on Sample Tests and tests set by their instructors. At the core of MyEconLab are the following features:

- Sample Tests, two per chapter
- Personal Study Plan
- Tutorial Instruction
- Graphing Tool

Sample Tests   Two Sample Tests for each chapter are preloaded in MyEconLab, enabling students to practice what they have learned, test their understanding, and identify areas in which they need further work. Students can study on their own, or they can complete assignments created by their instructor.

Personal Study Plan   Based on a student's performance on tests, MyEconLab generates a personal Study Plan that shows where the student needs further study. The Study Plan consists of a series of additional practice exercises with detailed feedback and guided solutions and keyed to other tutorial resources.

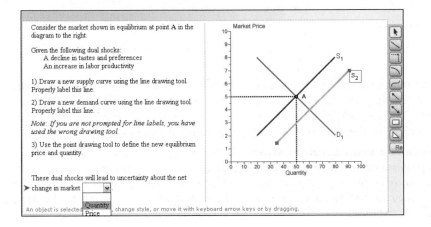

Tutorial Instruction   Launched from many of the exercises in the Study Plan, MyEconLab provides tutorial instruction in the form of step-by-step solutions and other media-based explanations.

Graphing Tool   A graphing tool is integrated into the Tests and Study Plan exercises to enable students to make and manipulate graphs. This feature helps students understand how concepts, numbers, and graphs connect.

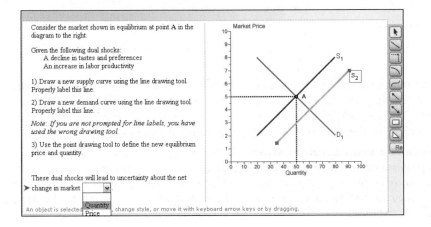

Additional MyEconLab Tools   MyEconLab includes the following additional features:

1. **Economics in the News**—This feature provides weekly updates during the school year of news items with links to sources for further reading and discussion questions. Instructors can assign these articles with related, auto-graded questions to assess students' understanding of what they've read.

2. **eText**—While students are working in the Study Plan or completing homework assignments, part of the tutorial resources available is a direct link to the relevant page of the text so that students can review the appropriate material to help them complete the exercise.

3. **Glossary**—This searchable version of the textbook glossary provides additional examples and links to related terms.

4. **Glossary Flashcards**—Every key term is available as a flashcard, allowing students to quiz themselves on vocabulary from one or more chapters at a time.

5. **Ask the Author**—Students can e-mail economics-related questions to the author.

6. **Research Navigator (CourseCompass™ version only)**—This feature offers extensive help on the research process and provides four exclusive databases of credible and reliable source material, including *The New York Times*, the *Financial Times*, and peer-reviewed journals.

MyEconLab content has been created through the efforts of: Charles Baum, Middle Tennessee State University; Sarah Ghosh, University of Scranton; Russell Kellogg, University of Colorado–Denver; Bert G. Wheeler, Cedarville University; and Noel Lotz and Douglas A. Ruby, Pearson Education.

Resources for the Instructor

The following supplements are designed to make teaching and testing flexible and easy.

Instructor's Manual

Prepared by Tony Lima of California State University, Hayward, the Instructor's Manual is designed to provide the utmost teaching support for instructors. It includes the following content:

- Detailed *Chapter Outlines* include key terminology, teaching notes, and lecture suggestions.
- *Topics for Class Discussion* provide topics and real-world situations that help ensure that economic concepts resonate with students.
- Unique *Economics in Practice* features that are not in the main text provide extra real-world examples to present and discuss in class.
- *Teaching Tips* provide alternative ways to cover the material and brief reminders on additional help to provide students. These tips include suggestions for exercises and experiments to complete in class.
- *Extended Applications* include exercises, activities, and experiments to help make economics relevant to students.
- *Solutions* are provided for all problems in the book.

Three Test Item Files

We have tailored the Test Item Files to help instructors easily and efficiently assess student understanding of economic concepts and analyses. Test questions are annotated with the following information:

- **Difficulty:** 1 for straight recall, 2 for some analysis, 3 for complex analysis
- **Type:** multiple-choice, true/false, short-answer, essay
- **Topic:** the term or concept the question supports
- **Skill:** fact, definition, analytical, conceptual
- **AACSB** (see description that follows)
- **Special feature in the main book:** *Economics in Practice*

The Test Item Files include questions with tables that students must analyze to solve for numerical answers. The Test Item Files also contain questions based on the graphs that appear in the book. The questions ask students to interpret the information presented in the graph. Many questions in the Test Item Files require students to sketch a graph on their own and interpret curve movements.

Macroeconomics Test Item File 1, by Randy Methenitis of Richland College: Test Item File 1 (TIF1) includes over 2,200 questions. All questions are machine-gradable and are either multiple-choice or true-false. TIF 1 is for use with the ninth edition of *Principles of Macroeconomics* in the first year of publication. This Test Item File is available in a computerized format using TestGen EQ test-generating software.

Macroeconomics Test Item File 2, by Randy Methenitis of Richland College: This additional Test Item File contains another 2,200 machine-gradable questions based on the TIF1 but regenerated to provide instructors with fresh questions when using the book the second year. This Test Item File is available in a computerized format using TestGen EQ test-generating software.

Macroeconomics Test Item File 3, by Richard Gosselin of Houston Community College: This third Test Item File includes 1,000 conceptual problems, essay questions, and short-answer questions. Application-type problems ask students to draw graphs and analyze tables. The Word files are available on the Instructor's Resource Center (www.prenhall.com/casefair).

The Test Item Files were checked for accuracy by: Leon J. Battista, Bronx Community College; Margaret Brooks, Bridgewater State College; Mike Cohick, Collin County Community College; Dennis Debrecht, Carroll College; Amrik Dua, California State Polytechnic University, Pomona; Mitchell Dudley, The College of William & Mary; Ann Eike, University of Kentucky; Connel Fullencamp, Duke University; Craig Gallet, California State University, Sacramento; Michael Goode, Central Piedmont Community College; Steve Hamilton, California State Polytechnic University; James R. Irwin, Central Michigan University; Aaron Jackson, Bentley College; Rus Janis, University of Massachusetts, Amherst; Jonatan Jelen, The City College of New York; Kathy A. Kelly, University of Texas, Arlington; Kate Krause, University of New Mexico; Gary F. Langer, Roosevelt University; Leonard Lardaro, University of Rhode Island; Ross LaRoe, Denison University; Melissa Lind, University of Texas, Arlington; Solina Lindahl, California State Polytechnic University; Pete Mavrokordatos, Tarrant County College; Roberto Mazzoleni, Hofstra University; Kimberly Mencken, Baylor University; Ida Mirzaie, Ohio State University; Shahruz Mohtadi, Suffolk University; Mary Pranzo, California State University, Fresno; Ed Price, Oklahoma State University; Robert Shoffner, Central Piedmont Community College; James Swofford, University of South Alabama; Helen Tauchen, University of North Carolina, Chapel Hill; Eric Taylor, Central Piedmont Community College; Henry Terrell, University of Maryland; John Tommasi, Bentley College; Mukti Upadhyay, Eastern Illinois University; Robert Whaples, Wake Forest University; and Timothy Wunder, University of Texas, Arlington.

The Association to Advance Collegiate Schools of Business (AACSB)   The authors of the Test Item Files have connected select questions to the general knowledge and skill guidelines found in the AACSB assurance of learning standards.

What Is the AACSB?   AACSB is a not-for-profit corporation of educational institutions, corporations, and other organizations devoted to the promotion and improvement of higher education in business administration and accounting. A collegiate institution offering degrees in business administration or accounting may volunteer for AACSB accreditation review. The AACSB makes initial accreditation decisions and conducts periodic reviews to promote continuous quality improvement in management education. Pearson Education is a proud member of the AACSB and is pleased to provide advice to help you apply AACSB assurance of learning standards.

What Are AACSB Assurance of Learning Standards?   One of the criteria for AACSB accreditation is quality of the curricula. Although no specific courses are required, the AACSB expects a curriculum to include learning experiences in areas such as the following:

- Communication
- Ethical Reasoning
- Analytic Skills
- Use of Information Technology
- Multicultural and Diversity
- Reflective Thinking

Questions that test skills relevant to these guidelines are appropriately tagged. For example, a question testing the moral questions associated with externalities would receive the Ethical Reasoning tag.

How Can Instructors Use the AACSB Tags? Tagged questions help you measure whether students are grasping the course content that aligns with the AACSB guidelines noted. In addition, the tagged questions may help instructors identify potential applications of these skills. This in turn may suggest enrichment activities or other educational experiences to help students achieve these skills.

TestGen

The computerized TestGen package allows instructors to customize, save, and generate classroom tests. The test program permits instructors to edit, add, or delete questions from the Test Item Files; edit existing graphics and create new graphics; analyze test results; and organize a database of tests and student results. This software allows for extensive flexibility and ease of use. It provides many options for organizing and displaying tests, along with search and sort features. The software and the Test Item Files can be downloaded from the Instructor's Resource Center (www.prenhall.com/casefair).

PowerPoint® Lecture Presentation

Three sets of PowerPoint® slides, prepared by Fernando and Yvonn Quijano, are available for instructors to use:

1. A comprehensive set of PowerPoint® slides that can be used by instructors for class presentations or by students for lecture preview or review. The presentation includes all the graphs, tables, and equations in the textbook. It displays figures in step-by-step, automated mode with a single click per graph curve.
2. A comprehensive set of PowerPoint® slides with Classroom Response Systems (CRS) questions built in so that instructors can incorporate CRS "clickers" into their classroom lectures. For more information on Prentice Hall's partnership with CRS, see the description below. Instructors may download these PowerPoint presentations from the Instructor's Resource Center (www.prenhall.com/casefair).
3. A student version of the PowerPoint® slides is available as .pdf files from the book's companion website at www.prenhall.com/case. This version allows students to print the slides and bring them to class for note taking.

Instructor's Resource CD-ROM

The Instructor's Resource CD-ROM contains all the faculty and student resources that support this text. Instructors have the ability to access and edit the following three supplements:

- Instructor's Manual
- Three Test Item Files
- PowerPoint® presentations

By clicking on a chapter or searching for a key word, faculty can access an interactive library of resources. Faculty can pick and choose from the various supplements and export them to their hard drives.

Classroom Response Systems

Classroom Response Systems (CRS) is an exciting new wireless polling technology that makes large and small classrooms even more interactive because it enables instructors to pose questions to their students, record results, and display the results instantly. Students can answer questions easily by using compact remote-control transmitters. Prentice Hall has partnerships with leading providers of classroom response systems and can show you everything you need to know about setting up and using a CRS system. We provide the classroom hardware, text-specific PowerPoint® slides, software, and support; and we show you how your students can benefit. Learn more at www.prenhall.com/crs.

Blackboard® and WebCT® Course Content

Prentice Hall offers fully customizable course content for the Blackboard® and WebCT® Course Management Systems.

Resources for the Student

The following supplements are designed to help students understand and retain the key concepts of each chapter.

MyEconLab

MyEconLab allows students to practice what they learn, test their understanding, and pursue a personalized Study Plan generated from their performance on Sample Tests and tests set by their instructors. Here are MyEconLab's key features. (See page xv of this preface for more details on MyEconLab.)

- Sample Tests, two per chapter
- Personal Study Plan
- Tutorial Instruction
- Graphing Tool

Study Guide

The study guide, prepared by Thomas M. Beveridge of Durham Technical Community College, provides students with additional applications and exercises.

Each chapter contains the following elements:

- **Point-by-Point Chapter Objectives** A list of learning goals for the chapter. Each objective is followed up with a summary of the material, learning tips for each concept, and practice questions with solutions.

- *Economics in Practice* **Questions** A question that requires students to apply concepts of the chapter to the *Economics in Practice* feature. The answer accompanies the question.

- **Practice Tests** Approximately 20 multiple-choice questions and answers and application questions that require students to use graphic or numerical analysis to solve economic problems.

- **Solutions** Worked-out solutions to all questions in the *Study Guide*

- **Comprehensive Part Exams** Multiple-choice and application questions to test students' overall comprehension. Solutions to all questions are also provided.

CourseSmart

CourseSmart is an exciting new *choice* for students looking to save money. As an alternative to purchasing the print textbook, students can purchase an electronic version of the same content and save up to 50 percent off the suggested list price of the print text. With a CourseSmart eTextbook, students can search the text, make notes online, print out reading assignments that incorporate lecture notes, and bookmark important passages for later review. For more information or to purchase access to the CourseSmart eTextbook, visit **www.coursesmart.com**.

Student Subscriptions

Staying on top of current economic issues is critical to understanding and applying economic theory in and out of class. Keep students engaged by packaging, at a discount, a semester-long subscription to *The Wall Street Journal*, the *Financial Times*, or Economist.com with each student text. Contact your local Prentice Hall representative for more information about benefits of these subscriptions and how to order one for your students.

Acknowledgments

We are grateful to the many people who helped us prepare the ninth edition. We thank Jodi Bolognese, our editor, and Virginia Guariglia, our project manager , for their help and enthusiasm. We are also grateful to Lena Buonanno, Developmental Editor, for overseeing the entire project. The quality of the book owes much to her guidance. Steve Deitmer, Director of Development, brought sound judgment to many decisions required during a revision.

Lori DeShazo, Executive Marketing Manager, carefully crafted the marketing message. Lynne Breitfeller, Production Editor, and Cynthia Zonneveld, our production managing editor, ensured that the production process of the book went smoothly. In addition, we also want to thank Marisa Taylor of GEX Publishing Services, who kept us on schedule, and Sheila Norman, who researched the many photographs that appear in the book.

We want to give special thanks to Patsy Balin, Murielle Dawdy, and Tracy Waldman for their research assistance.

We also owe a debt of gratitude to those who reviewed and accuracy-checked the ninth edition. They provided us with valuable insight as we prepared this edition and its supplement package.

Consultant Board

The guidance and recommendations of the following professors helped us develop our revision plan and select *Economics in Practice* features for each chapter.

Brett Katzman, Kennesaw State University
Margaret D. Ledyard, University of Texas, Austin
Nathan Perry, University of Utah
Joseph A. Petry, University of Illinois
Chris Phillips, Somerset Community College
Jeff Rubin, Rutgers University
William Walsh, University of St. Thomas
Robert Whaples, Wake Forest University

Accuracy Reviewers

A dedicated team of economics professors accuracy-checked the text for the ninth edition:

Fatma Abdel-Raouf, Goldey-Beacom College
Charles Callahan, III, State University of New York, Brockport
Tisha Emerson, Baylor University
Daniel Lawson, Drew University
Randy Methenitis, Richland College
Robert Whaples, Wake Forest University

Reviewers of the Current Edition

The guidance and recommendations of the following professors helped us develop the revision plans for our new edition and shape the content of the new chapters:

Cynthia Abadie, Southwest Tennessee Community College
Shawn Abbott, College of the Siskiyous

Rebecca Abraham, Nova Southeastern University
Basil Adams, Notre Dame de Namur University
Carlos Aguilar, El Paso Community College
Ehsan Ahmed, James Madison University
Ferhat Akbas, Texas A&M University
Terence Alexander, Iowa State University
Hassan Aly, Ohio State University
David Anderson, Centre College
Joan Anderssen, Arapahoe Community College
Bevin Ashenmiller, Occidental College
Birjees Ashraf, Houston Community College Southwest
Musa Ayar, University of Texas, Austin
Asatar Bair, City College of San Francisco
Nick Barcia, Baruch College
Laurie Bates, Bryant University
Diana Bajrami, College of Alameda
Rita Balaban, University of North Carolina, Chapel Hill
Henry Barker, Tiffin University
Robin Bartlett, Denison University
Leon Battista, City University of New York
Amanda Bayer, Swarthmore College
Klaus Becker, Texas Tech University
Clive Belfield, Queens College
Richard Beil, Auburn University
Emil Berendt, Siena Heights University
Kurt Beron, University of Texas, Dallas
Derek Berry, Calhoun Community College
Tibor Besedes, Georgia Institute of Technology
Thomas Beveridge, Durham Technical Community College
Anoop Bhargava, Finger Lakes Community College
Eugenie Bietry, Pace University
Kelly Blanchard, Purdue University
Mark Bock, Loyola College in Maryland
Howard Bodenhorn, Lafayette College
Jeff Bookwalter, University of Montana
Antonio Bos, Tusculum College
Barry Brown, Murray State University

Bruce Brown, California State Polytechnic University, Pomona
Jennifer Brown, Eastern Connecticut State University
Don Brunner, Spokane Falls Community College
Jeff Bruns, Bacone College
David Bunting, Eastern Washington University
Barbara Burnell, College of Wooster
Alison Butler, Willamette University
Fred Campano, Fordham University
Douglas Campbell, University of Memphis
Beth Cantrell, Central Baptist College
Kevin Carlson, University of Massachusetts, Boston
Leonard Carlson, Emory University
Arthur Schiller Casimir, Western New England College
Cesar Corredor, Texas A&M University
Suparna Chakraborty, Baruch College of the City University of New York
David Ching, University of Hawaii, Honolulu
Dmitriy Chulkov, Indiana University, Kokomo
Karen Conway, University of New Hampshire
Tyler Cowen, George Mason University
Amy Cramer, Pima Community College, West Campus
Jerry Crawford, Arkansas State University
James Cunningham, Chapman University
Barbara Craig, Oberlin College
James D'Angelo, University of Cincinnati
David Dahl, University of St. Thomas
Sonia Dalmia, Grand Valley State University
Sheryll Dahlke, Lees-McRae College
Joseph Dahms, Hood College
Rosa Lea Danielson, College of DuPage
David Danning, University of Massachusetts, Boston
Amlan Datta, Cisco Junior College
David Davenport, McLennan Community College

Stephen Davis, Southwest Minnesota State University

Dale DeBoer, Colorado University, Colorado Springs

Dennis Debrecht, Carroll College

Juan J. DelaCruz, Fashion Institute of Technology and Lehman College

Greg Delemeester, Marietta College

Amy Diduch, Mary Baldwin College

Yanan Di, State University of New York, Stony Brook

Timothy Diette, Washington and Lee University

Alan Dobrowolksi, Manchester Community College

Eric Dodge, Hanover College

Carol Dole, Jacksonville University

Shahpour Dowlatshahi, Fayetteville Technical Community College

Kevin Duncan, Colorado State University

Ann Eike, University of Kentucky

Eugene Elander, Plymouth State University

Tisha Emerson, Baylor University

Michael Enz, Western New England College

Erwin Erhardt III, University of Cincinnati

William Even, Miami University

Dr. Ali Faegh, Houston Community College, Northwest

Deborah Figart, Richard Stockton College

Fred Foldvary, Santa Clara University

Kevin Foster, The City College of New York

Johanna Francis, Fordham University

Mark Frascatore, Clarkson University

Amanda Freeman, Kansas State University

Morris Frommer, Owens Community College

Brandon Fuller, University of Montana

David Fuller, University of Iowa

Mark Funk, University of Arkansas, Little Rock

Craig Gallet, California State University, Sacramento

Bill Ganley, Buffalo State College

Jeff Gerlach, Sungkyunkwan Graduate School of Business

Lynn G. Gillette, Spalding University

Donna Ginther, University of Kansas

Amy Glass, Texas A&M University

Bill Godair, Landmark College

Joshua Goodman, New York University

Ophelia Goma, DePauw University

John Gonzales, University of San Francisco

David Gordon, Illinois Valley College

Eugene Gotwalt, Sweet Briar College

Osman Gulseven, North Carolina State University

Mike Gumpper, Millersville University

Thomas A. Gresik, University of Notre Dame

Wayne Grove, Le Moyne College

Daryl Gruver, Mount Vernon Nazarene University

Anthony Gyapong, Penn State University, Abington

Bradley Hansen, University of Mary Washington

Mehdi Haririan, Bloomsburg University of Pennsylvania

David Harris, Benedictine College

David Harris, San Diego State University

James Hartley, Mount Holyoke College

Bruce Hartman, California Maritime Academy of California State University

Dewey Heinsma, Mt. San Jacinto College

Sara Helms, University of Alabama, Birmingham

Brian Hill, Salisbury University

Arleen Hoag, Owens Community College

Carol Hogan, University of Michigan, Dearborn

Ward Hooker, Orangeburg-Calhoun Technical College

Daniel Horton, Cleveland State University

Ying Huang, Manhattan College

Creed Hyatt, Lehigh Carbon Community College

Ana Ichim, Louisiana State University

Aaron Iffland, Rocky Mountain College

Aaron Jackson, Bentley College

Brian Jacobsen, Wisconsin Lutheran College

Russell Janis, University of Massachusetts, Amherst

Jonatan Jelen, The City College of New York

Aaron Johnson, Missouri State University

Paul Johnson, University of Alaska Anchorage

Donn Johnson, Quinnipiac University

Dennis Kaufman, University of Wisconsin, Parkside

Pavel Kapinos, Carleton College

Russell Kashian, University of Wisconsin, Whitewater

Amoz Kats, Virginia Technical University

David Kaun, University of California, Santa Cruz

Brett Katzman, Kennesaw State University

Fred Keast, Portland State University

Stephanie Kelton, University of Missouri, Kansas City

Deborah Kelly, Palomar College

Erasmus Kersting, Texas A&M University

Randall Kesselring, Arkansas State University

Alan Kessler, Providence College

Gary Kikuchi, University of Hawaii, Manoa

Keon-Ho Kim, University of Utah

Kil-Joong Kim, Austin Peay State University

Sang W. Kim, Hood College

Janet Koscianski, Shippensburg University

Vani Kotcherlakota, University of Nebraska, Kearney

Barry Kotlove, Edmonds Community College

Kate Krause, University of New Mexico

David Kroeker, Tabor College

Stephan Kroll, California State University, Sacramento

Joseph Kubec, Park University

Jacob Kurien, Helzberg School of Management

Sally Kwak, University of Hawaii- Manoa

David Lang, California State University, Sacramento

Gary Langer, Roosevelt University

Anthony Laramie, Merrimack College

Leonard Lardaro, University of Rhode Island

Ross LaRoe, Denison University

Pareena Lawrence, Unversity of Minnesota, Morris

Mary Rose Leacy, Wagner College

Alan Leonard, Wilson Technical Community College

Ding Li, Northern State University

Zhe Li, Stony Brook University

Benjamin Liebman, Saint Joseph's University

Larry Lichtenstein, Canisius College

Jesse Liebman, Kennesaw State University

Melissa Lind, University of Texas, Arlington

Charles Link, University of Delaware

Samuel Liu, West Valley College

Jeffrey Livingston, Bentley College

Ming Chien Lo, Saint Cloud University

Alina Luca, Drexel University

Adrienne Lucas, Wellesley College

Nancy Lutz, Virginia Tech

Kristina Lybecker, Colorado College

Ann E. Lyon, University of Alaska Anchorage

Bruce Madariaga, Montgomery College

Tim Mason, Eastern Illinois University

Don Mathews, Coastal Georgia Community College

Roberto Mazzoleni, Hofstra University

Patrick McEwan, Wellesley College

Dawn McLaren, Mesa Community College

B. Starr McMullen, Oregon State University

Martin Melkonian, Hofstra University

Alice Melkumian, Western Illinois University

William Mertens, University of Colorado, Boulder

Randy Methenitis, Richland College

Carrie A. Meyer, George Mason University

David Mitchell, Missouri State University

Ida Mirzaie, The Ohio State University

Bijan Moeinian, Osceola Campus

Robert Mohr, University of New Hampshire

Shahruz Mohtadi, Suffolk University

Amyaz Moledina, College of Wooster

Gary Mongiovi, St. John's University

Terry Monson, Michigan Technological University

Barbara A. Moore, University of Central Florida

W. Douglas Morgan, University of California, Santa Barbara

David Murphy, Boston College

Ellen Mutari, Richard Stockton College of New Jersey

Steven C. Myers, University of Akron

Doug Nelson, Spokane Community College

Sung No, Southern University and A&M College

Albert Okunade, University of Memphis

Constantin Ogloblin, Georgia Southern University

David O'Hara, Metropolitan State University

Ronald Olive, University of Massachusetts, Lowell

Martha Olney, University of California, Berkeley

Mete Ozcan, Brooklyn College

Alexandre Padilla, Metropolitan State College of Denver

Aaron Pankratz, Fresno City College

Spiro Patton, Rasmussen College

Andrew Pearlman, Bard College

Richard Peck, University of Illinois at Chicago

Don Peppard, Connecticut College

Elizabeth Perry, Randolph College

Nathan Perry, University of Utah

Chris Phillips, Somerset Community College

Frankie Pircher, University of Missouri, Kansas City

Dennis Placone, Clemson University

Linnea Polgreen, University of Iowa

Bob Potter, University of Central Florida

Ed Price, Oklahoma State University

Ramkishen S. Rajan, George Mason University

James Rakowski, University of Notre Dame

Amy Ramirez-Gay, Eastern Michigan University

Artatrana Ratha, St. Cloud State University

Brian Roberson, Miami University

Michael Robinson, Mount Holyoke College

Juliette Roddy, University of Michigan, Dearborn

Belinda Roman, Palo Alto College

Paul Roscelli, Canada College

Charles Roussel, Louisiana State University

Brian Rosario, University of California, Davis

Greg Rose, Sacramento City College

Howard Ross, Baruch College

Robert Rosenthal, Stonehill College

Jeff Rubin, Rutgers University, Rutgers

Luz A. Saavedra, University of St. Thomas

William Samuelson, Boston University School of Management

Allen Sanderson, University of Chicago

David Saner, Springfield College – Benedictine University

Ahmad Saranjam, Bridgewater State College

Eric Schansberg, Indiana University, Southeast

Robert Schenk, Saint Joseph's College

Adina Schwartz, Lakeland College

Amy Scott, DeSales University

Atindra Sen, Miami University

Chad Settle, University of Tulsa

Ronald Shadbegian, University of Massachusetts, Dartmouth

Paul Shea, University of Oregon

Gerald Shilling, Eastfield College

Dongsoo Shin, Santa Clara University

William Simeone, Providence College

Larry Singell, University of Oregon

Dennis Shannon, Southwestern Illinois College

David Shideler, Murray State University

Elias Shukralla, St. Louis Community College, Meramec

Anne Shugars, Harford Community College

Richard Sicotte, University of Vermont

Priyanka Singh, University of Texas, Dallas

Edward Skelton, Southern Methodist University

Ken Slaysman, York College

John Smith, New York University

Donald Snyder, Utah State University

Marcia Snyder, College of Charleston

John Solow, University of Iowa

Angela Sparkman, Itawamba Community College

Martin Spechler, Indiana University

Arun Srinivasa, Indiana University, Southeast

Sarah Stafford, College of William and Mary

Richard Stahl, Louisiana State University

Mary Stevenson, University of Massachusetts, Boston

Courtenay Stone, Ball State University

Edward Stuart, Northeastern Illinois University

Chuck Stull, Kalamazoo College

Della Sue, Marist College

Abdulhamid Sukar, Cameron University

Christopher Surfield, Saginaw Valley State University

Bernica Tackett, Pulaski Technical College

William Taylor, New Mexico Highlands University

Samia Costa Tavares, Rochester Institute of Technology

Henry Terrell, University of Maryland

Jennifer Thacher, University of New Mexico

Donna Thompson, Brookdale Community College

David Tolman, Boise State University

Susanne Toney, Hampton University

Boone Turchi, University of North Carolina, Chapel Hill

Kristin Van Gaasbeck, California State University, Sacramento

HuiKuan Tseng, University of North Carolina at Charlotte

Amy Vander Laan, Hastings College

William Walsh, University of St. Thomas

Chunbei Wang, University of St. Thomas

Bruce Webb, Gordon College

Ross Weiner, The City College of New York

Elaine Wendt, Milwaukee Area Technical College

Christopher Westley, Jacksonville State University

Robert Whaples, Wake Forest University

Alex Wilson, Rhode Island College

Wayne Winegarden, Marymount University

Jennifer Wissink, Cornell University

Arthur Woolf, University of Vermont

Bill Yang, Georgia Southern University

Jay Zagorsky, Boston University

Alexander Zampieron, Bentley College

Sourushe Zandvakili, University of Cincinnati

Walter J. Zeiler, University of Michigan

Reviewers of Previous Editions

The following individuals were of immense help in reviewing all or part of previous editions of this book and the teaching/learning package in various stages of development:

Lew Abernathy, University of North Texas

Jack Adams, University of Maryland

Douglas K. Adie, Ohio University

Douglas Agbetsiafa, Indiana University, South Bend

Sheri Aggarwal, University of Virginia

Sam Alapati, Rutgers University

John W. Allen, Texas A&M University

Polly Allen, University of Connecticut

Stuart Allen, University of North Carolina at Greensboro

Alex Anas, University at Buffalo, The State University of New York

Jim Angresano, Hampton-Sydney College

Kenneth S. Arakelian, University of Rhode Island

Harvey Arnold, Indian River Community College

Nick Apergis, Fordham University

Richard Ashley, Virginia Technical University

Kidane Asmeron, Pennsylvania State University

James Aylesworth, Lakeland Community College

Moshen Bahmani, University of Wisconsin-Milwaukee

Mohammad Bajwa, Northampton Community College

A. Paul Ballantyne, University of Colorado, Colorado Springs

Richard J. Ballman, Jr., Augustana College

King Banaian, St. Cloud State University

Kari Battaglia, University of North Texas

Leon Battista, Bronx Community College

Willie J. Belton, Jr., Georgia Institute of Technology

Daniel K. Benjamin, Clemson University

Charles A. Bennett, Gannon University

Daniel Berkowitz, University of Pittsburgh

Bruce Bolnick, Northeastern University

Frank Bonello, University of Notre Dame

Jeffrey Bookwalter, University of Montana

Maristella Botticini, Boston University

G. E. Breger, University of South Carolina

Dennis Brennan, William Rainey Harper Junior College

Anne E. Bresnock, California State Polytechnic University, Pomona, and the University of California, Los Angeles

David Brownstone, University of California, Irvine

Charles Callahan, III, State University of New York at Brockport

Lindsay Caulkins, John Carroll University

Atreya Chakraborty, Boston College

Winston W. Chang, University at Buffalo, The State University of New York

Janie Chermak, University of New Mexico

Harold Christensen, Centenary College

Daniel Christiansen, Albion College

Susan Christoffersen, Philadelphia University

Samuel Kim-Liang Chuah, Walla Walla College

David Colander, Middlebury College

Daniel Condon, University of Illinois at Chicago; Moraine Valley Community College

David Cowen, University of Texas, Austin

Peggy Crane, Southwestern College

Minh Quang Dao, Eastern Illinois University

Vernon J. Dixon, Haverford College

Michael Donihue, Colby College

Joanne M. Doyle, James Madison University

Robert Driskill, Ohio State University

James Dulgeroff, San Bernardino Valley College

Yvonne Durham, Western Washington University

Debra Sabatini Dwyer, State University of New York, Stony Brook

Gary Dymski, University of Southern California

David Eaton, Murray State University

Jay Egger, Towson State University

Ronald D. Elkins, Central Washington University

Noel J. J. Farley, Bryn Mawr College

Mosin Farminesh, Temple University

Dan Feaster, Miami University of Ohio

Susan Feiner, Virginia Commonwealth University

Getachew Felleke, Albright College

Lois Fenske, South Puget Sound Community College

William Field, DePauw University

Mary Flannery, Santa Clara University

Bill Foeller, State University of New York, Fredonia

Roger Nils Folsom, San Jose State University

Mathew Forstater, University of Missouri-Kansas City

Richard Fowles, University of Utah

Sean Fraley, College of Mount Saint Joseph

Roger Frantz, San Diego State University

Alejandro Gallegos, Winona State University

N. Galloro, Chabot College

Martin A. Garrett, Jr., College of William & Mary

Tom Gausman, Northern Illinois University

Shirley J. Gedeon, University of Vermont

Lisa Giddings, University of Wisconsin, La Crosse

Gary Gigliotti, Rutgers University

Lynn Gillette, Texas A&M University

Donna Ginther, University of Kansas

James N. Giordano, Villanova University

Sarah L. Glavin, Boston College

Roy Gobin, Loyola University, Chicago

Bill Goffe, University of Mississippi

Devra Golbe, Hunter College

Roger Goldberg, Ohio Northern University

Richard Gosselin, Houston Community College

John W. Graham, Rutgers University

Douglas Greenley, Morehead State University

Thomas A. Gresik, University of Notre Dame

Lisa M. Grobar, California State University, Long Beach

Wayne A. Grove, Syracuse University

Benjamin Gutierrez, Indiana University, Bloomington

A. R. Gutowsky, California State University, Sacramento

David R. Hakes, University of Missouri, St. Louis

Stephen Happel, Arizona State University

Mitchell Harwitz, University at Buffalo, The State University of New York

David Hoaas, Centenary College

Harry Holzer, Michigan State University

Bobbie Horn, University of Tulsa

John Horowitz, Ball State University

Janet Hunt, University of Georgia

E. Bruce Hutchinson, University of Tennessee, Chattanooga

Fred Inaba, Washington State University

Richard Inman, Boston College

Russell A. Janis, University of Massachusetts, Amherst

Eric Jensen, The College of William & Mary

Shirley Johnson, Vassar College

Farhoud Kafi, Babson College

R. Kallen, Roosevelt University

Arthur E. Kartman, San Diego State University

Hirshel Kasper, Oberlin College

Brett Katzman, Kennesaw State University

Bruce Kaufman, Georgia State University

Fred Keast, Portland State University

Stephanie Kelton, University of Missouri-Kansas City

Dominique Khactu, The University of North Dakota

Hwagyun Kim, State University of New York, Buffalo

Phillip King, San Francisco State University

Barbara Kneeshaw, Wayne County Community College

Inderjit Kohli, Santa Clara University

Heather Kohls, Marquette University

Barry Kotlove, Elmira College

David Kraybill, University of Georgia

Rosung Kwak, University of Texas at Austin

Steven Kyle, Cornell University

Anil K. Lal, Pittsburg State University

Melissa Lam, Wellesley College

Micheal Lawlor, Wake Forest University

Jim Lee, Fort Hays State University

Judy Lee, Leeward Community College

Sang H. Lee, Southeastern Louisiana University

Don Leet, California State University, Fresno

Robert J. Lemke, Lake Forest College

Gary Lemon, DePauw University

Alan Leonard, Northern Illinois University

Mary Lesser, Iona College

George Lieu, Tuskegee University

Stephen E. Lile, Western Kentucky University

Jane Lillydahl, University of Colorado at Boulder

Anthony K. Lima, California State University at Hayward

Al Link, University of North Carolina Greensboro

Charles R. Link, University of Delaware

Robert Litro, U.S. Air Force Academy

Ming Chien Lo, St. Cloud State University

Burl F. Long, University of Florida

Gerald Lynch, Purdue University

Karla Lynch, University of North Texas

Michael Magura, University of Toledo

Marvin S. Margolis, Millersville University of Pennsylvania

Don Maxwell, Central State University

Nan Maxwell, California State University
at Hayward

Cynthia S. McCarty, Jacksonville State
University

J. Harold McClure, Jr., Villanova University

Rick McIntyre, University of Rhode Island

James J. McLain, University of New Orleans

K. Mehtaboin, College of St. Rose

Art Meyer, Lincoln Land Community
College

Carrie Meyer, George Mason University

Meghan Millea, Mississippi State University

Jenny Minier, University of Miami

Shahruz Mohtadi, Suffolk University

Terry D. Monson, Michigan Tech University

Barbara A. Moore, University of Central
Florida

Joe L. Moore, Arkansas Technical University

Myra Moore, University of Georgia

Robert Moore, Occidental College

Norma C. Morgan, Curry College

W. Douglas Morgan, University of
California, Santa Barbara

John Murphy, North Shore Community
College, Massachusetts

Veena Nayak, University at Buffalo, The
State University of New York

Ron Necoechea, Robert Wesleyan College

Randy Nelson, Colby College

David Nickerson, University of British
Columbia

Rachel Nugent, Pacific Lutheran University

Akorlie A. Nyatepe-Coo, University of
Wisconsin LaCrosse

Norman P. Obst, Michigan State University

William C. O'Connor, Western Montana
College

Martha L. Olney, University of California,
Berkeley

Kent Olson, Oklahoma State University

Jaime Ortiz, Florida Atlantic University

Theresa Osborne, Hunter College

Donald J. Oswald, California State
University, Bakersfield

Niki Papadopoulou, University of Cyprus

Walter Park, American University

Carl Parker, Fort Hays State University

Spirog Patton, Neumann College

Mary Ann Pevas, Winona State University

Tony Pizelo, Spokane Community College

Mike Pogodzinski, San Jose State
University

Elizabeth Porter, University of North
Florida

Abe Qastin, Lakeland College

Kevin Quinn, St. Norbert College

Paul Rappoport, Temple University

Michael Rendich, Westchester
Community College

Lynn Rittenoure, University of Tulsa

Michael Rolleigh, University of Minnesota

S. Scanlon Romer, Delta College

David C. Rose, University of
Missouri-St. Louis

Greg Rose, Sacramento City College

Richard Rosenberg, Pennsylvania State
University

Robert Rosenman, Washington State
University

Paul Rothstein, Washington University

Jeff Rubin, Rutgers University

Mark Rush, University of Florida

Dereka Rushbrook, Ripon College

Jerard Russo, University of Hawaii

David L. Schaffer, Haverford College

Ramon Schreffler, Houston Community
College System (retired)

Jerry Schwartz, Broward Community
College

Gary Sellers, University of Akron

Jean Shackleford, Bucknell University

Linda Shaffer, California State University,
Fresno

Stephen L Shapiro, University of
North Florida

Geoff Shepherd, University of
Massachusetts Amherst

Bih-Hay Sheu, University of Texas at Austin

Alden Shiers, California Polytechnic State
University

Scott Simkins, North Carolina Agricultural
and Technical State University

Sue Skeath, Wellesley College

Paula Smith, Central State University,
Oklahoma

David Sobiechowski, Wayne State
University

John Solow, University of Iowa

David J. St. Clair, California State
University at Hayward

Rebecca Stein, University of Pennsylvania

Susan Stojanovic, Washington University,
St. Louis

Ernst W. Stromsdorfer, Washington State
University

Chris Stufflebean, Southwestern
Oklahoma State University

Rodney B. Swanson, University of
California, Los Angeles

James Swofford, University of Alabama

Michael Taussig, Rutgers University

Samia Tavares, Rochester Institute of
Technology

Timothy Taylor, Stanford University

Sister Beth Anne Tercek, SND, Notre
Dame College of Ohio

Henry Terrell, University of Maryland,
College Park

Robert Tokle, Idaho State University

Karen M. Travis, Pacific Lutheran
University

Jack Trierweler, Northern State University

Brian M. Trinque, University of Texas at
Austin

Ann Velenchik, Wellesley College

Lawrence Waldman, University of New
Mexico

Chris Waller, Indiana University,
Bloomington

Walter Wessels, North Carolina State
University

Joan Whalen-Ayyappan, DeVry Institute
of Technology

Robert Whaples, Wake Forest University

Leonard A. White, University of Arkansas

Paula Worthington, Northwestern
University

Ben Young, University of Missouri,
Kansas City

Darrel Young, University of Texas

Michael Youngblood, Rock Valley College

Abera Zeyege, Ball State University

James Ziliak, Indiana University,
Bloomington

Jason Zimmerman, South Dakota State
University

We welcome comments about the ninth edition. Please write to us care of Economics Editor, Prentice Hall Higher Education Division, One Lake Street, Upper Saddle River, NJ 07458.

Karl E. Case

Ray C. Fair

Sharon M. Oster

Save a Tree!
Many of the components of the teaching and learning package are available online. Online supplements conserve paper and allow you to select and print only the material you plan to use. For more information, please contact your Prentice Hall sales representative.

The Scope and Method of Economics

1

The study of economics should begin with a sense of wonder. Pause for a moment and consider a typical day in your life. It might start with a bagel made in a local bakery with flour produced in Minnesota from wheat grown in Kansas and bacon from pigs raised in Ohio packaged in plastic made in New Jersey. You spill coffee from Colombia on your shirt made in Texas from textiles shipped from South Carolina.

After class you drive with a friend on an interstate highway that is part of a system that took

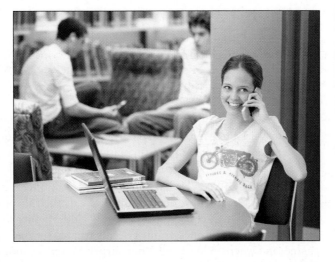

20 years and billions of dollars to build. You stop for gasoline refined in Louisiana from Saudi Arabian crude oil brought to the United States on a supertanker that took 3 years to build at a shipyard in Maine.

Later you log onto the Web with a laptop computer assembled in Indonesia from parts made in China and send an e-mail to your brother in Mexico City, and you call a buddy on a cell phone made by a company in Finland. Your call is picked up by a microwave dish hidden in a church steeple rented from the church by a cellular company that was just bought by a European conglomerate.

You use or consume tens of thousands of things, both tangible and intangible, every day: buildings, rock music, iPods, telephone services, staples, paper, toothpaste, tweezers, pizza, soap, digital watches, fire protection, banks, electricity, eggs, insurance, football fields, computers, buses, rugs, subways, health services, sidewalks, and so forth. Somebody made all these things. Somebody organized men and women and materials to produce and distribute them. Thousands of decisions went into their completion. Somehow they got to you.

In the United States, over 146 million people—almost half the total population—work at hundreds of thousands of different jobs producing over $14 trillion worth of goods and services every year. Some cannot find work; some choose not to work. Some are rich; others are poor.

The United States imports over $257 billion worth of automobiles and parts and about $229 billion worth of petroleum and petroleum products each year; it exports around $62 billion worth of agricultural products, including food. High-rise office buildings go up in central cities. Condominiums and homes are built in the suburbs. In other places, homes are abandoned and boarded up.

Some countries are wealthy. Others are impoverished. Some are growing. Some are not. Some businesses are doing well. Others are going bankrupt.

At any moment in time, every society faces constraints imposed by nature and by previous generations. Some societies are handsomely endowed by nature with fertile land, water, sunshine, and natural resources. Others have deserts and few mineral resources. Some societies receive much from previous generations—art, music, technical knowledge, beautiful buildings, and productive factories. Others are left with overgrazed, eroded land, cities leveled by war, or polluted natural environments. *All* societies face limits.

economics The study of
how individuals and societies
choose to use the scarce
resources that nature and
previous generations have
provided.

Economics is the study of how individuals and societies choose to use the scarce resources that nature and previous generations have provided. The key word in this definition is *choose*. Economics is a behavioral, or social, science. In large measure, it is the study of how people make choices. The choices that people make, when added up, translate into societal choices.

The purpose of this chapter and the next is to elaborate on this definition and to introduce the subject matter of economics. What is produced? How is it produced? Who gets it? Why? Is the result good or bad? Can it be improved?

Why Study Economics?

There are four main reasons to study economics: to learn a way of thinking, to understand society, to understand global affairs, and to be an informed citizen.

To Learn a Way of Thinking

Probably the most important reason for studying economics is to learn a way of thinking. Economics has three fundamental concepts that, once absorbed, can change the way you look at everyday choices: opportunity cost, marginalism, and the working of efficient markets.

Opportunity Cost What happens in an economy is the outcome of thousands of individual decisions. People must decide how to divide their incomes among all the goods and services available in the marketplace. They must decide whether to work, whether to go to school, and how much to save. Businesses must decide what to produce, how much to produce, how much to charge, and where to locate. It is not surprising that economic analysis focuses on the process of decision making.

Nearly all decisions involve trade-offs. A key concept that recurs in analyzing the decision-making process is the notion of *opportunity cost*. The full "cost" of making a specific choice includes what we give up by not making the alternative choice. The best alternative that we forgo, or give up, when we make a choice or a decision is called the **opportunity cost** of that decision.

opportunity cost The
best alternative that we forgo,
or give up, when we make a
choice or a decision.

When asked how much a movie costs, most people cite the ticket price. For an economist, this is only part of the answer: to see a movie takes not only a ticket but also time. The opportunity cost of going to a movie is the value of the other things you could have done with the same money and time. If you decide to take time off from work, the opportunity cost of your leisure is the pay that you would have earned had you worked. Part of the cost of a college education is the income you could have earned by working full-time instead of going to school. If a firm purchases a new piece of equipment for $3,000, it does so because it expects that equipment to generate more profit. There is an opportunity cost, however, because that $3,000 could have been deposited in an interest-earning account. To a society, the opportunity cost of using resources to launch astronauts on a space shuttle is the value of the private/civilian or other government goods that could have been produced with the same resources.

scarce Limited.

Opportunity costs arise because resources are scarce. **Scarce** simply means limited. Consider one of our most important resources—time. There are only 24 hours in a day, and we must live our lives under this constraint. A farmer in rural Brazil must decide whether it is better to continue to farm or to go to the city and look for a job. A hockey player at the University of Vermont must decide whether to play on the varsity team or spend more time studying.

marginalism The process
of analyzing the additional or
incremental costs or benefits
arising from a choice or
decision.

Marginalism A second key concept used in analyzing choices is the notion of **marginalism**. In weighing the costs and benefits of a decision, it is important to weigh only the costs and benefits that arise from the decision. Suppose, for example, that you live in New Orleans and that you are weighing the costs and benefits of visiting your mother in Iowa. If business required that you travel to Kansas City, the cost of visiting Mom would be only the additional, or *marginal*, time and money cost of getting to Iowa from Kansas City.

Consider the music business. To produce a typical CD, music labels spend approximately $300,000 on recording the music and music video, developing marketing materials, and distributing the album. Once the label has made this investment, physically producing another copy of the CD for sale typically costs about $2. When the music label is deciding whether to sign a new artist and produce a CD, the $300,000 investment is important. Companies such as EMI and Columbia Records spend a great deal of time thinking about whether a new CD by a newly discovered artist will sell enough copies to make a profit. But once an artist is signed and the investment is made and the music label is trying to decide whether to manufacture the 100,001st copy of a new CD, the key cost number is $2. Every new copy costs only $2, and as long as EMI can sell that copy for more than $2, it is better off making the copy. The original investment made to create the music is irrelevant—a **sunk cost**. Sunk costs are costs that cannot be avoided because they have already been incurred.

Technically, we call the incremental cost of producing one more unit of a good or service the *marginal cost*. One of the interesting changes in the music business is what has happened to the marginal cost of producing another copy of a CD given the introduction of iTunes as an alternative to the physical CD. While it is not always easy to figure out what the marginal cost is (and we will spend some time in this text honing your skills in this area), understanding the idea of marginalism when thinking about choices is critical.

There are numerous examples in which the concept of marginal cost is useful. For an airplane that is about to take off with empty seats, the marginal cost of an extra passenger is essentially zero; the total cost of the trip is roughly unchanged by the addition of an extra passenger. Thus, setting aside a few seats to be sold at big discounts through www.priceline.com or other Web sites can be profitable even if the fare for those seats is far below the average cost per seat of making the trip. As long as the airline succeeds in filling seats that would otherwise have been empty, doing so is profitable.

> **sunk costs** Costs that cannot be avoided because they have already been incurred.

Efficient Markets—No Free Lunch

Suppose you are ready to check out of a busy grocery store on the day before a storm and seven checkout registers are open with several people in each line. Which line should you choose? Usually, the waiting time is approximately the same no matter which register you choose (assuming you have more than 12 items). If one line is much shorter than the others, people will quickly move into it until the lines are equalized again.

As you will see later, the term *profit* in economics has a very precise meaning. Economists, however, often loosely refer to "good deals" or risk-free ventures as *profit opportunities*. Using the term loosely, a profit opportunity exists at the checkout lines when one line is shorter than the others. In general, such profit opportunities are rare. At any time, many people are searching for them; as a consequence, few exist. Markets like this, where any profit opportunities are eliminated almost instantaneously, are said to be **efficient markets**. (We discuss *markets*, the institutions through which buyers and sellers interact and engage in exchange, in detail in Chapter 2.)

> **efficient market** A market in which profit opportunities are eliminated almost instantaneously.

The common way of expressing the efficient markets concept is "there's no such thing as a free lunch." How should you react when a stockbroker calls with a hot tip on the stock market? With skepticism. Thousands of individuals each day are looking for hot tips in the market. If a particular tip about a stock is valid, there will be an immediate rush to buy the stock, which will quickly drive up its price. This view that very few profit opportunities exist can, of course, be carried too far. There is a story about two people walking along, one an economist and one not. The noneconomist sees a $20 bill on the sidewalk and says, "There's a $20 bill on the sidewalk." The economist replies, "That is not possible. If there were, somebody would already have picked it up."

There are clearly times when profit opportunities exist. Someone has to be first to get the news, and some people have quicker insights than others. Nevertheless, news travels fast and there are thousands of people with quick insights. The general view that large profit opportunities are rare is close to the mark.

The study of economics teaches us a way of thinking and helps us make decisions.

To Understand Society

Another reason for studying economics is to understand society better. Past and present economic decisions have an enormous influence on the character of life in a society. The current state of the physical environment, the level of material well-being, and the nature and number of jobs are all products of the economic system.

To get a sense of the ways in which economic decisions have shaped our environment, imagine looking out a top-floor window of an office tower in any large city. The workday is about to begin. All around you are other tall glass and steel buildings full of workers. In the distance, you see the smoke of factories. Looking down, you see thousands of commuters pouring off trains and buses and cars backed up on freeway exit ramps. You see trucks carrying goods from one place to another. You also see the face of urban poverty: Just beyond the freeway is a large public housing project and, beyond that, burned-out and boarded-up buildings.

What you see before you is the product of millions of economic decisions made over hundreds of years. People at some point decided to spend time and money building those buildings and factories. Somebody cleared the land, laid the tracks, built the roads, and produced the cars and buses.

Economic decisions not only have shaped the physical environment but also have determined the character of society. At no time has the impact of economic change on a society been more evident than in England during the late eighteenth and early nineteenth centuries, a period that we now call the **Industrial Revolution**. Increases in the productivity of agriculture, new manufacturing technologies, and development of more efficient forms of transportation led to a massive movement of the British population from the countryside to the city. At the beginning of the eighteenth century, approximately 2 out of 3 people in Great Britain worked in agriculture. By 1812, only 1 in 3 remained in agriculture; by 1900, the figure was fewer than 1 in 10. People jammed into overcrowded cities and worked long hours in factories. England had changed completely in two centuries—a period that in the run of history was nothing more than the blink of an eye.

It is not surprising that the discipline of economics began to take shape during this period. Social critics and philosophers looked around and knew that their philosophies must expand to accommodate the changes. Adam Smith's *Wealth of Nations* appeared in 1776. It was followed by the writings of David Ricardo, Karl Marx, Thomas Malthus, and others. Each tried to make sense out of what was happening. Who was building the factories? Why? What determined the level of wages paid to workers or the price of food? What would happen in the future, and what *should* happen? The people who asked these questions were the first economists.

Similar changes continue to affect the character of life in more recent times. In fact, many argue that the late 1990s marked the beginning of a new Industrial Revolution. As we turned the corner into the new millennium, the "e" revolution was clearly having an impact on virtually every aspect of our lives: the way we buy and sell products, the way we get news, the way we plan vacations, the way we communicate with each other, the way we teach and take classes, and on and on. These changes have had and will clearly continue to have profound impacts on societies across the globe, from Beijing to Calcutta to New York.

These changes have been driven by economics. Although the government was involved in the early years of the World Wide Web, private firms that exist to make a profit (such as Facebook, YouTube, Yahoo!, Microsoft, Google, Monster.com, Amazon.com, and E-Trade) created almost all the new innovations and products. How does one make sense of all this? What will the effects of these innovations be on the number of jobs, the character of those jobs, the family incomes, the structure of our cities, and the political process both in the United States and in other countries?

During the last days of August 2005, Hurricane Katrina slammed into the coasts of Louisiana and Mississippi, causing widespread devastation, killing thousands, and leaving hundreds of thousands homeless. The economic impact of this catastrophic storm was huge. Thinking about various markets involved helps frame the problem.

For example, the labor market was massively affected. By some estimates, over 400,000 jobs were lost as the storm hit. Hotels, restaurants, small businesses, and oil refineries, to name just a few, were destroyed. All the people who worked in those establishments instantly lost their jobs and their incomes. The cleanup and rebuilding process took time to organize, and it eventually created a great deal of employment.

The storm created a major disruption in world oil markets. Loss of refinery capacity sent gasoline prices up immediately, nearly 40 percent to over $4 per gallon in some locations. The

Industrial Revolution
The period in England during the late eighteenth and early nineteenth centuries in which new manufacturing technologies and improved transportation gave rise to the modern factory system and a massive movement of the population from the countryside to the cities.

price per gallon of crude oil rose to over $70 per barrel. Local governments found their tax bases destroyed, with no resources to pay teachers and local officials. Hundreds of hospitals were destroyed, and colleges and universities were forced to close their doors, causing tens of thousands of students to change their plans.

While the horror of the storm hit all kinds of people, the worst hit were the very poor, who could not get out of the way because they had no cars or other means of escape. The storm raised fundamental issues of fairness, which we will be discussing for years to come.

The study of economics is an essential part of the study of society.

To Understand Global Affairs

A third reason for studying economics is to understand global affairs. News headlines are filled with economic stories. International events often have enormous economic consequences. The destruction of the World Trade Center towers in New York City in 2001 and the subsequent war on terror in Afghanistan and elsewhere led to a huge decline in both tourism and business travel. Several major airlines, including U.S. Airways and Swissair, went bankrupt. Hotel operators worldwide suffered huge losses. The war in Iraq and a strike in Venezuela, a major oil exporter, in 2003 sent oil markets gyrating dramatically, initially increasing the cost of energy across the globe. The rapid spread of HIV and AIDS across Africa will continue to have terrible economic consequences for the continent and ultimately for the world.

Some claim that economic considerations dominate international relations. Certainly, politicians place the economic well-being of their citizens near the top of their priority lists. It would be surprising if that were not so. Thus, the economic consequences of things such as environmental policy, free trade, and immigration play a huge role in international negotiations and policies.

Great Britain and the other countries of the European Union have struggled with the agreement among most members to adopt a common currency, the euro. In 2005, France and the Netherlands rejected a proposed European constitution that would have gone a long way toward a completely open economy in Europe. The nations of the former Soviet Union are wrestling with a growing phenomenon that clouds their efforts to "privatize" formerly state-owned industries: organized crime.

Another important issue in today's world is the widening gap between rich and poor nations. In 2007, world population was over 6.5 billion. Of that number, over 2.4 billion lived in low-income (less than $900 annually per capita) countries and just over 1 billion lived in high-income (over $11,000 per capita per year) countries. The 37 percent of the world's population that lives in the low-income countries receives less than 3.3 percent of the world's income. In dozens of countries, per capita income is only a few hundred dollars a year. The 15 percent of the population in high-income countries earn 75 percent of the world's income.

An understanding of economics is essential to an understanding of global affairs.

To Be an Informed Citizen

A knowledge of economics is essential to being an informed citizen. During the last 35 years, the U.S. economy has been on a roller coaster. In 1973–1974, the Organization of Petroleum Exporting Countries (OPEC) succeeded in raising the price of crude oil by 400 percent. Simultaneously, a sequence of events in the world food market drove food prices up by 25 percent. By mid-1974, prices in the United States were rising across the board at a very rapid rate. Partially as a result of government policy to fight runaway inflation, the economy went into a recession in 1975. (An *inflation* is an increase in the overall price level in the economy; a *recession* is a period of decreasing output and rising unemployment.) The recession succeeded in slowing price increases, but in the process, millions found themselves unemployed.

From 1979 through 1983, it happened all over again. Prices rose rapidly, the government reacted with more policies designed to stop prices from rising, and the United States ended up with an even worse recession in 1982. By the end of that year, 10.8 percent of the work force was unemployed. Then, in mid-1990—after almost 8 years of strong economic performance—the

iPod and the World

It is impossible to understand the workings of an economy without first understanding the ways in which economies are connected across borders. The United States was importing goods and services at a rate of over $2 trillion per year in 2007 and was exporting at a rate of over $1.5 trillion per year.

For literally hundreds of years, the virtues of free trade have been the subject of heated debate. Opponents have argued that buying foreign-produced goods costs Americans jobs and hurts American producers. Proponents argue that there are gains from trade—that all countries can gain from specializing in the production of the goods and services that they produce best.

But in today's global economy, it is often unclear what is an import and what is an export. Consider the following column in *The New York Times* in 2007:

An iPod Has Global Value. Ask the (Many) Countries That Make It.

The New York Times

Who makes the Apple iPod? Here's a hint: It is not Apple. The company outsources the entire manufacture of the device to a number of Asian enterprises, among them Asustek, Inventec Appliances, and Foxconn.

But this list of companies isn't a satisfactory answer either: They only do final assembly. What about the 451 parts that go into the iPod? Where are they made and by whom?

Three researchers at the University of California, Irvine—Greg Linden, Kenneth L. Kraemer, and Jason Dedrick—applied some investigative cost accounting to this question, using a report from Portelligent Inc. that examined all the parts that went into the iPod.

Their study, sponsored by the Sloan Foundation, offers a fascinating illustration of the complexity of the global economy, and how difficult it is to understand that complexity by using only conventional trade statistics.

The retail value of the 30-gigabyte video iPod that the authors examined was $299. The most expensive component in it was the hard drive, which was manufactured by Toshiba and costs about $73. The next most costly components were the display module (about $20), the video/multimedia processor chip ($8), and the controller chip ($5). They estimated that the final assembly, done in China, cost only about $4 a unit.

The researchers estimated that $163 of the iPod's $299 retail value in the United States was captured by American companies and workers, breaking it down to $75 for distribution and retail costs, $80 to Apple, and $8 to various domestic component makers. Japan contributed about $26 to the value added (mostly via the Toshiba disk drive), while Korea contributed less than $1.

The real value of the iPod doesn't lie in its parts or even in putting those parts together. The bulk of the iPod's value is in the conception and design of the iPod. That is why Apple gets $80 for each of these video iPods it sells, which is by far the largest piece of value added in the entire supply chain.

Those clever folks at Apple figured out how to combine 451 mostly generic parts into a valuable product. They may not make the iPod, but they created it. In the end, that's what really matters.

Source: Hal R. Varian, Published: June 28, 2007, The New York Times, *reprinted with permission.*

U.S. economy went into another recession. During the third and fourth quarters of 1990 and the first quarter of 1991, *gross domestic product (GDP*, a measure of the total output of the U.S. economy) fell and unemployment again increased sharply. The election of Bill Clinton late in 1992 was no doubt in part influenced by the so-called "jobless recovery."

From the second quarter of 1991 through the early part of the new millennium, the U.S. economy experienced the longest expansion in its history. More than 24 million new jobs were created, pushing unemployment below 4 percent by the year 2000. The stock market boomed to historic levels, and the biggest worry facing the American economy was that things were too good!

The presidential election of 2000 was close, to say the least, with the outcome not known until early December. In mid-December, President-elect George W. Bush and his economic advisers began to worry about the possibility of a recession occurring in 2001. The stock market was below its highs for the year, corporate profits were not coming in as well as expected, and there were some signs that demand for goods was slowing.

Indeed, following the election, the economy slipped into a recession and economic conditions were made worse by the September 11, 2001, attacks on the World Trade Center and on the Pentagon. The stock market, which suffered losses as early as 2000, fell for 3 consecutive years, reducing people's wealth by trillions of dollars. Total employment dropped by nearly 2.7 million. But by 2002, the economy began to grow again, slowly, and by 2005, nearly 3.5 million jobs had been created.

The war in Iraq and the threat of international terrorism following the 9/11 attacks increased military expenditures in the United States substantially. At the same time, tax cuts proposed by President Bush and passed by Congress led to large deficits in the federal budget.

The housing market began to boom in 2001. Fueled by lower interest rates that made borrowing less expensive, foreign demand, and a highly competitive mortgage market that made mortgage credit available to virtually any applicant, house prices rose substantially around the country. Housing starts, the number of new housing units begun each period, rose steadily to a record high by 2005 of over 2 million annually. Sales of existing homes at the same time rose above 7 million per year. In addition, as house values rose, home owners had higher wealth and increased their spending. Much spending was driven by borrowing against the house. When you add all the services surrounding house sales, the huge spending on new units, and the purchases at stores such as Home Depot that go with new house sales, the economy was strongly stimulated by the housing market until the middle of 2006, when housing began to slow.

One of the key factors that fueled the housing boom was the expansion of mortgage credit to borrowers who in earlier years would have not have qualified. Some borrowers had bad credit histories, low incomes, or other substantial debts. These mortgages came to be called subprime loans. In addition, mortgage loans that carried low monthly payments for a few years that were later followed by substantially higher payments became prevalent.

In the summer of 2007, the housing market stalled, prices began to fall, and the huge amount of mortgage debt outstanding (over $10 trillion by 2007) experienced rising delinquency and default. Losses were huge and sent financial markets, including the stock market, into a sharp decline. The question at the start of 2008 was whether the sharp slowdown of the housing market combined with the problems of the credit markets would lead the economy as a whole into a recession.

To be an informed citizen requires a basic understanding of economics.

The Scope of Economics

Most students taking economics for the first time are surprised by the breadth of what they study. Some think that economics will teach them about the stock market or what to do with their money. Others think that economics deals exclusively with problems such as inflation and unemployment. In fact, it deals with all those subjects, but they are pieces of a much larger puzzle.

Economics has deep roots in and close ties to social philosophy. An issue of great importance to philosophers, for example, is distributional justice. Why are some people rich and others poor? And whatever the answer, is this fair? A number of nineteenth-century social philosophers wrestled with these questions, and out of their musings, economics as a separate discipline was born.

The easiest way to get a feel for the breadth and depth of what you will be studying is to explore briefly the way economics is organized. First of all, there are two major divisions of economics: microeconomics and macroeconomics.

Microeconomics and Macroeconomics

microeconomics The branch of economics that examines the functioning of individual industries and the behavior of individual decision-making units—that is, firms and households.

Microeconomics deals with the functioning of individual industries and the behavior of individual economic decision-making units: firms and households. Firms' choices about what to produce and how much to charge and households' choices about what and how much to buy help to explain why the economy produces the goods and services it does.

Another big question addressed by microeconomics is who gets the goods and services that are produced. Wealthy households get more than poor households, and the forces that determine this distribution of output are the province of microeconomics. Why does poverty exist? Who is poor? Why do some jobs pay more than others?

Think again about what you consume in a day and then think back to that view over a big city. Somebody decided to build those factories. Somebody decided to construct the roads, build the housing, produce the cars, and smoke the bacon. Why? What is going on in all those buildings? It is easy to see that understanding individual microdecisions is very important to any understanding of society.

macroeconomics The branch of economics that examines the economic behavior of aggregates—income, employment, output, and so on—on a national scale.

Macroeconomics looks at the economy as a whole. Instead of trying to understand what determines the output of a single firm or industry or what the consumption patterns are of a single household or group of households, macroeconomics examines the factors that determine national output, or national product. Microeconomics is concerned with *household* income; macroeconomics deals with *national* income.

Whereas microeconomics focuses on individual product prices and relative prices, macroeconomics looks at the overall price level and how quickly (or slowly) it is rising (or falling). Microeconomics questions how many people will be hired (or fired) this year in a particular industry or in a certain geographic area and focuses on the factors that determine how much labor a firm or an industry will hire. Macroeconomics deals with *aggregate* employment and unemployment: how many jobs exist in the economy as a whole and how many people who are willing to work are not able to find work.

To summarize:

> Microeconomics looks at the individual unit—the household, the firm, the industry. It sees and examines the "trees." Macroeconomics looks at the whole, the aggregate. It sees and analyzes the "forest."

Table 1.1 summarizes these divisions of economics and some of the subjects with which they are concerned.

TABLE 1.1 Examples of Microeconomic and Macroeconomic Concerns

Division of Economics	Production	Prices	Income	Employment
Microeconomics	*Production/output in individual industries and businesses* How much steel How much office space How many cars	*Prices of individual goods and services* Price of medical care Price of gasoline Food prices Apartment rents	*Distribution of income and wealth* Wages in the auto industry Minimum wage Executive salaries Poverty	*Employment by individual businesses and industries* Jobs in the steel industry Number of employees in a firm Number of accountants
Macroeconomics	*National production/output* Total industrial output Gross domestic product Growth of output	*Aggregate price level* Consumer prices Producer prices Rate of inflation	*National income* Total wages and salaries Total corporate profits	*Employment and unemployment in the economy* Total number of jobs Unemployment rate

The Diverse Fields of Economics

Individual economists focus their research and study in many diverse areas. Many of these specialized fields are reflected in the advanced courses offered at most colleges and universities. Some are concerned with economic history or the history of economic thought. Others focus on international economics or growth in less developed countries. Still others study the economics of cities (urban economics) or the relationship between economics and law. These fields are summarized in Table 1.2.

Economists also differ in the emphasis they place on theory. Some economists specialize in developing new theories, whereas other economists spend their time testing the theories of others. Some economists hope to expand the frontiers of knowledge, whereas other economists are more interested in applying what is already known to the formulation of public policies.

TABLE 1.2 The Fields of Economics

Comparative economic systems	examines the ways alternative economic systems function. What are the advantages and disadvantages of different systems?
Econometrics	applies statistical techniques and data to economic problems in an effort to test hypotheses and theories. Most schools require economics majors to take at least one course in statistics or econometrics.
Economic development	focuses on the problems of low-income countries. What can be done to promote development in these nations? Important concerns of development economists include population growth and control, provision for basic needs, and strategies for international trade.
Economic history	traces the development of the modern economy. What economic and political events and scientific advances caused the Industrial Revolution? What explains the tremendous growth and progress of post—World War II Japan? What caused the Great Depression of the 1930s?
Economics of race and gender	examines the role of race and gender in economic theory, in economic life, and in policymaking. How has discrimination by race or gender affected the well-being of households and the distribution of income and wealth?
Environmental economics	studies the potential failure of the market system to account fully for the impacts of production and consumption on the environment and on natural resource depletion. Have alternative public policies and new economic institutions been effective in correcting these potential failures?
Finance	examines the ways in which households and firms actually pay for, or finance, their purchases. It involves the study of capital markets (including the stock and bond markets), futures and options, capital budgeting, and asset valuation.
The history of economic thought,	which is grounded in philosophy, studies the development of economic ideas and theories over time, from Adam Smith in the eighteenth century to the works of economists such as Thomas Malthus, Karl Marx, and John Maynard Keynes. Because economic theory is constantly developing and changing, studying the history of ideas helps give meaning to modern theory and puts it in perspective.
Industrial organization	looks carefully at the structure and performance of industries and firms within an economy. How do businesses compete? Who gains and who loses?
International economics	studies trade flows among countries and international financial institutions. What are the advantages and disadvantages for a country that allows its citizens to buy and sell freely in world markets? Why is the dollar strong or weak?
Labor economics	deals with the factors that determine wage rates, employment, and unemployment. How do people decide whether to work, how much to work, and at what kind of job? How have the roles of unions and management changed in recent years?
Law and economics	analyzes the economic function of legal rules and institutions. How does the law change the behavior of individuals and businesses? Do different liability rules make accidents and injuries more or less likely? What are the economic costs of crime?
Public economics	examines the role of government in the economy. What are the economic functions of government, and what should they be? How should the government finance the services that it provides? What kinds of government programs should confront the problems of poverty, unemployment, and pollution? What problems does government involvement create?
Urban and regional economics	studies the spatial arrangement of economic activity. Why do we have cities? Why are manufacturing firms locating farther and farther from the center of urban areas?

As you begin your study of economics, look through your school's course catalog and talk to the faculty about their interests. You will discover that economics encompasses a broad range of inquiry and is linked to many other disciplines.

The Method of Economics

positive economics An approach to economics that seeks to understand behavior and the operation of systems without making judgments. It describes what exists and how it works.

normative economics An approach to economics that analyzes outcomes of economic behavior, evaluates them as good or bad, and may prescribe courses of action. Also called *policy economics.*

Economics asks and attempts to answer two kinds of questions: positive and normative. **Positive economics** attempts to understand behavior and the operation of economic systems *without making judgments* about whether the outcomes are good or bad. It strives to describe what exists and how it works. What determines the wage rate for unskilled workers? What would happen if we abolished the corporate income tax? The answers to such questions are the subject of positive economics.

In contrast, **normative economics** looks at the outcomes of economic behavior and asks whether they are good or bad and whether they can be made better. Normative economics involves judgments and prescriptions for courses of action. Should the government subsidize or regulate the cost of higher education? Should medical benefits to the elderly under Medicare be available only to those with incomes below some threshold? Should the United States allow importers to sell foreign-produced goods that compete with U.S.-produced products? Should we reduce or eliminate inheritance taxes? Normative economics is often called *policy economics.*

Of course, most normative questions involve positive questions. To know whether the government *should* take a particular action, we must know first if it *can* and second what the consequences are likely to be. (For example, if we lower import fees, will there be more competition and lower prices?)

Some claim that positive, value-free economic analysis is impossible. They argue that analysts come to problems with biases that cannot help but influence their work. Furthermore, even in choosing what questions to ask or what problems to analyze, economists are influenced by political, ideological, and moral views.

Although this argument has some merit, it is nevertheless important to distinguish between analyses that attempt to be positive and those that are intentionally and explicitly normative. Economists who ask explicitly normative questions should be forced to specify their grounds for judging one outcome superior to another.

Descriptive Economics and Economic Theory

descriptive economics The compilation of data that describe phenomena and facts.

Positive economics is often divided into descriptive economics and economic theory. **Descriptive economics** is simply the compilation of data that describe phenomena and facts. Examples of such data appear in the *Statistical Abstract of the United States*, a large volume of data published by the Department of Commerce every year that describes many features of the U.S. economy. Massive volumes of data can now be found on the World Wide Web. As an example, look at www.bls.gov (Bureau of Labor Statistics).

Where do all these data come from? The Census Bureau collects an enormous amount of raw data every year, as do the Bureau of Labor Statistics, the Bureau of Economic Analysis, and nongovernment agencies such as the University of Michigan Survey Research Center. One important study now published annually is the *Survey of Consumer Expenditure*, which asks individuals to keep careful records of all their expenditures over a long period of time. Another is the *National Longitudinal Survey of Labor Force Behavior*, conducted over many years by the Center for Human Resource Development at The Ohio State University.

economic theory A statement or set of related statements about cause and effect, action and reaction.

Economic theory attempts to generalize about data and interpret them. An **economic theory** is a statement or set of related statements about cause and effect, action and reaction. One of the first theories you will encounter in this text is the *law of demand*, which was most clearly stated by Alfred Marshall in 1890: When the price of a product rises, people tend to buy less of it; when the price of a product falls, people tend to buy more.

Theories do not always arise out of formal numerical data. All of us have been collecting observations of people's behavior and their responses to economic stimuli for most of our lives. We may have observed our parents' reaction to a sudden increase—or decrease—in income or to the loss of a job or the acquisition of a new one. We all have seen people standing in line waiting for a bargain. Of course, our own actions and reactions are another important source of data.

Theories and Models

In many disciplines, including physics, chemistry, meteorology, political science, and economics, theorists build formal models of behavior. A **model** is a formal statement of a theory. It is usually a mathematical statement of a presumed relationship between two or more variables.

A **variable** is a measure that can change from time to time or from observation to observation. Income is a variable—it has different values for different people and different values for the same person at different times. The rental price of a movie on a DVD is a variable; it has different values at different stores and at different times. There are countless other examples.

Because all models simplify reality by stripping part of it away, they are abstractions. Critics of economics often point to abstraction as a weakness. Most economists, however, see abstraction as a real strength.

The easiest way to see how abstraction can be helpful is to think of a map. A map is a representation of reality that is simplified and abstract. A city or state appears on a piece of paper as a series of lines and colors. The amount of reality that the mapmaker can strip away before the map loses something essential depends on what the map will be used for. If you want to drive from St. Louis to Phoenix, you need to know only the major interstate highways and roads. You lose absolutely nothing and gain clarity by cutting out the local streets and roads. However, if you need to get around Phoenix, you may need to see every street and alley.

Most maps are two-dimensional representations of a three-dimensional world; they show where roads and highways go but do not show hills and valleys along the way. Trail maps for hikers, however, have "contour lines" that represent changes in elevation. When you are in a car, changes in elevation matter very little; they would make a map needlessly complex and more difficult to read. However, if you are on foot carrying a 50-pound pack, a knowledge of elevation is crucial.

Like maps, economic models are abstractions that strip away detail to expose only those aspects of behavior that are important to the question being asked. The principle that irrelevant detail should be cut away is called the principle of **Ockham's razor** after the fourteenth-century philosopher William of Ockham.

Be careful—although abstraction is a powerful tool for exposing and analyzing specific aspects of behavior, it is possible to oversimplify. Economic models often strip away a good deal of social and political reality to get at underlying concepts. When an economic theory is used to help formulate actual government or institutional policy, political and social reality must often be reintroduced if the policy is to have a chance of working.

The key here is that the appropriate amount of simplification and abstraction depends on the use to which the model will be put. To return to the map example: you do not want to walk around San Francisco with a map made for drivers—there are too many very steep hills.

All Else Equal: *Ceteris Paribus* It is usually true that whatever you want to explain with a model depends on more than one factor. Suppose, for example, that you want to explain the total number of miles driven by automobile owners in the United States. The number of miles driven will change from year to year or month to month; it is a variable. The issue, if we want to understand and explain changes that occur, is what factors cause those changes.

Obviously, many things might affect total miles driven. First, more or fewer people may be driving. This number, in turn, can be affected by changes in the driving age, by population growth, or by changes in state laws. Other factors might include the price of gasoline, the household's income, the number and age of children in the household, the distance from home to work, the location of shopping facilities, and the availability and quality of public transport. When any of these variables change, the members of the household may drive more or less. If changes in any of these variables affect large numbers of households across the country, the total number of miles driven will change.

model A formal statement of a theory, usually a mathematical statement of a presumed relationship between two or more variables.

variable A measure that can change from time to time or from observation to observation.

Ockham's razor The principle that irrelevant detail should be cut away.

Very often we need to isolate or separate these effects. For example, suppose we want to know the impact on driving of a higher tax on gasoline. This change would raise the price of gasoline at the pump but would not (at least in the short run) affect income, workplace location, number of children, and so on.

ceteris paribus, *or* all else equal A device used to analyze the relationship between two variables while the values of other variables are held unchanged.

To isolate the impact of one single factor, we use the device of **ceteris paribus**, or **all else equal**. We ask: What is the impact of a change in gasoline price on driving behavior, *ceteris paribus*, or assuming that nothing else changes? If gasoline prices rise by 10 percent, how much less driving will there be, assuming no simultaneous change in anything else—that is, assuming that income, number of children, population, laws, and so on, all remain constant? Using the device of *ceteris paribus* is one part of the process of abstraction. In formulating economic theory, the concept helps us simplify reality to focus on the relationships that interest us.

Expressing Models in Words, Graphs, and Equations Consider the following statements: Lower airline ticket prices cause people to fly more frequently. Higher interest rates slow the rate of home sales. When firms produce more output, employment increases. Higher gasoline prices cause people to drive less and to buy more fuel-efficient cars.

Each of those statements expresses a relationship between two variables that can be quantified. In each case, there is a stimulus and a response, a cause and an effect. Quantitative relationships can be expressed in a variety of ways. Sometimes words are sufficient to express the essence of a theory, but often it is necessary to be more specific about the nature of a relationship or about the size of a response. The most common method of expressing the quantitative relationship between two variables is *graphing* that relationship on a two-dimensional plane. In fact, we will use graphic analysis extensively in Chapter 2 and beyond. Because it is essential that you be familiar with the basics of graphing, the Appendix to this chapter presents a careful review of graphing techniques.

Quantitative relationships between variables can also be presented through *equations*. For example, suppose we discovered that over time, U.S. households collectively spend, or consume, 90 percent of their income and save 10 percent of their income. We could then write:

$$C = .90\, Y \text{ and } S = .10Y$$

where C is consumption spending, Y is income, and S is saving. Writing explicit algebraic expressions like these helps us understand the nature of the underlying process of decision making. Understanding this process is what economics is all about.

Cautions and Pitfalls In formulating theories and models, it is especially important to avoid two pitfalls: the *post hoc* fallacy and the fallacy of composition.

The* Post Hoc *Fallacy Theories often make statements or sets of statements about cause and effect. It can be quite tempting to look at two events that happen in sequence and assume that the first caused the second to happen. This is not always the case. This common error is called the ***post hoc, ergo propter hoc*** (or "after this, therefore because of this") fallacy.

post hoc, ergo propter hoc Literally, "after this (in time), therefore because of this." A common error made in thinking about causation: If Event A happens before Event B, it is not necessarily true that A caused B.

There are thousands of examples. The Colorado Rockies have won seven games in a row. Last night you went to the game and they lost. You must have jinxed them. They lost *because* you went to the game.

Stock market analysts indulge in what is perhaps the most striking example of the *post hoc* fallacy in action. Every day the stock market goes up or down, and every day some analyst on some national news program singles out one or two of the day's events as *the* cause of some change in the market: "Today the Dow Jones industrial average rose 5 points on heavy trading; analysts say that the increase was due to progress in talks between Israel and Syria." Research has shown that daily changes in stock market averages are very largely random. Although major news events clearly have a direct influence on certain stock prices, most daily changes cannot be linked directly to specific news stories.

Very closely related to the *post hoc* fallacy is the often erroneous link between correlation and causation. Two variables are said to be *correlated* if one variable changes when the other variable changes. However, correlation does not imply causation. Cities that have high crime rates also have many automobiles, so there is a very high degree of correlation between number of cars and crime rates. Can we argue, then, that cars *cause* crime? No. The reason for the correlation may have nothing to do with cause and effect. Big cities have many people, many people have many cars; therefore, big cities have many cars. Big cities also have high crime rates for many reasons—crowding, poverty, anonymity, unequal distribution of wealth, and readily available drugs, to mention only a few. However, the presence of cars is probably not one of them.

This caution must also be viewed in reverse. Sometimes events that seem entirely unconnected actually *are* connected. In 1978, Governor Michael Dukakis of Massachusetts ran for reelection. Still quite popular, Dukakis was nevertheless defeated in the Democratic primary that year by a razor-thin margin. The weekend before, the Boston Red Sox, in the thick of the division championship race, had been badly beaten by the New York Yankees in four straight games. Some very respectable political analysts believe that hundreds of thousands of Boston sports fans vented their anger on the incumbent governor the following Tuesday.

The Fallacy of Composition   To conclude that what is true for a part is necessarily true for the whole is to fall into the **fallacy of composition**. Suppose that a large group of cattle ranchers graze their cattle on the same range. To an individual rancher, more cattle and more grazing mean a higher income. However, because its capacity is limited, the land can support only so many cattle. If every cattle rancher increased the number of cattle sent out to graze, the land would become overgrazed and barren; as a result, everyone's income would fall. In short, theories that seem to work well when applied to individuals or households often break down when they are applied to the whole.

fallacy of composition
The erroneous belief that what is true for a part is necessarily true for the whole.

Testing Theories and Models: Empirical Economics   In science, a theory is rejected when it fails to explain what is observed or when another theory better explains what is observed. Prior to the sixteenth century, almost everyone believed that Earth was the center of the universe and that the sun and stars rotated around it. The astronomer Ptolemy (A.D. 127 to 151) built a model that explained and predicted the movements of the heavenly bodies in a geocentric (Earth-centered) universe. Early in the sixteenth century, however, the Polish astronomer Nicholas Copernicus found himself dissatisfied with the Ptolemaic model and proposed an alternative theory or model, placing the sun at the center of the known universe and relegating Earth to the status of one planet among many. The battle between the competing models was waged, at least in part, with data based on observations—actual measurements of planetary movements. The new model ultimately predicted much better than the old, and in time it came to be accepted.

In the seventeenth century, building on the works of Copernicus and others, Sir Isaac Newton constructed yet another body of theory that seemed to predict planetary motion with still more accuracy. Newtonian physics became the accepted body of theory, relied on for almost 300 years. Then, in the early twentieth century, Albert Einstein's theory of relativity replaced Newtonian physics for particular types of problems because it was able to explain some problems that earlier theories could not.

Economic theories are also confronted with new and often conflicting data from time to time. The collection and use of data to test economic theories is called **empirical economics**.

Numerous large data sets are available to facilitate economic research. For example, economists studying the labor market can now test behavioral theories against the actual working experiences of thousands of randomly selected people who have been surveyed continuously since the 1960s by economists at The Ohio State University. Macroeconomists continuously monitoring and studying the behavior of the national economy pass thousands of items of data, collected by both government agencies and private companies, back and forth over the Internet.

empirical economics
The collection and use of data to test economic theories.

Scientific research often seeks to isolate and measure the responsiveness of one variable to a change in another variable, *ceteris paribus*. Physical scientists such as physicists and geologists can often impose the condition of *ceteris paribus* by conducting controlled experiments. They can, for example, measure the effect of one chemical on another while literally holding all else constant in an environment that they control completely. Social scientists, who study people, rarely have this luxury.

Although controlled experiments are difficult in economics and other social sciences, they are not impossible. During recent presidential and congressional elections, many candidates pointed to dramatic declines in crime rates in most American cities. Of course, incumbent candidates took credit, claiming that the decline was due to their policies. In fact, careful analysis shows that the decline in crime was largely due to two factors essentially beyond the control of political leaders: fewer people in the age groups that tend to commit crimes and a very strong economy with low unemployment. How do researchers know this? They look at data over time on crimes committed by people of various ages, they look at crime rates across states with different economic conditions, and they look at the pattern of crime rates nationally over time under different economic conditions. Even though economists cannot generally do controlled experiments, fluctuations in economic conditions and factors such as birthrate patterns in a way set up natural experiments.

Economic Policy

Economic theory helps us understand how the world works, but the formulation of *economic policy* requires a second step. We must have objectives. What do we want to change? Why? What is good and what is bad about the way the system is operating? Can we make it better?

Such questions force us to be specific about the grounds for judging one outcome superior to another. What does it mean to be better? Four criteria are frequently applied in judging economic outcomes:

1. Efficiency
2. Equity
3. Growth
4. Stability

Efficiency In physics, "efficiency" refers to the ratio of useful energy delivered by a system to the energy supplied to it. An efficient automobile engine, for example, is one that uses a small amount of fuel per mile for a given level of power.

efficiency In economics, allocative efficiency. An efficient economy is one that produces what people want at the least possible cost.

In economics, **efficiency** means *allocative efficiency*. An efficient economy is one that produces what people want at the least possible cost. If the system allocates resources to the production of goods and services that nobody wants, it is inefficient. If all members of a particular society were vegetarians and somehow half of all that society's resources were used to produce meat, the result would be inefficient. It is inefficient when steel beams lie in the rain and rust because somebody fouled up a shipping schedule. If a firm could produce its product using 25 percent less labor and energy without sacrificing quality, it too is inefficient.

The clearest example of an efficient change is a voluntary exchange. If you and I each want something that the other has and we agree to exchange, we are both better off and no one loses. When a company reorganizes its production or adopts a new technology that enables it to produce more of its product with fewer resources, without sacrificing quality, it has made an efficient change. At least potentially, the resources saved could be used to produce more of something.

Inefficiencies can arise in numerous ways. Sometimes they are caused by government regulations or tax laws that distort otherwise sound economic decisions. Suppose that land in Ohio is best suited for corn production and that land in Kansas is best suited for wheat production. A law that requires Kansas to produce only corn and Ohio to produce only wheat would be inefficient. If firms that cause environmental damage are not held accountable for their actions, the incentive to minimize those damages is lost and the result is inefficient.

equity Fairness.

Equity While efficiency has a fairly precise definition that can be applied with some degree of rigor, **equity** (fairness) lies in the eye of the beholder. To many, fairness implies a more equal distribution of income and wealth. Fairness may imply alleviating poverty, but the extent to which the poor should receive cash benefits from the government is the subject of enormous disagreement. For thousands of years, philosophers have wrestled with the principles of justice that should guide social decisions. They will probably wrestle with such questions for thousands of years to come.

Despite the impossibility of defining equity or fairness universally, public policy makers judge the fairness of economic outcomes all the time. Rent control laws were passed because some legislators thought that landlords treated low-income tenants unfairly. Certainly, most social welfare programs are created in the name of equity.

Growth As the result of technological change, the building of machinery, and the acquisition of knowledge, societies learn to produce new goods and services and to produce old ones better. In the early days of the U.S. economy, it took nearly half the population to produce the required food supply. Today less than 2.5 percent of the country's population works in agriculture.

When we devise new and better ways of producing the goods and services we use now and when we develop new goods and services, the total amount of production in the economy increases. **Economic growth** is an increase in the total output of an economy. If output grows faster than the population, output per capita rises and standards of living increase. Presumably, when an economy grows, it produces more of what people want. Rural and agrarian societies become modern industrial societies as a result of economic growth and rising per capita output.

economic growth An increase in the total output of an economy.

Some policies discourage economic growth, and others encourage it. Tax laws, for example, can be designed to encourage the development and application of new production techniques. Research and development in some societies are subsidized by the government. Building roads, highways, bridges, and transport systems in developing countries may speed up the process of economic growth. If businesses and wealthy people invest their wealth outside their country rather than in their country's industries, growth in their home country may be slowed.

Stability Economic **stability** refers to the condition in which national output is growing steadily, with low inflation and full employment of resources. During the 1950s and 1960s, the U.S. economy experienced a long period of relatively steady growth, stable prices, and low unemployment. Between 1951 and 1969, consumer prices never rose more than 5 percent in a single year and in only 2 years did the number of unemployed exceed 6 percent of the labor force. From the end of the Gulf War in 1991 to the beginning of 2001, the U.S. economy enjoyed price stability and strong economic growth with rising employment. It was the longest expansion in American history.

stability A condition in which national output is growing steadily, with low inflation and full employment of resources.

The decades of the 1970s and 1980s, however, were not as stable. The United States experienced two periods of rapid price inflation (over 10 percent) and two periods of severe unemployment. In 1982, for example, 12 million people (10.8 percent of the workforce) were looking for work. The beginning of the 1990s was another period of instability, with a recession occurring in 1990–1991. Around the world, economic fluctuations have been severe in recent years. During the late 1990s, many economies in Asia fell into recessions with falling incomes and rising unemployment. The transition economies of Eastern Europe and the former Soviet Union have experienced periods of decline as well as periods of rapidly rising prices since the fall of the Berlin Wall in 1989.

The causes of instability and the ways in which governments have attempted to stabilize the economy are the subject matter of macroeconomics.

An Invitation

This chapter has prepared you for your study of economics. The first part of the chapter invited you into an exciting discipline that deals with important issues and questions. You cannot begin to understand how a society functions without knowing something about its economic history and its economic system.

The second part of the chapter introduced the method of reasoning that economics requires and some of the tools that economics uses. We believe that learning to think in this very powerful way will help you better understand the world.

As you proceed, it is important that you keep track of what you have learned in earlier chapters. This book has a plan; it proceeds step-by-step, each section building on the last. It would be a good idea to read each chapter's table of contents at the start of each chapter and scan each chapter before you read it to make sure you understand where it fits in the big picture.

SUMMARY

1. *Economics* is the study of how individuals and societies choose to use the scarce resources that nature and previous generations have provided.

WHY STUDY ECONOMICS? *p. 2*

2. There are many reasons to study economics, including (a) to learn a way of thinking, (b) to understand society, (c) to understand global affairs, and (d) to be an informed citizen.

3. The best alternative that we forgo when we make a choice or a decision is the *opportunity cost* of that decision.

THE SCOPE OF ECONOMICS *p. 7*

4. *Microeconomics* deals with the functioning of individual markets and industries and with the behavior of individual decision-making units: business firms and households.

5. *Macroeconomics* looks at the economy as a whole. It deals with the economic behavior of aggregates—national output, national income, the overall price level, and the general rate of inflation.

6. Economics is a broad and diverse discipline with many special fields of inquiry. These include economic history, international economics, and urban economics.

THE METHOD OF ECONOMICS *p. 10*

7. Economics asks and attempts to answer two kinds of questions: positive and normative. *Positive economics* attempts to understand behavior and the operation of economies without making judgments about whether the outcomes are good or bad. *Normative economics* looks at the results of economic behavior and asks whether they are good or bad and whether they can be improved.

8. Positive economics is often divided into two parts. *Descriptive economics* involves the compilation of data that accurately describe economic facts and events. *Economic theory* attempts to generalize and explain what is observed. It involves statements of cause and effect—of action and reaction.

9. An economic *model* is a formal statement of an economic theory. Models simplify and abstract from reality.

10. It is often useful to isolate the effects of one variable on another while holding "all else constant." This is the device of *ceteris paribus*.

11. Models and theories can be expressed in many ways. The most common ways are in words, in graphs, and in equations.

12. Because one event happens before another, the second event does not necessarily happen as a result of the first. To assume that "after" implies "because" is to commit the fallacy of *post hoc, ergo propter hoc*. The erroneous belief that what is true for a part is necessarily true for the whole is the *fallacy of composition*.

13. *Empirical economics* involves the collection and use of data to test economic theories. In principle, the best model is the one that yields the most accurate predictions.

14. To make policy, one must be careful to specify criteria for making judgments. Four specific criteria are used most often in economics: *efficiency, equity, growth,* and *stability*.

REVIEW TERMS AND CONCEPTS

ceteris paribus, or all else equal, *p. 12*

descriptive economics, *p. 10*

economic growth, *p. 15*

economic theory, *p. 10*

economics, *p. 2*

efficiency, *p. 14*

efficient market, *p. 3*

empirical economics, *p. 13*

equity, *p. 14*

fallacy of composition, *p. 13*

Industrial Revolution, *p. 4*

macroeconomics, *p. 8*

marginalism, *p. 2*

microeconomics, *p. 8*

model, *p. 11*

normative economics, *p. 10*

Ockham's razor, *p. 11*

opportunity cost, *p. 2*

positive economics, *p. 10*

post hoc, ergo propter hoc, p. 12

scarce, *p. 2*

stability, *p. 15*

sunk costs, *p. 3*

variable, *p. 11*

PROBLEMS

1. One of the scarce resources that constrain our behavior is time. Each of us has only 24 hours in a day. How do you go about allocating your time in a given day among competing alternatives? How do you go about weighing the alternatives? Once you choose a most important use of time, why do you not spend all your time on it? Use the notion of opportunity cost in your answer.

2. In the summer of 2007, the housing market and the mortgage market were both in decline. Housing prices in most U.S. cities began to decline in mid-2006. With prices falling and the inventory of unsold houses rising, the production of new homes fell to around 1.5 million in 2007 from 2.3 million in 2005. With new construction falling dramatically, it was expected that construction *employment* would fall and that this would have the potential of slowing the national economy and increasing the general unemployment rate. Go to www.bls.gov and check out the recent data on total employment and construction employment. Have they gone up or down from their levels in August 2007? What has happened to the unemployment rate? Go to www.ofheo.gov and look at the housing price index. Have home prices risen or fallen since August 2007? Finally, look at the latest GDP release at www.bea.gov. Look at residential and nonresidential investment (Table 1.1.5) during the last 2 years. Do you see a pattern? Does it explain the employment numbers? Explain your answer.

3. Which of the following statements are examples of positive economic analysis? Which are examples of normative analysis?
   a. The inheritance tax should be repealed because it is unfair.
   b. Allowing Chile to join NAFTA would cause wine prices in the United States to drop.
   c. The first priorities of the new regime in the Democratic Republic of Congo (DRC, formerly Zaire) should be to rebuild schools and highways and to provide basic health care.

4. Selwyn signed up with an Internet provider for a fixed fee of $19.95 per month. For this fee, he gets unlimited access to the World Wide Web. During the average month in 2007, he was logged onto the Web for 17 hours. What is the average cost of an hour of Web time to Selwyn? What is the marginal cost of an additional hour?

5. A question facing many U.S. states is whether to allow casino gambling. States with casino gambling have seen a substantial increase in tax revenue flowing to state government. This revenue can be used to finance schools, repair roads, maintain social programs, or reduce other taxes.
   a. Recall that efficiency means producing what people want at the least cost. Can you make an efficiency argument in favor of allowing casinos to operate?
   b. What nonmonetary costs might be associated with gambling? Would these costs have an impact on the efficiency argument you presented in part **a**?
   c. Using the concept of equity, argue for or against the legalization of casino gambling.

6. For each of the following situations, identify the full cost (opportunity cost) involved:
   a. A worker earning an hourly wage of $8.50 decides to cut back to part-time to attend Houston Community College.
   b. Sue decides to drive to Los Angeles from San Francisco to visit her son, who attends UCLA.
   c. Tom decides to go to a wild fraternity party and stays out all night before his physics exam.
   d. Annie spends $200 on a new dress.
   e. The Confab Company spends $1 million to build a new branch plant that will probably be in operation for at least 10 years.
   f. Alex's father owns a small grocery store in town. Alex works 40 hours a week in the store but receives no compensation.

7. [Related to the *Economics in Practice* on *p. 6*] Log onto www.census.gov. Click on "Foreign Trade," then on "Statistics," and finally on "State Export Data." There you will find a list of the products produced in your state and exported to countries around the world. In looking over that list, are you surprised by anything? Do you know of any firms that produce these items? Search the Web to find a company that does. Do some research and write a paragraph about your company: what it produces, how many people it employs, and whatever else you can learn about the firm. You might even call the company to obtain the information.

APPENDIX

HOW TO READ AND UNDERSTAND GRAPHS

Economics is the most quantitative of the social sciences. If you flip through the pages of this or any other economics text, you will see countless tables and graphs. These serve a number of purposes. First, they illustrate important economic relationships. Second, they make difficult problems easier to understand and analyze. Finally, they can show patterns and regularities that may not be discernible in simple lists of numbers.

A **graph** is a two-dimensional representation of a set of numbers, or data. There are many ways that numbers can be illustrated by a graph.

TIME SERIES GRAPHS

It is often useful to see how a single measure or variable changes over time. One way to present this information is to plot the values of the variable on a graph, with each value corresponding to a different time period. A graph of this kind is called a **time series graph.** On a time series graph, time is measured along the horizontal scale and the variable being graphed is measured along the vertical scale. Figure 1A.1 is a time series graph that presents the total disposable personal income in the U.S. economy for each year between 1975 and 2006.[1] This graph is based on the data found in Table 1A.1. By displaying these data graphically, we can see that (1) total disposable personal income has increased steadily since 1975 and (2) during certain periods, income has increased at a faster rate than during other periods.

---

[1] The measure of income presented in Table 1A.1 and in Figure 1A.1 is disposable personal income in billions of dollars. It is the total personal income received by all households in the United States minus the taxes that they pay.

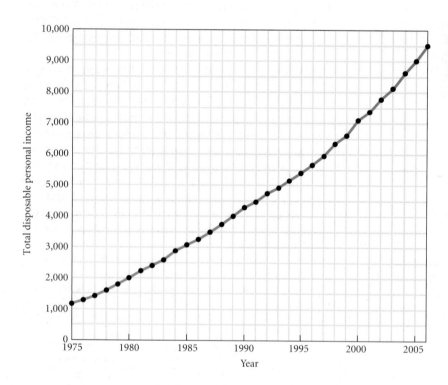

▲ FIGURE 1A.1 **Total Disposable Personal Income in the United States: 1975–2006 (in billions of dollars)**

Source: See Table 1A.1.

TABLE 1A.1	Total Disposable Personal Income in the United States, 1975–2006 (in billions of dollars)		
Year	Total Disposable Personal Income	Year	Total Disposable Personal Income
1975	1,181.4	1991	4,474.8
1976	1,299.9	1992	4,754.6
1977	1,436.0	1993	4,935.3
1978	1,614.8	1994	5,165.4
1979	1,808.2	1995	5,422.6
1980	2,019.8	1996	5,677.7
1981	2,247.9	1997	5,968.2
1982	2,406.8	1998	6,355.6
1983	2,586.0	1999	6,627.4
1984	2,887.6	2000	7,120.2
1985	3,086.5	2001	7,393.2
1986	3,262.5	2002	7,827.7
1987	3,459.5	2003	8,159.9
1988	3,752.4	2004	8,646.9
1989	4,016.3	2005	9,019.1
1990	4,293.6	2006	9,501.5

Source: U.S. Department of Commerce, Bureau of Economic Analysis.

GRAPHING TWO VARIABLES ON A CARTESIAN COORDINATE SYSTEM

More important than simple graphs of one variable are graphs that contain information on two variables at the same time. The most common method of graphing two variables is the **Cartesian coordinate system**. This system is constructed by drawing two perpendicular lines: a horizontal line, or **X-axis**, and a vertical line, or **Y-axis**. The axes contain measurement scales that intersect at 0 (zero). This point is called the **origin**. On the vertical scale, positive numbers lie above the horizontal axis (that is, above the origin) and negative numbers lie below it. On the horizontal scale, positive numbers lie to the right of the vertical axis (to the right of the origin) and negative numbers lie to the left of it. The point at which the graph intersects the Y-axis is called the **Y-intercept**. The point at which the graph intersects the X-axis is called the **X-intercept**.

When two variables are plotted on a single graph, each point represents a pair of numbers. The first number is measured on the X-axis, and the second number is measured on the Y-axis. For example, the following points (X, Y) are plotted on the set of axes drawn in Figure 1A.2: (4, 2), (2, −1), (−3, 4), (−3, −2). Most, but not all, of the graphs in this book are plots of two variables where both values are positive numbers [such as (4, 2) in Figure 1A.2]. On these graphs, only the upper right quadrant of the coordinate system (that is, the quadrant in which all X and Y values are positive) will be drawn.

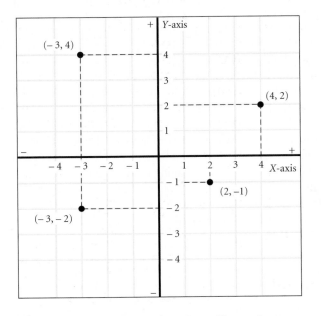

▲ **FIGURE 1A.2 A Cartesian Coordinate System**

A Cartesian coordinate system is constructed by drawing two perpendicular lines: a vertical axis (the Y-axis) and a horizontal axis (the X-axis). Each axis is a measuring scale.

PLOTTING INCOME AND CONSUMPTION DATA FOR HOUSEHOLDS

Table 1A.2 presents data collected by the Bureau of Labor Statistics (BLS). In a recent survey, 5,000 households were asked to keep track of all their expenditures. This table shows average income and average spending for those households, ranked by income. For example, the average income for the top fifth (20 percent) of the households was $147,737. The average spending for the top 20 percent was $90,469.

Figure 1A.3 presents the numbers from Table 1A.2 graphically using the Cartesian coordinate system. Along the horizontal scale, the X-axis, we measure average income. Along the vertical scale, the Y-axis, we measure average consumption spending. Each of the five pairs of numbers from the table is represented by a point on the graph. Because all numbers are positive numbers, we need to show only the upper right quadrant of the coordinate system.

To help you read this graph, we have drawn a dotted line connecting all the points where consumption and income would be equal. *This 45° line does not represent any data.* Instead, it represents the line along which all variables on the X-axis correspond exactly to the variables on the Y-axis, for example, [10,000, 10,000], [20,000, 20,000], and [37,000, 37,000]. The heavy blue line traces the data; the purpose of the dotted line is to help you read the graph.

There are several things to look for when reading a graph. The first thing you should notice is whether the line slopes upward or downward as you move from left to right. The blue line in Figure 1A.3 slopes upward, indicating that there seems to be a **positive relationship** between income and spending: The higher a household's income, the more a household tends to consume. If we had graphed the percentage of each group receiving welfare payments along the Y-axis, the line would presumably slope downward, indicating that welfare payments are lower at higher income levels. The income level/welfare payment relationship is thus a **negative relationship**.

TABLE 1A.2	Consumption Expenditures and Income, 2005	
	Average Income Before Taxes	Average Consumption Expenditures
Bottom fifth	$ 9,676	$19,120
2nd fifth	25,546	28,921
3rd fifth	42,622	39,098
4th fifth	67,813	54,354
Top fifth	147,737	90,469

Source: Consumer Expenditures in 2005, U.S. Bureau of Labor Statistics; Report 998, Feb. 2007.

▶ **FIGURE 1A.3**

Household Consumption and Income

A graph is a simple two-dimensional geometric representation of data. This graph displays the data from Table 1A.2. Along the horizontal scale (*X*-axis), we measure household income. Along the vertical scale (*Y*-axis), we measure household consumption. *Note*: At point *A*, consumption equals $19,120 and income equals $9,676. At point *B*, consumption equals $28,921 and income equals $25,546.

Source: See Table 1A.2.

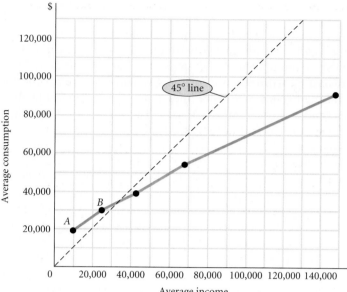

SLOPE

The **slope** of a line or curve is a measure that indicates whether the relationship between the variables is positive or negative and how much of a response there is in *Y* (the variable on the vertical axis) when *X* (the variable on the horizontal axis) changes. The slope of a line between two points is the change in the quantity measured on the *Y*-axis divided by the change in the quantity measured on the *X*-axis. We will normally use Δ (the Greek letter *delta*) to refer to a change in a variable. In Figure 1A.4, the slope of the line between points *A* and *B* is Δ*Y* divided by Δ*X*. Sometimes it is easy to remember slope as "the rise over the run," indicating the vertical change over the horizontal change.

To be precise, Δ*X* between two points on a graph is simply X_2 minus X_1, where X_2 is the *X* value for the second point and X_1 is the *X* value for the first point. Similarly, Δ*Y* is defined as Y_2 minus Y_1, where Y_2 is the *Y* value for the second point and Y_1 is the *Y* value for the first point. Slope is equal to

$$\frac{\Delta Y}{\Delta X} = \frac{Y_2 - Y_1}{X_2 - X_1}$$

As we move from *A* to *B* in Figure 1A.4(a), both *X* and *Y* increase; the slope is thus a positive number. However, as we move from *A* to *B* in Figure 1A.4(b), *X* increases [$(X_2 - X_1)$ is a positive number], but *Y* decreases [$(Y_2 - Y_1)$ is a negative number]. The slope in Figure 1A.4(b) is thus a negative number, because a negative number divided by a positive number results in a negative quotient.

To calculate the numerical value of the slope between points *A* and *B* in Figure 1A.3, we need to calculate Δ*Y* and Δ*X*. Because consumption is measured on the *Y*-axis, Δ*Y* is 9,801 [$(Y_2 - Y_1) = (28,921 - 19,120)$]. Because income is measured along the *X*-axis, Δ*X* is 15,870 [$(X_2 - X_1) = (25,546 - 9,676)$]. The slope between *A* and *B* is Δ*Y*/Δ*X* = 9,801/15,870 = + 0.62.

Another interesting thing to note about the data graphed in Figure 1A.3 is that all the points lie roughly along a straight line. (If you look very closely, however, you can see that the slope declines as you move from left to right; the line becomes slightly less steep.) A straight line has a constant slope. That is, if you pick any two points along it and calculate the slope, you will always get the same number. A horizontal line has a zero slope (Δ*Y* is zero); a vertical line has an "infinite" slope because Δ*Y* is too big to be measured.

▶ **FIGURE 1A.4 A Curve with (a) Positive Slope and (b) Negative Slope**

A *positive* slope indicates that increases in *X* are associated with increases in *Y* and that decreases in *X* are associated with decreases in *Y*. A *negative* slope indicates the opposite—when *X* increases, *Y* decreases; and when *X* decreases, *Y* increases.

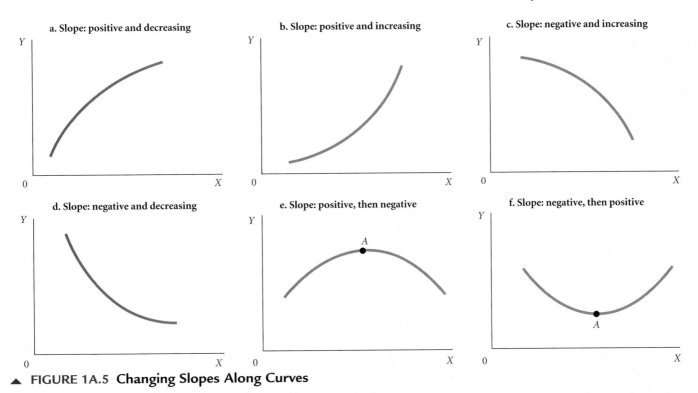

a. Slope: positive and decreasing

b. Slope: positive and increasing

c. Slope: negative and increasing

d. Slope: negative and decreasing

e. Slope: positive, then negative

f. Slope: negative, then positive

▲ **FIGURE 1A.5 Changing Slopes Along Curves**

Unlike the slope of a straight line, the slope of a *curve* is continually changing. Consider, for example, the curves in Figure 1A.5. Figure 1A.5(a) shows a curve with a positive slope that decreases as you move from left to right. The easiest way to think about the concept of increasing or decreasing slope is to imagine what it is like walking up a hill from left to right. If the hill is steep, as it is in the first part of Figure 1A.5(a), you are moving more in the Y direction for each step you take in the X direction. If the hill is less steep, as it is further along in Figure 1A.5(a), you are moving less in the Y direction for every step you take in the X direction. Thus, when the hill is steep, slope $(\Delta Y/\Delta X)$ is a larger number than it is when the hill is flatter. The curve in Figure 1A.5(b) has a positive slope, but its slope *increases* as you move from left to right.

The same analogy holds for curves that have a negative slope. Figure 1A.5(c) shows a curve with a negative slope that increases (in absolute value) as you move from left to right. This time think about skiing down a hill. At first, the descent in Figure 1A.5(c) is gradual (low slope); but as you proceed down the hill (to the right), you descend more quickly (high slope). Figure 1A.5(d) shows a curve with a negative slope that *decreases* (in absolute value) as you move from left to right.

In Figure 1A.5(e), the slope goes from positive to negative as X increases. In Figure 1A.5(f), the slope goes from negative to positive. At point A in both, the slope is zero. [Remember, slope is defined as $\Delta Y/\Delta X$. At point A, Y is not changing $(\Delta Y = 0)$. Therefore, slope at point A is zero.]

SOME PRECAUTIONS

When you read a graph, it is important to think carefully about what the points in the space defined by the axes represent. Table 1A.3 and Figure 1A.6 present a graph of consumption and income that is very different from the one in Table 1A.2 and Figure 1A.3. First, each point in Figure 1A.6 represents a different year; in Figure 1A.3, each point represented a different group of households at the *same* point in time (2005). Second, the points in Figure 1A.6 represent *aggregate* consumption and income for the whole nation measured in *billions* of dollars; in Figure 1A.3, the points represented average *household* income and consumption measured in dollars.

It is interesting to compare these two graphs. All points on the aggregate consumption curve in Figure 1A.6 lie below the 45° line, which means that aggregate consumption is always less than aggregate income. However, the graph of average household income and consumption in Figure 1A.3 crosses the 45° line, implying that for some households, consumption is larger than income.

TABLE 1A.3	Aggregate National Income and Consumption for the United States, 1930–2006 (in billions of dollars)	
	Aggregate National Income	**Aggregate Consumption**
1930	75.6	70.2
1940	81.1	71.2
1950	241.0	192.7
1960	427.5	332.3
1970	837.5	648.9
1980	2,243.0	1,762.9
1990	4,642.1	3,831.5
2000	7,984.4	6,683.7
2004	10,306.8	8,195.9
2005	10,887.6	8,707.8
2006	11,655.6	9,224.5

Source: U.S. Department of Commerce, Bureau of Economic Analysis.

▶ **FIGURE 1A.6 National Income and Consumption**

It is important to think carefully about what is represented by points in the space defined by the axes of a graph. In this graph, we have graphed income with consumption, as in Figure 1A.3, but here each observation point is national income and aggregate consumption in *different years*, measured in billions of dollars.

Source: See Table 1A.3.

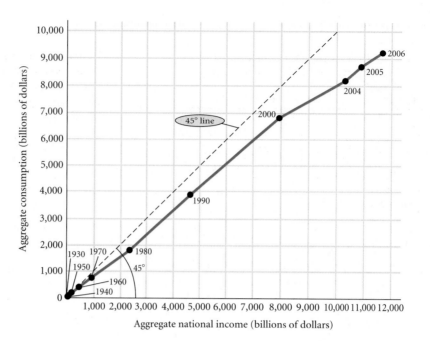

SUMMARY

1. A *graph* is a two-dimensional representation of a set of numbers, or data. A *time series graph* illustrates how a single variable changes over time.

2. The most common method of graphing two variables on one graph is the *Cartesian coordinate system*, which includes an *X* (horizontal)-*axis* and a *Y* (vertical)-*axis*. The points at which the two axes intersect is called the *origin*. The point at which a graph intersects the *Y*-axis is called the *Y-intercept*. The point at which a graph intersects the *X*-axis is called the *X-intercept*.

3. The *slope* of a line or curve indicates whether the relationship between the two variables graphed on a Cartesian coordinate system is positive or negative and how much of a response there is in *Y* (the variable on the vertical axis) when *X* (the variable on the horizontal axis) changes. The slope of a line between two points is the change in the quantity measured on the *Y*-axis divided by the change in the quantity measured on the *X*-axis.

REVIEW TERMS AND CONCEPTS

Cartesian coordinate system A common method of graphing two variables that makes use of two perpendicular lines against which the variables are plotted. *p. 19*

graph A two-dimensional representation of a set of numbers, or data. *p. 18*

negative relationship A relationship between two variables, *X* and *Y*, in which a decrease in *X* is associated with an increase in *Y* and an increase in *X* is associated with a decrease in *Y*. *p. 19*

origin On a Cartesian coordinate system, the point at which the horizontal and vertical axes intersect. *p. 19*

positive relationship A relationship between two variables, *X* and *Y*, in which a decrease in *X* is associated with a decrease in *Y*, and an increase in *X* is associated with an increase in *Y*. *p. 19*

slope A measurement that indicates whether the relationship between variables is positive or negative and how much of a response there is in *Y* (the variable on the vertical axis) when *X* (the variable on the horizontal axis) changes. *p. 20*

time series graph A graph illustrating how a variable changes over time. *p. 18*

X-axis On a Cartesian coordinate system, the horizontal line against which a variable is plotted. *p. 19*

X-intercept The point at which a graph intersects the *X*-axis. *p. 19*

Y-axis On a Cartesian coordinate system, the vertical line against which a variable is plotted. *p. 19*

Y-intercept The point at which a graph intersects the *Y*-axis. *p. 19*

PROBLEMS

1. Graph each of the following sets of numbers. Draw a line through the points and calculate the slope of each line.

1		2		3		4		5		6	
X	Y	X	Y	X	Y	X	Y	X	Y	X	Y
1	5	1	25	0	0	0	40	0	0	0.1	100
2	10	2	20	10	10	10	30	10	10	0.2	75
3	15	3	15	20	20	20	20	20	20	0.3	50
4	20	4	10	30	30	30	10	30	10	0.4	25
5	25	5	5	40	40	40	0	40	0	0.5	0

2. For each of the graphs in Figure 1, determine whether the curve has a positive or negative slope. Give an intuitive explanation for what is happening with the slope of each curve.

3. For each of the following equations, graph the line and calculate its slope.
  a. $P = 10 - 2q_D$ (Put q_D on the X-axis.)
  b. $P = 100 - 4q_D$ (Put q_D on the X-axis.)
  c. $P = 50 + 6q_S$ (Put q_S on the X-axis.)
  d. $I = 10,000 - 500r$ (Put I on the X-axis.)

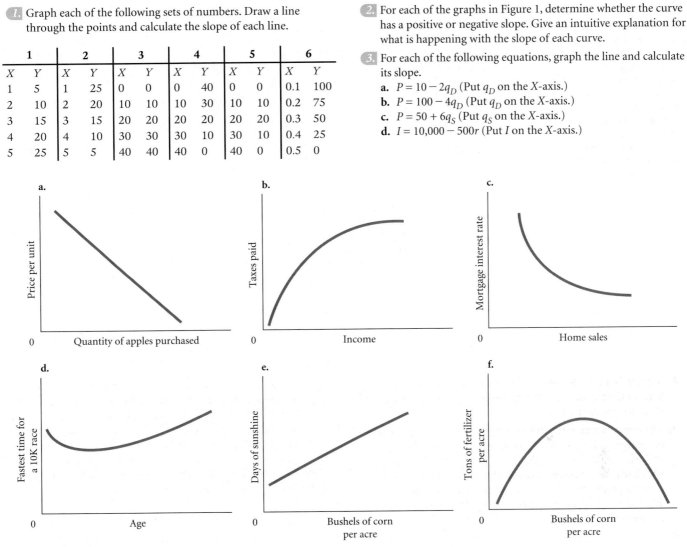

▲ **FIGURE 1**

The Economic Problem: Scarcity and Choice

2

Chapter 1 began with a very broad definition of economics. Every society, no matter how small or large, no matter how simple or complex, has a system or process that works to transform the resources that nature and previous generations provide into useful form. Economics is the study of that process and its outcomes.

Figure 2.1 illustrates three basic questions that must be answered to understand the functioning of the economic system:

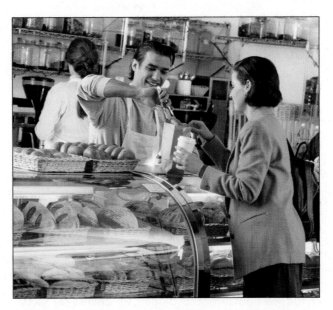

- What gets produced?
- How is it produced?
- Who gets what is produced?

This chapter explores these questions in detail. In a sense, this entire chapter *is* the definition of economics. It lays out the central problems addressed by the discipline and presents a framework that will guide you through the rest of the book. The starting point is the presumption that *human wants are unlimited but resources are not.* Limited or scarce resources force individuals and societies to choose among competing uses of resources—alternative combinations of produced goods and services—and among alternative final distributions of what is produced among households.

These questions are *positive* or *descriptive.* That is, they ask how the system functions without passing judgment about whether the result is good or bad. They must be answered first before we ask more normative questions such as these:

- Is the outcome good or bad?
- Can it be improved?

The term *resources* is very broad. The sketch on the left side of Figure 2.1 shows several categories of resources. Some resources are the products of nature: land, wildlife, fertile soil, minerals, timber, energy, and even the rain and wind. In addition, the resources available to an economy include things such as buildings and equipment that have been produced in the past but are now being used to produce other things. And perhaps the most important resource of a society is its human workforce with people's talents, skills, and knowledge.

Things that are produced and then used in the production of other goods and services are called capital resources, or simply **capital**. Buildings, equipment, desks, chairs, software, roads, bridges, and highways are a part of the nation's stock of capital.

The basic resources available to a society are often referred to as **factors of production**, or simply **factors**. The three key factors of production are land, labor, and capital. The process that transforms scarce resources into useful goods and services is called **production**. In many societies, most of the production of goods and services is done by private firms. Private airlines in

capital Things that are produced and then used in the production of other goods and services.

factors of production (or factors) The inputs into the process of production. Another term for resources.

production The process that transforms scarce resources into useful goods and services.

The three basic questions:

1. What gets produced?   **2. How is it produced?**   **3. Who gets what is produced?**

Mix of output

Resources   **Producers**   **Households**

Allocation of resources   Distribution of output

▲ **FIGURE 2.1 The Three Basic Questions**
Every society has some system or process that transforms its scarce resources into useful goods and services. In doing so, it must decide what gets produced, how it is produced, and to whom it is distributed. The primary resources that must be allocated are land, labor, and capital.

the United States use land (runways), labor (pilots and mechanics), and capital (airplanes) to produce transportation services. But in all societies, some production is done by the public sector, or government. Examples of government-produced or government-provided goods and services include national defense, public education, police protection, and fire protection.

Resources or factors of production are the **inputs** into the process of production; goods and services of value to households are the **outputs** of the process of production.

inputs *or* **resources**
Anything provided by nature or previous generations that can be used directly or indirectly to satisfy human wants.

outputs Goods and services of value to households.

Scarcity, Choice, and Opportunity Cost

In the second half of this chapter we discuss the global economic landscape. Before you can understand the different types of economic systems, it is important to master the basic economic concepts of scarcity, choice, and opportunity cost.

Scarcity and Choice in a One-Person Economy

The simplest economy is one in which a single person lives alone on an island. Consider Bill, the survivor of a plane crash, who finds himself cast ashore in such a place. Here individual and society are one; there is no distinction between social and private. *Nonetheless, nearly all the same basic decisions that characterize complex economies must also be made in a simple economy.* That is, although Bill will get whatever he produces, he still must decide how to allocate the island's resources, what to produce, and how and when to produce it.

First, Bill must decide *what* he wants to produce. Notice that the word *needs* does not appear here. Needs are absolute requirements; but beyond just enough water, basic nutrition, and shelter to survive, needs are very difficult to define. What is an "absolute necessity" for one person may not be for another person. In any case, Bill must put his wants in some order of priority and make some choices.

Next, he must look at the *possibilities*. What can he do to satisfy his wants given the limits of the island? In every society, no matter how simple or complex, people are constrained in what they can do. In this society of one, Bill is constrained by time, his physical condition, his knowledge, his skills, and the resources and climate of the island.

Given that resources are limited, Bill must decide *how* to best use them to satisfy his hierarchy of wants. Food would probably come close to the top of his list. Should he spend his time gathering fruits and berries? Should he hunt for game? Should he clear a field and plant seeds? The answers to those questions depend on the character of the island, its climate, its flora and fauna (*are* there any fruits and berries?), the extent of his skills and knowledge (does he know anything about farming?), and his preferences (he may be a vegetarian).

Opportunity Cost The concepts of *constrained choice* and *scarcity* are central to the discipline of economics. They can be applied when discussing the behavior of individuals such as Bill and when analyzing the behavior of large groups of people in complex societies.

Given the scarcity of time and resources, if Bill decides to hunt, he will have less time to gather fruits and berries. He faces a trade-off between meat and fruit. There is a trade-off between food and shelter too. If Bill likes to be comfortable, he may work on building a nice place to live, but that may require giving up the food he might have produced. As we noted in Chapter 1, the best alternative that we give up, or forgo, when we make a choice is the **opportunity cost** of that choice.

Bill may occasionally decide to rest, to lie on the beach, and to enjoy the sun. In one sense, that benefit is free—he does not have to buy a ticket to lie on the beach. In reality, however, relaxing does have an opportunity cost. The true cost of that leisure is the value of the other things Bill could have produced, but did not, during the time he spent on the beach.

The Houston Dynamos are a championship soccer team currently playing in an old arena on the University of Houston campus. In the summer of 2007, the Harris County Houston Sports Authority and local politicians were actively debating whether to spend taxpayers money on a new arena for the team. An important part of that debate was the opportunity cost of the taxpayers' dollars: what else could tax dollars be spent on, and how much value would the alternatives bring to the local taxpayers? Perhaps without the new arena, taxes could be lower. Here the opportunity cost would include the value taxpayers receive from goods and services they would consume with the earnings that are no longer taxed. Most discussions of public expenditures at all levels of government include active considerations of opportunity costs.

In making everyday decisions, it is often helpful to think about opportunity costs. Should you go to the dorm party or not? First, it costs $4 to attend. When you pay money for anything, you give up the other things you could have bought with that money. Second, it costs 2 or 3 hours. Time is a valuable commodity for a college student. You have exams next week, and you need to study. You could go to a movie instead of the party. You could go to another party. You could sleep. Just as Bill must weigh the value of sunning on the beach against more food or better housing, so you must weigh the value of the fun you may have at the party against everything else you might otherwise do with the time and money.

opportunity cost The best alternative that we give up, or forgo, when we make a choice or decision.

Scarcity and Choice in an Economy of Two or More

Now suppose that another survivor of the crash, Colleen, appears on the island. Now that Bill is not alone, things are more complex and some new decisions must be made. Bill's and Colleen's preferences about what things to produce are likely to be different. They will probably not have the same knowledge or skills. Perhaps Colleen is very good at tracking animals and Bill has a knack for building things. How should they split the work that needs to be done? Once things are produced, the two castaways must decide how to divide them. How should their products be distributed?

The mechanism for answering these fundamental questions is clear when Bill is alone on the island. The "central plan" is his; he simply decides what he wants and what to do about it. The minute someone else appears, however, a number of decision-making arrangements immediately become possible. One or the other may take charge, in which case that person will decide for both of them. The two may agree to cooperate, with each having an equal say, and come up with a joint plan; or they may agree to split the planning as well as the production duties. Finally, they may go off to live alone at opposite ends of the island. Even if they live apart, however, they may take advantage of each other's presence by specializing and trading.

Modern industrial societies must answer the same questions that Colleen and Bill must answer, but the mechanics of larger economies are more complex. Instead of two people living together, the United States has over 300 million people. Still, decisions must be made about what to produce, how to produce it, and who gets it.

Specialization, Exchange, and Comparative Advantage The idea that members of society benefit by specializing in what they do best has a long history and is one of the most important and powerful ideas in all of economics. David Ricardo, a major nineteenth-century British economist, formalized the point precisely. According to Ricardo's **theory of comparative advantage**, specialization and free trade will benefit all trading parties, even

theory of comparative advantage Ricardo's theory that specialization and free trade will benefit all trading parties, even those that may be "absolutely" more efficient producers.

ECONOMICS IN PRACTICE

Frozen Foods and Opportunity Costs

In 2007, $27 billion of frozen foods were sold in U.S. grocery stores, one quarter of it in the form of frozen dinners and entrees. In the mid-1950s, sales of frozen foods amounted to only $1 billion, a tiny fraction of the overall grocery store sales. One industry observer attributes this growth to the fact that frozen food tastes much better than it did in the past. Can you think of anything else that might be occurring?

The growth of the frozen dinner entrée market in the last 50 years is a good example of the role of opportunity costs in our lives. One of the most significant social changes in the U.S. economy in this period has been the increased participation of women in the labor force. In 1950, only 24 percent of married women worked; by 2000, that fraction had risen to 61 percent. Producing a meal takes two basic ingredients: food and time. When both husbands and wives work, the opportunity cost of time for housework—including making meals—goes up. This tells us that making a home-cooked meal became more expensive in the last 50 years. A natural result is to shift people toward labor-saving ways to make meals. Frozen foods are an obvious solution to the problem of increased opportunity costs.

Another, somewhat more subtle, opportunity cost story is at work encouraging the consumption of frozen foods. In 1960, the first microwave oven was introduced. The spread of this device into America's kitchens was rapid. The microwave turned out to be a quick way to defrost and cook those frozen entrées. So this technology lowered the opportunity cost of making frozen dinners, reinforcing the advantage these meals had over home-cooked meals. Microwaves made cooking with frozen foods cheaper once opportunity cost was considered while home-cooked meals were becoming more expensive.

The entrepreneurs among you also might recognize that the rise we described in the opportunity cost of the home-cooked meal *contributed* in part to the spread of the microwave, creating a reinforcing cycle. In fact, many entrepreneurs find that the simple tools of economics—like the idea of opportunity costs—help them anticipate what products will be profitable for them to produce in the future. The growth of the two-worker family has stimulated many entrepreneurs to search for labor-saving solutions to family tasks.

The public policy students among you might be interested to know that some researchers attribute part of the growth in obesity in the United States to the lower opportunity costs of making meals associated with the growth of the markets for frozen foods and the microwave. (See David M. Cutler, Edward L. Glaeser, and Jesse M. Shapiro, "Why Have Americans Become More Obese?" *Journal of Economic Perspectives*, Summer 2003, 93–118.)

when some are "absolutely" more efficient producers than others. Ricardo's basic point applies just as much to Colleen and Bill as it does to different nations.

To keep things simple, suppose that Colleen and Bill have only two tasks to accomplish each week: gathering food to eat and cutting logs to burn. If Colleen could cut more logs than Bill in 1 day and Bill could gather more nuts and berries than Colleen could, specialization would clearly lead to more total production. Both would benefit if Colleen only cuts logs and Bill only gathers nuts and berries, as long as they can trade. Suppose that Bill is slow and somewhat clumsy in his nut gathering and that Colleen is better at cutting logs *and* gathering food.

At first, it might seem that since Colleen is better at everything, she should do everything. But that cannot be right. Colleen's time is limited after all, and even though Bill is clumsy and not very clever, he must be able to contribute something.

One of Ricardo's lasting contributions to economics has been his analysis of exactly this situation. His analysis, which is illustrated in Figure 2.2, shows both how Colleen and Bill should divide the work of the island and how much they will gain from specializing and exchanging even if, as in this example, one party is absolutely better at everything than the other party.

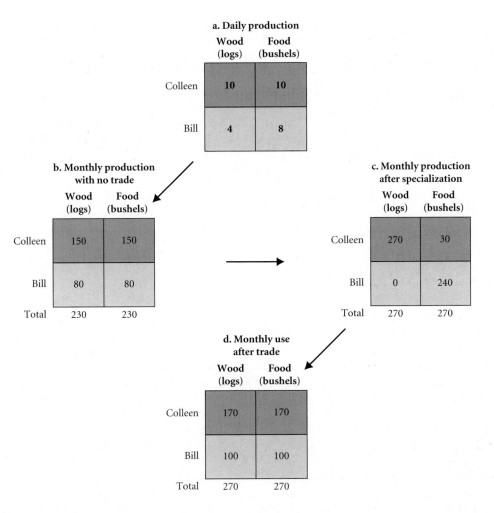

a. Daily production

	Wood (logs)	Food (bushels)
Colleen	10	10
Bill	4	8

b. Monthly production with no trade

	Wood (logs)	Food (bushels)
Colleen	150	150
Bill	80	80
Total	230	230

c. Monthly production after specialization

	Wood (logs)	Food (bushels)
Colleen	270	30
Bill	0	240
Total	270	270

d. Monthly use after trade

	Wood (logs)	Food (bushels)
Colleen	170	170
Bill	100	100
Total	270	270

◀ **FIGURE 2.2**
Comparative Advantage and the Gains from Trade

In this figure, (a) shows the number of logs and bushels of food that Colleen and Bill can produce for every day spent at the task and (b) shows how much output they could produce in a month, assuming they wanted an equal number of logs and bushels. Colleen would split her time 50/50, devoting 15 days to each task and achieving total output of 150 logs and 150 bushels of food. Bill would spend 20 days cutting wood and 10 days gathering food. As shown in (c) and (d), by specializing and trading, both Colleen and Bill will be better off. Going from (c) to (d), Colleen trades 100 logs to Bill in exchange for 140 bushels of food.

Suppose Colleen can cut 10 logs per day and Bill can cut only 4. Also suppose Colleen can gather 10 bushels of food per day and Bill can gather only 8. A producer has an **absolute advantage** over another in the production of a good or service if he or she can produce the good or service using fewer resources, including time. Since Colleen can cut more logs per day than Bill, we say that she has an absolute advantage in the production of logs. Similarly, Colleen has an absolute advantage over Bill in the production of food.

Thinking just about productivity and the output of food and logs, you might conclude that it would benefit Colleen to move to the other side of the island and be by herself. Since she is more productive in cutting logs and gathering food, would she not be better off on her own? How could she benefit by hanging out with Bill and sharing what they produce?

To answer that question we must remember that Colleen's time is limited: This limit creates opportunity cost. A producer has a **comparative advantage** over another in the production of a good or service if he or she can produce the good or service at a lower opportunity cost. First, think about Bill. He can produce 8 bushels of food per day, or he can cut 4 logs. To get 8 additional bushels of food, he must give up cutting 4 logs. Thus, *for Bill, the opportunity cost of 8 bushels of food is 4 logs*. Think next about Colleen. She can produce 10 bushels of food per day, or she can cut 10 logs. She thus gives up 1 log for each additional bushel; so *for Colleen, the opportunity cost of 8 bushels of food is 8 logs*. Bill has a comparative advantage over Colleen in the production of food because he gives up only 4 logs for an additional 8 bushels, whereas Colleen gives up 8 logs.

Think now about what Colleen must give up in terms of food to get 10 logs. To produce 10 logs she must work a whole day. If she spends a day cutting 10 logs, she gives up a day of gathering 10 bushels of food. Thus, *for Colleen, the opportunity cost of 10 logs is 10 bushels of food*. What must Bill give up to get 10 logs? To produce 4 logs, he must work 1 day. For each day he cuts logs, he gives up 8 bushels of food. He thus gives up 2 bushels of food for each log; so *for Bill, the*

absolute advantage
A producer has an absolute advantage over another in the production of a good or service if he or she can produce that product using fewer resources.

comparative advantage
A producer has a comparative advantage over another in the production of a good or service if he or she can produce that product at a lower *opportunity cost*.

opportunity cost of 10 logs is 20 bushels of food. Colleen has a comparative advantage over Bill in the production of logs since she gives up only 10 bushels of food for an additional 10 logs, whereas Bill gives up 20 bushels.

Ricardo then argues that two parties can benefit from specialization and trade even if one party has an absolute advantage in the production of both goods. Suppose Colleen and Bill both want equal numbers of logs and bushels of food. If Colleen goes off on her own, in a 30-day month, she can produce 150 logs and 150 bushels, devoting 15 days to each task. For Bill to produce equal numbers of logs and bushels on his own requires that he spend 10 days on food and 20 days on logs. This yields 80 bushels of food (10 days × 8 bushels per day) and 80 logs (20 days × 4 logs per day). Between the two, they produce 230 logs and 230 bushels of food.

Let's see if specialization and trade can work. If Bill spends all his time on food, he produces 240 bushels in a month (30 days × 8 bushels per day). If Colleen spends 3 days on food and 27 days on logs, she produces 30 bushels of food (3 days × 10 bushels per day) and 270 logs (27 days × 10 logs per day). Between the two, they produce 270 logs and 270 bushels of food, which is more than the 230 logs and 230 bushels they produced when not specializing. Thus, by specializing in the production of the good in which they enjoyed a comparative advantage, there are more of both goods. We see in this example how the fundamental concept of opportunity cost covered earlier in this chapter relates to the theory of comparative advantage.

Even if Colleen were to live at another place on the island, she could specialize, producing 30 bushels of food and 270 logs, then trading 100 of her logs to Bill for 140 bushels of food. This would leave her with 170 logs and 170 bushels of food, which is more than the 150 of each she could produce on her own. Bill would specialize completely in food, producing 240 bushels. Trading 140 bushels of food to Colleen for 100 logs leaves him with 100 of each, which is more than the 80 of each he could produce on his own.

The simple example of Bill and Colleen should begin to give you some insight into why most economists see value in free trade. Even if one country is absolutely better than another country at producing everything, our example has shown that there are gains to specializing and trading.

A Graphical Presentation of Comparative Advantage and Gains from Trade
Graphs can also be used to show the benefits from specialization and trade in the example of Colleen and Bill. To construct a graph reflecting Colleen's production choices (Figure 2.3 (a)), we start with the end points. If she were to devote an entire month (30 days) to log production, she could cut 300 logs—10 logs per day × 30 days. Similarly, if she were to devote an entire month to food gathering, she could produce 300 bushels. If she chose to split her time evenly (15 days to logs and 15 days to food), she would have 150 bushels and 150 logs. Her production possibilities are illustrated by the straight line between *A* and *B* and illustrate the trade-off that she faces between logs and food: By reducing her time spent in food gathering, Colleen is able to devote more time to logs; and for every 10 bushels of food that she gives up, she gets 10 logs.

In Figure 2.3(b), we construct a graph of Bill's production possibilities. Recall that Bill can produce 8 bushels of food per day, but he can cut only 4 logs. Again, starting with the end points, if Bill devoted all his time to food production, he could produce 240 bushels—8 bushels of food per day × 30 days. Similarly, if he were to devote the entire 30 days to log cutting, he could cut 120 logs—4 logs per day × 30 days. By splitting his time, with 20 days spent on log cutting and 10 days spent gathering food, Bill could produce 80 logs and 80 bushels of food. His production possibilities are illustrated by the straight line between *D* and *E*. By shifting his resources and time from logs to food, he gets 2 bushels for every log.

Figures 2.3(a) and 2.3(b) illustrate the maximum amounts of food and logs that Bill and Colleen can produce acting independently with no specialization or trade, which is 230 logs and 230 bushels. Now let us have each specialize in producing the good in which he or she has a comparative advantage. Back in Figure 2.2 on p. 29, we showed that if Bill devoted all his time to food production, producing 240 bushels (30 days × 8 bushels per day), and Colleen devoted the vast majority of her time to cutting logs (27 days) and just a few days to gathering food (3 days), their combined total would be 270 logs and 270 bushels of food. Colleen would produce 270 logs and 30 bushels of food to go with Bill's 240 bushels of food.

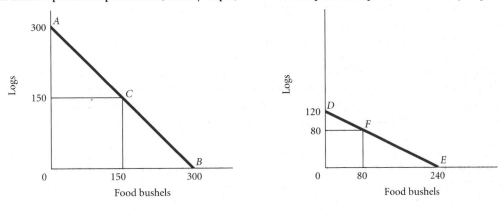

a. Colleen's production possibilities (monthly output)

b. Bill's production possibilities (monthly output)

▲ FIGURE 2.3 Production Possibilities with No Trade

The figure in (a) shows all of the combinations of logs and bushels of food that Colleen can produce by herself. If she spends all 30 days each month on logs, she produces 300 logs and no food (point A). If she spends all 30 days on food, she produces 300 bushels of food and no logs (point B). If she spends 15 days on logs and 15 days on food, she produces 150 of each (point C).

The figure in (b) shows all of the combinations of logs and bushels of food that Bill can produce by himself. If he spends all 30 days each month on logs, he produces 120 logs and no food (point D). If he spends all 30 days on food, he produces 240 bushels of food and no logs (point E). If he spends 20 days on logs and 10 days on food, he produces 80 of each (point F).

Finally, we arrange a trade, and the result is shown in Figures 2.4(a) and 2.4(b). Bill trades 140 bushels of food to Colleen for 100 logs; and he ends up with 100 logs and 100 bushels of food, 20 more of each than he would have had before the specialization and trade.

Colleen ends up with 170 logs and 170 bushels, again 20 more of each than she would have had before the specialization and trade. Both are better off. Both move beyond their individual production possibilities.

a. Colleen moves beyond her original production possibilties

b. Bill moves beyond his original production possibilties

▲ FIGURE 2.4 Colleen and Bill Gain from Trade

By specializing and engaging in trade, Colleen and Bill can move beyond their own production possibilities. If Bill spends all his time producing food, he will produce 240 bushels of food and no logs. If he can trade 140 of his bushels of food to Colleen for 100 logs, he will end up with 100 logs and 100 bushels of food. The figure in (b) shows that he can move from point F to point F'.

If Colleen spends 27 days cutting logs and 3 days producing food, she will produce 270 logs and 30 bushels of food. If she can trade 100 of her logs to Bill for 140 bushels of food, she will end up with 170 logs and 170 bushels of food. The figure in (a) shows that she can move from point C to point C'.

Weighing Present and Expected Future Costs and Benefits   Very often we find ourselves weighing benefits available today against benefits available tomorrow. Here, too, the notion of opportunity cost is helpful.

While alone on the island, Bill had to choose between cultivating a field and just gathering wild nuts and berries. Gathering nuts and berries provides food now; gathering seeds and clearing a field for planting will yield food tomorrow if all goes well. Using today's time to farm may well be worth the effort if doing so will yield more food than Bill would otherwise have in the future. By planting, Bill is trading present value for future value.

The simplest example of trading present for future benefits is the act of saving. When you put income aside today for use in the future, you give up some things that you could have had today in exchange for something tomorrow. Because nothing is certain, some judgment about future events and expected values must be made. What will your income be in 10 years? How long are you likely to live?

We trade off present and future benefits in small ways all the time. If you decide to study instead of going to the dorm party, you are trading present fun for the expected future benefits of higher grades. If you decide to go outside on a very cold day and run 5 miles, you are trading discomfort in the present for being in better shape later.

Capital Goods and Consumer Goods   A society trades present for expected future benefits when it devotes a portion of its resources to research and development or to investment in capital. As we said earlier in this chapter, *capital* in its broadest definition is anything that has already been produced that will be used to produce other valuable goods or services over time.

Building capital means trading present benefits for future ones. Bill and Colleen might trade gathering berries or lying in the sun for cutting logs to build a nicer house in the future. In a modern society, resources used to produce capital goods could have been used to produce **consumer goods**—that is, goods for present consumption. Heavy industrial machinery does not directly satisfy the wants of anyone, but producing it requires resources that could instead have gone into producing things that do satisfy wants directly—for example, food, clothing, toys, or golf clubs.

Capital is everywhere. A road is capital. Once a road is built, we can drive on it or transport goods and services over it for many years to come. A house is also capital. Before a new manufacturing firm can start up, it must put some capital in place. The buildings, equipment, and inventories that it uses comprise its capital. As it contributes to the production process, this capital yields valuable services over time.

In Chapter 1, we talked about the enormous amount of capital—buildings, factories, housing, cars, trucks, telephone lines, and so on—that you might see from a window high in a skyscraper. Much of that capital was put in place by previous generations, yet it continues to provide valuable services today; it is part of this generation's endowment of resources. To build every building, every road, every factory, every house, and every car or truck, society must forgo using resources to produce consumer goods today. To get an education, you pay tuition and put off joining the workforce for a while.

Capital does not need to be tangible. When you spend time and resources developing skills or getting an education, you are investing in human capital—your own human capital. This capital will continue to exist and yield benefits to you for years to come. A computer program produced by a software company may come on a CD that costs 75¢ to make, but its true intangible value comes from the ideas embodied in the program itself, which will drive computers to do valuable, time-saving tasks over time. It too is capital.

The process of using resources to produce new capital is called **investment**. (In everyday language, the term *investment* often refers to the act of buying a share of stock or a bond, as in "I invested in some Treasury bonds." In economics, however, investment *always* refers to the creation of capital: the purchase or putting in place of buildings, equipment, roads, houses, and the like.) A wise investment in capital is one that yields future benefits that are more valuable than the present cost. When you spend money for a house, for example, presumably you value its future benefits. That is, you expect to gain more from living in it than you would from the things you could buy today with the same money. Because resources are scarce, the opportunity cost of every investment in capital is forgone present consumption.

consumer goods Goods produced for present consumption.

investment The process of using resources to produce new capital.

production possibility frontier (ppf) A graph that shows all the combinations of goods and services that can be produced if all of society's resources are used efficiently.

The Production Possibility Frontier

A simple graphic device called the **production possibility frontier (ppf)** illustrates the principles of constrained choice, opportunity cost, and scarcity. The ppf is a graph that shows all the combinations of goods and services that can be produced if all of a society's resources are used efficiently. Figure 2.5 shows a ppf for a hypothetical economy.

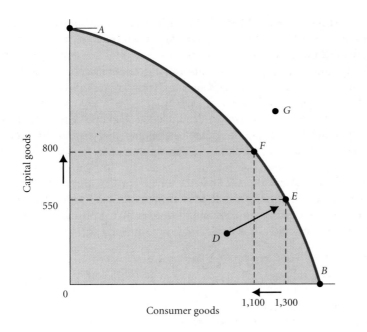

◀ **FIGURE 2.5**
Production Possibility Frontier
The ppf illustrates a number of economic concepts. One of the most important is *opportunity cost*. The opportunity cost of producing more capital goods is fewer consumer goods. Moving from *E* to *F*, the number of capital goods increases from 550 to 800, but the number of consumer goods decreases from 1,300 to 1,100.

On the *Y*-axis, we measure the quantity of capital goods produced. On the *X*-axis, we measure the quantity of consumer goods. All points below and to the left of the curve (the shaded area) represent combinations of capital and consumer goods that are possible for the society given the resources available and existing technology. Points above and to the right of the curve, such as point *G*, represent combinations that cannot be reached. If an economy were to end up at point *A* on the graph, it would be producing no consumer goods at all; all resources would be used for the production of capital. If an economy were to end up at point *B*, it would be devoting all its resources to the production of consumer goods and none of its resources to the formation of capital.

While all economies produce some of each kind of good, different economies emphasize different things. About 17.1 percent of gross output in the United States in 2005 was new capital. In Japan, capital historically accounted for a much higher percent of gross output, while in the Congo, the figure was 7 percent. Japan is closer to point *A* on its ppf, the Congo is closer to *B*, and the United States is somewhere in between.

Points that are actually on the ppf are points of both full resource employment and production efficiency. (Recall from Chapter 1 that an efficient economy is one that produces the things that people want at the least cost. *Production efficiency* is a state in which a given mix of outputs is produced at the least cost.) Resources are not going unused, and there is no waste. Points that lie within the shaded area but that are not on the frontier represent either unemployment of resources or production inefficiency. An economy producing at point *D* in Figure 2.5 can produce more capital goods and more consumer goods, for example, by moving to point *E*. This is possible because resources are not fully employed at point *D* or are not being used efficiently.

Unemployment   During the Great Depression of the 1930s, the U.S. economy experienced prolonged unemployment. Millions of workers found themselves without jobs. In 1933, 25 percent of the civilian labor force was unemployed. This figure stayed above 14 percent until 1940, when increased defense spending by the United States created millions of jobs. In June 1975, the unemployment rate went over 9 percent for the first time since the 1930s. In December 1982, when the unemployment rate hit 10.8 percent, nearly 12 million people were looking for work. In 2007, the figure was 7.1 million.

In addition to the hardship that falls on the unemployed, unemployment of labor means unemployment of capital. During economic downturns or recessions, industrial plants run at less than their total capacity. When there is unemployment of labor and capital, we are not producing all that we can.

Periods of unemployment correspond to points inside the ppf, points such as *D* in Figure 2.5. Moving onto the frontier from a point such as *D* means achieving full employment of resources.

Inefficiency   Although an economy may be operating with full employment of its land, labor, and capital resources, it may still be operating inside its ppf (at a point such as *D* in Figure 2.5). It could be using those resources *inefficiently*.

Waste and mismanagement are the results of a firm operating below its potential. If you are the owner of a bakery and you forget to order flour, your workers and ovens stand idle while you figure out what to do.

Sometimes inefficiency results from mismanagement of the economy instead of misman-agement of individual private firms. Suppose, for example, that the land and climate in Ohio are best suited for corn production and that the land and climate in Kansas are best suited for wheat production. If Congress passes a law forcing Ohio farmers to plant 50 percent of their acreage with wheat and Kansas farmers to plant 50 percent with corn, neither corn nor wheat production will be up to potential. The economy will be at a point such as *A* in Figure 2.6—inside the ppf. Allowing each state to specialize in producing the crop that it produces best increases the pro-duction of both crops and moves the economy to a point such as *B* in Figure 2.6.

▶ **FIGURE 2.6**
Inefficiency from Misallocation of Land in Farming

Society can end up inside its ppf at a point such as *A* by using its resources inefficiently. If, for example, Ohio's climate and soil were best suited for corn produc-tion and those of Kansas were best suited for wheat produc-tion, a law forcing Kansas farm-ers to produce corn and Ohio farmers to produce wheat would result in less of both. In such a case, society might be at point *A* instead of point *B*.

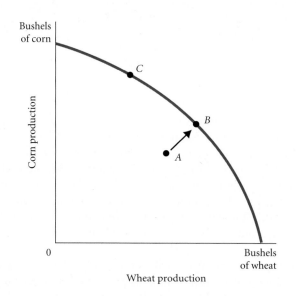

The Efficient Mix of Output   To be efficient, an economy must produce what people want. This means that in addition to operating *on* the ppf, the economy must be operating at the *right point* on the ppf. This is referred to as *output efficiency*, in contrast to production efficiency. Suppose that an economy devotes 100 percent of its resources to beef production and that the beef industry runs efficiently using the most modern techniques. Also suppose that everyone in the society is a vegetarian. The result is a total waste of resources (assuming that the society can-not trade its beef for vegetables produced in another country).

Points *B* and *C* in Figure 2.6 are points of production efficiency and full employment. Whether *B* is more or less efficient than *C*, however, depends on the preferences of members of society and is not shown in the ppf graph.

Negative Slope and Opportunity Cost   As we have seen, points that lie on the ppf rep-resent points of full resource employment and production efficiency. Society can choose only one point on the curve. Because a society's choices are constrained by available resources and existing technology, when those resources are fully and efficiently employed, it can produce more capital goods only by reducing production of consumer goods. The opportunity cost of the additional capital is the forgone production of consumer goods.

The fact that scarcity exists is illustrated by the negative slope of the ppf. (If you need a review of slope, see the Appendix to Chapter 1.) In moving from point *E* to point *F* in Figure 2.5, capital production *increases* by 800 − 550 = 250 units (a positive change), but that increase in capital can be achieved only by shifting resources out of the production of consumer goods. Thus, in moving from point *E* to point *F* in Figure 2.5, consumer goods production *decreases* by

1,300 − 1,100 = 200 units (a negative change). The slope of the curve, the ratio of the change in capital goods to the change in consumer goods, is negative.

The value of the slope of a society's ppf is called the **marginal rate of transformation (MRT)**. In Figure 2.5, the MRT between points *E* and *F* is simply the ratio of the change in capital goods (a positive number) to the change in consumer goods (a negative number).

marginal rate of transformation (MRT)
The slope of the production possibility frontier (ppf).

The Law of Increasing Opportunity Cost The negative slope of the ppf indicates the trade-off that a society faces between two goods. We can learn something further about the shape of the frontier and the terms of this trade-off. Let's look at the trade-off between corn and wheat production in Ohio and Kansas. In a recent year, Ohio and Kansas together produced 510 million bushels of corn and 380 million bushels of wheat. Table 2.1 presents these two numbers, plus some hypothetical combinations of corn and wheat production that might exist for Ohio and Kansas together. Figure 2.7 graphs the data from Table 2.1.

TABLE 2.1	Production Possibility Schedule for Total Corn and Wheat Production in Ohio and Kansas	
Point on ppf	Total Corn Production (Millions of Bushels Per Year)	Total Wheat Production (Millions of Bushels Per Year)
A	700	100
B	650	200
C	510	380
D	400	500
E	300	550

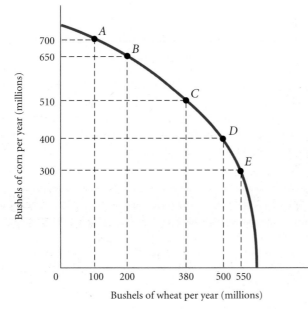

◀ **FIGURE 2.7 Corn and Wheat Production in Ohio and Kansas**
The ppf illustrates that the opportunity cost of corn production increases as we shift resources from wheat production to corn production. Moving from point *E* to *D*, we get an additional 100 million bushels of corn at a cost of 50 million bushels of wheat. Moving from point *B* to *A*, we get only 50 million bushels of corn at a cost of 100 million bushels of wheat. The *cost per bushel* of corn—measured in lost wheat—has increased.

Suppose that society's demand for corn dramatically increases. If this happens, farmers would probably shift some of their acreage from wheat production to corn production. Such a shift is represented by a move from point *C* (where corn = 510 and wheat = 380) up and to the left along the ppf toward points *A* and *B* in Figure 2.7. As this happens, it becomes more difficult to produce additional corn. The best land for corn production was presumably already in corn, and the best land for wheat production was already in wheat. As we try to produce more corn, the land is less well suited to that crop. As we take more land out of wheat production, we are taking increasingly better wheat-producing land. In other words, the opportunity cost of more corn, measured in terms of wheat, increases.

Moving from point *E* to *D*, Table 2.1 shows that we can get 100 million bushels of corn (400 − 300) by sacrificing only 50 million bushels of wheat (550 − 500)—that is, we get

2 bushels of corn for every bushel of wheat. However, when we are already stretching the ability of the land to produce corn, it becomes harder to produce more and the opportunity cost increases. Moving from point *B* to *A*, we can get only 50 million bushels of corn (700 − 650) by sacrificing 100 million bushels of wheat (200 − 100). For every bushel of wheat, we now get only half a bushel of corn. However, if the demand for *wheat* were to increase substantially and we were to move down and to the right along the ppf, it would become increasingly difficult to produce wheat and the opportunity cost of wheat, in terms of corn, would increase. This is the *law of increasing opportunity cost*.

If you think about the example we discussed earlier of Colleen and Bill producing logs and food on an island, you will recognize that the production possibilities described were highly simplified. In that example, we drew a downward slope, *straight line ppf*, to make the problem easier; we assume constant opportunity costs. In a real economy, ppf's would be expected to look like Figure 2.5.

Although it exists only as an abstraction, the ppf illustrates a number of very important concepts that we will use throughout the rest of this book: scarcity, unemployment, inefficiency, opportunity cost, the law of increasing opportunity cost, economic growth, and the gains from trade.

It is important to remember that the ppf represents choices available within the constraints imposed by the current state of agricultural technology. In the long run, technology may improve, and when that happens, we have *growth*.

economic growth An increase in the total output of an economy. It occurs when a society acquires new resources or when it learns to produce more using existing resources.

Economic Growth **Economic growth** is characterized by an increase in the total output of an economy. It occurs when a society acquires new resources or learns to produce more with existing resources. New resources may mean a larger labor force or an increased capital stock. The production and use of new machinery and equipment (capital) increase workers' productivity. (Give a man a shovel, and he can dig a bigger hole; give him a steam shovel, and wow!) Improved productivity also comes from technological change and *innovation*, the discovery and application of new, more efficient production techniques.

In the past few decades, the productivity of U.S. agriculture has increased dramatically. Based on data compiled by the Department of Agriculture, Table 2.2 shows that yield per acre in corn production has increased fivefold since the late 1930s, while the labor required to produce it has dropped significantly. Productivity in wheat production has also increased, at only a slightly less remarkable rate: Output per acre has more than tripled, while labor requirements are down nearly 90 percent. These increases are the result of more efficient farming techniques, more and better capital (tractors, combines, and other equipment), and advances in scientific knowledge and technological change (hybrid seeds, fertilizers, and so on). As you can see in Figure 2.8, increases such as these shift the ppf up and to the right.

TABLE 2.2 Increasing Productivity in Corn and Wheat Production in the United States, 1935–2007

	Corn		Wheat	
	Yield Per Acre (Bushels)	Labor Hours Per 100 Bushels	Yield Per Acre (Bushels)	Labor Hours Per 100 Bushels
1935–1939	26.1	108	13.2	67
1945–1949	36.1	53	16.9	34
1955–1959	48.7	20	22.3	17
1965–1969	78.5	7	27.5	11
1975–1979	95.3	4	31.3	9
1981–1985	107.2	3	36.9	7
1985–1990	112.8	NA[a]	38.0	NA[a]
1990–1995	120.6	NA[a]	38.1	NA[a]
1998	134.4	NA[a]	43.2	NA[a]
2001	138.2	NA[a]	43.5	NA[a]
2006	145.6	NA[a]	42.3	NA[a]
2007	152.8	NA[a]	40.6	NA[a]

[a]Data not available.

Source: U.S. Department of Agriculture, Economic Research Service, Agricultural Statistics, Crop Summary. August 2007.

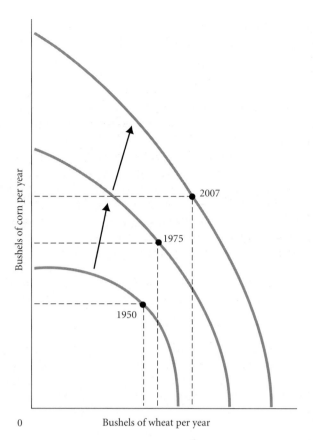

◀ **FIGURE 2.8 Economic Growth Shifts the PPF Up and to the Right**
Productivity increases have enhanced the ability of the United States to produce both corn and wheat. As Table 2.2 shows, productivity increases were more dramatic for corn than for wheat. Thus, the shifts in the ppf were not parallel.

Note: The ppf also shifts if the amount of land or labor in corn and wheat production changes. Although we emphasize productivity increases here, the actual shifts between years were due in part to land and labor changes.

Sources of Growth and the Dilemma of Poor Countries Economic growth arises from many sources, the two most important over the years having been the accumulation of capital and technological advances. For poor countries, capital is essential; they must build the communication networks and transportation systems necessary to develop industries that function efficiently. They also need capital goods to develop their agricultural sectors.

Recall that capital goods are produced only at a sacrifice of consumer goods. The same can be said for technological advances. Technological advances come from research and development that use resources; thus, they too must be paid for. The resources used to produce capital goods—to build a road, a tractor, or a manufacturing plant—*and* to develop new technologies could have been used to produce consumer goods.

When a large part of a country's population is very poor, taking resources out of the production of consumer goods (such as food and clothing) is very difficult. In addition, in some countries, people wealthy enough to invest in domestic industries choose instead to invest abroad because of political turmoil at home. As a result, it often falls to the governments of poor countries to generate revenues for capital production and research out of tax collections.

All these factors have contributed to the growing gap between some poor and rich nations. Figure 2.9 shows the result using ppf's. On the left, the rich country devotes a larger portion of its production to capital while the poor country produces mostly consumer goods. On the right, you see the results: the ppf of the rich country shifts up and out farther and faster.

The importance of capital goods and technological developments to the position of workers in less developed countries is well illustrated by Robert Jensen's study of South India's industry. Conventional telephones require huge investments in wires and towers and, as a result, many less developed areas are without landlines. Mobile phones, on the other hand, require a less expensive investment; thus, in many areas, people upgraded from no phones directly to cell phones. Jensen found that in small fishing villages, the advent of cell phones allowed fishermen to determine on any given day where to take their catch to sell, resulting in a large decrease in fish wasted and an increase in fishing profits. The ability of newer communication technology to aid development is one of the exciting features of our times. (See Robert Jensen, "The Digital Provide: Information Technology, Market Performance, and Welfare in the South Indian Fisheries Sector," *Quarterly Journal of Economics*, August 2007, 879–924.)

▶ **FIGURE 2.9 Capital Goods and Growth in Poor and Rich Countries**
Rich countries find it easier than poor countries to devote resources to the production of capital, and the more resources that flow into capital production, the faster the rate of economic growth. Thus, the gap between poor and rich countries has grown over time.

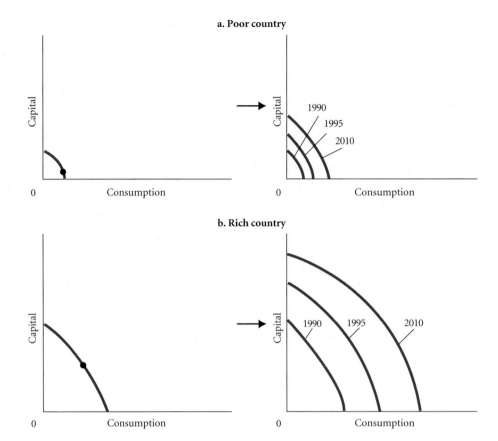

The Economic Problem

Recall the three basic questions facing all economic systems: (1) What gets produced? (2) How is it produced? and (3) Who gets it?

When Bill was alone on the island, the mechanism for answering those questions was simple: He thought about his own wants and preferences, looked at the constraints imposed by the resources of the island and his own skills and time, and made his decisions. As Bill set about his work, he allocated available resources quite simply, more or less by dividing up his available time. Distribution of the output was irrelevant. Because Bill was the society, he got it all.

Introducing even one more person into the economy—in this case, Colleen—changed all that. With Colleen on the island, resource allocation involves deciding not only how each person spends his or her time but also who does what; and now there are two sets of wants and preferences. If Bill and Colleen go off on their own and form two separate self-sufficient economies, there will be lost potential. Two people can do more things together than each person can do alone. They may use their comparative advantages in different skills to specialize. Cooperation and coordination may give rise to gains that would otherwise not be possible.

When a society consists of millions of people, the problem of coordination and cooperation becomes enormous, but so does the potential for gain. In large, complex economies, specialization can go wild, with people working in jobs as different in their detail as an impressionist painting is from a blank page. The range of products available in a modern industrial society is beyond anything that could have been imagined a hundred years ago, and so is the range of jobs.

The amount of coordination and cooperation in a modern industrial society is almost impossible to imagine. Yet something seems to drive economic systems, if sometimes clumsily and inefficiently, toward producing the goods and services that people want. Given scarce resources, how do large, complex societies go about answering the three basic economic questions? This is the economic problem, which is what this text is about.

Economic Systems

Now that you understand the economic problem, we can explore how different economic systems go about answering the three basic questions.

In the long struggle between the United States and the USSR in the post–World War II period, there was a general view that authoritarian political systems went hand in hand with highly centralized and governmentally controlled economic systems. The recent explosive growth in China and the structure of the Chinese economy have created some debate over that connection.

China has become a magnet for private capital and entrepreneurship and has one of the most rapidly growing economies in the world. For the last decade, China has been growing at double-digit rates. Between 2001 and 2004, China's national output went up almost 50 percent. In the single month of June 2005, the Chinese sold $21 billion worth of goods and services to the United States, while the United States sold only $3.4 billion to China. While the Chinese political system is still highly controlled, the economy has many hallmarks of a free market system. Exciting new work is taking place to help better understand the connections between the economic system and the political system.

Command Economies

In a pure **command economy**, the basic economic questions are answered by a central government. Through a combination of government ownership of state enterprises and central planning, the government, either directly or indirectly, sets output targets, incomes, and prices.

> **command economy** An economy in which a central government either directly or indirectly sets output targets, incomes, and prices.

While the extremes of central planning have been rejected, so too has the idea that "markets solve all problems." The real debate is not about whether we have government at all, it is about the extent and the character of a limited government role in the economy. One of the major themes of this book is that government involvement, in theory, may improve the efficiency and fairness of the allocation of a nation's resources. At the same time, a poorly functioning government can destroy incentives, lead to corruption, and result in the waste of a society's resources.

Laissez-Faire Economies: The Free Market

At the opposite end of the spectrum from the command economy is the **laissez-faire economy**. The term *laissez-faire*, which translated literally from French means "allow [them] to do," implies a complete lack of government involvement in the economy. In this type of economy, individuals and firms pursue their own self-interest without any central direction or regulation; the sum total of millions of individual decisions ultimately determines all basic economic outcomes. The central institution through which a laissez-faire system answers the basic questions is the **market**, a term that is used in economics to mean an institution through which buyers and sellers interact and engage in exchange.

> **laissez-faire economy** Literally from the French: "allow [them] to do." An economy in which individual people and firms pursue their own self-interest without any central direction or regulation.
>
> **market** The institution through which buyers and sellers interact and engage in exchange.

The interactions between buyers and sellers in any market range from simple to complex. Early explorers of the North American Midwest who wanted to exchange with Native Americans did so simply by bringing their goods to a central place and trading them. Today the World Wide Web is revolutionizing exchange. A jewelry maker in upstate Maine can exhibit wares through digital photographs on the Web. Buyers can enter orders or make bids and pay by credit card. Companies such as eBay facilitate the worldwide interaction of tens of thousands of buyers and sellers sitting at their computers.

In short:

> Some markets are simple and others are complex, but they all involve buyers and sellers engaging in exchange. The behavior of buyers and sellers in a laissez-faire economy determines what gets produced, how it is produced, and who gets it.

The following chapters explore market systems in great depth. A quick preview is worthwhile here, however.

Consumer Sovereignty In a free, unregulated market, goods and services are produced and sold only if the supplier can make a profit. In simple terms, making a *profit* means selling goods or services for more than it costs to produce them. You cannot make a profit unless someone wants the product that you are selling. This logic leads to the notion of **consumer sovereignty**: The mix of output found in any free market system is dictated ultimately by the

> **consumer sovereignty** The idea that consumers ultimately dictate what will be produced (or not produced) by choosing what to purchase (and what not to purchase).

tastes and preferences of consumers who "vote" by buying or not buying. Businesses rise and fall in response to consumer demands. No central directive or plan is necessary.

Individual Production Decisions: Free Enterprise   Under a free market system, individual producers must also determine how to organize and coordinate the actual production of their products or services. The owner of a small shoe repair shop must alone buy the needed equipment and tools, hang signs, and set prices. In a big corporation, so many people are involved in planning the production process that in many ways, corporate planning resembles the planning in a command economy. In a free market economy, producers may be small or large. One person who hand-paints eggshells may start to sell them as a business; a person good with computers may start a business designing Web sites. On a larger scale, a group of furniture designers may put together a large portfolio of sketches, raise several million dollars, and start a bigger business. At the extreme are huge corporations such as Microsoft, Mitsubishi, and Intel, each of which sells tens of billions of dollars' worth of products every year. Whether the firms are large or small, however, production decisions in a market economy are made by separate private organizations acting in what they perceive to be their own interests.

free enterprise The freedom of individuals to start and operate private businesses in search of profits.

Often the market system is called a free enterprise system. **Free enterprise** means the freedom of individuals to start private businesses in search of profits. Because new businesses require capital investment before they can begin operation, starting a new business involves risk. A well-run business that produces a product for which demand exists is likely to succeed; a poorly run business or one that produces a product for which little demand exists now or in the future is likely to fail. It is through free enterprise that new products and new production techniques find their way into use.

Proponents of free market systems argue that free enterprise leads to more efficient production and better response to diverse and changing consumer preferences. If a producer produces inefficiently, competitors will come along, fight for the business, and eventually take it away. Thus, in a free market economy, competition forces producers to use efficient techniques of production. It is competition, then, that ultimately dictates how output is produced.

Distribution of Output   In a free market system, the distribution of output—who gets what—is also determined in a decentralized way. The amount that any one household gets depends on its income and wealth. *Income* is the amount that a household earns each year. It comes in a number of forms: wages, salaries, interest, and the like. *Wealth* is the amount that households have accumulated out of past income through saving or inheritance.

To the extent that income comes from working for a wage, it is at least in part determined by individual choice. You will work for the wages available in the market only if these wages (and the products and services they can buy) are sufficient to compensate you for what you give up by working. Your leisure certainly has a value also. You may discover that you can increase your income by getting more education or training. You *cannot* increase your income, however, if you acquire a skill that no one wants.

Price Theory   The basic coordinating mechanism in a free market system is price. A price is the amount that a product sells for per unit, and it reflects what society is willing to pay. Prices of inputs—labor, land, and capital—determine how much it costs to produce a product. Prices of various kinds of labor, or *wage rates*, determine the rewards for working in different jobs and professions. Many of the independent decisions made in a market economy involve the weighing of prices and costs, so it is not surprising that much of economic theory focuses on the factors that influence and determine prices. This is why microeconomic theory is often simply called *price theory*.

In sum:

> In a free market system, the basic economic questions are answered without the help of a central government plan or directives. This is what the "free" in free market means—the system is left to operate on its own with no outside interference. Individuals pursuing their own self-interest will go into business and produce the products and services that people want. Other individuals will decide whether to acquire skills; whether to work; and whether to buy, sell, invest, or save the income that they earn. The basic coordinating mechanism is price.

Mixed Systems, Markets, and Governments

The differences between command economies and laissez-faire economies in their pure forms are enormous. In fact, these pure forms do not exist in the world; all real systems are in some sense "mixed." That is, individual enterprise exists and independent choice is exercised even in economies in which the government plays a major role.

Conversely, no market economies exist without government involvement and government regulation. The United States has basically a free market economy, but government purchases accounted for about 19.4 percent of the country's total production in 2007. Governments in the United States (local, state, and federal) directly employ about 16 percent of all workers, counting the military. They also redistribute income by means of taxation and social welfare expenditures, and they regulate many economic activities.

One of the major themes in this book, and indeed in economics, is the tension between the advantages of free, unregulated markets and the desire for government involvement. Advocates of free markets argue that such markets work best when left to themselves. They produce only what people want; without buyers, sellers go out of business. Competition forces firms to adopt efficient production techniques. Wage differentials lead people to acquire needed skills. Competition also leads to innovation in both production techniques and products. The result is quality and variety, but market systems have problems too. Even staunch defenders of the free enterprise system recognize that market systems are not perfect. First, they do not always produce what people want at the lowest cost—there are inefficiencies. Second, rewards (income) may be unfairly distributed and some groups may be left out. Third, periods of unemployment and inflation recur with some regularity.

Many people point to these problems as reasons for government involvement. Indeed, for some problems, government involvement may be the only solution. However, government decisions are made by people who presumably, like the rest of us, act in their own self-interest. While governments may be called on to improve the functioning of the economy, there is no guarantee that they will do so. Just as markets may fail to produce an allocation of resources that is perfectly efficient and fair, governments may fail to improve matters. We return to this debate many times throughout this text.

Looking Ahead

This chapter described the economic problem in broad terms. We outlined the questions that all economic systems must answer. We also discussed very broadly the two kinds of economic systems. In the next chapter, we analyze the way market systems work.

SUMMARY

1. Every society has some system or process for transforming into useful form what nature and previous generations have provided. Economics is the study of that process and its outcomes.

2. *Producers* are those who take resources and transform them into usable products, or *outputs*. Private firms, households, and governments all produce something.

SCARCITY, CHOICE, AND OPPORTUNITY COST p. 26

3. All societies must answer *three basic questions*: What gets produced? How is it produced? Who gets what is produced? These three questions make up the *economic problem*.

4. One person alone on an island must make the same basic decisions that complex societies make. When a society consists of more than one person, questions of distribution, cooperation, and specialization arise.

5. Because resources are scarce relative to human wants in all societies, using resources to produce one good or service implies *not* using them to produce something else. This concept of *opportunity cost* is central to an understanding of economics.

6. Using resources to produce *capital* that will in turn produce benefits in the future implies *not* using those resources to produce consumer goods in the present.

7. Even if one individual or nation is absolutely more efficient at producing goods than another, all parties will gain if they specialize in producing goods in which they have a *comparative advantage*.

8. A *production possibility frontier* (ppf) is a graph that shows all the combinations of goods and services that can be produced if all of society's resources are used efficiently. The ppf illustrates a number of important economic concepts: scarcity, unemployment, inefficiency, increasing opportunity cost, and economic growth.

9. *Economic growth* occurs when society produces more, either by acquiring more resources or by learning to produce more with existing resources. Improved productivity may come from additional capital or from the discovery and application of new, more efficient techniques of production.

ECONOMIC SYSTEMS *p. 38*

10. In some modern societies, government plays a big role in answering the three basic questions. In pure *command economies*, a central authority directly or indirectly sets output targets, incomes, and prices.

11. A *laissez-faire economy* is one in which individuals independently pursue their own self-interest, without any central direction or regulation, and ultimately determine all basic economic outcomes.

12. A *market* is an institution through which buyers and sellers interact and engage in exchange. Some markets involve simple face-to-face exchange; others involve a complex series of transactions, often over great distances or through electronic means.

13. There are no purely planned economies and no pure laissez-faire economies; all economies are mixed. Individual enterprise, independent choice, and relatively free markets exist in centrally planned economies; and there is significant government involvement in market economies such as that of the United States.

14. One of the great debates in economics revolves around the tension between the advantages of free, unregulated markets and the desire for government involvement in the economy. Free markets produce what people want, and competition forces firms to adopt efficient production techniques. The need for government intervention arises because free markets are characterized by inefficiencies and an unequal distribution of income and experience regular periods of inflation and unemployment.

REVIEW TERMS AND CONCEPTS

absolute advantage, *p. 29*

capital, *p. 25*

command economy, *p. 39*

comparative advantage, *p. 29*

consumer goods, *p. 32*

consumer sovereignty, *p. 39*

economic growth, *p. 36*

factors of production (*or* factors), *p. 25*

free enterprise, *p. 40*

inputs *or* resources, *p. 26*

investment, *p. 32*

laissez-faire economy, *p. 39*

marginal rate of transformation (MRT), *p. 35*

market, *p. 39*

opportunity cost, *p. 27*

outputs, *p. 26*

production, *p. 25*

production possibility frontier (ppf), *p. 32*

theory of comparative advantage, *p. 27*

PROBLEMS

Visit www.myeconlab.com to complete the problems marked in orange online. You will receive instant feedback on your answers, tutorial help, and access to additional practice problems.

1. For each of the following, describe some of the potential opportunity costs:
   a. Studying for your economics test
   b. Spending 2 hours playing computer games
   c. Buying a new car instead of keeping the old one
   d. A local community voting to raise property taxes to increase school expenditures and to reduce class size
   e. A number of countries working together to build a space station
   f. Going to graduate school

2. "As long as all resources are fully employed and every firm in the economy is producing its output using the best available technology, the result will be efficient." Do you agree or disagree with this statement? Explain your answer.

3. You are an intern to the editor of a small-town newspaper in Mallsburg, Pennsylvania. Your boss, the editor, asks you to write the first draft of an editorial for this week's paper. Your assignment is to describe the costs and the benefits of building a new bridge across the railroad tracks in the center of town. Currently, most people who live in this town must drive 2 miles through thickly congested traffic to the existing bridge to get to the main shopping and employment center. The bridge will cost the citizens of Mallsburg $25 million, which will be paid for with a tax on their incomes over the next 20 years. What are the opportunity costs of building this bridge? What are the benefits that citizens will likely receive if the bridge is built? What other factors might you consider in writing this editorial?

4. Kristen and Anna live in the beach town of Santa Monica. They own a small business in which they make wristbands and pot holders and sell them to people on the beach. As shown in the table on the following page, Kristen can make 15 wristbands per hour but only 3 pot holders. Anna is a bit slower and can make only 12 wristbands or 2 pot holders in an hour.

	OUTPUT PER HOUR	
	WRISTBANDS	POT HOLDERS
Kristen	15	3
Anna	12	2

a. For Kristen and for Anna, what is the opportunity cost of a pot holder? Who has a comparative advantage in the production of pot holders? Explain your answer.

b. Who has a comparative advantage in the production of wristbands? Explain your answer.

c. Assume that Kristen works 20 hours per week in the business. Assuming Kristen is in business on her own, graph the possible combinations of pot holders and wristbands that she could produce in a week. Do the same for Anna.

d. If Kristen devoted half of her time (10 out of 20 hours) to wristbands and half of her time to pot holders, how many of each would she produce in a week? If Anna did the same, how many of each would she produce? How many wristbands and pot holders would be produced in total?

e. Suppose that Anna spent all 20 hours of her time on wristbands and Kristen spent 17 hours on pot holders and 3 hours on wristbands. How many of each item would be produced?

f. Suppose that Kristen and Anna can sell all their wristbands for $1 each and all their pot holders for $5.50 each. If each of them worked 20 hours per week, how should they split their time between wristbands and pot holders? What is their maximum joint revenue?

5. Briefly describe the trade-offs involved in each of the following decisions. Specifically, list some of the opportunity costs associated with each decision, paying particular attention to the trade-offs between present and future consumption.

a. After a stressful senior year in high school, Sherice decides to take the summer off instead of working before going to college.

b. Frank is overweight and decides to work out every day and to go on a diet.

c. Mei is diligent about taking her car in for routine maintenance even though it takes 2 hours of her time and costs $100 four times each year.

d. Jim is in a hurry. He runs a red light on the way to work.

*6. The countries of Figistan and Blah are small island countries in the South Pacific. Both produce fruit and timber. Each island has a labor force of 1,200. The following table gives production per month for each worker in each country.

	BASKETS OF FRUIT	BOARD FEET OF TIMBER
Figistan workers	10	5
Blah workers	30	10

Productivity of one worker for one month

a. Which country has an absolute advantage in the production of fruit? Which country has an absolute advantage in the production of timber?

b. Which country has a comparative advantage in the production of fruit? of timber?

c. Sketch the ppf's for both countries.

d. Assuming no trading between the two, if both countries wanted to have equal numbers of feet of timber and baskets of fruit, how would they allocate workers to the two sectors?

e. Show that specialization and trade can move both countries beyond their ppf's.

7. Suppose that a simple society has an economy with only one resource, labor. Labor can be used to produce only two commodities—X, a necessity good (food), and Y, a luxury good (music and merriment). Suppose that the labor force consists of 100 workers. One laborer can produce either 5 units of necessity per month (by hunting and gathering) or 10 units of luxury per month (by writing songs, playing the guitar, dancing, and so on).

a. On a graph, draw the economy's ppf. Where does the ppf intersect the Y-axis? Where does it intersect the X-axis? What meaning do those points have?

b. Suppose the economy produced at a point *inside* the ppf. Give at least two reasons why this could occur. What could be done to move the economy to a point *on* the ppf?

c. Suppose you succeeded in lifting your economy to a point on its ppf. What point would you choose? How might your small society decide the point at which it wanted to be?

d. Once you have chosen a point on the ppf, you still need to decide how your society's production will be divided. If you were a dictator, how would you decide? What would happen if you left product distribution to the free market?

*8. Match each diagram in Figure 1 on the next page with its description here. Assume that the economy is producing or attempting to produce at point A and that most members of society like meat and not fish. Some descriptions apply to more than one diagram, and some diagrams have more than one description.

a. Inefficient production of meat and fish

b. Productive efficiency

c. An inefficient mix of output

d. Technological advances in the production of meat and fish

e. The law of increasing opportunity cost

f. An impossible combination of meat and fish

9. A nation with fixed quantities of resources is able to produce any of the following combinations of bread and ovens:

LOAVES OF BREAD (MILLIONS)	OVENS (THOUSANDS)
75	0
60	12
45	22
30	30
15	36
0	40

These figures assume that a certain number of previously produced ovens are available in the current period for baking bread.

a. Using the data in the table, graph the ppf (with ovens on the vertical axis).

b. Does the principle of "increasing opportunity cost" hold in this nation? Explain briefly. (*Hint:* What happens to the opportunity cost of bread—measured in number of ovens—as bread production increases?)

c. If this country chooses to produce both ovens and bread, what will happen to the ppf over time? Why?

Now suppose that a new technology is discovered that allows twice as many loaves of bread to be baked in each existing oven.

d. Illustrate (on your original graph) the effect of this new technology on the ppf.

e. Suppose that before the new technology is introduced, the nation produces 22 ovens. After the new technology is

*Note: Problems marked with an asterisk are more challenging.

introduced, the nation produces 30 ovens. What is the effect of the new technology on the production of bread? (Give the number of loaves before and after the change.)

10. [Related to the *Economics in Practice* on *p. 28*] An analysis of a large-scale survey of consumer food purchases by Mark Aguiar and Erik Hurst indicates that retired people spend less *for the same market basket of food* than working people do. Use the concept of opportunity cost to explain this fact.

*11. Dr. Falk is a dentist who performs two basic procedures: filling cavities and whitening teeth. Falk charges $50 per cavity filled, a process that takes him 15 minutes per tooth and requires no help or materials. For tooth whitening, a process requiring 30 minutes, Falk charges $150 net of materials. Again, no help is required. Is anything puzzling about Falk's pricing pattern? Explain your answer.

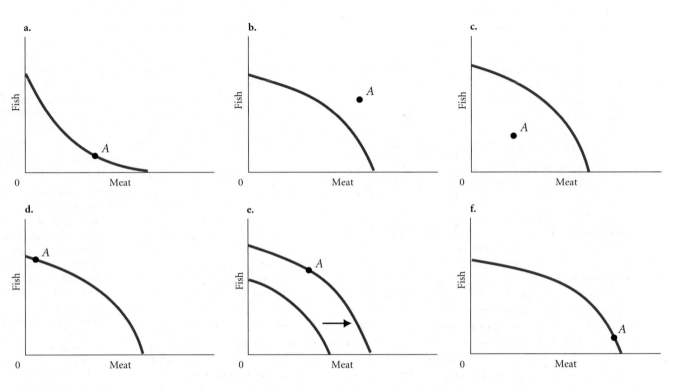

▲ FIGURE 1

Demand, Supply, and Market Equilibrium

3

Chapters 1 and 2 introduced the discipline, methodology, and subject matter of economics. We now begin the task of analyzing how a market economy actually works. This chapter and the next present an overview of the way individual markets work. They introduce some of the concepts needed to understand both microeconomics and macroeconomics.

As we proceed to define terms and make assumptions, it is important to keep in mind what we are doing. In Chapter 1 we explained what economic theory

attempts to do. Theories are abstract representations of reality, like a map that represents a city. We believe that the models presented here will help you understand the workings of the economy just as a map helps you find your way around a city. Just as a map presents one view of the world, so too does any given theory of the economy. Alternatives exist to the theory that we present. We believe, however, that the basic model presented here, while sometimes abstract, is useful in gaining an understanding of how the economy works.

In the simple island society discussed in Chapter 2, Bill and Colleen solved the economic problem directly. They allocated their time and used the island's resources to satisfy their wants. Bill might be a farmer, Colleen a hunter and carpenter. He might be a civil engineer, she a doctor. Exchange occurred, but complex markets were not necessary.

In societies of many people, however, production must satisfy wide-ranging tastes and preferences. Producers therefore specialize. Farmers produce more food than they can eat so that they can sell it to buy manufactured goods. Physicians are paid for specialized services, as are attorneys, construction workers, and editors. When there is specialization, there must be exchange, and *markets* are the institutions through which exchange takes place.

This chapter begins to explore the basic forces at work in market systems. The purpose of our discussion is to explain how the individual decisions of households and firms together, without any central planning or direction, answer the three basic questions: What gets produced? How is it produced? Who gets what is produced? We begin with some definitions.

Firms and Households: The Basic Decision-Making Units

Throughout this book, we discuss and analyze the behavior of two fundamental decision-making units: *firms*—the primary producing units in an economy—and *households*—the consuming units in an economy. Both are made up of people performing different functions and playing different roles. In essence, what we are developing is a theory of human behavior.

firm An organization that transforms resources (inputs) into products (outputs). Firms are the primary producing units in a market economy.

A **firm** exists when a person or a group of people decides to produce a product or products by transforming *inputs*—that is, resources in the broadest sense—into *outputs*, the products that are sold in the market. Some firms produce goods; others produce services. Some are large, many are small, and some are in between. All firms exist to transform resources into goods and services that people want. The Colorado Symphony Orchestra takes labor, land, a building, musically talented people, instruments, and other inputs and combines them to produce concerts. The production process can be extremely complicated. For example, the first flautist in the orchestra uses training, talent, previous performance experience, score, instrument, conductor's interpretation, and personal feelings about the music to produce just one contribution to an overall performance.

Most firms exist to make a profit for their owners, but some do not. Columbia University, for example, fits the description of a firm: It takes inputs in the form of labor, land, skills, books, and buildings and produces a service that we call education. Although the university sells that service for a price, it does not exist to make a profit; instead, it exists to provide education of the highest quality possible.

Still, most firms exist to make a profit. They engage in production because they can sell their product for more than it costs to produce it. The analysis of a firm's behavior that follows rests on the assumption that *firms make decisions in order to maximize profits.*

entrepreneur A person who organizes, manages, and assumes the risks of a firm, taking a new idea or a new product and turning it into a successful business.

An **entrepreneur** is a person who organizes, manages, and assumes the risks of a firm. When a new firm is created, someone must organize the new firm, arrange financing, hire employees, and take risks. That person is an entrepreneur. Sometimes existing firms introduce new products, and sometimes new firms develop or improve on an old idea, but at the root of it all is entrepreneurship, which some see as the core of the free enterprise system.

At the heart of the debate about the potential of free enterprise in formerly socialist Eastern Europe is the question of entrepreneurship. Does an entrepreneurial spirit exist in that part of the world? If not, can it be developed? Without it, the free enterprise system breaks down.

households The consuming units in an economy.

The consuming units in an economy are **households**. A household may consist of any number of people: a single person living alone, a married couple with four children, or 15 unrelated people sharing a house. Household decisions are presumably based on individual tastes and preferences. The household buys what it wants and can afford. In a large, heterogeneous, and open society such as the United States, wildly different tastes find expression in the marketplace. A six-block walk in any direction on any street in Manhattan or a drive from the Chicago Loop south into rural Illinois should be enough to convince someone that it is difficult to generalize about what people do and do not like.

Even though households have wide-ranging preferences, they also have some things in common. All—even the very rich—have ultimately limited incomes, and all must pay in some way for the goods and services that they consume. Although households may have some control over their incomes—they can work more hours or fewer hours—they are also constrained by the availability of jobs, current wages, their own abilities, and their accumulated and inherited wealth (or lack thereof).

Input Markets and Output Markets: The Circular Flow

Households and firms interact in two basic kinds of markets: product (or output) markets and input (or factor) markets. Goods and services that are intended for use by households are exchanged in **product or output markets**. In output markets, firms *supply* and households *demand*.

product or output markets The markets in which goods and services are exchanged.

input or factor markets The markets in which the resources used to produce goods and services are exchanged.

To produce goods and services, firms must buy resources in **input or factor markets**. Firms buy inputs from households, which supply these inputs. When a firm decides how much to produce (supply) in output markets, it must simultaneously decide how much of each input it needs to produce the desired level of output. To produce automobiles, Ford Motor Company must use many inputs, including tires, steel, complicated machinery, and many different kinds of labor.

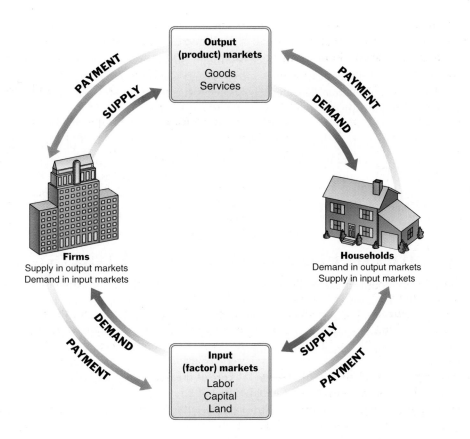

Firms
Supply in output markets
Demand in input markets

Households
Demand in output markets
Supply in input markets

Output (product) markets
Goods
Services

Input (factor) markets
Labor
Capital
Land

◀ **FIGURE 3.1 The Circular Flow of Economic Activity**
Diagrams like this one show the circular flow of economic activity, hence the name *circular flow diagram*. Here goods and services flow clockwise: Labor services supplied by households flow to firms, and goods and services produced by firms flow to households. Payment (usually money) flows in the opposite (counterclockwise) direction: Payment for goods and services flows from households to firms, and payment for labor services flows from firms to households.

Note: Color Guide—In Figure 3.1 households are depicted in *blue* and firms are depicted in *red*. From now on all diagrams relating to the behavior of households will be blue or shades of blue and all diagrams relating to the behavior of firms will be red or shades of red.

Figure 3.1 shows the *circular flow* of economic activity through a simple market economy. Note that the flow reflects the direction in which goods and services flow through input and output markets. For example, goods and services flow from firms to households through output markets. Labor services flow from households to firms through input markets. Payment (most often in money form) for goods and services flows in the opposite direction.

In input markets, households *supply* resources. Most households earn their incomes by working—they supply their labor in the **labor market** to firms that demand labor and pay workers for their time and skills. Households may also loan their accumulated or inherited savings to firms for interest or exchange those savings for claims to future profits, as when a household buys shares of stock in a corporation. In the **capital market**, households supply the funds that firms use to buy capital goods. Households may also supply land or other real property in exchange for rent in the **land market**.

Inputs into the production process are also called **factors of production**. Land, labor, and capital are the three key factors of production. Throughout this text, we use the terms *input* and *factor of production* interchangeably. Thus, input markets and factor markets mean the same thing.

Early economics texts included entrepreneurship as a type of input, just like land, labor, and capital. Treating entrepreneurship as a separate factor of production has fallen out of favor, however, partially because it is unmeasurable. Most economists today implicitly assume that entrepreneurship is in plentiful supply. That is, if profit opportunities exist, it is likely that entrepreneurs will crop up to take advantage of them. This assumption has turned out to be a good predictor of actual economic behavior and performance.

The supply of inputs and their prices ultimately determine household income. Thus, the amount of income a household earns depends on the decisions it makes concerning what types of inputs it chooses to supply. Whether to stay in school, how much and what kind of training to get, whether to start a business, how many hours to work, whether to work at all, and how to invest savings are all household decisions that affect income.

labor market The input/factor market in which households supply work for wages to firms that demand labor.

capital market The input/factor market in which households supply their savings, for interest or for claims to future profits, to firms that demand funds to buy capital goods.

land market The input/factor market in which households supply land or other real property in exchange for rent.

factors of production The inputs into the production process. Land, labor, and capital are the three key factors of production.

As you can see:

> Input and output markets are connected through the behavior of both firms and households. Firms determine the quantities and character of outputs produced and the types and quantities of inputs demanded. Households determine the types and quantities of products demanded and the quantities and types of inputs supplied.[1]

The following analysis of demand and supply will lead up to a theory of how market prices are determined. Prices are determined by the interaction between demanders and suppliers. To understand this interaction, we first need to know how product prices influence the behavior of demanders and suppliers *separately*. Therefore, we discuss output markets by focusing first on demanders, then on suppliers, and finally on their interaction.

Demand in Product/Output Markets

In real life, households make many decisions at the same time. To see how the forces of demand and supply work, however, let us focus first on the amount of a *single* product that an *individual* household decides to consume within some given period of time, such as a month or a year.

A household's decision about what quantity of a particular output, or product, to demand depends on a number of factors, including:

- The *price of the product* in question.
- The *income available* to the household.
- The household's *amount of accumulated wealth*.
- The *prices of other products* available to the household.
- The household's *tastes and preferences*.
- The household's *expectations* about future income, wealth, and prices.

quantity demanded The amount (number of units) of a product that a household would buy in a given period if it could buy all it wanted at the current market price.

Quantity demanded is the amount (number of units) of a product that a household would buy in a given period *if it could buy all it wanted at the current market price*. Of course, the amount of a product that households finally purchase depends on the amount of product actually available in the market. The expression *if it could buy all it wanted* is critical to the definition of quantity demanded because it allows for the possibility that quantity supplied and quantity demanded are unequal.

Changes in Quantity Demanded versus Changes in Demand

The most important relationship in individual markets is that between market price and quantity demanded. For this reason, we need to begin our discussion by analyzing the likely response of households to changes in price using the device of *ceteris paribus*, or "all else equal." That is, we will attempt to derive a relationship between the quantity demanded of a good per time period and the price of that good, holding income, wealth, other prices, tastes, and expectations constant.

It is very important to distinguish between price changes, which affect the quantity of a good demanded, and changes in other factors (such as income), which change the entire relationship between price and quantity. For example, if a family begins earning a higher income, it might buy more of a good at every possible price. To be sure that we distinguish between changes in price

---

[1] Our description of markets begins with the behavior of firms and households. Modern orthodox economic theory essentially combines two distinct but closely related theories of behavior. The "theory of household behavior," or "consumer behavior," has its roots in the works of nineteenth century utilitarians such as Jeremy Bentham, William Jevons, Carl Menger, Leon Walras, Vilfredo Parcto, and F. Y. Edgeworth. The "theory of the firm" developed out of the earlier classical political economy of Adam Smith, David Ricardo, and Thomas Malthus. In 1890, Alfred Marshall published the first of many editions of his *Principles of Economics*. That volume pulled together the main themes of both the classical economists and the utilitarians into what is now called *neoclassical economics*. While there have been many changes over the years, the basic structure of the model that we build can be found in Marshall's work.

and other changes that affect demand, throughout the rest of the text, we will be very precise about terminology. Specifically:

> Changes in the price of a product affect the *quantity demanded* per period. Changes in any other factor, such as income or preferences, affect *demand*. Thus, we say that an increase in the price of Coca-Cola is likely to cause a decrease in the *quantity of Coca-Cola demanded*. However, we say that an increase in income is likely to cause an increase in the *demand* for most goods.

Price and Quantity Demanded: The Law of Demand

A **demand schedule** shows the quantities of a product that a household would be willing to buy at different prices. Table 3.1 presents a hypothetical demand schedule for Anna, a student who goes off to college to study economics while her boyfriend goes to art school. If telephone calls were free (a price of zero), Anna would call her boyfriend every day, or 30 times a month. At a price of $0.50 per call, she makes 25 calls a month. When the price hits $3.50, she cuts back to seven calls a month. This same information presented graphically is called a **demand curve**. Anna's demand curve is presented in Figure 3.2.

You will note in Figure 3.2 that *quantity* (*q*) is measured along the horizontal axis and *price* (*P*) is measured along the vertical axis. This is the convention we follow throughout this book.

demand schedule A table showing how much of a given product a household would be willing to buy at different prices.

demand curve A graph illustrating how much of a given product a household would be willing to buy at different prices.

TABLE 3.1	Anna's Demand Schedule for Telephone Calls
Price (Per Call)	Quantity Demanded (Calls Per Month)
$ 0.00	30
0.50	25
3.50	7
7.00	3
10.00	1
15.00	0

◀ **FIGURE 3.2 Anna's Demand Curve**

The relationship between price (*P*) and quantity demanded (*q*) presented graphically is called a demand curve. Demand curves have a negative slope, indicating that lower prices cause quantity demanded to increase. Note that Anna's demand curve is blue; demand in product markets is determined by household choice.

Demand Curves Slope Downward The data in Table 3.1 show that at lower prices, Anna calls her boyfriend more frequently; at higher prices, she calls less frequently. Thus, there is a *negative, or inverse, relationship between quantity demanded and price*. When price rises, quantity demanded falls, and when price falls, quantity demanded rises. Thus, demand curves always slope downward. This negative relationship between price and quantity demanded is often referred to as the **law of demand**, a term first used by economist Alfred Marshall in his 1890 textbook.

law of demand The negative relationship between price and quantity demanded: As price rises, quantity demanded decreases; as price falls, quantity demanded increases.

Some people are put off by the abstraction of demand curves. Of course, we do not actually draw our own demand curves for products. When we want to make a purchase, we usually face only a single price and how much we would buy at other prices is irrelevant. However, demand curves help analysts understand the kind of behavior that households are *likely* to exhibit if they are actually faced with a higher or lower price. We know, for example, that if the price of a good rises enough, the quantity demanded must ultimately drop to zero. The demand curve is thus a tool that helps us explain economic behavior and predict reactions to possible price changes.

Marshall's definition of a social "law" captures the idea:

> The term "law" means nothing more than a general proposition or statement of tendencies, more or less certain, more or less definite . . . a *social law* is a statement of social tendencies; that is, that a certain course of action may be expected from the members of a social group under certain conditions.[2]

It seems reasonable to expect that consumers will demand more of a product at a lower price and less of it at a higher price. Households must divide their incomes over a wide range of goods and services. If you spend $4.50 for a pound of prime beef, you are sacrificing the other things that you might have bought with that $4.50. If the price of prime beef were to jump to $7 per pound while chicken breasts remained at $1.99 (remember *ceteris paribus*—we are holding all else constant), you would have to give up more chicken and/or other items to buy that pound of beef. So you would probably eat more chicken and less beef. Anna calls her boyfriend three times when phone calls cost $7 each. A fourth call would mean sacrificing $7 worth of other purchases. At a price of $3.50, however, the opportunity cost of each call is lower and she calls more frequently.

Another explanation for the fact that demand curves slope downward rests on the notion of *utility*. Economists use the concept of *utility* to mean happiness or satisfaction. Presumably, we consume goods and services because they give us utility. As we consume more of a product within a given period of time, it is likely that each additional unit consumed will yield successively less satisfaction. The utility you gain from a second ice cream cone is likely to be less than the utility you gained from the first, the third is worth even less, and so on. This *law of diminishing marginal utility* is an important concept in economics. If each successive unit of a good is worth less to you, you are not going to be willing to pay as much for it. Thus, it is reasonable to expect a downward slope in the demand curve for that good.

The idea of diminishing marginal utility also helps to explain Anna's behavior. The demand curve is a way of representing what she is willing to pay per phone call. At a price of $7, she calls her boyfriend three times per month. A fourth call, however, is worth less than the third—that is, the fourth call is worth less than $7 to her—so she stops at three. If the price were only $3.50, however, she would continue calling. Even at $3.50, she would stop at seven calls per month. This behavior reveals that the eighth call has less value to Anna than the seventh.

Thinking about the ways that people are affected by price changes also helps us see what is behind the law of demand. Consider this example: Luis lives and works in Mexico City. His elderly mother lives in Santiago, Chile. Last year the airlines servicing South America got into a price war, and the price of flying between Mexico City and Santiago dropped from 20,000 pesos to 10,000 pesos. How might Luis's behavior change?

First, he is better off. Last year he flew home to Chile three times at a total cost of 60,000 pesos. This year he can fly to Chile the same number of times, buy exactly the same combination of other goods and services that he bought last year, and have 30,000 pesos left over. Because he is better off—his income can buy more—he may fly home more frequently. Second, the opportunity cost of flying home has changed. Before the price war, Luis had to sacrifice 20,000 pesos worth of other goods and services each time he flew to Chile. After the price war, he must sacrifice only 10,000 pesos worth of other goods and services for each trip. The trade-off has changed. Both of these effects are likely to lead to a higher quantity demanded in response to the lower price.

In sum:

> It is reasonable to expect quantity demanded to fall when price rises, *ceteris paribus*, and to expect quantity demanded to rise when price falls, *ceteris paribus*. Demand curves have a negative slope.

---

[2] Alfred Marshall, *Principles of Economics*, 8th ed. (New York: Macmillan, 1948), p. 33. (The first edition was published in 1890.)

Other Properties of Demand Curves   Two additional things are notable about Anna's demand curve. First, it intersects the *Y*-, or price, axis. This means that there is a price above which no calls will be made. In this case, Anna simply stops calling when the price reaches $15 per call. As long as households have limited incomes and wealth, all demand curves will intersect the price axis. For any commodity, there is always a price above which a household will not or cannot pay. Even if the good or service is very important, all households are ultimately constrained, or limited, by income and wealth.

Second, Anna's demand curve intersects the *X*-, or quantity, axis. Even at a zero price, there is a limit to the number of phone calls Anna will make. If telephone calls were free, she would call 30 times a month, but not more. That demand curves intersect the quantity axis is a matter of common sense. Demand in a given period of time is limited, if only by time, even at a zero price.

To summarize what we know about the shape of demand curves:

1. They have a negative slope. An increase in price is likely to lead to a decrease in quantity demanded, and a decrease in price is likely to lead to an increase in quantity demanded.
2. They intersect the quantity (*X*-) axis, a result of time limitations and diminishing marginal utility.
3. They intersect the price (*Y*-) axis, a result of limited income and wealth.

That is all we can say; it is not possible to generalize further. The actual shape of an individual household demand curve—whether it is steep or flat, whether it is bowed in or bowed out—depends on the unique tastes and preferences of the household and other factors. Some households may be very sensitive to price changes; other households may respond little to a change in price. In some cases, plentiful substitutes are available; in other cases, they are not. Thus, to fully understand the shape and position of demand curves, we must turn to the other determinants of household demand.

Other Determinants of Household Demand

Of the many factors likely to influence a household's demand for a specific product, we have considered only the price of the product. Other determining factors include household income and wealth, the prices of other goods and services, tastes and preferences, and expectations.

Income and Wealth   Before we proceed, we need to define two terms that are often confused, *income* and *wealth*. A household's **income** is the sum of all the wages, salaries, profits, interest payments, rents, and other forms of earnings received by the household *in a given period of time*. Income is thus a *flow* measure: We must specify a time period for it—income *per month* or *per year*. You can spend or consume more or less than your income in any given period. If you consume less than your income, you save. To consume more than your income in a period, you must either borrow or draw on savings accumulated from previous periods.

Wealth is the total value of what a household owns minus what it owes. Another word for wealth is **net worth**—the amount a household would have left if it sold all of its possessions and paid all of its debts. Wealth is a *stock* measure: It is measured at a given point in time. If, in a given period, you spend less than your income, you save; the amount that you save is added to your wealth. Saving is the flow that affects the stock of wealth. When you spend more than your income, you *dissave*—you reduce your wealth.

Households with higher incomes and higher accumulated savings or inherited wealth can afford to buy more goods and services. In general, we would expect higher demand at higher levels of income/wealth and lower demand at lower levels of income/wealth. Goods for which demand goes up when income is higher and for which demand goes down when income is lower are called **normal goods**. Movie tickets, restaurant meals, telephone calls, and shirts are all normal goods.

However, generalization in economics can be hazardous. Sometimes demand for a good falls when household income rises. Consider, for example, the various qualities of meat available. When a household's income rises, it is likely to buy higher-quality meats—its demand for filet mignon is likely to rise—but its demand for lower-quality meats—chuck steak, for example—is likely to fall. Transportation is another example. At higher incomes, people can afford to fly. People who can afford to fly are less likely to take the bus long distances. Thus, higher income

income   The sum of all a household's wages, salaries, profits, interest payments, rents, and other forms of earnings in a given period of time. It is a flow measure.

wealth *or* **net worth**   The total value of what a household owns minus what it owes. It is a stock measure.

normal goods   Goods for which demand goes up when income is higher and for which demand goes down when income is lower.

inferior goods Goods for which demand tends to fall when income rises.

may *reduce* the number of times someone takes a bus. Goods for which demand tends to fall when income rises are called **inferior goods**.

Prices of Other Goods and Services No consumer decides in isolation on the amount of any one commodity to buy. Instead, each decision is part of a larger set of decisions that are made simultaneously. Households must apportion their incomes over many different goods and services. As a result, the price of any one good can and does affect the demand for other goods.

This is most obviously the case when goods are substitutes for one another. To return to our lonesome first-year student: If the price of a telephone call rises to $10, Anna will call her boyfriend only once a month. (See Table 3.1 on p. 49.) Of course, she can get in touch with him in other ways. Presumably she substitutes some other, less costly form of communication, such as writing more letters or sending more e-mails.

substitutes Goods that can serve as replacements for one another; when the price of one increases, demand for the other increases.

When an *increase* in the price of one good causes demand for another good to *increase* (a positive relationship), we say that the goods are **substitutes**. A *fall* in the price of a good causes a *decline* in demand for its substitutes. Substitutes are goods that can serve as replacements for one another.

perfect substitutes Identical products.

To be substitutes, two products do not need to be identical. Identical products are called **perfect substitutes**. Japanese cars are not identical to American cars. Nonetheless, all have four wheels, are capable of carrying people, and run on gasoline. Thus, significant changes in the price of one country's cars can be expected to influence demand for the other country's cars. Restaurant meals are substitutes for meals eaten at home, and flying from New York to Washington, D.C., is a substitute for taking the train.

complements, complementary goods Goods that "go together"; a decrease in the price of one results in an increase in demand for the other and vice versa.

Often two products "go together"—that is, they complement each other. Our lonesome letter writer, for example, will find her demand for stamps and stationery rising as she writes more letters and her demand for Internet access rising as she sends more e-mails. Bacon and eggs are **complementary goods**, as are cars and gasoline, and cameras and film. When two goods are **complements**, a *decrease* in the price of one results in an *increase* in demand for the other and vice versa. In mid-2007, Microsoft coordinated the release of its wildly popular game *Halo 3* for the Xbox 360 with the introduction of its new, improved wireless headset because Microsoft understood that the game was a complement to the headset and would thus increase the demand for that product.

Because any one good may have many potential substitutes and complements at the same time, a single price change may affect a household's demands for many goods simultaneously; the demand for some of these products may rise while the demand for others may fall. For example, consider the compact disc read-only memory (CD-ROM). Massive amounts of data can be stored digitally on CDs that can be read by personal computers with a CD-ROM drive. When these drives first came on the market, they were quite expensive, selling for several hundred dollars each. Now they are much less expensive, and most new computers have them built in. As a result, the demand for CD-ROM discs (complementary goods) has soared. As more students adopted the CD technology and the price of CDs and CD hardware fell, fewer students bought printed reference books such as encyclopedias and dictionaries (substitute goods).

Tastes and Preferences Income, wealth, and prices of goods available are the three factors that determine the combinations of goods and services that a household is *able* to buy. You know that you cannot afford to rent an apartment at $1,200 per month if your monthly income is only $400, but within these constraints, you are more or less free to choose what to buy. Your final choice depends on your individual tastes and preferences.

Changes in preferences can and do manifest themselves in market behavior. Thirty years ago the major big-city marathons drew only a few hundred runners. Now tens of thousands enter and run. The demand for running shoes, running suits, stopwatches, and other running items has greatly increased. For many years, people drank soda for refreshment. Today convenience stores are filled with a dizzying array of iced teas, fruit juices, natural beverages, and mineral waters.

Within the constraints of prices and incomes, preference shapes the demand curve, but it is difficult to generalize about tastes and preferences. First, they are volatile: Five years ago more people smoked cigarettes and fewer people had computers. Second, tastes are idiosyncratic: Some people like to talk on the telephone, whereas others prefer to use e-mail; some people prefer dogs, whereas others are crazy about cats; some people like chicken wings, whereas others prefer drumsticks. The diversity of individual demands is almost infinite.

One of the interesting questions in economics is why, in some markets, diverse consumer tastes give rise to a variety of styles, while in other markets, despite a seeming diversity in tastes, we find only one or two varieties. All sidewalks in the United States are a similar gray color, yet houses are painted a rainbow of colors. Yet it is not obvious on the face of it that people would not prefer as much variety in their sidewalks as in their houses. To answer this type of question, we need to move beyond the demand curve. We will revisit this question in a later chapter.

Expectations   What you decide to buy today certainly depends on today's prices and your current income and wealth. You also have expectations about what your position will be in the future. You may have expectations about future changes in prices too, and these may affect your decisions today.

There are many examples of the ways expectations affect demand. When people buy a house or a car, they often must borrow part of the purchase price and repay it over a number of years. In deciding what kind of house or car to buy, they presumably must think about their income today, as well as what their income is likely to be in the future.

As another example, consider a student in the final year of medical school living on a scholarship of $12,000. Compare that student with another person earning $6 an hour at a full-time job, with no expectation of a significant change in income in the future. The two have virtually identical incomes because there are about 2,000 working hours in a year (40 hours per week × 50 work weeks per year). But even if they have the same tastes, the medical student is likely to demand different goods and services, simply because of the expectation of a major increase in income later on.

Increasingly, economic theory has come to recognize the importance of expectations. We will devote a good deal of time to discussing how expectations affect more than just demand. For the time being, however, it is important to understand that demand depends on more than just *current* incomes, prices, and tastes.

Shift of Demand versus Movement Along a Demand Curve

Recall that a demand curve shows the relationship between quantity demanded and the price of a good. Demand curves are derived while holding income, tastes, and other prices constant. If income, tastes, or other prices change, we would have to derive an entirely new relationship between price and quantity.

Let us return once again to Anna. (See Table 3.1 and Figure 3.2 on p. 49.) Suppose that when we derived the demand schedule in Table 3.1, Anna had a part-time job that paid $300 per month. Now suppose that her parents inherit some money and begin sending her an additional $300 per month. Assuming that she keeps her job, Anna's income is now $600 per month.

With her higher income, Anna would probably call her boyfriend more frequently, regardless of the price of a call. Table 3.2 and Figure 3.3 present Anna's original income schedule (D_0) and increased income demand schedule (D_1). Our models tell us that with a higher income, Anna likely makes more calls at each price level. In Table 3.2, we have drawn an example that illustrates this pattern. At $0.50 per call, the frequency of her calls (the quantity she demands) increases from 25 to 33 calls per month; at $3.50 per call, frequency increases from 7 to 18 calls per month; at $10.00 per call, frequency increases from 1 to 7 calls per month. (Note in Figure 3.3 that even if calls are free, Anna's income matters; at zero price, her demand increases. With a higher income, she may visit her boyfriend more, for example, and more visits might mean more phone calls to organize and plan.)

The fact that demand *increased* when income increased implies that telephone calls are *normal goods* to Anna.

The conditions that were in place at the time we drew the original demand curve have now changed. In other words, a factor that affects Anna's demand for telephone calls (in this case, her income) has changed, and there is now a new relationship between price and quantity demanded. Such a change is referred to as a **shift of a demand curve**.

It is very important to distinguish between a change in quantity demanded—that is, some movement *along* a demand curve—and a shift of demand. Demand schedules and demand curves show the relationship between the price of a good or service and the quantity demanded per period, *ceteris paribus*. If price changes, quantity demanded will change—this is a

shift of a demand curve
The change that takes place in a demand curve corresponding to a new relationship between quantity demanded of a good and price of that good. The shift is brought about by a change in the original conditions.

TABLE 3.2 Shift of Anna's Demand Schedule Due to Increase in Income

Price (Per Call)	Schedule D_0 Quantity Demanded (Calls per Month at an Income of $300 per Month)	Schedule D_1 Quantity Demanded (Calls per Month at an Income of $600 per Month)
$ 0.00	30	35
0.50	25	33
3.50	7	18
7.00	3	12
10.00	1	7
15.00	0	2
20.00	0	0

movement along a demand curve The change in quantity demanded brought about by a change in price.

movement along a demand curve. When any of the *other* factors that influence demand change, however, a new relationship between price and quantity demanded is established—this is a *shift of a demand curve*. The result, then, is a *new* demand curve. Changes in income, preferences, or prices of other goods cause a demand curve to shift:

Change in price of a good or service leads to
└─────▶ Change in *quantity demanded* (**movement along a demand curve**).

Change in income, preferences, or prices of other goods or services leads to
└─────▶ Change in *demand* (**shift of a demand curve**).

Figure 3.4 illustrates the differences between movement along a demand curve and shifting demand curves. In Figure 3.4(a), an increase in household income causes demand for hamburger (an inferior good) to decline, or shift to the left from D_0 to D_1. (Because quantity is measured on the horizontal axis, a decrease means a *shift to the left*.) In contrast, demand for steak (a normal good) increases, or *shifts to the right*, when income rises.

In Figure 3.4(b), an increase in the price of hamburger from $1.49 to $3.09 a pound causes a household to buy less hamburger each month. In other words, the higher price causes the *quantity demanded* to decline from 10 pounds to 5 pounds per month. This change represents a movement *along* the demand curve for hamburger. In place of hamburger, the household buys more chicken. The household's demand for chicken (a substitute for hamburger) rises—the demand curve shifts to the right. At the same time, the demand for ketchup (a good that complements hamburger) declines—its demand curve shifts to the left.

▶ **FIGURE 3.3 Shift of a Demand Curve Following a Rise in Income**
When the price of a good changes, we move *along* the demand curve for that good. When any other factor that influences demand changes (income, tastes, and so on), the relationship between price and quantity is different; there is a *shift* of the demand curve, in this case from D_0 to D_1. Telephone calls are normal goods.

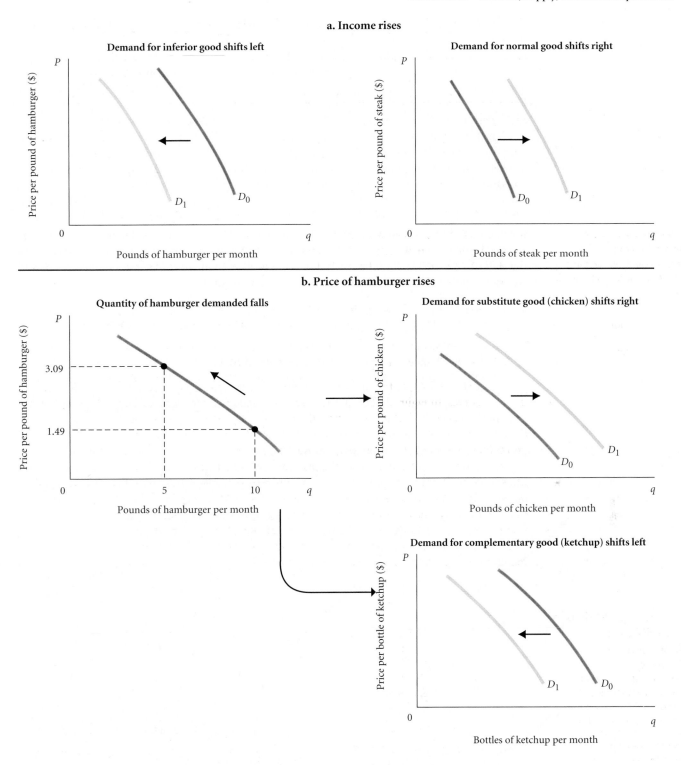

▲ **FIGURE 3.4 Shifts versus Movement Along a Demand Curve**
a. When income increases, the demand for inferior goods *shifts to the left* and the demand for normal goods *shifts to the right*. **b.** If the price of hamburger rises, the quantity of hamburger demanded declines—this is a movement along the demand curve. The same price rise for hamburger would shift the demand for chicken (a substitute for hamburger) to the right and the demand for ketchup (a complement to hamburger) to the left.

From Household Demand to Market Demand

Market demand is simply the sum of all the quantities of a good or service demanded per period by all the households buying in the market for that good or service. Figure 3.5 shows the derivation of a market demand curve from three individual demand curves. (Although this

market demand The sum of all the quantities of a good or service demanded per period by all the households buying in the market for that good or service.

market demand curve is derived from the behavior of only three people, most markets have thousands, or even millions of demanders.) As the table in Figure 3.5 shows, when the price of a pound of coffee is $3.50, both household A and household C would purchase 4 pounds per month, while household B would buy none. At that price, presumably, B drinks tea. Market demand at $3.50 would thus be a total of 4 + 4, or 8 pounds. At a price of $1.50 per pound, however, A would purchase 8 pounds per month; B, 3 pounds; and C, 9 pounds. Thus, at $1.50 per pound, market demand would be 8 + 3 + 9, or 20 pounds of coffee per month.

The total quantity demanded in the marketplace at a given price is simply the sum of all the quantities demanded by all the individual households shopping in the market *at that price*. A market demand curve shows the total amount of a product that would be sold at each price if households could buy all they wanted at that price. As Figure 3.5 shows, the market demand curve is the sum of all the individual demand curves—that is, the sum of all the individual quantities demanded at each price. Thus, the market demand curve takes its shape and position from the shapes, positions, and number of individual demand curves. If more people decide to shop in a market, more demand curves must be added and the market demand curve will shift to the right. Market demand curves may also shift as a result of preference changes, income changes, or changes in the number of demanders.

An interesting fact about the market demand curve in Figure 3.5 is that at different prices, not only the number of people demanding the product may change but also the *type* of people demanding the product. When Apple halved the price of its iPhone in fall 2007, it announced that it wanted to make the iPhone available to a broader group of people. When prices fall, people like those in household B in Figure 3.5 move into markets that are otherwise out of their reach.

As a general rule throughout this book, capital letters refer to the entire market and lower-case letters refer to individual households or firms. Thus, in Figure 3.5, Q refers to total quantity demanded in the market, while q refers to the quantity demanded by individual households.

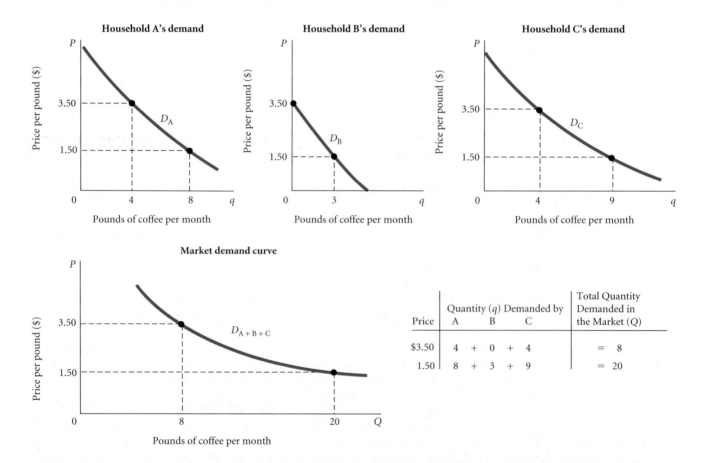

▲ FIGURE 3.5 Deriving Market Demand from Individual Demand Curves

Total demand in the marketplace is simply the sum of the demands of all the households shopping in a particular market. It is the sum of all the individual demand curves—that is, the sum of all the individual quantities demanded at each price.

Supply in Product/Output Markets

In addition to dealing with household demands for outputs, economic theory deals with the behavior of business firms, which supply in output markets and demand in input markets. (See Figure 3.1 on p. 47 again.) Firms engage in production, and we assume that they do so for profit. Successful firms make profits because they are able to sell their products for more than it costs to produce them.

Thus, supply decisions can be expected to depend on profit potential. Because **profit** is the difference between revenues and costs, supply is likely to react to changes in revenues and changes in production costs. The amount of revenue that a firm earns depends on what the price of its product in the market is and on how much it sells. Costs of production depend on many factors, the most important of which are (1) the kinds of inputs needed to produce the product, (2) the amount of each input required, and (3) the prices of inputs.

The supply decision is just one of several decisions that firms make to maximize profit. There are usually a number of ways to produce any given product. A golf course can be built by hundreds of workers with shovels and grass seed or by a few workers with heavy earth-moving equipment and sod blankets. Hamburgers can be fried individually by a short-order cook or grilled by the hundreds on a mechanized moving grill. Firms must choose the production technique most appropriate to their products and projected levels of production. The best method of production is the one that minimizes cost, thus maximizing profit.

Which production technique is best, in turn, depends on the prices of inputs. Where labor is cheap and machinery is expensive and difficult to transport, firms are likely to choose production techniques that use a great deal of labor. Where machines or resources to produce machines are readily available and labor is scarce or expensive, firms are likely to choose more capital-intensive methods. Obviously, the technique ultimately chosen determines input requirements. Thus, by choosing an output supply target and the most appropriate technology, firms determine which inputs to demand.

With the caution that no decision exists in a vacuum, let us begin our examination of firm behavior by focusing on the output supply decision and the relationship between quantity supplied and output price, *ceteris paribus*.

profit The difference between revenues and costs.

Price and Quantity Supplied: The Law of Supply

Quantity supplied is the amount of a particular product that firms would be willing and able to offer for sale at a particular price during a given time period. A **supply schedule** shows how much of a product firms will sell at alternative prices.

Let us look at an agricultural market as an example. Table 3.3 itemizes the quantities of soybeans that an individual representative farmer such as Clarence Brown might sell at various prices. If the market paid $1.50 or less for a bushel for soybeans, Brown would not supply any soybeans: When Farmer Brown looks at the costs of growing soybeans, including the opportunity cost of his time and land, $1.50 per bushel will not compensate him for those costs. At $1.75 per bushel, however, at least some soybean production takes place on Brown's farm, and a price increase from $1.75 to $2.25 per bushel causes the quantity supplied by Brown to increase from 10,000 to 20,000 bushels per year. The higher price may justify shifting land from wheat to soybean production or putting previously fallow land into soybeans, or it may lead to more intensive farming of land already in soybeans, using expensive fertilizer or equipment that was not cost-justified at the lower price.

Generalizing from Farmer Brown's experience, we can reasonably expect an increase in market price, *ceteris paribus*, to lead to an increase in quantity supplied for Brown and farmers like him. In other words, there is a positive relationship between the quantity of a good supplied and price. This statement sums up the **law of supply**: An increase in market price will lead to an increase in quantity supplied, and a decrease in market price will lead to a decrease in quantity supplied.

The information in a supply schedule may be presented graphically in a **supply curve**. Supply curves slope upward. The upward, or positive, slope of Brown's curve in Figure 3.6 reflects this positive relationship between price and quantity supplied.

quantity supplied The amount of a particular product that a firm would be willing and able to offer for sale at a particular price during a given time period.

supply schedule A table showing how much of a product firms will sell at alternative prices.

law of supply The positive relationship between price and quantity of a good supplied: An increase in market price will lead to an increase in quantity supplied, and a decrease in market price will lead to a decrease in quantity supplied.

supply curve A graph illustrating how much of a product a firm will sell at different prices.

TABLE 3.3	Clarence Brown's Supply Schedule for Soybeans
Price (Per Bushel)	Quantity Supplied (Bushels Per Year)
$1.50	0
1.75	10,000
2.25	20,000
3.00	30,000
4.00	45,000
5.00	45,000

▶ **FIGURE 3.6 Clarence Brown's Individual Supply Curve**
A producer will supply more when the price of output is higher. The slope of a supply curve is positive. Note that the supply curve is red: Supply is determined by choices made by firms.

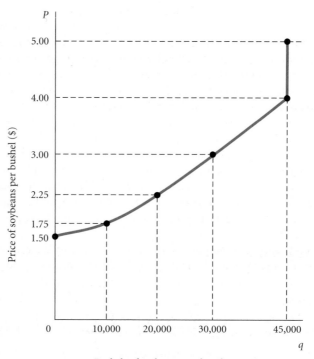

Bushels of soybeans produced per year

Note in Brown's supply schedule, however, that when price rises from $4 to $5, quantity supplied no longer increases. Often an individual firm's ability to respond to an increase in price is constrained by its existing scale of operations, or capacity, in the short run. For example, Brown's ability to produce more soybeans depends on the size of his farm, the fertility of his soil, and the types of equipment he has. The fact that output stays constant at 45,000 bushels per year suggests that he is running up against the limits imposed by the size of his farm, the quality of his soil, and his existing technology.

In the longer run, however, Brown may acquire more land or technology may change, allowing for more soybean production. The terms *short run* and *long run* have very precise meanings in economics; we will discuss them in detail later. Here it is important only to understand that time plays a critical role in supply decisions. When prices change, firms' immediate response may be different from what they are able to do after a month or a year. Short-run and long-run supply curves are often different.

Other Determinants of Supply

Of the factors we have listed that are likely to affect the quantity of output supplied by a given firm, we have thus far discussed only the price of output. Other factors that affect supply include the cost of producing the product and the prices of related products.

The Cost of Production In order for a firm to make a profit, its revenue must exceed its costs. As an individual producer, like Farmer Brown, thinks about how much to supply at a particular price, the producer will be looking at his or her costs. Brown's supply decision is likely to change in response to changes in the cost of production. Cost of production depends on a number of factors, including the available technologies and the prices and quantities of the inputs needed by the firm (labor, land, capital, energy, and so on).

Technological change can have an enormous impact on the cost of production over time. Consider agriculture. The introduction of fertilizers, the development of complex farm machinery, and the use of bioengineering to increase the yield of individual crops have all powerfully affected the cost of producing agricultural products. Farm productivity in the United States has been increasing dramatically for decades. Yield per acre of corn production has increased fivefold since the late 1930s, and the amount of labor required to produce 100 bushels of corn has fallen from 108 hours in the late 1930s to 20 hours in the late 1950s to less than 3 hours today. (See Table 2.2 on p. 36.)

When a technological advance lowers the cost of production, output is likely to increase. When yield per acre increases, individual farmers can and do produce more. The output of the Ford Motor Company increased substantially after the introduction of assembly-line techniques. The production of electronic calculators, and later personal computers, boomed with the development of inexpensive techniques to produce microprocessors.

Cost of production is also directly affected by the price of the factors of production. In the spring of 2008, the world price of oil rose to more than $100 per barrel from below $20 in 2002. As a result, cab drivers faced higher gasoline prices, airlines faced higher fuel costs, and manufacturing firms faced higher heating bills. The result: Cab drivers probably spent less time driving around looking for customers, airlines cut a few low-profit routes, and some manufacturing plants stopped running extra shifts. The moral of this story: Increases in input prices raise costs of production and are likely to reduce supply.

The Prices of Related Products Firms often react to changes in the prices of related products. For example, if land can be used for either corn or soybean production, an increase in soybean prices may cause individual farmers to shift acreage out of corn production into soybeans. Thus, an increase in soybean prices actually affects the amount of corn supplied.

Similarly, if beef prices rise, producers may respond by raising more cattle. However, leather comes from cowhide. Thus, an increase in beef prices may actually increase the supply of leather.

To summarize:

Assuming that its objective is to maximize profits, a firm's decision about what quantity of output, or product, to supply depends on:

1. The price of the good or service.
2. The cost of producing the product, which in turn depends on:
   - The price of required inputs (labor, capital, and land).
   - The technologies that can be used to produce the product.
3. The prices of related products.

Shift of Supply versus Movement Along a Supply Curve

A supply curve shows the relationship between the quantity of a good or service supplied by a firm and the price that good or service brings in the market. Higher prices are likely to lead to an increase in quantity supplied, *ceteris paribus*. Remember: The supply curve is derived holding everything constant except price. When the price of a product changes *ceteris paribus*, a change in the quantity supplied follows—that is, a **movement along a supply curve** takes place. As you have seen, supply decisions are also influenced by factors other than price. New relationships between price and quantity supplied come about when factors other than price change, and the result is a **shift of a supply curve**. When factors other than price cause supply curves to shift, we say that there has been a *change in supply*.

movement along a supply curve The change in quantity supplied brought about by a change in price.

shift of a supply curve The change that takes place in a supply curve corresponding to a new relationship between quantity supplied of a good and the price of that good. The shift is brought about by a change in the original conditions.

Recall that the cost of production depends on the price of inputs and the technologies of production available. Now suppose that a major breakthrough in the production of soybeans has occurred: Genetic engineering has produced a superstrain of disease- and pest-resistant seed. Such a technological change would enable individual farmers to supply more soybeans at *any* market price. Table 3.4 and Figure 3.7 describe this change. At $3 a bushel, farmers would have produced 30,000 bushels from the old seed (schedule S_0 in Table 3.4); with the lower cost of production and higher yield resulting from the new seed, they produce 40,000 bushels (schedule S_1 in Table 3.4). At $1.75 per bushel, they would have produced 10,000 bushels from the old seed; but with the lower costs and higher yields, output rises to 23,000 bushels.

TABLE 3.4	Shift of Supply Schedule for Soybeans Following Development of a New Disease-Resistant Seed Strain	
	Schedule S_0	Schedule S_1
Price (per Bushel)	Quantity Supplied (Bushels per Year Using Old Seed)	Quantity Supplied (Bushels per Year Using New Seed)
$1.50	0	5,000
1.75	10,000	23,000
2.25	20,000	33,000
3.00	30,000	40,000
4.00	45,000	54,000
5.00	45,000	54,000

▶ **FIGURE 3.7 Shift of the Supply Curve for Soybeans Following Development of a New Seed Strain**

When the price of a product changes, we move *along* the supply curve for that product; the quantity supplied rises or falls. When any other factor affecting supply changes, the supply curve *shifts*.

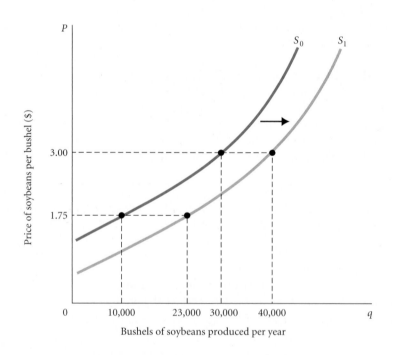

Increases in input prices may also cause supply curves to shift. If Farmer Brown faces higher fuel costs, for example, his supply curve will shift to the left—that is, he will produce less at any given market price. If Brown's soybean supply curve shifted far enough to the left, it would intersect the price axis at a higher point, meaning that it would take a higher market price to induce Brown to produce any soybeans at all.

As with demand, it is very important to distinguish between *movements along* supply curves (changes in quantity supplied) and *shifts in* supply curves (changes in supply):

Change in price of a good or service leads to
└──▶ Change in *quantity supplied* (**movement along a supply curve**).

Change in costs, input prices, technology, or prices of related goods and services leads to
└──▶ Change in *supply* (**shift of a supply curve**).

From Individual Supply to Market Supply

Market supply is determined in the same fashion as market demand. It is simply the sum of all that is supplied each period by all producers of a single product. Figure 3.8 derives a market supply curve from the supply curves of three individual firms. (In a market with more firms, total market supply would be the sum of the amounts produced by each of the firms in that market.) As the table in Figure 3.8 shows, at a price of $3, farm A supplies 30,000 bushels of soybeans, farm B supplies 10,000 bushels, and farm C supplies 25,000 bushels. At this price, the total amount supplied in the market is 30,000 + 10,000 + 25,000, or 65,000 bushels. At a price of $1.75, however, the total amount supplied is only 25,000 bushels (10,000 + 5,000 + 10,000). Thus, the market supply curve is the simple addition of the individual supply curves of all the firms in a particular market—that is, the sum of all the individual quantities supplied at each price.

The position and shape of the market supply curve depends on the positions and shapes of the individual firms' supply curves from which it is derived. The market supply curve also depends on the number of firms that produce in that market. If firms that produce for a particular market are earning high profits, other firms may be tempted to go into that line of business. When the technology to produce computers for home use became available, literally hundreds of new firms got into the act. The popularity and profitability of professional football has, three times, led to the formation of new leagues. When new firms enter an industry, the supply curve shifts to the right. When firms go out of business, or "exit" the market, the supply curve shifts to the left.

market supply The sum of all that is supplied each period by all producers of a single product.

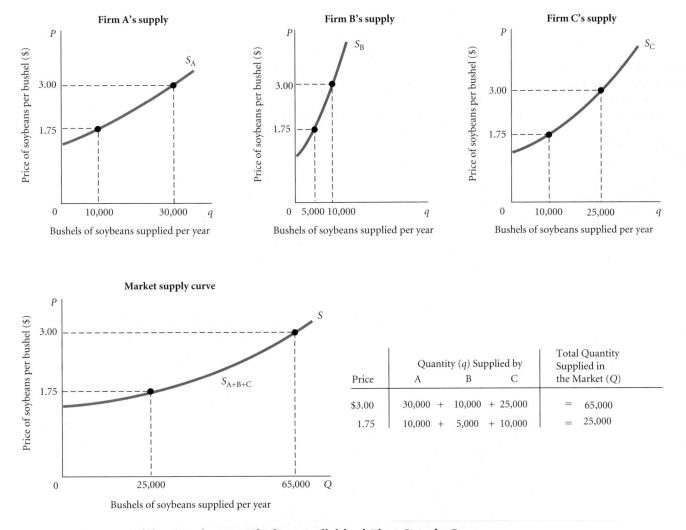

▲ **FIGURE 3.8 Deriving Market Supply from Individual Firm Supply Curves**
Total supply in the marketplace is the sum of all the amounts supplied by all the firms selling in the market. It is the sum of all the individual quantities supplied at each price.

Market Equilibrium

So far, we have identified a number of factors that influence the amount that households demand and the amount that firms supply in product (output) markets. The discussion has emphasized the role of market price as a determinant of both quantity demanded and quantity supplied. We are now ready to see how supply and demand in the market interact to determine the final market price.

We have been very careful in our discussions thus far to separate household decisions about how much to demand from firm decisions about how much to supply. The operation of the market, however, clearly depends on the interaction between suppliers and demanders. At any moment, one of three conditions prevails in every market: (1) The quantity demanded exceeds the quantity supplied at the current price, a situation called *excess demand*; (2) the quantity supplied exceeds the quantity demanded at the current price, a situation called *excess supply*; or (3) the quantity supplied equals the quantity demanded at the current price, a situation called **equilibrium**. At equilibrium, no tendency for price to change exists.

equilibrium The condition that exists when quantity supplied and quantity demanded are equal. At equilibrium, there is no tendency for price to change.

Excess Demand

Excess demand, or a **shortage**, exists when quantity demanded is greater than quantity supplied at the current price. Figure 3.9, which plots both a supply curve and a demand curve on the same graph, illustrates such a situation. As you can see, market demand at $1.75 per bushel (50,000 bushels) exceeds the amount that farmers are currently supplying (25,000 bushels).

excess demand *or* **shortage** The condition that exists when quantity demanded exceeds quantity supplied at the current price.

When excess demand occurs in an unregulated market, there is a tendency for price to rise as demanders compete against each other for the limited supply. The adjustment mechanisms may differ, but the outcome is always the same. For example, consider the mechanism of an auction. In an auction, items are sold directly to the highest bidder. When the auctioneer starts the bidding at a low price, many people bid for the item. At first, there is a shortage: Quantity demanded exceeds quantity supplied. As would-be buyers offer higher and higher prices, bidders drop out until the one who offers the most ends up with the item being auctioned. Price rises until quantity demanded and quantity supplied are equal.

At a price of $1.75 (see Figure 3.9 again), farmers produce soybeans at a rate of 25,000 bushels per year, but at that price, the demand is for 50,000 bushels. Most farm products are sold to local dealers who in turn sell large quantities in major market centers, where bidding would push prices up if quantity demanded exceeded quantity supplied. As price rises above $1.75, two things happen: (1) The quantity demanded falls as buyers drop out of the market and perhaps choose a substitute, and (2) the quantity supplied increases as farmers find themselves receiving a higher price for their product and shift additional acres into soybean production.[3]

▶ **FIGURE 3.9 Excess Demand, or Shortage**
At a price of $1.75 per bushel, quantity demanded exceeds quantity supplied. When excess *demand* exists, there is a tendency for price to rise. When quantity demanded equals quantity supplied, excess demand is eliminated and the market is in equilibrium. Here the equilibrium price is $2.50 and the equilibrium quantity is 35,000 bushels.

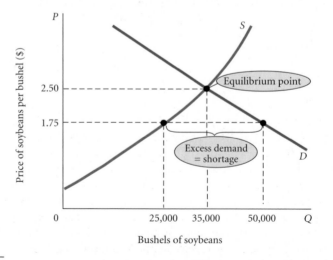

³ Once farmers have produced in any given season, they cannot change their minds and produce more, of course. When we derived Clarence Brown's supply schedule in Table 3.3, we imagined him reacting to prices that existed at the time he decided how much land to plant in soybeans. In Figure 3.9, the upward slope shows that higher prices justify shifting land from other crops. Final price may not be determined until final production figures are in. For our purposes here, however, we have ignored this timing problem. The best way to think about it is that demand and supply are *flows*, or *rates*, of production—that is, we are talking about the number of bushels produced *per production period*. Adjustments in the rate of production may take place over a number of production periods.

This process continues until the shortage is eliminated. In Figure 3.9, this occurs at $2.50, where quantity demanded has fallen from 50,000 to 35,000 bushels per year and quantity supplied has increased from 25,000 to 35,000 bushels per year. When quantity demanded and quantity supplied are equal and there is no further bidding, the process has achieved an equilibrium, a situation in which *there is no natural tendency for further adjustment*. Graphically, the point of equilibrium is the point at which the supply curve and the demand curve intersect.

Increasingly, items are auctioned over the Internet. Companies such as eBay connect buyers and sellers of everything from automobiles to wine and from computers to airline tickets. Auctions are occurring simultaneously with participants located across the globe. The principles through which prices are determined in these auctions are the same: When excess demand exists, prices rise.

While the principles are the same, the process through which excess demand leads to higher prices is different in different markets. Consider the market for houses in the hypothetical town of Boomville with a population of 25,000 people, most of whom live in single-family homes. Normally, about 75 homes are sold in the Boomville market each year. However, last year a major business opened a plant in town, creating 1,500 new jobs that pay good wages. This attracted new residents to the area, and real estate agents now have more buyers than there are properties for sale. Quantity demanded now exceeds quantity supplied. In other words, there is a shortage.

Auctions are not unheard of in the housing market, but they are rare. This market usually works more subtly, but the outcome is the same. Properties are sold very quickly, and housing prices begin to rise. Boomville sellers soon learn that there are more buyers than usual, and they begin to hold out for higher offers. As prices for Boomville houses rise, quantity demanded eventually drops off and quantity supplied increases. Quantity supplied increases in at least two ways: (1) Encouraged by the high prices, builders begin constructing new houses, and (2) some people, attracted by the higher prices their homes will fetch, put their houses on the market. Discouraged by higher prices, however, some potential buyers (demanders) may begin to look for housing in neighboring towns and settle on commuting. Eventually, equilibrium will be reestablished, with the quantity of houses demanded just equal to the quantity of houses supplied.

Although the mechanics of price adjustment in the housing market differ from the mechanics of an auction, the outcome is the same:

> When quantity demanded exceeds quantity supplied, price tends to rise. When the price in a market rises, quantity demanded falls and quantity supplied rises until an equilibrium is reached at which quantity demanded and quantity supplied are equal.

This process is called *price rationing*. When a shortage exists, some people will be satisfied and some will not. When the market operates without interference, price increases will distribute what is available to those who are willing and able to pay the most. As long as there is a way for buyers and sellers to interact, those who are willing to pay more will make that fact known somehow. (We discuss the nature of the price system as a rationing device in detail in Chapter 4.)

Excess Supply

Excess supply, or a **surplus**, exists when the quantity supplied exceeds the quantity demanded at the current price. As with a shortage, the mechanics of price adjustment in the face of a surplus can differ from market to market. For example, if automobile dealers find themselves with unsold cars in the fall when the new models are coming in, you can expect to see price cuts. Sometimes dealers offer discounts to encourage buyers; sometimes buyers themselves simply offer less than the price initially asked. In any event, products do no one any good sitting in dealers' lots or on warehouse shelves. The auction metaphor introduced earlier can also be applied here: If the initial asking price is too high, no one bids and the auctioneer tries a lower price. It is almost always true, and 2007 was no exception, that certain items do not sell as well as anticipated during the Christmas holidays. After Christmas, most stores have big sales during which they lower the prices of overstocked items. Quantities supplied exceeded quantities demanded at the current prices, so stores cut prices.

Across the state from Boomville is Bustville, where last year a drug manufacturer shut down its operations and 1,500 people found themselves out of work. With no other prospects for work,

excess supply *or* **surplus**
The condition that exists when quantity supplied exceeds quantity demanded at the current price.

many residents decided to pack up and move. They put their houses up for sale, but there were few buyers. The result was an excess supply, or surplus, of houses: The quantity of houses supplied exceeded the quantity demanded at the current prices.

As houses sit unsold on the market for months, sellers start to cut their asking prices. Potential buyers begin offering considerably less than sellers are asking. As prices fall, two things are likely to happen. First, the low housing prices may attract new buyers. People who might have bought in a neighboring town see that housing bargains are to be had in Bustville, and quantity demanded rises in response to price decline. Second, some of those people who put their houses on the market may be discouraged by the lower prices and decide to stay in Bustville. Developers are certainly not likely to be building new housing in town. Thus, lower prices lead to a decline in quantity supplied as potential sellers pull their houses from the market. This was the situation in New England and California in the early 1990s.

Figure 3.10 illustrates another excess supply/surplus situation. At a price of $3 per bushel, suppose farmers are supplying soybeans at a rate of 40,000 bushels per year, but buyers are demanding only 20,000. With 20,000 (40,000 minus 20,000) bushels of soybeans going unsold, the market price falls. As price falls from $3.00 to $2.50, quantity supplied decreases from 40,000 bushels per year to 35,000. The lower price causes quantity demanded to rise from 20,000 to 35,000. At $2.50, quantity demanded and quantity supplied are equal. For the data shown here, $2.50 and 35,000 bushels are the equilibrium price and quantity, respectively.

Although oil prices rose to record levels in 2008, back in 2001, crude oil production worldwide exceeded the quantity demanded and prices fell significantly as competing producer countries tried to maintain their share of world markets. Although the mechanism by which price is adjusted is different for automobiles, housing, soybeans, and crude oil, the outcome is the same:

> When quantity supplied exceeds quantity demanded at the current price, the price tends to fall. When price falls, quantity supplied is likely to decrease and quantity demanded is likely to increase until an equilibrium price is reached where quantity supplied and quantity demanded are equal.

▶ **FIGURE 3.10 Excess Supply, or Surplus**
At a price of $3.00, quantity supplied exceeds quantity demanded by 20,000 bushels. This excess supply will cause the price to fall.

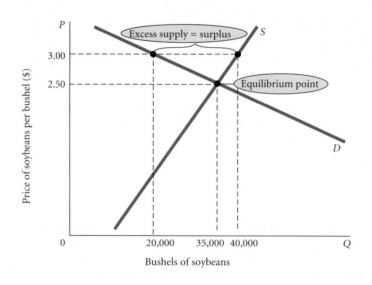

Changes in Equilibrium

When supply and demand curves shift, the equilibrium price and quantity change. The following example will help to illustrate this point.

South America is a major producer of coffee beans. A cold snap there can reduce the coffee harvest enough to affect the world price of coffee beans. In the mid-1990s, a major freeze hit Brazil and Colombia and drove up the price of coffee on world markets to a record $2.40 per pound. Severe hurricanes in the Caribbean caused a similar shift of supply in 2005.

Figure 3.11 illustrates how the freeze pushed up coffee prices. Initially, the market was in equilibrium at a price of $1.20. At that price, the quantity demanded was equal to quantity supplied (13.2 billion pounds). At a price of $1.20 and a quantity of 13.2 billion pounds, the demand curve (labeled D) intersected the initial supply curve (labeled S_0). (Remember that equilibrium exists when quantity demanded equals quantity supplied—the point at which the supply and demand curves intersect.)

The freeze caused a decrease in the supply of coffee beans. That is, the freeze caused the supply curve to shift to the left. In Figure 3.11, the new supply curve (the supply curve that shows the relationship between price and quantity supplied after the freeze) is labeled S_1.

At the initial equilibrium price, $1.20, there is now a shortage of coffee. If the price were to remain at $1.20, quantity demanded would not change; it would remain at 13.2 billion pounds. However, at that price, quantity supplied would drop to 6.6 billion pounds. At a price of $1.20, quantity demanded is greater than quantity supplied.

When excess demand exists in a market, price can be expected to rise, and rise it did. As the figure shows, price rose to a new equilibrium at $2.40. At $2.40, quantity demanded is again equal to quantity supplied, this time at 9.9 billion pounds—the point at which the new supply curve (S_1) intersects the demand curve.

Notice that as the price of coffee rose from $1.20 to $2.40, two things happened. First, the quantity demanded declined (a movement along the demand curve) as people shifted to substitutes such as tea and hot cocoa. Second, the quantity supplied began to rise, but within the limits imposed by the damage from the freeze. (It might also be that some countries or areas with high costs of production, previously unprofitable, came into production and shipped to the world market at the higher price.) That is, the quantity supplied increased in response to the higher price *along* the new supply curve, which lies to the left of the old supply curve. The final result was a higher price ($2.40), a smaller quantity finally exchanged in the market (9.9 billion pounds), and coffee bought only by those willing to pay $2.40 per pound.

Since many market prices are driven by the interaction of millions of buyers and sellers, it is often difficult to predict how they will change. A series of events in the mid-1990s led to the leftward shift in supply, thus driving up the price of coffee, but the opposite occurred more recently. Today coffee beans are exported by over 50 countries, with Brazil being the largest producer with about 30 percent of the market. Large increases in production have kept prices low. In July 2007, the average price per pound was $1.06.

Figure 3.12 summarizes the possible supply and demand shifts that have been discussed and the resulting changes in equilibrium price and quantity. Study the graphs carefully to ensure that you understand them.

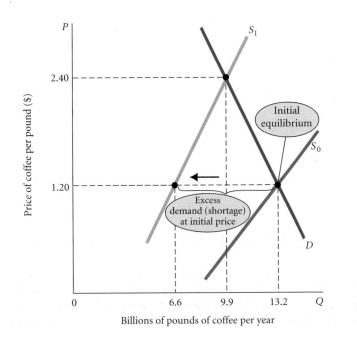

◀ **FIGURE 3.11 The Coffee Market: A Shift of Supply and Subsequent Price Adjustment**
Before the freeze, the coffee market was in equilibrium at a price of $1.20 per pound. At that price, quantity demanded equaled quantity supplied. The freeze shifted the supply curve to the left (from S_0 to S_1), increasing the equilibrium price to $2.40.

▲ FIGURE 3.12 Examples of Supply and Demand Shifts for Product X

Demand and Supply in Product Markets: A Review

As you continue your study of economics, you will discover that it is a discipline full of controversy and debate. There is, however, little disagreement about the basic way that the forces of supply and demand operate in free markets. If you hear that a freeze in Florida has destroyed a good portion of the citrus crop, you can bet that the price of oranges will rise.

ECONOMICS IN PRACTICE

Bad News for Orange Juice Fanatics

This article once again shows the way in which the laws of supply and demand end up affecting our lives. In this article, the bad weather in California caused the supply of oranges—an essential input into orange juice (OJ)—to drop dramatically. This shift in the supply curve to the left raised the price of those oranges for companies such as Tropicana as we see in the graph below. The most likely result is the one described here: an increase in the price of orange juice.

For those of you interested in this topic, you might enjoy Eddie Murphy in the movie *Trading Places*. In the movie, a freeze in Florida and the resulting change in the price of orange juice futures contracts play an important role.

We should also note that while the story told in the article is most likely the case in practice, in theory a freeze has the potential to actually lower frozen orange juice prices. Frozen oranges are useless as fresh fruit, but some fraction can typically be salvaged for frozen juice. Thus while the overall supply of oranges falls with a freeze, we may also see a shift in the remaining oranges from fresh to frozen. In theory this could shift the supply to frozen OJ firms to the right, lowering price. In Florida, most oranges are currently used for frozen orange juice, and so the story told in the article is most likely the case in practice.

Orange Juice Prices Could Skyrocket After Freeze Destroys Most of California Output

City News

It's not a place where they often talk about the cold.

But farmers in California aren't thinking about much else this week, and you may soon be sharing their distress.

The freak cold snap that has left oranges from the Golden State frozen amid icicles on the trees could send the cost of your morning glass of OJ skyrocketing.

New figures show that three days of below freezing temperatures have destroyed as much as three quarters of the state's $1 billion citrus crop, a devastating blow unseen since a similar spell in December 1998 left growers with a $700 million loss.

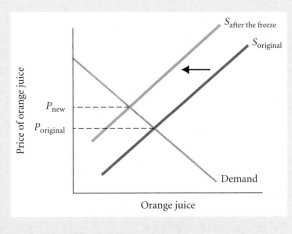

It's believed 50–75 percent of all crops were lost to the weather, and while the farmers tried to save what they could before the big blast hit, a labour shortage kept them from getting too much of it.

"When you're already cutting the ice within the oranges, you know those are gone," laments Philip LoBue, who represents a growers' trade organization.

It's believed the loss could total some $960 million.

It's some bad weather in a place 3,000 miles away, so what does it mean to you? A lot if you buy fresh fruit or juice.

Last November, the makers of Tropicana warned they might have to raise prices on their popular orange juice by 12.5 percent in 2007, because of a devastating disease that ravaged much of Florida's citrus crop.

With the California output now also in doubt, it's possible the cost of your next morning glass of fruit juice could soar at local supermarkets in the coming weeks.

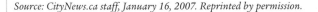

Source: CityNews.ca staff, January 16, 2007. Reprinted by permission.

If you read that the weather in the Midwest has been good and a record corn crop is expected, you can bet that corn prices will fall. When fishermen in Massachusetts go on strike and stop bringing in the daily catch, you can bet that the price of fish will go up.

Here are some important points to remember about the mechanics of supply and demand in product markets:

1. A demand curve shows how much of a product a household would buy if it could buy all it wanted at the given price. A supply curve shows how much of a product a firm would supply if it could sell all it wanted at the given price.

2. Quantity demanded and quantity supplied are always per time period—that is, per day, per month, or per year.

3. The demand for a good is determined by price, household income and wealth, prices of other goods and services, tastes and preferences, and expectations.

4. The supply of a good is determined by price, costs of production, and prices of related products. Costs of production are determined by available technologies of production and input prices.

5. Be careful to distinguish between movements along supply and demand curves and shifts of these curves. When the price of a good changes, the quantity of that good demanded or supplied changes—that is, a movement occurs along the curve. When any other factor changes, the curve shifts, or changes position.

6. Market equilibrium exists only when quantity supplied equals quantity demanded at the current price.

Looking Ahead: Markets and the Allocation of Resources

You can already begin to see how markets answer the basic economic questions of what is produced, how it is produced, and who gets what is produced. A firm will produce what is profitable to produce. If the firm can sell a product at a price that is sufficient to ensure a profit after production costs are paid, it will in all likelihood produce that product. Resources will flow in the direction of profit opportunities.

- Demand curves reflect what people are willing and able to pay for products; demand curves are influenced by incomes, wealth, preferences, prices of other goods, and expectations. Because product prices are determined by the interaction of supply and demand, prices reflect what people are willing to pay. If people's preferences or incomes change, resources will be allocated differently. Consider, for example, an increase in demand—a shift in the market demand curve. Beginning at an equilibrium, households simply begin buying more. At the equilibrium price, quantity demanded becomes greater than quantity supplied. When there is excess demand, prices will rise, and higher prices mean higher profits for firms in the industry. Higher profits, in turn, provide existing firms with an incentive to expand and new firms with an incentive to enter the industry. Thus, the decisions of independent private firms responding to prices and profit opportunities determine *what* will be produced. No central direction is necessary.

  Adam Smith saw this self-regulating feature of markets more than 200 years ago:

  > Every individual . . . by pursuing his own interest . . . promotes that of society. He is led . . . by an invisible hand to promote an end which was no part of his intention.[4]

  The term Smith coined, the *invisible hand*, has passed into common parlance and is still used by economists to refer to the self-regulation of markets.

- Firms in business to make a profit have a good reason to choose the best available technology—lower costs mean higher profits. Thus, individual firms determine *how* to produce their products, again with no central direction.

---

[4] Adam Smith, *The Wealth of Nations*, Modern Library Edition (New York: Random House, 1937), p. 456 (1st ed., 1776).

ECONOMICS IN PRACTICE

Why Do the Prices of Newspapers Rise?

In 2006, the average price for a daily edition of a Baltimore newspaper was $0.50. In 2007, the average price had risen to $0.75. Three different analysts have three different explanations for the higher equilibrium price.

Analyst 1: The higher price for Baltimore newspapers is good news because it means the population is better informed about public issues. These data clearly show that the citizens of Baltimore have a new, increased regard for newspapers.

Analyst 2: The higher price for Baltimore newspapers is bad news for the citizens of Baltimore. The higher cost of paper, ink, and distribution reflected in these higher prices will further diminish the population's awareness of public issues.

Analyst 3: The higher price for Baltimore newspapers is an unfortunate result of newspapers trying to make money as many consumers have turned to the Internet to access news coverage for free.

As economists, we are faced with two tasks in looking at these explanations: Do they make sense based on what we know about economic principles? And if they do make sense, can we figure out which explanation applies to the case of rising newspaper prices in Baltmore?

What is Analyst 1 saying? Her observation about consumers' new increased regard for newspapers tells us something about the demand curve. Analyst 1 seems to be arguing that tastes have changed in favor of newspapers, which would mean a shift in the demand curve to the right. With upward-sloping supply, such a shift would produce a price increase. So Analyst 1's story is plausible.

Analyst 2 refers to an increased cost of newsprint. This would cause production costs of newspapers to rise, shifting the supply curve to the left. A downward-sloping demand curve also results in increased prices. So Analyst 2 also has a plausible story.

Since Analyst 1 and Analyst 2 have plausible stories based on economic principles, we can look at evidence to see who is in fact right. If you go back to the graphs in Figure 3.12 on p. 66, you will find a clue. When demand shifts to the right (as in Analyst 1's story) the price rises, but so does the quantity as shown in Figure (a) below. When supply shifts to the left (as in Analyst 2's story) the price rises, but the quantity falls as shown in Figure (b) below. So we would look at what happened to newspaper circulation during this period to see whether the price increase is from the demand side or the supply side. In fact, in most markets, including Baltimore, quantities of newspapers bought have been falling, so Analyst 2 is most likely correct.

But be careful. Both analysts may be correct. If demand shifts to the right and supply shifts to the left by a greater amount, the price will rise and the quantity sold will fall.

What about Analyst 3? Analyst 3 clearly never had an economics course! Free Internet access to news is a substitute for print media. A decrease in the price of this substitute should shift the demand for newspapers to the left. The result should be a lower price, not a price increase. The fact that the newspaper publishers are "trying to make money" faced with this new competition does not change the laws of supply and demand.

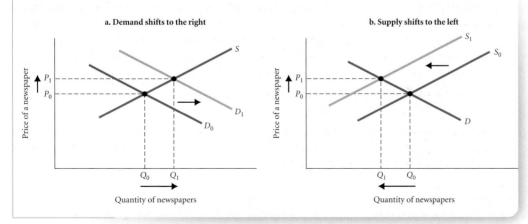

a. Demand shifts to the right   b. Supply shifts to the left

■ So far, we have barely touched on the question of distribution—*who* gets what is produced? You can see part of the answer in the simple supply and demand diagrams. When a good is in short supply, price rises. As it does, those who are willing and able to continue buying do so; others stop buying.

The next chapter begins with a more detailed discussion of these topics. How, exactly, is the final allocation of resources (the mix of output and the distribution of output) determined in a market system?

SUMMARY

1. In societies with many people, production must satisfy wide-ranging tastes and preferences, and producers must therefore specialize.

FIRMS AND HOUSEHOLDS: THE BASIC DECISION-MAKING UNITS *p. 45*

2. A *firm* exists when a person or a group of people decides to produce a product or products by transforming resources, or *inputs*, into *outputs*—the products that are sold in the market. Firms are the primary producing units in a market economy. We assume that firms make decisions to try to maximize profits.

3. *Households* are the primary consuming units in an economy. All households' incomes are subject to constraints.

INPUT MARKETS AND OUTPUT MARKETS: THE CIRCULAR FLOW *p. 46*

4. Households and firms interact in two basic kinds of markets: *product* or *output markets* and *input* or *factor markets*. Goods and services intended for use by households are exchanged in output markets. In output markets, competing firms supply and competing households demand. In input markets, competing firms demand and competing households supply.

5. Ultimately, firms choose the quantities and character of outputs produced, the types and quantities of inputs demanded, and the technologies used in production. Households choose the types and quantities of products demanded and the types and quantities of inputs supplied.

DEMAND IN PRODUCT/OUTPUT MARKETS *p. 48*

6. The quantity demanded of an individual product by an individual household depends on (1) price, (2) income, (3) wealth, (4) prices of other products, (5) tastes and preferences, and (6) expectations about the future.

7. *Quantity demanded* is the amount of a product that an individual household would buy in a given period if it could buy all that it wanted at the current price.

8. A *demand schedule* shows the quantities of a product that a household would buy at different prices. The same information can be presented graphically in a *demand curve*.

9. The *law of demand* states that there is a negative relationship between price and quantity demanded: As price rises, quantity demanded decreases and vice versa. Demand curves slope downward.

10. All demand curves eventually intersect the price axis because there is always a price above which a household cannot or will not pay. Also, all demand curves eventually intersect the quantity axis because demand for most goods is limited, if only by time, even at a zero price.

11. When an increase in income causes demand for a good to rise, that good is a *normal good*. When an increase in income causes demand for a good to fall, that good is an *inferior good*.

12. If a rise in the price of good X causes demand for good Y to increase, the goods are *substitutes*. If a rise in the price of X causes demand for Y to fall, the goods are *complements*.

13. *Market demand* is simply the sum of all the quantities of a good or service demanded per period by all the households buying in the market for that good or service. It is the sum of all the individual quantities demanded at each price.

SUPPLY IN PRODUCT/OUTPUT MARKETS *p. 57*

14. *Quantity supplied* by a firm depends on (1) the price of the good or service; (2) the cost of producing the product, which includes the prices of required inputs and the technologies that can be used to produce the product; and (3) the prices of related products.

15. *Market supply* is the sum of all that is supplied in each period by all producers of a single product. It is the sum of all the individual quantities supplied at each price.

16. It is very important to distinguish between *movements* along demand and supply curves and *shifts* of demand and supply curves. The demand curve shows the relationship between price and quantity demanded. The supply curve shows the relationship between price and quantity supplied. A change in price is a movement along the curve. Changes in tastes, income, wealth, expectations, or prices of other goods and services cause demand curves to shift; changes in costs, input prices, technology, or prices of related goods and services cause supply curves to shift.

MARKET EQUILIBRIUM *p. 62*

17. When quantity demanded exceeds quantity supplied at the current price, *excess demand* (or a *shortage*) exists and the price tends to rise. When prices in a market rise, quantity demanded falls and quantity supplied rises until an equilibrium is reached at which quantity supplied and quantity demanded are equal. At *equilibrium*, there is no further tendency for price to change.

18. When quantity supplied exceeds quantity demanded at the current price, *excess supply* (or a *surplus*) exists and the price tends to fall. When price falls, quantity supplied decreases and quantity demanded increases until an equilibrium price is reached where quantity supplied and quantity demanded are equal.

REVIEW TERMS AND CONCEPTS

capital market, *p. 47*

complements, complementary goods, *p. 52*

demand curve, *p. 49*

demand schedule, *p. 49*

entrepreneur, *p. 46*

equilibrium, *p. 62*

excess demand *or* shortage, *p. 62*

excess supply *or* surplus, *p. 63*

factors of production, *p. 47*

firm, *p. 46*

households, *p. 46*

income, *p. 51*

inferior goods, *p. 52*

input *or* factor markets, *p. 46*

labor market, *p. 47*

land market, *p. 47*

law of demand, *p. 49*

law of supply, *p. 57*

market demand, *p. 55*

market supply, *p. 61*

movement along a demand curve, *p. 54*

movement along a supply curve, *p. 59*

normal goods, *p. 51*

perfect substitutes, *p. 52*

product *or* output markets, *p. 46*

profit, *p. 57*

quantity demanded, *p. 48*

quantity supplied, *p. 57*

shift of a demand curve, *p. 53*

shift of a supply curve, *p. 59*

substitutes, *p. 52*

supply curve, *p. 57*

supply schedule, *p. 57*

wealth *or* net worth, *p. 51*

PROBLEMS

Visit www.myeconlab.com to complete the problems marked in orange online. You will receive instant feedback on your answers, tutorial help, and access to additional practice problems.

1. Illustrate the following with supply and demand curves:
   a. With increased access to wireless technology and lighter weight, the demand for laptop computers has increased substantially. Laptops have also become easier and cheaper to produce as new technology has come online. Despite the shift of demand, prices have fallen.
   b. Cranberry production in Massachusetts totaled 1.97 million barrels in 2006, a 39 percent increase from the previous year's production. This year's crop yield averaged 140.9 barrels per acre, an increase of over 40 barrels per acre from the 2005 crop. But demand increased by even more than supply, actually pushing 2006 prices above 2005 prices.
   c. During the high-tech boom in the late 1990s, San Jose office space was in very high demand and rents were very high. With the national recession that began in March 2001, however, the market for office space in San Jose (Silicon Valley) was hit very hard, with rents per square foot falling. In 2005, the employment numbers from San Jose were rising slowly and rents began to rise again. Assume for simplicity that no new office space was built during the period.
   d. Before economic reforms were implemented in the countries of Eastern Europe, regulation held the price of bread substantially below equilibrium. When reforms were implemented, prices were deregulated and the price of bread rose dramatically. As a result, the quantity of bread demanded fell and the quantity of bread supplied rose sharply.
   e. The steel industry has been lobbying for high taxes on imported steel. Russia, Brazil, and Japan have been producing and selling steel on world markets at $610 per metric ton, well below what equilibrium would be in the United

States with no imports. If no imported steel was permitted into the country, the equilibrium price would be $970 per metric ton. Show supply and demand curves for the United States, assuming no imports; then show what the graph would look like if U.S. buyers could purchase all the steel that they wanted from world markets at $610 per metric ton; show the quantity of imported steel.

2. On Sunday, August 19, the Detroit Tigers and the New York Yankees played baseball at Yankee Stadium. Both teams were in pursuit of league championships. Tickets to the game were sold out, and many more fans would have attended if additional tickets had been available. On that same day, the Cleveland Indians and the Tampa Bay Devil Rays played each other and sold tickets to only 22,500 people in Tampa.

   The Devil Rays stadium, Tropicana Field, holds 43,772. Yankee Stadium holds 57,478. Assume for simplicity that tickets to all regular-season games are priced at $40.
   a. Draw supply and demand curves for the tickets to each of the two games. (*Hint:* Supply is fixed. It does not change with price.) Draw one graph for each game.
   b. Is there a pricing policy that would have filled the ballpark for the Tampa game? If the Devil Rays adopted such a strategy, would it bring in more or less revenue?
   c. The price system was not allowed to work to ration the New York tickets when they were initially sold to the public. How do you know? How do you suppose the tickets were rationed?

3. During the last 10 years, Orlando, Florida grew rapidly, with new jobs luring young people into the area. Despite increases in population and income growth that expanded demand for housing, the price of existing houses barely increased. Why? Illustrate your answer with supply and demand curves.

4. Do you agree or disagree with each of the following statements? Briefly explain your answers and illustrate each with supply and demand curves.
   a. The price of a good rises, causing the demand for another good to fall. Therefore, the two goods are substitutes.
   b. A shift in supply causes the price of a good to fall. The shift must have been an increase in supply.
   c. During 2007, incomes rose sharply for most Americans. This change would likely lead to an increase in the prices of both normal and inferior goods.
   d. Two normal goods cannot be substitutes for each other.
   e. If demand increases and supply increases at the same time, price will clearly rise.
   f. The price of good A falls. This causes an increase in the price of good B. Therefore, goods A and B are complements.

5. The U.S. government administers two programs that affect the market for cigarettes. Media campaigns and labeling requirements are aimed at making the public aware of the health dangers of cigarettes. At the same time, the Department of Agriculture maintains price supports for tobacco. Under this program, the supported price is above the market equilibrium price and the government limits the amount of land that can be devoted to tobacco production. Are these two programs at odds with the goal of reducing cigarette consumption? As part of your answer, illustrate graphically the effects of both policies on the market for cigarettes.

6. Housing prices in Boston and Los Angeles have been on a roller-coaster ride. Illustrate each of the following situations with supply and demand curves:
   a. In both cities, an increase in income combined with expectations of a strong market shifted demand and caused prices to rise rapidly during the mid- to late 1980s.
   b. By 1990, the construction industry boomed as more developers started new residential projects. Those new projects expanded the supply of housing just as demand was shifting as a result of falling incomes and expectations during the 1990–1991 recession.

7. The following sets of statements contain common errors. Identify and explain each error:
   a. Demand increases, causing prices to rise. Higher prices cause demand to fall. Therefore, prices fall back to their original levels.
   b. The supply of meat in Russia increases, causing meat prices to fall. Lower prices always mean that Russian households spend more on meat.

8. For each of the following statements, draw a diagram that illustrates the likely effect on the market for eggs. Indicate in each case the impact on equilibrium price and equilibrium quantity.
   a. A surgeon general warns that high-cholesterol foods cause heart attacks.
   b. The price of bacon, a complementary product, decreases.
   c. An increase in the price of chicken feed occurs.
   d. Caesar salads become trendy at dinner parties. (The dressing is made with raw eggs.)
   e. A technological innovation reduces egg breakage during packing.

*9. Suppose the demand and supply curves for eggs in the United States are given by the following equations:

$$Q_d = 100 - 20P$$
$$Q_s = 10 + 40P$$

where Q_d = millions of dozens of eggs Americans would like to buy each year; Q_s = millions of dozens of eggs U.S. farms would like to sell each year; P = price per dozen of eggs.
   a. Fill in the following table:

PRICE (PER DOZEN)	QUANTITY DEMANDED (Q_d)	QUANTITY SUPPLIED (Q_s)
$ .50	_____	_____
$1.00	_____	_____
$1.50	_____	_____
$2.00	_____	_____
$2.50	_____	_____

   b. Use the information in the table to find the equilibrium price and quantity.
   c. Graph the demand and supply curves and identify the equilibrium price and quantity.

*10. Housing policy analysts debate the best way to increase the number of housing units available to low-income households. One strategy—the demand-side strategy—is to provide people with housing vouchers, paid for by the government, that can be used to rent housing supplied by the private market. Another—a supply-side strategy—is to have the government subsidize housing suppliers or to build public housing.
   a. Illustrate supply- and demand-side strategies using supply and demand curves. Which results in higher rents?
   b. Critics of housing vouchers (the demand-side strategy) argue that because the supply of housing to low-income households is limited and does not respond to higher rents, demand vouchers will serve only to drive up rents and make landlords better off. Illustrate their point with supply and demand curves.

*11. Suppose the market demand for pizza is given by $Q_d = 300 - 20P$ and the market supply for pizza is given by $Q_s = 20P - 100$, where P = price (per pizza).
   a. Graph the supply and demand schedules for pizza using $5 through $15 as the value of P.
   b. In equilibrium, how many pizzas would be sold and at what price?
   c. What would happen if suppliers set the price of pizza at $15? Explain the market adjustment process.
   d. Suppose the price of hamburgers, a substitute for pizza, doubles. This leads to a doubling of the demand for pizza. (At each price, consumers demand twice as much pizza as before.) Write the equation for the new market demand for pizza.
   e. Find the new equilibrium price and quantity of pizza.

12. [Related to the *Economics in Practice* on p. 67] In the winter, which is the peak season for coats, the price of coats is typically higher than it is in the summer. In the case of strawberries, however, the reverse is true: The price of strawberries is lower in the peak season than it is in the winter season. How do we explain this seeming contradiction?

13. [Related to the *Economics in Practice* on p. 69] Analyst 1 suggested that the demand curve for newspapers in Baltimore might have shifted to the right because people were becoming more literate. Think of two other plausible stories that would result in this demand curve shifting to the right.

---

*Note: Problems marked with an asterisk are more challenging.

Demand and Supply Applications

4

Every society has a system of institutions that determines what is produced, how it is produced, and who gets what is produced. In some societies, these decisions are made centrally, through planning agencies or by government directive. However, in every society, many decisions are made in a *decentralized* way, through the operation of markets.

Markets exist in all societies, and Chapter 3 provided a barebones description of how markets operate. In this chapter, we continue our examination of demand, supply, and the price system.

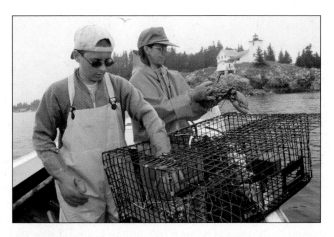

price rationing The process by which the market system allocates goods and services to consumers when quantity demanded exceeds quantity supplied.

The Price System: Rationing and Allocating Resources

The market system, also called the *price system*, performs two important and closely related functions. First, it provides an automatic mechanism for distributing scarce goods and services. That is, it serves as a **price rationing** device for allocating goods and services to consumers when the quantity demanded exceeds the quantity supplied. Second, the price system ultimately determines both the allocation of resources among producers and the final mix of outputs.

Price Rationing

Consider the simple process by which the price system eliminates a shortage. Figure 4.1 shows hypothetical supply and demand curves for lobsters caught off the coast of New England.

Lobsters are considered a delicacy. Maine produces most of the lobster catch in the United States, and anyone who drives up the Maine coast cannot avoid the hundreds of restaurants selling lobster rolls, steamed lobster, and baked stuffed lobster.

As Figure 4.1 shows, the equilibrium price of live New England lobsters was $11.50 per pound in the summer of 2007. At this price, lobster boats brought in lobsters at a rate of 81 million pounds per year—an amount that was just enough to satisfy demand.

Market equilibrium existed at $11.50 per pound because at that price, quantity demanded was equal to quantity supplied. (Remember that equilibrium occurs at the point where the supply and demand curves intersect. In Figure 4.1, this occurs at point C.)

Now suppose in 2008 that the waters off a section of the Maine coast become contaminated with a poisonous parasite. As a result, the Department of Agriculture is forced to close 15,000 square miles of the most productive lobstering areas. Even though many of the lobster boats shift their trapping activities to other waters, there is a sharp reduction in the quantity of lobster available for trapping. The supply curve shifts to the left, from S_{2007} to S_{2008}. This shift in

▶ **FIGURE 4.1** **The Market for Lobsters**

Suppose in 2008 that 15,000 square miles of lobstering waters off the coast of Maine are closed. The supply curve shifts to the left. Before the waters are closed, the lobster market is in equilibrium at the price of $11.50 and a quantity of 81 million pounds. The decreased supply of lobster leads to higher prices, and a new equilibrium is reached at $16.10 and 60 million pounds (point *B*).

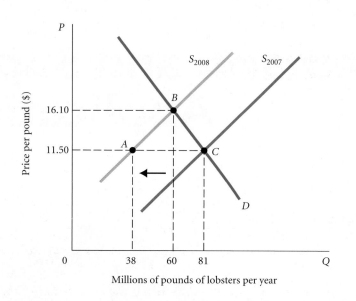

the supply curve creates a situation of excess demand at $11.50. At that price, the quantity demanded is 81 million pounds and the quantity supplied is 38 million pounds. Quantity demanded exceeds quantity supplied by 43 million pounds.

The reduced supply causes the price of lobster to rise sharply. As the price rises, the available supply is "rationed." Those who are willing and able to pay the most get it.

You can see the market's price rationing function clearly in Figure 4.1. As the price rises from $11.50, the quantity demanded declines along the demand curve, moving from point *C* (81 million pounds) toward point *B* (60 million pounds). The higher prices mean that restaurants must charge more for lobster rolls and stuffed lobsters. As a result, many people stop buying lobster or order it less frequently when they dine out. Some restaurants drop lobster from the menu entirely, and some shoppers at the fish counter turn to lobster substitutes such as swordfish and salmon.

As the price rises, lobster trappers (suppliers) also change their behavior. They stay out longer and put out more traps than they did when the price was $11.50 per pound. Quantity supplied increases from 38 million pounds to 60 million pounds. This increase in price brings about a movement along the 2008 supply curve from point *A* to point *B*.

Finally, a new equilibrium is established at a price of $16.10 per pound and a total output of 60 million pounds. The market has determined who gets the lobsters: *The lower total supply is rationed to those who are willing and able to pay the higher price.*

This idea of "willingness to pay" is central to the distribution of available supply, and willingness depends on both desire (preferences) and income/wealth. Willingness to pay does not necessarily mean that only the very rich will continue to buy lobsters when the price increases. For anyone to continue to buy lobster at a higher price, his or her enjoyment comes at a higher cost in terms of other goods and services.

In sum:

> The adjustment of price is the rationing mechanism in free markets. Price rationing means that whenever there is a need to ration a good—that is, when a shortage exists—in a free market, the price of the good will rise until quantity supplied equals quantity demanded—that is, until the market clears.

There is some price that will clear any market you can think of. Consider the market for a famous painting such as Jackson Pollock's *No. 5, 1948*, illustrated in Figure 4.2. At a low price, there would be an enormous excess demand for such an important painting. The price would be bid up until there was only one remaining demander. Presumably, that price would be very high. In fact, the Pollock painting sold for a record $140 million in 2006. If the product is in strictly scarce supply, as a single painting is, its price is said to be *demand-determined*. That is, its price is determined solely and exclusively by the amount that the highest bidder or highest bidders are willing to pay.

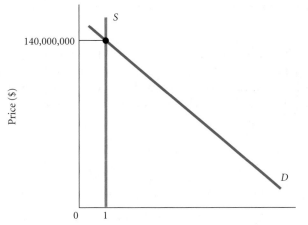

◀ FIGURE 4.2 Market for a Rare Painting
There is some price that will clear any market, even if supply is strictly limited. In an auction for a unique painting, the price (bid) will rise to eliminate excess demand until there is only one bidder willing to purchase the single available painting. Some estimate that the *Mona Lisa* would sell for $600 million if auctioned.

One might interpret the statement that "there is some price that will clear any market" to mean "everything has its price," but that is not exactly what it means. Suppose you own a small silver bracelet that has been in your family for generations. It is quite possible that you would not sell it for *any* amount of money. Does this mean that the market is not working, or that quantity supplied and quantity demanded are not equal? Not at all. It simply means that *you* are the highest bidder. By turning down all bids, you must be willing to forgo what anybody offers for it.

Constraints on the Market and Alternative Rationing Mechanisms

On occasion, both governments and private firms decide to use some mechanism other than the market system to ration an item for which there is excess demand at the current price. Policies designed to stop price rationing are commonly justified in a number of ways.

The rationale most often used is fairness. It is not "fair" to let landlords charge high rents, not fair for oil companies to run up the price of gasoline, not fair for insurance companies to charge enormous premiums, and so on. After all, the argument goes, we have no choice but to pay— housing and insurance are necessary, and one needs gasoline to get to work. Although it is not precisely true that price rationing allocates goods and services solely on the basis of income and wealth, income and wealth do constrain our wants. Why should all the gasoline or all the tickets to the World Series go just to the rich?

Various schemes to keep price from rising to equilibrium are based on several perceptions of injustice, among them (1) that price-gouging is bad, (2) that income is unfairly distributed, and (3) that some items are necessities and everyone should be able to buy them at a "reasonable" price. Regardless of the rationale, the following examples will make two things clear:

1. Attempts to bypass price rationing in the market and to use alternative rationing devices are more difficult and more costly than they would seem at first glance.
2. Very often such attempts distribute costs and benefits among households in unintended ways.

Oil, Gasoline, and OPEC In 1973 and 1974, OPEC imposed an embargo on shipments of crude oil to the United States. What followed was a drastic reduction in the quantity of gasoline available at local gas pumps.

Had the market system been allowed to operate, refined gasoline prices would have increased dramatically until quantity supplied was equal to quantity demanded. However, the government decided that rationing gasoline only to those who were willing and able to pay the most was unfair, and Congress imposed a **price ceiling**, or maximum price, of $0.57 per gallon of leaded regular gasoline. That price ceiling was intended to keep gasoline "affordable," but it also perpetuated the shortage. At the restricted price, quantity demanded remained greater than

price ceiling A maximum price that sellers may charge for a good, usually set by government.

quantity supplied and the available gasoline had to be divided up somehow among all potential demanders.

You can see the effects of the price ceiling by looking carefully at Figure 4.3. If the price had been set by the interaction of supply and demand, it would have increased to approximately $1.50 per gallon. Instead, Congress made it illegal to sell gasoline for more than $0.57 per gallon. At that price, quantity demanded exceeded quantity supplied and a shortage existed. Because the price system was not allowed to function, an alternative rationing system had to be found to distribute the available supply of gasoline.

▶ **FIGURE 4.3 Excess Demand (Shortage) Created by a Price Ceiling**

In 1974, a ceiling price of $0.57 cents per gallon of leaded regular gasoline was imposed. If the price had been set by the interaction of supply and demand instead, it would have increased to approximately $1.50 per gallon. At $0.57 per gallon, the quantity demanded exceeded the quantity supplied. Because the price system was not allowed to function, an alternative rationing system had to be found to distribute the available supply of gasoline.

queuing   Waiting in line as a means of distributing goods and services: a nonprice rationing mechanism.

favored customers   Those who receive special treatment from dealers during situations of excess demand.

ration coupons   Tickets or coupons that entitle individuals to purchase a certain amount of a given product per month.

Several devices were tried. The most common of all nonprice rationing systems is **queuing**, a term that means waiting in line. During 1974, very long lines formed daily at gas stations, starting as early as 5 A.M. Under this system, gasoline went to those people who were willing to pay the most, but the sacrifice was measured in hours and aggravation instead of dollars.[1]

A second nonprice rationing device used during the gasoline crisis was that of **favored customers**. Many gas station owners decided not to sell gasoline to the general public, but to reserve their scarce supplies for friends and favored customers. Not surprisingly, many customers tried to become "favored" by offering side payments to gas station owners. Owners also charged high prices for service. By doing so, they increased the real price of gasoline but hid it in service overcharges to get around the ceiling.

Yet another method of dividing up available supply is the use of **ration coupons**. It was suggested in both 1974 and 1979 that families be given ration tickets or coupons that would entitle them to purchase a certain number of gallons of gasoline each month. That way, everyone would get the same amount regardless of income. Such a system had been employed in the United States

---

[1] You can also show formally that the result is inefficient—that there is a resulting net loss of total value to society. First, there is the cost of waiting in line. Time has a value. With price rationing, no one has to wait in line and the value of that time is saved. Second, there may be additional lost value if the gasoline ends up in the hands of someone who places a lower value on it than someone else who gets no gas. Suppose, for example, that the market price of gasoline if unconstrained would rise to $2 but that the government has fixed at $1. There will be long lines to get gas. Imagine that to motorist A, 10 gallons of gas is worth $35 but that she fails to get gas because her time is too valuable to wait in line. To motorist B, 10 gallons is worth only $15, but his time is worth much less; so he gets the gas. In the end, A could pay B for the gas and both would be better off. If A pays B $30 for the gas, A is $5 better off and B is $15 better off. In addition, A does not have to wait in line. Thus, the allocation that results from nonprice rationing involves a net loss of value. Such losses are called *deadweight losses*. See p. 84 of this chapter.

during the 1940s when wartime price ceilings on meat, sugar, butter, tires, nylon stockings, and many other items were imposed.

When ration coupons are used with no prohibition against trading them, however, the result is almost identical to a system of price rationing. Those who are willing and able to pay the most buy up the coupons and use them to purchase gasoline, chocolate, fresh eggs, or anything else that is sold at a restricted price.[2] This means that the price of the restricted good will effectively rise to the market-clearing price. For instance, suppose that you decide not to sell your ration coupon. You are then forgoing what you would have received by selling the coupon. Thus, the "real" price of the good you purchase will be higher (if only in opportunity cost) than the restricted price. Even when trading coupons is declared illegal, it is virtually impossible to stop black markets from developing. In a **black market**, illegal trading takes place at market-determined prices.

black market A market in which illegal trading takes place at market-determined prices.

Rationing Mechanisms for Concert and Sports Tickets On September 16, 2007, Justin Timberlake performed at the Staples Center in Los Angeles. The day before the concert, you could buy a front row ticket for $16,000 on the StubHub Web site. Tickets for sporting events such as the World Series, the Super Bowl, and the World Cup command huge prices in the open market. In many cases, the prices are substantially above the original issue price.

The Staples Center seats 20,000 for concerts. Figure 4.4 illustrates the situation. The supply of tickets is fixed. Of course, there are good seats and bad seats; but to keep things simple, let's assume that all the seats are the same and that the promoters originally charged $50 for all tickets. Supply is represented by a vertical line at 20,000. A higher price does not increase the supply of seats. At the original issue price, the quantity demanded is 38,000, which is greater than the quantity supplied.

The first question is why would a profit-maximizing enterprise not charge the highest price it could charge? The answer depends on the event. If the Chicago Cubs got into the World Series,

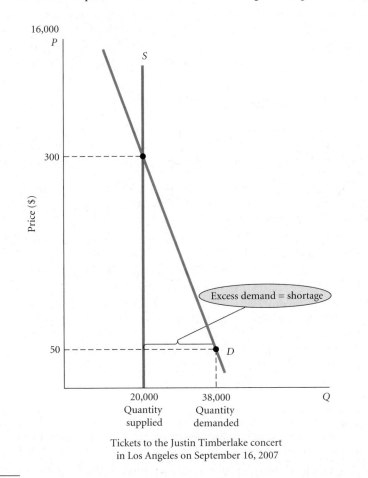

Tickets to the Justin Timberlake concert
in Los Angeles on September 16, 2007

◀ **FIGURE 4.4 Supply of and Demand for a Concert in 2007**

The face value of a ticket to the Justin Timberlake concert on September 16, 2007, at the Staples Center in Los Angeles was $50. The Staples Center holds 20,000. The supply curve is vertical at 20,000. At $50, the quantity supplied is below the quantity demanded. The diagram shows that the quantity demanded and the quantity supplied would be equal at $300. The Web shows that one ticket could be worth $16,000.

---

[2] Of course, if you are assigned a number of tickets and you sell them, you are better off than you would be with price rationing. Ration coupons thus serve as a way of redistributing income.

the people of Chicago would buy all the tickets available for thousands of dollars each. But if the Cubs actually *charged* $2,000 a ticket, the hard-working fans would be furious: "Greedy Cubs Gouge Fans" the headlines would scream. Ordinary loyal fans earning reasonable salaries would not be able to afford those prices. Next season, perhaps some of those irate fans would change loyalties, supporting the White Sox over the Cubs. In part to keep from alienating loyal fans, prices for championship games are held down.

Not every concert promoter or sports team behaves that way. In 2000, Barbra Streisand gave a concert in Sydney, Australia. Tickets were issued with a *face value* of $1,530, a record for a concert that still stands today.

If all the Justin Timberlake tickets were sold for $50, the sold-out concert would take in $1 million dollars. But who would get the tickets? As in the case of gasoline, a variety of rationing mechanisms might be used. The most common is queuing, waiting in line. The tickets would go on sale at a particular time, and people would show up and wait. Now ticket sellers have virtual waiting rooms online. Tickets for the World Series go on sale at a particular time in September, and the people who log on to team Web sites at the right moment get into an electronic queue and can buy tickets. Often tickets are sold out in a matter of minutes.

Again there are also favored customers. Those who get tickets without queuing are local politicians, sponsors, and friends of the artist or friends of the players.

But "once the dust settles," the power of technology and the concept of *opportunity cost* take over. Even if you get the Timberlake ticket for the (relatively) low price of $50, that is not the true cost. The true cost is what you give up to sit in the seat. If people on eBay, StubHub, or Ticketmaster are willing to pay $500 for your ticket, that's what you must pay, or sacrifice, to go to the concert. Many people—even strong fans—will choose to sell that ticket. Once again, it is difficult to stop the market from rationing the tickets to those people who are willing and able to pay the most.

No matter how good the intentions of private organizations and governments, it is very difficult to prevent the price system from operating and to stop people's willingness to pay from asserting itself. Every time an alternative is tried, the price system seems to sneak in the back door. With favored customers and black markets, the final distribution may be even more unfair than that which would result from simple price rationing.

Prices and the Allocation of Resources

Thinking of the market system as a mechanism for allocating scarce goods and services among competing demanders is very revealing, but the market determines more than just the distribution of final outputs. It also determines what gets produced and how resources are allocated among competing uses.

Consider a change in consumer preferences that leads to an increase in demand for a specific good or service. During the 1980s, for example, people began going to restaurants more frequently than before. Researchers think that this trend, which continues today, is partially the result of social changes (such as a dramatic rise in the number of two-earner families) and partially the result of rising incomes. The market responded to this change in demand by shifting resources, both capital and labor, into more and better restaurants.

With the increase in demand for restaurant meals, the price of eating out rose and the restaurant business became more profitable. The higher profits attracted new businesses and provided old restaurants with an incentive to expand. As new capital, seeking profits, flowed into the restaurant business, so did labor. New restaurants need chefs. Chefs need training, and the higher wages that came with increased demand provided an incentive for them to get it. In response to the increase in demand for training, new cooking schools opened and existing schools began to offer courses in the culinary arts. This story could go on and on, but the point is clear:

Price changes resulting from shifts of demand in output markets cause profits to rise or fall. Profits attract capital; losses lead to disinvestment. Higher wages attract labor and encourage workers to acquire skills. At the core of the system, supply, demand, and prices in input and output markets determine the allocation of resources and the ultimate combinations of goods and services produced.

ECONOMICS IN PRACTICE

The Price Mechanism at Work for Shakespeare

Every summer, New York City puts on free performances of Shakespeare in the Park. Tickets are distributed on a first-come-first-serve basis at the Delacorte Theatre in the Park beginning at 1 P.M. on the day of the show. People usually begin lining up at 6 A.M. when the park opens; and by 10 A.M. the line has typically reached a length sufficient to give away all available tickets.

When you examine the people standing in line for these tickets, most of them seem to be fairly young. Many carry book bags identifying them as students in one of New York's many colleges. Of course, all college students may be fervent Shakespeare fans, but can you think of another reason for the composition of the line? Further, when you attend one of the plays and look around, the audience appears much older and much sleeker than the people who were standing in line. What is going on?

While the tickets are "free" in terms of financial costs, their true price includes the value of the time spent standing in line. Thus, the tickets are cheaper for people (for example, students) whose time value is lower than they are for high-wage earners, like an investment banker from Goldman Sachs. The true cost of a ticket is $0 plus the opportunity cost of the time spent in line. If the average person spends 4 hours in line, as is done in the Central Park case, for someone with a high wage, the true cost of the ticket might be very high. For example, a lawyer who earns $300 an hour would be giving up $1,200 to wait in line. It should not surprise you to see more people waiting in line for whom the tickets are inexpensive.

What about the people who are at the performance? Think about our discussion of the power of entrepreneurs. In this case, the students who stand in line as consumers of the tickets also can play a role as producers. In fact, the students can produce tickets relatively cheaply by waiting in line. They can then turn around and sell those tickets to the high-wage Shakespeare lovers. These days eBay is a great source of tickets to free events, sold by individuals with low opportunity costs of their time who queued up. Craigslist even provides listings for people who are willing to wait in line for you.

Of course, now and again we do encounter a busy businessperson in one of the Central Park lines. Recently, one of the authors encountered one and asked him why he was waiting in line rather than using eBay, and he replied that it reminded him of when he was young, waiting in line for rock concerts.

Price Floors

As we have seen, price ceilings, often imposed because price rationing is viewed as unfair, result in alternative rationing mechanisms that are inefficient and may be equally unfair. Some of the same arguments can be made for price floors. A **price floor** is a minimum price below which exchange is not permitted. If a price floor is set above the equilibrium price, the result will be excess supply; quantity supplied will be greater than quantity demanded.

The most common example of a price floor is the **minimum wage**, which is a floor set for the price of labor. Employers (who demand labor) are not permitted under federal law to pay a wage less than $6.55 per hour (in 2008) to workers (who supply labor). Critics argue that since the minimum wage is above equilibrium, the result will be wasteful unemployment. At the wage of $6.55, the quantity of labor demanded is less than the quantity of labor supplied. Whenever a price floor is set above equilibrium, there will be an excess supply.

price floor A minimum price below which exchange is not permitted.

minimum wage A price floor set for the price of labor.

Supply and Demand Analysis: An Oil Import Fee

The basic logic of supply and demand is a powerful tool of analysis. As an extended example of the power of this logic, we will consider a recent proposal to impose a tax on imported oil. The idea of taxing imported oil is hotly debated, and the tools we have learned thus far will show us the effects of such a tax.

Consider the facts. Between 1985 and 1989, the United States increased its dependence on oil imports dramatically. In 1989, total U.S. demand for crude oil was 13.6 million barrels per day. Of that amount, only 7.7 million barrels per day (57 percent) were supplied by U.S. producers, with the remaining 5.9 million barrels per day (43 percent) imported. The price of oil on world markets that year averaged about $18. This heavy dependence on foreign oil left the United States vulnerable to the price shock that followed the Iraqi invasion of Kuwait in August 1990. In the months following the invasion, the price of crude oil on world markets shot up to $40 per barrel.

Even before the invasion, many economists and some politicians had recommended a stiff oil import fee (or tax) that would, it was argued, reduce the U.S. dependence on foreign oil by (1) reducing overall consumption and (2) providing an incentive for increased domestic production. An added bonus would be improved air quality from the reduction in driving.

Supply and demand analysis makes the arguments of the import fee proponents easier to understand. Figure 4.5(a) shows the U.S. market for oil. The world price of oil is assumed to be $18, and the United States is assumed to be able to buy *all the oil that it wants* at this price. This

▶ **FIGURE 4.5 The U.S. Market for Crude Oil, 1989**

At a world price of $18, domestic production is 7.7 million barrels per day and the total quantity of oil demanded in the United States is 13.6 million barrels per day. The difference is total imports (5.9 million barrels per day).

If the government levies a 33 1/3 percent tax on imports, the price of a barrel of oil rises to $24. The quantity demanded falls to 12.2 million barrels per day. At the same time, the quantity supplied by domestic producers increases to 9.0 million barrels per day and the quantity imported falls to 3.2 million barrels per day.

a. U.S. market, 1989

b. Effects of an oil import fee in the United States

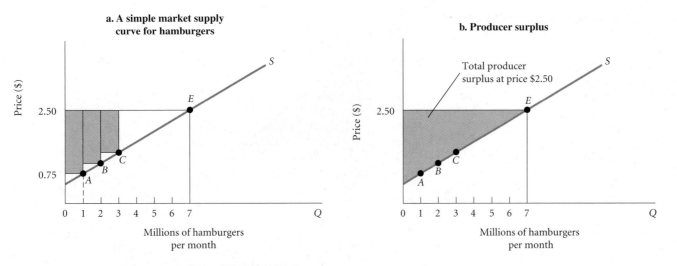

a. A simple market supply curve for hamburgers

b. Producer surplus

▲ **FIGURE 4.7 Market Supply and Producer Surplus**

As illustrated in Figure 4.7(a), some producers are willing to produce hamburgers for a price of $0.75 each. Since they are paid $2.50, they earn a producer surplus equal to $1.75. Other producers are willing to supply hamburgers at a price of $1.00; they receive a producer surplus equal to $1.50. Since the market price of hamburgers is $2.50, the area of the shaded triangle in Figure 4.7(b) is equal to total producer surplus.

Notice, however, that if the price were just $0.75 (75 cents), although production would be much lower—most producers would be out of business at that price—a few producers would actually be supplying burgers. In fact, producers would supply about 1 million burgers to the market. These firms must have lower costs: They are more efficient or they have access to raw beef at a lower price or perhaps they can hire low-wage labor.

If these efficient, low-cost producers are able to charge $2.50 for each hamburger, they are earning what is called a **producer surplus**. Producer surplus is the difference between the current market price and the full cost of production for the firm. The first 1 million hamburgers would generate a producer surplus of $2.50 minus $0.75, or $1.75 per hamburger: a total of $1.75 million. The second million hamburgers would also generate a producer surplus because the price of $2.50 exceeds the producers' total cost of producing these hamburgers, which is above $0.75 but much less than $2.50.

The total value of the producer surplus received by producers of hamburgers at a price of $2.50 per burger is roughly equal to the shaded triangle in Figure 4.7(b). Those producers just able to make a profit producing burgers will be near point *E* on the supply curve and will earn very little in the way of surplus.

producer surplus The difference between the current market price and the full cost of production for the firm.

Competitive Markets Maximize the Sum of Producer and Consumer Surplus

In the preceding example, the quantity of hamburgers supplied and the quantity of hamburgers demanded are equal at $2.50. Figure 4.8 shows the total net benefits to consumers and producers resulting from the production of 7 million hamburgers. Consumers receive benefits in excess of the price they pay and equal to the blue shaded area between the demand curve and the price line at $2.50; the area is equal to the amount of consumer surplus being earned. Producers receive compensation in excess of costs and equal to the red shaded area between the supply curve and the price line at $2.50; the area is equal to the amount of producer surplus being earned.

Now consider the result to consumers and producers if production were to be reduced to 4 million burgers. Look carefully at Figure 4.9(a). At 4 million burgers, consumers are willing to pay $3.75 for hamburgers and there are firms whose cost makes it worthwhile to supply at a price as low as $1.50, yet something is stopping production at 4 million. The result is a loss of both consumer and producer surplus. You can see in Figure 4.9(a) that if production were expanded from 4 million to 7 million, the market would yield more consumer surplus and more producer surplus.

▶ **FIGURE 4.8 Total Producer and Consumer Surplus**

Total producer and consumer surplus is greatest where supply and demand curves intersect at equilibrium.

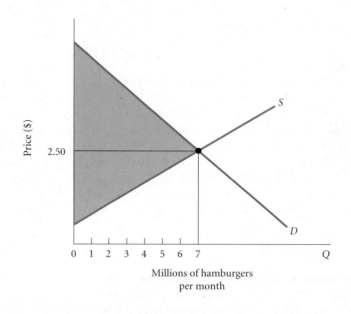

deadweight loss The total loss of producer and consumer surplus from underproduction or overproduction.

The total loss of producer and consumer surplus from *underproduction* and, as we will see shortly, from overproduction is referred to as a **deadweight loss**. In Figure 4.9(a) the deadweight loss is equal to the area of triangle *ABC* shaded in yellow.

Figure 4.9(b) illustrates how a deadweight loss of both producer and consumer surplus can result from *overproduction* as well. For every hamburger produced above 7 million, consumers are willing to pay less than the cost of production. The cost of the resources needed to produce hamburgers above 7 million exceeds the benefits to consumers, resulting in a net loss of producer and consumer surplus equal to the yellow shaded area *ABC*.

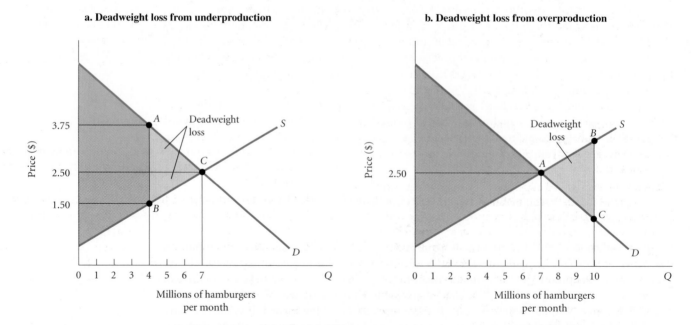

▲ **FIGURE 4.9 Deadweight Loss**

Figure 4.9(a) shows the consequences of producing 4 million hamburgers per month instead of 7 million hamburgers per month. Total producer and consumer surplus is reduced by the area of triangle *ABC* shaded in yellow. This is called the deadweight loss from underproduction. Figure 4.9(b) shows the consequences of producing 10 million hamburgers per month instead of 7 million hamburgers per month. As production increases from 7 million to 10 million hamburgers, the full cost of production rises above consumers' willingness to pay, resulting in a deadweight loss equal to the area of triangle *ABC*.

Potential Causes of Deadweight Loss From Under- and Overproduction

Most of the next few chapters will discuss perfectly competitive markets in which prices are determined by the free interaction of supply and demand. As you will see, when supply and demand interact freely, competitive markets produce what people want at the least cost, that is, they are efficient. Beginning in Chapter 13, however, we will begin to relax assumptions and will discover a number of naturally occurring sources of market failure. Monopoly power gives firms the incentive to underproduce and overprice, taxes and subsidies may distort consumer choices, external costs such as pollution and congestion may lead to over- or underproduction of some goods, and artificial price floors and price ceilings may have the same effects.

Looking Ahead

We have now examined the basic forces of supply and demand and discussed the market/price system. These fundamental concepts will serve as building blocks for what comes next. Whether you are studying microeconomics or macroeconomics, you will be studying the functions of markets and the behavior of market participants in more detail in the following chapters.

Because the concepts presented in the first four chapters are so important to your understanding of what is to come, this might be a good time for you to review this material.

SUMMARY

THE PRICE SYSTEM: RATIONING AND ALLOCATING RESOURCES *p. 73*

1. In a market economy, the market system (or price system) serves two functions. It determines the allocation of resources among producers and the final mix of outputs. It also distributes goods and services on the basis of willingness and ability to pay. In this sense, it serves as a *price rationing* device.

2. Governments as well as private firms sometimes decide not to use the market system to ration an item for which there is excess demand. Examples of nonprice rationing systems include *queuing, favored customers,* and *ration coupons.* The most common rationale for such policies is "fairness."

3. Attempts to bypass the market and use alternative nonprice rationing devices are more difficult and costly than it would seem at first glance. Schemes that open up opportunities for favored customers, black markets, and side payments often end up less "fair" than the free market.

SUPPLY AND DEMAND ANALYSIS: AN OIL IMPORT FEE *p. 80*

1. The basic logic of supply and demand is a powerful tool for analysis. For example, supply and demand analysis shows that an oil import tax will reduce quantity of oil demanded,

increase domestic production, and generate revenues for the government.

SUPPLY AND DEMAND AND MARKET EFFICIENCY *p. 81*

1. Supply and demand curves can also be used to illustrate the idea of market efficiency, an important aspect of normative economics.

2. *Consumer surplus* is the difference between the maximum amount a person is willing to pay for a good and the current market price.

3. *Producer surplus* is the difference between the current market price and the full cost of production for the firm.

4. At free market equilibrium with competitive markets, the sum of consumer surplus and producer surplus is maximized.

5. The total loss of producer and consumer surplus from underproduction or overproduction is referred to as a *deadweight loss.*

REVIEW TERMS AND CONCEPTS

black market, *p. 77*

consumer surplus, *p. 82*

deadweight loss, *p. 84*

favored customers, *p. 76*

minimum wage, *p. 79*

price ceiling, *p. 75*

price floor, *p. 79*

price rationing, *p. 73*

producer surplus, *p. 83*

queuing, *p. 76*

ration coupons, *p. 76*

PROBLEMS

Visit **www.myeconlab.com** to complete the problems marked in orange online. You will receive instant feedback on your answers, tutorial help, and access to additional practice problems.

1. Illustrate the following with supply and demand curves:
   a. In the summer of 2006, Viennese artist Gustav Klimt's Portrait of Adele Bloch-Bauer was sold in New York for $135 million.
   b. In 2008, hogs in the United States were selling for $67 each, down from $75 a year before. This was due primarily to the fact that supply had increased during the period to 1.8 million hogs per week.
   c. Early in 2009, a survey of greenhouses indicated that the demand for houseplants was rising sharply. At the same time, large numbers of low-cost producers started growing plants for sale. The overall result was a drop in the average price of houseplants and an increase in the number of plants sold.

2. Every demand curve must eventually hit the quantity axis because with limited incomes, there is always a price so high that there is no demand for the good. Do you agree or disagree? Why?

3. When excess demand exists for tickets to a major sporting event or a concert, profit opportunities exist for scalpers. Explain briefly using supply and demand curves to illustrate. Some argue that scalpers work to the advantage of everyone and are "efficient." Do you agree or disagree? Explain briefly.

4. In an effort to "support" the price of some agricultural goods, the Department of Agriculture pays farmers a subsidy in cash for every acre that they leave *unplanted*. The Agriculture Department argues that the subsidy increases the "cost" of planting and that it will reduce supply and increase the price of competitively produced agricultural goods. Critics argue that because the subsidy is a payment to farmers, it will reduce costs and lead to lower prices. Which argument is correct? Explain.

5. The rent for apartments in New York City has been rising sharply. Demand for apartments in New York City has been rising sharply as well. This is hard to explain because the law of demand says that higher prices should lead to lower demand. Do you agree or disagree? Explain your answer.

6. Illustrate the following with supply and/or demand curves:
   a. The federal government "supports" the price of wheat by paying farmers not to plant wheat on some of their land.
   b. An increase in the price of chicken has an impact on the price of hamburger.
   c. Incomes rise, shifting the demand for gasoline. Crude oil prices rise, shifting the supply of gasoline. At the new equilibrium, the quantity of gasoline sold is less than it was before. (Crude oil is used to produce gasoline.)

7. Illustrate the following with supply and/or demand curves:
   a. A situation of excess labor supply (unemployment) caused by a "minimum wage" law.
   b. The effect of a sharp increase in heating oil prices on the demand for insulation material.

8. Suppose that the world price of oil is $70 per barrel and that the United States can buy all the oil it wants at this price. Suppose also that the demand and supply schedules for oil in the United States are as follows:

PRICE ($ PER BARREL)	U.S. QUANTITY DEMANDED	U.S. QUANTITY SUPPLIED
68	16	4
70	15	6
72	14	8
74	13	10
76	12	12

   a. On graph paper, draw the supply and demand curves for the United States.
   b. With free trade in oil, what price will Americans pay for their oil? What quantity will Americans buy? How much of this will be supplied by American producers? How much will be imported? Illustrate total imports on your graph of the U.S. oil market.
   c. Suppose the United States imposes a tax of $4 per barrel on imported oil. What quantity would Americans buy? How much of this would be supplied by American producers? How much would be imported? How much tax would the government collect?
   d. Briefly summarize the impact of an oil import tax by explaining who is helped and who is hurt among the following groups: domestic oil consumers, domestic oil producers, foreign oil producers, and the U.S. government.

9. Use the data in the preceding problem to answer the following questions. Now suppose that the United States allows no oil imports.
   a. What are the equilibrium price and quantity for oil in the United States?
   b. If the United States imposed a price ceiling of $74 per barrel on the oil market and prohibited imports, would there be an excess supply or an excess demand for oil? If so, how much?
   c. Under the price ceiling, quantity supplied and quantity demanded differ. Which of the two will determine how much oil is purchased? Briefly explain why.

10. Use the following diagram to calculate total consumer surplus at a price of $8 and production of 6 million meals per day. For the same equilibrium, calculate total producer surplus. Assuming price remained at $8 but production was cut to 3 million meals per day, calculate producer surplus and consumer surplus. Calculate the deadweight loss from underproduction.

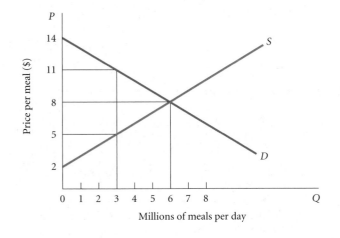

11. In early 2008, many predicted that in a relatively short period of time, unleaded regular gasoline at the pump would be selling for over $4. Do some research on the price of gasoline. Have those dire predictions materialized? What is the price of unleaded regular today in your city or town? If it is below $4 per gallon, what are the reasons? Similarly, if it is higher than $4, what has happened to drive up the price? Illustrate with supply and demand curves.

12. [Related to the *Economics in Practice* on p. 79] Many cruise lines offer 5-day trips. A disproportionate number of these trips leave port on Thursday and return late Monday. Why might this be true?

13. [Related to the *Economics in Practice* on p. 79] Lines for free tickets to see Shakespeare in Central Park are often long. A local politician has suggested that it would be a great service if the Park provided music to entertain those who are waiting in line. What do you think of this suggestion?

Introduction to Macroeconomics

5

Macroeconomics is part of our everyday lives. If the macroeconomy is doing well, few people do not have a job who want one, people's incomes are generally rising, and profits of corporations are generally high. In this type of an economy, it is relatively easy for new entrants into the labor force, such as students who have just graduated, to find jobs. On the other hand, if the macroeconomy is in a slump, new jobs are hard to find, incomes are not growing well, and profits are low. Students who entered the job market in the boom of the late 1990s in the United States, on average, had an easier time finding a job than did those who entered in the recession of 2001. Given the large effect that the macroeconomy can have on our lives, it is important that we understand how it works.

We begin by discussing the differences between microeconomics and macroeconomics that we glimpsed in Chapter 1. **Microeconomics** examines the functioning of individual industries and the behavior of individual decision-making units, typically firms and households. With a few assumptions about how these units behave (firms maximize profits; households maximize utility), we can derive useful conclusions about how markets work, how resources are allocated, and so on.

Macroeconomics, instead of focusing on the factors that influence the production of particular products and the behavior of individual industries, focuses on the determinants of total national output. Macroeconomics studies not household income but *national* income, not individual prices but the *overall* price level. It does not analyze the demand for labor in the automobile industry but instead total employment in the economy.

Both microeconomics and macroeconomics are concerned with the decisions of households and firms. Microeconomics deals with individual decisions; macroeconomics deals with the sum of these individual decisions. *Aggregate* is used in macroeconomics to refer to sums. When we speak of **aggregate behavior**, we mean the behavior of all households and firms together. We also speak of aggregate consumption and aggregate investment, which refer to total consumption and total investment in the economy, respectively.

Because microeconomists and macroeconomists look at the economy from different perspectives, you might expect that they would reach somewhat different conclusions about the way the economy behaves. This is true to some extent. Microeconomists generally conclude that markets work well. They see prices as flexible, adjusting to maintain equality between quantity supplied and quantity demanded. Macroeconomists, however, observe that important prices in the economy—for example, the wage rate (or price of labor)—often seem "sticky." **Sticky prices** are prices that do not always adjust rapidly to maintain equality between quantity supplied and quantity demanded. Microeconomists do not expect to see the quantity of apples supplied exceeding the

microeconomics
Examines the functioning of individual industries and the behavior of individual decision-making units—firms and households.

macroeconomics Deals with the economy as a whole. Macroeconomics focuses on the determinants of total national income, deals with aggregates such as aggregate consumption and investment, and looks at the overall level of prices instead of individual prices.

aggregate behavior
The behavior of all households and firms together.

sticky prices Prices that do not always adjust rapidly to maintain equality between quantity supplied and quantity demanded.

quantity of apples demanded because the price of apples is not sticky. On the other hand, macro-economists—who analyze aggregate behavior—examine periods of high unemployment, where the quantity of labor supplied appears to exceed the quantity of labor demanded. At such times, it appears that wage rates do not adjust fast enough to equate the quantity of labor supplied and the quantity of labor demanded.

Macroeconomic Concerns

Three of the major concerns of macroeconomics are

- Output growth
- Unemployment
- Inflation and deflation

Government policy makers would like to have high output growth, low unemployment, and low inflation. We will see that these goals may conflict with one another and that an important point in understanding macroeconomics is understanding these conflicts.

Output Growth

business cycle The cycle of short-term ups and downs in the economy.

aggregate output The total quantity of goods and services produced in an economy in a given period.

recession A period during which aggregate output declines. Conventionally, a period in which aggregate output declines for two consecutive quarters.

depression A prolonged and deep recession.

expansion *or* boom The period in the business cycle from a trough up to a peak during which output and employment grow.

contraction, recession, *or* slump The period in the business cycle from a peak down to a trough during which output and employment fall.

Instead of growing at an even rate at all times, economies tend to experience short-term ups and downs in their performance. The technical name for these ups and downs is the **business cycle**. The main measure of how an economy is doing is **aggregate output**, the total quantity of goods and services produced in the economy in a given period. When less is produced (in other words, when aggregate output decreases), there are fewer goods and services to go around and the average standard of living declines. When firms cut back on production, they also lay off workers, increasing the rate of unemployment.

Recessions are periods during which aggregate output declines. It has become conventional to classify an economic downturn as a "recession" when aggregate output declines for two consecutive quarters. A prolonged and deep recession is called a **depression**, although economists do not agree on when a recession becomes a depression. Since the beginning of the twentieth century, the United States has experienced one depression (during the 1930s), three severe recessions (1946, 1974–1975, and 1980–1982), and a number of less severe and shorter recessions (1954, 1958, 1990–1991, and 2001). Other countries also experienced recessions in the twentieth century, some roughly coinciding with U.S. recessions and some not.

A typical business cycle is illustrated in Figure 5.1. Since most economies, on average, grow over time, the business cycle in Figure 5.1 shows a positive trend—the *peak* (the highest point) of a new business cycle is higher than the peak of the previous cycle. The period from a *trough*, or bottom of the cycle, to a peak is called an **expansion** or a **boom**. During an expansion, output and employment grow. The period from a peak to a trough is called a **contraction**, **recession**, or **slump**, when output and employment fall.

In judging whether an economy is expanding or contracting, note the difference between the level of economic activity and its rate of change. If the economy has just left a trough (point *A* in Figure 5.1), it will be growing (rate of change is positive), but its level of output will still be low. If the economy has just started to decline from a peak (point *B*), it will be contracting (rate of change is negative), but its level of output will still be high.

The business cycle in Figure 5.1 is symmetrical, which means that the length of an expansion is the same as the length of a contraction. Most business cycles are not symmetrical, however. It is possible, for example, for the expansion phase to be longer than the contraction phase. When contraction comes, it may be fast and sharp, while expansion may be slow and gradual. Moreover, the economy is not nearly as regular as the business cycle in Figure 5.1 indicates. The ups and downs in the economy tend to be erratic.

Figure 5.2 shows the actual business cycles in the United States between 1900 and 2007. Although many business cycles have occurred in the last 108 years, each has been unique. The economy is not so simple that it has regular cycles.

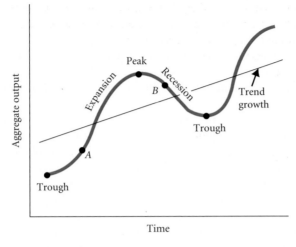

◀ **FIGURE 5.1 A Typical Business Cycle**

In this business cycle, the economy is expanding as it moves through point *A* from the trough to the peak. When the economy moves from a peak down to a trough, through point *B*, the economy is in recession.

The periods of the Great Depression and World Wars I and II show the largest fluctuations in Figure 5.2, although other large contractions and expansions have taken place. Note the expansion in the 1960s and the recessions at the beginning of the 1980s and 1990s. Some of the cycles have been long; some have been very short. Note also that aggregate output actually increased between 1933 and 1937, even though it was still quite low in 1937. The economy did not come out of the Depression until the defense buildup prior to the start of World War II. Note also that business cycles were more extreme before World War II than they have been since then.

▲ **FIGURE 5.2 U.S. Aggregate Output (Real GDP), 1900–2007**

The periods of the Great Depression and World Wars I and II show the largest fluctuations in aggregate output.

Unemployment

You cannot listen to the news or read a newspaper without noticing that data on the unemployment rate are released each month. The **unemployment rate**—the percentage of the labor force that is unemployed—is a key indicator of the economy's health. Because the unemployment rate is usually closely related to the economy's aggregate output, announcements of each month's new figure are followed with great interest by economists, politicians, and policy makers.

unemployment rate The percentage of the labor force that is unemployed.

Although macroeconomists are interested in learning why the unemployment rate has risen or fallen in a given period, they also try to answer a more basic question: Why is there any unemployment at all? We do not expect to see zero unemployment. At any time, some firms may go bankrupt due to competition from rivals, bad management, or bad luck. Employees of such firms typically are not able to find new jobs immediately, and while they are looking for work, they will be unemployed. Also, workers entering the labor market for the first time may require a few weeks or months to find a job.

If we base our analysis on supply and demand, we would expect conditions to change in response to the existence of unemployed workers. Specifically, when there is unemployment beyond some minimum amount, there is an excess supply of workers—at the going wage rates, there are people who want to work who cannot find work. In microeconomic theory, the response to excess supply is a decrease in the price of the commodity in question and therefore an increase in the quantity demanded, a reduction in the quantity supplied, and the restoration of equilibrium. With the quantity supplied equal to the quantity demanded, the market clears.

The existence of unemployment seems to imply that the aggregate labor market is not in equilibrium—that something prevents the quantity supplied and the quantity demanded from equating. Why do labor markets not clear when other markets do, or is it that labor markets are clearing and the unemployment data are reflecting something different? This is another main concern of macroeconomists.

Inflation and Deflation

inflation An increase in the overall price level.

hyperinflation A period of very rapid increases in the overall price level.

Inflation is an increase in the overall price level. Keeping inflation low has long been a goal of government policy. Especially problematic are **hyperinflations**, or periods of very rapid increases in the overall price level.

Most Americans are unaware of what life is like under very high inflation. In some countries at some times, people were accustomed to prices rising by the day, by the hour, or even by the minute. During the hyperinflation in Bolivia in 1984 and 1985, the price of one egg rose from 3,000 pesos to 10,000 pesos in 1 week. In 1985, three bottles of aspirin sold for the same price as a luxury car had sold for in 1982. At the same time, the problem of handling money became a burden. Banks stopped counting deposits—a $500 deposit was equivalent to about 32 million pesos, and it just did not make sense to count a huge sack full of bills. Bolivia's currency, printed in West Germany and England, was the country's third biggest import in 1984, surpassed only by wheat and mining equipment.

Skyrocketing prices in Bolivia are a small part of the story. When inflation approaches rates of 2,000 percent per year, the economy and the whole organization of a country begin to break down. Workers may go on strike to demand wage increases in line with the high inflation rate, and firms may find it hard to secure credit.

Hyperinflations are rare. Nonetheless, economists have devoted much effort to identifying the costs and consequences of even moderate inflation. Does anyone gain from inflation? Who loses? What costs does inflation impose on society? How severe are they? What causes inflation? What is the best way to stop it? These are some of the main concerns of macroeconomists.

deflation A decrease in the overall price level.

A decrease in the overall price level is called **deflation**. In some periods in U.S. history and recently in Japan, deflation has occurred over an extended period of time. The goal of policy makers is to avoid prolonged periods of deflation as well as inflation in order to pursue the macroeconomic goal of stability.

The Components of the Macroeconomy

Understanding how the macroeconomy works can be challenging because a great deal is going on at one time. Everything seems to affect everything else. To see the big picture, it is helpful to divide the participants in the economy into four broad groups: (1) *households*, (2) *firms*, (3) the *government*, and (4) the *rest of the world*. Households and firms make up the private sector, the government is the public sector, and the rest of the world is the foreign sector. These four groups interact in the economy in a variety of ways, many involving either receiving or paying income.

The Circular Flow Diagram

A useful way of seeing the economic interactions among the four groups in the economy is a **circular flow** diagram, which shows the income received and payments made by each group. A simple circular flow diagram is pictured in Figure 5.3.

circular flow A diagram showing the income received and payments made by each sector of the economy.

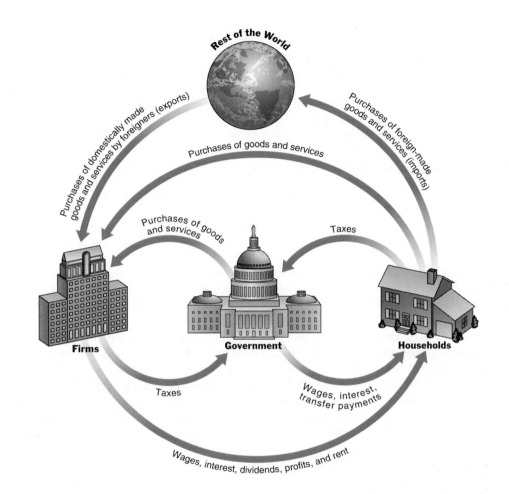

◀ **FIGURE 5.3 The Circular Flow of Payments**

Households receive income from firms and the government, purchase goods and services from firms, and pay taxes to the government. They also purchase foreign-made goods and services (imports). Firms receive payments from households and the government for goods and services; they pay wages, dividends, interest, and rents to households and taxes to the government. The government receives taxes from firms and households, pays firms and households for goods and services—including wages to government workers—and pays interest and transfers to households. Finally, people in other countries purchase goods and services produced domestically (exports).

Note: Although not shown in this diagram, firms and governments also purchase imports.

Let us walk through the circular flow step by step. Households work for firms and the government, and they receive wages for their work. Our diagram shows a flow of wages *into* households as payment for those services. Households also receive interest on corporate and government bonds and dividends from firms. Many households receive other payments from the government, such as Social Security benefits, veterans' benefits, and welfare payments. Economists call these kinds of payments from the government (for which the recipients do not supply goods, services, or labor) **transfer payments**. Together, these receipts make up the total income received by the households.

Households spend by buying goods and services from firms and by paying taxes to the government. These items make up the total amount paid out by the households. The difference between the total receipts and the total payments of the households is the amount that the households save or dissave. If households receive more than they spend, they *save* during the period. If they receive less than they spend, they *dissave*. A household can dissave by using up some of its previous savings or by borrowing. In the circular flow diagram, household spending is shown as a flow *out* of households. Saving by households is sometimes termed a "leakage" from the circular flow because it withdraws income, or current purchasing power, from the system.

Firms sell goods and services to households and the government. These sales earn revenue, which shows up in the circular flow diagram as a flow *into* the firm sector. Firms pay wages, interest, and dividends to households, and firms pay taxes to the government. These payments are shown flowing *out* of firms.

transfer payments Cash payments made by the government to people who do not supply goods, services, or labor in exchange for these payments. They include Social Security benefits, veterans' benefits, and welfare payments.

The government collects taxes from households and firms. The government also makes payments. It buys goods and services from firms, pays wages and interest to households, and makes transfer payments to households. If the government's revenue is less than its payments, the government is dissaving.

Finally, households spend some of their income on *imports*—goods and services produced in the rest of the world. Similarly, people in foreign countries purchase *exports*—goods and services produced by domestic firms and sold to other countries.

One lesson of the circular flow diagram is that everyone's expenditure is someone else's receipt. If you buy a personal computer from Dell, you make a payment to Dell and Dell receives revenue. If Dell pays taxes to the government, it has made a payment and the government has received revenue. Everyone's expenditures go somewhere. It is impossible to sell something without there being a buyer, and it is impossible to make a payment without there being a recipient. Every transaction must have two sides.

The Three Market Arenas

Another way of looking at the ways households, firms, the government, and the rest of the world relate to one another is to consider the markets in which they interact. We divide the markets into three broad arenas: (1) the goods-and-services market, (2) the labor market, and (3) the money (financial) market.

Goods-and-Services Market Households and the government purchase goods and services from firms in the *goods-and-services market*. In this market, firms also purchase goods and services from each other. For example, Levi Strauss buys denim from other firms to make its blue jeans. In addition, firms buy capital goods from other firms. If General Motors needs new robots on its assembly lines, it may buy them from another firm instead of making them. The *Economics in Practice* in Chapter 1 describes how Apple, in constructing its iPod, buys parts from a number of other firms.

Firms *supply* to the goods-and-services market. Households, the government, and firms *demand* from this market. Finally, the rest of the world buys from and sells to the goods-and-services market. The United States imports hundreds of billions of dollars' worth of automobiles, DVDs, oil, and other goods. In the case of Apple's iPod, inputs come from other firms located in countries all over the world. At the same time, the United States exports hundreds of billions of dollars' worth of computers, airplanes, and agricultural goods.

Labor Market Interaction in the *labor market* takes place when firms and the government purchase labor from households. In this market, households *supply* labor and firms and the government *demand* labor. In the U.S. economy, firms are the largest demanders of labor, although the government is also a substantial employer. The total supply of labor in the economy depends on the sum of decisions made by households. Individuals must decide whether to enter the labor force (whether to look for a job at all) and how many hours to work.

Labor is also supplied to and demanded from the rest of the world. In recent years, the labor market has become an international market. For example, vegetable and fruit farmers in California would find it very difficult to bring their product to market if it were not for the labor of migrant farm workers from Mexico. For years, Turkey has provided Germany with "guest workers" who are willing to take low-paying jobs that more prosperous German workers avoid. Call centers run by major U.S. corporations are sometimes staffed by labor in India and other developing countries.

Money Market In the *money market*—sometimes called the *financial market*—households purchase stocks and bonds from firms. Households *supply* funds to this market in the expectation of earning income in the form of dividends on stocks and interest on bonds. Households also *demand* (borrow) funds from this market to finance various purchases. Firms borrow to build new facilities in the hope of earning more in the future. The government borrows by issuing bonds. The rest of the world borrows from and lends to the money market. Every morning there are reports on TV and radio about the Japanese and British stock markets. Much of the borrowing and lending of households, firms, the government, and the rest of the world are coordinated by financial institutions—commercial banks, savings and loan associations, insurance companies, and the like. These institutions take deposits from one group and lend them to others.

When a firm, a household, or the government borrows to finance a purchase, it has an obligation to pay that loan back, usually at some specified time in the future. Most loans also involve payment of interest as a fee for the use of the borrowed funds. When a loan is made, the borrower usually signs a "promise to repay," or *promissory note*, and gives it to the lender. When the federal government borrows, it issues "promises" called **Treasury bonds**, **notes**, or **bills** in exchange for money. Firms can borrow by issuing **corporate bonds**.

Instead of issuing bonds to raise funds, firms can also issue shares of stock. A **share of stock** is a financial instrument that gives the holder a share in the firm's ownership and therefore the right to share in the firm's profits. If the firm does well, the value of the stock increases and the stockholder receives a *capital gain*[1] on the initial purchase. In addition, the stock may pay **dividends**—that is, the firm may return some of its profits directly to its stockholders instead of retaining the profits to buy capital. If the firm does poorly, so does the stockholder. The capital value of the stock may fall, and dividends may not be paid.

Stocks and bonds are simply contracts, or agreements, between parties. I agree to loan you a certain amount, and you agree to repay me this amount plus something extra at some future date, or I agree to buy part ownership in your firm, and you agree to give me a share of the firm's future profits.

A critical variable in the money market is the *interest rate*. Although we sometimes talk as if there is only one interest rate, there is never just one interest rate at any time. Instead, the interest rate on a given loan reflects the length of the loan and the perceived risk to the lender. A business that is just getting started must pay a higher rate than General Motors pays. A 30-year mortgage has a different interest rate than a 90-day loan. Nevertheless, interest rates tend to move up and down together, and their movement reflects general conditions in the financial market.

> **Treasury bonds, notes,** *and* **bills** Promissory notes issued by the federal government when it borrows money.
>
> **corporate bonds** Promissory notes issued by firms when they borrow money.
>
> **shares of stock** Financial instruments that give to the holder a share in the firm's ownership and therefore the right to share in the firm's profits.
>
> **dividends** The portion of a firm's profits that the firm pays out each period to its shareholders.

The Role of the Government in the Macroeconomy

The government plays a major role in the macroeconomy, so a useful way of learning how the macroeconomy works is to consider how the government uses policy to affect the economy. The two main policies are (1) fiscal policy and (2) monetary policy. Much of the study of macroeconomics is learning how fiscal and monetary policies work.

Fiscal policy refers to the government's decisions about how much to tax and spend. The federal government collects taxes from households and firms and spends those funds on goods and services ranging from missiles to parks to Social Security payments to interstate highways. Taxes take the form of personal income taxes, Social Security taxes, and corporate profits taxes, among others. An *expansionary* fiscal policy is a policy in which taxes are cut and/or government spending increases. A *contractionary* fiscal policy is the reverse.

Monetary policy in the United States is controlled by the Federal Reserve, the nation's central bank. The Fed, as it is usually called, determines the quantity of money in the economy, which in turn affects interest rates. The Fed's decisions have important effects on the economy. In fact, the task of trying to smooth out business cycles in the United States is primarily left to the Fed (that is, to monetary policy). The chair of the Federal Reserve is sometimes said to be the second most powerful person in the United States after the president.

> **fiscal policy** Government policies concerning taxes and spending.
>
> **monetary policy** The tools used by the Federal Reserve to control the quantity of money, which in turn affects interest rates.

A Brief History of Macroeconomics

The severe economic contraction and high unemployment of the 1930s, the decade of the **Great Depression**, spurred a great deal of thinking about macroeconomic issues, especially unemployment. Figure 5.2 shows that this period had the largest and longest aggregate output contraction in the twentieth century in the United States. The 1920s had been prosperous years for the U.S. economy. Virtually everyone who wanted a job could get one, incomes rose substantially, and prices were stable. Beginning in late 1929, things took a sudden turn for the worse. In 1929, 1.5 million people were unemployed. By 1933, that had increased to 13 million out of a labor force of 51 million. In 1933, the United States produced about 27 percent fewer goods and services than it had in 1929. In October 1929, when stock prices collapsed on Wall Street, billions of

> **Great Depression** The period of severe economic contraction and high unemployment that began in 1929 and continued throughout the 1930s.

---

[1] A *capital gain* occurs whenever the value of an asset increases. If you bought a stock for $1,000 and it is now worth $1,500, you have earned a capital gain of $500. A capital gain is "realized" when you sell the asset. Until you sell, the capital gain is *accrued* but not *realized*.

dollars of personal wealth were lost. Unemployment remained above 14 percent of the labor force until 1940. (See the *Economics in Practice*, p. 97, "Macroeconomics in Literature," for Fitzgerald's and Steinbeck's take on the 1920s and 1930s.)

Before the Great Depression, economists applied microeconomic models, sometimes referred to as "classical" or "market clearing" models, to economy-wide problems. For example, classical supply and demand analysis assumed that an excess supply of labor would drive down wages to a new equilibrium level; as a result, unemployment would not persist.

In other words, classical economists believed that recessions were self-correcting. As output falls and the demand for labor shifts to the left, the argument went, the wage rate will decline, thereby raising the quantity of labor demanded by firms that will want to hire more workers at the new lower wage rate. However, during the Great Depression, unemployment levels remained very high for nearly 10 years. In large measure, the failure of simple classical models to explain the prolonged existence of high unemployment provided the impetus for the development of macroeconomics. It is not surprising that what we now call macroeconomics was born in the 1930s.

One of the most important works in the history of economics, *The General Theory of Employment, Interest and Money*, by John Maynard Keynes, was published in 1936. Building on what was already understood about markets and their behavior, Keynes set out to construct a theory that would explain the confusing economic events of his time.

Much of macroeconomics has roots in Keynes's work. According to Keynes, it is not prices and wages that determine the level of employment, as classical models had suggested; instead, it is the level of aggregate demand for goods and services. Keynes believed that governments could intervene in the economy and affect the level of output and employment. The government's role during periods when private demand is low, Keynes argued, is to stimulate aggregate demand and, by so doing, to lift the economy out of recession. (Keynes was a larger-than-life figure, one of the Bloomsbury group in England that included, among others, Virginia Woolf and Clive Bell. See the *Economics in Practice*, p. 99, "John Maynard Keynes.")

After World War II and especially in the 1950s, Keynes's views began to gain increasing influence over both professional economists and government policy makers. Governments came to believe that they could intervene in their economies to attain specific employment and output goals. They began to use their powers to tax and spend as well as their ability to affect interest rates and the money supply for the explicit purpose of controlling the economy's ups and downs. This view of government policy became firmly established in the United States with the passage of the Employment Act of 1946. This act established the President's Council of Economic Advisers, a group of economists who advise the president on economic issues. The act also committed the federal government to intervening in the economy to prevent large declines in output and employment.

The notion that the government could and should act to stabilize the macroeconomy reached the height of its popularity in the 1960s. During these years, Walter Heller, the chairman of the Council of Economic Advisers under both President Kennedy and President Johnson, alluded to **fine-tuning** as the government's role in regulating inflation and unemployment. During the 1960s, many economists believed the government could use the tools available to manipulate unemployment and inflation levels fairly precisely.

In the 1970s and early 1980s, the U.S. economy had wide fluctuations in employment, output, and inflation. In 1974–1975 and again in 1980–1982, the United States experienced a severe recession. Although not as catastrophic as the Great Depression of the 1930s, these two recessions left millions without jobs and resulted in billions of dollars of lost output and income. In 1974–1975 and again in 1979–1981, the United States also saw very high rates of inflation.

The 1970s was thus a period of stagnation and high inflation, which came to be called stagflation. **Stagflation** is defined as a situation in which there is high inflation at the same time there are slow or negative output growth and high unemployment. Until the 1970s, high inflation had been observed only in periods when the economy was prospering and unemployment was low. The problem of stagflation was vexing both for macroeconomic theorists and policy makers concerned with the health of the economy.

It was clear by 1975 that the macroeconomy was more difficult to control than Heller's words or textbook theory had led economists to believe. The events of the 1970s and early 1980s had an important influence on macroeconomic theory. Much of the faith in the simple Keynesian model and the "conventional wisdom" of the 1960s was lost. Although we are now 30 years past the

fine-tuning The phrase used by Walter Heller to refer to the government's role in regulating inflation and unemployment.

stagflation A situation of both high inflation and high unemployment.

ECONOMICS IN PRACTICE

Macroeconomics in Literature

As you know, the language of economics includes a heavy dose of graphs and equations. But the underlying phenomena that economists study are the stuff of novels as well as graphs and equations. The following two passages, from *The Great Gatsby* by F. Scott Fitzgerald and *The Grapes of Wrath* by John Steinbeck, capture in graphic, although not graphical, form the economic growth and spending of the Roaring Twenties and the human side of the unemployment of the Great Depression.

The Great Gatsby, written in 1925, is set in the 1920s, while *The Grapes of Wrath*, written in 1939, is set in the early 1930s. If you look at Figure 5.2 for these two periods, you will see the translation of Fitzgerald and Steinbeck into macroeconomics.

From *The Great Gatsby*

At least once a fortnight a corps of caterers came down with several hundred feet of canvas and enough colored lights to make a Christmas tree of Gatsby's enormous garden. On buffet tables, garnished with glistening hors d'œuvre, spiced baked hams crowded against salads of harlequin designs and pastry pigs and turkeys bewitched to a dark gold. In the main hall a bar with a real brass rail was set up, and stocked with gins and liquors and with cordials so long forgotten that most of his female guests were too young to know one from another.

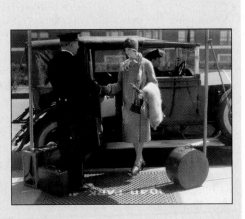

By seven o'clock the orchestra has arrived—no thin five piece affair but a whole pit full of oboes and trombones and saxophones and viols and cornets and piccolos and low and high drums. The last swimmers have come in from the beach now and are dressing upstairs; the cars from New York are parked five deep in the drive, and already the halls and salons and verandas are gaudy with primary colors and hair shorn in strange new ways and shawls beyond the dreams of Castile.

From *The Grapes of Wrath*

The moving, questing people were migrants now. Those families who had lived on a little piece of land, who had lived and died on forty acres, had eaten or starved on the produce of forty acres, had now the whole West to rove in. And they scampered about, looking for work; and the highways were streams of people, and the ditch banks were lines of people. Behind them more were coming. The great highways streamed with moving people.

And the migrants streamed in on the highways and their hunger was in their eyes, and their need was in their eyes. They had no argument, no system, nothing but their numbers and their needs. When there was work for a man, ten men fought for it—fought with a low wage. If that fella'll work for thirty cents, I'll work for twenty-five.

1970s, the discipline of macroeconomics is still in flux and there is no agreed-upon view of how the macroeconomy works. Many important issues have yet to be resolved. This makes macroeconomics hard to teach but exciting to study.

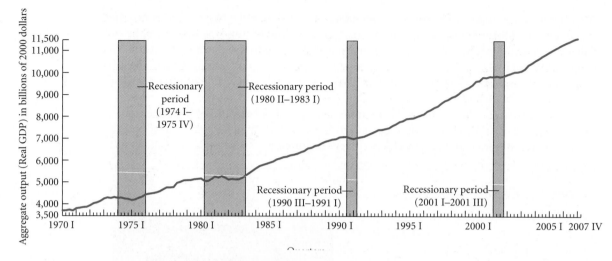

▲ FIGURE 5.4 **Aggregate Output (Real GDP), 1970 I–2007 IV**

Aggregate output in the United States since 1970 has risen overall, but there have been four recessionary periods: 1974 I–1975 IV, 1980 II–1983 I, 1990 III–1991 I, and 2001 I–2001 III.

The U.S Economy Since 1970

In the following chapters, it will be useful to have a picture of how the U.S. economy has performed in recent history. Since 1970, the U.S. economy has experienced four recessions and two periods of high inflation. The period since 1970 is illustrated in Figures 5.4, 5.5, and 5.6. These figures are based on quarterly data (that is, data for each quarter of the year). The first quarter consists of January, February, and March; the second quarter consists of April, May, and June; and so on. The Roman numerals I, II, III, and IV denote the four quarters. For example, 1972 III refers to the third quarter of 1972. The measurement of aggregate output, real GDP, in Figure 5.4 is discussed in the next chapter. In Figure 5.6, the measurement of inflation, the percentage change in the GDP deflator, is also discussed in the next chapter.

Figure 5.4 plots aggregate output for 1970 I–2007 IV. The four recessionary periods are 1974 I–1975 IV, 1980 II–1983 I, 1990 III–1991 I, and 2001 I–2001 III.[2] These four periods are shaded in the figure. Figure 5.5 plots the unemployment rate for the same overall period with the same shading for the recessionary periods. Note that unemployment rose in all four recessions. In the 1974–1975 recession, the unemployment rate reached a maximum of 8.8 percent in the second quarter of 1975. During the 1980–1982 recession, it reached a maximum of 10.7 percent in the fourth quarter of 1982. The unemployment rate continued to rise after the 1990–1991 recession and reached a peak of 7.6 percent in 1992 III. By the end of 1994, the unemployment rate had fallen to 5.6 percent, and by the second quarter of 2000, it had fallen to 4.0 percent. It then rose to 5.8 percent by the second quarter of 2002. It began falling again in the fourth quarter of 2003.

Figure 5.6 plots the inflation rate for 1970 I–2007 IV. The two high inflation periods are 1973 IV–1975 IV and 1979 I–1981 IV, which are shaded. In the first high inflation period, the inflation rate peaked at 11 percent in the first quarter of 1975. In the second high inflation period, inflation peaked at 10.1 percent in the first quarter of 1981. Since 1983, the inflation rate has been quite low by the standards of the 1970s. Since 1994, it has been between about 2 and 3 percent.

---

[2] As Figure 5.4 shows, output rose in the middle of 1981 before falling again in the last quarter of 1981. Given this fact, one possibility would be to treat the 1980 II–1983 I period as if it included two separate recessionary periods: 1980 II–1981 I and 1981 IV–1983 I. Because expansion in 1981 was so short-lived, however, we have chosen not to separate the period into two parts.

ECONOMICS IN PRACTICE

John Maynard Keynes

Much of the framework of modern macroeconomics comes from the works of John Maynard Keynes, whose *General Theory of Employment, Interest and Money* was published in 1936. The following excerpt by Robert L. Heilbroner provides some insights into Keynes's life and work.

By 1933 the nation was virtually prostrate. On street corners, in homes, in Hoovervilles (communities of makeshift shacks), 14 million unemployed sat, haunting the land....

It was the unemployment that was hardest to bear. The jobless millions were like an embolism in the nation's vital circulation; and while their indisputable existence argued more forcibly than any text that something was wrong with the system, the economists wrung their hands and racked their brains... but could offer neither diagnosis nor remedy. Unemployment—this kind of unemployment—was simply not listed among the possible ills of the system: it was absurd, impossible, unreasonable, and paradoxical. But it was there.

It would seem logical that the man who would seek to solve this impossible paradox of not enough production existing side by side with men fruitlessly seeking work would be a Left-winger, an economist with strong sympathies for the proletariat, an angry man. Nothing could be further from the fact. The man who tackled it was almost a dilettante with nothing like a chip on his shoulder. The simple truth was that his talents inclined in every direction. He had, for example, written a most recondite book on mathematical probability, a book that Bertrand Russell had declared "impossible to praise too highly"; then he had gone on to match his skill in abstruse logic with a flair for making money—he accumulated a fortune of £500,000 by way of the most treacherous of all roads to riches: dealing in international currencies and commodities. More impressive yet, he had written his mathematics treatise on the side, as it were, while engaged in Government service, and he piled up his private wealth by applying himself for only half an hour a day while still abed.

But this is only a sample of his many-sidedness. He was an economist, of course—a Cambridge don with all the dignity and erudition that go with such an appointment.... He managed to be simultaneously the darling of the Bloomsbury set, the cluster of Britain's most avant-garde intellectual brilliants, and also the chairman of a life insurance company, a niche in life rarely noted for its intellectual abandon. He was a pillar of stability in delicate matters of international diplomacy, but his official correctness did not prevent him from acquiring a knowledge of other European politicians that included their... neuroses and financial prejudices.... He ran a theater, and he came to be a Director of the Bank of England. He knew Roosevelt and Churchill and also Bernard Shaw and Pablo Picasso....

His name was John Maynard Keynes, an old British name (pronounced to rhyme with "rains") that could be traced back to one William de Cahagnes and 1066. Keynes was a traditionalist; he liked to think that greatness ran in families, and it is true that his own father was John Neville Keynes, an illustrious enough economist in his own right. But it took more than the ordinary gifts of heritage to account for the son; it was as if the talents that would have sufficed half a dozen men were by happy accident crowded into one person.

By a coincidence he was born in 1883, in the very year that Karl Marx passed away. But the two economists who thus touched each other in time, although each was to exert the profoundest influence on the philosophy of the capitalist system, could hardly have differed from one another more. Marx was bitter, at bay, heavy and disappointed; as we know, he was the draftsman of Capitalism Doomed. Keynes loved life and sailed through it buoyant, at ease, and consummately successful to become the architect of Capitalism Viable.

Source: Reprinted with the permission of Simon & Schuster Adult Group from The Worldly Philosophers 7th edition *by Robert L. Heilbroner. Copyright © 1953, 1961, 1967, 1972, 1980, 1986, 1999 by Robert L. Heilbroner. Copyright renewed © 1981, 1989, 1995, 2000 by Robert L. Heilbroner.*

▲ **FIGURE 5.5** **Unemployment Rate, 1970 I–2007 IV**

The U.S. unemployment rate since 1970 shows wide variations. The four recessionary reference periods show increases in the unemployment rate.

In the following chapters, we will explain the behavior of and the connections among variables such as output, unemployment, and inflation. When you understand the forces at work in creating the movements shown in Figures 5.4, 5.5, and 5.6, you will have come a long way in understanding how the macroeconomy works.

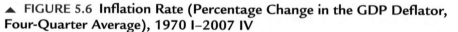

▲ **FIGURE 5.6** **Inflation Rate (Percentage Change in the GDP Deflator, Four-Quarter Average), 1970 I–2007 IV**

Since 1970, inflation has been high in two periods: 1973 IV–1975 IV and 1979 I–1981 IV. Inflation between 1983 and 1992 was moderate. Since 1992, it has been fairly low.

The Economy and the Election in 2008

On November 4, 2008, Democrat Barak Obama was victorious over Republican John McCain in the U.S. presidential election, winning over 53 percent of the popular vote.

At the time of the 2008 election, the economy was not doing well. Output was falling and unemployment was rising. Indeed, in the fall of 2008, the United States was in the midst of a worldwide financial crisis in which large financial institutions around the globe were faltering. In the United States, fiscal policy and monetary policy were expansive in 2008 as policy makers tried to help the economy. These policies are discussed in future *Economics in Practice* boxes. The policies were not enough, however, to prevent a contraction.

The economy and election outcomes are closely linked. The state of the economy is almost always an important issue in U.S. presidential elections. Voters appear to hold the party that is in power in the White House accountable for the economy. Voters tend to favor the incumbent-party candidate if the economy is good (high output and low inflation) and vote against the incumbent-party candidate if the economy is bad (low output and high inflation). In fact, it is possible to quantify the relationship between the economy and election outcomes using the tools of econometrics, one of the fields listed in Table 1.2 on p. 9. One of the authors of this text (Fair, *Predicting Presidential Elections and Other Things*, Stanford University Press, 2002) has an equation that explains the incumbent-party vote share for president based on output and inflation (and some non-economic incumbency information). Economic performances and election outcomes back to the 1916 election are used for the analysis. Given predictions of output and inflation before an election, this equation can be used to predict each party's vote share.

Two years ahead of the 2008 election, on November 1, 2006, the equation was predicting, given economic forecasts that were available at the time, that the Democratic challenger, whoever he or she might be, would get 53.5 percent of the vote. During the next two years the economic forecasts changed as new economic information became available, which allowed a new vote prediction to be made. The final vote prediction before the election, on October 30, 2008, was 51.9 percent for the Democratic challenger (Obama). In fact, Obama got 53.3 percent of the vote, so the predictions from the vote equation were quite close to what actually occurred. Two years ahead the equation was predicting that the Democrats would win and by roughly the amount by which they did! Not all economic and political predictions are this accurate, but it is important to realize that the economy is generally very important in influencing elections. The economy was struggling at the time of the 2008 election, and the incumbent-party candidate lost.

SUMMARY

1. *Microeconomics* examines the functioning of individual industries and the behavior of individual decision-making units. *Macroeconomics* is concerned with the sum, or aggregate, of these individual decisions—the consumption of *all* households in the economy, the amount of labor supplied and demanded by *all* individuals and firms, and the total amount of *all* goods and services produced.

MACROECONOMIC CONCERNS *p. 90*

2. The three topics of primary concern to macroeconomists are the growth rate of aggregate output; the level of unemployment; and increases in the overall price level, or *inflation*.

THE COMPONENTS OF THE MACROECONOMY *p. 92*

3. The *circular flow* diagram shows the flow of income received and payments made by the four groups in the economy—households, firms, the government, and the rest of the world. Everybody's expenditure is someone else's receipt—every transaction must have two sides.

4. Another way of looking at how households, firms, the government, and the rest of the world relate is to consider the markets in which they interact: the goods-and-services market, labor market, and money (financial) market.

5. Among the tools that the government has available for influencing the macroeconomy are *fiscal policy* (decisions on

taxes and government spending) and *monetary policy* (control of the money supply, which affects interest rates).

A BRIEF HISTORY OF MACROECONOMICS *p. 95*

6. Macroeconomics was born out of the effort to explain the *Great Depression* of the 1930s. Since that time, the discipline has evolved, concerning itself with new issues as the problems facing the economy have changed. Through the late

1960s, it was believed that the government could "fine-tune" the economy to keep it running on an even keel at all times. The poor economic performance of the 1970s, however, showed that *fine-tuning* does not always work.

THE U.S. ECONOMY SINCE 1970 *p. 99*

7. Since 1970, the U.S. economy has seen four *recessions* and two periods of high inflation.

REVIEW TERMS AND CONCEPTS

aggregate behavior, *p. 89*

aggregate output, *p. 90*

business cycle, *p. 90*

circular flow, *p. 93*

contraction, recession, *or* slump, *p. 90*

corporate bonds, *p. 95*

deflation, *p. 92*

depression, *p. 90*

dividends, *p. 95*

expansion *or* boom, *p. 90*

fine-tuning, *p. 96*

fiscal policy, *p. 95*

Great Depression, *p. 95*

hyperinflation, *p. 92*

inflation, *p. 92*

macroeconomics, *p. 89*

microeconomics, *p. 89*

monetary policy, *p. 95*

recession, *p. 90*

shares of stock, *p. 95*

stagflation, *p. 96*

sticky prices, *p. 89*

transfer payments, *p. 93*

Treasury bonds, notes, *and* bills, *p. 95*

unemployment rate, *p. 91*

PROBLEMS

Visit **www.myeconlab.com** to complete the problems marked in orange online. You will receive instant feedback on your answers, tutorial help, and access to additional practice problems.

1. Define inflation. Assume that you live in a simple economy in which only three goods are produced and traded: fish, fruit, and meat. Suppose that on January 1, 2007, fish sold for $2.50 per pound, meat was $3.00 per pound, and fruit was $1.50 per pound. At the end of the year, you discover that the catch was low and that fish prices had increased to $5.00 per pound, but fruit prices stayed at $1.50 and meat prices had actually fallen to $2.00. Can you say what happened to the overall "price level"? How might you construct a measure of the "change in the price level"? What additional information might you need to construct your measure?

2. Define *unemployment*. Should everyone who does not hold a job be considered "unemployed"? To help with your answer, draw a supply and demand diagram depicting the labor market. What is measured along the demand curve? What factors determine the quantity of labor demanded during a given period? What is measured along the labor supply curve? What factors determine the quantity of labor supplied by households during a given period? What is the opportunity cost of holding a job?

3. [Related to the *Economics in Practice* on p. 97] The *Economics in Practice* describes prosperity and recession as they are depicted in literature. At the beginning of 2008, there was a debate about whether the U.S. economy was in recession. Look at the data on real GDP growth and unemployment and describe the pattern since 2007. You can find raw data on employment and unemployment at www.bls.gov, and you can find raw data on real GDP growth at www.bea.gov. (In both

cases, use the data described in "Current Releases.") Summarize what happened during 2008. Did we have a recession? Explain.

4. A recession occurred in the U.S. economy during the first three quarters of 2001. National output of goods and services fell during this period. But during the fourth quarter of 2001, output began to increase and it increased at a slow rate through the first quarter of 2003. At the same time, between March 2001 and April 2003, employment declined almost continuously with a loss of over 2 million jobs. How is it possible that output rises while at the same time employment is falling?

5. Describe the economy of your state. What is the most recently reported unemployment rate? How has the number of payroll jobs changed over the last 3 months and over the last year? How does your state's performance compare to the U.S. economy's performance over the last year? What explanations have been offered in the press? How accurate are they?

6. Explain briefly how macroeconomics is different from microeconomics. How can macroeconomists use microeconomic theory to guide them in their work, and why might they want to do so?

7. During 1993 when the economy was growing very slowly, President Clinton recommended a series of spending cuts and tax increases designed to reduce the deficit. These were passed by Congress in the Omnibus Budget Reconciliation Act of 1993. Some who opposed the bill argue that the United States was pursuing a "contractionary fiscal policy" at precisely the wrong time. Explain their logic.

8. Many of the expansionary periods during the twentieth century occurred during wars. Why do you think this is true?

9. In the 1940s, you could buy a soda for 5 cents, eat dinner at a restaurant for less than $1, and purchase a house for $10,000. From this statement, it follows that consumers today are worse off than consumers in the 1940s. Comment.

10. [Related to *Economics in Practice* on *p. 99*] John Maynard Keynes was the first to show that government policy could be used to change aggregate output and prevent recessions by stabilizing the economy. Describe the economy of the world at the time Keynes was writing. Describe the economy of the United States today. What measures were being proposed by the Presidential candidates in the election of 2008 to prevent or end a recession in 2008-2009? Where the actions taken appropriate

from the standpoint of John Maynard Keynes? Did they have the desired effect?

11. [Related to *Economics in Practice* on *p. 101*] Presidential elections are often influenced by the current state of the economy. The state of the U.S economy was a major campaign issue in the 2008 presidential election. Go to www.bls.gov to find the quarterly data on the unemployment rate in 2008, and www.bea.gov to find the quarterly GDP data for 2008. Based on this data, was the economy in a recession prior to the 2008 presidential election? Does there appear to be any link between the election results and the state of the economy? Briefly explain how the election results may or may not have been influenced by the state of the economy in 2008. For more information, see fairmodel.econ.yale.edu/vote2008/index2.htm.

Measuring National Output and National Income

6

We saw in the last chapter that three main concerns of macroeconomics are aggregate output, unemployment, and inflation. In this chapter, we discuss the measurement of aggregate output and inflation. In the next chapter, we discuss the measurement of unemployment. Accurate measures of these variables are critical for understanding the economy. Without good measures, economists would have a hard time analyzing how the economy works and policy makers

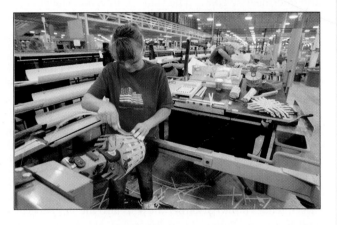

would have little to guide them on which policies are best for the economy.

Much of the macroeconomic data are from the **national income and product accounts**, which are compiled by the Bureau of Economic Analysis (BEA) of the U.S. Department of Commerce. It is hard to overestimate the importance of these accounts. They are, in fact, one of the great inventions of the twentieth century. (See the *Economics in Practice*, p. 113.) They not only convey data about the performance of the economy but also provide a conceptual framework that macroeconomists use to think about how the pieces of the economy fit together. When economists think about the macroeconomy, the categories and vocabulary they use come from the national income and product accounts.

The national income and product accounts can be compared with the mechanical or wiring diagrams for an automobile engine. The diagrams do not explain how an engine works, but they identify the key parts of an engine and show how they are connected. Trying to understand the macroeconomy without understanding national income accounting is like trying to fix an engine without a mechanical diagram and with no names for the engine parts.

There are literally thousands of variables in the national income and product accounts. In this chapter, we discuss only the most important. This chapter is meant to convey the way the national income and product accounts represent or organize the economy and the *sizes* of the various pieces of the economy.

Gross Domestic Product

The key concept in the national income and product accounts is **gross domestic product (GDP)**.

> GDP is the total market value of a country's output. It is the market value of all final goods and services produced within a given period of time by factors of production located within a country.

U.S. GDP for 2007—the value of all output produced by factors of production in the United States in 2007—was $13,841.3 billion.

national income and product accounts Data collected and published by the government describing the various components of national income and output in the economy.

gross domestic product (GDP) The total market value of all final goods and services produced within a given period by factors of production located within a country.

GDP is a critical concept. Just as an individual firm needs to evaluate the success or failure of its operations each year, so the economy as a whole needs to assess itself. GDP, as a measure of the total production of an economy, provides us with a country's economic report card. Because GDP is so important, we need to take time to explain exactly what its definition means.

Final Goods and Services

final goods and services Goods and services produced for final use.

intermediate goods Goods that are produced by one firm for use in further processing by another firm.

First, note that the definition refers to **final goods and services**. Many goods produced in the economy are not classified as *final* goods, but instead as intermediate goods. **Intermediate goods** are produced by one firm for use in further processing by another firm. For example, tires sold to automobile manufacturers are intermediate goods. The parts that go in Apple's iPod are also intermediate goods. The value of intermediate goods is not counted in GDP.

Why are intermediate goods not counted in GDP? Suppose that in producing a car, General Motors (GM) pays $200 to Goodyear for tires. GM uses these tires (among other components) to assemble a car, which it sells for $24,000. The value of the car (including its tires) is $24,000, not $24,000 + $200. The final price of the car already reflects the value of all its components. To count in GDP both the value of the tires sold to the automobile manufacturers and the value of the automobiles sold to the consumers would result in double counting.

value added The difference between the value of goods as they leave a stage of production and the cost of the goods as they entered that stage.

Double counting can also be avoided by counting only the value added to a product by each firm in its production process. The **value added** during some stage of production is the difference between the value of goods as they leave that stage of production and the cost of the goods as they entered that stage. Value added is illustrated in Table 6.1. The four stages of the production of a gallon of gasoline are: (1) oil drilling, (2) refining, (3) shipping, and (4) retail sale. In the first stage, value added is the value of the crude oil. In the second stage, the refiner purchases the oil from the driller, refines it into gasoline, and sells it to the shipper. The refiner pays the driller $3.00 per gallon and charges the shipper $3.30. The value added by the refiner is thus $0.30 per gallon. The shipper then sells the gasoline to retailers for $3.60. The value added in the third stage of production is $0.30. Finally, the retailer sells the gasoline to consumers for $4.00. The value added at the fourth stage is $0.40; and the total value added in the production process is $4.00, the same as the value of sales at the retail level. Adding the total values of sales at each stage of production ($3.00 + $3.30 + $3.60 + $4.00 = $13.90) would significantly overestimate the value of the gallon of gasoline.

In calculating GDP, we can sum up the value added at each stage of production or we can take the value of final sales. We do not use the value of total sales in an economy to measure how much output has been produced.

TABLE 6.1 Value Added in the Production of a Gallon of Gasoline (Hypothetical Numbers)

Stage of Production	Value of Sales	Value Added
(1) Oil drilling	$3.00	$3.00
(2) Refining	3.30	0.30
(3) Shipping	3.60	0.30
(4) Retail sale	4.00	0.40
Total value added		$4.00

Exclusion of Used Goods and Paper Transactions

GDP is concerned only with new, or current, production. Old output is not counted in current GDP because it was already counted when it was produced. It would be double counting to count sales of used goods in current GDP. If someone sells a used car to you, the transaction is not counted in GDP because no new production has taken place. Similarly, a house is counted in GDP only at the time it is built, not each time it is resold. In short:

GDP does not count transactions in which money or goods changes hands but in which no new goods and services are produced.

Sales of stocks and bonds are not counted in GDP. These exchanges are transfers of ownership of assets, either electronically or through paper exchanges, and do not correspond to current production. However, what if you sell the stock or bond for more than you originally paid for it? Profits from the stock or bond market have nothing to do with current production, so they are not counted in GDP. However, if you pay a fee to a broker for selling a stock of yours to someone else, this fee is counted in GDP because the broker is performing a service for you. This service is part of current production. Be careful to distinguish between exchanges of stocks and bonds for money (or for other stocks and bonds), which do not involve current production, and fees for performing such exchanges, which do.

Exclusion of Output Produced Abroad by Domestically Owned Factors of Production

GDP is the value of output produced by factors of production *located within a country*.

The three basic factors of production are land, labor, and capital. The labor of U.S. citizens counts as a domestically owned factor of production for the United States. The output produced by U.S. citizens abroad—for example, U.S. citizens working for a foreign company—is *not* counted in U.S. GDP because the output is not produced within the United States. Likewise, profits earned abroad by U.S. companies are not counted in U.S. GDP. However, the output produced by foreigners working in the United States is counted in U.S. GDP because the output is produced within the United States. Also, profits earned in the United States by foreign-owned companies are counted in U.S. GDP.

It is sometimes useful to have a measure of the output produced by factors of production owned by a country's citizens regardless of where the output is produced. This measure is called **gross national product (GNP)**. For most countries, including the United States, the difference between GDP and GNP is small. In 2007, GNP for the United States was $13,937.1 billion, which is close to the $13,841.3 billion value for U.S. GDP.

The distinction between GDP and GNP can be tricky. Consider the Honda plant in Marysville, Ohio. The plant is owned by the Honda Corporation, a Japanese firm, but most of the workers employed at the plant are U.S. workers. Although all the output of the plant is included in U.S. GDP, only part of it is included in U.S. GNP. The wages paid to U.S. workers are part of U.S. GNP, while the profits from the plant are not. The profits from the plant are counted in Japanese GNP because this is output produced by Japanese-owned factors of production (Japanese capital in this case). The profits, however, are not counted in Japanese GDP because they were not earned in Japan.

gross national product (GNP) The total market value of all final goods and services produced within a given period by factors of production owned by a country's citizens, regardless of where the output is produced.

Calculating GDP

GDP can be computed two ways. One way is to add up the total amount spent on all final goods and services during a given period. This is the **expenditure approach** to calculating GDP. The other way is to add up the income—wages, rents, interest, and profits—received by all factors of production in producing final goods and services. This is the **income approach** to calculating GDP. These two methods lead to the same value for GDP for the reason we discussed in the previous chapter: *Every payment (expenditure) by a buyer is at the same time a receipt (income) for the seller*. We can measure either income received or expenditures made, and we will end up with the same total output.

Suppose the economy is made up of just one firm and the firm's total output this year sells for $1 million. Because the total amount spent on output this year is $1 million, this year's GDP is $1 million. (Remember: The expenditure approach calculates GDP on the basis of the total amount spent on final goods and services in the economy.) However, *every one* of the million dollars of GDP either is paid to someone or remains with the owners of the firm as profit. Using the income approach, we add up the wages paid to employees of the firm, the interest paid to those who lent money to the firm, and the rents paid to those who leased land, buildings, or equipment to the firm. What is left over is profit, which is, of course, income to the owners of the firm. If we add up the incomes of all the factors of production, including profits to the owners, we get a GDP of $1 million.

expenditure approach A method of computing GDP that measures the total amount spent on all final goods and services during a given period.

income approach A method of computing GDP that measures the income—wages, rents, interest, and profits—received by all factors of production in producing final goods and services.

The Expenditure Approach

Recall from the previous chapter the four main groups in the economy: households, firms, the government, and the rest of the world. There are also four main categories of expenditure:

- Personal consumption expenditures (C): household spending on consumer goods
- Gross private domestic investment (I): spending by firms and households on new capital, that is, plant, equipment, inventory, and new residential structures
- Government consumption and gross investment (G)
- Net exports (EX − IM): net spending by the rest of the world, or exports (EX) minus imports (IM)

The expenditure approach calculates GDP by adding together these four components of spending. It is shown here in equation form:

$$GDP = C + I + G + (EX - IM)$$

U.S. GDP was $13,841.3 billion in 2007. The four components of the expenditure approach are shown in Table 6.2, along with their various categories.

TABLE 6.2 Components of U.S. GDP, 2007: The Expenditure Approach

	Billions of Dollars	Percentage of GDP
Personal consumption expenditures (C)	9,734.2	70.3
Durable goods	1,078.2	7.8
Nondurable goods	2,833.2	20.5
Services	5,822.8	42.1
Gross private domestic investment (I)	2,125.4	15.4
Nonresidential	1,481.8	10.7
Residential	640.7	4.6
Change in business inventories	2.9	0.0
Government consumption and gross investment (G)	2,689.8	19.4
Federal	976.0	7.1
State and local	1,713.8	12.4
Net exports (EX − IM)	−708.0	−5.1
Exports (EX)	1,643.0	11.9
Imports (IM)	2,351.0	17.0
Gross domestic product	13,841.3	100.0

Note: Numbers may not add exactly because of rounding.

Source: U.S. Department of Commerce, Bureau of Economic Analysis.

personal consumption expenditures (C)
Expenditures by consumers on goods and services.

durable goods Goods that last a relatively long time, such as cars and household appliances.

nondurable goods Goods that are used up fairly quickly, such as food and clothing.

services The things we buy that do not involve the production of physical things, such as legal and medical services and education.

Personal Consumption Expenditures (C) The largest part of GDP consists of **personal consumption expenditures (C)**. Table 6.2 shows that in 2007, the amount of personal consumption expenditures accounted for 70.3 percent of GDP. These are expenditures by consumers on goods and services.

There are three main categories of consumer expenditures: durable goods, nondurable goods, and services. **Durable goods**, such as automobiles, furniture, and household appliances, last a relatively long time. **Nondurable goods**, such as food, clothing, gasoline, and cigarettes, are used up fairly quickly. Payments for **services**—those things we buy that do not involve the production of physical items—include expenditures for doctors, lawyers, and educational institutions. As Table 6.2 shows, in 2007, durable goods expenditures accounted for 7.8 percent of GDP, nondurables for 20.5 percent, and services for 42.1 percent.

Gross Private Domestic Investment (I) *Investment*, as we use the term in economics, refers to the purchase of new capital—housing, plants, equipment, and inventory. The economic use of the term is in contrast to its everyday use, where *investment* often refers to purchases of stocks, bonds, or mutual funds.

ECONOMICS IN PRACTICE

Where Does eBay Get Counted?

eBay runs an online marketplace with over 220 million registered users who buy and sell 2.4 billion items a year, ranging from children's toys to oil paintings. In December 2007, one eBay user auctioned off a 1933 Chicago World's Fair pennant. The winning bid was just over $20.

eBay is traded on the New York Stock Exchange, employs hundreds of people, and has a market value of about $40 billion. With regard to eBay, what do you think gets counted as part of current GDP?

That 1933 pennant, for example, does not get counted. The production of that pennant was counted back in 1933. The many cartons of K'nex bricks sent from one home to another don't count either. Their value was counted when the bricks were first produced. What about a newly minted Scrabble game? One of the interesting features of eBay is that it has changed from being a market in which individuals market their hand-me-downs to a place that small and even large businesses use as a sales site. The value of the new Scrabble game would be counted as part of this year's GDP if it were produced in the year.

So do any of eBay's services count as part of GDP? eBay's business is to provide a marketplace for exchange. In doing so, it uses labor and capital and creates value. In return for creating this value, eBay charges fees to the sellers that use its site. The value of these fees do enter into GDP. So while the old knickknacks that people sell on eBay do not contribute to current GDP, the cost of finding an interested buyer for those old goods does indeed get counted.

Total investment in capital by the private sector is called **gross private domestic investment (I)**. Expenditures by firms for machines, tools, plants, and so on make up **nonresidential investment**.[1] Because these are goods that firms buy for their own final use, they are part of "final sales" and counted in GDP. Expenditures for new houses and apartment buildings constitute **residential investment**. The third component of gross private domestic investment, the **change in business inventories**, is the amount by which firms' inventories change during a period. Business inventories can be looked at as the goods that firms produce now but intend to sell later. In 2007, gross private domestic investment accounted for 15.4 percent of GDP. Of that, 10.7 percent was nonresidential investment, 4.6 percent was residential investment, and 0.0 percent (rounded to one decimal point) was change in business inventories.

Change in Business Inventories It is sometimes confusing to students that inventories are counted as capital and that changes in inventory are counted as part of gross private domestic investment, but conceptually it makes sense. The inventory a firm owns has a value, and it serves a purpose (or provides a service) to the firm. That inventory has value is obvious. Think of the inventory of a new car dealer or of a clothing store or stocks of newly produced but unsold computers awaiting shipment. All these have value.

gross private domestic investment (I) Total investment in capital—that is, the purchase of new housing, plants, equipment, and inventory by the private (or nongovernment) sector.

nonresidential investment Expenditures by firms for machines, tools, plants, and so on.

residential investment Expenditures by households and firms on new houses and apartment buildings.

change in business inventories The amount by which firms' inventories change during a period. Inventories are the goods that firms produce now but intend to sell later.

---

[1] The distinction between what is considered investment and what is considered consumption is sometimes fairly arbitrary. A firm's purchase of a car or a truck is counted as investment, but a household's purchase of a car or a truck is counted as consumption of durable goods. In general, expenditures by firms for items that last longer than a year are counted as investment expenditures. Expenditures for items that last less than a year are seen as purchases of intermediate goods.

However, what *service* does inventory provide? Firms keep stocks of inventory for a number of reasons. One is to meet unforeseen demand. Firms are never sure how much they will sell from period to period. Sales go up and down. To maintain the goodwill of their customers, firms need to be able to respond to unforeseen increases in sales. The only way to do that is with inventory.

Some firms use inventory to provide direct services to customers—the main function of a retail store. A grocery store provides a service—convenience. The store itself does not produce any food. It simply assembles a wide variety of items and puts them on display so consumers with varying tastes can come and shop in one place for what they want. The same is true for clothing and hardware stores. To provide their services, such stores need light fixtures, counters, cash registers, buildings, and stocks of inventory. Capital stocks are made up of plant, equipment, and inventory. Inventory accumulation is part of the change in capital stocks, or investment.

Remember that GDP is not the market value of total final *sales* during a period—it is the market value of total *production*. The relationship between total production and total sales is as follows:

$$\text{GDP} = \text{Final sales} + \text{Change in business inventories}$$

Total production (GDP) equals final sales of domestic goods plus the change in business inventories. In 2007, production in the United States exceeded sales by $2.9 billion. Inventories at the end of 2007 were $2.9 billion *greater* than they were at the end of 2006.

Gross Investment versus Net Investment During the process of production, capital (especially machinery and equipment) produced in previous periods gradually wears out. GDP does not give us a true picture of the real production of an economy. GDP includes newly produced capital goods but does not take account of capital goods "consumed" in the production process.

Capital assets decline in value over time. The amount by which an asset's value falls each period is called its **depreciation**.[2] A personal computer purchased by a business today may be expected to have a useful life of 4 years before becoming worn out or obsolete. Over that period, the computer steadily depreciates.

What is the relationship between gross investment (I) and depreciation? **Gross investment** is the total value of all newly produced capital goods (plant, equipment, housing, and inventory) produced in a given period. It takes no account of the fact that some capital wears out and must be replaced. **Net investment** is equal to gross investment minus depreciation. Net investment is a measure of how much the stock of capital *changes* during a period. Positive net investment means that the amount of new capital produced exceeds the amount that wears out, and negative net investment means that the amount of new capital produced is less than the amount that wears out. Therefore, if net investment is positive, the capital stock has increased, and if net investment is negative, the capital stock has decreased. Put another way, the capital stock at the end of a period is equal to the capital stock that existed at the beginning of the period plus net investment:

$$\text{capital}_{\text{end of period}} = \text{capital}_{\text{beginning of period}} + \text{net investment}$$

depreciation The amount by which an asset's value falls in a given period.

gross investment The total value of all newly produced capital goods (plant, equipment, housing, and inventory) produced in a given period.

net investment Gross investment minus depreciation.

government consumption and gross investment (G) Expenditures by federal, state, and local governments for final goods and services.

Government Consumption and Gross Investment (G)
Government consumption and gross investment (G) include expenditures by federal, state, and local governments for final goods (bombs, pencils, school buildings) and services (military salaries, congressional salaries, school teachers' salaries). Some of these expenditures are counted as government consumption, and some are counted as government gross investment. Government transfer payments (Social Security benefits, veterans' disability stipends, and so on) are not included in G because these transfers are not purchases of anything currently produced. The payments are not made in exchange for any goods or services. Because interest payments on the government debt are also counted as transfers, they are excluded from GDP on the grounds that they are not payments for current goods or services.

As Table 6.2 shows, government consumption and gross investment accounted for $2,689.8 billion, or 19.4 percent of U.S. GDP, in 2007. Federal government consumption and gross investment in 2007 accounted for 7.1 percent of GDP, and state and local government consumption and gross investment accounted for 12.4 percent.

---

[2] This is the formal definition of economic depreciation. Because depreciation is difficult to measure precisely, accounting rules allow firms to use shortcut methods to approximate the amount of depreciation that they incur each period. To complicate matters even more, the U.S. tax laws allow firms to deduct depreciation for tax purposes under a different set of rules.

Net Exports (EX − IM) The value of **net exports (EX − IM)** is the difference between *exports* (sales to foreigners of U.S.-produced goods and services) and *imports* (U.S. purchases of goods and services from abroad). This figure can be positive or negative. In 2007, the United States exported less than it imported, so the level of net exports was negative (−$708.0 billion). Before 1976, the United States was generally a net exporter—exports exceeded imports, so the net export figure was positive.

The reason for including net exports in the definition of GDP is simple. Consumption, investment, and government spending (*C*, *I*, and *G*, respectively) include expenditures on goods produced at home and abroad. Therefore, *C + I + G* overstates domestic production because it contains expenditures on foreign-produced goods—that is, imports (*IM*), which have to be subtracted from GDP to obtain the correct figure. At the same time, *C + I + G* understates domestic production because some of what a nation produces is sold abroad and therefore is not included in *C*, *I*, or *G*—exports (*EX*) have to be added in. If a U.S. firm produces computers and sells them in Germany, the computers are part of U.S. production and should be counted as part of U.S. GDP.

net exports (EX − IM) The difference between exports (sales to foreigners of U.S.-produced goods and services) and imports (U.S. purchases of goods and services from abroad). The figure can be positive or negative.

The Income Approach

We now turn to calculating GDP using the income approach, which looks at GDP in terms of who receives it as income rather than as who purchases it.

We begin with the concept of **national income**, which is defined in Table 6.3. National income is the sum of eight income items. **Compensation of employees**, the largest of the eight items by far, includes wages and salaries paid to households by firms and by the government, as well as various supplements to wages and salaries such as contributions that employers make to social insurance and private pension funds. **Proprietors' income** is the income of unincorporated businesses. **Rental income**, a minor item, is the income received by property owners in the form of rent. **Corporate profits**, the second-largest item of the eight, is the income of corporations. **Net interest** is the interest paid by business. (Interest paid by households and the government is not counted in GDP because it is not assumed to flow from the production of goods and services.)

national income The total income earned by the factors of production owned by a country's citizens.

compensation of employees Includes wages, salaries, and various supplements—employer contributions to social insurance and pension funds, for example—paid to households by firms and by the government.

proprietors' income The income of unincorporated businesses.

rental income The income received by property owners in the form of rent.

corporate profits The income of corporations.

net interest The interest paid by business.

TABLE 6.3 National Income, 2007		
	Billions of Dollars	Percentage of National Income
National income	12,221.1	100.0
Compensation of employees	7,874.2	64.4
Proprietors' income	1,042.6	8.5
Rental income	65.4	0.5
Corporate profits	1,598.2	13.1
Net interest	602.6	4.9
Indirect taxes minus subsidies	961.4	7.9
Net business transfer payments	94.2	0.8
Surplus of government enterprises	−14.5	−0.1

Source: See Table 6.2.

The sixth item, **indirect taxes minus subsidies**, includes taxes such as sales taxes, customs duties, and license fees less subsidies that the government pays for which it receives no goods or services in return. (Subsidies are like negative taxes.) The value of indirect taxes minus subsidies is thus net income received by the government. **Net business transfer payments** are net transfer payments by businesses to others and are thus income of others. The final item is the **surplus of government enterprises**, which is the income of government enterprises. Table 6.3 shows that this item was negative in 2007: government enterprises on net ran at a loss.

National income is the total income of the country, but it is not quite GDP. Table 6.4 shows what is involved in going from national income to GDP. Table 6.4 first shows that in moving from gross domestic product (GDP) to gross national product (GNP), we need to add receipts of factor income from the rest of the world and subtract payments of factor income to the rest of the world. National income is income of the country's citizens, not the income of the residents of the country. So we first need to move from GDP to GNP. This, as discussed earlier, is a minor adjustment.

indirect taxes minus subsidies Taxes such as sales taxes, customs duties, and license fees less subsidies that the government pays for which it receives no goods or services in return.

net business transfer payments Net transfer payments by businesses to others.

surplus of government enterprises Income of government enterprises.

TABLE 6.4 GDP, GNP, NNP, and National Income, 2007

	Dollars (Billions)
GDP	13,841.3
Plus: Receipts of factor income from the rest of the world	+817.5
Less: Payments of factor income to the rest of the world	−721.8
Equals: **GNP**	13,937.1
Less: Depreciation	−1,686.6
Equals: **Net national product (NNP)**	12,250.5
Less: Statistical discrepancy	−29.4
Equals: **National income**	12,221.1

Source: See Table 6.2

net national product (NNP) Gross national product minus depreciation; a nation's total product minus what is required to maintain the value of its capital stock.

We then need to subtract depreciation from GNP, which is a large adjustment. GNP less depreciation is called **net national product (NNP)**. Why is depreciation subtracted? To see why, go back to the example earlier in this chapter in which the economy is made up of just one firm and total output (GDP) for the year is $1 million. Assume that after the firm pays wages, interest, and rent, it has $100,000 left. Assume also that its capital stock depreciated by $40,000 during the year. National income includes corporate profits (see Table 6.3); and in calculating corporate profits, the $40,000 depreciation is subtracted from the $100,000, leaving profits of $60,000. When we calculate GDP using the expenditure approach, depreciation is not subtracted. We simply add consumption, investment, government spending, and net exports. In our simple example, this is just $1 million. We thus must subtract depreciation from GDP (actually GNP when there is a rest-of-the-world sector) to get national income.

statistical discrepancy Data measurement error.

Table 6.4 shows that net national product and national income are the same except for a **statistical discrepancy**, a data measurement error. If the government were completely accurate in its data collection, the statistical discrepancy would be zero. The data collection, however, is not perfect, and the statistical discrepancy is the measurement error in each period. Table 6.4 shows that in 2007, this error was −$29.4 billion, which is small compared to national income of $12,221.1 billion.

personal income The total income of households.

We have so far seen from Table 6.3 the various income items that make up total national income, and we have seen from Table 6.4 how GDP and national income are related. A useful way to think about national income is to consider how much of it goes to households. The total income of households is called **personal income**, and it turns out that almost all of national income is personal income. Table 6.5 shows that of the $12,221.1 billion in national income in 2007, $11,659.5 billion was personal income. Although not shown in Table 6.5, one of the differences between national income and personal income is the profits of corporations not paid to households in the form of dividends, called the *retained earnings* of corporations. This is income that goes to corporations rather than to households, and so it is part of national income but not personal income.

TABLE 6.5 National Income, Personal Income, Disposable Personal Income, and Personal Saving, 2007

	Dollars (Billions)
National income	12,221.1
Less: Amount of national income not going to households	−561.6
Equals: **Personal income**	11,659.5
Less: Personal income taxes	−1,482.5
Equals: **Disposable personal income**	10,177.0
Less: Personal consumption expenditures	−9,734.2
Personal interest payments	−262.8
Transfer payments made by households	−137.1
Equals: **Personal saving**	42.9
Personal saving as a percentage of disposable personal income:	0.4%

Source: See Table 6.2

ECONOMICS IN PRACTICE

GDP: One of the Great Inventions of the 20th Century

As the 20th century drew to a close, the U.S. Department of Commerce embarked on a review of its achievements. At the conclusion of this review, the Department named the development of the national income and product accounts as "its achievement of the century."

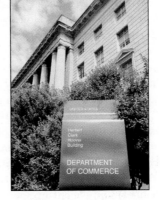

J. Steven Landefeld *Director, Bureau of Economic Analysis*

While the GDP and the rest of the national income accounts may seem to be arcane concepts, they are truly among the great inventions of the twentieth century.

Paul A. Samuelson and William D. Nordhaus

GDP! The right concept of economy-wide output, accurately measured. The U.S. and the world rely on it to tell where we are in the business cycle and to estimate long-run growth. It is the centerpiece of an elaborate and indispensable system of social accounting, the national income and product accounts. This is surely the single most innovative achievement of the Commerce Department in the 20th century. I was fortunate to become an economist in the 1930's when Kuznets, Nathan, Gilbert, and Jaszi were creating this most important set of economic time series. In economic theory, macroeconomics was just beginning at the same time. Complementary, these two innovations deserve much credit for the improved performance of the economy in the second half of the century.

James Tobin

FROM THE *SURVEY OF CURRENT BUSINESS*

Prior to the development of the NIPAs [national income and product accounts], policymakers had to guide the economy using limited and fragmentary information about the state of the economy. The Great Depression underlined the problems of incomplete data and led to the development of the national accounts:

One reads with dismay of Presidents Hoover and then Roosevelt designing policies to combat the Great Depression of the 1930's on the basis of such sketchy data as stock price indices, freight car loadings, and incomplete indices of industrial production. The fact was that comprehensive measures of national income and output did not exist at the time. The Depression, and with it the growing role of government in the economy, emphasized the need for such measures and led to the development of a comprehensive set of national income accounts.

Richard T. Froyen

In response to this need in the 1930's, the Department of Commerce commissioned Nobel laureate Simon Kuznets of the National Bureau of Economic Research to develop a set of national economic accounts....Professor Kuznets coordinated the work of researchers at the National Bureau of Economic Research in New York and his staff at Commerce. The original set of accounts was presented in a report to Congress in 1937 and in a research report, *National Income, 1929–35*....

The national accounts have become the mainstay of modern macroeconomic analysis, allowing policymakers, economists, and the business community to analyze the impact of different tax and spending plans, the impact of oil and other price shocks, and the impact of monetary policy on the economy as a whole and on specific components of final demand, incomes, industries, and regions....

Source: U.S. Department of Commerce, Bureau of Economics, "GDP: One of the Great Inventions of the 20th Century," Survey of Current Business, *January 2000, pp. 6–9.*

disposable personal income *or* after-tax income Personal income minus personal income taxes. The amount that households have to spend or save.

Personal income is the income received by households before they pay personal income taxes. The amount of income that households have to spend or save is called **disposable personal income**, or **after-tax income**. It is equal to personal income minus personal income taxes, as shown in Table 6.5.

Because disposable personal income is the amount of income that households can spend or save, it is an important income concept. Table 6.5 on p. 112 shows there are three categories of spending: (1) personal consumption expenditures, (2) personal interest payments, and (3) transfer payments made by households. The amount of disposable personal income left after total personal spending is **personal saving**. If your monthly disposable income is $500 and you spend $450, you have $50 left at the end of the month. Your personal saving is $50 for the month. Your personal saving level can be negative: If you earn $500 and spend $600 during the month, you have *dissaved* $100. To spend $100 more than you earn, you will have to borrow the $100 from someone, take the $100 from your savings account, or sell an asset you own.

personal saving The amount of disposable income that is left after total personal spending in a given period.

The **personal saving rate** is the percentage of disposable personal income saved, an important indicator of household behavior. A low saving rate means households are spending a large amount of their income. A high saving rate means households are cautious in their spending. As Table 6.5 shows, the U.S. personal saving rate in 2007 was 0.4 percent. Saving rates tend to rise during recessionary periods, when consumers become anxious about their future, and fall during boom times, as pent-up spending demand gets released.

personal saving rate The percentage of disposable personal income that is saved. If the personal saving rate is low, households are spending a large amount relative to their incomes; if it is high, households are spending cautiously.

Nominal versus Real GDP

Although we have finished discussing the measurement of GDP, we are not yet close to being done. We have thus far looked at GDP measured in **current dollars**, or the current prices we pay for goods and services. When we measure something in current dollars, we refer to it as a *nominal* value. **Nominal GDP** is GDP measured in current dollars—all components of GDP valued at their current prices.

current dollars The current prices that we pay for goods and services.

In most applications in macroeconomics, however, nominal GDP is not what we are after. It is not a good measure of aggregate output over time. Why? Assume that there is only one good—say, pizza, which is the same quality year after year. In each year 1 and 2, 100 units (slices) of pizza were produced. Production thus remained the same for year 1 and year 2. Suppose the price of pizza increased from $1.00 per slice in year 1 to $1.10 per slice in year 2. Nominal GDP in year 1 is $100 (100 units × $1.00 per unit), and nominal GDP in year 2 is $110 (100 units × $1.10 per unit). Nominal GDP has increased by $10 even though no more slices of pizza were produced. If we use nominal GDP to measure growth, we can be misled into thinking production has grown when all that has really happened is a rise in the price level (inflation).

nominal GDP Gross domestic product measured in current dollars.

If there were only one good in the economy—for example, pizza—it would be easy to measure production and compare one year's value to another's. We would add up all the pizza slices produced each year. In the example, production is 100 in both years. If the number of slices had increased to 105 in year 2, we would say production increased by 5 slices between year 1 and year 2, which is a 5 percent increase. Alas, however, there is more than one good in the economy.

The following is a discussion of how the BEA adjusts nominal GDP for price changes. As you read the discussion, keep in mind that this adjustment is not easy. Even in an economy of just apples and oranges, it would not be obvious how to add up apples and oranges to get an overall measure of output. The BEA's task is to add up thousands of goods, each of whose price is changing over time.

weight The importance attached to an item within a group of items.

In the following discussion, we will use the concept of a **weight**, either price weights or quantity weights. What is a weight? It is easiest to define the term by an example. Suppose in your economics course there is a final exam and two other tests. If the final exam counts for one-half of the grade and the other two tests for one-fourth each, the "weights" are one-half, one-fourth, and one-fourth. If instead the final exam counts for 80 percent of the grade and the other two tests for 10 percent each, the weights are .8, .1, and .1. The more important an item is in a group, the larger its weight.

Calculating Real GDP

Nominal GDP adjusted for price changes is called *real GDP*. All the main issues involved in computing real GDP can be discussed using a simple three-good economy and 2 years. Table 6.6 presents all the data that we will need. The table presents price and quantity data for 2 years and three goods. The goods are labeled *A*, *B*, and *C*, and the years are labeled 1 and 2. *P* denotes price, and *Q* denotes quantity. Keep in mind that everything in the following discussion, including the discussion of the GDP deflation, is based on the numbers in Table 6.6. Nothing has been brought in from the outside. The table is the entire economy.

The first thing to note from Table 6.6 is that *nominal output*—in current dollars—in year 1 for good *A* is the price of good *A* in year 1 ($0.50) times the number of units of good *A* produced in year 1 (6), which is $3.00. Similarly, nominal output in year 1 is $7 \times \$0.30 = \$2.10$ for good *B* and $10 \times \$0.70 = \$7.00$ for good *C*. The sum of these three amounts, $12.10 in column 5, is nominal GDP in year 1 in this simple economy. Nominal GDP in year 2—calculated by using the year 2 quantities and the year 2 prices—is $19.20 (column 8). Nominal GDP has risen from $12.10 in year 1 to $19.20 in year 2, an increase of 58.7 percent.[3]

TABLE 6.6 A Three-Good Economy

	(1)	(2)	(3)	(4)	(5) GDP in Year 1 in Year 1 Prices	(6) GDP in Year 2 in Year 1 Prices	(7) GDP in Year 1 in Year 2 Prices	(8) GDP in Year 2 in Year 2 Prices
	Production		Price per Unit					
	Year 1 Q_1	Year 2 Q_2	Year 1 P_1	Year 2 P_2	$P_1 \times Q_1$	$P_1 \times Q_2$	$P_2 \times Q_1$	$P_2 \times Q_2$
Good *A*	6	11	$0.50	$0.40	$3.00	$5.50	$2.40	$4.40
Good *B*	7	4	0.30	1.00	2.10	1.20	7.00	4.00
Good *C*	10	12	0.70	0.90	7.00	8.40	9.00	10.80
Total					$12.10 Nominal GDP in year 1	$15.10	$18.40	$19.20 Nominal GDP in year 2

You can see that the price of each good changed between year 1 and year 2—the price of good *A* fell (from $0.50 to $0.40) and the prices of goods *B* and *C* rose (*B* from $0.30 to $1.00; *C* from $0.70 to $0.90). Some of the change in nominal GDP between years 1 and 2 is due to price changes and not production changes. How much can we attribute to price changes and how much to production changes? Here things get tricky. The procedure that the BEA used prior to 1996 was to pick a **base year** and to use the prices in that base year as weights to calculate real GDP. This is a **fixed-weight procedure** because the weights used, which are the prices, are the same for all years—namely, the prices that prevailed in the base year.

Let us use the fixed-weight procedure and year 1 as the base year, which means using year 1 prices as the weights. Then in Table 6.6, real GDP in year 1 is $12.10 (column 5) and real GDP in year 2 is $15.10 (column 6). Note that both columns use year 1 prices and that nominal and real GDP are the same in year 1 because year 1 is the base year. Real GDP has increased from $12.10 to $15.10, an increase of 24.8 percent.

Let us now use the fixed-weight procedure and year 2 as the base year, which means using year 2 prices as the weights. In Table 6.6, real GDP in year 1 is $18.40 (column 7) and real GDP in year 2 is $19.20 (column 8). Note that both columns use year 2 prices and that nominal and real GDP are the same in year 2 because year 2 is the base year. Real GDP has increased from $18.40 to $19.20, an increase of 4.3 percent.

This example shows that growth rates can be sensitive to the choice of the base year— 24.8 percent using year 1 prices as weights and 4.3 percent using year 2 prices as weights. The old

base year The year chosen for the weights in a fixed-weight procedure.

fixed-weight procedure A procedure that uses weights from a given base year.

---

[3] The percentage change is calculated as $[(19.20 - 12.10)/12.10] \times 100 = .587 \times 100 = 58.7$ percent.

BEA procedure simply picked one year as the base year and did all the calculations using the prices in that year as weights. The new procedure makes two important changes. The first (using the current example) is to "split the difference" between 24.8 percent and 4.3 percent. What does "splitting the difference" mean? One way is to take the average of the two numbers, which is 14.55 percent. What the BEA does is to take the *geometric* average, which for the current example is 14.09 percent.[4] These two averages (14.55 percent and 14.09 percent) are quite close, and the use of either would give similar results. The point here is not that the geometric average is used, but that the first change is to split the difference using some average. Note that this new procedure requires two "base" years because 24.8 percent was computed using year 1 prices as weights and 4.3 percent was computed using year 2 prices as weights.

The second BEA change is to use years 1 and 2 as the base years when computing the percentage change between years 1 and 2, then use years 2 and 3 as the base years when computing the percentage change between years 2 and 3, and so on. The two base years change as the calculations move through time. The series of percentage changes computed this way is taken to be the series of growth rates of real GDP. So in this way, nominal GDP is adjusted for price changes. To make sure you understand this, review the calculations in Table 6.6, which provides all the data you need to see what is going on.

Calculating the GDP Deflator

We now switch gears from real GDP, a quantity measure, to the GDP deflator, a price measure. One of economic policy makers' goals is to keep changes in the overall price level small. For this reason, policy makers not only need good measures of how real output is changing but also good measures of how the overall price level is changing. The GDP deflator is one measure of the overall price level. We can use the data in Table 6.6 to show how the BEA computes the GDP deflator.

In Table 6.6, the price of good *A* fell from $0.50 in year 1 to $0.40 in year 2, the price of good *B* rose from $0.30 to $1.00, and the price of good *C* rose from $0.70 to $0.90. If we are interested only in how individual prices change, this is all the information we need. However, if we are interested in how the overall price *level* changes, we need to weight the individual prices in some way. The obvious weights to use are the quantities produced, but which quantities—those of year 1 or year 2? The same issues arise here for the quantity weights as for the price weights in computing real GDP.

Let us first use the fixed-weight procedure and year 1 as the base year, which means using year 1 quantities as the weights. Then in Table 6.6, the "bundle" price in year 1 is $12.10 (column 5) and the bundle price in year 2 is $18.40 (column 7). Both columns use year 1 quantities. The bundle price has increased from $12.10 to $18.40, an increase of 52.1 percent.

Next, use the fixed-weight procedure and year 2 as the base year, which means using year 2 quantities as the weights. Then the bundle price in year 1 is $15.10 (column 6), and the bundle price in year 2 is $19.20 (column 8). Both columns use year 2 quantities. The bundle price has increased from $15.10 to $19.20, an increase of 27.2 percent.

This example shows that overall price increases can be sensitive to the choice of the base year: 52.1 percent using year 1 quantities as weights and 27.2 percent using year 2 quantities as weights. Again, the old BEA procedure simply picked one year as the base year and did all the calculations using the quantities in the base year as weights. First, the new procedure splits the difference between 52.1 percent and 27.2 percent by taking the geometric average, which is 39.1 percent. Second, it uses years 1 and 2 as the base years when computing the percentage change between years 1 and 2, years 2 and 3 as the base years when computing the percentage change between years 2 and 3, and so on. The series of percentage changes computed this way is taken to be the series of percentage changes in the GDP deflator, that is, a series of inflation rates.

The Problems of Fixed Weights

To see why the BEA switched to the new procedure, let us consider a number of problems using fixed-price weights to compute real GDP. First, 1987 price weights, the last price weights the BEA used before it changed procedures, are not likely to be very accurate for, say, the 1950s. Many

---

[4] The geometric average is computed as the square root of 124.8×104.3, which is 114.09.

structural changes have taken place in the U.S. economy in the last 40 to 50 years, and it seems unlikely that 1987 prices are good weights to use for the 1950s.

Another problem is that the use of fixed-price weights does not account for the responses in the economy to supply shifts. Perhaps bad weather leads to a lower production of oranges in year 2. In a simple supply-and-demand diagram for oranges, this corresponds to a shift of the supply curve to the left, which leads to an increase in the price of oranges and a decrease in the quantity demanded. As consumers move up the demand curve, they are substituting away from oranges. If technical advances in year 2 result in cheaper ways of producing computers, the result is a shift of the computer supply curve to the right, which leads to a decrease in the price of computers and an increase in the quantity demanded. Consumers are substituting toward computers. (You should be able to draw supply-and-demand diagrams for both cases.) Table 6.6 on p. 115 shows this tendency. The quantity of good *A* rose between years 1 and 2 and the price decreased (the computer case), whereas the quantity of good *B* fell and the price increased (the orange case). The computer supply curve has been shifting to the right over time, due primarily to technical advances. The result has been large decreases in the price of computers and large increases in the quantity demanded.

To see why these responses pose a problem for the use of fixed-price weights, consider the data in Table 6.6. Because the price of good *A* was higher in year 1, the increase in production of good *A* is weighted more if we use year 1 as the base year than if we used year 2 as the base year. Also, because the price of good *B* was lower in year 1, the decrease in production of good *B* is weighted less if we use year 1 as the base year. These effects make the overall change in real GDP larger if we use year 1 price weights than if we use year 2 price weights. Using year 1 price weights ignores the kinds of substitution responses discussed in the previous paragraph and leads to what many believe are too-large estimates of real GDP changes. In the past, the BEA tended to move the base year forward about every 5 years, resulting in the past estimates of real GDP growth being revised downward. It is undesirable to have past growth estimates change simply because of the change to a new base year. The new BEA procedure avoids many of these fixed-weight problems.

Similar problems arise when using fixed-quantity weights to compute price indexes. For example, the fixed-weight procedure ignores the substitution away from goods whose prices are increasing and toward goods whose prices are decreasing or increasing less rapidly. The procedure tends to overestimate the increase in the overall price level. As discussed in the next chapter, there are still a number of price indexes that are computed using fixed weights. The GDP deflator differs because it does not use fixed weights. It is also a price index for all the goods and services produced in the economy. Other price indexes cover fewer domestically produced goods and services but also include some imported (foreign-produced) goods and services.

It should finally be stressed that there is no "right" way of computing real GDP. The economy consists of many goods, each with its own price, and there is no exact way of adding together the production of the different goods. We can say that the BEA's new procedure for computing real GDP avoids the problems associated with the use of fixed weights, and it seems to be an improvement over the old procedure. We will see in the next chapter, however, that the consumer price index (CPI)—a widely used price index—is still computed using fixed weights.

Limitations of the GDP Concept

We generally think of increases in GDP as good. Increasing GDP (or preventing its decrease) is usually considered one of the chief goals of the government's macroeconomic policy. Because some serious problems arise when we try to use GDP as a measure of happiness or well-being, we now point out some of the limitations of the GDP concept as a measure of welfare.

GDP and Social Welfare

If crime levels went down, society would be better off, but a decrease in crime is not an increase in output and is not reflected in GDP. Neither is an increase in leisure time. Yet to the extent that households want extra leisure time (instead of having it forced on them by a lack of jobs in the economy), an increase in leisure is also an increase in social welfare. Furthermore, some increases in social welfare are associated with a *decrease* in GDP. An increase in leisure during a time of full employment, for example, leads to a decrease in GDP because less time is spent on producing output.

Most nonmarket and domestic activities, such as housework and child care, are not counted in GDP even though they amount to real production. However, if I decide to send my children to day care or hire someone to clean my house or drive my car for me, GDP increases. The salaries of day care staff, cleaning people, and chauffeurs are counted in GDP; but the time I spend doing the same things is not counted. A mere change of institutional arrangements, even though no more output is being produced, can show up as a change in GDP.

Furthermore, GDP seldom reflects losses or social ills. GDP accounting rules do not adjust for production that pollutes the environment. The more production there is, the larger the GDP, regardless of how much pollution results in the process.

GDP also has nothing to say about the distribution of output among individuals in a society. It does not distinguish, for example, between the case in which most output goes to a few people and the case in which output is evenly divided among all people. We cannot use GDP to measure the effects of redistributive policies (which take income from some people and give income to others). Such policies have no direct impact on GDP. GDP is also neutral about the kinds of goods an economy produces. Symphony performances, handguns, cigarettes, professional football games, Bibles, soda pop, milk, economics textbooks, and comic books all get counted similarly without regard to their differing value to society.

The Underground Economy

Many transactions are missed in the calculation of GDP even though, in principle, they should be counted. Most illegal transactions are missed unless they are "laundered" into legitimate business. Income that is earned but not reported as income for tax purposes is usually missed, although some adjustments are made in the GDP calculations to take misreported income into account. The part of the economy that should be counted in GDP but is not is sometimes called the **underground economy**.

underground economy The part of the economy in which transactions take place and in which income is generated that is unreported and therefore not counted in GDP.

Tax evasion is usually thought to be the major incentive for people to participate in the underground economy. Studies estimate that the size of the U.S. underground economy, ranging from 5 percent to 30 percent of GDP,[5] is comparable to the size of the underground economy in most European countries and probably much smaller than the size of the underground economy in the Eastern European countries. Estimates of Italy's underground economy range from 10 percent to 35 percent of Italian GDP. At the lower end of the scale, estimates for Switzerland range from 3 percent to 5 percent.

Why should we care about the underground economy? To the extent that GDP reflects only a part of economic activity instead of a complete measure of what the economy produces, it is misleading. Unemployment rates, for example, may be lower than officially measured if people work in the underground economy without reporting this fact to the government. Also, if the size of the underground economy varies among countries—as it does—we can be misled when we compare GDP among countries. For example, Italy's GDP would be much higher if we considered its underground sector as part of the economy, while Switzerland's GDP would change very little.

Gross National Income per Capita

gross national income (GNI) GNP converted into dollars using an average of currency exchange rates over several years adjusted for rates of inflation.

Making comparisons across countries is difficult because such comparisons need to be made in a single currency, generally U.S. dollars. Converting GNP numbers for Japan into dollars requires converting from yen into dollars. Since exchange rates can change quite dramatically in short periods of time, such conversions are tricky. Recently, the World Bank adopted a new measuring system for international comparisons. The concept of **gross national income (GNI)** is GNP converted into dollars using an average of currency exchange rates over several years adjusted for

[5] See, for example, Edgar L. Feige, "Defining and Estimating Underground and Informal Economies: The New Industrial Economic Approach," *World Development* 19(7), 1990, and "The Underground Economy in the United States," Occasional Paper No. 2, U.S. Department of Labor, September 1992.

rates of inflation. Figure 6.1 lists the gross national income per capita (GNI divided by population) for various countries in 2006. Norway has the highest per capita GNI followed by Switzerland, Denmark, Ireland, and the United States. Ethiopia was estimated to have per capita GNI of only $180 in 2006.

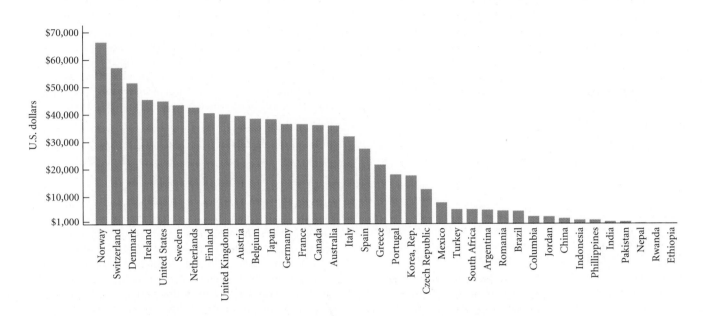

▲ **FIGURE 6.1 Per Capita Gross National Income for Selected Countries, 2006**

Source: World Bank, September 2007.

Looking Ahead

This chapter has introduced many key variables in which macroeconomists are interested, including GDP and its components. There is much more to be learned about the data that macroeconomists use. In the next chapter, we will discuss the data on employment, unemployment, and the labor force. In Chapters 10 and 11, we will discuss the data on money and interest rates. Finally, in Chapter 20, we will discuss in more detail the data on the relationship between the United States and the rest of the world.

— S U M M A R Y —

1. One source of data on the key variables in the macroeconomy is the *national income and product accounts*. These accounts provide a conceptual framework that macroeconomists use to think about how the pieces of the economy fit together.

GROSS DOMESTIC PRODUCT *p. 105*

2. *Gross domestic product* (*GDP*) is the key concept in national income accounting. GDP is the total market value of all final goods and services produced within a given period by factors of production located within a country. GDP excludes *intermediate goods*. To include goods when they are purchased as inputs and when they are sold as final products

would be double counting and would result in an overstatement of the value of production.

3. GDP excludes all transactions in which money or goods change hands but in which no new goods and services are produced. GDP includes the income of foreigners working in the United States and the profits that foreign companies earn in the United States. GDP excludes the income of U.S. citizens working abroad and profits earned by U.S. companies in foreign countries.

4. *Gross national product* (*GNP*) is the market value of all final goods and services produced during a given period by factors of production owned by a country's citizens.

CALCULATING GDP p. 107

5. The *expenditure approach* to GDP adds up the amount spent on all final goods and services during a given period. The four main categories of expenditures are *personal consumption expenditures* (*C*), *gross private domestic investment* (*I*), *government consumption and gross investment* (*G*), and *net exports* (*EX − IM*). The sum of these categories equals GDP.

6. The three main components of *personal consumption expenditures* (*C*) are *durable goods, nondurable goods*, and *services*.

7. *Gross private domestic investment* (*I*) is the total investment made by the private sector in a given period. There are three kinds of investment: *nonresidential investment, residential investment*, and *changes in business inventories*. Gross investment does not take *depreciation*—the decrease in the value of assets—into account. *Net investment* is equal to gross investment minus depreciation.

8. *Government consumption and gross investment* (*G*) include expenditures by state, federal, and local governments for final goods and services. The value of *net exports* (*EX − IM*) equals the differences between exports (sales to foreigners of U.S.-produced goods and services) and imports (U.S. purchases of goods and services from abroad).

9. Because every payment (expenditure) by a buyer is a receipt (income) for the seller, GDP can be computed in terms of who receives it as income—the *income approach* to calculating gross domestic product.

10. GNP minus depreciation is *net national product* (*NNP*). *National income* is the total amount earned by the factors of production in the economy. It is equal to NNP except for a statistical discrepancy. *Personal income* is the total income of

households. *Disposable personal income* is what households have to spend or save after paying their taxes. The *personal saving rate* is the percentage of disposable personal income saved instead of spent.

NOMINAL VERSUS REAL GDP p. 114

11. GDP measured in current dollars (the current prices that one pays for goods) is *nominal GDP*. If we use nominal GDP to measure growth, we can be misled into thinking that production has grown when all that has happened is a rise in the price level, or inflation. A better measure of production is *real GDP*, which is nominal GDP adjusted for price changes.

12. The GDP deflator is a measure of the overall price level.

LIMITATIONS OF THE GDP CONCEPT p. 117

13. We generally think of increases in GDP as good, but some problems arise when we try to use GDP as a measure of happiness or well-being. The peculiarities of GDP accounting mean that institutional changes can change the value of GDP even if real production has not changed. GDP ignores most social ills, such as pollution. Furthermore, GDP tells us nothing about what kinds of goods are being produced or how income is distributed across the population. GDP also ignores many transactions of the *underground economy*.

14. The concept of *gross national income* (*GNI*) is GNP converted into dollars using an average of currency exchange rates over several years adjusted for rates of inflation.

REVIEW TERMS AND CONCEPTS

base year, *p. 115*

change in business inventories, *p. 109*

compensation of employees, *p. 111*

corporate profits, *p. 111*

current dollars, *p. 114*

depreciation, *p. 110*

disposable personal income, *or after-tax income, p. 114*

durable goods, *p. 108*

expenditure approach, *p. 107*

final goods and services, *p. 106*

fixed-weight procedure, *p. 115*

government consumption and gross investment (*G*), *p. 110*

gross domestic product (GDP), *p. 105*

gross investment, *p. 110*

gross national income (GNI), *p. 118*

gross national product (GNP), *p. 107*

gross private domestic investment (*I*), *p. 109*

income approach, *p. 107*

indirect taxes minus subsidies, *p. 111*

intermediate goods, *p. 106*

national income, *p. 111*

national income and product accounts, *p. 105*

net business transfer payments, *p. 111*

net exports (*EX − IM*), *p. 111*

net interest, *p. 111*

net investment, *p. 110*

net national product (NNP), *p. 112*

nominal GDP, *p. 114*

nondurable goods, *p. 108*

nonresidential investment, *p. 109*

personal consumption expenditures (*C*), *p. 108*

personal income, *p. 112*

personal saving, *p. 114*

personal saving rate, *p. 114*

proprietors' income, *p. 111*

rental income, *p. 111*

residential investment, *p. 109*

services, *p. 108*

statistical discrepancy, *p. 112*

surplus of government enterprises, *p. 111*

underground economy, *p. 118*

value added, *p. 106*

weight, *p. 114*

Expenditure approach to GDP: GDP = *C* + *I* + *G* + (*EX − IM*), *p. 108*

GDP = Final sales + Change in business inventories, *p. 110*

Net investment = Capital end of period − Capital beginning of period, *p. 110*

PROBLEMS

Visit **www.myeconlab.com** to complete the problems marked in orange online. You will receive instant feedback on your answers, tutorial help, and access to additional practice problems.

1. **[Related to the *Economics in Practice* on *p. 109*]** In a simple economy suppose that all income is either compensation of employees or profits. Suppose also that there are no indirect taxes. Calculate gross domestic product from the following set of numbers. Show that the expenditure approach and the income approach add up to the same figure.

Consumption	$5,000
Investment	1,000
Depreciation	600
Profits	900
Exports	500
Compensation of employees	5,300
Government purchases	1,000
Direct taxes	800
Saving	1,100
Imports	700

2. How do we know that calculating GDP by the expenditure approach yields the same answer as calculating GDP by the income approach?

3. As the following table indicates, GNP and real GNP were almost the same in 1972, but there was a $300 billion difference by mid-1975. Explain why. Describe what the numbers here suggest about conditions in the economy at the time. How do the conditions compare with conditions today?

DATE	GNP (BILLIONS OF DOLLARS)	REAL GNP (BILLIONS OF DOLLARS)	REAL GNP (% CHANGE)	GNP DEFLATOR (% CHANGE)
72:2	1,172	1,179	7.62	2.93
72:3	1,196	1,193	5.11	3.24
72:4	1,233	1,214	7.41	5.30
73:1	1,284	1,247	10.93	5.71
73:2	1,307	1,248	.49	7.20
73:3	1,338	1,256	2.44	6.92
73:4	1,377	1,266	3.31	8.58
74:1	1,388	1,253	−4.00	7.50
74:2	1,424	1,255	.45	10.32
74:3	1,452	1,247	−2.47	10.78
74:4	1,473	1,230	−5.51	12.03
75:1	1,480	1,204	−8.27	10.86
75:2	1,517	1,219	5.00	5.07

4. What are some of the problems in using fixed weights to compute real GDP and the GDP price index? How does the BEA's approach attempt to solve these problems?

5. Explain what double counting is and discuss why GDP is not equal to total sales.

6. The following table gives some figures from a forecast of real GDP (in 2000 dollars) and population done in 2008. According to the forecast, approximately how much real growth will there be between 2009 and 2010? What is per capita GDP projected to be in 2009 and in 2010? Compute the forecast rate of change in real GDP and per capita real GDP between 2009 and 2010.

Real GDP 2009 (billions)	$12,043
Real GDP 2010 (billions)	$12,464
Population 2009 (millions)	306.4
Population 2010 (millions)	308.8

7. Look at a recent edition of *The Economist*. Go to the section on economic indicators. Go down the list of countries and make a list of the ones with the fastest and slowest GDP growth. Look also at the forecast rates of GDP growth. Go back to the table of contents at the beginning of the journal to see if there are articles about any of these countries. Write a paragraph or two describing the events or the economic conditions in one of the countries. Explain why they are growing or not growing rapidly.

8. During 2002, real GDP in Japan rose about 1.3 percent. During the same period, retail sales in Japan fell 1.8 percent in real terms. What are some possible explanations for retail sales to consumers falling when GDP rises? (*Hint:* Think of the composition of GDP using the expenditure approach.)

9. **[Related to the *Economics in Practice* on *p. 113*]** Which of the following transactions would not be counted in GDP? Explain your answers.
   a. General Motors issues new shares of stock to finance the construction of a plant.
   b. General Motors builds a new plant.
   c. Company A successfully launches a hostile takeover of company B, in which company A purchases all the assets of company B.
   d. Your grandmother wins $10 million in the lottery.
   e. You buy a new copy of this textbook.
   f. You buy a used copy of this textbook.
   g. The government pays out Social Security benefits.
   h. A public utility installs new antipollution equipment in its smokestacks.
   i. Luigi's Pizza buys 30 pounds of mozzarella cheese, holds it in inventory for 1 month, and then uses it to make pizza (which it sells).
   j. You spend the weekend cleaning your apartment.
   k. A drug dealer sells $500 worth of illegal drugs.

10. If you buy a new car, the entire purchase is counted as consumption in the year in which you make the transaction. Explain briefly why this is in one sense an "error" in national income accounting. (*Hint:* How is the purchase of a car different from the purchase of a pizza?) How might you correct this error?

11. Explain why imports are subtracted in the expenditure approach to calculating GDP.

12. GDP calculations do not directly include the economic costs of environmental damage—for example, global warming and acid rain. Do you think these costs should be included in GDP? Why or why not? How could GDP be amended to include environmental damage costs?

13. Beginning in 2005, the housing market, which had been booming for years, turned. Housing construction dropped sharply in 2006. Go to www.bea.gov. Look at the GDP release and at past releases from 2002 onward. In real dollars, how much private residential fixed investment (houses, apartments, condominiums, and cooperatives) took place in each quarter from 2002 through 2008? What portion of GDP did housing construction represent? After 2006, residential fixed investment was declining sharply, yet GDP was growing. What categories of aggregate output kept the economy growing into 2008?

14. At the beginning of 2008, most people were convinced that the U.S. economy was in a recession. Define *recession*. Go to www.bea.gov and look at the growth of GDP during 2008. In addition, go to www.bls.gov and look at payroll employment and the unemployment rate. Was the United States in a recession? What do you see in the data? Can you tell by reading the newspapers or watching CNN whether the country was in a recession? Explain.

Unemployment, Inflation, and Long-Run Growth

7

Each month the U.S. Bureau of Labor Statistics (BLS) announces the value of the unemployment rate for the previous month. For example, on February 1, 2008, it announced that the unemployment rate for January 2008 was 4.9 percent. The unemployment rate is a key measure of how the economy is doing. This announcement is widely watched, and if the announced unemployment rate is different from what the financial markets expect, there can be large move-

ments in those markets. It is thus important to know how the BLS computes the unemployment rate. The first part of this chapter describes how the unemployment rate is computed and discusses its various components.

Inflation is another key macroeconomic variable. The previous chapter discussed how the GDP deflator, the price deflator for the entire economy, is computed. The percentage change in the GDP deflator is a measure of inflation. There are, however, other measures of inflation, each pertaining to some part of the economy. The most widely followed price index is the consumer price index (CPI), and its measurement is discussed next in this chapter. The CPI is also announced monthly by the BLS, and this announcement is widely followed by the financial markets as well. For example, on February 20, 2008, the BLS announced that the percentage change in the CPI for January was 4.9 percent at an annual rate. After discussing the measurement of the CPI, this chapter discusses various costs of inflation.

The last topic considered in this chapter is long-run growth. Although much of macroeconomics is concerned with explaining business cycles, long-run growth is also a major concern. The average yearly growth rate of U.S. real GDP depicted in Figure 5.2 on p. 91 is 3.4 percent. So while there were many ups and downs during the 108 years depicted in Figure 5.2, on average, the economy was growing at a 3.4 percent rate. In the last part of this chapter, we discuss the sources of this growth.

Keep in mind that this chapter is still descriptive. We begin our analysis of how the economy works in the next chapter.

Unemployment

We begin our discussion of unemployment with its measurement.

Measuring Unemployment

The unemployment data released each month by the BLS are based on a survey of households. Each month the BLS draws a sample of 65,000 households and completes interviews with all but about 2,500 of them. Each interviewed household answers questions concerning the work

employed Any person 16 years old or older (1) who works for pay, either for someone else or in his or her own business for 1 or more hours per week, (2) who works without pay for 15 or more hours per week in a family enterprise, or (3) who has a job but has been temporarily absent with or without pay.

unemployed A person 16 years old or older who is not working, is available for work, and has made specific efforts to find work during the previous 4 weeks.

not in the labor force A person who is not looking for work because he or she does not want a job or has given up looking.

labor force The number of people employed plus the number of unemployed.

unemployment rate The ratio of the number of people unemployed to the total number of people in the labor force.

activity of household members 16 years of age or older during the calendar week that contains the twelfth of the month. (The survey is conducted in the week that contains the twelfth of the month.)

If a household member 16 years of age or older worked 1 hour or more as a paid employee, either for someone else or in his or her own business or farm, the person is classified as **employed**. A household member is also considered employed if he or she worked 15 hours or more without pay in a family enterprise. Finally, a household member is counted as employed if the person held a job from which he or she was temporarily absent due to illness, bad weather, vacation, labor-management disputes, or personal reasons, regardless of whether he or she was paid.

Those who are not employed fall into one of two categories: (1) unemployed or (2) not in the labor force. To be considered **unemployed**, a person must be 16 years old or older, available for work, and have made specific efforts to find work during the previous 4 weeks. A person not looking for work because he or she does not want a job or has given up looking is classified as **not in the labor force**. People not in the labor force include full-time students, retirees, individuals in institutions, and those staying home to take care of children or elderly parents.

The total **labor force** in the economy is the number of people employed plus the number of unemployed:

$$\text{labor force} = \text{employed} + \text{unemployed}$$

The total population 16 years of age or older is equal to the number of people in the labor force plus the number not in the labor force:

$$\text{population} = \text{labor force} + \text{not in labor force}$$

With these numbers, several ratios can be calculated. The **unemployment rate** is the ratio of the number of people unemployed to the total number of people in the labor force:

$$\text{unemployment rate} = \frac{\text{unemployed}}{\text{employed} + \text{unemployed}}$$

In January 2008, the labor force contained 153.824 million people, 146.248 million of whom were employed and 7.576 million of whom were unemployed and looking for work. The unemployment rate was 4.9 percent:

$$\frac{7.576}{146.248 + 7.576} = 4.9\%$$

labor force participation rate The ratio of the labor force to the total population 16 years old or older.

The ratio of the labor force to the population 16 years old or over is called the **labor force participation rate**:

$$\text{labor force participation rate} = \frac{\text{labor force}}{\text{population}}$$

In January 2008, the population of 16 years old or over was 232.616 million. So the labor force participation rate was .66 (= 153.824/232.616).

Table 7.1 shows values of these variables for selected years since 1953. The year 1982 shows the effects of the recession. Although the unemployment rate has gone up and down, the labor force participation rate has grown steadily since 1953. Much of this increase is due to the growth in the participation rate of women between the ages of 25 and 54. Column 3 in Table 7.1 shows how many new workers the U.S. economy has absorbed in recent years. The number of employed workers increased by about 38 million between 1953 and 1982 and by about 47 million between 1982 and 2007.

TABLE 7.1	Employed, Unemployed, and the Labor Force, 1953–2007					
	(1)	(2)	(3)	(4)	(5)	(6)
	Population 16 Years Old or Over (Millions)	Labor Force (Millions)	Employed (Millions)	Unemployed (Millions)	Labor Force Participation Rate (Percentage Points)	Unemployment Rate (Percentage Points)
1953	107.1	63.0	61.2	1.8	58.9	2.9
1960	117.2	69.6	65.8	3.9	59.4	5.5
1970	137.1	82.8	78.7	4.1	60.4	4.9
1980	167.7	106.9	99.3	7.6	63.8	7.1
1982	172.3	110.2	99.5	10.7	64.0	9.7
1990	189.2	125.8	118.8	7.0	66.5	5.6
2000	212.6	142.6	136.9	5.7	67.1	4.0
2007	231.9	153.1	146.0	7.1	66.0	4.6

Note: Figures are civilian only (military excluded).
Source: Economic Report of the President, 2008, Table B-35.

Components of the Unemployment Rate

The unemployment rate by itself conveys some but not all information about the unemployment picture. To get a better picture, it is useful to look at unemployment rates across groups of people, regions, and industries.

Unemployment Rates for Different Demographic Groups   There are large differences in rates of unemployment across demographic groups. Table 7.2 shows the unemployment rate for November 1982—the worst month of the recession in 1982—and for March 2008, broken down by race, sex, and age. In November 1982, when the overall unemployment rate hit 10.8 percent, the rate for whites was 9.6 percent while the rate for African Americans was more than twice that—20.2 percent.

TABLE 7.2	Unemployment Rates by Demographic Group, 1982 and 2008		
	Years	Nov. 1982	March 2008
Total		<u>10.8</u>	<u>5.1</u>
White		9.6	4.5
Men	20+	9.0	4.1
Women	20+	8.1	4.1
Both sexes	16–19	21.3	13.2
African American		20.2	9.0
Men	20+	19.3	8.4
Women	20+	16.5	7.5
Both sexes	16–19	49.5	31.3

Source: U.S. Department of Labor, Bureau of Labor Statistics. Data are seasonally adjusted.

During the recession in 1982, men fared worse than women. In November 1982, 9.0 percent of white men 20 years and over but only 8.1 percent of white women 20 years and over were unemployed. For African Americans, 19.3 percent of men 20 years and over and 16.5 percent of women 20 years and over were unemployed. Teenagers between 16 and 19 years of age fared worst. African Americans between 16 and 19 experienced an unemployment rate of 49.5 percent in November 1982. For whites between 16 and 19, the unemployment rate was 21.3 percent. Although the rates were lower for all groups in March 2008, the pattern was similar. The highest unemployment rates were for African-American teenagers—31.3 percent. The main point of Table 7.2 is that an unemployment rate of, say, 5.1 percent does not mean every group in society has a 5.1 percent unemployment rate. There are large differences in unemployment rates across demographic groups.

Unemployment Rates in States and Regions   Unemployment rates vary by geographic location. For a variety of reasons, not all states and regions have the same level of unemployment. States and regions have different combinations of industries, which do not all grow and decline at the same time and at the same rate. Also, the labor force is not completely mobile—workers often cannot or do not want to pack up and move to take advantage of job opportunities in other parts of the country.

As Table 7.3 shows, in the last 30 years remarkable changes have occurred in the relative prosperity of regions, particularly in the Northeast and the oil-rich Southwest. During the early 1970s, the Northeast (New England, in particular) was hit by a serious decline in its industrial base. Textile mills, leather goods plants, and furniture factories closed in the face of foreign competition or moved south to states with lower wages. During the recession of 1975, Massachusetts and Michigan had very high unemployment rates (11.2 percent and 12.5 percent, respectively). Riding the crest of rising oil prices, Texas had one of the lowest unemployment rates at that time (5.6 percent).

During the recession of 1982, Texas continued to do well and Massachusetts took a sharp turn for the better. The unemployment rate in Massachusetts went from nearly three points above the national average during the 1975 recession to nearly two points below during the 1982 recession.

By 1987, things had changed. Although not shown in Table 7.3, Massachusetts had one of the lowest unemployment rates in the country in 1987 (an amazing 2.8 percent) and Texas (at 8.5 percent) had one of the highest. In Massachusetts, high-tech firms such as Wang Laboratories and Digital Equipment, two firms that employed a total of over 100,000 people, had grown dramatically. In contrast, the fall in crude oil prices from over $30 per barrel to under $15 per barrel in the early 1980s forced the oil-based economy of Texas into a deep and prolonged recession. Then, in 1991, Massachusetts experienced yet another reversal with an unemployment rate of 9 percent.

TABLE 7.3	Regional Differences in Unemployment, 1975, 1982, 1991, and 2003			
	1975	1982	1991	2003
U.S. avg.	8.5	9.7	6.7	6.0
Cal.	9.9	9.9	7.5	6.7
Fla.	10.7	8.2	7.3	5.1
Ill.	7.1	11.3	7.1	6.7
Mass.	11.2	7.9	9.0	5.8
Mich.	12.5	15.5	9.2	7.3
N.J.	10.2	9.0	6.6	5.9
N.Y.	9.5	8.6	7.2	6.3
N.C.	8.6	9.0	5.8	6.5
Ohio	9.1	12.5	6.4	6.1
Tex.	5.6	6.9	6.6	6.8

Source: Statistical Abstract of the United States, various editions.

The economy of Michigan is heavily tied to the fortunes of the automobile industry. During the recession of 1982, Michigan had the highest unemployment rate in the country at 15.5 percent. The automobile industry not only suffered from the decline in the U.S. economy but also faced stiff foreign competition, primarily from Japan. Michigan also suffered in 1991, with an unemployment rate of 9.2 percent.

The recession of 2001 was mild by comparison, and the impact was more uniform around the country. By the second quarter of 2003, the national unemployment rate had risen to 6.1 percent from 3.9 percent in the fourth quarter of 2000. For the states listed in Table 7.3, the unemployment rate in 2003 varied from 5.1 percent for Florida to 7.3 percent for Michigan. Again, the national unemployment rate does not tell the whole story. A low national rate of unemployment does not mean that the entire nation is growing and producing at the same rate.

ECONOMICS IN PRACTICE

A Quiet Revolution: Women Join the Labor Force

Table 7.1 shows that the labor force participation rate in the United States increased from 58.9 percent in 1953 to 66.0 percent in 2007. Much of this increase was due to the increased participation of women in the labor force. In 1955, the labor force participation rate of women was 36 percent. For married women, the rate was even lower at 29 percent. By the 1990s, these numbers shifted considerably. In 1996, the labor force participation

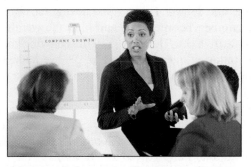

rate was 60 percent for all women and 62 percent for married women. The reasons for these changes are complex. Certainly, in the 1960s, there was a change in society's attitude toward women and paid work. In addition, the baby boom became the baby bust as greater availability of birth control led to fewer births.

By comparison, the participation rate for men declined over this period—from 85 percent in 1955 to 75 percent in 1996. Why the labor force participation rate for men fell is less clear than why the women's rate rose. No doubt, some men dropped out to assume more traditional women's roles, such as child care. Whatever the causes, the economy grew in a way that absorbed virtually all the new entrants during the period in question.

As women began joining the labor force in greater numbers in the 1970s and 1980s, their wages relative to men's wages actually fell. Most economists attribute this decline to the fact that less experienced women were entering the labor force, pointing out the importance of correcting for factors such as experience and education when we analyze labor markets.

At least some of the women entering the labor force at this time hired housecleaners and child care workers to perform tasks they had once done themselves. As we learned in Chapter 6, the salaries of daycare staff and cleaning people are counted in GDP, while the value of these tasks when done by a husband or wife in a household is not part of GDP.

If you are interested in learning more about the economic history of American women, read the book *Understanding the Gender Gap: An Economic History of American Women* by Harvard University economist Claudia Goldin.

Discouraged-Worker Effects   Remember, people who stop looking for work are classified as having dropped out of the labor force instead of being unemployed. During recessions, people may become discouraged about finding a job and stop looking. This lowers the unemployment rate because those no longer looking for work are no longer counted as unemployed.

To demonstrate how this **discouraged-worker effect** lowers the unemployment rate, suppose there are 10 million unemployed out of a labor force of 100 million. This means an unemployment rate of 10/100 = .10, or 10 percent. If 1 million of these 10 million unemployed people stopped looking for work and dropped out of the labor force, 9 million would be unemployed out of a labor force of 99 million. The unemployment rate would then drop to 9/99 = .091, or 9.1 percent.

The BLS survey provides some evidence on the size of the discouraged-worker effect. Respondents who indicate that they have stopped searching for work are asked why they stopped. If the respondent cites inability to find employment as the sole reason for not searching, that person might be classified as a discouraged worker.

The number of discouraged workers seems to hover around 1 percent of the size of the labor force in normal times. During the 1980–1982 recession, the number of discouraged workers increased steadily to a peak of 1.5 percent. By the end of the first quarter of 1991, the recession of

discouraged-worker effect   The decline in the measured unemployment rate that results when people who want to work but cannot find jobs grow discouraged and stop looking, thus dropping out of the ranks of the unemployed and the labor force.

1990–1991 had produced 997,000 discouraged workers. Some economists argue that adding the number of discouraged workers to the number who are now classified as unemployed gives a better picture of the unemployment situation.

The Duration of Unemployment   The unemployment rate measures unemployment at a given point in time. It tells us nothing about how long the average unemployed worker is out of work. Table 7.4 shows that during recessionary periods, the average duration of unemployment rises. Between 1979 and 1983, the average duration of unemployment rose from 10.8 weeks to 20.0 weeks. The slow growth following the 1990–1991 recession resulted in an increase in duration of unemployment to 17.7 weeks in 1992 and to 18.8 weeks in 1994. In 2000, average duration was down to 12.6 weeks, which then rose to 19.6 weeks in 2004. In 2006 and 2007, it was 16.8 weeks.

TABLE 7.4 Average Duration of Unemployment, 1979–2007			
	Weeks		Weeks
1979	10.8	1993	18.0
1980	11.9	1994	18.8
1981	13.7	1995	16.6
1982	15.6	1996	16.7
1983	20.0	1997	15.8
1984	18.2	1998	14.5
1985	15.6	1999	13.4
1986	15.0	2000	12.6
1987	14.5	2001	13.1
1988	13.5	2002	16.6
1989	11.9	2003	19.2
1990	12.0	2004	19.6
1991	13.7	2005	18.4
1992	17.7	2006	16.8
		2007	16.8

Sources: U.S. Department of Labor, Bureau of Labor Statistics.

The Costs of Unemployment

In the Employment Act of 1946, Congress declared that it was the

> continuing policy and responsibility of the federal government to use all practicable means...to promote maximum employment, production, and purchasing power.

In 1978, Congress passed the Full Employment and Balanced Growth Act, commonly referred to as the *Humphrey-Hawkins Act*, which formally established a specific unemployment target of 4 percent. Why should full employment be a policy objective of the federal government? What costs does unemployment impose on society?

Some Unemployment Is Inevitable   Before we discuss the costs of unemployment, we must realize that some unemployment is simply part of the natural workings of the labor market. Remember, to be classified as unemployed, a person must be looking for a job. Every year thousands of people enter the labor force for the first time. Some have dropped out of high school, some are high school or college graduates, and still others are finishing graduate programs. At the same time, new firms are starting up and others are expanding and creating new jobs while other firms are contracting or going out of business.

At any moment, there is a set of job seekers and a set of jobs that must be matched with one another. It is important that the right people end up in the right jobs. The right job for a person will depend on that person's skills, preferences concerning work environment (large firm or small, formal or informal), location of the individual's home, and willingness to commute. At the same time, firms want workers who can meet the requirements of the job and grow with the company.

To make a good match, workers must acquire information on job availability, wage rates, location, and work environment. Firms must acquire information on worker availability and skills. Information gathering consumes time and resources. The search may involve travel, interviews, preparation of a résumé, telephone calls, and hours going through the newspaper. To the extent that these efforts lead to a better match of workers and jobs, they are well spent. As long as the gains to firms and workers exceed the costs of search, the result is efficient.

When we consider the various costs of unemployment, it is useful to categorize unemployment into three types:

- Frictional unemployment
- Structural unemployment
- Cyclical unemployment

Frictional, Structural, and Cyclical Unemployment

When the BLS does its survey about work activity for the week containing the twelfth of each month, it interviews many people who are involved in the normal search for work. Some are either entering the labor force or switching jobs. This unemployment is both natural and beneficial for the economy.

The portion of unemployment due to the normal working of the labor market is called **frictional unemployment**. The frictional unemployment rate can never be zero. It may, however, change over time. As jobs become more differentiated and the number of required skills increases, matching skills and jobs becomes more complex and the frictional unemployment rate may rise.

The concept of frictional unemployment is somewhat abstract because it is hard to know what "the normal working of the labor market" means. The industrial structure of the U.S. economy is continually changing. Manufacturing, for instance, has yielded part of its share of total employment to services and to finance, insurance, and real estate. Within the manufacturing sector, the steel and textile industries have contracted sharply, while high-technology sectors such as electronic components have expanded.

Although the unemployment that arises from such structural shifts could be classified as frictional, it is usually called **structural unemployment**. The term *frictional unemployment* is used to denote short-run job/skill matching problems, problems that last a few weeks. *Structural unemployment* denotes longer-run adjustment problems—those that tend to last for years. Although structural unemployment is expected in a dynamic economy, it is painful to the workers who experience it. In some ways, those who lose their jobs because their skills are obsolete experience the greatest pain. The fact that structural unemployment is natural and inevitable does not mean that it costs society nothing.

Economists sometimes use the term **natural rate of unemployment** to refer to unemployment that occurs as a normal part of the functioning of the economy. This concept is also somewhat vague because *natural* is not a precise word. It is probably best to think of the natural rate as the sum of the frictional rate and the structural rate. Estimates of the natural rate range from 4 percent to 6 percent.

Although some unemployment is natural, there are times when the unemployment rate seems to be above the natural rate. In 1979, the unemployment rate was 5.8 percent, but it did not fall below 6 percent again until 1987, 8 years later. In the meantime, the United States experienced a major recession, during which the unemployment rate rose substantially. The increase in unemployment that occurs during recessions and depressions is called **cyclical unemployment**.

Social Consequences

The costs of unemployment are neither evenly distributed across the population nor easily quantified. The social consequences of the Depression of the 1930s are perhaps the hardest to comprehend. Most people alive today did not live through the Great Depression and can only read about it in books or hear stories told by parents and grandparents. Few emerged from this period unscathed. At the bottom were the poor and the fully unemployed, about 25 percent of the labor force. Even those who kept their jobs found themselves working part-time. Many people lost all or part of their savings as the stock market crashed and thousands of banks failed.

frictional unemployment The portion of unemployment that is due to the normal working of the labor market; used to denote short-run job/skill matching problems.

structural unemployment The portion of unemployment that is due to changes in the structure of the economy that result in a significant loss of jobs in certain industries.

natural rate of unemployment The unemployment that occurs as a normal part of the functioning of the economy. Sometimes taken as the sum of frictional unemployment and structural unemployment.

cyclical unemployment The increase in unemployment that occurs during recessions and depressions.

Congressional committees heard story after story. In Cincinnati, where the labor force totaled about 200,000, about 48,000 were wholly unemployed, 40,000 more were on short time, and relief payments to the needy averaged $7 to $8 per week:

> Relief is given to a family one week and then they are pushed off for a week in the hope that somehow or other the breadwinner may find some kind of work....We are paying no rent at all. That, of course, is a very difficult problem because we are continually having evictions, and social workers...are hard put to find places for people whose furniture has been put out on the street.[1]

From Birmingham, Alabama, in 1932:

> ...we have about 108,000 wage and salary workers in my district. Of that number, it is my belief that not exceeding 8000 have their normal incomes. At least 25,000 men are altogether without work. Some of them have not had a stroke of work for more than 12 months. Perhaps 60,000 or 70,000 are working from one to five days a week, and practically all have had serious cuts in wages and many of them do not average over $1.50 per day.[2]

Economic hardship accompanied the 1980–1982 recession as well. Between 1979 and 1983, the number of people officially classified as living in poverty in the United States rose from 26.1 million (11.7 percent of the population) to 35.5 million (15.3 percent). In addition to economic hardship, prolonged unemployment may also bring with it social and personal ills: anxiety, depression, deterioration of physical and psychological health, drug abuse (including alcoholism), and suicide.

Inflation

It is important to note that not all price increases constitute inflation. Prices of individual goods and services are determined in many ways. In competitive markets, the interaction of many buyers and many sellers—the operation of supply and demand—determines prices. In imperfectly competitive markets, prices are determined by producers' decisions. (This is the core of microeconomic theory.) In any economy, prices are continuously changing as markets adjust to changing conditions. Lack of rain may dry up corn and wheat fields, reducing supply and pushing up the price of agricultural products. At the same time, high levels of production by oil producers may be driving down the price of oil and petroleum products. Simultaneously, the United Auto Workers may be negotiating a contract with the Ford Motor Company that raises (or lowers) wage rates.

When prices of some goods are rising and others are falling, these are *relative* price changes. Inflation, on the other hand, occurs when there is an increase in the overall price level and deflation occurs when there is a decrease in the overall price level. We measure overall price levels by looking at all or a large number of goods and services in the economy. The GDP deflator, which was discussed in the last chapter, is the price deflator for all goods and services in the economy. The consumer price index, on the other hand, covers a smaller market basket of goods. We turn to this topic now.

The Consumer Price Index

consumer price index (CPI) A price index computed each month by the Bureau of Labor Statistics using a bundle that is meant to represent the "market basket" purchased monthly by the typical urban consumer.

The **consumer price index (CPI)** is the most widely followed price index. Unlike the GDP deflator, it is a fixed-weight index. It was first constructed during World War I as a basis for adjusting shipbuilders' wages, which the government controlled during the war. Currently, the CPI is computed by the BLS each month using a bundle of goods meant to represent the "market basket" purchased monthly by the typical urban consumer. The quantities of each good in the bundle that are used for the weights are based on extensive surveys of consumers. In fact, the BLS

---

[1] U.S. Senate Hearings before a subcommittee of the Committee of Manufacturers, 72nd Congress, first session (1931), p. 239. Cited in Lester Chandler, *America's Greatest Depression, 1929–1941* (New York: Harper & Row, 1970), p. 43.
[2] Senate Hearings, in Lester Chandler, *America's Greatest Depression, 1929–1941* (New York: Harper & Row, 1970), p. 43.

collects prices each month for about 71,000 goods and services from about 22,000 outlets in 44 geographic areas. For example, the cost of housing is included in the data collection by surveying about 5,000 renters and 1,000 homeowners each month. Figure 7.1 shows the CPI market basket for December 2007.

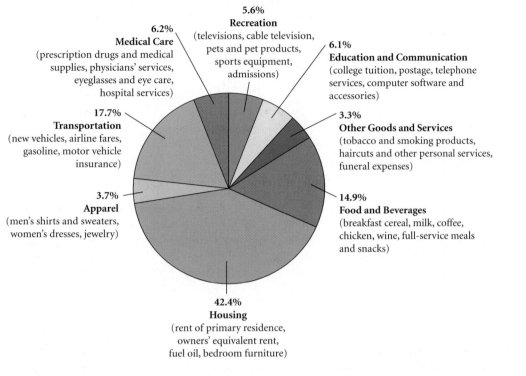

5.6%
Recreation
(televisions, cable television, pets and pet products, sports equipment, admissions)

6.2%
Medical Care
(prescription drugs and medical supplies, physicians' services, eyeglasses and eye care, hospital services)

6.1%
Education and Communication
(college tuition, postage, telephone services, computer software and accessories)

17.7%
Transportation
(new vehicles, airline fares, gasoline, motor vehicle insurance)

3.3%
Other Goods and Services
(tobacco and smoking products, haircuts and other personal services, funeral expenses)

3.7%
Apparel
(men's shirts and sweaters, women's dresses, jewelry)

14.9%
Food and Beverages
(breakfast cereal, milk, coffee, chicken, wine, full-service meals and snacks)

42.4%
Housing
(rent of primary residence, owners' equivalent rent, fuel oil, bedroom furniture)

◀ **FIGURE 7.1**
The CPI Market Basket
The CPI market basket shows how a typical consumer divides his or her money among various goods and services. Most of a consumer's money goes toward housing, transportation, and food and beverages.

Source: The Bureau of Labor Statistics

Table 7.5 shows values of the CPI since 1950. The base period for this index is 1982–1984, which means that the index is constructed to have a value of 100.0 when averaged across these three years. The percentage change for a given year in the table is a measure of inflation in that year. For example, from 1970 to 1971, the CPI increased from 38.8 to 40.5, a percentage change of 4.9 percent. [The percentage change is (40.5 − 38.8)/38.8 times 100.] The table shows the high inflation rates in the 1970s and early 1980s and the fairly low inflation rates since 1992.

Since the CPI is a fixed-weight price index (with the current base period 1982–1984), it suffers from the substitution problem discussed in the last chapter. With fixed weights, it does not account for consumers' substitution away from high-priced goods. The CPI thus has a tendency to overestimate the rate of inflation. This problem has important policy implications because government transfers such as Social Security payments are tied to the CPI. If inflation as measured by percentage changes in the CPI is biased upward, Social Security payments will grow more rapidly than they would with a better measure: The government is spending more than it otherwise would.

In response to the fixed-weight problem, in August 2002, the BLS began publishing a version of the CPI called the Chained Consumer Price Index, which uses changing weights. Although this version is not yet the main version, it may be that within a few years the BLS completely moves away from the fixed-weight version of the CPI. Remember, however, that even if this happens, the CPI will still differ in important ways from the GDP deflator, discussed in the last chapter. The CPI covers only consumer goods and services—those listed in Figure 7.1—whereas the GDP deflator covers all goods and services produced in the economy. Also, the CPI includes prices of imported goods, which the GDP deflator does not.

Other popular price indexes are **producer price indexes (PPIs)**, once called *wholesale price indexes*. These are indexes of prices that producers receive for products at all stages in the production process, not just the final stage. The indexes are calculated separately for various stages in the production process. The three main categories are *finished goods, intermediate materials,* and *crude materials,* although there are subcategories within each of these categories.

producer price indexes (PPIs) Measures of prices that producers receive for products at all stages in the production process.

TABLE 7.5 The CPI, 1950–2007					
	Percentage Change			Percentage Change	
	in CPI	CPI		in CPI	CPI
1950	1.3	24.1	1979	11.3	72.6
1951	7.9	26.0	1980	13.5	82.4
1952	1.9	26.5	1981	10.3	90.9
1953	0.8	26.7	1982	6.2	96.5
1954	0.7	26.9	1983	3.2	99.6
1955	−0.4	26.8	1984	4.3	103.9
1956	1.5	27.2	1985	3.6	107.6
1957	3.3	28.1	1986	1.9	109.6
1958	2.8	28.9	1987	3.6	113.6
1959	0.7	29.1	1988	4.1	118.3
1960	1.7	29.6	1989	4.8	124.0
1961	1.0	29.9	1990	5.4	130.7
1962	1.0	30.2	1991	4.2	136.2
1963	1.3	30.6	1992	3.0	140.3
1964	1.3	31.0	1993	3.0	144.5
1965	1.6	31.5	1994	2.6	148.2
1966	2.9	32.4	1995	2.8	152.4
1967	3.1	33.4	1996	3.0	156.9
1968	4.2	34.8	1997	2.3	160.5
1969	5.5	36.7	1998	1.6	163.0
1970	5.7	38.8	1999	2.2	166.6
1971	4.4	40.5	2000	3.4	172.2
1972	3.2	41.8	2001	2.8	177.1
1973	6.2	44.4	2002	1.6	179.9
1974	11.0	49.3	2003	2.3	184.0
1975	9.1	53.8	2004	2.7	188.9
1976	5.8	56.9	2005	3.4	195.3
1977	6.5	60.6	2006	3.2	201.6
1978	7.6	65.2	2007	2.8	207.3

Sources: Bureau of Labor Statistics, U.S. Department of Labor.

One advantage of some of the PPIs is that they detect price increases early in the production process. Because their movements sometimes foreshadow future changes in consumer prices, they are considered to be leading indicators of future consumer prices.

The Costs of Inflation

If you asked most people why inflation is bad, they would tell you that it lowers the overall standard of living by making goods and services more expensive. That is, it cuts into people's purchasing power. People are fond of recalling the days when a bottle of Coca-Cola cost a dime and a hamburger cost a quarter. Just think what we could buy today if prices had not changed. What people usually do not think about is what their incomes were in the "good old days." The fact that the cost of a Coke has increased from 10 cents to a dollar does not mean anything in real terms if people who once earned $5,000 now earn $50,000. Why? The reason is simple: People's income from wages and salaries, profits, interest, and rent increases during inflations. The wage rate is the price of labor, rent is the price of land, and so on. During inflations, most prices—including input prices—tend to rise together; and input prices determine both the incomes of workers and the incomes of owners of capital and land.

Inflation May Change the Distribution of Income Whether you gain or lose during a period of inflation depends on whether your income rises faster or slower than the prices of the things you buy. The group most often mentioned when the impact of inflation is discussed is people living on fixed incomes. If your income is fixed and prices rise, your ability to purchase goods and services falls proportionately.

Although the elderly are often thought of as living on fixed incomes, many pension plans pay benefits that are *indexed* to inflation. The benefits these plans provide automatically increase when the general price level rises. If prices rise 10 percent, benefits also rise 10 percent. The biggest source of income for the elderly is Social Security. These benefits are fully indexed; when prices rise—that is, when the CPI rises—by 5 percent, Social Security benefits also increase by 5 percent.

Wages are also sometimes indexed to inflation through cost of living adjustments (COLAs) written into labor contracts. These contracts usually stipulate that future wage increases will be larger the larger is the rate of inflation. If wages are fully indexed, workers do not suffer a fall in real income when inflation rises, although wages are not always fully indexed.

One way of thinking about the effects of inflation on the distribution of income is to distinguish between *anticipated* and *unanticipated* inflation. If inflation is anticipated and contracts are made and agreements written with the anticipated value of inflation in mind, there need not be any effects of inflation on income distribution. Take, for example, debtors versus creditors. It is commonly believed that debtors benefit at the expense of creditors during an inflation because with inflation they pay back less in the future in real terms than they borrowed. But this is not the case if the inflation is anticipated and the loan contract is written with this in mind.

Suppose that you want to borrow $100 from me to be paid back in a year and that we both agree that if there is no inflation the appropriate interest rate is 5 percent. Suppose also that we both anticipate that the inflation rate will be 10 percent. In this case we will agree on a 15 percent interest rate—you will pay me back $115 at the end of the year. By charging you 15 percent I have taken into account the fact that you will be paying me back with dollars worth 10 percent less in real terms than when you borrowed them. I am then not hurt by inflation and you are not helped if the actual inflation rate turns out to equal our anticipated rate. I am earning a 5 percent **real interest rate**—the difference between the interest rate on a loan and the inflation rate.

Unanticipated inflation, on the other hand, is a different story. If the actual inflation rate during the year turns out to be 20 percent, I as a creditor will be hurt. I charged you 15 percent interest, expecting to get a 5 percent real rate of return, when I needed to charge you 25 percent to get the same 5 percent real rate of return. Because inflation was higher than anticipated, I got a negative real return of 5 percent. Inflation that is higher than anticipated benefits debtors; inflation that is lower than anticipated benefits creditors.

To summarize, the effects of anticipated inflation on the distribution of income are likely to be fairly small, since people and institutions will adjust to the anticipated inflation. Unanticipated inflation, on the other hand, may have large effects, depending, among other things, on how much indexing to inflation there is. If many contracts are not indexed and are based on anticipated inflation rates that turn out to be wrong, there can be big winners and losers. In general, there is more uncertainty and risk when inflation is unanticipated. This uncertainty may prevent people from signing long-run contracts that would otherwise be beneficial for both parties.

real interest rate The difference between the interest rate on a loan and the inflation rate.

Administrative Costs and Inefficiencies There may also be costs associated even with anticipated inflation. One is the administrative cost associated with simply keeping up. During the rapid inflation in Israel in the early 1980s, a telephone hotline was set up to give the hourly price index. Store owners had to recalculate and repost prices frequently, and this took time that could have been used more efficiently. In Zimbabwe, where the inflation rate in June 2008 was estimated by some to be over 1 million percent at an annual rate, the government was forced to print ever-increasing denominations of money.

More frequent banking transactions may also be required when anticipated inflation is high. For example, interest rates tend to rise with anticipated inflation. When interest rates are high, the opportunity costs of holding cash outside of banks is high. People therefore hold less cash and need to stop at the bank more often. (We discuss this effect in more detail in the next part of this book.)

Public Enemy Number One? Economists have debated the seriousness of the costs of inflation for decades. Some, among them Alan Blinder, say, "Inflation, like every teenager, is grossly misunderstood, and this gross misunderstanding blows the political importance of inflation out of all proportion to its economic importance."[3] Others such as Phillip Cagan and Robert Lipsey argue, "It was once thought that the economy would in time make all the necessary adjustments [to inflation], but many of them are proving to be very difficult.... For financial institutions and markets, the effects of inflation have been extremely unsettling."[4]

No matter what the real economic cost of inflation, people do not like it. It makes us uneasy and unhappy. In 1974, President Ford verbalized some of this discomfort when he said, "Our inflation, our public enemy number one, will unless whipped destroy our country, our homes, our liberties, our property, and finally our national pride, as surely as any well-armed wartime enemy."[5] In this belief, our elected leaders have vigorously pursued policies designed to stop inflation.

Long-Run Growth

output growth The growth rate of the output of the entire economy.

per-capita output growth The growth rate of output per person in the economy.

productivity growth The growth rate of output per worker.

In discussing long-run growth, it will be useful to begin with a few definitions. **Output growth** is the growth rate of the output of the entire economy. **Per-capita output growth** is the growth rate of output per person in the economy. If the population of a country is growing at the same rate as output, then per-capita output is not growing: Output growth is simply keeping up with population growth. Not everyone in a country works, and so output per worker is not the same as output per person. Output per worker is larger than output per person, and it is called productivity. **Productivity growth** is thus the growth rate of output per worker.

If we take as the measure of economic welfare of a country its per-capita output, a rapid growth rate of output does not necessarily improve individual welfare. If population is growing as rapidly as output, per-capita output is not growing, which means that the economic welfare of the average person is not growing. If the fraction of the population that is working remains the same and productivity increases, per-capita output will increase because more output is being produced per person. Per-capita output will also increase if productivity does not change but the fraction of the population that is working increases. In this case, more output is also being produced per person, although this is so because more people are working.

Output and Productivity Growth

We have pointed out that aggregate output in the United States has grown at an annual rate of 3.4 percent since 1900. Some years are better than this and some years worse, but, on average, the growth rate has been 3.4 percent. An area of economics called *growth theory* is concerned with the question of what determines this rate. Why 3.4 percent and not 2 percent or 4 percent? We take up this question in Chapter 17, but a few points are useful to make now.

Before we begin our discussion of economic growth, it is important to review what is meant by *capital*. Capital is anything that is produced that is then used as an input to produce other goods and services. Capital can be tangible, such as buildings and equipment, or intangible. The knowledge and skills acquired through education and training can be thought of as intangible *human capital*. Capital can be private or public. The roads and bridges that we drive on are a part of the public capital stock. Capital, thus, can take many forms. To simplify the discussion, however, we will sometimes refer to capital as simply "machines."

In a simplified economy, machines (capital) and workers (labor) are needed to produce output. Suppose that an economy consists of six machines and 60 workers, with 10 workers working on each machine, and that the length of the workweek is 40 hours, with this workweek resulting in 50 units of output per month per machine. Total output (GDP) for the month is thus 300 units (6 machines times 50 units per machine) in this simple economy.

How can output increase in this economy? There are a number of ways. One way is to add more workers. If, for example, 12 workers are added, 2 extra per machine, more output can be produced per machine per hour worked because there are more workers helping out on each machine. Another way is to add more machines. For example, if 4 machines are added, the

---

[3] Alan Blinder, *Hard Heads, Soft Hearts: Tough-Minded Economics for a Just Society* (Reading, MA: Addison-Wesley, 1987).
[4] Phillip Cagan and Robert Lipsey, "The Financial Effects of Inflation," National Bureau of Economic Research (Cambridge, MA: General Series No. 103, 1978), pp. 67–68.
[5] U.S. President, *Weekly Compilation of Presidential Documents*, vol. 10, no. 41, p. 1247. Cited in Blinder, *Hard Heads*.

60 workers have a total of 10 machines to work with instead of 6 and more output can be produced per worker per hour worked. A third way is to increase the length of the workweek (for example, from 40 hours to 45 hours). With workers and machines working more hours, more output can be produced. Output can thus increase if labor or capital increases or if the amount of time that labor and capital are working per week increases.

Another way for output to increase in our economy is for the quality of the workers to increase. If, for example, the education of the workers increases, this may add to their skills and thus increase their ability to work on the machines. Output per machine might then rise from 50 units per month to some larger number per month. Also, if workers become more physically fit by exercising more and eating less fat and more whole grains and fresh fruits and vegetables, their greater fitness may increase their output on the machines. People are sometimes said to be adding to their *human capital* when they increase their mental or physical skills.

The quality of the machines may also increase. In particular, new machines that replace old machines may allow more output to be produced per hour with the same number of workers. In our example, it may be that 55 instead of 50 units of output can be produced per month per new machine with 10 workers per machine and a 40-hour workweek. An obvious example is the replacement of an old computer with a new, faster one that allows more to be done per minute of work on the computer.

To summarize, output can increase when there are more workers, more skills per worker, more machines, better machines, or a longer workweek.

Turning now to the actual economy, an interesting variable to look at is the ratio of total output to the total number of worker hours. Output per worker hour is called *labor productivity* or sometimes just *productivity*. Output per worker hour is plotted in Figure 7.2 for the 1952 I–2007 IV period. Two features are immediately clear from the figure. First, there is an upward trend. Second, there are fairly sizable short-run fluctuations around the trend. We will see in Chapter 16 why there are short-run fluctuations. This has to do with the possibility that the employed workforce is not always fully utilized. For now, however, the main interest is the long-run trend.

To smooth out the short-run fluctuations in Figure 7.2, we have added straight-line segments to the figure, where the segments roughly go through the high values. The slope of each line segment is the growth rate of productivity along the segment. The growth rates are listed in the figure. The different productivity growth rates in the figure tell an interesting story. From the 1950s through the mid-1960s, the growth rate was 3.1 percent. The rate then fell to 2.5 percent in the last half of the 1960s and early 1970s. Between the early 1970s and the early 1990s, the growth rate was much lower at 1.5 percent. Since the early 1990s, it has been 1.9 percent.

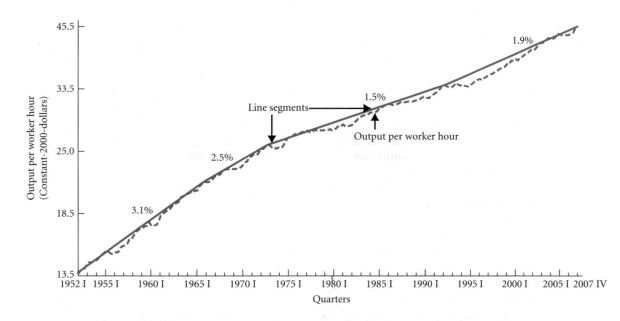

▲ **FIGURE 7.2 Output per Worker Hour (Productivity), 1952 I–2007 IV**
Productivity grew much faster in the 1950s and 1960s than since.

Why are the growth rates positive in Figure 7.2? In other words, why has the amount of output that a worker can produce per hour risen in the last half century? Part of the answer is that the amount of capital per worker has increased. In Figure 7.3 capital per worker is plotted for the same 1952 I–2007 IV period. It is clear from the figure that the amount of capital per worker has generally been rising. Therefore, with more capital per worker, more output can be produced per worker. The other part of the answer is that the quality of labor and capital has been increasing. Both the average skill of workers and the average quality of capital have been increasing. This means that more output can be produced per worker for a given quantity of capital because both workers and capital are getting better.

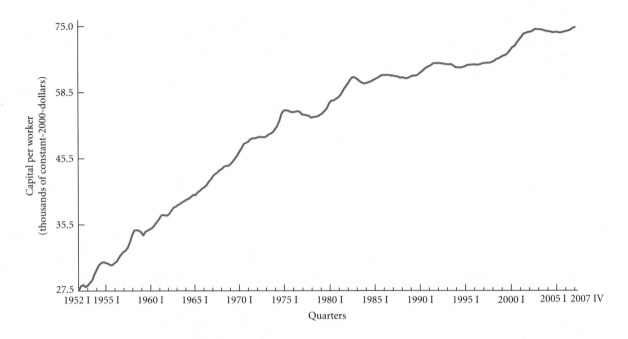

▲ **FIGURE 7.3 Capital per Worker, 1952 I–2007 IV**
Capital per worker grew until about 1980 and then leveled off somewhat.

A harder question to answer concerning Figure 7.2 is why the growth rate of productivity was much higher in the 1950s and 1960s than it has been since the early 1970s. Again, part of the answer is that the amount of capital per worker rose more rapidly in the 1950s and 1960s than it has since then. This can be seen in Figure 7.3. The other part of the answer is, of course, that the quality of labor and capital must have increased more in the 1950s and 1960s than later, although this, to some extent, begs the question. The key question is why the quality of labor and capital has grown more slowly since the early 1970s. We take up this question in Chapter 17, where we will see that there seems to be no one obvious answer. An interesting question for the future is whether the continued growth of the Internet will lead to a much larger productivity growth rate, perhaps as large as the growth rate in the 1950s and 1960s. In the present context, you can think about the growth of the Internet as an increase in physical capital (wires, servers, switchers, and so on) and an increase in the quality of capital (an increase in what can be done per minute using the Internet). Time will tell whether the Internet will lead to a "new age" of productivity growth.

Looking Ahead

This ends our introduction to the basic concepts and problems of macroeconomics. The first chapter of this part introduced the field; the second chapter discussed the measurement of national product and national income; and this chapter discussed unemployment, inflation and long-run growth. We are now ready to begin the analysis of how the macroeconomy works.

S U M M A R Y

UNEMPLOYMENT *p. 123*

1. The *unemployment rate* is the ratio of the number of *unemployed* people to the number of people in the *labor force*. To be considered unemployed and in the labor force, a person must be looking for work.

2. Big differences in rates of unemployment exist across demographic groups, regions, and industries. African Americans, for example, experience much higher unemployment rates than whites.

3. A person who decides to stop looking for work is considered to have dropped out of the labor force and is no longer classified as unemployed. People who stop looking because they are discouraged about finding a job are sometimes called *discouraged workers*.

4. Some unemployment is inevitable. Because new workers are continually entering the labor force, because industries and firms are continuously expanding and contracting, and because people switch jobs, there is a constant process of job search as workers and firms try to match the best people to the available jobs. This unemployment is both natural and beneficial for the economy.

5. The unemployment that occurs because of short-run job/skill-matching problems is called *frictional unemployment*. The unemployment that occurs because of longer-run structural changes in the economy is called *structural unemployment*. The *natural rate of unemployment*

is the sum of the frictional rate and the structural rate. The increase in unemployment that occurs during recessions and depressions is called *cyclical unemployment*.

INFLATION *p. 130*

6. The *consumer price index* (*CPI*) is a fixed-weight price index. It represents the "market basket" purchased by the typical urban consumer.

7. Whether people gain or lose during a period of inflation depends on whether their income rises faster or slower than the prices of the things they buy. The elderly are more insulated from inflation than most people think because Social Security benefits and many pensions are indexed to inflation.

8. Inflation is likely to have a larger effect on the distribution of income when it is unanticipated than when it is anticipated.

LONG-RUN GROWTH *p. 134*

9. Output growth depends on: (1) the growth rate of the capital stock, (2) the growth rate of output per unit of the capital stock, (3) the growth rate of labor, and (4) the growth rate of output per unit of labor.

10. Output per worker hour (labor productivity) rose faster in the 1950s and 1960s than it rose from the 1970s to 2007. An interesting question is whether labor productivity will rise faster in the future because of the Internet.

R E V I W   T E R M S   A N D   C O N C E P T S

consumer price index (CPI), *p. 130*

cyclical unemployment, *p. 129*

discouraged-worker effect, *p. 127*

employed, *p. 124*

frictional unemployment, *p. 129*

labor force, *p. 124*

labor force participation rate, *p. 124*

natural rate of unemployment, *p. 129*

not in the labor force, *p. 124*

output growth, *p. 134*

per-capita output growth, *p. 134*

producer price indexes (PPIs), *p. 131*

productivity growth, *p. 134*

real interest rate, *p. 133*

structural unemployment, *p. 129*

unemployed, *p. 124*

unemployment rate, *p. 124*

1. labor force = employed + unemployed

2. population = labor force + not in labor force

3. unemployment rate = $\dfrac{\text{unemployed}}{\text{employed} + \text{unemployed}}$

4. labor force participation rate = $\dfrac{\text{labor force}}{\text{population}}$

P R O B L E M S

Visit **www.myeconlab.com** to complete the problems marked in orange online. You will receive instant feedback on your answers, tutorial help, and access to additional practice problems.

1. In early 2008, economists were debating whether the U.S. economy was in a recession even though the unemployment rate was close to full employment at only 5.1 percent. How can they make this assertion?

2. When an inefficient firm or a firm producing a product that people no longer want goes out of business, people are unemployed, but that is part of the normal process of economic growth and development. The unemployment is part of the natural rate and need not concern policy makers. Discuss that statement and its relevance to the economy today.

3. What is the unemployment rate in your state today? What was it in 1970, 1975, 1982, and 2008? How has your state done relative to the national average? Do you know or can you determine why?

4. Suppose all wages, salaries, welfare benefits, and other sources of income were indexed to inflation. Would inflation still be considered a problem? Why or why not?

5. [Related to the *Economics in Practice* on p. *127*] Go to www.bls.gov and click on the links for state and area employment and unemployment. Look at your home state and describe what changes have taken place in the workforce. Has the labor force participation rate gone up or down? Provide an explanation for the rate change. Are your state's experiences the same as the rest of the country? Provide an explanation of why your state's experiences are the same as or different from the rest of the country.

6. What do the CPI and the PPI measure? Why do we need both of these price indexes? (Think about what purpose you would use each one for.)

7. The consumer price index (CPI) is a fixed-weight index. It compares the price of a fixed bundle of goods in one year with the price of the same bundle of goods in some base year. Calculate the price of a bundle containing 100 units of good *X*, 150 units of good *Y*, and 25 units of good *Z* in 2006, 2007, and 2008. Convert the results into an index by dividing each bundle price figure by the bundle price in 2006. Calculate the percentage change in your index between 2006 and 2007 and again between 2007 and 2008. Was there inflation between 2007 and 2008?

GOOD	QUANTITY CONSUMED	PRICES 2006	PRICES 2007	PRICES 2008
X	100	$1.00	$1.50	$1.75
Y	150	1.50	2.00	2.00
Z	25	3.00	3.25	3.00

8. Consider the following statements:
   a. More people are employed in Tappania now than at any time in the past 50 years.
   b. The unemployment rate in Tappania is higher now than it has been in 50 years.

   Can both of those statements be true at the same time? Explain.

9. Policy makers talk about the "capacity" of the economy to grow. What specifically is meant by the "capacity" of the economy? How might capacity be measured? In what ways is capacity limited by labor constraints and by capital constraints? What are the consequences if demand in the economy exceeds capacity? What signs would you look for?

10. What was the rate of growth in real GDP during the most recent quarter? You can find the answer in publications such as the *Survey of Current Business, The Economist,* and *Business Week.* Has growth been increasing or decreasing? What policies might you suggest for increasing the economy's potential long-run rate of growth?

11. Suppose the stock of capital and the workforce are both increasing at 3 percent annually in the country of Wholand. At the same time, real output is growing at 6 percent. How is that possible in the short run and in the long run?

part **III**

The Core of Macroeconomic Theory

We now begin our discussion of the theory of how the macroeconomy works. We know how to calculate gross domestic product (GDP), but what factors *determine* it? We know how to define and measure inflation and unemployment, but what circumstances *cause* inflation and unemployment? What, if anything, can government do to reduce unemployment and inflation?

Analyzing the various components of the macroeconomy is a complex undertaking. The level of GDP, the overall price level, and the level of employment—three chief concerns of macroeconomists—are influenced by events in three broadly defined "markets":

- Goods-and-services market
- Financial (money) market
- Labor market

We will explore each market, as well as the links between them, in our discussion of macroeconomic theory. Figure III.1 presents the plan of the next seven chapters, which form the

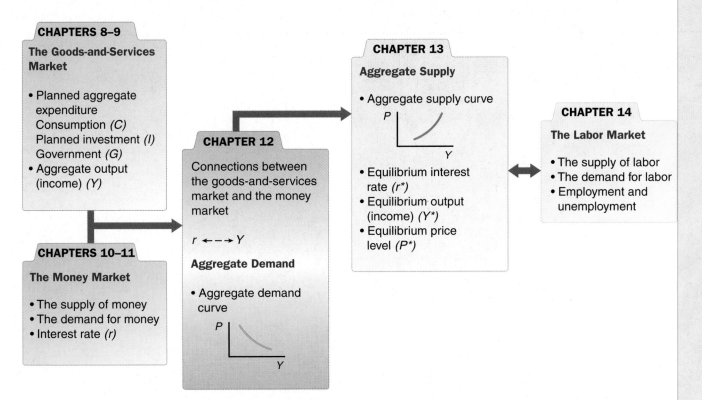

▲ FIGURE III.1 **The Core of Macroeconomic Theory**

We build up the macroeconomy slowly. In Chapters 8 and 9, we examine the market for goods and services. In Chapters 10 and 11, we examine the money market. Then in Chapter 12, we bring the two markets together, in so doing explaining the links between aggregate output (Y) and the interest rate (r), and derive the aggregate demand curve. In Chapter 13, we introduce the aggregate supply curve and determine the price level (P). We then explain in Chapter 14 how the labor market fits into the macroeconomic picture.

core of macroeconomic theory. In Chapters 8 and 9, we describe the market for goods and services, often called the *goods market*. In Chapter 8, we explain several basic concepts and show how the equilibrium level of output is determined in a simple economy with no government and no imports or exports. In Chapter 9, we add the government to the economy.

In Chapters 10 and 11, we focus on the *money market*. Chapter 10 introduces the money market and the banking system and discusses the way the U.S. central bank (the Federal Reserve) controls the money supply. Chapter 11 analyzes the demand for money and the way interest rates are determined. Chapter 12 then examines the relationship between the goods market and the money market and derives the aggregate demand curve. At the end of Chapter 12, the equilibrium values of aggregate output and the interest rate are determined for a given price level. Chapter 13 then uses the analysis from Chapter 12, adds the aggregate supply curve, and determines the price level. Having then determined output, the interest rate, and the price level, we are ready to analyze the effects of fiscal and monetary policies on the economy. This is done in the second half of Chapter 13. Finally, Chapter 14 discusses the supply of and demand for labor and the functioning of the *labor market* in the macroeconomy. This material is essential to understanding employment and unemployment.

Before we begin our discussion of aggregate output and income, we need to stress that production, consumption, and other activities that we will be discussing in the following chapters are ongoing activities. Nonetheless, it is helpful to think about these activities as if they took place in a series of *production periods*. A period might be a month long or 3 months long. During each period, output is produced, income is generated, and spending takes place. At the end of each period, we can examine the results. Was everything that was produced in the economy sold? What percentage of income was spent? What percentage was saved? Is output (income) likely to rise or fall in the next period?

Aggregate Expenditure and Equilibrium Output

8

In this chapter, we explain how equilibrium output is determined in an economy with no government. We build slowly, and the only theory we use is that consumption depends on income and that the goods market is in equilibrium. Having determined equilibrium output, we then discuss how an economy that is out of equilibrium adjusts back to equilibrium.

In Chapter 6, we introduced real gross domestic product as a measure of the total quantity of

output produced in the economy in a given period. Output includes the production of services, consumer goods, and investment goods. We saw that GDP can be calculated in terms of income or expenditures. Because every dollar of expenditure is received by someone as income, we can compute total GDP by adding up the total spent on all final goods and services during a period *or* by adding up all the income—wages, rents, interest, and profits—received by all factors of production.

We will use the variable Y to refer to both **aggregate output** and **aggregate income** because they are the same seen from two different points of view. When output increases, additional income is generated. More workers may be hired and paid, workers may put in and be paid for more hours, and owners may earn more profits. When output is cut, income falls, workers may be laid off or work fewer hours (and be paid less), and profits may fall.

> In any given period, there is an exact equality between aggregate output (production) and aggregate income. You should be reminded of this fact whenever you encounter the combined term **aggregate output (income) (Y)**.

Aggregate output can also be considered the aggregate quantity supplied because it is the amount that firms are supplying (producing) during a period. In the discussions that follow, we use the term *aggregate output (income)* instead of *aggregate quantity supplied*, but keep in mind that the two are equivalent. Also remember that *aggregate output* means "real GDP."

From the outset, you must think in "real terms." For example, when we talk about output (Y), we mean real output, not nominal output. Although we discussed in Chapter 6 that the calculation of real GDP is complicated, you can ignore these complications in the following analysis. To help make things easier to read, we will frequently use dollar values for Y. But do not confuse Y with nominal output. The main point is to think of Y as being in real terms—the quantities of goods and services produced, not the dollars circulating in the economy.

aggregate output The total quantity of goods and services produced (or supplied) in an economy in a given period.

aggregate income The total income received by all factors of production in a given period.

aggregate output (income) (Y) A combined term used to remind you of the exact equality between aggregate output and aggregate income.

The Keynesian Theory of Consumption

In 2005, the average American family spent about $1,350 on clothing. For high-income families earning more than $148,000, the amount spent on clothing was substantially higher, at $3,700. We all recognize that for consumption as a whole, as well as for consumption of most specific categories of goods and services, consumption rises with income. This relationship between consumption and income is central to Keynes's model of the economy. While Keynes recognized that many factors, including wealth and interest rates, play a role in determining consumption levels in the economy, in his classic *The General Theory of Employment, Interest and Money*, current income played the key role:

> The fundamental psychological law, upon which we are entitled to depend with great confidence both *a priori* from our knowledge of human nature and from the detailed facts of experience, is that men [and women, too] are disposed, as a rule and on average, to increase their consumption as their incomes increase, but not by as much as the increase in their income.[1]

Keynes is telling us two things in this quote. First, if you find your income going up, you will spend more than you did before. But Keynes is also saying something about how much more you will spend: He predicts—based on his looking at the data and his understanding of people—that the rise in consumption will be less than the full rise in income. This simple observation plays a large role in helping us understand the workings of the aggregate economy.

The relationship between consumption and income is called a **consumption function**. Figure 8.1 shows a hypothetical consumption function for an individual household. The curve is labeled $c(y)$, which is read "c is a function of y," or "consumption is a function of income." Note that we have drawn the line with an upward slope, reflecting that consumption increases with income. To reflect Keynes's view that consumption increases less than one for one with income, we have drawn the consumption function with a slope of less than 1. The consumption function in Figure 8.1 is a straight line, telling us that an increase in income of $1 leads to the same increase in consumption regardless of the initial value of income. In practice, the consumption function may be curved, with the slope decreasing as income increases. This would tell us that the typical consumer spends less of the incremental income received as his or her income rises.

consumption function
The relationship between consumption and income.

▶ **FIGURE 8.1 A Consumption Function for a Household**

A consumption function for an individual household shows the level of consumption at each level of household income.

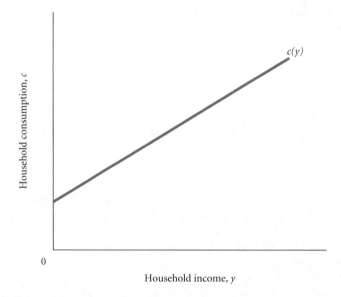

The consumption function in Figure 8.1 represents an individual household. In macroeconomics, however, we are interested in the behavior of the economy as a whole, the aggregate consumption of all households in the economy in relation to aggregate income. Figure 8.2 shows this

[1] John Maynard Keynes, *The General Theory of Employment, Interest, and Money* (1936), First Harbinger Ed. (New York: Harcourt Brace Jovanovich, 1964), p. 96.

aggregate consumption function, again using a straight line, or constant slope, for simplicity. With a straight line consumption curve, we can use the following equation to describe the curve:

$$C = a + bY$$

Y is aggregate output (income), C is aggregate consumption, and a is the point at which the consumption function intersects the C-axis—a constant. The letter b is the slope of the line, in this case $\Delta C/\Delta Y$ [because consumption (C) is measured on the vertical axis and income (Y) is measured on the horizontal axis].[2] Every time income increases (say by ΔY), consumption increases by b times ΔY. Thus, $\Delta C = b \times \Delta Y$ and $\Delta C/\Delta Y = b$. Suppose, for example, that the slope of the line in Figure 8.2 is .75 (that is, $b = .75$). An increase in income (ΔY) of $1,000 would then increase consumption by $b\Delta Y = .75 \times \$1,000$, or $750.

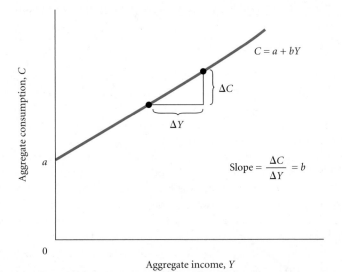

◀ **FIGURE 8.2 An Aggregate Consumption Function**

The aggregate consumption function shows the level of aggregate consumption at each level of aggregate income. The upward slope indicates that higher levels of income lead to higher levels of consumption spending.

The **marginal propensity to consume (MPC)** is the fraction of a change in income that is consumed. In the consumption function here, b is the MPC. An MPC of .75 means consumption changes by .75 of the change in income. The slope of the consumption function is the MPC. An MPC less than 1 tells us that individuals spend less than 100 percent of their income increase, just as Keynes suggested.

marginal propensity to consume (MPC) That fraction of a change in income that is consumed, or spent.

$$\text{marginal propensity to consume} \equiv \text{slope of consumption function} \equiv \frac{\Delta C}{\Delta Y}$$

Aggregate saving (S) in the economy, denoted S, is the difference between aggregate income and aggregate consumption:

aggregate saving (S) The part of aggregate income that is not consumed.

$$S \equiv Y - C$$

The triple equal sign means that this equation is an **identity**, or something that is always true by definition. This equation simply says that income that is not consumed must be saved. If $0.75 of a $1.00 increase in income goes to consumption, $0.25 must go to saving. If income decreases by $1.00, consumption will decrease by $0.75 and saving will decrease by $0.25. The **marginal propensity to save (MPS)** is the fraction of a change in income that is saved: $\Delta S/\Delta Y$, where ΔS is the change in saving. Because everything not consumed is saved, the MPC and the MPS must add up to 1.

identity Something that is always true.

marginal propensity to save (MPS) That fraction of a change in income that is saved.

$$MPC + MPS \equiv 1$$

---

[2] The Greek letter Δ (delta) means "change in." For example, ΔY (read "delta Y") means the "change in income." If income (Y) in 2007 is $100 and income in 2008 is $110, then ΔY for this period is $110 - \$100 = \$10$. For a review of the concept of slope, see Appendix, Chapter 1.

┆ Because the *MPC* and the *MPS* are important concepts, it may help to review their definitions. The marginal propensity to consume (*MPC*) is the fraction of an increase in income that is consumed (or the fraction of a decrease in income that comes out of consumption). The marginal propensity to save (*MPS*) is the fraction of an increase in income that is saved (or the fraction of a decrease in income that comes out of saving).

The numerical examples used in the rest of this chapter are based on the following consumption function:

$$C = \underbrace{100}_{a} + \underbrace{.75Y}_{b}$$

This equation is simply an extension of the generic $C = a + bY$ consumption function we have been discussing, where *a* is 100 and *b* is .75. This function is graphed in Figure 8.3.

▶ **FIGURE 8.3 The Aggregate Consumption Function Derived from the Equation $C = 100 + .75Y$**

In this simple consumption function, consumption is 100 at an income of zero. As income rises, so does consumption. For every 100 increase in income, consumption rises by 75. The slope of the line is .75.

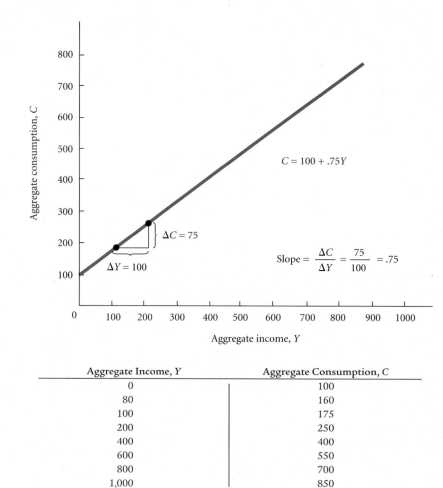

Aggregate Income, Y	Aggregate Consumption, C
0	100
80	160
100	175
200	250
400	400
600	550
800	700
1,000	850

Since saving and consumption by definition add up to income, we can use the consumption curve to tell us about both consumption and saving. We do this in Figure 8.4. In this figure, we have drawn a 45° line from the origin. Everywhere along this line aggregate consumption is equal to aggregate income. Therefore, saving is zero. Where the consumption curve is *above* the 45° line, consumption exceeds income and saving is negative. Where the consumption function *crosses* the 45° line, consumption is equal to income and saving is zero. Where the consumption function is *below* the 45° line, consumption is less than income and saving is positive. Note that the slope of the saving function is $\Delta S/\Delta Y$, which is equal to the marginal propensity to save (*MPS*). The consumption function and the saving function are mirror images of each other. No information appears in one that does not appear in the other. These functions tell us how households in the aggregate will divide income between consumption spending and saving at every possible income level. In other words, they embody aggregate household behavior.

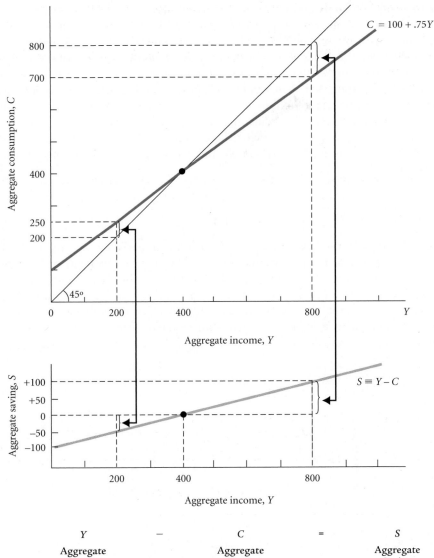

▲ **FIGURE 8.4 Deriving the Saving Function from the Consumption Function in Figure 8.3**

Because $S \equiv Y - C$, it is easy to derive the saving function from the consumption function. A 45° line drawn from the origin can be used as a convenient tool to compare consumption and income graphically. At $Y = 200$, consumption is 250. The 45° line shows us that consumption is larger than income by 50. Thus, $S \equiv Y - C = -50$. At $Y = 800$, consumption is less than income by 100. Thus, $S = 100$ when $Y = 800$.

Y	$-$	C	$=$	S
Aggregate Income		Aggregate Consumption		Aggregate Saving
0		100		−100
80		160		−80
100		175		−75
200		250		−50
400		400		0
600		550		50
800		700		100
1,000		850		150

Other Determinants of Consumption

The assumption that consumption depends only on income is obviously a simplification. In practice, the decisions of households on how much to consume in a given period are also affected by their wealth, by the interest rate, and by their expectations of the future. Households with higher wealth are likely to spend more, other things being equal, than households with less wealth.

In 2007, Steve Schwarzman, CEO of Blackstone, a private equity firm, spent $3 million on a lavish 60th birthday party for himself, considerably more than most people would spend. While Schwarzman's spending is likely influenced by his income ($750 million in 2006/2007 combined), it also reflects his enormous wealth.

For many households, interest rates also figure in to consumption and saving decisions. Lower interest rates reduce the cost of borrowing, so lower interest rates are likely to stimulate spending. (Conversely, higher interest rates increase the cost of borrowing and are likely to decrease spending.)

Finally, as households think about what fraction of incremental income to consume versus save, their expectations about the future may also play a role. If households are optimistic and expect to do better in the future, they may spend more at present than if they think the future will be bleak.

Household expectations are also important regarding households' responses to changes in their income. If, for example, the government announces a tax cut, which increases after-tax income, households' responses to the tax cut will likely depend on whether the tax cut is expected to be temporary or permanent. If households expect that the tax cut will be in effect for only two years, their responses are likely to be smaller than if they expect the tax cut to be permanent.

We examine these issues in Chapter 16, where we take a closer look at household behavior regarding both consumption and labor supply. But for now, we will focus only on income as affecting consumption.

Planned Investment (*I*)

In Chapter 12, we present a theory as to why the investment decisions of firms are likely to be affected by the interest rate, where low interest rates stimulate investment and high interest rates discourage investment. Then in Chapter 16, we look more carefully at firms' decisions, including their investment decisions. For now, however, we are treating firms' investment decisions in a very simple way. We assume that the investment that firms plan to make, denoted *I*, is fixed. In particular, it does not depend on income. This assumption is depicted in Figure 8.5. In this figure, planned investment is 25 for all values of income.

▶ **FIGURE 8.5 The Planned Investment Function**

For the time being, we will assume that planned investment is fixed. It does not change when income changes, so its graph is a horizontal line.

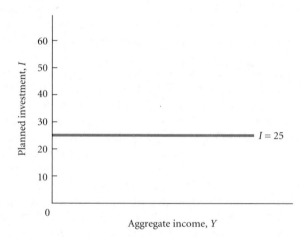

We know from Chapter 6 that investment includes both plant and equipment investment as well as the change in inventories. If a firm buys a machine, its stock of capital increases since machines are part of the capital stock. Part of the capital stock, however, also includes the stock of inventories. If an automobile firm has 10,000 cars in inventory, these cars are considered part of the firm's capital stock. If in the current period the firm produces 20,000 cars and sells 18,000, its change in inventories is the value of 2,000 cars and its capital stock has increased by the value of 2,000 cars.

The difference between planned investment and actual investment plays a major role in this chapter in the discussion of equilibrium. We will use *I* to refer to planned investment only. **Planned investment (*I*)** is the investment that firms plan to make. Remember that investment includes investment in plant and equipment as well as the change in inventories. **Actual investment** is the actual amount of investment that takes place. How can planned and actual investment differ? Consider the automobile firm again. Assume that it plans to buy $5 million in machines and to have no change in inventories. Assume that it buys the $5 million in machines, produces 20,000 cars expecting to sell all of them, and sells only 18,000. The firm's actual investment is the $5 million plus the value of 2,000 cars. So its actual investment was larger than its planned investment. Actual investment can differ from planned investment if a firm misestimates how much it will sell in the period. Any misestimation means that the change in its inventories, which is part of its actual investment, will be different from what it planned the change to be. We will see that the economy is in equilibrium only when planned investment is equal to actual investment. Otherwise, the actual change in inventories is different from planned: Firms have misestimated their sales.

planned investment (*I*) Those additions to capital stock and inventory that are planned by firms.

actual investment The actual amount of investment that takes place; it includes items such as unplanned changes in inventories.

Behavioral Biases in Saving Behavior

This chapter has described how saving is related to income. Economists have generally assumed that people make their saving decisions rationally, just as they make other decisions about choices in consumption and the labor market. Saving decisions involve thinking about trade-offs between present and future consumption. Recent work in behavioral economics has highlighted the role of psychological biases in saving behavior and has demonstrated that seemingly small changes in the way saving programs are designed can result in big behavioral changes.

Many retirement plans are designed with an opt-in feature. That is, you need to take some action to enroll. Typically, when you begin a job, you need to check yes on the retirement plan enrollment form. Recent work in economics by James Choi of Yale University and Bridget Madrian and Dennis Shea of the University of Chicago suggests that simply changing the enrollment process from the opt-in structure just described to an opt-out system in which people are automatically enrolled unless they check the no box dramatically increases enrollment in retirement pension plans. In one study, the change from an opt-in to an opt-out system increased pension plan enrollment after 3 months of work from 65 percent to 98 percent of workers.

Behavioral economists have administered a number of surveys suggesting that people, on average, think they save too little of their income for retirement. Shlomo Benartzi, from the University of California, Los Angeles, and Richard Thaler, from the University of Chicago, devised a retirement program to try to increase saving rates. Under this plan, called Save More Tomorrow, employees are offered a program that allows them to precommit to save more whenever they get a pay raise. Behavioral economists argue that people find this option attractive because it is easier for them to commit to making sacrifices tomorrow than it is for them to make those sacrifices today. (This is why many people resolve to diet some time in the future but continue to overeat today.) The Save More Tomorrow retirement plans have been put in place in a number of companies, including Vanguard, T. Rowe Price, and TIAA-CREF. Early results suggest dramatic increases in the saving rates of those enrolled, with saving rates quadrupling after 4 years and 4 pay raises.

The Determination of Equilibrium Output (Income)

Thus far, we have described the behavior of firms and households. We now discuss the nature of equilibrium and explain how the economy achieves equilibrium.

A number of definitions of **equilibrium** are used in economics. They all refer to the idea that at equilibrium, there is no tendency for change. In microeconomics, equilibrium is said to exist in a particular market (for example, the market for bananas) at the price for which the quantity demanded is equal to the quantity supplied. At this point, both suppliers and demanders are satisfied. The equilibrium price of a good is the price at which suppliers want to furnish the amount that demanders want to buy.

equilibrium Occurs when there is no tendency for change. In the macroeconomic goods market, equilibrium occurs when planned aggregate expenditure is equal to aggregate output.

planned aggregate expenditure (AE) The total amount the economy plans to spend in a given period. Equal to consumption plus planned investment: $AE \equiv C + I$.

To define equilibrium, we start with a new variable, **planned aggregate expenditure (AE)**. Planned aggregate expenditure is, by definition, consumption plus planned investment:

$$AE \equiv C + I$$

Note that I is planned investment spending only. It does not include any unplanned increases or decreases in inventory. Note also that this is a definition. Aggregate expenditure is always equal to $C + I$, and we write it with the triple equal sign.

The economy is defined to be in equilibrium when aggregate output (Y) is equal to planned aggregate expenditure (AE).

$$\text{Equilibrium: } Y = AE$$

Because AE is, by definition, $C + I$, equilibrium can also be written:

$$\text{Equilibrium: } Y = C + I$$

It will help in understanding the equilibrium concept to consider what happens if the economy is out of equilibrium. First, suppose aggregate output is greater than planned aggregate expenditure:

$$Y > C + I$$

aggregate output $>$ planned aggregate expenditure

When output is greater than planned spending, there is unplanned inventory investment. Firms planned to sell more of their goods than they sold, and the difference shows up as an unplanned increase in inventories.

Next, suppose planned aggregate expenditure is greater than aggregate output:

$$C + I > Y$$

planned aggregate expenditure $>$ aggregate output

When planned spending exceeds output, firms have sold more than they planned to. Inventory investment is smaller than planned. Planned and actual investment are not equal. Only when output is exactly matched by planned spending will there be no unplanned inventory investment. If there is unplanned inventory investment, this will be a state of disequilibrium. The mechanism by which the economy returns to equilibrium will be discussed later. Equilibrium in the goods market is achieved only when aggregate output (Y) and planned aggregate expenditure ($C + I$) are equal, or when actual and planned investment are equal.

Table 8.1 derives a planned aggregate expenditure schedule and shows the point of equilibrium for our numerical example. (Remember, all our calculations are based on $C = 100 + .75Y$.) To determine planned aggregate expenditure, we add consumption spending (C) to planned investment spending (I) at every level of income. Glancing down columns 1 and 4, we see one and only one level at which aggregate output and planned aggregate expenditure are equal: $Y = 500$.

TABLE 8.1 Deriving the Planned Aggregate Expenditure Schedule and Finding Equilibrium. The Figures in Column 2 are Based on the Equation $C = 100 + .75Y$.

(1) Aggregate Output (Income) (Y)	(2) Aggregate Consumption (C)	(3) Planned Investment (I)	(4) Planned Aggregate Expenditure (AE) C + I	(5) Unplanned Inventory Change Y − (C + I)	(6) Equilibrium? (Y = AE?)
100	175	25	200	−100	No
200	250	25	275	−75	No
400	400	25	425	−25	No
500	475	25	500	0	Yes
600	550	25	575	+25	No
800	700	25	725	+75	No
1,000	850	25	875	+125	No

Figure 8.6 illustrates the same equilibrium graphically. Figure 8.6a adds planned investment, constant at 25, to consumption at every level of income. Because planned investment is a constant, the planned aggregate expenditure function is simply the consumption function displaced vertically by that constant amount. Figure 8.6b shows the planned aggregate expenditure function with the 45° line. The 45° line represents all points on the graph where the variables on the horizontal and vertical axes are equal. Any point on the 45° line is a potential equilibrium point. The planned aggregate expenditure function crosses the 45° line at a single point, where $Y = 500$. (The point at which the two lines cross is sometimes called the *Keynesian cross*.) At that point, $Y = C + I$.

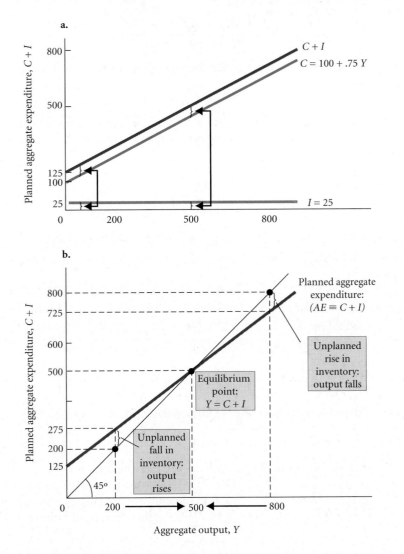

◀ **FIGURE 8.6**

Equilibrium Aggregate Output

Equilibrium occurs when planned aggregate expenditure and aggregate output are equal. Planned aggregate expenditure is the sum of consumption spending and planned investment spending.

Now let us look at some other levels of aggregate output (income). First, consider $Y = 800$. Is this an equilibrium output? Clearly, it is not. At $Y = 800$, planned aggregate expenditure is 725 (see Table 8.1). This amount is less than aggregate output, which is 800. Because output is greater than planned spending, the difference ends up in inventory as unplanned inventory investment. In this case, unplanned inventory investment is 75. In the aggregate, firms have more inventory than desired. As a result, firms have an incentive to change their production plans going forward. In this sense, the economy will not be in equilibrium.

Next, consider $Y = 200$. Is this an equilibrium output? No. At $Y = 200$, planned aggregate expenditure is 275. Planned spending (AE) is greater than output (Y), and there is unplanned inventory disinvestment of 75. Again, firms in the aggregate will experience a different result from what they expected.

At $Y = 200$ and $Y = 800$, planned investment and actual investment are unequal. There is unplanned investment, and the system is out of balance. Only at $Y = 500$, where planned aggregate expenditure and aggregate output are equal, will planned investment equal actual investment.

Finally, let us find the equilibrium level of output (income) algebraically. Recall that we know the following:

$$(1) \ Y = C + I \qquad \text{(equilbrium)}$$
$$(2) \ C = 100 + .75Y \qquad \text{(consumption function)}$$
$$(3) \ I = 25 \qquad \text{(planned investment)}$$

By substituting (2) and (3) into (1), we get:

$$Y = \underbrace{100 + .75Y}_{C} + \underbrace{25.}_{I}$$

There is only one value of Y for which this statement is true, and we can find it by rearranging terms:

$$Y - .75Y = 100 + 25$$
$$Y - .75Y = 125$$
$$.25Y = 125$$
$$Y = \frac{125}{.25} = 500$$

The equilibrium level of output is 500, as shown in Table 8.1 and Figure 8.6.

The Saving/Investment Approach to Equilibrium

Because aggregate income must be saved or spent, by definition, $Y \equiv C + S$, which is an identity. The equilibrium condition is $Y = C + I$, but this is not an identity because it does not hold when we are out of equilibrium.[3] By substituting $C + S$ for Y in the equilibrium condition, we can write:

$$C + S = C + I$$

Because we can subtract C from both sides of this equation, we are left with:

$$S = I$$

Thus, only when planned investment equals saving will there be equilibrium.

Figure 8.7 reproduces the saving schedule derived in Figure 8.4 and the horizontal investment function from Figure 8.5. Notice that $S = I$ at one and only one level of aggregate output, $Y = 500$. At $Y = 500$, $C = 475$ and $I = 25$. In other words, $Y = C + I$; therefore, equilibrium exists.

▶ **FIGURE 8.7 The $S = I$ Approach to Equilibrium**

Aggregate output is equal to planned aggregate expenditure only when saving equals planned investment ($S = I$). Saving and planned investment are equal at $Y = 500$.

[3] It would be an identity if I included unplanned inventory accumulations—in other words, if I were actual investment instead of planned investment.

Adjustment to Equilibrium

We have defined equilibrium and learned how to find it, but we have said nothing about how firms might react to *disequilibrium*. Let us consider the actions firms might take when planned aggregate expenditure exceeds aggregate output (income).

We already know the only way firms can sell more than they produce is by selling some inventory. This means that when planned aggregate expenditure exceeds aggregate output, unplanned inventory reductions have occurred. It seems reasonable to assume that firms will respond to unplanned inventory reductions by increasing output. If firms increase output, income must also increase. (Output and income are two ways of measuring the same thing.) As GM builds more cars, it hires more workers (or pays its existing workforce for working more hours), buys more steel, uses more electricity, and so on. These purchases by GM represent income for the producers of labor, steel, electricity, and so on. When firms try to keep their inventories intact by increasing production, this will generate more income in the economy as a whole. This will lead to more consumption. Remember, when income rises, so does consumption. The adjustment process will continue as long as output (income) is below planned aggregate expenditure. If firms react to unplanned inventory reductions by increasing output, an economy with planned spending greater than output will adjust to equilibrium, with Y higher than before. If planned spending is less than output, there will be unplanned increases in inventories. In this case, firms will respond by reducing output. As output falls, income falls, consumption falls, and so on, until equilibrium is restored, with Y lower than before.

As Figure 8.6 shows, at any level of output above $Y = 500$, such as $Y = 800$, output will fall until it reaches equilibrium at $Y = 500$, and at any level of output below $Y = 500$, such as $Y = 200$, output will rise until it reaches equilibrium at $Y = 500$.[4]

The Multiplier

Now that we know how the equilibrium value of income is determined, we ask: How does the equilibrium level of output change when planned investment changes? If there is a sudden change in planned investment, how will output respond, if it responds at all? Suppose firms in aggregate decide that instead of a desired or planned investment of 25 as in the example we have been using, planned investment rises to 50. What will this do to the level of aggregate output in the economy? We also will see that, the change in equilibrium output is *greater* than the initial change in planned investment. Output changes by a *multiple* of the change in planned investment.

The **multiplier** is defined as the ratio of the change in the equilibrium level of output to a change in some exogenous variable. An **exogenous variable** is a variable that is assumed not to depend on the state of the economy—that is, a variable is exogenous if it does not change in response to changes in the economy. In this chapter, we consider planned investment to be exogenous. This simplifies our analysis and provides a foundation for later discussions.

With planned investment exogenous, we can ask how much the equilibrium level of output changes when planned investment changes. Remember that we are not trying to explain *why* planned investment changes; we are simply asking how much the equilibrium level of output changes when (for whatever reason) planned investment changes. (Beginning in Chapter 12, we will no longer take planned investment as given and will explain how planned investment is determined.)

Consider a sustained increase in planned investment of 25—that is, suppose I increases from 25 to 50 and stays at 50. If equilibrium existed at $I = 25$, an increase in planned investment of 25 will cause a disequilibrium, with planned aggregate expenditure greater than aggregate output by 25. Firms immediately see unplanned reductions in their inventories. As a result, firms begin to increase output.

multiplier The ratio of the change in the equilibrium level of output to a change in some exogenous variable.

exogenous variable A variable that is assumed not to depend on the state of the economy—that is, it does not change when the economy changes.

---

[4] In discussing simple supply and demand equilibrium in Chapters 3 and 4, we saw that when quantity supplied exceeds quantity demanded, the price falls and the quantity supplied declines. Similarly, when quantity demanded exceeds quantity supplied, the price rises and the quantity supplied increases. In the analysis here, we are ignoring potential changes in prices or in the price level and focusing on changes in the level of real output (income). Later, after we have introduced money and the price level into the analysis, prices will be very important. At this stage, however, only aggregate output (income) (Y) adjusts when aggregate expenditure exceeds aggregate output (with inventory falling) or when aggregate output exceeds aggregate expenditure (with inventory rising).

Let us say the increase in planned investment comes from an anticipated increase in travel that leads airlines to purchase more airplanes, car rental companies to increase purchases of automobiles, and bus companies to purchase more buses (all capital goods). The firms experiencing unplanned inventory declines will be automobile manufacturers, bus producers, and aircraft producers—GM, Ford, Boeing, and so on. In response to declining inventories of planes, buses, and cars, these firms will increase output.

Now suppose these firms raise output by the full 25 increase in planned investment. Does this restore equilibrium? No, it does not because when output goes up, people earn more income and a part of that income will be spent. This increases planned aggregate expenditure even further. In other words, an increase in I also leads indirectly to an increase in C. To produce more airplanes, Boeing has to hire more workers or ask its existing employees to work more hours. It also must buy more engines from General Electric, more tires from Goodyear, and so on. Owners of these firms will earn more profits, produce more, hire more workers, and pay out more in wages and salaries. This added income does not vanish into thin air. It is paid to households that spend some of it and save the rest. The added production leads to added income, which leads to added consumption spending.

If planned investment (I) goes up by 25 initially *and is sustained at this higher level*, an increase of output of 25 will *not* restore equilibrium because it generates even more consumption spending (C). People buy more consumer goods. There are unplanned reductions of inventories of basic consumption items—washing machines, food, clothing, and so on—and this prompts other firms to increase output. The cycle starts all over again.

Output and income can rise significantly more than the initial increase in planned investment, but how much and how large is the multiplier? This is answered graphically in Figure 8.8. Assume that the economy is in equilibrium at point A, where equilibrium output is 500. The increase in I of 25 shifts the $AE \equiv C + I$ curve up by 25 because I is higher by 25 at every level of income. The new equilibrium occurs at point B, where the equilibrium level of output is 600. Like point A, point B is on the 45° line and is an equilibrium value. Output (Y) has increased by 100 (600 − 500), or four times the initial increase in planned investment of 25, between point A and point B. The multiplier in this example is 4. At point B, aggregate spending is also higher by 100. If 25 of this additional 100 is investment (I), as we know it is, the remaining 75 is added consumption (C). From point A to point B then, $\Delta Y = 100$, $\Delta I = 25$, and $\Delta C = 75$.

▶ **FIGURE 8.8**

The Multiplier as Seen in the Planned Aggregate Expenditure Diagram

At point A, the economy is in equilibrium at $Y = 500$. When I increases by 25, planned aggregate expenditure is initially greater than aggregate output. As output rises in response, additional consumption is generated, pushing equilibrium output up by a multiple of the initial increase in I. The new equilibrium is found at point B, where $Y = 600$. Equilibrium output has increased by 100 (600 − 500), or *four times* the amount of the increase in planned investment.

Why doesn't the multiplier process go on forever? The answer is that only a fraction of the increase in income is consumed in each round. Successive increases in income become smaller and smaller in each round of the multiplier process, due to leakage as saving, until equilibrium is restored.

The size of the multiplier depends on the slope of the planned aggregate expenditure line. The steeper the slope of this line, the greater the change in output for a given change in investment. When planned investment is fixed, as in our example, the slope of the $AE \equiv C + I$ line is just the marginal propensity to consume ($\Delta C/\Delta Y$). The greater the MPC, the greater the multiplier. This should not be surprising. A large MPC means that consumption increases a great deal when income increases. The more consumption changes, the more output has to change to achieve equilibrium.

The Multiplier Equation

Is there a way to determine the size of the multiplier without using graphic analysis? Yes, there is.

Assume that the market is in equilibrium at an income level of $Y = 500$. Now suppose planned investment (I)—thus, planned aggregate expenditure (AE)—increases and remains higher by 25. Planned aggregate expenditure is greater than output, there is an unplanned inventory reduction, and firms respond by increasing output (income) (Y). This leads to a second round of increases, and so on.

What will restore equilibrium? Look at Figure 8.7 and recall: Planned aggregate expenditure ($AE \equiv C + I$) is not equal to aggregate output (Y) unless $S = I$; the leakage of saving must exactly match the injection of planned investment spending for the economy to be in equilibrium. Recall also that we assumed that planned investment jumps to a new, higher level and stays there; it is a *sustained* increase of 25 in planned investment spending. As income rises, consumption rises and so does saving. Our $S = I$ approach to equilibrium leads us to conclude that equilibrium will be restored only when saving has increased by exactly the amount of the initial increase in I. Otherwise, I will continue to be greater than S and $C + I$ will continue to be greater than Y. (The $S = I$ approach to equilibrium leads to an interesting paradox in the macroeconomy. See the following Economics in Practice, "The Paradox of Thrift.")

It is possible to figure how much Y must increase in response to the additional planned investment before equilibrium will be restored. Y will rise, pulling S up with it until the change in saving is exactly equal to the change in planned investment—that is, until S is again equal to I at its new higher level. Because added saving is a *fraction* of added income (the MPS), the increase in *income* required to restore equilibrium must be a *multiple* of the increase in planned investment.

Recall that the marginal propensity to save (MPS) is the fraction of a change in income that is saved. It is defined as the change in S (ΔS) over the change in income (ΔY):

$$MPS = \frac{\Delta S}{\Delta Y}$$

Because ΔS must be equal to ΔI for equilibrium to be restored, we can substitute ΔI for ΔS and solve:

$$MPS = \frac{\Delta I}{\Delta Y}$$

Therefore,

$$\Delta Y = \Delta I \times \frac{1}{MPS}$$

As you can see, the change in equilibrium income (ΔY) is equal to the initial change in planned investment (ΔI) times $1/MPS$. The multiplier is $1/MPS$:

$$\text{multiplier} \equiv \frac{1}{MPS}$$

Because $MPS + MPC \equiv 1$, $MPS \equiv 1 - MPC$. It follows that the multiplier is equal to

$$\text{multiplier} \equiv \frac{1}{1 - MPC}$$

ECONOMICS IN PRACTICE

The Paradox of Thrift

An interesting paradox can arise when households attempt to increase their saving. What happens if households become concerned about the future and want to save more today to be prepared for hard times tomorrow? If households increase their planned saving, the saving schedule in the graph below shifts upward from S_0 to S_1. The plan to save more is a plan to consume less, and the resulting drop in spending leads to a drop in income. Income drops by a multiple of the initial shift in the saving schedule. Before the increase in saving, equilibrium exists at point A, where $S_0 = I$ and $Y = 500$. Increased saving shifts the equilibrium to point B, the point at which $S_1 = I$. New equilibrium output is 300—a 200 decrease (ΔY) from the initial equilibrium.

By consuming less, households have actually *caused* the hard times about which they were apprehensive. Worse, the new equilibrium finds saving at the same level as it was before consumption dropped (25). In their attempt to save more, households have caused a contraction in output, and thus in income. They end up consuming less, but they have not saved any more.

It should be clear why saving at the new equilibrium is equal to saving at the old equilibrium. Equilibrium requires that saving equals planned investment, and because planned investment is unchanged, saving must remain unchanged for equilibrium to exist. This paradox shows that the interactions among sectors in the economy can be of crucial importance.

The paradox of thrift is "paradoxical" because it contradicts the widely held belief that "a penny saved is a penny earned." This may be true for an individual, but when society as a whole saves more, the result is a drop in income but no increased saving.

Does the paradox of thrift always hold? Recall our assumption that planned investment is fixed. Let us drop this assumption for a moment. If the extra saving that households want to do to ward off hard times is channeled into additional investment through financial markets, there is a shift up in the I schedule. The paradox could then be averted. If investment increases, a new equilibrium can be achieved at a higher level of saving and income. This result, however, depends critically on the existence of a channel through which additional household saving finances additional investment.

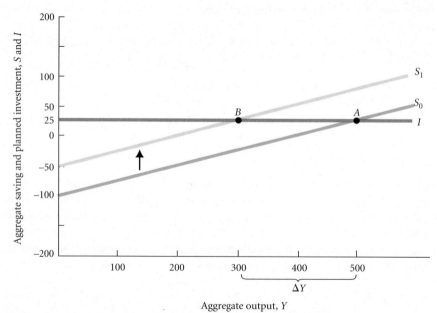

The Paradox of Thrift

An increase in planned saving from S_0 to S_1 causes equilibrium output to decrease from 500 to 300. The decreased consumption that accompanies increased saving leads to a contraction of the economy and to a reduction of income. But at the new equilibrium, saving is the same as it was at the initial equilibrium. Increased efforts to save have caused a drop in income but no overall change in saving.

In our example, the *MPC* is .75; so the *MPS* must equal 1 − .75, or .25. Thus, the multiplier is 1 divided by .25, or 4. The change in the equilibrium level of *Y* is 4 × 25, or 100.[5] Also note that the same analysis holds when planned investment falls. If planned investment falls by a certain amount and is sustained at this lower level, output will fall by a multiple of the reduction in *I*. As the initial shock is felt and firms cut output, they lay people off. The result: Income, and subsequently consumption, falls.

The Size of the Multiplier in the Real World

In considering the size of the multiplier, it is important to realize that the multiplier we derived in this chapter is based on a *very* simplified picture of the economy. First, we have assumed that planned investment is exogenous and does not respond to changes in the economy. Second, we have thus far ignored the role of government, financial markets, and the rest of the world in the macroeconomy. For these reasons, it would be a mistake to move on from this chapter thinking that national income can be increased by $100 billion simply by increasing planned investment spending by $25 billion.

As we relax these assumptions in the following chapters, you will see that most of what we add to make our analysis more realistic has the effect of *reducing* the size of the multiplier. For example:

1. The Appendix to Chapter 9 shows that when tax payments depend on income (as they do in the real world), the size of the multiplier is reduced. As the economy expands, tax payments increase and act as a drag on the economy. The multiplier effect is smaller.
2. We will see in Chapter 12 that planned investment (*I*) is not exogenous; instead, it depends on the interest rate in the economy. This too has the effect of reducing the size of the multiplier.
3. Thus far we have not discussed how the overall price level is determined in the economy. When we do (in Chapter 13), we will see that part of an expansion of the economy is likely to take the form of an increase in the price level instead of an increase in output. When this happens, the size of the multiplier is reduced.
4. The multiplier is also reduced when imports are introduced (in Chapter 20), because some domestic spending leaks into foreign markets.

These juicy tidbits give you something to look forward to as you proceed through the rest of this book. For now, however, it is enough to point out that in reality the size of the multiplier is about 1.4. That is, a sustained increase in exogenous spending of $10 billion into the U.S. economy can be expected to raise real GDP over time by about $14 billion. This is a far cry from the value of 4.0 that we used in this chapter.

Looking Ahead

In this chapter, we took the first step toward understanding how the economy works. We assumed that consumption depends on income, that planned investment is fixed, and that there is equilibrium. We discussed how the economy might adjust back to equilibrium when it is out of equilibrium. We also discussed the effects on equilibrium output from a change in planned investment and derived the multiplier. In the next chapter, we retain these assumptions and add the government to the economy.

---

[5] The multiplier can also be derived algebraically, as the Appendix to this chapter demonstrates.

SUMMARY

THE KEYNESIAN THEORY OF CONSUMPTION *p. 142*

1. Aggregate consumption is assumed to be a function of aggregate income.

2. The *marginal propensity to consume (MPC)* is the fraction of a change in income that is consumed, or spent. The *marginal propensity to save (MPS)* is the fraction of a change in income that is saved. Because all income must be saved or spent, $MPS + MPC \equiv 1$.

PLANNED INVESTMENT *p. 146*

3. Planned investment is assumed to be fixed. Planned investment may differ from actual investment because of unanticipated changes in inventories.

THE DETERMINATION OF EQUILIBRIUM OUTPUT (INCOME) *p. 147*

4. *Planned aggregate expenditure (AE)* equals consumption plus planned investment: $AE \equiv C + I$. *Equilibrium* in the goods market is achieved when planned aggregate expenditure equals aggregate output: $C + I = Y$. This holds if and only if planned investment and actual investment are equal.

5. Because aggregate income must be saved or spent, the equilibrium condition $Y = C + I$ can be rewritten as $C + S = C + I$, or $S = I$. Only when planned investment equals saving will

there be equilibrium. This approach to equilibrium is the *saving/ investment approach* to equilibrium.

6. When planned aggregate expenditure exceeds aggregate output (*income*), there is an unplanned fall in inventories. Firms will increase output. This increased output leads to increased income and even more consumption. This process will continue as long as output (income) is below planned aggregate expenditure. If firms react to unplanned inventory reductions by increasing output, an economy with planned spending greater than output will adjust to a new equilibrium, with Y higher than before.

THE MULTIPLIER *p. 151*

7. Equilibrium output changes by a multiple of the change in planned investment or any other *exogenous variable*. The *multiplier* is $1/MPS$.

8. When households increase their planned saving, income decreases and saving does not change. Saving does not increase because in equilibrium, saving must equal planned investment and planned investment is fixed. If planned investment also increased, this *paradox of thrift* could be averted and a new equilibrium could be achieved at a higher level of saving and income. This result depends on the existence of a channel through which additional household saving finances additional investment.

REVIEW TERMS AND CONCEPTS

actual investment, *p. 146*
aggregate income, *p. 141*
aggregate output, *p. 141*
aggregate output (income) (*Y*), *p. 141*
aggregate saving (*S*), *p. 143*
consumption function, *p. 142*
equilibrium, *p. 147*
exogenous variable, *p. 151*

identity, *p. 143*
marginal propensity to consume (*MPC*), *p. 143*
marginal propensity to save (*MPS*), *p. 143*

multiplier, *p. 151*
planned aggregate expenditure (*AE*), *p. 148*
planned investment (*I*), *p. 146*

1. $S \equiv Y - C$
2. $MPC \equiv$ slope of consumption function $\equiv \dfrac{\Delta C}{\Delta Y}$
3. $MPC + MPS \equiv 1$
4. $AE \equiv C + I$
5. Equilibrium condition: $Y = AE$ or $Y = C + I$
6. Saving/investment approach to equilibrium: $S = I$
7. Multiplier $\equiv \dfrac{1}{MPS} \equiv \dfrac{1}{1 - MPC}$

PROBLEMS

Visit **www.myeconlab.com** to complete the problems marked in orange online. You will receive instant feedback on your answers, tutorial help, and access to additional practice problems.

myeconlab

1. Briefly define the following terms and explain the relationship between them:

MPC . . . . Multiplier
Actual investment . . . . Planned investment
Aggregate expenditure . . . . Real GDP
Aggregate output . . . . Aggregate income

2. Expert econometricians in the Republic of Yuck estimate the following:

Real GNP (Y) . . . . 200 billion Yuck dollars
Planned investment spending . . . . 75 billion Yuck dollars

Yuck is a simple economy with no government, no taxes, and no imports or exports. Yuckers (citizens of Yuck) are creatures of habit. They have a rule that everyone saves exactly 25 percent of income. Assume that planned investment is fixed and remains at 75 billion Yuck dollars.

You are asked by the business editor of the *Weird Herald*, the local newspaper, to predict the economic events of the next few months. By using the data given, can you make a forecast? What is likely to happen to inventories? What is likely to happen to the level of real GDP? Is the economy at an equilibrium? When will things stop changing?

3. Go to www.commerce.gov. Click on "Bureau of Economic Analysis." Click next on "National" and then on the latest GDP release. Look through the report. Which of the components of aggregate expenditure appear to be growing or falling the fastest? What story can you tell about the current economic events from the data?

4. The following questions refer to this table:

AGGREGATE OUTPUT/INCOME	CONSUMPTION	PLANNED INVESTMENT
2,000	2,100	300
2,500	2,500	300
3,000	2,900	300
3,500	3,300	300
4,000	3,700	300
4,500	4,100	300
5,000	4,500	300
5,500	4,900	300

a. At each level of output, calculate saving. At each level of output, calculate unplanned investment (inventory change). What is likely to happen to aggregate output if the economy produces at each of the levels indicated? What is the equilibrium level of output?

b. Over each range of income (2,000 to 2,500, 2,500 to 3,000, and so on), calculate the marginal propensity to consume. Calculate the marginal propensity to save. What is the multiplier?

c. By assuming there is no change in the level of the *MPC* and the *MPS* and planned investment jumps by 200 and is sustained at that higher level, recompute the table. What is the new equilibrium level of *Y*? Is this consistent with what you compute using the multiplier?

5. Explain the multiplier intuitively. Why is it that an increase in planned investment of $100 raises equilibrium output by more than $100? Why is the effect on equilibrium output finite? How do we know that the multiplier is 1/*MPS*?

6. You are given the following data concerning Freedonia, a legendary country:
(1) Consumption function: $C = 200 + 0.8Y$
(2) Investment function: $I = 100$
(3) $AE \equiv C + I$
(4) $AE = Y$

a. What is the marginal propensity to consume in Freedonia, and what is the marginal propensity to save?

b. Graph equations (3) and (4) and solve for equilibrium income.

c. Suppose equation (2) is changed to (2′) $I = 110$. What is the new equilibrium level of income? By how much does the $10 increase in planned investment change equilibrium income? What is the value of the multiplier?

d. Calculate the saving function for Freedonia. Plot this saving function on a graph with equation (2). Explain why the equilibrium income in this graph must be the same as in part b.

7. This chapter argued that saving and spending behavior depended in part on wealth (accumulated savings and inheritance), but our simple model does not incorporate this effect. Consider the following model of a very simple economy:

$$C = 10 + .75Y + .04W$$
$$I = 100$$
$$W = 1,000$$
$$Y = C + I$$
$$S = Y - C$$

If you assume that wealth (*W*) and investment (*I*) remain constant (we are ignoring the fact that saving adds to the stock of wealth), what are the equilibrium levels of GDP (*Y*), consumption (*C*), and saving (*S*)? Now suppose that wealth increases by 50 percent to 1,500. Recalculate the equilibrium levels of *Y, C,* and *S*. What impact does wealth accumulation have on GDP? Many were concerned with the very large increase in stock values in the late 1990s. Does this present a problem for the economy? Explain.

8. You learned earlier that expenditures and income should always be equal. In this chapter, you learned that *AE* and aggregate output (income) can be different. Is there an inconsistency here? Explain.

9. [Related to the *Economics in Practice* on p. 147] The *Economics in Practice* describes some of the difficulties that households have with regard to decisions involving trade-offs between the present and the future. Explain briefly how the problem of global warming and the problem of adequate household saving are similar. Describe ways in which the concept of opportunity costs can be used to frame these two problems. What barriers might prevent households or societies from achieving satisfactory outcomes?

10. [Related to the *Economics in Practice* on p. 154] If households decide to save more, saving in the aggregate may fall. Explain this in words.

APPENDIX

DERIVING THE MULTIPLIER ALGEBRAICALLY

In addition to deriving the multiplier using the simple substitution we used in the chapter, we can also derive the formula for the multiplier by using simple algebra.

Recall that our consumption function is:

$$C = a + bY$$

where b is the marginal propensity to consume. In equilibrium:

$$Y = C + I$$

Now we solve these two equations for Y in terms of I. By substituting the first equation into the second, we get:

$$Y = \underbrace{a + bY}_{C} + I$$

This equation can be rearranged to yield:

$$Y - bY = a + I$$
$$Y(1 - b) = a + I$$

We can then solve for Y in terms of I by dividing through by $(1 - b)$:

$$Y = (a + I)\left(\frac{1}{1 - b}\right)$$

Now look carefully at this expression and think about increasing I by some amount, ΔI, with a held constant. If I increases by ΔI, income will increase by

$$\Delta Y = \Delta I \times \frac{1}{1 - b}$$

Because $b \equiv MPC$, the expression becomes

$$\Delta Y = \Delta I \times \frac{1}{1 - MPC}$$

The multiplier is

$$\frac{1}{1 - MPC}$$

Finally, because $MPS + MPC \equiv 1$, MPS is equal to $1 - MPC$, making the alternative expression for the multiplier $1/MPS$, just as we saw in this chapter.

The Government and Fiscal Policy

9

Nothing in macroeconomics or microeconomics arouses as much controversy as the role of government in the economy.

In microeconomics, the active presence of government in regulating competition, providing roads and education, and redistributing income is applauded by those who believe a free market simply does not work well when left to its own devices. Opponents of government intervention say it is the government, not the market, that performs badly. They say bureaucracy and inefficiency could be eliminated or reduced if the government played a smaller role in the economy.

In macroeconomics, the debate over what the government can and should do has a similar flavor, although the issues are somewhat different. At one end of the spectrum are the Keynesians and their intellectual descendants who believe that the macroeconomy is likely to fluctuate too much if left on its own and that the government should smooth out fluctuations in the business cycle. These ideas can be traced to Keynes's analysis in *The General Theory*, which suggests that governments can use their taxing and spending powers to increase aggregate expenditure (and thereby stimulate aggregate output) in recessions or depressions. At the other end of the spectrum are those who claim that government spending is incapable of stabilizing the economy, or worse, is destabilizing and harmful.

Perhaps the one thing most people can agree on is that, like it or not, governments are important actors in the economies of virtually all countries. For this reason alone, it is worth our while to analyze the way government influences the functioning of the macroeconomy.

The government has a variety of powers—including regulating firms' entry into and exit from an industry, setting standards for product quality, setting minimum wage levels, and regulating the disclosure of information—but in macroeconomics, we study a government with general but limited powers. Specifically, government can affect the macroeconomy through two policy channels: fiscal policy and monetary policy. **Fiscal policy**, the focus of this chapter, refers to the government's spending and taxing behavior—in other words, its budget policy. (The word *fiscal* comes from the root *fisc*, which refers to the "treasury" of a government.) Fiscal policy is generally divided into three categories: (1) policies concerning government purchases of goods and services, (2) policies concerning taxes, and (3) policies concerning transfer payments (such as unemployment compensation, Social Security benefits, welfare payments, and veterans' benefits) to households. **Monetary policy**, which we consider in the next two chapters, refers to the behavior of the nation's central bank, the Federal Reserve, concerning the nation's money supply.

fiscal policy The government's spending and taxing policies.

monetary policy The behavior of the Federal Reserve concerning the nation's money supply.

discretionary fiscal policy Changes in taxes or spending that are the result of deliberate changes in government policy.

net taxes (T) Taxes paid by firms and households to the government minus transfer payments made to households by the government.

disposable, *or* **after-tax, income (Y_d)** Total income minus net taxes: Y − T.

Government in the Economy

Given the scope and power of local, state, and federal governments, there are some matters over which they exert great control and some matters beyond their control. We need to distinguish between variables that a government controls directly and variables that are a consequence of government decisions *combined with the state of the economy.*

For example, tax rates are controlled by the government. By law, Congress has the authority to decide who and what should be taxed and at what rate. Tax *revenue,* on the other hand, is not subject to complete control by the government. Revenue from the personal income tax system depends on personal tax rates (which Congress sets) *and* on the income of the household sector (which depends on many factors not under direct government control, such as how much households decide to work). Revenue from the corporate profits tax depends on both corporate profits tax rates and the size of corporate profits. The government controls corporate tax rates but not the size of corporate profits.

Some government spending also depends on government decisions and on the state of the economy. For example, in the United States, the unemployment insurance program pays benefits to unemployed people. When the economy goes into a recession, the number of unemployed workers increases and so does the level of government unemployment insurance payments.

Because taxes and spending often go up or down in response to changes in the economy instead of as the result of deliberate decisions by policy makers, we will occasionally use **discretionary fiscal policy** to refer to changes in taxes or spending that are the result of deliberate changes in government policy.

Government Purchases (G), Net Taxes (T), and Disposable Income (Y_d)

We now add the government to the simple economy in Chapter 8. To keep things simple, we will combine two government activities—the collection of taxes and the payment of transfer payments—into a category we call **net taxes (T)**. Specifically, net taxes are equal to the tax payments made to the government by firms and households minus transfer payments made to households by the government. The other variable we will consider is government purchases of goods and services (G).

Our earlier discussions of household consumption did not take taxes into account. We assumed that all the income generated in the economy was spent or saved by households. When we take into account the role of government, as Figure 9.1 does, we see that as income (Y) flows toward households, the government takes income from households in the form of net taxes (T). The income that ultimately gets to households is called **disposable, or after-tax, income (Y_d)**:

$$\text{disposable income} \equiv \text{total income} - \text{net taxes}$$
$$Y_d \equiv Y - T$$

Y_d excludes taxes paid by households and includes transfer payments made to households by the government. For now, we are assuming that T does not depend on Y—that is, net taxes do not depend on income. This assumption is relaxed in Appendix B to this chapter. Taxes that do not depend on income are sometimes called *lump-sum taxes.*

As Figure 9.1 shows, the disposable income (Y_d) of households must end up as either consumption (C) or saving (S). Thus,

$$Y_d \equiv C + S$$

This equation is an identity—something that is always true.

Because disposable income is aggregate income (Y) minus net taxes (T), we can write another identity:

$$Y - T \equiv C + S$$

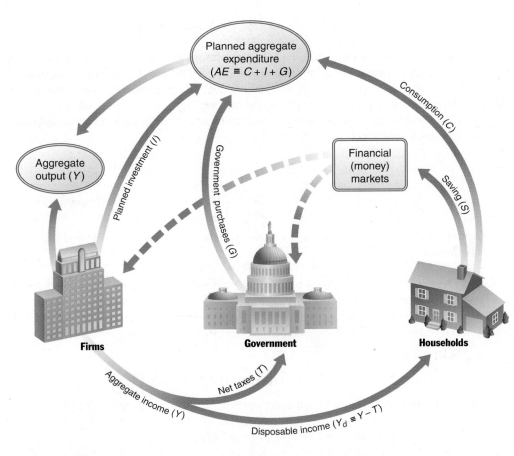

Adding Net Taxes (T) and Government Purchases (G) to the Circular Flow of Income

By adding T to both sides:

$$Y \equiv C + S + T$$

This identity says that aggregate income gets cut into three pieces. Government takes a slice (net taxes, T), and then households divide the rest between consumption (C) and saving (S).

Because governments spend money on goods and services, we need to expand our definition of planned aggregate expenditure. Planned aggregate expenditure (AE) is the sum of consumption spending by households (C), planned investment by business firms (I), *and* government purchases of goods and services (G).

$$AE \equiv C + I + G$$

A government's **budget deficit** is the difference between what it spends (G) and what it collects in taxes (T) in a given period:

$$\text{budget deficit} \equiv G - T$$

If G exceeds T, the government must borrow from the public to finance the deficit. It does so by selling Treasury bonds and bills (more on this later). In this case, a part of household saving (S) goes to the government. The dashed lines in Figure 9.1 mean that some S goes to firms to finance investment projects and some goes to the government to finance its deficit. If G is less than T, which means that the government is spending less than it is collecting in taxes, the government is running a *surplus*. A budget surplus is simply a negative budget deficit.

budget deficit The difference between what a government spends and what it collects in taxes in a given period: $G - T$.

Adding Taxes to the Consumption Function

In Chapter 8, we assumed that aggregate consumption (C) depends on aggregate income (Y), and for the sake of illustration, we used a specific linear consumption function:

$$C = a + bY$$

where b is the marginal propensity to consume. We need to modify this consumption function because we have added government to the economy. With taxes a part of the picture, it makes sense to assume that disposable income (Y_d), instead of before-tax income (Y), determines consumption behavior. If you earn a million dollars but have to pay $950,000 in taxes, you have no more disposable income than someone who earns only $50,000 but pays no taxes. What you have available for spending on current consumption is your disposable income, not your before-tax income.

To modify our aggregate consumption function to incorporate disposable income instead of before-tax income, instead of $C = a + bY$, we write

$$C = a + bY_d$$

or

$$C = a + b(Y - T)$$

Our consumption function now has consumption depending on disposable income instead of before-tax income.

Planned Investment   What about planned investment? The government can affect investment behavior through its tax treatment of depreciation and other tax policies. Investment may also vary with economic conditions and interest rates, as we will see later. For our present purposes, however, we continue to assume that planned investment (I) is fixed.

The Determination of Equilibrium Output (Income)

We know from Chapter 8 that equilibrium occurs where $Y = AE$—that is, where aggregate output equals planned aggregate expenditure. Remember that planned aggregate expenditure in an economy with a government is $AE \equiv C + I + G$, so equilibrium is

$$Y = C + I + G$$

The equilibrium analysis in Chapter 8 applies here also. If output (Y) exceeds planned aggregate expenditure $(C + I + G)$, there will be an unplanned increase in inventories—actual investment will exceed planned investment. Conversely, if $C + I + G$ exceeds Y, there will be an unplanned decrease in inventories.

An example will illustrate the government's effect on the macroeconomy and the equilibrium condition. First, our consumption function, $C = 100 + .75Y$ before we introduced the government sector, now becomes

$$C = 100 + .75Y_d$$

or

$$C = 100 + .75(Y - T)$$

Second, we assume that G is 100 and T is 100.[1] In other words, the government is running a balanced budget, financing all of its spending with taxes. Third, we assume that planned investment (I) is 100.

Table 9.1 calculates planned aggregate expenditure at several levels of disposable income. For example, at $Y = 500$, disposable income is $Y - T$, or 400. Therefore, $C = 100 + .75(400) = 400$. Assuming that I is fixed at 100 and assuming that G is fixed at 100, planned aggregate expenditure is 600 ($C + I + G = 400 + 100 + 100$). Because output (Y) is only 500, planned spending is greater than output by 100. As a result, there is an unplanned inventory decrease of 100, giving firms an incentive to raise output. Thus, output of 500 is below equilibrium.

---

[1] As we pointed out earlier, the government does not have complete control over tax revenues and transfer payments. We ignore this problem here, however, and set T, tax revenues minus transfers, at a fixed amount. Things will become more realistic later in this chapter and in Appendix B.

TABLE 9.1 Finding Equilibrium for $I = 100$, $G = 100$, and $T = 100$

(1) Output (Income) Y	(2) Net Taxes T	(3) Disposable Income $Y_d \equiv Y - T$	(4) Consumption Spending $C = 100 + .75 Y_d$	(5) Saving S $Y_d - C$	(6) Planned Investment Spending I	(7) Government Purchases G	(8) Planned Aggregate Expenditure $C + I + G$	(9) Unplanned Inventory Change $Y - (C + I + G)$	(10) Adjustment to Disequilibrium
300	100	200	250	−50	100	100	450	−150	Output ↑
500	100	400	400	0	100	100	600	−100	Output ↑
700	100	600	550	50	100	100	750	−50	Output ↑
900	100	800	700	100	100	100	900	0	Equilibrium
1,100	100	1,000	850	150	100	100	1,050	+50	Output ↓
1,300	100	1,200	1,000	200	100	100	1,200	+100	Output ↓
1,500	100	1,400	1,150	250	100	100	1,350	+150	Output ↓

If $Y = 1,300$, then $Y_d = 1,200$, $C = 1,000$, and planned aggregate expenditure is 1,200. Here planned spending is *less* than output, there will be an unplanned inventory increase of 100, and firms have an incentive to cut back output. Thus, output of 1,300 is above equilibrium. Only when output is 900 are output and planned aggregate expenditure equal, and only at $Y = 900$ does equilibrium exist.

In Figure 9.2, we derive the same equilibrium level of output graphically. First, the consumption function is drawn, taking into account net taxes of 100. The old function was $C = 100 + .75Y$. The new function is $C = 100 + .75(Y - T)$ or $C = 100 + .75(Y - 100)$, rewritten as $C = 100 + .75Y - 75$, or $C = 25 + .75Y$. For example, consumption at an income of zero is 25 ($C = 25 + .75Y = 25 + .75(0) = 25$). The marginal propensity to consume has not changed—we assume that it remains .75. Note that the consumption function in Figure 9.2 plots the points in columns 1 and 4 of Table 9.1.

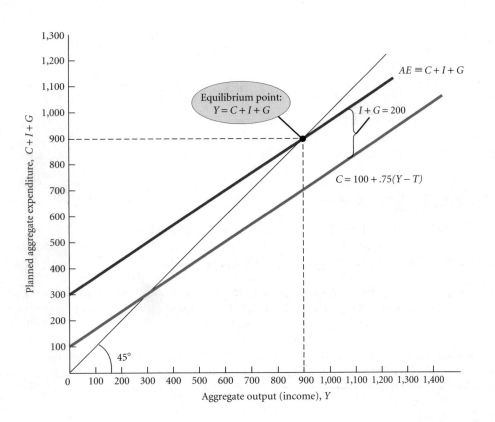

◀ **FIGURE 9.2**

Finding Equilibrium Output/Income Graphically

Because G and I are both fixed at 100, the aggregate expenditure function is the new consumption function displaced upward by $I + G = 200$. Equilibrium occurs at $Y = C + I + G = 900$.

Planned aggregate expenditure, recall, adds planned investment to consumption. Now in addition to 100 in investment, we have government purchases of 100. Because I and G are constant at 100 each at all levels of income, we add $I + G = 200$ to consumption at every level of income. The result is the new AE curve. This curve is just a plot of the points in columns 1 and 8 of Table 9.1. The 45° line helps us find the equilibrium level of real output, which, we already know, is 900. If you examine any level of output above or below 900, you will find disequilibrium. Look, for example, at $Y = 500$ on the graph. At this level, planned aggregate expenditure is 600, but output is only 500. Inventories will fall below what was planned, and firms will have an incentive to increase output.

The Saving/Investment Approach to Equilibrium   As in the last chapter, we can also examine equilibrium using the saving/investment approach. Look at the circular flow of income in Figure 9.1. The government takes out net taxes (T) from the flow of income—a leakage—and households save (S) some of their income—also a leakage from the flow of income. The planned spending injections are government purchases (G) and planned investment (I). If leakages ($S + T$) equal planned injections ($I + G$), there is equilibrium:

> saving/investment approach to equilibrium: $S + T = I + G$

To derive this, we know that in equilibrium, aggregate output (income) (Y) equals planned aggregate expenditure (AE). By definition, AE equals $C + I + G$; and by definition, Y equals $C + S + T$. Therefore, at equilibrium

$$C + S + T = C + I + G$$

Subtracting C from both sides leaves:

$$S + T = I + G$$

Note that equilibrium does *not* require that $G = T$ (a balanced government budget) or that $S = I$. It is only necessary that the sum of S and T equals the sum of I and G.

Column 5 of Table 9.1 calculates aggregate saving by subtracting consumption from disposal income at every level of disposable income ($S \equiv Y_d - C$). Because I and G are fixed, $I + G$ equals 200 at every level of income. Using the table to add saving and taxes ($S + T$), we see that $S + T$ equals 200 only at $Y = 900$. Thus, the equilibrium level of output (income) is 900, the same answer we arrived at through numerical and graphic analysis.

Fiscal Policy at Work: Multiplier Effects

You can see from Figure 9.2 that if the government were able to change the levels of either G or T, it would be able to change the equilibrium level of output (income). At this point, we are assuming that the government controls G and T. In this section, we will review three multipliers:

- Government spending multiplier
- Tax multiplier
- Balanced-budget multiplier

The Government Spending Multiplier

Suppose you are the chief economic adviser to the president and the economy is sitting at the equilibrium output pictured in Figure 9.2. Output and income are 900, and the government is currently buying 100 worth of goods and services each year and is financing them with 100 in taxes. The budget is balanced. In addition, firms are investing (producing capital goods) 100. The president calls you into the Oval Office and says, "Unemployment is too high. We need to lower unemployment by increasing output and income." After some research, you determine that an acceptable unemployment rate can be achieved only if aggregate output increases to 1,100.

You now need to determine how the government can use taxing and spending policy—fiscal policy—to increase the equilibrium level of national output. Suppose the president has let it be known that taxes must remain at present levels—Congress just passed a major tax reform package—so adjusting T is out of the question for several years. That leaves you with G. Your only option is to increase government spending while holding taxes constant.

To increase spending without raising taxes (which provides the government with revenue to spend), the government must borrow. When G is bigger than T, the government runs a deficit and the difference between G and T must be borrowed. For the moment, we will ignore the possible effect of the deficit and focus only on the effect of a higher G with T constant.

Meanwhile, the president is awaiting your answer. How much of an increase in spending would be required to generate an increase of 200 in the equilibrium level of output, pushing it from 900 to 1,100 and reducing unemployment to the president's acceptable level? You might be tempted to say that because we need to increase income by 200 (1,100 − 900), we should increase government spending by the same amount—but what will happen? The increased government spending will throw the economy out of equilibrium. Because G is a component of aggregate spending, planned aggregate expenditure will increase by 200. Planned spending will be greater than output, inventories will be lower than planned, and firms will have an incentive to increase output. Suppose output rises by the desired 200. You might think, "We increased spending by 200 and output by 200, so equilibrium is restored."

There is more to the story than this. The moment output rises, the economy is generating more income. This was the desired effect: the creation of more employment. The newly employed workers are also consumers, and some of their income gets spent. With higher consumption spending, planned spending will be greater than output, inventories will be lower than planned, and firms will raise output (and thus raise income) again. This time firms are responding to the new consumption spending. Already, total income is over 1,100.

This story should sound familiar. It is the multiplier in action. Although this time it is government spending (G) that is changed rather than planned investment (I), the effect is the same as the multiplier effect we described in Chapter 8. An increase in government spending has the same impact on the equilibrium level of output and income as an increase in planned investment. A dollar of extra spending from either G or I is identical with respect to its impact on equilibrium output. The equation for the government spending multiplier is the same as the equation for the multiplier for a change in planned investment.

$$\text{government spending multiplier} \equiv \frac{1}{MPS}$$

We derive the government spending multiplier algebraically in Appendix A to this chapter.

Formally, the **government spending multiplier** is defined as the ratio of the change in the equilibrium level of output to a change in government spending. This is the same definition we used in the previous chapter, but now the autonomous variable is government spending instead of planned investment.

Remember that we were thinking of increasing government spending (G) by 200. We can use the multiplier analysis to see what the new equilibrium level of Y would be for an increase in G of 200. The multiplier in our example is 4. (Because b—the MPC—is .75, the MPS must be 1 − .75 = .25; and 1/.25 = 4.) Thus, Y will increase by 800 (4 × 200). Because the initial level of Y was 900, the new equilibrium level of Y is 900 + 800 = 1,700 when G is increased by 200.

The level of 1,700 is much larger than the level of 1,100 that we calculated as being necessary to lower unemployment to the desired level. Let us back up then. If we want Y to increase by 200 and if the multiplier is 4, we need G to increase by only 200/4 = 50. If G changes by 50, the equilibrium level of Y will change by 200 and the new value of Y will be 1,100 (900 + 200), as desired.

Looking at Table 9.2, we can check our answer to make sure it is an equilibrium. Look first at the old equilibrium of 900. When government purchases (G) were 100, aggregate output (income) was equal to planned aggregate expenditure ($AE \equiv C + I + G$) at $Y = 900$. Now G has increased to 150. At $Y = 900$, ($C + I + G$) is greater than Y, there is an unplanned fall in inventories, and output will rise but by how much? The multiplier told us that equilibrium income

government spending multiplier The ratio of the change in the equilibrium level of output to a change in government spending.

would rise by four times the 50 change in G. Y should rise by $4 \times 50 = 200$, from 900 to 1,100, before equilibrium is restored. Let us check. If $Y = 1,100$, consumption is $C = 100 + .75Y_d = 100 + .75(1,000) = 850$. Because I equals 100 and G now equals 100 (the original level of G) + 50 (the additional G brought about by the fiscal policy change) = 150, $C + I + G = 850 + 100 + 150 = 1,100$. $Y = AE$, and the economy is in equilibrium.

TABLE 9.2 Finding Equilibrium After a Government Spending Increase of 50 (G Has Increased from 100 in Table 9.1 to 150 Here)

(1) Output (Income) Y	(2) Net Taxes T	(3) Disposable Income $Y_d \equiv Y - T$	(4) Consumption Spending $C = 100 + .75\,Y_d$	(5) Saving S $Y_d - C$	(6) Planned Investment Spending I	(7) Government Purchases G	(8) Planned Aggregate Expenditure $C + I + G$	(9) Unplanned Inventory Change $Y - (C + I + G)$	(10) Adjustment to Disequilibrium
300	100	200	250	−50	100	150	500	−200	Output ↑
500	100	400	400	0	100	150	650	−150	Output ↑
700	100	600	550	50	100	150	800	−100	Output ↑
900	100	800	700	100	100	150	950	−50	Output ↑
1,100	100	1,000	850	150	100	150	1,100	0	Equilibrium
1,300	100	1,200	1,000	200	100	150	1,250	+50	Output ↓

The graphic solution to the president's problem is presented in Figure 9.3. An increase of 50 in G shifts the planned aggregate expenditure function up by 50. The new equilibrium income occurs where the new AE line (AE_2) crosses the 45° line, at $Y = 1,100$.

▶ **FIGURE 9.3**

The Government Spending Multiplier

Increasing government spending by 50 shifts the AE function up by 50. As Y rises in response, additional consumption is generated. Overall, the equilibrium level of Y increases by 200, from 900 to 1,100.

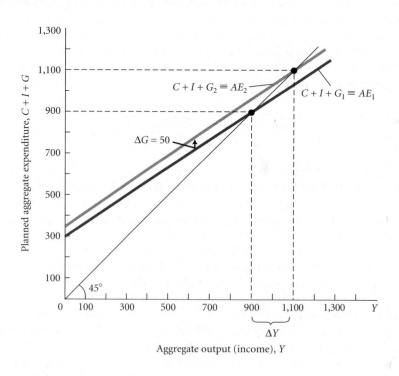

The Tax Multiplier

Remember that fiscal policy comprises policies concerning government spending *and* policies concerning taxation. To see what effect a change in tax policy has on the economy, imagine the following. You are still chief economic adviser to the president, but now you are instructed to devise a plan to reduce unemployment to an acceptable level *without* increasing the level of government spending (*G*), you decide to cut taxes and maintain the current level of spending. A tax cut increases disposable income, which is likely to lead to added consumption spending. (Remember our general rule that increased income leads to increased consumption.) Would the decrease in taxes affect aggregate output (income) the same as an increase in G?

A decrease in taxes would increase income. The government spends no less than it did before the tax cut, and households find that they have a larger after-tax (or disposable) income than they had before. This leads to an increase in consumption. Planned aggregate expenditure will increase, which will lead to inventories being lower than planned, which will lead to a rise in output.\When output rises, more workers will be employed and more income will be generated, causing a second-round increase in consumption, and so on. Thus, income will increase by a multiple of the decrease in taxes, but there is a "wrinkle." The multiplier for a change in taxes is *not the same* as the multiplier for a change in government spending. Why does the **tax multiplier**—the ratio of change in the equilibrium level of output to a change in taxes—differ from the spending multiplier? To answer that question, we need to compare the ways in which a tax cut and a spending increase work their way through the economy.

tax multiplier The ratio of change in the equilibrium level of output to a change in taxes.

Look at Figure 9.1 on p. 161. When the government increases spending, there is an immediate and direct impact on the economy's *total* spending. Because G is a component of planned aggregate expenditure, an increase in G leads to a dollar-for-dollar increase in planned aggregate expenditure. When taxes are cut, there is no direct impact on spending. Taxes enter the picture only because they have an effect on the household's disposable income, which influences household's consumption (which is part of total spending). As Figure 9.1 shows, the tax cut flows through households before affecting aggregate expenditure.

Let us assume that the government decides to cut taxes by $1. By how much would spending increase? We already know the answer. The marginal propensity to consume (MPC) tells us how much consumption spending changes when disposable income changes. In the example running through this chapter, the marginal propensity to consume out of disposable income is .75. This means that if households' after-tax incomes rise by $1.00, they will increase their consumption not by the full $1.00, but by only $0.75.[2]

In summary, when government spending increases by $1, planned aggregate expenditure increases initially by the full amount of the rise in G, or $1. When taxes are cut, however, the initial increase in planned aggregate expenditure is only the MPC times the change in taxes. Because the initial increase in planned aggregate expenditure is smaller for a tax cut than for a government spending increase, the final effect on the equilibrium level of income will be smaller.

We figure the size of the tax multiplier in the same way we derived the multiplier for an increase in investment and an increase in government purchases. The final change in the equilibrium level of output (income) (Y) is

$$\Delta Y = (\text{initial increase in aggregate expenditure}) \times \left(\frac{1}{MPS} \right)$$

Because the initial change in aggregate expenditure caused by a tax change of ΔT is ($-\Delta T \times MPC$), we can solve for the tax multiplier by substitution:

$$\Delta Y = (-\Delta T \times MPC) \times \left(\frac{1}{MPS} \right) = -\Delta T \times \left(\frac{MPC}{MPS} \right)$$

Because a tax cut will cause an *increase* in consumption expenditures and output and a tax increase will cause a *reduction* in consumption expenditures and output, the tax multiplier is a negative multiplier:

$$\text{tax multiplier} \equiv -\left(\frac{MPC}{MPS} \right)$$

We derive the tax multiplier algebraically in Appendix A to this chapter.

---

[2] What happens to the other $0.25? Remember that whatever households do not consume is, by definition, saved. The other $0.25 thus gets allocated to saving.

If the *MPC* is .75, as in our example, the multiplier is −.75/.25 = −3. A tax cut of 100 will increase the equilibrium level of output by −100 × −3 = 300. This is very different from the effect of our government spending multiplier of 4. Under those same conditions, a 100 increase in *G* will increase the equilibrium level of output by 400 (100 × 4).

The Balanced-Budget Multiplier

We have now discussed (1) changing government spending with no change in taxes and (2) changing taxes with no change in government spending. What if government spending and taxes are increased by the same amount? That is, what if the government decides to pay for its extra spending by increasing taxes by the same amount? The government's budget deficit would not change because the increase in expenditures would be matched by an increase in tax income.

You might think in this case that equal increases in government spending and taxes have no effect on equilibrium income. After all, the extra government spending equals the extra amount of tax revenues collected by the government. This is not so. Take, for example, a government spending increase of $40 billion. We know from the preceding analysis that an increase in *G* of 40, with taxes (*T*) held constant, should increase the equilibrium level of income by 40 × the government spending multiplier. The multiplier is 1/*MPS* or 1/.25 = 4. The equilibrium level of income should rise by 160 (40 × 4).

Now suppose that instead of keeping tax revenues constant, we finance the 40 increase in government spending with an equal increase in taxes so as to maintain a balanced budget. What happens to aggregate spending as a result of the rise in *G* and the rise in *T*? There are two initial effects. First, government spending rises by 40. This effect is direct, immediate, and positive. Now the government also collects 40 more in taxes. The tax increase has a *negative* impact on overall spending in the economy, but it does not fully offset the increase in government spending.

The final impact of a tax increase on aggregate expenditure depends on how households respond to it. The only thing we know about household behavior so far is that households spend 75 percent of their added income and save 25 percent. We know that when disposable income falls, both consumption and saving are reduced. A tax *increase* of 40 reduces disposable income by 40, and that means consumption falls by 40 × *MPC*. Because *MPC* = .75, consumption falls by 30 (40 × .75). The net result in the beginning is that government spending rises by 40 and consumption spending falls by 30. Aggregate expenditure increases by 10 right after the simultaneous balanced-budget increases in *G* and *T*.

So a balanced-budget increase in *G* and *T* will raise output, but by how much? How large is this **balanced-budget multiplier**? The answer may surprise you:

balanced-budget multiplier The ratio of change in the equilibrium level of output to a change in government spending where the change in government spending is balanced by a change in taxes so as not to create any deficit. The balanced-budget multiplier is equal to 1: The change in *Y* resulting from the change in *G* and the equal change in *T* are exactly the same size as the initial change in *G* or *T*.

> balanced-budget multiplier ≡ 1

Let us combine what we know about the tax multiplier and the government spending multiplier to explain this. To find the final effect of a simultaneous increase in government spending and increase in net taxes, we need to add the multiplier effects of the two. The government spending multiplier is 1/*MPS*. The tax multiplier is −*MPC*/*MPS*. Their sum is (1/*MPS*) + (−*MPC*/*MPS*) ≡ (1 − *MPC*)/*MPS*. Because *MPC* + *MPS* ≡ 1, 1 − *MPC* ≡ *MPS*. This means that (1 − *MPC*)/*MPS* ≡ *MPS*/*MPS* ≡ 1. (We also derive the balanced-budget multiplier in Appendix A to this chapter.)

Returning to our example, recall that by using the government spending multiplier, a 40 increase in *G* would *raise* output at equilibrium by 160 (40 × the government spending multiplier of 4). By using the tax multiplier, we know that a tax hike of 40 will *reduce* the equilibrium level of output by 120 (40 × the tax multiplier, −3). The net effect is 160 minus 120, or 40. It should be clear then that the effect on equilibrium *Y* is equal to the balanced increase in *G* and *T*. In other words, the net increase in the equilibrium level of *Y* resulting from the change in *G* and the change in *T* are exactly the size of the initial change in *G* or *T*.

If the president wanted to raise *Y* by 200 without increasing the deficit, a simultaneous increase in *G* and *T* of 200 would do it. To see why, look at the numbers in Table 9.3. In Table 9.1, we saw an equilibrium level of output at 900. With both *G* and *T* up by 200, the new equilibrium is 1,100—higher by 200. At no other level of *Y* do we find (*C* + *I* + *G*) = *Y*. An increase in government spending has a direct initial effect on planned aggregate expenditure; a tax increase does not. The initial effect of the tax increase is that households cut consumption by the MPC times the change in taxes. This change in consumption is less than the change in taxes because the MPC is less than 1. The positive stimulus from the government spending increase is thus greater than the negative stimulus from the tax increase. The net effect is that the balanced-budget multiplier is 1.

TABLE 9.3 Finding Equilibrium After a Balanced-Budget Increase in G and T of 200 Each (Both G and T Have Increased from 100 in Table 9.1 to 300 Here)

(1) Output (Income) Y	(2) Net Taxes T	(3) Disposable Income $Y_d \equiv Y - T$	(4) Consumption Spending $C = 100 + .75\,Y_d$	(5) Planned Investment Spending I	(6) Government Purchases G	(7) Planned Aggregate Expenditure $C + I + G$	(8) Unplanned Inventory Change $Y - (C + I + G)$	(9) Adjustment to Disequilibrium
500	300	200	250	100	300	650	−150	Output ↑
700	300	400	400	100	300	800	−100	Output ↑
900	300	600	550	100	300	950	−50	Output ↑
1,100	300	800	700	100	300	1,100	0	Equilibrium
1,300	300	1,000	850	100	300	1,250	+50	Output ↓
1,500	300	1,200	1,000	100	300	1,400	+100	Output ↓

Table 9.4 summarizes everything we have said about fiscal policy multipliers.

TABLE 9.4 Summary of Fiscal Policy Multipliers

	Policy Stimulus	Multiplier	Final Impact on Equilibrium Y
Government spending multiplier	Increase or decrease in the level of government purchases: ΔG	$\dfrac{1}{MPS}$	$\Delta G \times \dfrac{1}{MPS}$
Tax multiplier	Increase or decrease in the level of net taxes: ΔT	$\dfrac{-MPC}{MPS}$	$\Delta T \times \dfrac{-MPC}{MPS}$
Balanced-budget multiplier	Simultaneous balanced-budget increase or decrease in the level of government purchases and net taxes: $\Delta G = \Delta T$	1	ΔG

A Warning Although we have added government, the story told about the multiplier is still incomplete and oversimplified. For example, we have been treating net taxes (T) as a lump-sum, fixed amount, whereas in practice, taxes depend on income. Appendix B to this chapter shows that the size of the multiplier is reduced when we make the more realistic assumption that taxes depend on income. We continue to add more realism and difficulty to our analysis in the chapters that follow.

The Federal Budget

Because fiscal policy is the manipulation of items in the federal budget, we need to consider those aspects of the budget relevant to our study of macroeconomics. The **federal budget** is an enormously complicated document, up to thousands of pages each year. It lists in detail all the things the government plans to spend money on and all the sources of government revenues for the coming year. It is the product of a complex interplay of social, political, and economic forces.

The "budget" is really three different budgets. First, it is a *political document* that dispenses favors to certain groups or regions (the elderly benefit from Social Security, farmers from agricultural price supports, students from federal loan programs, and so on) and places burdens (taxes) on others. Second, it is a *reflection of goals* the government wants to achieve. For example, in addition to assisting farmers, agricultural price supports are meant to preserve the "family farm." Tax

federal budget The budget of the federal government.

breaks for corporations engaging in research and development of new products are meant to encourage research. Finally, the budget may be an *embodiment of some beliefs about how (if at all) the government should manage the macroeconomy*. The macroeconomic aspects of the budget are only a part of a more complicated story, a story that may be of more concern to political scientists than to economists.

The Budget in 2007

A highly condensed version of the federal budget is shown in Table 9.5. In 2007, the government had total receipts of $2,671.4 billion, largely from personal income taxes ($1,162.1 billion) and contributions for social insurance ($953.0 billion). (Contributions for social insurance are employer and employee Social Security taxes.) Receipts from corporate income taxes accounted for $380.8 billion, or only 14.3 percent of total receipts. Not everyone is aware of the fact that corporate income taxes as a percentage of government receipts are quite small relative to personal income taxes and Social Security taxes.

TABLE 9.5 Federal Government Receipts and Expenditures, 2007 (Billions of Dollars)

	Amount	Percentage of Total
Current receipts		
Personal income taxes	1,162.1	43.5
Excise taxes and customs duties	99.9	3.7
Corporate income taxes	380.8	14.3
Taxes from the rest of the world	13.4	0.5
Contributions for social insurance	953.0	35.7
Interest receipts and rents and royalties	25.1	0.9
Current transfer receipts from business and persons	39.4	1.5
Current surplus of government enterprises	−2.3	−0.0
Total	2,671.4	100.0
Current expenditures		
Consumption expenditures	856.0	29.6
Transfer payments to persons	1,270.7	43.9
Transfer payments to the rest of the world	38.6	1.3
Grants-in-aid to state and local governments	377.5	13.1
Interest payments	302.4	10.5
Subsidies	46.7	1.6
Total	2,892.0	100.0
Net federal government saving—surplus (+) or deficit (−)		
(Total current receipts − Total current expenditures)	−220.6	

Source: U.S. Department of Commerce, Bureau of Economic Analysis.

The federal government also spent $2,892.0 billion in expenditures in 2007. Of this, $1,270.7 billion represented transfer payments to persons (Social Security benefits, military retirement benefits, and unemployment compensation).[3] Consumption ($856.0 billion) was the next-largest component, followed by grants-in-aid to state and local governments ($377.5 billion), which are grants given to the state and local governments by the federal government, and interest payments on the federal debt ($302.4 billion).

The difference between the federal government's receipts and its expenditures is the **federal surplus (+)** or **deficit (−)**, which is federal government saving. Table 9.5 shows that the federal government spent more than it took in during 2007, resulting in a deficit of $220.6 billion.

federal surplus (+) *or* **deficit (−)** Federal government receipts minus expenditures.

[3] Remember that there is an important difference between transfer payments and government purchases of goods and services (consumption expenditures). Much of the government budget goes for things that an economist would classify as transfers (payments that are grants or gifts) instead of purchases of goods and services. Only the latter are included in our variable G. Transfers are counted as part of net taxes.

Fiscal Policy Since 1993: The Clinton and Bush Administrations

Since 1993, there have been large fluctuations in many fiscal policy variables. These fluctuations reflect the different behavior of the two Clinton administrations (1993–2000) and the two Bush administrations (2001–2007). Figure 9.4 plots total federal personal income taxes as a percentage of total taxable income for the 1993 I–2007 IV period. This is a graph of the average personal income tax rate. As the figure shows, the average tax rate increased substantially during the Clinton administrations. Much of this increase was due to a tax bill that was passed in 1993 during the first Clinton administration. The figure then shows the dramatic effects of the tax cuts during the first Bush administration. The large fall in the average tax rate in 2001 III was due to a tax rebate passed after the 9/11 terrorist attacks. Although the average tax rate went back up in 2001 IV, it then fell substantially as the Bush tax cuts began to be felt. The overall tax policy of the federal government since 1993 is thus clear from Figure 9.4. The average tax rate rose sharply under President Clinton and fell sharply under President Bush.

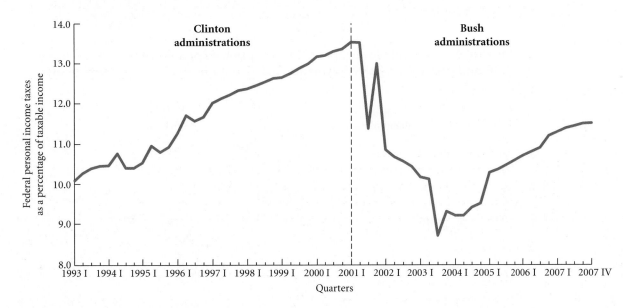

▲ **FIGURE 9.4 Federal Personal Income Taxes as a Percentage of Taxable Income, 1993 I–2007 IV**

Table 9.5 shows that the three most important spending variables of the federal government are consumption expenditures, transfer payments to persons, and grants-in-aid to state and local governments. Consumption expenditures, which are government expenditures on goods and services, are part of GDP. Transfer payments and grants-in-aid are not spending on current output (GDP), but just transfers from the federal government to people and state and local governments. Figure 9.5 plots two spending ratios. One is federal government consumption expenditures as a percentage of GDP, and the other is transfer payments to persons plus grants-in-aid to state and local governments as a percentage of GDP. The figure shows that consumption expenditures as a percentage of GDP generally fell during the Clinton administrations and generally rose during the Bush administrations. The increase during the Bush administrations reflects primarily the spending on the Iraq war. The figure also shows that transfer payments as a percentage of GDP generally rose during the Bush administrations. The figure was flat or slightly falling during the Clinton administrations. Some of the fall between 1996 and 2000 was due to President Clinton's welfare reform legislation. Some of the rise from 2001 on is due to increased Medicare payments.

Figure 9.6 plots the federal government surplus (+) or deficit (−1) as a percentage of GDP for the 1993 I–2007 IV period. The figure shows that during the Clinton administrations the federal budget moved from substantial deficit to noticeable surplus. This, of course, should not be surprising since the average tax rate generally rose during this period and spending as a percentage of GDP generally fell. Figure 9.6 then shows that the surplus turned into a substantial deficit during the first Bush administration. This also should not be surprising since the average tax rate generally fell during this period and spending as a percentage of GDP generally rose.

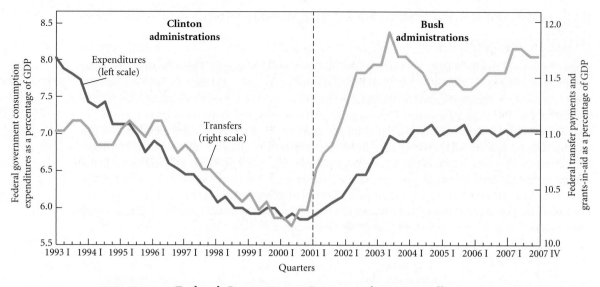

▲ **FIGURE 9.5** **Federal Government Consumption Expenditures as a Percentage of GDP and Federal Transfer Payments and Grants-in-Aid as a Percentage of GDP, 1993 I–2007 IV**

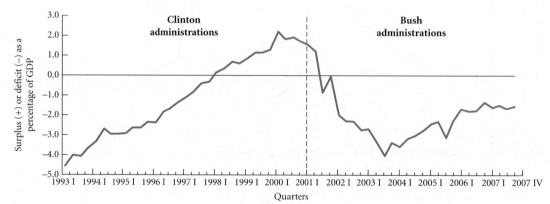

▲ **FIGURE 9.6**

The Federal Government Surplus (+) or Deficit (–) as a Percentage of GDP, 1993 I–2007 IV

To summarize, Figures 9.4, 9.5, and 9.6 show clearly the large differences in the fiscal policies of the Clinton and Bush administrations. Tax rates generally rose and spending as a percentage of GDP generally fell during the Clinton administrations, and the opposite generally happened during the Bush administrations.

As you look at these differences, you should remember that the decisions that governments make about levels of spending and taxes reflect not only macroeconomic concerns but also microeconomic issues and political philosophy. President Clinton's welfare reform program resulted in a decrease in government transfer payments but was motivated in part by interest in improving market incentives. President Bush's early tax cuts were based less on macroeconomic concerns than on political philosophy, while the increased spending came from international relations. Even when tax and spending policies are not motivated by macroeconomic concerns, however, they have macroeconomic consequences.

The Federal Government Debt

federal debt The total amount owed by the federal government.

When the government runs a deficit, it must borrow to finance it. To borrow, the federal government sells government securities to the public. It issues pieces of paper promising to pay a certain amount, with interest, in the future. In return, it receives funds from the buyers of the paper and uses these funds to pay its bills. This borrowing increases the **federal debt**, the total amount owed by the federal government. The federal debt is the total of all accumulated deficits minus surpluses over time. Conversely, if the government runs a surplus, the federal debt falls.

Some of the securities that the government issues end up being held by the federal government at the Federal Reserve or in government trust funds, the largest of which is Social Security. The term **privately held federal debt** refers only to the *privately held* debt of the U.S. government. At the beginning of December 2007, the federal debt was $9.2 trillion, of which $5.2 trillion was privately held.

The federal government debt (privately held) as a percentage of GDP is plotted in Figure 9.7 for the 1993 I–2007 IV period. The percentage fell during the second Clinton administration, when the budget was in surplus, and it mostly rose during the Bush administrations, when the budget was in deficit. In 2007 IV, the percentage was 36.5 percent.

privately held federal debt The privately held (non-government-owned) debt of the U.S. government.

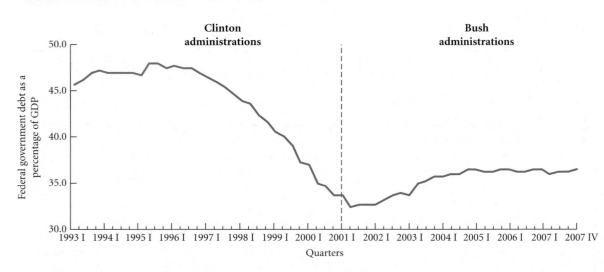

▲ FIGURE 9.7

The Federal Government Debt as a Percentage of GDP, 1993 I–2007 IV

The Economy's Influence on the Government Budget

Some parts of the government's budget depend on the state of the economy, over which the government has no direct control. Following are some of the ways in which the economy affects the budget.

Tax Revenues Depend on the State of the Economy

Consider the revenue side of the budget. The government passes laws that set tax rates and tax brackets, variables the government does control. Tax revenue, on the other hand, depends on taxable income, and income depends on the state of the economy, which the government does *not* completely control. The government can set a personal income tax rate of 20 percent, but the revenue that the tax brings in will depend on the average income that households earn. The government will collect more revenue when average income is $60,000 than when average income is $40,000.

Some Government Expenditures Depend on the State of the Economy

Some items on the expenditure side of the government budget also depend on the state of the economy. As the economy expands, unemployment falls. The result is a decrease in unemployment benefits. Welfare payments and food stamp allotments also decrease somewhat. Some of the people who receive these benefits during bad times are able to find jobs when the state of the economy improves, and they begin earning enough income that they no longer qualify. Transfer payments

ECONOMICS IN PRACTICE

Fiscal Policy In 2008

At the beginning of 2008, many worried that the economy was slipping into a recession. The Bureau of Labor Statistics reported that the number of payroll jobs was falling and GDP growth stalled from over 4 percent annually in the third quarter of 2007 to under 1 percent in the fourth quarter. A decline in house prices and a huge drop in new construction was leading the way. Against this backdrop, Congress and the president agreed on expansionary fiscal policy. Specifically, they passed a rapid-fire tax cut that is described in the following article.

Congress Approves Economic-Stimulus Bill

Wall Street Journal

WASHINGTON—Congress approved a $168 billion bill to boost the economy, paving the way for more than 130 million households to start receiving rebate checks this spring.

The measure passed the Senate, 81-16, after Democrats dropped demands for billions in extra spending and tax breaks, which were opposed by most Republicans. The House quickly adopted the Senate's changes last night, in a 380-34 vote.

The speedy action on the legislation marked a rare bipartisan effort in an election year, as lawmakers more accustomed to fighting decided to work together on the economy, a top concern for many voters. The last hurdle for the bill was cleared earlier yesterday, as Senate leaders agreed to a compromise that closely mirrored a bipartisan House agreement worked out with the Bush administration last month.

In a statement, President Bush made clear he intends to sign the legislation, calling it "an example of bipartisan cooperation at a time when the American people most expect it."

The new Senate bill disappointed many Democrats in that chamber, who had tried unsuccessfully to pick up enough Republican votes for a more-expansive package that would have extended unemployment-insurance benefits, boosted funding for home-heating subsidies for the poor, and supplied $500 checks to millions of Social Security recipients.

Under the final bill, most taxpayers would receive checks of up to $600 for individuals, or $1,200 for married couples, amounts that would begin to phase out at incomes above $75,000 for individuals and $150,000 for married couples. Millions of people who don't pay income taxes but have incomes of at least $3,000 would receive smaller rebates of $300, or $600 for married couples. This group would include Social Security recipients and military veterans receiving disability payments, as well as their surviving spouses—a provision generated by the Senate. People receiving rebates would receive $300 credits for each child.

Source: Sarah Lueck, February 8, 2008.

tend to go down automatically during an expansion. (During a slump, transfer payments tend to increase because there are more people without jobs and more poor people generally.)

Another reason that government spending is not completely controllable is that inflation often picks up when the economy is expanding. This can lead the government to spend more than it had planned to spend. Suppose the government has ordered 20 planes at $2 million each and inflation causes the actual price to be higher than expected. If the government decides to go ahead and buy the planes anyway, it will be forced to increase its spending. Finally, any change in the interest rate changes government interest payments. An increase in interest rates means that the government spends more in interest payments.

Automatic Stabilizers

As the economy expands, the government's tax receipts increase. Also, transfer payments fall as the economy expands, which leads to a decrease in government expenditures. The revenue and expenditure items that change in response to changes in economic activity in such a way as to moderate changes in GDP are known as **automatic stabilizers**. As the economy expands or contracts, "automatic" changes in government revenues and expenditures take place that tend to reduce the change in, or to stabilize, GDP.

The fact that some revenues *automatically* tend to rise and some expenditures *automatically* tend to fall in an expansion means that the government surplus is larger (or the deficit is smaller) in an expansion than it otherwise would be. Suppose we wanted to assess whether a government is practicing a policy designed to increase spending and income. If we looked only at the size of the government budget deficit, we might be fooled into thinking that the government is trying to stimulate the economy when, in fact, the real source of the deficit is a slump in the economy that caused revenues to fall and transfer payments to increase.

automatic stabilizers Revenue and expenditure items in the federal budget that automatically change with the state of the economy in such a way as to stabilize GDP.

Fiscal Drag

If the economy is doing well, income will be high and so will tax revenue. Tax revenue rises with increases in income for two reasons. First, there is more income to be taxed when people are earning more. Second, as people earn more income, they move into higher tax brackets and the average tax rate that they pay increases. This type of increase in tax rates is a **fiscal drag** because the increase in average tax rates that results when people move into higher brackets acts as a "drag" on the economy. As the economy expands and income increases, the automatic tax increase mechanism built into the system goes to work. Tax rates go up, reducing the after-tax wage, which slows down the expansion.

Before 1982, people found themselves pushed into higher tax brackets by inflation alone. Suppose my income rose 10 percent in 1981 but the price level also rose by 10 percent that year. My income did not increase at all in real terms; but because the tax brackets were not legislated in real terms, I ended up paying more taxes. Since 1982, however, tax brackets have been indexed—that is, adjusted for inflation—and this change has substantially reduced the automatic fiscal drag built into the system.

fiscal drag The negative effect on the economy that occurs when average tax rates increase because taxpayers have moved into higher income brackets during an expansion.

Full-Employment Budget

Because the condition of the economy affects the budget deficit so strongly, we cannot accurately judge either the intent or the success of fiscal policies just by looking at the surplus or deficit. Instead of looking simply at the size of the surplus or deficit, economists have developed an alternative way to measure how effective fiscal policy actually is. By examining what the budget would be like if the economy were producing at the full-employment level of output—the so-called **full-employment budget**—we can establish a benchmark for evaluating fiscal policy.

The distinction between the actual and full-employment budget is important. Suppose the economy is in a slump and the deficit is $250 billion. Also suppose that if there were full employment, the deficit would fall to $75 billion. The $75 billion deficit that would remain even with full employment would be due to the structure of tax and spending programs instead of the state of the economy. This deficit—the deficit that remains at full employment—is sometimes called the **structural deficit**. The $175 billion ($250 billion − $75 billion) part of the deficit caused by the fact the economy is in a slump is known as the **cyclical deficit**. The existence of the cyclical deficit depends on where the economy is in the business cycle, and it ceases to exist when full employment is reached. By definition, the cyclical deficit of the full-employment budget is zero.

full-employment budget What the federal budget would be if the economy were producing at the full-employment level of output.

structural deficit The deficit that remains at full employment.

cyclical deficit The deficit that occurs because of a downturn in the business cycle.

Looking Ahead

We have now seen how households, firms, and the government interact in the goods market, how equilibrium output (income) is determined, and how the government uses fiscal policy to influence the economy. In the following two chapters, we analyze the money market and monetary policy—the government's other major tool for influencing the economy.

SUMMARY

1. The government can affect the macroeconomy through two specific policy channels. *Fiscal policy* refers to the government's taxing and spending behavior. *Discretionary fiscal policy* refers to changes in taxes or spending that are the result of deliberate changes in government policy. *Monetary policy* refers to the behavior of the Federal Reserve concerning the nation's money supply.

GOVERNMENT IN THE ECONOMY *p. 160*

2. The government does not have complete control over tax revenues and certain expenditures, which are partially dictated by the state of the economy.

3. As a participant in the economy, the government makes purchases of goods and services (G), collects taxes, and makes transfer payments to households. *Net taxes* (T) is equal to the tax payments made to the government by firms and households minus transfer payments made to households by the government.

4. *Disposable*, or *after-tax, income* (Y_d) is equal to the amount of income received by households after taxes: $Y_d \equiv Y - T$. After-tax income determines households' consumption behavior.

5. The *budget deficit* is equal to the difference between what the government spends and what it collects in taxes: $G - T$. When G exceeds T, the government must borrow from the public to finance its deficit.

6. In an economy in which government is a participant, planned aggregate expenditure equals consumption spending by households (C) plus planned investment spending by firms (I) plus government spending on goods and services (G): $AE \equiv C + I + G$. Because the condition $Y = AE$ is necessary for the economy to be in equilibrium, it follows that $Y = C + I + G$ is the macroeconomic equilibrium condition. The economy is also in equilibrium when leakages out of the system equal injections into the system. This occurs when saving and net taxes (the leakages) equal planned investment and government purchases (the injections): $S + T = I + G$.

FISCAL POLICY AT WORK: MULTIPLIER EFFECTS *p. 164*

7. Fiscal policy has a multiplier effect on the economy. A change in government spending gives rise to a multiplier equal to $1/MPS$. A change in taxation brings about a multiplier equal to $-MPC/MPS$. A simultaneous equal increase or decrease in government spending and taxes has a multiplier effect of 1.

THE FEDERAL BUDGET *p. 169*

8. During the two Clinton administrations, the federal budget went from being in deficit to being in surplus. This was reversed during the two Bush administrations, driven by tax rate decreases and government spending increases.

THE ECONOMY'S INFLUENCE ON THE GOVERNMENT BUDGET *p. 173*

9. *Automatic stabilizers* are revenue and expenditure items in the federal budget that automatically change with the state of the economy and tend to stabilize GDP. For example, during expansions, the government automatically takes in more revenue because people are making more money that is taxed. Higher income and tax brackets also mean fewer transfer payments.

10. *Fiscal drag* is the negative effect on the economy that occurs when average tax rates increase because taxpayers have moved into higher income brackets during an expansion. These higher taxes reduce disposable income and slow down the expansion. Since 1982, tax brackets have been indexed to inflation. This change has reduced the fiscal drag built into the tax system.

11. The *full-employment budget* is an economist's construction of what the federal budget would be if the economy were producing at a full-employment level of output. The *structural deficit* is the federal deficit that remains even at full employment. A *cyclical deficit* occurs when there is a downturn in the business cycle.

REVIEW TERMS AND CONCEPTS

automatic stabilizers, *p. 175*

balanced-budget multiplier, *p. 168*

budget deficit, *p. 161*

cyclical deficit, *p. 175*

discretionary fiscal policy, *p. 160*

disposable, *or after-tax, income* (Y_d), *p. 160*

federal budget, *p. 169*

federal debt, *p. 172*

federal surplus (+) *or* deficit (−), *p. 170*

fiscal drag, *p. 175*

fiscal policy, *p. 160*

full-employment budget, *p. 175*

government spending multiplier, *p. 165*

monetary policy, *p. 160*

net taxes (T), *p. 160*

privately held federal debt, *p. 173*

structural deficit, *p. 175*

tax multiplier, *p. 167*

4. Equilibrium in an economy with a government: $Y = C + I + G$

5. Saving/investment approach to equilibrium in an economy with a government: $S + T = I + G$

6. Government spending multiplier
$$\equiv \frac{1}{MPS}$$

1. Disposable income $Y_d \equiv Y - T$

2. $AE \equiv C + I + G$

3. Government budget deficit $\equiv G - T$

7. Tax multiplier $\equiv -\left(\dfrac{MPC}{MPS}\right)$

8. Balanced-budget multiplier $\equiv 1$

PROBLEMS

Visit **www.myeconlab.com** to complete the problems marked in orange online. You will receive instant feedback on your answers, tutorial help, and access to additional practice problems.

1. You are appointed secretary of the treasury of a recently independent country called Rugaria. The currency of Rugaria is the lav. The new nation began fiscal operations this year, and the budget situation is that the government will spend 10 million lavs and taxes will be 9 million lavs. The 1-million-lav difference will be borrowed from the public by selling 10-year government bonds paying 5 percent interest. The interest on the outstanding bonds must be added to spending each year, and we assume that additional taxes are raised to cover that interest. Assuming that the budget stays the same except for the interest on the debt for 10 years, what will be the accumulated debt? What will the size of the budget be after 10 years?

2. Suppose that the government of Lumpland is enjoying a fat budget surplus with fixed government expenditures of $G = 150$ and fixed taxes of $T = 200$. Assume that consumers of Lumpland behave as described in the following consumption function:

$$C = 150 + 0.75(Y - T)$$

Suppose further that investment spending is fixed at 100. Calculate the equilibrium level of GDP in Lumpland. Solve for equilibrium levels of Y, C, and S. Next, assume that the Republican Congress in Lumpland succeeds in reducing taxes by 20 to a new fixed level of 180. Recalculate the equilibrium level of GDP using the tax multiplier. Solve for equilibrium levels of Y, C, and S after the tax cut and check to ensure that the multiplier worked. What arguments are likely to be used in support of such a tax cut? What arguments might be used to oppose such a tax cut?

3. For each of the following statements, decide whether you agree or disagree and explain your answer:
   a. During periods of budget surplus (when $G < T$), the government debt grows.
   b. A tax cut will increase the equilibrium level of GDP if the budget is in deficit but will decrease the equilibrium level of GDP if the budget is in surplus.
   c. If the $MPS = .90$, the tax multiplier is actually larger than the expenditure multiplier.

4. Define *saving* and *investment*. Data for the simple economy of Newt show that in 2005, saving exceeded investment and the government is running a balanced budget. What is likely to happen? What would happen if the government were running a deficit and saving were equal to investment?

5. Expert economists in the economy of Yuk estimate the following:

	BILLION YUKS
Real output/income	1,000
Government purchases	200
Total net taxes	200
Investment spending (planned)	100

Assume that Yukkers consume 75 percent of their disposable incomes and save 25 percent.
   a. You are asked by the business editor of the *Yuk Gazette* to predict the events of the next few months. By using the data given, make a forecast. (Assume that investment is constant.)

   b. If no changes were made, at what level of GDP (Y) would the economy of Yuk settle?
   c. Some local conservatives blame Yuk's problems on the size of the government sector. They suggest cutting government purchases by 25 billion Yuks. What effect would such cuts have on the economy? (Be specific.)

6. A $1 increase in government spending will raise equilibrium income more than a $1 tax cut will, yet both have the same impact on the budget deficit. So if we care about the budget deficit, the best way to stimulate the economy is through increases in spending, not cuts in taxes. Comment.

7. Assume that in 2008, the following prevails in the Republic of Nurd:

$Y = \$200$	$G = \$0$
$C = \$160$	$T = \$0$
$S = \$40$	
I (planned) = 30	

Assume that households consume 80 percent of their income, they save 20 percent of their income, $MPC = .8$, and $MPS = .2$. That is, $C = .8Y_d$ and $S = .2Y_d$.
   a. Is the economy of Nurd in equilibrium? What is Nurd's equilibrium level of income? What is likely to happen in the coming months if the government takes no action?
   b. If $200 is the "full-employment" level of Y, what fiscal policy might the government follow if its goal is full employment?
   c. If the full-employment level of Y is $250, what fiscal policy might the government follow?
   d. Suppose $Y = \$200$, $C = \$160$, $S = \$40$, and $I = \$40$. Is Nurd's economy in equilibrium?
   e. Starting with the situation in part d, suppose the government starts spending $30 each year with no taxation and continues to spend $30 every period. If I remains constant, what will happen to the equilibrium level of Nurd's domestic product (Y)? What will the new levels of C and S be?
   f. Starting with the situation in part d, suppose the government starts taxing the population $30 each year without spending anything and continues to tax at that rate every period. If I remains constant, what will happen to the equilibrium level of Nurd's domestic product (Y)? What will be the new levels of C and S? How does your answer to part f differ from your answer to part e? Why?

8. Some economists claim World War II ended the Great Depression of the 1930s. The war effort was financed by borrowing massive sums of money from the public. Explain how a war could end a recession. Look at recent and back issues of the *Economic Report of the President* or the *Statistical Abstract of the United States*. How large was the federal government's debt as a percentage of GDP in 1946? How large is it today?

9. Suppose all tax collections are fixed (instead of dependent on income) and all spending and transfer programs are fixed (in the sense that they do not depend on the state of the economy, as, for example, unemployment benefits now do). In this case, would there be any automatic stabilizers in the government budget? Would there be any distinction between the full-employment deficit and the actual budget deficit? Explain.

10. Answer the following:

a. *MPS* = .4. What is the government spending multiplier?

b. *MPC* = .9. What is the government spending multiplier?

c. *MPS* = .5. What is the government spending multiplier?

d. *MPC* = .75. What is the tax multiplier?

e. *MPS* = .1. What is the tax multiplier?

f. If the government spending multiplier is 6, what is the tax multiplier?

g. If the tax multiplier is − 2, what is the government spending multiplier?

h. If government purchases and taxes are increased by $100 billion simultaneously, what will the effect be on equilibrium output (income)?

11. [Related to the *Economics in Practice* on *p. 174*] While many thought that the 2008 fiscal stimulus plan described in the feature on p. 174 was a good idea, some did not. Some even thought that Congress didn't go far enough. In retrospect, who was right? Did the economy experience a recession in 2008 or 2009? What happened to employment during the rest of 2008? What are some of the alternatives to a tax cut that might have been used?

APPENDIX A

DERIVING THE FISCAL POLICY MULTIPLIERS

THE GOVERNMENT SPENDING AND TAX MULTIPLIERS

In the chapter, we noted that the government spending multiplier is 1/*MPS*. (This is the same as the investment multiplier.) We can also derive the multiplier algebraically using our hypothetical consumption function:

$$C = a + b(Y - T)$$

where *b* is the marginal propensity to consume. As you know, the equilibrium condition is

$$Y = C + I + G$$

By substituting for *C*, we get

$$Y = a + b(Y - T) + I + G$$
$$Y = a + bY - bT + I + G$$

This equation can be rearranged to yield

$$Y - bY = a + I + G - bT$$
$$Y(1 - b) = a + I + G - bT$$

Now solve for *Y* by dividing through by $(1 - b)$:

$$Y = \frac{1}{(1 - b)} (a + I + G - bT)$$

We see from this last equation that if *G* increases by 1 with the other determinants of *Y* (*a*, *I*, and *T*) remaining constant, *Y* increases by $1/(1 - b)$. The multiplier is, as before, simply $1/(1 - b)$, where *b* is the marginal propensity to consume. Of course, $1 - b$ equals the marginal propensity to save, so the government spending multiplier is 1/*MPS*.

We can also derive the tax multiplier. The last equation says that when *T* increases by $1, holding *a*, *I*, and *G* constant, income decreases by $b/(1 - b)$ dollars. The tax multiplier is $- b/(1 - b)$, or $-MPC/(1 - MPC) = -MPC/MPS$. (Remember, the negative sign in the resulting tax multiplier shows that it is a *negative* multiplier.)

THE BALANCED-BUDGET MULTIPLIER

It is easy to show formally that the balanced-budget multiplier = 1. When taxes and government spending are simultaneously increased by the same amount, there are two effects on planned aggregate expenditure: one positive and one negative. The initial impact of a balanced-budget increase in government spending and taxes on aggregate expenditure would be the *increase* in government purchases (ΔG) minus the *decrease* in consumption (ΔC) caused by the tax increase. The decrease in consumption brought about by the tax increase is equal to $\Delta C = \Delta T (MPC)$.

increase in spending:	ΔG
− decrease in spending:	$\Delta C = \Delta T(MPC)$
= net increase in spending	$\Delta G - \Delta T(MPC)$

In a balanced-budget increase, $\Delta G = \Delta T$; so we can substitute:

net initial increase in spending:
$$\Delta G - \Delta G(MPC) = \Delta G (1 - MPC)$$

Because $MPS = (1 - MPC)$, the net initial increase in spending is:

$$\Delta G(MPS)$$

We can now apply the expenditure multiplier $\left(\dfrac{1}{MPS}\right)$ to this net initial increase in spending:

$$\Delta Y = \Delta G(MPS)\left(\frac{1}{MPS}\right) = \Delta G$$

Thus, the final total increase in the equilibrium level of Y is just equal to the initial balanced increase in G and T. That means the balanced-budget multiplier = 1, so the final increase in real output is of the same magnitude as the initial change in spending.

APPENDIX B

THE CASE IN WHICH TAX REVENUES DEPEND ON INCOME

In this chapter, we used the simplifying assumption that the government collects taxes in a lump sum. This made our discussion of the multiplier effects somewhat easier to follow. Now suppose that the government collects taxes not solely as a lump sum that is paid regardless of income but also partly in the form of a proportional levy against income. This is a more realistic assumption. Typically, tax collections either are based on income (as with the personal income tax) or follow the ups and downs in the economy (as with sales taxes). Instead of setting taxes equal to some fixed amount, let us say that tax revenues depend on income. If we call the amount of net taxes collected T, we can write $T = T_0 + tY$.

This equation contains two parts. First, we note that net taxes (T) will be equal to an amount T_0 if income (Y) is zero. Second, the tax rate (t) indicates how much net taxes change as income changes. Suppose T_0 is equal to -200 and t is 1/3. The resulting tax function is $T = -200 + 1/3Y$, which is graphed in Figure 9B.1. Note that when income is zero, the government collects "negative net taxes," which simply means that it makes transfer payments of 200. As income rises, tax collections increase because every extra dollar of income generates $0.33 in extra revenues for the government.

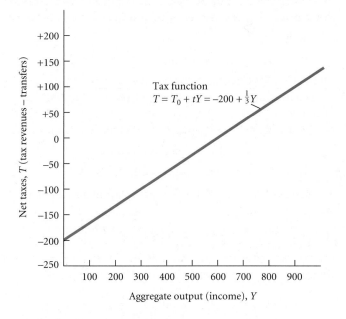

▲ FIGURE 9B.1 The Tax Function

This graph shows net taxes (taxes minus transfer payments) as a function of aggregate income.

How do we incorporate this new tax function into our discussion? All we do is replace the old value of T (in the example in the chapter, T was set equal to 100) with the new value, $-200 + 1/3Y$. Look first at the consumption equation. Consumption (C) still depends on disposable income, as it did before. Also,

disposable income is still $Y - T$, or income minus taxes. Instead of disposable income equaling $Y - 100$, however, the new equation for disposable income is

$$Y_d \equiv Y - T$$
$$Y_d \equiv Y - (-200 + 1/3Y)$$
$$Y_d \equiv Y + 200 - 1/3Y$$

Because consumption still depends on after-tax income, exactly as it did before, we have

$$C = 100 + .75Y_d$$
$$C = 100 + .75(Y + 200 - 1/3Y)$$

Nothing else needs to be changed. We solve for equilibrium income exactly as before, by setting planned aggregate expenditure equal to aggregate output. Recall that planned aggregate expenditure is $C + I + G$ and aggregate output is Y. If we assume, as before, that $I = 100$ and $G = 100$, the equilibrium is

$$Y = C + I + G$$
$$Y = \underbrace{100 + .75(Y + 200 - 1/3Y)}_{C} + \underbrace{100}_{I} + \underbrace{100}_{G}$$

This equation may look difficult to solve, but it is not. It simplifies to

$$Y = 100 + .75Y + 150 - .25Y + 100 + 100$$
$$Y = 450 + .5Y$$
$$.5Y = 450$$

This means that $Y = 450/.5 = 900$, the new equilibrium level of income.

Consider the graphic analysis of this equation as shown in Figure 9B.2, where you should note that when we make taxes a function of income (instead of a lump-sum amount), the AE function becomes *flatter* than it was before. Why? When tax collections do not depend on income, an increase in income of $1 means disposable income also increases by a dollar. Because taxes are a constant amount, adding more income does not raise the amount of taxes paid. Disposable income therefore changes dollar for dollar with any change in income.

When taxes depend on income, a $1 increase in income does not increase disposable income by a full dollar because some of the additional dollar goes to pay extra taxes. Under the modified tax function of Figure 9B.2, an extra dollar of income will increase disposable income by only $0.67 because $0.33 of the extra dollar goes to the government in the form of taxes.

No matter how taxes are calculated, the marginal propensity to consume out of disposable (or after-tax) income is the same—each extra dollar of disposable income will increase consumption spending by $0.75. However, a $1 change in before-tax income does not have the same effect on disposable income in each case. Suppose we were to increase income by $1. With the lump-sum tax function, disposable income would rise by $1.00, and consumption would increase by the MPC times the change

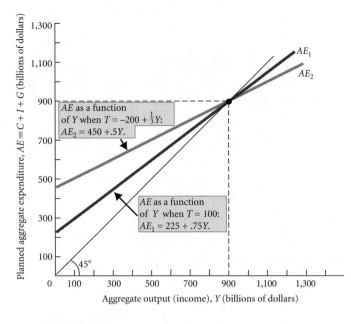

▲ **FIGURE 9B.2**

Different Tax Systems

When taxes are strictly lump-sum (T = 100) and do not depend on income, the aggregate expenditure function is steeper than when taxes depend on income.

in Y_d, or $0.75. When taxes depend on income, disposable income would rise by only $0.67 from the $1.00 increase in income and consumption would rise by only the MPC times the change in disposable income, or $0.75 × .67 = $0.50.

If a $1.00 increase in income raises expenditure by $0.75 in one case and by only $0.50 in the other, the second aggregate expenditure function must be flatter than the first.

THE GOVERNMENT SPENDING AND TAX MULTIPLIERS ALGEBRAICALLY

All this means that if taxes are a function of income, the three multipliers (investment, government spending, and tax) are less than they would be if taxes were a lump-sum amount. By using the same linear consumption function we used in Chapters 7 and 8, we can derive the multiplier:

$$C = a + b(Y - T)$$
$$C = a + b(Y - T_0 - tY)$$
$$C = a + bY - bT_0 - btY$$

We know that $Y = C + I + G$. Through substitution we get

$$Y = \underbrace{a + bY - bT_0 - btY}_{C} + I + G$$

Solving for Y:

$$Y = \frac{1}{1 - b + bt}(a + I + G - bT_0)$$

This means that a $1 increase in G or I (holding a and T_0 constant) will increase the equilibrium level of Y by

$$\frac{1}{1 - b + bt}$$

If $b = MPC = .75$ and $t = .20$, the spending multiplier is 2.5. (Compare this to 4, which would be the value of the spending multiplier if taxes were a lump sum, that is, if $t = 0$.)

Holding a, I, and G constant, a fixed or lump-sum tax cut (a cut in T_0) will increase the equilibrium level of income by

$$\frac{b}{1 - b + bt}$$

Thus, if $b = MPC = .75$ and $t = .20$, the tax multiplier is −1.875. (Compare this to −3, which would be the value of the tax multiplier if taxes were a lump sum.)

SUMMARY

1. When taxes depend on income, a $1 increase in income does not increase disposable income by a full dollar because some of the additional dollar must go to pay extra taxes. This means that if taxes are a function of income, the three multipliers (investment, government spending, and tax) are less than they would be if taxes were a lump-sum amount.

PROBLEMS

1. Assume the following for the economy of a country:
   a. Consumption function: $C = 85 + 0.5Y_d$
   b. Investment function: $I = 85$
   c. Government spending: $G = 60$
   d. Net taxes: $T = -40 + 0.25Y$
   e. Disposable income: $Y_d \equiv Y - T$
   f. Equilibrium: $Y = C + I + G$

Solve for equilibrium income. (*Hint*: Be very careful in doing the calculations. They are not difficult, but it is easy to make careless mistakes that produce wrong results.) How much does the government collect in net taxes when the economy is in equilibrium? What is the government's budget deficit or surplus?

The Money Supply and the Federal Reserve System

10

In the last two chapters, we explored how consumers, firms, and the government interact in the goods market. In this chapter and the next, we show how money markets work in the macroeconomy. We begin with what money is and what role it plays in the U.S. economy. We then discuss the forces that determine the supply of money and show how banks create money. Finally, we discuss the workings of the nation's central bank, the Federal Reserve (the Fed), and the tools at its disposal to control the money supply.

Microeconomics has little to say about money. Microeconomic theories and models are concerned primarily with *real* quantities (apples, oranges, hours of labor) and *relative* prices (the price of apples relative to the price of oranges or the price of labor relative to the prices of other goods). Most of the key ideas in microeconomics do not require that we know anything about money. As we shall see, this is not the case in macroeconomics.

An Overview of Money

You often hear people say things like, "He makes a lot of money" (in other words, "He has a high income") or "She's worth a lot of money" (meaning "She is very wealthy"). It is true that your employer uses money to pay you your income, and your wealth may be accumulated in the form of money. However, *money is not income, and money is not wealth.*

To see that money and income are not the same, think of a $20 bill. That bill may pass through a thousand hands in a year, yet never be used to pay anyone a salary. Suppose you get a $20 bill from an automatic teller machine, and you spend it on dinner. The restaurant puts that $20 bill in a bank in the next day's deposit. The bank gives it to a woman cashing a check the following day; she spends it at a baseball game that night. The bill has been through many hands but not as part of anyone's income.

What Is Money?

Most people take the ability to obtain and use money for granted. When the whole monetary system works well, as it generally does in the United States, the basic mechanics of the system are virtually invisible. People take for granted that they can walk into any store, restaurant, boutique, or gas station and buy whatever they want as long as they have enough green pieces of paper.

The idea that you can buy things with money is so natural and obvious that it seems absurd to mention it, but stop and ask yourself: "How is it that a store owner is willing to part with a steak and a loaf of bread that I can eat in exchange for some pieces of paper that are intrinsically worthless?" Why, on the other hand, are there times and places where it takes a shopping cart full of money to purchase a dozen eggs? The answers to these questions lie in what money is—a means of payment, a store of value, and a unit of account.

A Means of Payment, or Medium of Exchange Money is vital to the working of a market economy. Imagine what life would be like without it. The alternative to a monetary economy is **barter**, people exchanging goods and services for other goods and services directly instead of exchanging via the medium of money.

barter The direct exchange of goods and services for other goods and services.

How does a barter system work? Suppose you want bacon, eggs, and orange juice for breakfast. Instead of going to the store and buying these things with money, you would have to find someone who has the items and is willing to trade them. You would also have to have something the bacon seller, the orange juice purveyor, and the egg vendor want. Having pencils to trade will do you no good if the bacon, orange juice, and egg sellers do not want pencils.

A barter system requires a *double coincidence of wants* for trade to take place. That is, to effect a trade, you have to find someone who has what you want and that person must also want what you have. Where the range of goods traded is small, as it is in relatively unsophisticated economies, it is not difficult to find someone to trade with and barter is often used. In a complex society with many goods, barter exchanges involve an intolerable amount of effort. Imagine trying to find people who offer for sale all the things you buy in a typical trip to the supermarket and who are willing to accept goods that you have to offer in exchange for their goods.

medium of exchange, *or* means of payment What sellers generally accept and buyers generally use to pay for goods and services.

Some agreed-to **medium of exchange** (or **means of payment**) neatly eliminates the double-coincidence-of-wants problem. Under a monetary system, money is exchanged for goods or services when people buy things; goods or services are exchanged for money when people sell things. No one ever has to trade goods for other goods directly. Money is a lubricant in the functioning of a market economy.

A Store of Value Economists have identified other roles for money aside from its primary function as a medium of exchange. Money also serves as a **store of value**—an asset that can be used to transport purchasing power from one time period to another. If you raise chickens and at the end of the month sell them for more than you want to spend and consume immediately, you may keep some of your earnings in the form of money until the time you want to spend it.

store of value An asset that can be used to transport purchasing power from one time period to another.

There are many other stores of value besides money. You could have decided to hold your "surplus" earnings by buying such things as antique paintings, baseball cards, or diamonds, which you could sell later when you want to spend your earnings. Money has several advantages over these other stores of value. First, it comes in convenient denominations and is easily portable. You do not have to worry about making change for a Renoir painting to buy a gallon of gasoline. Second, because money is also a means of payment, it is easily exchanged for goods at all times. (A Renoir is not easily exchanged for other goods.) These two factors compose the **liquidity property of money**. Money is easily spent, flowing out of your hands like liquid. Renoirs and ancient Aztec statues are neither convenient nor portable and are not readily accepted as a means of payment.

liquidity property of money The property of money that makes it a good medium of exchange as well as a store of value: It is portable and readily accepted and thus easily exchanged for goods.

The main disadvantage of money as a store of value is that the value of money falls when the prices of goods and services rise. If the price of potato chips rises from $1 per bag to $2 per bag, the value of a dollar bill in terms of potato chips falls from one bag to half a bag. When this happens, it may be better to use potato chips (or antiques or real estate) as a store of value.

A Unit of Account Money also serves as a **unit of account**—a consistent way of quoting prices. All prices are quoted in monetary units. A textbook is quoted as costing $90, not 150 bananas or 5 DVDs, and a banana is quoted as costing 60 cents, not 1.4 apples or 6 pages of a textbook. Obviously, a standard unit of account is extremely useful when quoting prices. This function of money may have escaped your notice—what else would people quote prices in except money?

unit of account A standard unit that provides a consistent way of quoting prices.

Commodity and Fiat Monies

Introductory economics textbooks are full of stories about the various items that have been used as money by various cultures—candy bars, cigarettes (in World War II prisoner-of-war camps), huge wheels of carved stone (on the island of Yap in the South Pacific), cowrie shells (in West Africa), beads (among North American Indians), cattle (in southern Africa), and small green scraps of paper (in contemporary North America). The list goes on. These various kinds of money are generally divided into two groups, commodity monies and fiat money.

ECONOMICS IN PRACTICE

Dolphin Teeth as Currency

In most countries commodity monies are not used anymore, but the world is a big place and there are exceptions. The following article discusses the use of dolphin teeth as currency in the Solomon Islands. Dolphin teeth are being used as a means of payment and a store of value. Note that even with a currency like dolphin teeth there is a concern about counterfeit currency, namely fruit-bat teeth. Tooth decay is also a problem.

Shrinking Dollar Meets Its Match In Dolphin Teeth

Wall Street Journal

HONIARA, Solomon Islands—Forget the euro and the yen. In this South Pacific archipelago, people are pouring their savings into another appreciating currency: dolphin teeth.

Shaped like miniature ivory jalapeños, the teeth of spinner dolphins have facilitated commerce in parts of the Solomon Islands for centuries. This traditional currency is gaining in prominence now after years of ethnic strife that have undermined the country's economy and rekindled attachment to ancient customs.

Over the past year, one spinner tooth has soared in price to about two Solomon Islands dollars (26 U.S. cents), from as little as 50 Solomon Islands cents. The official currency, pegged to a global currency basket dominated by the U.S. dollar, has remained relatively stable in the period.

Even Rick Houenipwela, the governor of the Central Bank of the Solomon Islands, says he is an investor in teeth, having purchased a "huge amount" a few years ago. "Dolphin teeth are like gold," Mr. Houenipwela says. "You keep them as a store of wealth—just as if you'd put money in the bank."

Few Solomon Islanders share Western humane sensibilities about the dolphins. Hundreds of animals are killed at a time in regular hunts, usually off the large island of Malaita. Dolphin flesh provides protein for the villagers. The teeth are used like cash to buy local produce. Fifty teeth will purchase a pig; a handful are enough for some yams and cassava.

The tradition has deep roots. Dolphin teeth and other animal products were used as currency in the Solomon Islands and other parts of Melanesia long before European colonizers arrived here in the late nineteenth century.

An exhibit of traditional money in the central bank's lobby displays the now-worthless garlands of dog teeth. Curled pig tusks have played a similar role in the neighboring nation of Vanuatu and parts of Papua New Guinea. Whale, rather than dolphin, teeth were collected in Fiji. While the use of these traditional currencies is dying off elsewhere in the region, there is no sign of the boom in dolphin teeth abating here. Mr. Houenipwela, the central bank governor, says that some entrepreneurs have recently asked him for permission to establish a bank that would take deposits in teeth.

A dolphin-tooth bank with clean, insect-free vaults would solve the problem of tooth decay under inappropriate storage conditions, and would also deter counterfeiters who pass off fruit-bat teeth, which resemble dolphin teeth, for the genuine article. Mr. Houenipwela, however, says he had to turn down the request because only institutions accepting conventional currencies can call themselves banks under Solomon Islands law.

Source: Yaroslav Trofimov, April 30, 2008.

commodity monies
Items used as money that also have intrinsic value in some other use.

fiat, or token, money
Items designated as money that are intrinsically worthless.

legal tender Money that a government has required to be accepted in settlement of debts.

currency debasement
The decrease in the value of money that occurs when its supply is increased rapidly.

Commodity monies are those items used as money that also have an intrinsic value in some other use. For example, prisoners of war made purchases with cigarettes, quoted prices in terms of cigarettes, and held their wealth in the form of accumulated cigarettes. Of course, cigarettes could also be smoked—they had an alternative use apart from serving as money. Gold represents another form of commodity money. For hundreds of years gold could be used directly to buy things, but it also had other uses, ranging from jewelry to dental fillings.

By contrast, money in the United States today is mostly fiat money. **Fiat money**, sometimes called **token money**, is money that is intrinsically worthless. The actual value of a 1-, 10-, or 50-dollar bill is basically zero; what other uses are there for a small piece of paper with some green ink on it?

Why would anyone accept worthless scraps of paper as money instead of something that has some value, such as gold, cigarettes, or cattle? If your answer is "because the paper money is backed by gold or silver," you are wrong. There was a time when dollar bills were convertible directly into gold. The government backed each dollar bill in circulation by holding a certain amount of gold in its vaults. If the price of gold were $35 per ounce, for example, the government agreed to sell 1 ounce of gold for 35 dollar bills. However, dollar bills are no longer backed by any commodity—gold, silver, or anything else. They are exchangeable only for dimes, nickels, pennies, other dollars, and so on.

The public accepts paper money as a means of payment and a store of value because the government has taken steps to ensure that its money is accepted. The government declares its paper money to be **legal tender**. That is, the government declares that its money must be accepted in settlement of debts. It does this by fiat (hence *fiat money*). It passes laws defining certain pieces of paper printed in certain inks on certain plates to be legal tender, and that is that. Printed on every Federal Reserve note in the United States is "This note is legal tender for all debts, public and private." Often the government can get a start on gaining acceptance for its paper money by requiring that it be used to pay taxes. (Note that you cannot use chickens, baseball cards, or Renoir paintings to pay your taxes.)

Aside from declaring its currency legal tender, the government usually does one other thing to ensure that paper money will be accepted: It promises the public that it will not print paper money so fast that it loses its value. Expanding the supply of currency so rapidly that it loses much of its value has been a problem throughout history and is known as **currency debasement**. Debasement of the currency has been a special problem of governments that lack the strength to take the politically unpopular step of raising taxes. Printing money to be used on government expenditures of goods and services can serve as a substitute for tax increases, and weak governments have often relied on the printing press to finance their expenditures. A recent example is Zimbabwe. In 2007, faced with a need to improve the public water system, Zimbabwe's president, Robert Mugabe, said "Where money for projects cannot be found, we will print it" (reported in the *Washington Post*, July 29, 2007). In later chapters we will see the way in which this strategy for funding public projects can lead to serious inflation.

Measuring the Supply of Money in the United States

We now turn to the various kinds of money in the United States. Recall that money is used to buy things (a means of payment), to hold wealth (a store of value), and to quote prices (a unit of account). Unfortunately, these characteristics apply to a broad range of assets in the U.S. economy. As we will see, it is not at all clear where we should draw the line and say, "Up to this is money, beyond this is something else."

To solve the problem of multiple monies, economists have given different names to different measures of money. The two most common measures of money are transactions money, also called M1, and broad money, also called M2.

M1: Transactions Money What should be counted as money? Coins and dollar bills, as well as higher denominations of currency, must be counted as money—they fit all the requirements. What about checking accounts? Checks, too, can be used to buy things and can serve as a store of value. Debit cards provide even easier access to funds in checking accounts. In fact, bankers call checking accounts *demand deposits* because depositors have the right to go to the bank and cash in (demand) their entire checking account balance at any time. That makes your checking account balance virtually equivalent to bills in your wallet, and it should be included as part of the amount of money you hold.

If we take the value of all currency (including coins) held outside of bank vaults and add to it the value of all demand deposits, traveler's checks, and other checkable deposits, we have defined **M1**, or **transactions money**. As its name suggests, this is the money that can be directly used for transactions—to buy things.

$$\text{M1} \equiv \text{currency held outside banks} + \text{demand deposits} + \text{traveler's checks} + \text{other checkable deposits}$$

M1 at the end of February 2008 was $1,372.5 billion. M1 is a stock measure—it is measured at a point in time. It is the total amount of coins and currency outside of banks and the total dollar amount in checking accounts *on a specific day*. Until now, we have considered supply as a flow—a variable with a time dimension: the quantity of wheat supplied *per year*, the quantity of automobiles supplied to the market *per year*, and so on. However, M1 is a stock variable.

M2: Broad Money   Although M1 is the most widely used measure of the money supply, there are others. Should savings accounts be considered money? Many of these accounts cannot be used for transactions directly, but it is easy to convert them into cash or to transfer funds from a savings account into a checking account. What about money market accounts (which allow only a few checks per month but pay market-determined interest rates) and money market mutual funds (which sell shares and use the proceeds to purchase short-term securities)? These can be used to write checks and make purchases, although only over a certain amount.

If we add **near monies**, close substitutes for transactions money, to M1, we get **M2**, called **broad money** because it includes not-quite-money monies such as savings accounts, money market accounts, and other near monies.

$$\text{M2} \equiv \text{M1} + \text{Savings accounts} + \text{Money market accounts} + \text{Other near monies}$$

M2 at the end of February 2008 was $7,586.0 billion, considerably larger than the total M1 of $1,372.5 billion. The main advantage of looking at M2 instead of M1 is that M2 is sometimes more stable. For instance, when banks introduced new forms of interest-bearing checking accounts in the early 1980s, M1 shot up as people switched their funds from savings accounts to checking accounts. However, M2 remained fairly constant because the fall in savings account deposits and the rise in checking account balances were both part of M2, canceling each other out.

Beyond M2   Because a wide variety of financial instruments bear some resemblance to money, some economists have advocated including almost all of them as part of the money supply. In recent years, for example, credit cards have come to be used extensively in exchange. Everyone who has a credit card has a credit limit—you can charge only a certain amount on your card before you have to pay it off. Usually we pay our credit card bills with a check. One of the very broad definitions of money includes the amount of available credit on credit cards (your charge limit minus what you have charged but not paid) as part of the money supply.

There are no rules for deciding what is and is not money. This poses problems for economists and those in charge of economic policy. However, *for our purposes, "money" will always refer to transactions money, or M1*. For simplicity, we will say that M1 is the sum of two *general* categories: currency in circulation and deposits. Keep in mind, however, that M1 has *four* specific components: currency held outside banks, demand deposits, traveler's checks, and other checkable deposits.

The Private Banking System

Most of the money in the United States today is "bank money" of one sort or another. M1 is made up largely of checking account balances instead of currency, and currency makes up an even smaller part of M2 and other broader definitions of money. Any understanding of money requires some knowledge of the structure of the private banking system.

Banks and banklike institutions borrow from individuals or firms with excess funds and lend to those who need funds. For example, commercial banks receive funds in various forms, including

M1, *or* **transactions money**   Money that can be directly used for transactions.

near monies   Close substitutes for transactions money, such as savings accounts and money market accounts.

M2, *or* **broad money**   M1 plus savings accounts, money market accounts, and other near monies.

deposits in checking and savings accounts. They take these funds and loan them out in the form of car loans, mortgages, commercial loans, and so on. Banks and banklike institutions are called **financial intermediaries** because they "mediate," or act as a link between people who have funds to lend and those who need to borrow.

The main types of financial intermediaries are commercial banks, followed by savings and loan associations, life insurance companies, and pension funds. Since about 1970, the legal distinctions among the different types of financial intermediaries have narrowed considerably. It used to be, for example, that checking accounts could be held only in commercial banks and that commercial banks could not pay interest on checking accounts. Savings and loan associations were prohibited from offering certain kinds of deposits and were restricted primarily to making loans for mortgages.

The Depository Institutions Deregulation and Monetary Control Act, enacted by Congress in 1980, eliminated many of the previous restrictions on the behavior of financial institutions. Many types of institutions now offer checking accounts, and interest is paid on many types of checking accounts. Savings and loan associations now make loans for many things besides home mortgages.

How Banks Create Money

So far we have described the general way that money works and the way the supply of money is measured in the United States, but how much money is available at a given time? Who supplies it, and how does it get supplied? We are now ready to analyze these questions in detail. In particular, we want to explore a process that many find mysterious: the way banks *create money*.

A Historical Perspective: Goldsmiths

To begin to see how banks create money, consider the origins of the modern banking system. In the fifteenth and sixteenth centuries, citizens of many lands used gold as money, particularly for large transactions. Because gold is both inconvenient to carry around and susceptible to theft, people began to place their gold with goldsmiths for safekeeping. On receiving the gold, a goldsmith would issue a receipt to the depositor, charging him a small fee for looking after his gold. After a time, these receipts themselves, rather than the gold that they represented, began to be traded for goods. The receipts became a form of paper money, making it unnecessary to go to the goldsmith to withdraw gold for a transaction. The receipts of the de Medici's, who were both art patrons and goldsmith-bankers in Italy in the Renaissance period, were reputedly accepted in wide areas of Europe as currency.

At this point, all the receipts issued by goldsmiths were backed 100 percent by gold. If a goldsmith had 100 ounces of gold in his safe, he would issue receipts for 100 ounces of gold, and no more. Goldsmiths functioned as warehouses where people stored gold for safekeeping. The goldsmiths found, however, that people did not come often to withdraw gold. Why should they, when paper receipts that could easily be converted to gold were "as good as gold"? (In fact, receipts were better than gold—more portable, safer from theft, and so on.) As a result, goldsmiths had a large stock of gold continuously on hand.

Because they had what amounted to "extra" gold sitting around, goldsmiths gradually realized that they could lend out some of this gold without any fear of running out of gold. Why would they do this? Because instead of just keeping their gold idly in their vaults, they could earn interest on loans. Something subtle, but dramatic, happened at this point. The goldsmiths changed from mere depositories for gold into banklike institutions that had the power to create money. This transformation occurred as soon as goldsmiths began making loans. Without adding any more real gold to the system, the goldsmiths increased the amount of money in circulation by creating additional claims to gold—that is, receipts that entitled the bearer to receive a certain number of ounces of gold on demand.[1] Thus, there were more claims than there were ounces of gold.

---

[1] Remember, these receipts circulated as money, and people used them to make transactions without feeling the need to cash them in—that is, to exchange them for gold itself.

A detailed example may help to clarify this. Suppose you go to a goldsmith who is functioning only as a depository, or warehouse, and ask for a loan to buy a plot of land that costs 20 ounces of gold. Also suppose that the goldsmith has 100 ounces of gold on deposit in his safe and receipts for exactly 100 ounces of gold out to the various people who deposited the gold. If the goldsmith decides he is tired of being a mere goldsmith and wants to become a real bank, he will loan you some gold. You don't want the gold itself, of course; rather, you want a slip of paper that represents 20 ounces of gold. The goldsmith in essence "creates" money for you by giving you a receipt for 20 ounces of gold (even though his entire supply of gold already belongs to various other people).[2] When he does, there will be receipts for 120 ounces of gold in circulation instead of the 100 ounces worth of receipts before your loan and the supply of money will have increased.

People think the creation of money is mysterious. Far from it! The creation of money is simply an accounting procedure, among the most mundane of human endeavors. You may suspect the whole process is fundamentally unsound or somehow dubious. After all, the banking system began when someone issued claims for gold that already belonged to someone else. Here you may be on slightly firmer ground.

Goldsmiths-turned-bankers did face certain problems. Once they started making loans, their receipts outstanding (claims on gold) were greater than the amount of gold they had in their vaults at any given moment. If the owners of the 120 ounces worth of gold receipts all presented their receipts and demanded their gold at the same time, the goldsmith would be in trouble. With only 100 ounces of gold on hand, people could not get their gold at once.

In normal times, people would be happy to hold receipts instead of real gold, and this problem would never arise. If, however, people began to worry about the goldsmith's financial safety, they might begin to have doubts about whether their receipts really were as good as gold. Knowing there were more receipts outstanding than there were ounces of gold in the goldsmith's vault, they might start to demand gold for receipts.

This situation leads to a paradox. It makes perfect sense for people to hold paper receipts (instead of gold) if they know they can always get gold for their paper. In normal times, goldsmiths could feel perfectly safe in loaning out more gold than they actually had in their possession. But once people start to doubt the safety of the goldsmith, they are foolish not to demand their gold back from the vault.

A run on a goldsmith (or in our day, a **run on a bank**) occurs when many people present their claims at the same time. These runs tend to feed on themselves. If I see you going to the goldsmith to withdraw your gold, I may become nervous and decide to withdraw my gold as well. It is the *fear* of a run that usually causes the run. Runs on a bank can be triggered by a variety of causes: rumors that an institution may have made loans to borrowers who cannot repay, wars, failures of other institutions that have borrowed money from the bank, and so on. As you will see later in this chapter, today's bankers differ from goldsmiths—today's banks are subject to a "required reserve ratio." Goldsmiths had no legal reserve requirements, although the amount they loaned out was subject to the restriction imposed on them by their fear of running out of gold.

run on a bank Occurs when many of those who have claims on a bank (deposits) present them at the same time.

The Modern Banking System

To understand how the modern banking system works, you need to be familiar with some basic principles of accounting. Once you are comfortable with the way banks keep their books, the whole process of money creation will seem logical.

A Brief Review of Accounting Central to accounting practices is the statement that "the books always balance." In practice, this means that if we take a snapshot of a firm—any firm, including a bank—at a particular moment in time, then by definition:

$$\text{Assets} - \text{Liabilities} \equiv \text{Net Worth}$$
$$\text{or}$$
$$\text{Assets} \equiv \text{Liabilities} + \text{Net Worth}$$

---

[2] In return for lending you the receipt for 20 ounces of gold, the goldsmith expects to get an IOU promising to repay the amount (in gold itself or with a receipt from another goldsmith) with interest after a certain period of time.

Assets are things a firm owns that are worth something. For a bank, these assets include the bank building, its furniture, its holdings of government securities, cash in its vaults, bonds, stocks, and so on. Most important among a bank's assets, for our purposes at least, are the loans it has made. A borrower gives the bank an *IOU*, a promise to repay a certain sum of money on or by a certain date. This promise is an asset of the bank because it is worth something. The bank could (and sometimes does) sell the IOU to another bank for cash.

Other bank assets include cash on hand (sometimes called *vault cash*) and deposits with the U.S. central bank—the **Federal Reserve Bank (the Fed)**. As we will see later in this chapter, federal banking regulations require that banks keep a certain portion of their deposits on hand as vault cash or on deposit with the Fed.

A firm's *liabilities* are its debts—what it owes. A bank's liabilities are the promises to pay, or IOUs, that it has issued. A bank's most important liabilities are its deposits. *Deposits* are debts owed to the depositors because when you deposit money in your account, you are in essence making a loan to the bank.

The basic rule of accounting says that if we add up a firm's assets and then subtract the total amount it owes to all those who have lent it funds, the difference is the firm's net worth. *Net worth* represents the value of the firm to its stockholders or owners. How much would you pay for a firm that owns $200,000 worth of diamonds and had borrowed $150,000 from a bank to pay for them? The firm is worth $50,000—the difference between what it owns and what it owes. If the price of diamonds were to fall, bringing their value down to only $150,000, the firm would be worth nothing.

We can keep track of a bank's financial position using a simplified balance sheet called a T-account. By convention, the bank's assets are listed on the left side of the T-account and its liabilities and net worth are on the right side. By definition, the balance sheet always balances, so that the sum of the items on the left side of the T-account is equal to the sum of the items on the right side.

The T-account in Figure 10.1 shows a bank having $110 million in *assets*, of which $20 million are **reserves**, the deposits the bank has made at the Fed, and its cash on hand (coins and currency). Reserves are an asset to the bank because it can go to the Fed and get cash for them, the same way you can go to the bank and get cash for the amount in your savings account. Our bank's other asset is its loans, worth $90 million.

Federal Reserve Bank (the Fed) The central bank of the United States.

reserves The deposits that a bank has at the Federal Reserve bank plus its cash on hand.

▶ **FIGURE 10.1**

T-Account for a Typical Bank (millions of dollars)

The balance sheet of a bank must always balance, so that the sum of assets (reserves and loans) equals the sum of liabilities (deposits and net worth).

	Assets		Liabilities	
Reserves	20		100	Deposits
Loans	90		10	Net worth
Total	110		110	Total

Why do banks hold reserves/deposits at the Fed? There are many reasons, but perhaps the most important is the legal requirement that they hold a certain percentage of their deposit liabilities as reserves. The percentage of its deposits that a bank must keep as reserves is known as the **required reserve ratio**. If the reserve ratio is 20 percent, a bank with deposits of $100 million must hold $20 million as reserves, either as cash or as deposits at the Fed. To simplify, we will assume that banks hold all of their reserves in the form of deposits at the Fed.

On the liabilities side of the T-account, the bank has taken deposits of $100 million, so it owes this amount to its depositors. This means that the bank has a net worth of $10 million to its owners ($110 million in assets − $100 million in liabilities = $10 million net worth). The net worth of the bank is what "balances" the balance sheet. Remember that when some item on a bank's balance sheet changes, there must be at least one other change somewhere else to maintain balance. If a bank's reserves increase by $1, one of the following must also be true: (1) Its other assets (for example, loans) decrease by $1, (2) its liabilities (deposits) increase by $1, or (3) its net worth increases by $1. Various fractional combinations of these are also possible.

required reserve ratio
The percentage of its total deposits that a bank must keep as reserves at the Federal Reserve.

The Creation of Money

Like the goldsmiths, today's bankers seek to earn income by lending money out at a higher interest rate than they pay depositors for use of their money.

In modern times, the chances of a run on a bank are fairly small; and even if there is a run, the central bank protects the private banks in various ways. Therefore, banks usually make loans up to the point where they can no longer do so because of the reserve requirement restriction. A bank's required amount of reserves is equal to the required reserve ratio times the total deposits in the bank. If a bank has deposits of $100 and the required ratio is 20 percent, the required amount of reserves is $20. The difference between a bank's actual reserves and its required reserves is its **excess reserves**:

excess reserves   The difference between a bank's actual reserves and its required reserves.

$$\text{excess reserves} \equiv \text{actual reserves} - \text{required reserves}$$

If banks make loans up to the point where they can no longer do so because of the reserve requirement restriction, this means that banks make loans up to the point where their excess reserves are zero.

To see why, note that when a bank has excess reserves, it has credit available and it can make loans. Actually, a bank can make loans *only* if it has excess reserves. When a bank makes a loan, it creates a demand deposit for the borrower. This creation of a demand deposit causes the bank's excess reserves to fall because the extra deposits created by the loan use up some of the excess reserves the bank has on hand. An example will help demonstrate this.

Assume that there is only one private bank in the country, the required reserve ratio is 20 percent, and the bank starts off with nothing, as shown in panel 1 of Figure 10.2. Now suppose dollar bills are in circulation and someone deposits 100 of them in the bank. The bank deposits the $100 with the central bank, so it now has $100 in reserves, as shown in panel 2. The bank now has assets (reserves) of $100 and liabilities (deposits) of $100. If the required reserve ratio is 20 percent, the bank has excess reserves of $80.

Panel 1		Panel 2		Panel 3	
Assets	Liabilities	Assets	Liabilities	Assets	Liabilities
Reserves 0	0 Deposits	Reserves 100	100 Deposits	Reserves 100	500 Deposits
				Loans 400	

▲ **FIGURE 10.2 Balance Sheets of a Bank in a Single-Bank Economy**
In panel 2, there is an initial deposit of $100. In panel 3, the bank has made loans of $400.

How much can the bank lend and still meet the reserve requirement? For the moment, let us assume that anyone who gets a loan keeps the entire proceeds in the bank or pays them to someone else who does. Nothing is withdrawn as cash. In this case, the bank can lend $400 and still meet the reserve requirement. Panel 3 shows the balance sheet of the bank after completing the maximum amount of loans it is allowed with a 20 percent reserve ratio. With $80 of excess reserves, the bank can have up to $400 of additional deposits. The $100 in reserves plus $400 in loans (which are made as deposits) equals $500 in deposits. With $500 in deposits and a required reserve ratio of 20 percent, the bank must have reserves of $100 (20 percent of $500)—and it does. The bank can lend no more than $400 because its reserve requirement must not exceed $100. When a bank has no excess reserves and thus can make no more loans, it is said to be *loaned up*.

Remember, the money supply (M1) equals cash in circulation plus deposits. Before the initial deposit, the money supply was $100 ($100 cash and no deposits). After the deposit and the loans, the money supply is $500 (no cash outside bank vaults and $500 in deposits). It is clear then that when loans are converted into deposits, the supply of money can change.

The bank whose T-accounts are presented in Figure 10.2 is allowed to make loans of $400 based on the assumption that loans that are made *stay in the bank* in the form of deposits. Now suppose you borrow from the bank to buy a personal computer and you write a check to the computer store. If the store also deposits its money in the bank, your check merely results in a reduction in your account balance and an increase to the store's account balance within the bank. No cash has left the bank. As long as the system is closed in this way—remember that so far we have assumed that there is only one bank—the bank knows that it will never be called on to release any of its $100 in reserves. It can expand its loans up to the point where its total deposits are $500.

Of course, there are many banks in the country, a situation that is depicted in Figure 10.3. As long as the banking system as a whole is closed, it is still possible for an initial deposit of $100 to result in an expansion of the money supply to $500, but more steps are involved when there is more than one bank.

	Panel 1		Panel 2		Panel 3	
Bank 1	Assets	Liabilities	Assets	Liabilities	Assets	Liabilities
	Reserves 100	100 Deposits	Reserves 100 Loans 80	180 Deposits	Reserves 20 Loans 80	100 Deposits
Bank 2						
	Reserves 80	80 Deposits	Reserves 80 Loans 64	144 Deposits	Reserves 16 Loans 64	80 Deposits
Bank 3						
	Reserves 64	64 Deposits	Reserves 64 Loans 51.20	115.20 Deposits	Reserves 12.80 Loans 51.20	64 Deposits

Summary:	Loans	Deposits
Bank 1	80	100
Bank 2	64	80
Bank 3	51.20	64
Bank 4	40.96	51.20
⋮	⋮	⋮
Total	400.00	500.00

▲ **FIGURE 10.3 The Creation of Money When There Are Many Banks**
In panel 1, there is an initial deposit of $100 in bank 1. In panel 2, bank 1 makes a loan of $80 by creating a deposit of $80. A check for $80 by the borrower is then written on bank 1 (panel 3) and deposited in bank 2 (panel 1). The process continues with bank 2 making loans and so on. In the end, loans of $400 have been made and the total level of deposits is $500.

To see why, assume that Mary makes an initial deposit of $100 in bank 1 and the bank deposits the entire $100 with the Fed (panel 1 of Figure 10.3). All loans that a bank makes are withdrawn from the bank as the individual borrowers write checks to pay for merchandise. After Mary's deposit, bank 1 can make a loan of up to $80 to Bill because it needs to keep only $20 of its $100 deposit as reserves. (We are assuming a 20 percent required reserve ratio.) In other words, bank 1 has $80 in excess reserves.

Bank 1's balance sheet at the moment of the loan to Bill appears in panel 2 of Figure 10.3. Bank 1 now has loans of $80. It has credited Bill's account with the $80, so its total deposits are $180 ($80 in loans plus $100 in reserves). Bill then writes a check for $80 for a set of shock absorbers for his car. Bill wrote his check to Sam's Car Shop, and Sam deposits Bill's check in bank 2. When the check clears, bank 1 transfers $80 in reserves to bank 2. Bank 1's balance sheet now looks like the top of panel 3. Its assets include reserves of $20 and loans of $80; its liabilities are $100 in deposits. Both sides of the T-account balance: The bank's reserves are 20 percent of its deposits, as required by law, and it is fully loaned up.

Now look at bank 2. Because bank 1 has transferred $80 in reserves to bank 2, bank 2 now has $80 in deposits and $80 in reserves (panel 1, bank 2). Its reserve requirement is also 20 percent, so it has excess reserves of $64 on which it can make loans.

Now assume that bank 2 loans the $64 to Kate to pay for a textbook and Kate writes a check for $64 payable to the Manhattan College Bookstore. The final position of bank 2, after it honors

Kate's $64 check by transferring $64 in reserves to the bookstore's bank, is reserves of $16, loans of $64, and deposits of $80 (panel 3, bank 2).

The Manhattan College Bookstore deposits Kate's check in its account with bank 3. Bank 3 now has excess reserves because it has added $64 to its reserves. With a reserve ratio of 20 percent, bank 3 can loan out $51.20 (80 percent of $64, leaving 20 percent in required reserves to back the $64 deposit).

As the process is repeated over and over, the total amount of deposits created is $500, the sum of the deposits in each of the banks. Because the banking system can be looked on as one big bank, the outcome here for many banks is the same as the outcome in Figure 10.2 for one bank.[3]

The Money Multiplier

In practice, the banking system is not completely closed—there is some leakage out of the system. Still, the point here is that an increase in bank reserves leads to a greater than one-for-one increase in the money supply. Economists call the relationship between the final change in deposits and the change in reserves that caused this change the money multiplier. Stated somewhat differently, the **money multiplier** is the multiple by which deposits can increase for every dollar increase in reserves. Do not confuse the money multiplier with the spending multipliers we discussed in the last two chapters. They are not the same thing.

In the example we just examined, reserves increased by $100 when the $100 in cash was deposited in a bank and the amount of deposits increased by $500 ($100 from the initial deposit, $400 from the loans made by the various banks from their excess reserves). The money multiplier in this case is $500/$100 = 5. Mathematically, the money multiplier can be defined as follows:

money multiplier   The multiple by which deposits can increase for every dollar increase in reserves; equal to 1 divided by the required reserve ratio.

$$\text{money multiplier} \equiv \frac{1}{\text{required reserve ratio}}$$

In the United States, the required reserve ratio varies depending on the size of the bank and the type of deposit. For large banks and for checking deposits, the ratio is currently 10 percent, which makes the potential money multiplier $1/.10 = 10$. This means that an increase in reserves of $1 could cause an increase in deposits of $10 if there were no leakage out of the system.

The Federal Reserve System

We have seen how the private banking system creates money by making loans. However, private banks are not free to create money at will. Their ability to create money is controlled by the volume of reserves in the system, which is controlled by the Fed. The Fed therefore has the ultimate control over the money supply. We will now examine the structure and function of the Fed.

Founded in 1913 by an act of Congress (to which major reforms were added in the 1930s), the Fed is the central bank of the United States. The Fed is a complicated institution with many responsibilities, including the regulation and supervision of over 7,500 commercial banks. The organization of the Federal Reserve System is presented in Figure 10.4.

The *Board of Governors* is the most important group within the Federal Reserve System. The board consists of seven members, each appointed for 14 years by the president of the United States. The *chair* of the Fed, who is appointed by the president and whose term runs for 4 years, usually dominates the entire Federal Reserve System and is sometimes said to be the second most powerful person in the United States. The Fed is an independent agency in that it does not take orders from the president or from Congress.

The United States is divided into 12 Federal Reserve districts, each with its own Federal Reserve bank. These districts are indicated on the map in Figure 10.4. The district banks are like branch offices of the Fed in that they carry out the rules, regulations, and functions of the central system in their districts and report to the Board of Governors on local economic conditions.

---

[3] If banks create money when they make loans, does repaying a loan "destroy" money? The answer is yes.

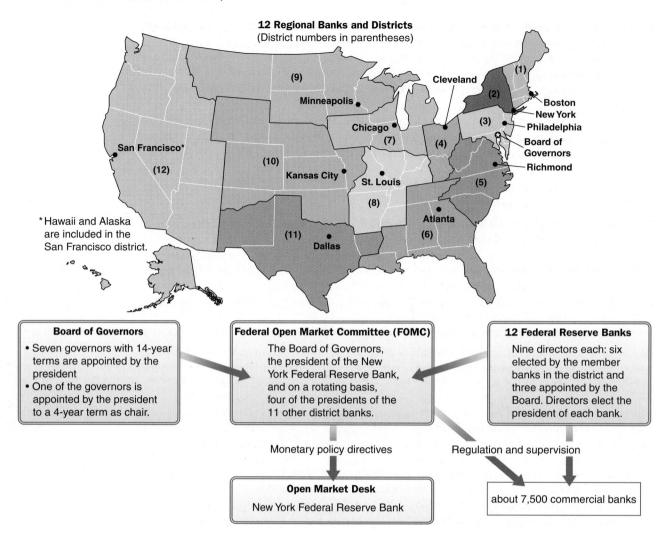

▲ FIGURE 10.4 **The Structure of the Federal Reserve System**

U.S. monetary policy—the behavior of the Fed concerning the money supply—is formally set by the **Federal Open Market Committee (FOMC)**. The FOMC consists of the seven members of the Fed's Board of Governors, the president of the New York Federal Reserve Bank and on a rotating basis, four of the presidents of the 11 other district banks. The FOMC sets goals concerning the money supply and interest rates, and it directs the **Open Market Desk** in the New York Federal Reserve Bank to buy and/or sell government securities. (We discuss the specifics of open market operations later in this chapter.)

Functions of the Federal Reserve

The Fed is the central bank of the United States. Central banks are sometimes known as "bankers' banks" because only banks (and occasionally foreign governments) can have accounts in them. As a private citizen, you cannot go to the nearest branch of the Fed and open a checking account or apply to borrow money.

Although from a macroeconomic point of view the Fed's crucial role is to control the money supply, the Fed also performs several important functions for banks. These functions include clearing interbank payments, regulating the banking system, and assisting banks in a difficult financial position. The Fed is also responsible for managing exchange rates and the nation's foreign exchange reserves.[4] In addition, it is often involved in intercountry negotiations on international economic issues.

---

[4] *Foreign exchange reserves* are holdings of the currencies of other countries—for example, Japanese yen—by the U.S. government. We discuss exchange rates and foreign exchange markets at length in Chapter 20.

Clearing Interbank Payments   Suppose you write a $100 check drawn on your bank, the First Bank of Fresno (FBF), to pay for tulip bulbs from Crockett Importers of Miami, Florida. Because Crockett Importers does not bank at FBF, but at Banco de Miami, how does your money get from your bank to the bank in Florida?

The answer: The Fed does it. Both FBF and Banco de Miami have accounts at the Fed. When Crockett Importers receives your check and deposits it at Banco de Miami, the bank submits the check to the Fed, asking it to collect the funds from FBF. The Fed presents the check to FBF and is instructed to debit FBF's account for the $100 and to credit the account of Banco de Miami. Accounts at the Fed count as reserves, so FBF loses $100 in reserves, and Banco de Miami gains $100 in reserves. The two banks effectively have traded ownerships of their deposits at the Fed. The *total* volume of reserves has not changed, nor has the money supply.

This function of clearing interbank payments allows banks to shift money around virtually instantaneously. All they need to do is wire the Fed and request a transfer, and the funds move at the speed of electricity from one computer account to another.

Other Duties of the Fed   Besides facilitating the transfer of funds between banks, the Fed performs several other important duties. It is responsible for many of the regulations governing banking practices and standards. For example, the Fed has the authority to control mergers between banks, and it is responsible for examining banks to ensure that they are financially sound and that they conform to a host of government accounting regulations. As we saw earlier, the Fed also sets reserve requirements for all financial institutions.

One of the most important responsibilities of the Fed is to act as the **lender of last resort** for the banking system. As our discussion of goldsmiths suggested, banks are subject to the possibility of runs on their deposits. In the United States, most deposits of less than $100,000 are insured by the Federal Deposit Insurance Corporation (FDIC), a U.S. government agency that was established in 1933 during the Great Depression. Deposit insurance makes panics less likely. Because depositors know they can always get their money, even if the bank fails, they are less likely to withdraw their deposits. Not all deposits are insured, so the possibility of bank panics remains. However, the Fed stands ready to provide funds to a troubled bank that cannot find any other sources of funds.

The Fed is the ideal lender of last resort for two reasons. First, providing funds to a bank that is in dire straits is risky and not likely to be very profitable, and it is hard to find private banks or other private institutions willing to do this. The Fed is a nonprofit institution whose function is to serve the overall welfare of the public. Thus, the Fed would certainly be interested in preventing catastrophic banking panics such as those that occurred in the late 1920s and the 1930s.

Second, the Fed has an essentially unlimited supply of funds with which to bail out banks facing the possibility of runs. The reason, as we shall see, is that the Fed can create reserves at will. A promise by the Fed that it will support a bank is very convincing. Unlike any other lender, the Fed can never run out of money. Therefore, the explicit or implicit support of the Fed should be enough to assure depositors that they are in no danger of losing their funds.

In March 2008, the Fed, in a major change in policy, began loaning money to financial institutions other than commercial banks. The change was in response to financial problems in the United States that resulted from falling housing prices and mortgage foreclosures. In an even larger change, the Fed guaranteed $30 billion of Bear Stearns' liabilities to JPMorgan in a deal that had JPMorgan buying Bear Stearns. It is hard to know how these changes in policy will play out, but it does suggest that the Fed may take a more active role in the private financial sector than merely as a lender of last resort.

lender of last resort
One of the functions of the Fed: It provides funds to troubled banks that cannot find any other sources of funds.

The Federal Reserve Balance Sheet

Although it is a special bank, the Fed is in some ways similar to an ordinary commercial bank. Like an ordinary bank, the Fed has a balance sheet that records its asset and liability position at any moment in time. The balance sheet for the Fed is presented in Table 10.1.

As the asset side of the balance sheet shows, the Fed owns about $11 billion of gold. *Do not think that this gold has anything to do with the supply of money.* Most of the gold was acquired during the 1930s, when it was purchased from the U.S. Treasury Department. Since 1934, the dollar has not been backed by (is not convertible into) gold. You cannot take a dollar bill to the Fed to

194 **PART III** The Core of Macroeconomic Theory

TABLE 10.1	Assets and Liabilities of the Federal Reserve System, October 24, 2007 (Millions of Dollars)		
Assets			**Liabilities**
Gold	$ 11,037	$776,701	Federal Reserve notes (outstanding)
Loans to banks	502		Deposits:
U.S. Treasury securities	779,574	21,107	Bank Reserves (from depository institutions)
All other assets	93,860	4,737	U.S. Treasury
Total	$884,973	82,428	All other liabilities and net worth
		$884,973	Total

Source: Board of Governors of the Federal Reserve System.

receive gold for it; all you can get for your old dollar bill is a new dollar bill.[5] Although it is unrelated to the money supply, the Fed's gold counts as an asset on its balance sheet because it is something of value the Fed owns.

The balance sheet mentions an asset called "loans to banks." These loans are an asset of the Fed in the same way a private commercial bank's loans are among its assets. The Fed sometimes makes loans to commercial banks that are short of reserves.[6] The $502 million in Table 10.1 represents these kinds of loans.

The largest of the Fed's assets by far consists of government (U.S. Treasury) securities: $779,574 million worth on October 24, 2007. Government securities such as Treasury bills and bonds are obligations of the federal government that the Fed has purchased over the years. The way in which these bonds are acquired has important implications for the Fed's control of the money supply. (We return to this topic after our survey of the Fed's balance sheet.)

The bulk of the Fed's liabilities are Federal Reserve notes. The dollar bill you use to buy a pack of gum is clearly an asset from your point of view—it is something you own that has value. Because every financial asset is by definition a liability of some other agent in the economy, whose liability is that dollar bill? That dollar bill, and bills of all other denominations in the economy, are a liability—an IOU—of the Fed. They are rather strange IOUs because all they can be redeemed for are other IOUs of exactly the same type. They are, nonetheless, classified as liabilities of the Fed.

The balance sheet shows that, like an ordinary commercial bank, the Fed has accepted deposits. These deposits are liabilities. The bulk of the Fed's deposits come from commercial banks. Remember, commercial banks are required to keep a certain share of their own deposits as deposits at the Fed. A bank's deposits at the Fed (its reserves) are an asset from the bank's point of view, and those same reserves must be a liability from the Fed's point of view.

Table 10.1 shows that the Fed has accepted a small volume of deposits from the U.S. Treasury. In effect, the Fed acts as the bank for the U.S. government. When the government needs to pay for something such as a new aircraft carrier, it may write a check to the supplier of the ship drawn on its "checking account" at the Fed. Similarly, when the government receives revenues from tax collections, fines, or sales of government assets, it may deposit these funds in its account at the Fed.

How the Federal Reserve Controls the Money Supply

To see how the Fed controls the supply of money in the U.S. economy, we need to understand the role of reserves. As we have said, the required reserve ratio establishes a link between the reserves of the commercial banks and the deposits (money) that commercial banks are allowed to create. The reserve requirement effectively determines how much a bank has available to lend. If the required reserve

[5] The fact that the Fed is not obliged to provide gold for currency means it can never go bankrupt. When the currency was backed by gold, it would have been possible for the Fed to run out of gold if too many of its depositors came to it at the same time and asked to exchange their deposits for gold. If depositors come to the Fed to withdraw their deposits today, all they can get is dollar bills. The dollar was convertible into gold internationally until August 15, 1971.
[6] Recall that commercial banks are required to keep a set percentage of their deposit liabilities on deposit at the Fed. If a bank suddenly finds itself short of reserves, one of its alternatives is to borrow the reserves it needs from the Fed.

ratio is 20 percent, each $1 of reserves can support $5 in deposits. A bank that has reserves of $100,000 cannot have more than $500,000 in deposits. If it did, it would fail to meet the required reserve ratio.

If you recall that the *money supply* is equal to the sum of deposits inside banks and the currency in circulation outside banks, you can see that reserves provide the leverage that the Fed needs to control the money supply. If the Fed wants to increase the supply of money, it creates more reserves, thereby freeing banks to create additional deposits by making more loans. If it wants to decrease the money supply, it reduces reserves.

Three tools are available to the Fed for changing the money supply: (1) changing the required reserve ratio, (2) changing the discount rate, and (3) engaging in open market operations. Although (3) is almost exclusively used to change the money supply, an understanding of how (1) and (2) work is useful in understanding how (3) works. We thus begin our discussion with the first two tools.

The Required Reserve Ratio

One way for the Fed to alter the supply of money is to change the required reserve ratio. This process is shown in Table 10.2. Let us assume the initial required reserve ratio is 20 percent.

In panel 1, a simplified version of the Fed's balance sheet (in billions of dollars) shows that reserves are $100 billion and currency outstanding is $100 billion. The total value of the Fed's assets is $200 billion, which we assume to be all in government securities. Assuming there are no excess reserves—banks stay fully loaned up—the $100 billion in reserves supports $500 billion in deposits at the commercial banks. ((Remember, the money multiplier equals 1/required reserve ratio = 1/.20 = 5. Thus, $100 billion in reserves can support $500 billion ($100 billion × 5) in deposits when the required reserve ratio is 20 percent.)) The supply of money (M1, or transactions money) is therefore $600 billion: $100 billion in currency and $500 billion in (checking account) deposits at the commercial banks.

TABLE 10.2 A Decrease in the Required Reserve Ratio from 20 Percent to 12.5 Percent Increases the Supply of Money (All Figures in Billions of Dollars)

Panel 1: Required Reserve Ratio = 20%

Federal Reserve			Commercial Banks			
Assets		Liabilities	Assets		Liabilities	
Government securities	$200	$100 Reserves	Reserves	$100	$500	Deposits
		$100 Currency	Loans	$400		

Note: Money supply (M1) = currency + deposits = $600.

Panel 2: Required Reserve Ratio = 12.5%

Federal Reserve			Commercial Banks			
Assets		Liabilities	Assets		Liabilities	
Government securities	$200	$100 Reserves	Reserves	$100	$800 (+$300)	Deposits
		$100 Currency	Loans (+$300)	$700		

Note: Money supply (M1) = currency + deposits = $900.

Now suppose the Fed wants to increase the supply of money to $900 billion. If it lowers the required reserve ratio from 20 percent to 12.5 percent (as in panel 2 of Table 10.2), the same $100 billion of reserves could support $800 billion in deposits instead of only $500 billion. In this case, the money multiplier is 1/.125, or 8. At a required reserve ratio of 12.5 percent, $100 billion in reserves can support $800 billion in deposits. The total money supply would be $800 billion in deposits plus the $100 billion in currency, for a total of $900 billion.[7]

---

[7] To find the maximum volume of deposits (D) that can be supported by an amount of reserves (R), divide R by the required reserve ratio. If the required reserve ratio is g, because R = gD, then D = R/g.

Put another way, with the new lower reserve ratio, banks have excess reserves of $37.5 billion. At a required reserve ratio of 20 percent, they needed $100 billion in reserves to back their $500 billion in deposits. At the lower required reserve ratio of 12.5 percent, they need only $62.5 billion of reserves to back their $500 billion of deposits; so the remaining $37.5 billion of the existing $100 billion in reserves is "extra." With that $37.5 billion of excess reserves, banks can lend out more money. If we assume the system loans money and creates deposits to the *maximum* extent possible, the $37.5 billion of reserves will support an additional $300 billion of deposits ($37.5 billion × the money multiplier of 8 = $300 billion). The change in the required reserve ratio has injected an additional $300 billion into the banking system, at which point the banks will be fully loaned up and unable to increase their deposits further. Decreases in the required reserve ratio allow banks to have more deposits with the existing volume of reserves. As banks create more deposits by making loans, the supply of money (currency + deposits) increases. The reverse is also true: If the Fed wants to restrict the supply of money, it can raise the required reserve ratio, in which case banks will find that they have insufficient reserves and must therefore reduce their deposits by "calling in" some of their loans.[8] The result is a decrease in the money supply.

For many reasons, the Fed has tended not to use changes in the reserve requirement to control the money supply. In part, this reluctance stems from the era when only some banks were members of the Fed and therefore subject to reserve requirements. The Fed reasoned that if it raised the reserve requirement to contract the money supply, banks might choose to stop being members. (Because reserves pay no interest, the higher the reserve requirement, the more the penalty imposed on those banks holding reserves.) This argument no longer applies. Since the passage of the Depository Institutions Deregulation and Monetary Control Act in 1980, all depository institutions are subject to Fed requirements.

It is also true that changing the reserve requirement ratio is a crude tool. Because of lags in banks' reporting to the Fed on their reserve and deposit positions, a change in the requirement today does not affect banks for about 2 weeks. (However, the fact that changing the reserve requirement expands or reduces credit in every bank in the country makes it a very powerful tool when the Fed does use it.)

The Discount Rate

discount rate The interest rate that banks pay to the Fed to borrow from it.

Banks may borrow from the Fed. The interest rate they pay the Fed is the **discount rate**. When banks increase their borrowing, the money supply increases. To see why this is true, assume that there is only one bank in the country and that the required reserve ratio is 20 percent. The initial position of the bank and the Fed appear in panel 1 of Table 10.3, where the money supply (currency + deposits) is $480 billion. In panel 2, the bank has borrowed $20 billion from the Fed. By using this $20 billion as a reserve, the bank can increase its loans by $100 billion, from $320 billion to $420 billion. (Remember, a required reserve ratio of 20 percent gives a money multiplier of 5; having excess reserves of $20 billion allows the bank to create an additional $20 billion × 5, or $100 billion, in deposits.) The money supply has thus increased from $480 billion to $580 billion. Bank borrowing from the Fed thus leads to an increase in the money supply.

The Fed can influence bank borrowing, and thus the money supply, through the discount rate. The higher the discount rate, the higher the cost of borrowing and the less borrowing banks will want to do. If the Fed wants to curtail the growth of the money supply, for example, it will raise the discount rate and discourages banks from borrowing from it, restricting the growth of reserves (and ultimately deposits).

Historically, the Fed has not used the discount rate to control the money supply. Prior to 2003 it usually set the discount rate lower than the rate that banks had to pay to borrow money in the private market. Although this provided an incentive for banks to borrow from the Fed, the Fed discouraged borrowing by putting pressure in various ways on the banks not to borrow. This

---

[8] To reduce the money supply, banks never really have to "call in" loans before they are due. First, the Fed is almost always expanding the money supply slowly because the real economy grows steadily and, as we shall see, growth brings with it the need for more circulating money. So when we speak of "contractionary monetary policy," we mean the Fed is slowing down the rate of money growth, not reducing the money supply. Second, even if the Fed were to cut reserves (instead of curb their expansion), banks would no doubt be able to comply by reducing the volume of new loans they make while old ones are coming due.

TABLE 10.3 The Effect on the Money Supply of Commercial Bank Borrowing from the Fed (All Figures in Billions of Dollars)

Panel 1: No Commercial Bank Borrowing from the Fed

Federal Reserve			Commercial Banks			
Assets		Liabilities	Assets		Liabilities	
Securities	$160	$80 Reserves	Reserves	$80	$400	Deposits
		$80 Currency	Loans	$320		

Note: Money supply (M1) = currency + deposits = $480.

Panel 2: Commercial Bank Borrowing $20 from the Fed

Federal Reserve			Commercial Banks			
Assets		Liabilities	Assets		Liabilities	
Securities	$160	$100 Reserves (+$20)	Reserves (+$20)	$100	$500	Deposits (+$300)
Loans	$20	$80 Currency	Loans (+$100)	$420	$20	Amount owed to Fed (+$20)

Note: Money supply (M1) = currency + deposits = $580.

pressure was sometimes called **moral suasion**. On January 9, 2003, the Fed announced a new procedure. Henceforth, the discount rate would be set above the rate that banks pay to borrow money in the private market and moral suasion would no longer be used. Although banks can now borrow from the Fed if they want to, they are unlikely to do so except in unusual circumstances because borrowing is cheaper in the private market. It is thus clear that the Fed is not using the discount rate as a tool to try to change the money supply on a regular basis.

moral suasion The pressure that in the past the Fed exerted on member banks to discourage them from borrowing heavily from the Fed.

Open Market Operations

By far the most significant of the Fed's tools for controlling the supply of money is **open market operations**. Congress has authorized the Fed to buy and sell U.S. government securities in the open market. When the Fed purchases a security, it pays for it by writing a check that, when cleared, *expands* the quantity of reserves in the system, increasing the money supply. When the Fed sells a bond, private citizens or institutions pay for it with a check that, when cleared, *reduces* the quantity of reserves in the system.

To see how open market operations and reserve controls work, we need to review several key ideas.

open market operations The purchase and sale by the Fed of government securities in the open market; a tool used to expand or contract the amount of reserves in the system and thus the money supply.

Two Branches of Government Deal in Government Securities The fact that the Fed is able to buy and sell government securities—bills and bonds—may be confusing. In fact, *two* branches of government deal in financial markets for different reasons; and you must keep the two separate in your mind.

First, keep in mind that the Treasury Department is responsible for collecting taxes and paying the federal government's bills. Salary checks paid to government workers, payments to General Dynamics for a new Navy ship, Social Security checks to retirees, and so on, are all written on accounts maintained by the Treasury. Tax receipts collected by the Internal Revenue Service, a Treasury branch, are deposited to these accounts.

If total government spending exceeds tax receipts, the law requires the Treasury to borrow the difference. Recall that the government deficit is $(G - T)$, or government purchases minus net taxes. $(G - T)$ is the amount the Treasury must borrow each year to finance the deficit. This means that the Treasury *cannot* print money to finance the deficit. The Treasury borrows by issuing bills, bonds, and notes that pay interest. These government securities, or IOUs, are sold to individuals and institutions. Often foreign countries as well as U.S. citizens buy them. As discussed in Chapter 9, the total amount of privately held government securities is the *privately held federal debt*.

The Fed is not the Treasury. Instead, it is a quasi-independent agency authorized by Congress to buy and sell *outstanding* (preexisting) U.S. government securities on the open market. The bonds and bills initially sold by the Treasury to finance the deficit are continuously resold and traded among ordinary citizens, firms, banks, pension funds, and so on. The Fed's participation in that trading affects the quantity of reserves in the system, as we will see.

Because the Fed owns some government securities, some of what the government owes it owes to itself. Recall that the Federal Reserve System's largest single asset is government securities. These securities are nothing more than bills and bonds initially issued by the Treasury to finance the deficit. They were acquired by the Fed over time through direct open market purchases that the Fed made to expand the money supply as the economy expanded.

The Mechanics of Open Market Operations How do open market operations affect the money supply? Look again at Table 10.1 on p. 194. As you can see, most of the Fed's assets consist of the government securities we have been talking about.

Suppose the Fed wants to decrease the supply of money. If it can reduce the volume of bank reserves on the liabilities side of its balance sheet, it will force banks, in turn, to reduce their own deposits (to meet the required reserve ratio). Since these deposits are part of the supply of money, the supply of money will contract.

What will happen if the Fed sells some of its holdings of government securities to the general public? The Fed's holdings of government securities must decrease because the securities it sold will now be owned by someone else. How do the purchasers of securities pay for what they have bought? They pay by writing checks drawn on their banks and payable to the Fed.

Let us look more carefully at how this works, with the help of Table 10.4. In panel 1, the Fed initially has $100 billion of government securities. Its liabilities consist of $20 billion of deposits (which are the reserves of commercial banks) and $80 billion of currency. With the required reserve ratio at 20 percent, the $20 billion of reserves can support $100 billion of deposits in the commercial banks. The commercial banking system is fully loaned up. Panel 1 also shows the financial position of a private citizen, Jane Q. Public. Jane has assets of $5 billion (a large checking account deposit in the bank) and no debts, so her net worth is $5 billion.

TABLE 10.4 Open Market Operations (The Numbers in Parentheses in Panels 2 and 3 Show the Differences Between Those Panels and Panel 1. All Figures in Billions of Dollars)

Panel 1

Federal Reserve			Commercial Banks			Jane Q. Public		
Assets	Liabilities		Assets	Liabilities		Assets	Liabilities	
Securities $100	$20	Reserves	Reserves $20	$100	Deposits	Deposits $5	$0	Debts
	$80	Currency	Loans $80				$5	Net Worth

Note: Money supply (M1) = currency + deposits = $180.

Panel 2

Federal Reserve			Commercial Banks			Jane Q. Public		
Assets	Liabilities		Assets	Liabilities		Assets	Liabilities	
Securities $95 (−$5)	$15 (−$5)	Reserves	Reserves $15 (−$5)	$95	Deposits (−$5)	Deposits $0 (−$5)	$0	Debts
	$80	Currency	Loans $80			Securities $5 (+$5)	$5	Net Worth

Note: Money supply (M1) = currency + deposits = $175.

Panel 3

Federal Reserve			Commercial Banks			Jane Q. Public		
Assets	Liabilities		Assets	Liabilities		Assets	Liabilities	
Securities $95 (−$5)	$15 (−$5)	Reserves	Reserves $15 (−$5)	$75	Deposits (−$25)	Deposits $0 (−$5)	$0	Debts
	$80	Currency	Loans $60 (−$20)			Securities $5 (+$5)	$5	Net Worth

Note: Money supply (M1) = currency + deposits = $155.

Now imagine that the Fed sells $5 billion in government securities to Jane. Jane pays for the securities by writing a check to the Fed, drawn on her bank. The Fed then reduces the reserve account of her bank by $5 billion. The balance sheets of all the participants after this transaction are shown in panel 2. Note that the supply of money (currency plus deposits) has fallen from $180 billion to $175 billion.

This is not the end of the story. As a result of the Fed's sale of securities, the amount of reserves has fallen from $20 billion to $15 billion, while deposits have fallen from $100 billion to $95 billion. With a required reserve ratio of 20 percent, banks must have .20 × $95 billion, or $19 billion, in reserves. Banks are under their required reserve ratio by $4 billion [$19 billion (the amount they should have) minus $15 billion (the amount they do have)]. To comply with the federal regulations, banks must decrease their loans and their deposits.[9]

The final equilibrium position is shown in panel 3, where commercial banks have reduced their loans by $20 billion. Notice that the change in deposits from panel 1 to panel 3 is $25 billion, which is five times the size of the change in reserves that the Fed brought about through its $5 billion open market sale of securities. This corresponds exactly to our earlier analysis of the money multiplier. The change in money (−$25 billion) is equal to the money multiplier (5) times the change in reserves (−$5 billion).

Now consider what happens when the Fed *purchases* a government security. Suppose you hold $100 in Treasury bills, which the Fed buys from you. The Fed writes you a check for $100, and you turn in your Treasury bills. You then take the $100 check and deposit it in your local bank. This increases the reserves of your bank by $100 and begins a new episode in the money expansion story. With a reserve requirement of 20 percent, your bank can now lend out $80. If that $80 is spent and ends up back in a bank, that bank can lend $64, and so on. (Review Figure 10.3.) The Fed can expand the money supply by buying government securities from people who own them, just the way it reduces the money supply by selling these securities.

Each business day the Open Market Desk in the New York Federal Reserve Bank buys or sells millions of dollars' worth of securities, usually to large security dealers who act as intermediaries between the Fed and the private markets. We can sum up the effect of these open market operations this way:

- An open market *purchase* of securities by the Fed results in an *increase* in reserves and an *increase* in the supply of money by an amount equal to the money multiplier times the change in reserves.
- An open market *sale* of securities by the Fed results in a *decrease* in reserves and a *decrease* in the supply of money by an amount equal to the money multiplier times the change in reserves.

Open market operations are the Fed's preferred means of controlling the money supply for several reasons. First, open market operations can be used with some precision. If the Fed needs to change the money supply by just a small amount, it can buy or sell a small volume of government securities. If it wants a larger change in the money supply, it can buy or sell a larger amount. Second, open market operations are extremely flexible. If the Fed decides to reverse course, it can easily switch from buying securities to selling them. Finally, open market operations have a fairly predictable effect on the supply of money. Because banks are obliged to meet their reserve requirements, an open market sale of $100 in government securities will reduce reserves by $100, which will reduce the supply of money by $100 times the money multiplier.

Where does the Fed get the money to buy government securities when it wants to expand the money supply? The Fed simply creates it! In effect, it tells the bank from which it has bought a $100 security that its reserve account (deposit) at the Fed now contains $100 more than it did previously. This is where the power of the Fed, or any central bank, lies. The Fed has the ability to create money at will. In the United States, the Fed exercises this power when it creates money to buy government securities.

---

[9] Once again, banks never really have to call in loans. Loans and deposits would probably be reduced by slowing the rate of new lending as old loans come due and are paid off.

The Supply Curve for Money

Thus far we know how the Fed can control the money supply by controlling the amount of reserves in the economy. If the Fed wants the quantity of money to be $1,350 billion on a given date, it can aim for this target by changing the discount rate by changing the required reserve ratio, or by engaging in open market operations. (As discussed earlier, the Fed almost always uses open market operations as its tool.) Because the Fed can choose whatever value of the money supply that it wants, it is useful to begin with the case in which the Fed picks a value independent of anything in the economy. In other words, we will assume for now that the Fed's choice of the value of the money supply does not depend on things like the interest rate, inflation, unemployment, and aggregate output. This assumption is relaxed in Chapter 13. We will see in Chapter 13 that in practice, the Fed chooses a value of the money supply to hit a particular value of the interest rate, where the Fed's choice for the target interest rate depends on things like inflation and unemployment. But this is jumping ahead of the story.

If the Fed's choice of the value for the money supply does not depend on the interest rate, then in Figure 10.5 we can draw the money supply curve as a vertical line. Therefore, until we get to Chapter 13, we will assume that the money supply curve is vertical.

▶ **FIGURE 10.5**

The Supply of Money

If the Fed's money supply behavior is not influenced by the interest rate, the money supply curve is a vertical line. Through open market operations, the Fed can have the money supply be whatever value it wants.

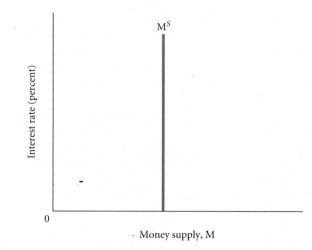

Looking Ahead

This chapter has discussed only the supply side of the money market. We have seen what money is, how banks create money by making loans, and how the Fed controls the money supply. In the next chapter, we turn to the demand side of the money market. We will examine the demand for money and see how the supply of and demand for money determine the equilibrium interest rate.

S U M M A R Y

AN OVERVIEW OF MONEY *p. 181*

1. Money has three distinguishing characteristics: (1) a *means of payment*, or *medium of exchange*; (2) *a store of value*; and (3) *a unit of account*. The alternative to using money is *barter*, in which goods are exchanged directly for other goods. Barter is costly and inefficient in an economy with many different kinds of goods.

2. *Commodity monies* are items that are used as money and that have an intrinsic value in some other use—for example, gold and cigarettes. *Fiat monies* are intrinsically worthless apart

from their use as money. To ensure the acceptance of fiat monies, governments use their power to declare money *legal tender* and promise the public they will not debase the currency by expanding its supply rapidly.

3. There are various definitions of money. Currency plus demand deposits plus traveler's checks plus other checkable deposits compose M1, or *transactions money*—money that can be used directly to buy things. The addition of savings accounts and money market accounts (*near monies*) to M1 gives M2, or *broad money*.

HOW BANKS CREATE MONEY p. 186

4. The *required reserve ratio* is the percentage of a bank's deposits that must be kept as *reserves* at the nation's central bank, the *Federal Reserve*.

5. Banks create money by making loans. When a bank makes a loan to a customer, it creates a deposit in that customer's account. This deposit becomes part of the money supply. Banks can create money only when they have *excess reserves*—reserves in excess of the amount set by the required reserve ratio.

6. The *money multiplier* is the multiple by which the total supply of money can increase for every dollar increase in reserves. The money multiplier is equal to 1/required reserve ratio.

THE FEDERAL RESERVE SYSTEM p. 191

7. The Fed's most important function is controlling the nation's money supply. The Fed also performs several other functions: It clears interbank payments, is responsible for many of the regulations governing banking practices and standards, and acts as a *lender of last resort* for troubled banks that cannot find any other sources of funds. The Fed also acts as the bank for the U.S. government.

HOW THE FEDERAL RESERVE CONTROLS THE MONEY SUPPLY p. 194

8. The key to understanding how the Fed controls the money supply is the role of reserves. If the Fed wants to increase the supply of money, it creates more reserves, freeing banks to create additional deposits. If it wants to decrease the money supply, it reduces reserves.

9. The Fed has three tools to control the money supply: (1) changing the required reserve ratio, (2) changing the *discount rate* (the interest rate member banks pay when they borrow from the Fed), and (3) engaging in *open market operations* (the buying and selling of already-existing government securities). To increase the money supply, the Fed can create additional reserves by lowering the discount rate or by buying government securities or the Fed can increase the number of deposits that can be created from a given quantity of reserves by lowering the required reserve ratio. To decrease the money supply, the Fed can reduce reserves by raising the discount rate or by selling government securities or it can raise the required reserve ratio.

10. If the Fed's money supply behavior is not influenced by the interest rate, the supply curve for money is a vertical line.

REVIEW TERMS AND CONCEPTS

barter, *p. 182*

commodity monies, *p. 184*

currency debasement, *p. 184*

discount rate, *p. 196*

excess reserves, *p. 189*

Federal Open Market Committee (FOMC), *p. 192*

Federal Reserve Bank (the Fed), *p. 188*

fiat, *or token, money, p. 184*

financial intermediaries, *p. 186*

legal tender, *p. 184*

lender of last resort, *p. 193*

liquidity property of money, *p. 182*

M1, *or transactions money, p. 185*

M2, *or broad money, p. 185*

medium of exchange, *or means of payment, p. 182*

money multiplier, *p. 191*

moral suasion, *p. 197*

near monies, *p. 185*

Open Market Desk, *p. 192*

open market operations, *p. 197*

required reserve ratio, *p. 188*

reserves, *p. 188*

run on a bank, *p. 187*

store of value, *p. 182*

unit of account, *p. 182*

1. M1 ≡ currency held outside banks + demand deposits + traveler's checks + other checkable deposits

2. M2 ≡ M1 + savings accounts + money market accounts + other near monies

3. Assets ≡ Liabilities + Net Worth

4. Excess reserves ≡ actual reserves − required reserves

5. Money multiplier $\equiv \dfrac{1}{\text{required reserve ratio}}$

PROBLEMS

Visit **www.myeconlab.com** to complete the problems marked in orange online. You will receive instant feedback on your answers, tutorial help, and access to additional practice problems.

1. In the Republic of Ragu, the currency is the rag. During 2009, the Treasury of Ragu sold bonds to finance the Ragu budget deficit. In all, the Treasury sold 50,000 10-year bonds with a face value of 100 rags each. The total deficit was 5 million rags. Further, assume that the Ragu Central Bank reserve requirement was 20 percent and that in the same year, the bank bought 500,000 rags' worth of outstanding bonds on the open market.

Finally, assume that all of the Ragu debt is held by either the private sector (the public) or the central bank.

a. What is the combined effect of the Treasury sale and the central bank purchase on the total Ragu debt outstanding? on the debt held by the private sector?

b. What is the effect of the Treasury sale on the money supply in Ragu?

c. Assuming no leakage of reserves out of the banking system, what is the effect of the central bank purchase of bonds on the money supply?

2. In 2000, the federal debt was being paid down because the federal budget was in surplus. Recall that surplus means that tax collections (T) exceed government spending (G). The surplus ($T - G$) was used to buy back government bonds from the public, reducing the federal debt. As we discussed in this chapter, the main method by which the Fed increases the money supply is to buy government bonds by using open market operations. What is the impact on the money supply of using the fiscal surplus to buy back bonds? In terms of their impacts on the money supply, what is the difference between Fed open market purchases of bonds and Treasury purchases of bonds using tax revenues?

3. For each of the following, determine whether it is an asset or a liability on the accounting books of a bank. Explain why in each case.

   Cash in the vault
   Demand deposits
   Savings deposits
   Reserves
   Loans
   Deposits at the Federal Reserve

4. [Related to the *Economics in Practice* on p. 183] It is well known that cigarettes served as money for prisoners of war in World War II. Do a Google search using the keyword *cigarettes* and write a description of how this came to be and how it worked.

5. If the head of the Central Bank of Japan wanted to expand the supply of money in Japan in 2009, which of the following would do it? Explain your answer.

   Increase the required reserve ratio
   Decrease the required reserve ratio
   Increase the discount rate
   Decrease the discount rate
   Buy government securities in the open market
   Sell government securities in the open market

6. Suppose in the Republic of Madison that the regulation of banking rested with the Madison Congress, including the determination of the reserve ratio. The Central Bank of Madison is charged with regulating the money supply by using open market operations. In April 2006, the money supply was estimated to be 52 million hurls. At the same time, bank reserves were 6.24 million hurls and the reserve requirement was 12 percent. The banking industry, being "loaned up," lobbied the Congress to cut the reserve ratio. The Congress yielded and cut required reserves to 10 percent. What is the potential impact on the money supply? Suppose the central bank decided that the money supply should not be increased. What countermeasures could it take to prevent the Congress from expanding the money supply?

7. The U.S. money supply (M1) at the beginning of 2000 was $1,148 billion broken down as follows: $523 billion in currency, $8 billion in traveler's checks, and $616 billion in checking deposits. Suppose the Fed decided to reduce the money supply by increasing the reserve requirement from 10 percent to 11 percent. Assuming all banks were initially loaned up (had no excess reserves) and currency held outside of banks did not change, how large a change in the money supply would have resulted from the change in the reserve requirement?

8. As king of Medivalia, you are constantly strapped for funds to pay your army. Your chief economic wizard suggests the following plan: "When you collect your tax payments from your subjects, insist on being paid in gold coins. Take those gold coins, melt them down, and remint them with an extra 10 percent of brass thrown in. You will then have 10 percent more money than you started with." What do you think of the plan? Will it work?

9. Why is M2 sometimes a more stable measure of money than M1? Explain in your own words using the definitions of M1 and M2.

10. Do you agree or disagree with each of the following statements? Explain your answers.
    a. When the Treasury of the United States issues bonds and sells them to the public to finance the deficit, the money supply remains unchanged because every dollar of money taken in by the Treasury goes right back into circulation through government spending. This is not true when the Fed sells bonds to the public.
    b. The money multiplier depends on the marginal propensity to save.

*11. When the Fed adds new reserves to the system, some of these new reserves find their way out of the country into foreign banks or foreign investment funds. In addition, some portion of the new reserves ends up in people's pockets and mattresses instead of bank vaults. These "leakages" reduce the money multiplier and sometimes make it very difficult for the Fed to control the money supply precisely. Explain why this is true.

12. You are given this account for a bank:

	ASSETS		LIABILITIES
Reserves	$ 500	$3,500	Deposits
Loans	3,000		

The required reserve ratio is 10 percent.
a. How much is the bank required to hold as reserves given its deposits of $3,500?
b. How much are its excess reserves?
c. By how much can the bank increase its loans?
d. Suppose a depositor comes to the bank and withdraws $200 in cash. Show the bank's new balance sheet, assuming the bank obtains the cash by drawing down its reserves. Does the bank now hold excess reserves? Is it meeting the required reserve ratio? If not, what can it do?

----

* Note: Problems marked with an asterisk are more challenging.

Money Demand and the Equilibrium Interest Rate

Having discussed the supply of money in the last chapter, we now turn to the *demand* for money. One goal of this and the previous chapter is to provide a theory of how the interest rate is determined in the macroeconomy. Once we have seen how the interest rate is determined, we can turn to how the Federal Reserve (Fed) affects the interest rate through its ability to change the money supply.

Interest Rates and Bond Prices

Interest is the fee that borrowers pay to lenders for the use of their funds. Firms and governments borrow funds by issuing bonds, and they pay interest to the lenders that purchase the bonds. Households also borrow, either directly from banks and finance companies or by taking out mortgages.

Some loans are very simple. You might borrow $1,000 from a bank to be paid back a year from the date you borrowed the funds. If the bank charged you, say, $100 for doing this, the interest rate on the loan would be 10 percent. You would receive $1,000 now and pay back $1,100 at the end of the year—the original $1,000 plus the interest of $100. In this simple case the interest rate is just the interest payment divided by the amount of the loan, namely 10 percent.

Bonds are more complicated loans. Bonds have several properties. First, they are issued with a face value, typically in denominations of $1,000. Second, they come with a maturity date, which is the date the borrower agrees to pay the lender the face value of the bond. Third, there is a fixed payment of a specified amount that is paid to the bondholder each year. This payment is known as a coupon.

Say that company XYZ on January 2, 2008, issued a 15-year bond that had a face value of $1,000 and paid a coupon of $100 per year. On this date the company sold the bond in the bond market. The price at which the bond sold would be whatever price the market determined it to be. Say that the market-determined price was in fact $1,000. (Firms when issuing bonds try to choose the coupon to be such that the price that the bond initially sells for is roughly equal to its face value.) The lender would give XYZ a check for $1,000 and every January for the next 14 years XYZ would send the lender a check for $100. Then on January 2, 2023, XYZ would send the lender a check for the face value of the bond—$1,000—plus the last coupon payment—$100— and that would square all accounts. In this example the interest rate that the lender receives each year on his or her $1,000 investment is 10 percent. If, on the other hand, the market-determined price of the XYZ bond at the time of issue were only $900, then the interest rate that the lender receives would be larger than 10 percent. The lender pays $900 and receives $100 each year. This is an interest rate of roughly 11.1 percent.

A key relationship that we will use in this chapter is that market-determined prices of existing bonds and interest rates are inversely related. The fact that the coupon on a bond is unchanged over

interest The fee that borrowers pay to lenders for the use of their funds.

Professor Serebryakov Makes an Economic Error

In Chekhov's play *Uncle Vanya*, Alexander Vladimirovitch Serebryakov, a retired professor, but apparently not of economics, calls his household together to make an announcement. He has retired to his country estate, but he does not like living there. Unfortunately, the estate does not derive enough income to allow him to live in town. To his gathered household, he thus proposes the following:

Omitting details, I will put it before you in rough outline. Our estate yields on an average not more than two per cent, on its capital value. I propose to sell it. If we invest the money in suitable securities, we should get from four to five per cent, and I think we might even have a few thousand roubles to spare for buying a small villa in Finland.

This idea was not well received by the household, especially by Uncle Vanya, who lost it for a while and tried to kill Professor Serebryakov, but no one pointed out that this was bad economics. As the beginning of this chapter discusses, if you buy a bond and interest rates rise, the price of your bond falls. What Professor Serebryakov does not realize is that what he is calling the capital value of the estate, on which he is earning 2 percent, is not the value for which he could sell the estate if the interest rate on "suitable" securities is 5 percent. If an investor in Russia can earn 5 percent on these securities, why would he or she buy an estate earning only 2 percent? The price of the estate would have to fall until the return to the investor was 5 percent. To make matters worse, it may have been that the estate was a riskier investment than the securities, and if this were so, a return higher than 5 percent would have been required on the estate purchase to compensate the investor for the extra risk. This would, of course, lower the price of the estate even more. In short, this is not a scheme by which the professor could earn more money than what the estate is currently yielding. Perhaps had Uncle Vanya taken an introductory economics course and known this, he would have been less agitated.

time does not mean that a bond's price is insulated from interest rate movements. Say that after XYZ issued its bond, interest rates went up so that a company similar to XYZ when issuing a 15-year bond had to choose a coupon of $200 to have its bond initially sell for $1,000. At $1,000 this bond is clearly a better deal than the XYZ bond at $1,000 because the coupon is larger. If the owner of the XYZ bond wanted to sell it, what price could he or she get? It should be obvious that he or she could not get $1,000 since people could buy the other bond for $1,000 and earn more. The price of the XYZ bond would have to fall to have investors be indifferent between buying it and buying the other bond. In other words, when interest rates rise, the prices of existing bonds fall.

It is important to realize that the bond market directly determines prices of bonds, not interest rates. Given a bond's market-determined price, its face value, its maturity, and its coupon, the interest rate, or yield, on that bond can be calculated. Interest rates are thus *indirectly* determined by the bond market. Although each bond generally has at least a slightly different interest rate, we will assume for simplicity in this and the following chapters that there is only one interest rate. (Appendix A to this chapter provides some detail on various types of interest rates.) In fact, we will assume in the following analysis that there is only one type of bond. The (one) interest rate is the market-determined interest rate on this bond.

The Demand for Money

What factors and what forces determine the demand for money are central issues in macroeconomics. As we shall see, the interest rate and the level of national income (Y) influence how much money households and firms choose to hold.

Before we proceed, we must stress one point that may be troublesome. When we speak of the demand for money, we are not asking these questions: How much cash would you like to have? How much income would you like to earn? How much wealth would you like? (The answer to these questions is presumably "as much as possible.") Instead, we are concerned with how much of your financial assets you want to hold *in the form of money*, which does not earn interest, versus how much you want to hold in interest-bearing securities such as bonds. We take as given the *total* amount of financial assets. Our concern here is with how these assets are divided between money and interest-bearing securities.

The Transaction Motive

How much money to hold involves a trade-off between the liquidity of money and the interest income offered by other kinds of assets. The main reason for holding money instead of interest-bearing assets is that money is useful for buying things. Economists call this the **transaction motive**. This rationale for holding money is at the heart of the discussion that follows.[1]

To keep our analysis of the demand for money clear, we need a few simplifying assumptions. First, we assume that there are only two kinds of assets available to households: bonds and money. By "bonds" we mean interest-bearing securities of all kinds. As noted above, we are assuming that there is only one type of bond and only one market-determined interest rate. By "money" we mean currency in circulation and deposits in checking accounts that do not pay interest.[2]

Second, we assume that income for the typical household is "bunched up." It arrives once a month at the beginning of the month. Spending, by contrast, is spread out over time; we assume that spending occurs at a completely uniform rate throughout the month—that is, that the same amount is spent each day (Figure 11.1). The mismatch between the timing of money inflow and the timing of money outflow is sometimes called the **nonsynchronization of income and spending**.

transaction motive The main reason that people hold money—to buy things.

nonsynchronization of income and spending The mismatch between the timing of money inflow to the household and the timing of money outflow for household expenses.

◀ **FIGURE 11.1**

The Nonsynchronization of Income and Spending

Income arrives only once a month, but spending takes place continuously.

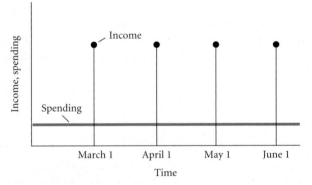

Finally, we assume that spending for the month is equal to income for the month. Because we are focusing on the transactions demand for money and not on its use as a store of value, this assumption is perfectly reasonable.

---

[1] The model that we discuss here is known in the economics profession as the Baumol/Tobin model, after the two economists who independently derived it, William Baumol and James Tobin.

[2] Although we are assuming that checking accounts do not pay interest, many do. Fortunately, all that we really need to assume here is that the interest rate on checking accounts is less than the interest rate on "bonds." Suppose bonds pay 10 percent interest and checking accounts pay 5 percent. (Checking accounts must pay less than bonds. Otherwise, everyone would hold all their wealth in checking accounts and none in bonds because checking accounts are more convenient.) When it comes to choosing whether to hold bonds or money, the difference in the interest rates on the two matters. People are concerned about how much extra interest they will earn from holding bonds instead of money. For simplicity, we are assuming in the following discussion that the interest rate on checking accounts is zero.

Given these assumptions, how would a rational person (household) decide how much of monthly income to hold as money and how much to hold as interest-bearing bonds? Suppose Jim decides to deposit his entire paycheck in his checking account. Let us say that Jim earns $1,200 per month. The pattern of Jim's bank account balance is illustrated in Figure 11.2. At the beginning of the month, Jim's balance is $1,200. As the month rolls by, Jim draws down his balance, writing checks or withdrawing cash to pay for the things he buys. At the end of the month, Jim's bank account balance is down to zero. Just in time, he receives his next month's paycheck, deposits it, and the process begins again.

▶ **FIGURE 11.2**

Jim's Monthly Checking Account Balances: Strategy 1

Jim could decide to deposit his entire paycheck ($1,200) into his checking account at the start of the month and run his balance down to zero by the end of the month. In this case, his average balance would be $600.

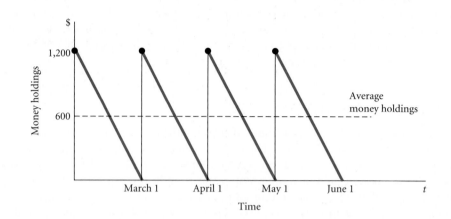

One useful statistic we need to calculate is the *average balance* in Jim's account. Jim spends his money at a constant $40 per day ($40 per day times 30 days per month = $1,200). His average balance is just his starting balance ($1,200) plus his ending balance (0) divided by 2, or ($1,200 + 0)/2 = $600. For the first half of the month, Jim has more than his average of $600 on deposit, and for the second half of the month, he has less than his average.

Is anything wrong with Jim's strategy? Yes. If he follows the plan described, Jim is giving up interest on his funds, interest he could be earning if he held some of his funds in interest-bearing bonds instead of in his checking account. How could he manage his funds to give himself more interest?

Instead of depositing his entire paycheck in his checking account at the beginning of the month, Jim could put half his paycheck into his checking account and buy a bond with the other half. By doing this, he would run out of money in his checking account halfway through the month. At a spending rate of $40 per day, his initial deposit of $600 would last only 15 days. Jim would have to sell his bond halfway through the month and deposit the $600 from the sale of the bond in his checking account to pay his bills during the second half of the month.

Jim's money holdings (checking account balances) if he follows this strategy are shown in Figure 11.3. When he follows the buy-a-$600-bond strategy, Jim reduces the average amount of money in his checking account. Comparing the dashed green lines (old strategy) with the solid green lines (buy-$600-bond strategy), his average bank balance is exactly half of what it was with the first strategy.[3]

The buy-a-$600-bond strategy seems sensible. The object of this strategy was to keep some funds in bonds, where they could earn interest, instead of being "idle" money. Why should he stop there? Another possibility would be for Jim to put only $400 into his checking account on the first of the month and buy two $400 bonds. The $400 in his account will last only 10 days if he spends $40 per day, so after 10 days he must sell one of the bonds and deposit the $400 from the sale in his checking account. This will last through the 20th of the month, at which point he must sell the second bond and deposit the other $400. This strategy lowers Jim's average money holding (checking account balance) even further, reducing his money holdings to an average of only $200 per month, with correspondingly higher average holdings of interest-earning bonds.

---

[3] Jim's average balance for the first half of the month is (starting balance + ending balance)/2, or ($600 + 0)/2 = $300. His average for the second half of the month is also $300. His average for the month as a whole is $300.

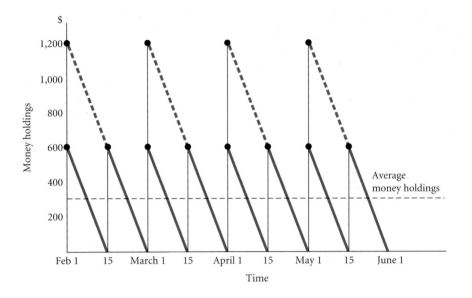

◀ FIGURE 11.3

Jim's Monthly Checking Account Balances: Strategy 2

Jim could also choose to put half of his paycheck into his checking account and buy a bond with the other half of his income. At mid-month, Jim would sell the bond and deposit the $600 into his checking account to pay the second half of the month's bills. Following this strategy, Jim's average money holdings would be $300.

You can imagine Jim going even further. Why not hold all wealth in the form of bonds (where it earns interest) and make transfers from bonds to money every time he makes a purchase? If selling bonds, transferring funds to checking accounts, and making trips to the bank were without cost, Jim would never hold money for more than an instant. Each time he needed to pay cash for something or to write a check, he would go to the bank or call the bank, transfer the exact amount of the transaction to his checking account, and withdraw the cash or write the check to complete the transaction. If he did this constantly, he would squeeze the most interest possible out of his funds because he would never hold assets that did not earn interest.

In practice, money management of this kind is costly. There are brokerage fees and other costs to buy or sell bonds, and time must be spent waiting in line at the bank or at an ATM. At the same time, it is costly to hold assets in non-interest-bearing form because they lose potential interest revenue.

We have a trade-off problem of the type that pervades economics. Switching more often from bonds to money raises the interest revenue Jim earns (because the more times he switches, the less, on average, he has to hold in his checking account and the more he can keep in bonds), but this increases his money management costs. Less switching means more interest revenue lost (because average money holdings are higher) but lower money management costs (fewer purchases and sales of bonds, less time spent waiting in bank lines, fewer trips to the bank, and so on). Given this trade-off, there is a level of average money balances that earns Jim the most profit, taking into account both the interest earned on bonds and the costs paid for switching from bonds to money. This level is his *optimal balance*.

How does the interest rate affect the number of switches that Jim makes and thus the average money balance he chooses to hold? It is easy to see why an increase in the interest rate lowers the optimal money balance. If the interest rate were only 2 percent, it would not be worthwhile to give up much liquidity by holding bonds instead of cash or checking balances. However, if the interest rate were 30 percent, the opportunity cost of holding money instead of bonds would be quite high and we would expect people to keep most of their funds in bonds and to spend considerable time managing their money balances. The interest rate represents the opportunity cost of holding money (and therefore not holding bonds, which pay interest). The higher the interest rate, the higher the opportunity cost of holding money and the less money people will want to hold. When interest rates are high, people want to take advantage of the high return on bonds, so they choose to hold very little money. Appendix B to this chapter provides a detailed example of this principle.

A demand curve for money, with the interest rate representing the "price" of money, would look like the curve labeled M^d in Figure 11.4. At higher interest rates, bonds are more attractive than money, so people hold less money because they must make a larger sacrifice in interest for each dollar of money they hold. The curve in Figure 11.4 slopes downward, just like an ordinary demand curve for oranges or shoes. There is an inverse relationship between the interest rate and the quantity of money demanded.[4]

▶ **FIGURE 11.4**

The Demand Curve for Money Balances

The quantity of money demanded (the amount of money households and firms want to hold) is a function of the interest rate. Because the interest rate is the opportunity cost of holding money balances, increases in the interest rate reduce the quantity of money that firms and households want to hold and decreases in the interest rate increase the quantity of money that firms and households want to hold.

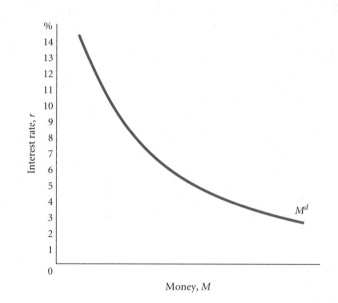

The Speculation Motive

A number of theories have been offered to explain why the quantity of money households want to hold may rise when interest rates fall and fall when interest rates rise. One theory involves household expectations and the fact, as discussed at the beginning of this chapter, that interest rates and bond prices are inversely related.

Consider your desire to hold money balances instead of bonds. If market interest rates are higher than normal, you may expect them to come down in the future. If and when interest rates fall, the bonds that you bought when interest rates were high will increase in price. When interest rates are high, the opportunity cost of holding cash balances is high and there is a **speculation motive** for holding bonds in lieu of cash. You are "speculating" that interest rates will fall in the future and thus that bond prices will rise.

speculation motive One reason for holding bonds instead of money: Because the market price of interest-bearing bonds is inversely related to the interest rate, investors may want to hold bonds when interest rates are high with the hope of selling them when interest rates fall.

Similarly, when market interest rates are lower than normal, you may expect them to rise in the future. Rising interest rates will bring about a decline in the price of existing bonds. Thus, when interest rates are low, it is a good time to be holding money and not bonds. When interest rates are low, not only is the opportunity cost of holding cash balances low, but also there is a speculative motive for holding a larger amount of money. Why should you put money into bonds now when you expect interest rates to rise in the future and thus bond prices to fall?

The Total Demand for Money

So far we have talked only about household demand for checking account balances. However, the total quantity of money demanded in the economy is the sum of the demand for checking account balances *and cash* by both households *and firms*.

The trade-off for firms is the same as it was for Jim. Like households, firms must manage their money. They have payrolls to meet and purchases to make, they receive cash and checks from sales, and many firms that deal with the public must make change—they need cash in the cash register. Thus, just like Jim, firms need money to engage in ordinary transactions.

---

[4] The theory of money demand presented here assumes that people know the exact timing of their income and spending. In practice, both have some uncertainty attached to them. For example, some income payments may be unexpectedly delayed a few days or weeks, and some expenditures may arise unexpectedly (such as the cost of repairing a plumbing problem). Because people know that this uncertainty exists, as a precaution against unanticipated delays in income receipts or unanticipated expenses, they may choose to hold more money than the strict transactions motive would suggest. This reason for holding money is sometimes called the *precautionary motive*.

ECONOMICS IN PRACTICE

ATMs and the Demand for Money

Twenty years ago the typical college student spent many a Friday afternoon visiting a bank to make sure he or she had enough cash for weekend activities. Today the typical student, whether in the United States or abroad, doesn't need to plan ahead. As a result of automated teller machines (ATMs), access to your bank account is available 24-7. What difference has the spread of ATMs made on the demand for money?

Italy makes a great case study of the effects of the spread of ATMs on the demand for money. In Italy, virtually all checking accounts pay interest. What doesn't pay interest is cash. So from the point of view of the model in this chapter, we can think of Italian checking accounts as (interest-earning) "bonds" and cash as (non-interest-earning) "money." In other words, in Italy there is an interest cost to carrying cash instead of depositing the cash in a checking account. A recent paper by three economists—Orazio Attansio from University College London, Luigi Guiso from the University

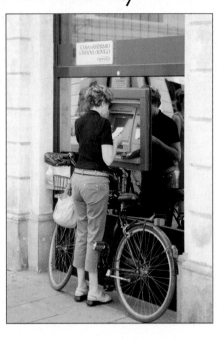

of Sassari, Italy, and Tullio Jappelli from the University of Salerno, Italy—took advantage of this institutional fact to see how the availability of ATMs influence the demand for cash (non-interest-earning money).[1]

Why do we think there might be an effect? Think back to the college student of 20 years ago. On Friday, he or she might have withdrawn cash in excess of expected weekly needs just in case. With ATMs everywhere, cash can be withdrawn as needed. This means that the amount of cash needed to support a given level of consumption should fall as ATMs proliferate. This is exactly what Attansio, Guiso, and Jappelli found in Italy in the first six years of ATM adoption. In 1989, ATM adoption in Italy was relatively low, about 15 percent of the population. By 1995, ATM use had risen to about 40 percent. What happened to cash holdings in this period? The amount of cash divided by total consumption fell from 3.8 percent to 2.8 percent. The study also found, as we would expect from our discussion in the text, that the demand for cash responds to changes in the interest rate paid on checking accounts. The higher the interest rate, the less cash held. In other words, when the interest rate on checking accounts rises, people go to ATM machines more often and take out less in cash each time, thereby keeping, on average, more in checking accounts earning the higher interest rate.

[1] *Orazio Attansio, Luigi Guiso, and Tullio Jappelli, "The Demand for Money, Financial Innovation and the Welfare Costs of Inflation: An Analysis with Household Data," Journal of Political Economy, April 2002.*

However, firms as well as households can hold their assets in interest-earning form. Firms manage their assets the same way households do, keeping some in cash, some in their checking accounts, and some in bonds. A higher interest rate raises the opportunity cost of money for firms as well as for households and thus reduces the demand for money.

The same trade-off holds for cash. We all walk around with some money in our pockets, but not thousands of dollars, for routine transactions. We carry, on average, about what we think we will need, not more, because there are costs—risks of being robbed and forgone interest. At any given moment, there is a demand for money—for cash and checking account balances. Although households and firms need to hold balances for everyday transactions, their demand has a limit. For both households and firms, the quantity of money demanded at any moment depends on the opportunity cost of holding money, a cost determined by the interest rate.

The Effects of Income and the Price Level on the Demand for Money

The money demand curve in Figure 11.4 is a function of the interest rate. There are, however, other factors besides the interest rate that influence total desired money holdings. One is the dollar value of transactions made during a given period of time. Suppose Jim's income were to increase. Instead of making $1,200 in purchases each month, he will now spend more. He thus needs to hold more money. The reason is simple: To buy more things, he needs more money.

What is true for Jim is true for the economy as a whole. The total demand for money in the economy depends on the total dollar volume of transactions made. The total dollar volume of transactions in the economy, in turn, depends on two things: the total *number* of transactions and the average transaction *amount*. Although there are no data on the actual number of transactions in the economy, a reasonable indicator is likely to be aggregate output (income) (Y). A rise in aggregate output—real gross domestic product (GDP)—means that there is more economic activity. Firms are producing and selling more output, more people are on payrolls, and household incomes are higher. In short, there are more transactions and firms, and households together will hold more money when they are engaging in more transactions. Thus, an increase in aggregate output (income) will increase the demand for money. Figure 11.5 shows a shift of the money demand curve resulting from an increase in Y. For a given interest rate, a higher level of output means an increase in the *number* of transactions and more demand for money. The money demand curve shifts to the right when Y rises. Similarly, a decrease in Y means a decrease in the number of transactions and a lower demand for money. The money demand curve shifts to the left when Y falls.

▶ **FIGURE 11.5**

An Increase in Aggregate Output (Income) (Y) Will Shift the Money Demand Curve to the Right

An increase in Y means that there is more economic activity. Firms are producing and selling more, and households are earning more income and buying more. There are more transactions, for which money is needed. As a result, both firms and households are likely to increase their holdings of money balances at a given interest rate.

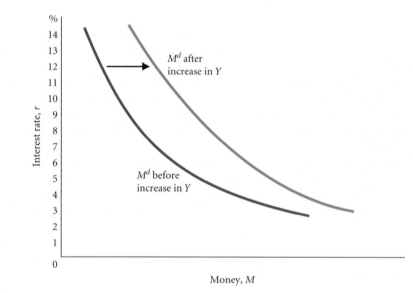

The amount of money that firms and households need to facilitate their day-to-day transactions also depends on the average *dollar amount* of each transaction. In turn, the average amount of each transaction depends on prices, or instead, on the *price level*. If all prices, including the price of labor (the wage rate) were to double, firms and households would need more money balances to carry out their day-to-day transactions—each transaction would require twice as much money. If the price of your lunch increases from $3.50 to $7.00, you will begin carrying more cash. If your end-of-the-month bills are twice as high as they used to be, you will keep more money in your checking account. Increases in the price level shift the money demand curve to the right, and decreases in the price level shift the money demand curve to the left. Even though the number of transactions may not have changed, the quantity of money needed to engage in them has.

Table 11.1 summarizes everything we have said about the demand for money. First, because the interest rate (r) is the opportunity cost of holding money balances for both firms and households, increases in the interest rate are likely to decrease the quantity of money demanded; decreases in the interest rate will increase the quantity of money demanded. Thus, the quantity of money demanded is a negative function of the interest rate.

The demand for money also depends on the dollar volume of transactions in a given period. The dollar volume of transactions depends on both aggregate output (income), Y, and the price level, P. The relationship of money demand to Y and the relationship of money demand to P are both positive. Increases in Y or in P will shift the money demand curve to the right; decreases in Y or P will shift the money demand curve to the left.

TABLE 11.1 Determinants of Money Demand

1. The interest rate: r (The quantity of money demanded is a negative function of the interest rate.)
2. The dollar volume of transactions
   a. Aggregate output (income): Y (An increase in Y shifts the money demand curve to the right.)
   b. The price level: P (An increase in P shifts the money demand curve to the right.)

The Equilibrium Interest Rate

We are now in a position to consider one of the key questions in macroeconomics: How is the interest rate determined in the economy?

Financial markets (what we call the money market) work very well in the United States. Almost all financial markets clear—that is, almost all reach an equilibrium where quantity demanded equals quantity supplied. In the money market, the point at which the quantity of money demanded equals the quantity of money supplied determines the equilibrium interest rate in the economy. This explanation sounds simple, but it requires elaboration.

Supply and Demand in the Money Market

We saw in Chapter 10 that the Fed controls the money supply through its manipulation of the amount of reserves in the economy. Because we are assuming that the Fed's money supply behavior does not depend on the interest rate, the money supply curve is a vertical line. (Review Figure 10.5 on p. 200.) In other words, we are assuming that the Fed uses its three tools (the required reserve ratio, the discount rate, and open market operations) to achieve its fixed target for the money supply.

Figure 11.6 superimposes the vertical money supply curve from Figure 10.5 on the downward-sloping money demand curve. Only at interest rate r^* is the quantity of money in circulation (the money supply) equal to the quantity of money demanded. To understand why r^* is an equilibrium, we need to ask what forces drive the interest rate to r^*. Keep in mind in the

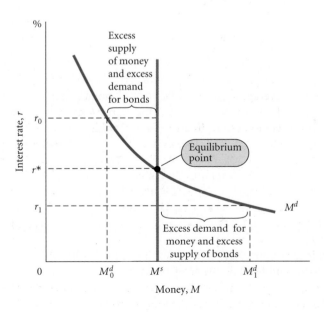

◀ **FIGURE 11.6**

Adjustments in the Money Market

Equilibrium exists in the money market when the supply of money is equal to the demand for money and thus when the supply of bonds is equal to the demand for bonds. At r_0 the price of bonds would be bid up (and thus the interest rate down), and at r_1 the price of bonds would be bid down (and thus the interest rate up).

following discussion that when the Fed fixes the money supply it also fixes the supply of bonds. The decision of households and firms is to decide what fraction of their funds to hold in non-interest-bearing money versus interest-bearing bonds. At the equilibrium interest rate r^* in Figure 11.6 the demand for bonds by households and firms is equal to the supply.

Consider r_0 in Figure 11.6, an interest rate higher than the equilibrium rate. At this interest rate households and firms would want to hold more bonds than the Fed is supplying (and less money than the Fed is supplying). They would bid the price of bonds up and thus the interest rate down. The bond market would clear when the price of bonds fell enough to correspond to an interest rate of r^*. At interest rate r_1 in Figure 11.6, which is lower than the equilibrium rate, households and firms would want to hold fewer bonds than the fed is supplying (and more money than the Fed is supplying). They would bid the price of bonds down and thus the interest rate up. The bond market would clear when the price of bonds rose enough to correspond to an interest rate of r^*.

Changing the Money Supply to Affect the Interest Rate

With an understanding of equilibrium in the money market, we now see how the Fed can affect the interest rate. Suppose the current interest rate is 7 percent and the Fed wants to reduce the interest rate. To do so, it would expand the money supply. Figure 11.7 shows how such an expansion would work. To expand M^s, the Fed can reduce the reserve requirement, cut the discount rate, or buy U.S. government securities on the open market. All these practices expand the quantity of reserves in the system. Banks can make more loans, and the money supply expands even more. (Review Chapter 10 if you are unsure why.) In Figure 11.7, the initial money supply curve, M_0^s, shifts to the right, to M_1^s. At M_1^s the supply of bonds is smaller than it was at M_0^s.

As the money supply expands from M_0^s to M_1^s, the supply of bonds is decreasing, which drives up the price of bonds. At M_1^s the equilibrium price of bonds corresponds to an interest rate of 4 percent. So the new equilibrium interest rate is 4 percent.

If the Fed wanted to increase the interest rate, it would contract the money supply. It could do so by increasing the reserve requirement, by raising the discount rate, or by selling U.S. government securities in the open market. Whichever tool the Fed chooses, the result would be lower reserves and a lower supply of money. The supply of money curve in Figure 11.7 would shift to the left, and the equilibrium interest rate would rise. (As an exercise, draw a graph of this situation and explain why the interest rate would rise.)

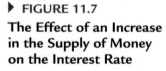

▶ **FIGURE 11.7**

The Effect of an Increase in the Supply of Money on the Interest Rate

An increase in the supply of money from M_0^s to M_1^s lowers the rate of interest from 7 percent to 4 percent.

Increases in Y and Shifts in the Money Demand Curve

Changes in the supply of money are not the only factors that influence the equilibrium interest rate. Shifts in money demand can do the same thing.

Recall that the demand for money depends on both the interest rate and the volume of transactions. As a rough measure of the volume of transactions, we use Y, the level of aggregate output (income). Remember that the relationship between money demand and Y is positive—increases in Y mean a higher level of real economic activity. More is being produced, income is higher, and there are more transactions in the economy. Consequently, the demand for money on the part of firms and households in aggregate is higher. An increase in Y shifts the money demand curve to the right.

Figure 11.8 illustrates such a shift. Y increases, causing money demand to shift from M_0^d to M_1^d. The result is an increase in the equilibrium level of the interest rate from 4 percent to 7 percent. A decrease in Y would shift M^d to the left, and the equilibrium interest rate would fall.

The money demand curve also shifts when the price level changes. If the price level rises, the money demand curve shifts to the right because people want more money to engage in their day-to-day transactions. In this case the equilibrium interest rate also rises. An increase in the price level is like an increase in Y in that both events increase the demand for money. The result is an increase in the equilibrium interest rate.

If the price level *falls*, the money demand curve shifts to the left because people want less money for their transactions. However, with the quantity of money supplied unchanged, the equilibrium interest rate falls. A decrease in the price level thus leads to a decrease in the equilibrium interest rate. We explore this relationship in more detail in Chapter 13.

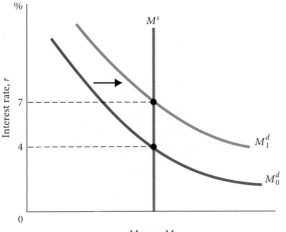

◀ **FIGURE 11.8**

The Effect of an Increase in Income on the Interest Rate

An increase in aggregate output (income) shifts the money demand curve from M_0^d to M_1^d, which raises the equilibrium interest rate from 4 percent to 7 percent.

Looking Ahead: The Federal Reserve and Monetary Policy

We now know that the Fed can change the interest rate by changing the quantity of money supplied. If the Fed increases the quantity of money, the interest rate falls. If the Fed decreases the quantity of money, the interest rate rises.

Nonetheless, we have not yet said *why* the Fed might want to change the interest rate or what happens to the economy when the interest rate changes. We have hinted at why: A low interest rate stimulates spending, particularly investment; a high interest rate reduces spending. By changing the interest rate, the Fed can change aggregate output (income). In the next chapter, we will combine our discussions of the goods and money markets and discuss how the interest rate affects the equilibrium level of aggregate output (income) (Y) in the goods market.

The Fed's use of its power to influence events in the goods market as well as in the money market is the center of the government's monetary policy. When the Fed moves to contract the money supply and thus raise interest rates in an effort to restrain the economy, economists call it a **tight monetary policy**. Conversely, when the Fed stimulates the economy by expanding the money supply and thus lower interest rates, it has an **easy monetary policy**. We will discuss the way in which the economy affects the Fed's behavior in Chapter 13.

tight monetary policy
Fed policies that contract the money supply and thus raise interest rates in an effort to restrain the economy.

easy monetary policy
Fed policies that expand the money supply and thus lower interest rates in an effort to stimulate the economy.

SUMMARY

INTEREST RATES AND BOND PRICES *p. 203*

1. *Interest* is the fee that borrowers pay to lenders for the use of their funds. Interest rates and bond prices are inversely related. Although there are many different interest rates in the United States, we assume for simplicity that there is only one interest rate in the economy.

THE DEMAND FOR MONEY *p. 205*

2. The demand for money depends negatively on the interest rate. The higher the interest rate, the higher the opportunity cost (more interest forgone) from holding money and the less money people will want to hold. An increase in the interest rate reduces the quantity demanded for money, and the money demand curve slopes downward.

3. The volume of transactions in the economy affects money demand. The total dollar volume of transactions depends on both the total number of transactions and the average transaction amount.

4. A reasonable measure of the number of transactions in the economy is aggregate output (income) (Y). When Y rises, there is more economic activity, more is being produced and sold, and more people are on payrolls—there are more transactions in the economy. An increase in Y causes the money demand curve to shift to the right. This effect follows because households and firms need more money when they are engaging in more transactions. A decrease in Y causes the money demand curve to shift to the left.

5. Changes in the price level affect the average dollar amount of each transaction. *Increases* in the price level increase the demand for money (shift the money demand curve to the right) because households and firms need more money for their expenditures. *Decreases* in the price level decrease the demand for money (shift the money demand curve to the left).

THE EQUILIBRIUM INTEREST RATE *p. 211*

6. The point at which the quantity of money supplied equals the quantity of money demanded determines the equilibrium interest rate in the economy. An excess supply of money will cause households and firms to buy more bonds, driving the interest rate down. An excess demand for money will cause households and firms to move out of bonds, driving the interest rate up.

7. The Fed can affect the equilibrium interest rate by changing the supply of money using one of its three tools—the required reserve ratio, the discount rate, or open market operations.

8. An increase in the price level is like an increase in Y in that both events cause an increase in money demand. The result is an increase in the equilibrium interest rate. A decrease in the price level leads to reduced money demand and a decrease in the equilibrium interest rate.

9. *Tight monetary policy* refers to Fed policies that contract the money supply and thus raise interest rates in an effort to restrain the economy. *Easy monetary policy* refers to Fed policies that expand the money supply and thus lower interest rates in an effort to stimulate the economy. The Fed chooses between these two types of policies for different reasons at different times.

REVIEW TERMS AND CONCEPTS

easy monetary policy, *p. 213*
interest, *p. 203*

nonsynchronization of income and spending, *p. 205*
speculation motive, *p. 208*

tight monetary policy, *p. 213*
transaction motive, *p. 205*

PROBLEMS

Visit **www.myeconlab.com** to complete the problems marked in orange online. You will receive instant feedback on your answers, tutorial help, and access to additional practice problems.

myeconlab

1. State whether you agree or disagree with the following statements and explain why.
   a. When the real economy expands (Y rises), the demand for money expands. As a result, households hold more cash and the supply of money expands.

   b. Inflation, a rise in the price level, causes the demand for money to decline. Because inflation causes money to be worth less, households want to hold less of it.
   c. If the Fed buys bonds in the open market and at the same time we experience a recession, interest rates will no doubt rise.

2. During 2003, we began to stop worrying that inflation was a problem. Instead, we began to worry about deflation, a decline in the price level. Assume that the Fed decided to hold the money supply constant. What impact would deflation have on interest rates?

3. [Related to *Economics in Practice* on *p. 209*] How many times a week do you use an ATM? If ATMs were not available, would you carry more cash? Would you keep more money in your checking account? How many times a day do you use cash?

4. What if, at a low level of interest rates, the money demand curve became nearly horizontal, as in the following graph. That is, with interest rates so low, the public would not find it attractive to hold bonds; thus, money demand would be very high. Many argue that this was the position of the U.S. economy in 2003. If the Fed decided to expand the money supply in the graph, what would be the impact on interest rates?

5. During the fourth quarter of 1993, real GDP in the United States grew at an annual rate of over 7 percent. During 1994, the economy continued to expand with modest inflation. (*Y* rose at a rate of 4 percent and *P* increased about 3 percent.) At the beginning of 1994, the prime interest rate (the interest rate that banks offer their best, least risky customers) stood at 6 percent, where it remained for over a year. By the beginning of 1995, the prime rate had increased to over 8.5 percent.
   a. By using money supply and money demand curves, show the effects of the increase in *Y* and *P* on interest rates, assuming *no change* in the money supply.
   b. On a separate graph, show that the interest rate can rise even if the Federal Reserve expands the money supply as long as it does so more slowly than money demand is increasing.

6. Illustrate the following situations using supply and demand curves for money:
   a. The Fed buys bonds in the open market during a recession.
   b. During a period of rapid inflation, the Fed increases the reserve requirement.
   c. The Fed acts to hold interest rates constant during a period of high inflation.
   d. During a period of no growth in GDP and zero inflation, the Fed lowers the discount rate.
   e. During a period of rapid real growth of GDP, the Fed acts to increase the reserve requirement.

7. During a recession, interest rates may fall even if the Fed takes no action to expand the money supply. Why? Use a graph to explain.

8. During the summer of 1997, Congress and the president agreed on a budget package to balance the federal budget. The "deal," signed into law by President Clinton in August as the Taxpayer Relief Act of 1997, contained substantial tax cuts and expenditure reductions. The tax reductions were scheduled to take effect immediately, however, while the expenditure cuts would come mostly in 1999 to 2002. Thus, in 1998, the package was seen by economists to be mildly expansionary. If the result is an increase in the growth of real output/income, what would you expect to happen to interest rates if the Fed holds the money supply (or the rate of growth of the money supply) constant? What would the Fed do if it wanted to raise interest rates? What if it wanted to lower interest rates? Illustrate with graphs.

9. The demand for money in a country is given by

$$M^d = 10,000 - 10,000r + Y$$

where M^d is money demand in dollars, r is the interest rate (a 10 percent interest rate means $r = 0.1$), and Y is national income. Assume that Y is initially 5,000.
   a. Graph the amount of money demanded (on the horizontal axis) against the interest rate (on the vertical axis).
   b. Suppose the money supply (M^s) is set by the central bank at $10,000. On the same graph you drew for part a., add the money supply curve. What is the equilibrium rate of interest? Explain how you arrived at your answer.
   c. Suppose income rises from $Y = 5,000$ to $Y = 7,500$. What happens to the money demand curve you drew in part a.? Draw the new curve if there is one. What happens to the equilibrium interest rate if the central bank does not change the supply of money?
   d. If the central bank wants to keep the equilibrium interest rate at the same value as it was in part b., by how much should it increase or decrease the supply of money given the new level of national income?
   e. Suppose the shift in part c. has occurred and the money supply remains at $10,000 but there is no observed change in the interest rate. What might have happened that could explain this?

10. [Related to *Economics in Practice* on *p. 204*] Between the end of 2007 and mid-2008, the Fed moved to cut interest rates to stimulate aggregate spending in the economy and to try and prevent a recession. Lower interest rates reduce the cost of borrowing and encourage firms to borrow and invest. They also have an effect on the value of the bonds (private and government) outstanding in the economy. Explain briefly but clearly why the value of bonds changes when interest rates change. Go to federalreserve.gov, click on "Economic Research & Data" and click on "Flow of Funds." Look at the most recent release and find balance sheet table B.100. How big is the value of Credit Market Instruments held by households?

APPENDIX A

THE VARIOUS INTEREST RATES IN THE U.S. ECONOMY

Although there are many different interest rates in the economy, they tend to move up or down with one another. Here we discuss some of their differences. We first look at the relationship between interest rates on securities with different *maturities*, or terms. We then briefly discuss some of the main interest rates in the U.S. economy.

THE TERM STRUCTURE OF INTEREST RATES

The *term structure of interest rates* is the relationship among the interest rates offered on securities of different maturities. The key here is understanding issues such as these: How are these different rates related? Does a 2-year security (an IOU that promises to repay principal, plus interest, after 2 years) pay a lower annual rate than a 1-year security (an IOU to be repaid, with interest, after 1 year)? What happens to the rate of interest offered on 1-year securities if the rate of interest on 2-year securities increases?

Assume that you want to invest some money for 2 years and at the end of the 2 years you want it back. Assume that you want to buy government securities. For this analysis, we restrict your choices to two: (1) You can buy a 2-year security today and hold it for 2 years, at which time you cash it in (we will assume that the interest rate on the 2-year security is 9 percent per year), or (2) you can buy a 1-year security today. At the end of 1 year, you must cash this security in; you can then buy another 1-year security. At the end of the second year, you will cash in the second security. Assume that the interest rate on the first 1-year security is 8 percent.

Which would you prefer? Currently, you do not have enough data to answer this question. To consider choice (2) sensibly, you need to know the interest rate on the 1-year security that you intend to buy in the second year. This rate will not be known until the second year. All you know now is the rate on the 2-year security and the rate on the current 1-year security. To decide what to do, you must form an *expectation* of the rate on the 1-year security a year from now. If you expect the 1-year rate (8 percent) to remain the same in the second year, you should buy the 2-year security. You would earn 9 percent per year on the 2-year security but only 8 percent per year on the two 1-year securities. If you expect the 1-year rate to rise to 12 percent a year from now, you should make the second choice. You would earn 8 percent in the first year, and you expect to earn 12 percent in the second year. The expected rate of return over the 2 years is about 10 percent, which is better than the 9 percent you can get on the 2-year security. If you expect the 1-year rate a year from now to be 10 percent, it does not matter very much which of the two choices you make. The rate of return over the 2-year period will be roughly 9 percent for both choices.

We now alter the focus of our discussion to get to the topic we are really interested in—how the 2-year rate is determined. Assume that the 1-year rate has been set by the Fed and it is 8 percent. Also assume that people expect the 1-year rate a year from now to be 10 percent. What is the 2-year rate? According to a theory called the *expectations theory of the term structure of interest rates*, the 2-year rate is equal to the average of the current 1-year rate and the 1-year rate expected a year from now. In this example, the 2-year rate would be 9 percent (the average of 8 percent and 10 percent).

If the 2-year rate were lower than the average of the two 1-year rates, people would not be indifferent as to which security they held. They would want to hold only the short-term 1-year securities. To find a buyer for a 2-year security, the seller would be forced to increase the interest rate it offers on the 2-year security until it is equal to the average of the current 1-year rate and the expected 1-year rate for next year. The interest rate on the 2-year security will continue to rise until people are once again indifferent between one 2-year security and two 1-year securities.[1]

Let us now return to Fed behavior. We know that the Fed can affect the short-term interest rate by changing the money supply, but does it also affect long-term interest rates? The answer is "somewhat." Because the 2-year rate is an average of the current 1-year rate and the expected 1-year rate a year from now, the Fed influences the 2-year rate to the extent that it influences the current 1-year rate. The same holds for 3-year rates and beyond. The current short-term rate is a means by which the Fed can influence longer-term rates.

In addition, Fed behavior may directly affect people's expectations of the future short-term rates, which will then affect long-term rates. If the chair of the Fed testifies before Congress that raising short-term interest rates is under consideration, people's expectations of higher future short-term interest rates are likely to increase. These expectations will then be reflected in current long-term interest rates.

TYPES OF INTEREST RATES

The following are some widely followed interest rates in the United States.

THREE-MONTH TREASURY BILL RATE

Government securities that mature in less than a year are called *Treasury bills*, or sometimes *T-bills*. The interest rate on 3-month Treasury bills is probably the most widely followed short-term interest rate.

GOVERNMENT BOND RATE

Government securities with terms of 1 year or more are called *government bonds*. There are 1-year bonds, 2-year bonds, and so on, up to 30-year bonds. Bonds of different terms have different interest rates. The relationship among the interest rates on the various maturities is the term structure of interest rates that we discussed in the first part of this Appendix.

FEDERAL FUNDS RATE

Banks borrow not only from the Fed but also from each other. If one bank has excess reserves, it can lend some of those reserves to other banks through the federal funds market. The

---

[1] For longer terms, additional future rates must be averaged in. For a 3-year security, for example, the expected 1-year rate a year from now and the expected 1-year rate 2 years from now are added to the current 1-year rate and averaged.

interest rate in this market is called the *federal funds rate*—the rate banks are charged to borrow reserves from other banks.

The federal funds market is really a desk in New York City. From all over the country, banks with excess reserves to lend and banks in need of reserves call the desk and negotiate a rate of interest. Account balances with the Fed are changed for the period of the loan without any physical movement of money.

This borrowing and lending, which takes place near the close of each working day, is generally for 1 day ("overnight"), so the federal funds rate is a 1-day rate. It is the rate on which the Fed has the most effect through its open market operations.

COMMERCIAL PAPER RATE

Firms have several alternatives for raising funds. They can sell stocks, issue bonds, or borrow from a bank. Large firms can also borrow directly from the public by issuing "commercial paper," which is essentially short-term corporate IOUs that offer a designated rate of interest. The interest rate offered on commercial paper depends on the financial condition of the firm and the maturity date of the IOU.

PRIME RATE

Banks charge different interest rates to different customers depending on how risky the banks perceive the customers to be. You would expect to pay a higher interest rate for a car loan than General Motors would pay for a $1 million loan to

finance investment. Also, you would pay more interest for an unsecured loan, a "personal" loan, than for one that was secured by some asset, such as a house or car, to be used as collateral.

The *prime rate* is a benchmark that banks often use in quoting interest rates to their customers. A very low-risk corporation might be able to borrow at (or even below) the prime rate. A less well-known firm might be quoted a rate of "prime plus three-fourths," which means that if the prime rate is, say, 10 percent, the firm would have to pay interest of 10.75 percent. The prime rate depends on the cost of funds to the bank; it moves up and down with changes in the economy.

AAA CORPORATE BOND RATE

Corporations finance much of their investment by selling bonds to the public. Corporate bonds are classified by various bond dealers according to their risk. Bonds issued by General Motors are in less risk of default than bonds issued by a new risky biotech research firm. Bonds differ from commercial paper in one important way: Bonds have a longer maturity.

Bonds are graded in much the same way students are. The highest grade is AAA, the next highest AA, and so on. The interest rate on bonds rated AAA is the *triple A corporate bond rate*, the rate that the least risky firms pay on the bonds that they issue.

PROBLEMS

1. The following table gives three key U.S. interest rates in 1980 and again in 1993:

	1980 (%)	1993 (%)
Three-month U.S. government bills	11.39	3.00
Long-term U.S. government bonds	11.27	6.59
Prime rate	15.26	6.00

Provide an explanation for the extreme differences that you see. Specifically, comment on (1) the fact that rates in 1980 were much higher than in 1993 and (2) the fact that the long-term rate was higher than the short-term rate in 1993 but lower in 1980.

APPENDIX B

THE DEMAND FOR MONEY: A NUMERICAL EXAMPLE

This Appendix presents a numerical example showing how optimal money management behavior can be derived.

We have seen that the interest rate represents the opportunity cost of holding funds in non-interest-bearing checking accounts (as opposed to bonds, which yield interest). We have also seen that costs are involved in switching from bonds to money. Given these costs, our objective is to determine the optimum amount of money for an individual to hold. The optimal average level of money holdings is the amount that maximizes the profits from money management. Interest is earned on average bond holdings, but the cost per switch multiplied by the

number of switches must be subtracted from interest revenue to obtain the net profit from money management.

Suppose the interest rate is .05 (5 percent), it costs $2 each time a bond is sold,[1] and the proceeds from the sale are deposited in one's checking account. Suppose also that the individual's income is $1,200 and that this income is spent evenly throughout the period. This situation is depicted in the top half of Table 11B.1. The optimum value for average money holdings is the value that achieves the largest possible profit in column 6 of the table. When the interest rate is 5 percent, the

---

[1] In this example, we will assume that the $2 cost does not apply to the original purchase of bonds.

TABLE 11B.1 Optimum Money Holdings

1 Number Of Switches[a]	2 Average Money Holdings[b]	3 Average Bond Holdings[c]	4 Interest Earned[d]	5 Cost Of Switching[e]	6 Net Profit[f]
			r = 5 percent		
0	$600.00	$ 0.00	$ 0.00	$0.00	$ 0.00
1	300.00	300.00	15.00	2.00	13.00
2	200.00	400.00	20.00	4.00	16.00
3	150.00*	450.00	22.50	6.00	16.50
4	120.00	480.00	24.00	8.00	16.00

Assumptions: Interest rate *r* = 0.05. Cost of switching from bonds to money equals $2 per transaction.

			r = 3 percent		
0	$600.00	$ 0.00	$ 0.00	$0.00	$0.00
1	300.00	300.00	9.00	2.00	7.00
2	200.00*	400.00	12.00	4.00	8.00
3	150.00	450.00	13.50	6.00	7.50
4	120.00	480.00	14.40	8.00	6.40

Assumptions: Interest rate *r* = 0.03. Cost of switching from bonds to money equals $2 per transaction.

*Optimum money holdings. [a]That is, the number of times you sell a bond. [b]Calculated as 600/(col. 1 + 1). [c]Calculated as 600 - col. 2. [d]Calculated as $r \times$ col. 3, where r is the interest rate. [e]Calculated as $t \times$ col. 1, where t is the cost per switch ($2). [f]Calculated as col. 4 − col. 5

optimum average money holdings are $150 (which means that the individual makes three switches from bonds to money).

In the bottom half of Table 11B.1, the same calculations are performed for an interest rate of 3 percent instead of 5 percent. In this case, the optimum average money holdings is $200 (which means the person/household makes two instead of three switches from bonds to money). The lower interest rate has led to an increase in the optimum average money holdings. Under the assumption that people behave optimally, the demand for money is a negative function of the interest rate: The lower the rate, the more money on average is held, and the higher the rate, the less money on average is held.

PROBLEMS

1. Sherman Peabody earns a monthly salary of $1,500, which he receives at the beginning of each month. He spends the entire amount each month at the rate of $50 per day. (Assume 30 days in a month.) The interest rate paid on bonds is 10 percent per month. It costs $4 every time Peabody sells a bond.
   a. Describe briefly how Mr. Peabody should decide how much money to hold.
   b. Calculate Peabody's optimal money holdings. (*Hint:* It may help to formulate a table such as Table 11B.1 in this Appendix.

You can round to the nearest $0.50, and you need to consider only average money holdings of more than $100.)
   c. Suppose the interest rate rises to 15 percent. Find Peabody's optimal money holdings at this new interest rate. What will happen if the interest rate increases to 20 percent?
   d. Graph your answers to b. and c. with the interest rate on the vertical axis and the amount of money demanded on the horizontal axis. Explain why your graph slopes downward.

Aggregate Demand in the Goods and Money Markets

12

In Chapters 8 and 9, we discussed the market for goods and services—the **goods market**—without mentioning money, the money market, or the interest rate. We described how the equilibrium level of aggregate output (income) (Y) is determined in the goods market. At given levels of planned investment spending (I), government spending (G), and net taxes (T), we were able to determine the equilibrium level of output in the economy.

In Chapters 10 and 11, we discussed the financial market, or **money market**, barely referring to the goods market, as we explained how the equilibrium level of the interest rate is determined in the money market.

The goods market and the money market do not operate independently, however. When the Fed increases the money supply and reduces the interest rate, this likely affects the demand for housing, autos, and a range of other goods. Similarly, when the rate of household formation increases the demand for housing, the equilibrium in the money market is likely changed. Events in the money market affect what goes on in the goods market, and events in the goods market affect what goes on in the money market. Only by analyzing the two markets together can we determine the values of aggregate output (income) (Y) and the interest rate (r) that are consistent with the existence of equilibrium in *both* markets.

Looking at both markets simultaneously also reveals how fiscal policy affects the money market and how monetary policy affects the goods market. This is what we will do in this chapter. By establishing how the two markets affect each other, we will show how open market purchases of government securities (which expand the money supply) affect the equilibrium level of aggregate output. Similarly, we will show how fiscal policy measures affect the interest rate.

The relationship between aggregate output and the price level that exists when the goods and money markets are combined can be summarized in a curve called the aggregate demand (AD) curve. Every point on the AD curve reflects equilibrium in both the goods and money markets for the given price level. In the last part of this chapter, we derive the AD curve from the relationships in the goods and money markets. The AD curve is then used in the next chapter in determining the price level.

Planned Investment and the Interest Rate

We have so far assumed for simplicity that planned investment is fixed, and we now must relax this assumption. In practice planned investment depends on many factors, but we focus here on just one: the interest rate. In the theory of household behavior in Chapter 8 we postulated that consumption depends only on income, and in the theory of firm behavior in this chapter we postulate that investment depends only on the interest rate. We will see that investment falls as the interest rate rises.

goods market　The market in which goods and services are exchanged and in which the equilibrium level of aggregate output is determined.

money market The market in which financial instruments are exchanged and in which the equilibrium level of the interest rate is determined.

Recall that investment refers to a firm's purchase of new capital—new machines and plants. Whether a firm decides to invest in a project depends on whether the expected profits from the project justify its costs. And one cost of an investment project is the interest cost. Consider a firm opening a new plant, or a new ice cream store. When a manufacturing firm builds a new plant, the contractor must be paid at the time the plant is built. When an entrepreneur decides to open a new ice cream parlor, freezers, tables, chairs, light fixtures, and signs are needed. These too must be paid for when they are installed. The money needed to carry out such projects is generally borrowed and paid back over an extended period. The real cost of an investment project thus depends in part on the interest rate—the cost of borrowing. When the interest rate rises, it becomes more expensive to borrow and fewer projects are likely to be undertaken; increasing the interest rate, *ceteris paribus*, is likely to reduce the level of planned investment spending. When the interest rate falls, it becomes less costly to borrow and more investment projects are likely to be undertaken; reducing the interest rate, *ceteris paribus*, is likely to increase the level of planned investment spending.

The relationship between the interest rate and planned investment is illustrated by the downward-sloping demand curve in Figure 12.1. The higher the interest rate, the lower the level of planned investment. At an interest rate of 3 percent, planned investment is I_0. When the interest rate rises from 3 to 6 percent, planned investment falls from I_0 to I_1. As the interest rate falls, however, more projects become profitable, so more investment is undertaken. The curve in Figure 12.1 is sometimes called the "marginal efficiency of investment" curve.

▶ **FIGURE 12.1**

Planned Investment Schedule

Planned investment spending is a negative function of the interest rate. An increase in the interest rate from 3 percent to 6 percent reduces planned investment from I_0 to I_1.

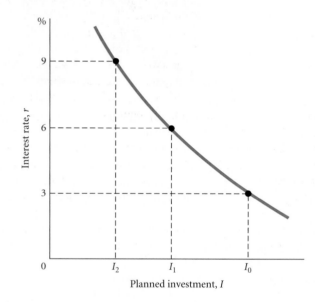

Other Determinants of Planned Investment

The assumption that planned investment depends only on the interest rate is obviously a simplification, just as is the assumption that consumption depends only on income. In practice, the decision of a firm on how much to invest depends on, among other things, its expectation of future sales. If a firm expects that its sales will increase in the future, it may begin to build up its capital stock—that is, to invest—now so that it will be able to produce more in the future to meet the increased level of sales. The optimism or pessimism of entrepreneurs about the future course of the economy can have an important effect on current planned investment. Keynes used the phrase *animal spirits* to describe the feelings of entrepreneurs, and he argued that these feelings affect investment decisions.

We come back to this issue in Chapter 16, where we take a closer look at firm behavior (and household behavior), but for now we will assume that planned investment simply depends on the interest rate.

Planned Aggregate Expenditure and the Interest Rate

We can use the fact that planned investment depends on the interest rate to consider how planned aggregate expenditure (*AE*) depends on the interest rate. Recall that planned aggregate expenditure is the sum of consumption, planned investment, and government purchases. That is,

ECONOMICS IN PRACTICE

Interest Rates and Investment Spending

The text discusses the idea that there is a negative relationship between the interest rate (r) and the investment spending of firms (I). A higher rate means a higher cost for firms that borrow to finance their capital expenditures and hence a higher cost of capital. Similarly, a lower interest rate is likely to stimulate additional investment spending.

A recent study by Simon Gilchrist, Fabio Natalucci, and Egon Zakrajsek finds that interest rates have a powerful effect on the behavior of firms.

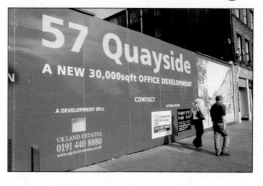

"The notion that business spending on fixed capital falls when interest rates rise is a theoretically unambiguous relationship that lies at the heart of the monetary transmission mechanism. Nonetheless, the presence of a robust negative relationship between investment expenditures has been difficult to document in actual data. In this paper we revisit this long-standing empirical anomaly. We do so by constructing a new data set . . . for more than 900 large U.S. non-financial corporations. Our results indicate that investment expenditures are highly sensitive—both economically and statistically—to changes in interest rates."[1]

According to their estimates, a one-percentage-point increase in the interest rate appropriate for a firm's borrowing leads to a drop in investment spending of more than one percentage point.

In 2007, interest rates were falling and many believed that the decline in interest rates would prevent a recession in 2008. The chairman of the President's Council for Economic Advisors, Ed Lazear, wrote in the annual Economics Report of the President:

"During the four quarters of 2007, real business investment on equipment and software grew at 3.7%. Its fastest growing components during 2007 included computer software and communication equipment. . . . Business investment growth is projected to remain solid during 2008. . . ."

[1] *Simon Gilchrist, Fabio Natalucci, and Egon Zakrajsek, "Interest Rate and Investment Redux," Federal Reserve Board of Governors, March 2007; Economic Report of the President, February 2008.*

$$AE \equiv C + I + G$$

We now know that there are many possible levels of I, each corresponding to a different interest rate. When the interest rate changes, planned investment changes. Therefore, a change in the interest rate (r) will lead to a change in total planned spending ($C + I + G$) as well.[1]

Figure 12.2 shows what happens to planned aggregate expenditure and output when the interest rate rises from 3 percent to 6 percent. At the higher interest rate, planned investment is lower; planned aggregate expenditure thus shifts *downward*. Recall from Chapters 8 and 9 that a fall in any component of aggregate spending has an even larger (or "multiplier") effect on equilibrium income (Y). When the interest rate rises, planned investment (and planned aggregate expenditure) falls and equilibrium output (income) falls by even more than the fall in planned investment. In Figure 12.2, equilibrium Y falls from Y_0 to Y_1 when the interest rate rises from 3 percent to 6 percent.

[1] When we look in detail in Chapter 16 at the behavior of households in the macroeconomy, we will see that consumption spending (C) is also stimulated by lower interest rates and discouraged by higher interest rates.

▶ **FIGURE 12.2**

The Effect of an Interest Rate Increase on Planned Aggregate Expenditure

An increase in the interest rate from 3 percent to 6 percent lowers planned aggregate expenditure and thus reduces equilibrium income from Y_0 to Y_1.

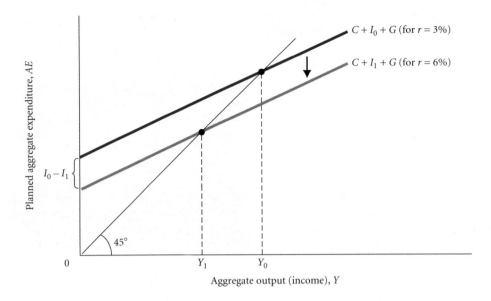

We can summarize the effects of a change in the interest rate on the equilibrium level of output. The effects of a change in the interest rate include:

- A high interest rate (r) discourages planned investment (I).
- Planned investment is a part of planned aggregate expenditure (AE).
- Thus, when the interest rate rises, planned aggregate expenditure (AE) at every level of income falls.
- Finally, a decrease in planned aggregate expenditure lowers equilibrium output (income) (Y) by a multiple of the initial decrease in planned investment.

Using a convenient shorthand:

$$r\uparrow \ \rightarrow \ I\downarrow \ \rightarrow \ AE\downarrow \ \rightarrow \ Y\downarrow$$
$$r\downarrow \ \rightarrow \ I\uparrow \ \rightarrow \ AE\uparrow \ \rightarrow \ Y\uparrow$$

Equilibrium in Both the Goods and Money Markets

It is now straightforward to see how the goods and money markets are linked. We have just seen that an increase in the interest rate (r) decreases output (Y) in the goods market because an increase in r lowers planned investment. This is the first link.

The second link can be seen from Figure 11.8 on p. 213. When income (Y) increase, this shifts the money demand curve to the right, which increases the interest rate (r) with a fixed money supply. We can thus write:

$$Y\uparrow \ \rightarrow \ M^d\uparrow \ \rightarrow \ r\uparrow$$
$$Y\downarrow \ \rightarrow \ M^d\downarrow \ \rightarrow \ r\downarrow$$

In other words, an increase in Y increases r in the money market and a decrease in Y decreases r.

Figure 12.3 summarize the links between the two markets. Given this figure, we are essentially done with the analysis. Given the interest rate, the equilibrium level of output can be determined from the goods market. Given output, the equilibrium interest rate can be determined from the money market. Putting both markets together allows the one pair of equilibrium values of Y and r to be determined. The equilibrium value of Y is the value that is consistent with the equilibrium value of r. There is equilibrium in both markets for the particular pair of values. This overall equilibrium is derived formally in the Appendix to this chapter.

Links Between the Goods Market and the Money Market

Planned investment depends on the interest rate, and money demand depends on aggregate output.

Policy Effects in the Goods and Money Markets

A useful way to examine the links between the goods and money markets is to consider the effects of changes in fiscal and monetary policy actions on the economy. We want to examine what happens to the equilibrium levels of output (Y) and interest rate (r) when policy changes. The three policy variables are government spending (G), net taxes (T), and the money supply (M^S).

Expansionary Policy Effects

Any government policy aimed at stimulating aggregate output (income) (Y) is said to be expansionary. An **expansionary fiscal policy** is an increase in government spending (G) or a reduction in net taxes (T) aimed at increasing aggregate output (income) (Y). An **expansionary monetary policy** is an increase in the money supply aimed at increasing aggregate output (income) (Y).

Expansionary Fiscal Policy: An Increase in Government Purchases (G) or a Decrease in Net Taxes (T)   As you know from Chapter 9, government purchases (G) and net taxes (T) are the two tools of government fiscal policy. The government can stimulate the economy—that is, it can increase aggregate output (income) (Y)—either by *increasing* government purchases or by *reducing* net taxes. Although the impact of a tax cut is somewhat smaller than the impact of an increase in G, both have a multiplier effect on the equilibrium level of Y.

Consider an increase in government purchases (G) of $10 billion. This increase in expenditure causes firms' inventories to be smaller than planned. Unplanned inventory reductions stimulate production, and firms increase output (Y). However, because added output means added income, some of which is subsequently spent, consumption spending (C) also increases. Again, inventories will be smaller than planned and output will rise even further. The final equilibrium level of output is higher by a multiple of the initial increase in government purchases.

This multiplier story is incomplete, however. Until this chapter, we have assumed that planned investment (I) is fixed at a certain level, but we now know that planned investment depends on the interest rate. We can now discuss what happens to the multiplier when investment varies because we have an understanding of the money market, in which the interest rate is determined.

Return to our multiplier story at the point that firms first begin to raise output in response to an increase in government purchases. As aggregate output (income) (Y) increases, an impact is felt in the money market—the increase in income (Y) increases the demand for money (M^d). (For the moment, assume that the Fed holds the quantity of money supplied [M^s] constant.) The resulting disequilibrium, with the quantity of money demanded greater than the quantity of money supplied, causes the interest rate to rise. The increase in G increases both Y and r.

The increase in r has a side effect—a higher interest rate causes planned investment spending (I) to decline. Because planned investment spending is a component of planned aggregate expenditure ($C + I + G$), the decrease in I works against the increase in G. An increase in government spending (G) increases planned aggregate expenditure and increases aggregate output, but a decrease in planned investment reduces planned aggregate expenditure and *decreases* aggregate output.

This tendency for increases in government spending to cause reductions in private investment spending is called the **crowding-out effect**. Without any expansion in the money supply to accommodate the rise in income and increased money demand, planned investment spending is partially crowded out by the higher interest rate. The extra spending created by the rise in

expansionary fiscal policy   An increase in government spending or a reduction in net taxes aimed at increasing aggregate output (income) (Y).

expansionary monetary policy   An increase in the money supply aimed at increasing aggregate output (income) (Y).

crowding-out effect   The tendency for increases in government spending to cause reductions in private investment spending.

government purchases is somewhat offset by the fall in planned investment spending. Income still rises, but the multiplier effect of the rise in G is lessened because of the higher interest rate's negative effect on planned investment.

This crowding-out effect is illustrated graphically in Figure 12.4. An increase in government purchases from G_0 to G_1 shifts the planned aggregate expenditure curve $(C + I_0 + G_0)$ upward. The increase in (Y) from Y_0 to Y_1 causes the demand for money to rise, which results in a disequilibrium in the money market. The excess demand for money raises the interest rate, causing I to decrease from I_0 to I_1. The fall in I pulls the planned aggregate expenditure curve back down, which lowers the equilibrium level of income to Y^*. (Remember that equilibrium is achieved when $Y = AE$.) The possibility of some crowding out of firm investment by increased government spending is a subject of political debate as well as economic analysis. To the extent that there is some crowding out, an increase in government spending as a way to increase aggregate output leads to a reduced share of private-sector (that is, firm) investment in GDP. There is considerable disagreement among voters and politicians in the United States about what constitutes the right mix of private investment and public spending in a healthy economy.

▶ **FIGURE 12.4**

The Crowding-Out Effect

An increase in government spending G from G_0 to G_1 shifts the planned aggregate expenditure schedule from 1 to 2. The crowding-out effect of the decrease in planned investment (brought about by the increased interest rate) then shifts the planned aggregate expenditure schedule from 2 to 3.

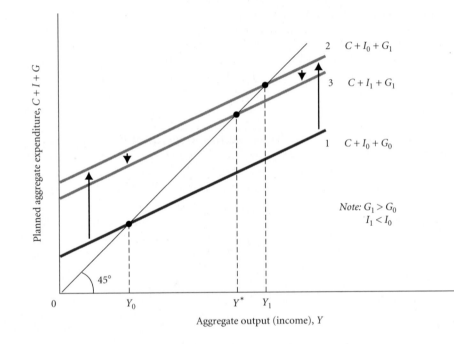

Note: $G_1 > G_0$
$I_1 < I_0$

Note that the size of the crowding-out effect and the ultimate size of the government spending multiplier depend on several things. First, we assumed that the Fed did not change the quantity of money supplied. If we were to assume instead that the Fed expanded the quantity of money to accommodate the increase in G, the multiplier would be larger. In this case, the higher demand for money would be satisfied with a higher quantity of money supplied and the interest rate would not rise. Without a higher interest rate, there would be no crowding out.

Second, the crowding-out effect depends on the **sensitivity** or **insensitivity of planned investment** spending to changes in the interest rate. Crowding out occurs because a higher interest rate reduces planned investment spending. Investment depends on factors other than the interest rate, however, and investment may at times be quite insensitive to changes in the interest rate. If planned investment does not fall when the interest rate rises, there is no crowding-out effect. These effects are summarized next.

interest sensitivity *or* **insensitivity of planned investment** The responsiveness of planned investment spending to changes in the interest rate. *Interest sensitivity* means that planned investment spending changes a great deal in response to changes in the interest rate; *interest insensitivity* means little or no change in planned investment as a result of changes in the interest rate.

Effects of an expansionary fiscal policy:

$$G \uparrow \rightarrow Y \uparrow \rightarrow M^d \uparrow \rightarrow r \uparrow \rightarrow I \downarrow$$

↳ Y increases less than if r did not increase

Exactly the same reasoning holds for changes in net taxes. The ultimate effect of a tax cut on the equilibrium level of output depends on how the money market reacts. The expansion of Y that a tax cut brings about will lead to an increase in the interest rate and thus a decrease in planned investment spending. The ultimate increase in Y will therefore be less than it would be if the interest rate did not rise.

Expansionary Monetary Policy: An Increase in the Money Supply   Now let us consider what will happen when the Fed decides to increase the supply of money through open market operations. At first, open market operations inject new reserves into the system and expand the quantity of money supplied (the money supply curve shifts to the right). Because the quantity of money supplied is now greater than the amount households want to hold, the equilibrium rate of interest falls. Planned investment spending (which is a component of planned aggregate expenditure) increases when the interest rate falls.

Increased planned investment spending means planned aggregate expenditure is now greater than aggregate output. Firms experience unplanned decreases in inventories, and they raise output (Y). An increase in the money supply decreases the interest rate and increases Y. However, the higher level of Y increases the demand for money (the demand for money curve shifts to the right), which keeps the interest rate from falling as far as it otherwise would.

If you review the sequence of events that follows the monetary expansion, you can see the links between the injection of reserves by the Fed into the economy and the increase in output. First, the increase in the quantity of money supplied pushes down the interest rate. Second, the lower interest rate causes planned investment spending to rise. Third, the increased planned investment spending means higher planned aggregate expenditure, which means increased output as firms react to unplanned decreases in inventories. Fourth, the increase in output (income) leads to an increase in the demand for money (the demand for money curve shifts to the right), which means the interest rate decreases less than it would have if the demand for money had not increased.

Effects of an expansionary monetary policy:

$$M^s\uparrow \;\rightarrow\; r\downarrow \;\rightarrow\; I\uparrow \;\rightarrow\; Y\uparrow \;\rightarrow\; M^d\uparrow$$

$\longrightarrow$ r decreases less than if M^d did not increase

The power of monetary policy to affect the goods market depends on how much of a reaction occurs at each link in this chain. Perhaps the most critical link is the link between r and I. Monetary policy can be effective *only* if I reacts to changes in r.[2] If firms sharply increase the number of investment projects undertaken when the interest rate falls, expansionary monetary policy works well at stimulating the economy. If, however, firms are reluctant to invest even at a low interest rate, expansionary monetary policy will have limited success. In other words, the effectiveness of monetary policy depends on the slope of the investment function. If it is nearly vertical, indicating very little responsiveness of investment to the interest rate, the middle link in this chain will be weak, rendering monetary policy ineffective.

Contractionary Policy Effects

Any government policy that is aimed at reducing aggregate output (income) (Y) is said to be *contractionary*. Where expansionary policy is used to boost the economy, contractionary policy is used to slow the economy.

Contractionary Fiscal Policy: A Decrease in Government Spending (G) or an Increase in Net Taxes (T)   A **contractionary fiscal policy** is a decrease in government spending (G) or an increase in net taxes (T) aimed at decreasing aggregate output (income) (Y). The effects of this policy are the opposite of the effects of an expansionary fiscal policy.

A decrease in government purchases or an increase in net taxes leads to a decrease in aggregate output (income) (Y), a decrease in the demand for money (M^d), and a decrease in

contractionary fiscal policy   A decrease in government spending or an increase in net taxes aimed at decreasing aggregate output (income) (Y).

---

[2] As we discuss in Chapter 16 , consumption (C) may also depend on r, which further increases the effectiveness of monetary policy.

the interest rate (r). The decrease in Y that accompanies a contractionary fiscal policy is less than it would be if we did not take the money market into account because the decrease in r also causes planned investment (I) to *increase*. This increase in I offsets some of the decrease in planned aggregate expenditure brought about by the decrease in G. (This also means the multiplier effect is smaller than it would be if we did not take the money market into account.) The effects of a decrease in G, or an increase in T, can be represented as shown.

Effects of a contractionary fiscal policy:

$$G\downarrow \ \text{or}\ T\uparrow \rightarrow Y\downarrow \rightarrow M^d\downarrow \rightarrow r\downarrow \rightarrow I\uparrow$$

$\longrightarrow$ Y decreases less than if r did not decrease

Contractionary Monetary Policy: A Decrease in the Money Supply

A **contractionary monetary policy** is a decrease in the money supply aimed at decreasing aggregate output (income) (Y). As you recall, the level of planned investment spending is a negative function of the interest rate: The higher the interest rate, the less planned investment there will be. The less planned investment there is, the lower planned aggregate expenditure will be and the lower the equilibrium level of output (income) (Y) will be. The lower equilibrium income results in a decrease in the demand for money, which means that the increase in the interest rate will be less than it would be if we did not take the goods market into account.

Effects of a contractionary monetary policy:

$$M^s\downarrow \ \rightarrow \ r\uparrow \ \rightarrow \ I\downarrow \ \rightarrow \ Y\downarrow \ \rightarrow \ M^d\downarrow$$

$\longrightarrow$ r increases less than if M^d did not decrease

The Macroeconomic Policy Mix

Although we have been treating fiscal and monetary policy separately, it should be clear that fiscal and monetary policy can be used simultaneously. For example, both government purchases (G) and the money supply (M^s) can be increased at the same time. We have seen that an increase in G by itself raises both Y and r, while an increase in M^s by itself raises Y but lowers r. Therefore, if the government wanted to increase Y without changing r, it could do so by increasing both G and M^s by the appropriate amounts.

policy mix The combination of monetary and fiscal policies in use at a given time.

Policy mix refers to the combination of monetary and fiscal policies in use at a given time. A policy mix that consists of a decrease in government spending and an increase in the money supply favors private investment spending over government spending. The reason is that both the increased money supply and the fall in government purchases cause the interest rate to fall, which leads to an increase in planned investment. The opposite is true for a mix that consists of an expansionary fiscal policy and a contractionary monetary policy. This mix favors government spending over investment spending. Such a policy has the effect of increasing government spending and reducing the money supply. Tight money and expanded government spending drives the interest rate up and planned investment down.

There is no rule about what constitutes the "best" policy mix or the "best" composition of output. On this issue, as on many other issues, economists (and others) disagree. In part, someone's preference for a certain composition of output—say, one weighted heavily toward private spending with relatively little government spending—depends on how that person stands on such issues as the proper role of government in the economy.

Table 12.1 summarizes the effects of various combinations of policies on several important macroeconomic variables. If you can explain the reasoning underlying each of the effects shown in the table, you can be satisfied that you have a good understanding of the links between the goods market and the money market.

TABLE 12.1 The Effects of the Macroeconomic Policy Mix

		Fiscal Policy	
		Expansionary ($\uparrow G$ or $\downarrow T$)	Contractionary ($\downarrow G$ or $\uparrow T$)
Monetary Policy	Expansionary ($\uparrow M^s$)	$Y\uparrow, r?, I?, C\uparrow$	$Y?, r\downarrow, I\uparrow, C?$
	Contractionary ($\downarrow M^s$)	$Y?, r\uparrow, I\downarrow, C?$	$Y\downarrow, r?, I?, C\downarrow$

Key:
$\uparrow$: Variable increases.
$\downarrow$: Variable decreases.
?: Forces push the variable in different directions. Without *ad*ditional information, we cannot specify which way the variable moves.

The Aggregate Demand (*AD*) Curve

Having determined equilibrium in the goods and money markets, we can now derive the aggregate demand (*AD*) curve. **Aggregate demand** is the total demand for goods and services in the economy. The *AD* curve shows the equilibrium levels of aggregate output associated with different price levels in the economy. The *AD* curve plays a key role in the next chapter in determining the price level (*P*). The aggregate demand curve is derived by assuming that the fiscal policy variables—government expenditures (*G*) and net taxes (*T*)—and the monetary policy variable (*M^s*) remain unchanged. In other words, the assumption is that the government does not take any action to affect the economy in response to changes in the price level.

To derive the aggregate demand curve, we examine what happens to aggregate output (*Y*) when the price level (*P*) changes, taking into account both the money and the goods markets. Begin with an exogenous increase in the price level. For now, you need not worry about where the price increase comes from. What happens as a result of this price increase? From the last chapter, we know that a price increase, all else equal, shifts the demand for money curve to the right. We have shown this in Figure 12.5(a). The supply of money curve is shown as a fixed vertical line since we have assumed that the Fed's money supply choice is independent of the interest rate. In the figure, we see that the price increase increases the interest rate from 6 percent to 9 percent as a result of the shift of the money demand curve. This new higher interest rate leads other things to change. Figure 12.5(b) shows the effect of the interest rate increase on planned investment. With higher borrowing costs, planned investment falls, from I_0 to I_1. But planned investment is one of the components of aggregate expenditure (*AE*), and so the fall in planned investment shifts the *AE* curve down, as we see in Figure 12.5(c). Lower *AE* means inventories are greater than planned, firms cut back on output, and *Y* falls from Y_0 to Y_1. An increase in the price level thus leads the level of aggregate output (income) to fall.

The situation is reversed when the price level declines. A lower price level shifts the money demand curve to the left, which leads to a lower interest rate. A lower interest rate stimulates planned investment spending, increasing planned aggregate expenditure, which leads to an increase in *Y*. A decrease in the price level thus leads the level of aggregate output (income) to rise.

This negative relationship between aggregate output (income) and the price level is called the **aggregate demand (*AD*) curve**, shown in Figure 12.6. Each point on the aggregate demand curve represents equilibrium in both the goods market *and* the money market. We have derived the *AD* curve using the analysis of the links between the goods market and the money market. Each value of *Y* on the aggregate demand curve corresponds to a value at which both the goods market and the money market are in equilibrium for the given value of the price level.

aggregate demand The total demand for goods and services in the economy.

aggregate demand (*AD*) curve A curve that shows the negative relationship between aggregate output (income) and the price level. Each point on the *AD* curve is a point at which both the goods market and the money market are in equilibrium.

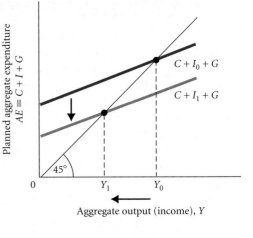

a. An increase in the price level (P) increases the demand for money from M_0^d to M_1^d. With the supply of money unchanged, the interest rate increases from 6 percent to 9 percent.

b. The higher interest rate decreases planned investment from I_0 to I_1.

c. Decreased planned investment reduces planned aggregate expenditure and causes equilibrium output (income) to fall from Y_0 to Y_1.

▲ **FIGURE 12.5 The Impact of an Increase in the Price Level on the Economy— Assuming No Changes in G, T, and M^s**

This figure shows that when P increases, Y decreases.

▶ **FIGURE 12.6**

The Aggregate Demand (AD) Curve

At all points along the *AD* curve, both the goods market and the money market are in equilibrium. The policy variables *G*, *T*, and *M^s* are fixed.

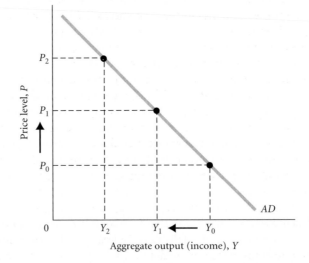

The Aggregate Demand Curve: A Warning

It is important that you realize what the aggregate demand curve represents. The aggregate demand curve is more complex than a simple individual or market demand curve. The *AD* curve is *not* a market demand curve, and it is *not* the sum of all market demand curves in the economy. To understand why, recall the logic behind a simple downward-sloping household demand curve. A demand curve shows the quantity of output demanded (by an individual household or in a single market) at every possible price, *ceteris paribus*. In drawing a simple demand curve, we are assuming that *other prices* and *income* are fixed. From these assumptions, it follows that one reason the quantity demanded of a particular good falls when its price rises is that other prices do *not* rise. The good in question therefore becomes more expensive relative to other goods, and households respond by substituting other goods for the good whose price increased. In addition, if income does not rise when the price of a good does, real income falls. This may also lead to a lower quantity demanded of the good whose price has risen.

Things are different when the *overall price level* rises. When the overall price level rises many prices—including many wage rates (many people's income)—rise together. For this reason, we cannot use the *ceteris paribus* assumption to draw the *AD* curve. The logic that explains why a simple demand curve slopes downward fails to explain why the *AD* curve also has a negative slope. Aggregate demand falls when the price level increases because the higher price level causes the demand for money (M^d) to rise. With the money supply constant, the interest rate will rise to reestablish equilibrium in the money market. *It is the higher interest rate that causes aggregate output to fall.* The *AD* curve traces the relationship between the overall price level and aggregate demand, taking into account the behavior of firms and households in the goods and money markets at the same time.

You do not need to understand anything about the money market to understand a simple individual or market demand curve. However, to understand what the *aggregate* demand curve represents, you must understand the interaction between the goods market and the money markets. The *AD* curve in Figure 12.6 embodies everything we have learned about the goods market and the money market up to now.

Other Reasons for a Downward-Sloping Aggregate Demand Curve

In addition to the effects of money supply and money demand on the interest rate, two other factors lie behind the downward slope of the *AD* curve. These are the consumption link and the real wealth effect.

The Consumption Link   We noted in Chapter 7 (and will discuss in detail in Chapter 16) that consumption (*C*) depends on the interest rate. Other things being equal, consumption expenditures tend to rise when the interest rate falls and to fall when the interest rate rises—just as planned investment does. This tendency is another link between the goods market and the money market. If something happens to change the interest rate in the money market, both consumption and planned investment are affected in the goods market.

The *consumption* link provides another reason for the *AD* curve's downward slope. An increase in the price level increases the demand for money, which leads to an increase in the interest rate, which leads to a decrease in consumption (as well as planned investment), which leads to a decrease in aggregate output (income). The initial decrease in consumption (brought about by the increase in the interest rate) contributes to the overall decrease in output. Planned investment does not bear all the burden of providing the link from a higher interest rate to a lower level of aggregate output. Decreased consumption brought about by a higher interest rate also contributes to this effect.

The Real Wealth Effect   We also noted in Chapter 8 (and will discuss in detail in Chapter 16) that consumption depends on wealth. Other things being equal, the more wealth households have, the more they consume. Wealth includes holdings of money, shares of stock, bonds, and housing, among other things. If household wealth decreases, the result will be less consumption now and in the future.

The price level has an effect on some kinds of wealth. Suppose you are holding $1,000 in a checking account or in a money market fund and the price level rises by 10 percent. Your holding is now worth 10 percent less because the prices of the goods that you could buy with your $1,000 have all increased by 10 percent. The purchasing power (or "real value") of your holding has decreased by 10 percent.

An increase in the price level may also lower the real value of stocks and housing, although whether it does depends on what happens to stock prices and housing prices when the overall price level rises. If stock prices and housing prices rise by the same percentage as the overall price level, the real value of stocks and housing will remain unchanged. If an increase in the price level does lower the real value of wealth, this is another reason for the downward slope of the *AD* curve. If real wealth falls, this leads to a decrease in consumption, which leads to a decrease in aggregate output (income). So if real wealth falls when there is an increase in the price level, there is a negative relationship between the price level and output through this **real wealth effect** or **real balance effect**.

real wealth, *or* **real balance, effect**   The change in consumption brought about by a change in real wealth that results from a change in the price level.

Aggregate Expenditure and Aggregate Demand

Throughout our discussion of macroeconomics so far, we have referred to the total planned spending by households (C), firms (I), and the government (G) as planned aggregate expenditure. At equilibrium, planned aggregate expenditure ($AE \equiv C + I + G$) and aggregate output (Y) are equal:

$$\text{equilibrium condition: } C + I + G = Y$$

How does planned aggregate expenditure relate to aggregate demand? At every point along the aggregate demand curve, the aggregate quantity demanded is exactly equal to planned aggregate expenditure, $C + I + G$. You can see this in Figures 12.5 and 12.6 on p. 228. When the price level rises, it is planned aggregate expenditure that decreases, moving us up the aggregate demand curve.

However, the aggregate demand curve represents more than just planned aggregate expenditure. Each point on the *AD* curve represents the *particular* level of planned aggregate expenditure that is consistent with equilibrium in the goods market and the money market at the given price level. Notice that the variable on the horizontal axis of the aggregate demand curve in Figure 12.6 is Y. At every point along the *AD* curve, $Y = C + I + G$.

Shifts of the Aggregate Demand Curve

The aggregate demand curve in Figure 12.6 is based on the assumption that the government policy variables G, T, and M^s are fixed. If any of these variables change, the aggregate demand curve will shift.

Consider an increase in the quantity of money supplied. If the quantity of money is expanded at any given price level, the interest rate will fall, causing planned investment spending (and planned aggregate expenditure) to rise. The result is an increase in output at the given price level. As Figure 12.7 shows, an increase in the quantity of money supplied at a given price level shifts the aggregate demand curve to the right.

▶ **FIGURE 12.7**

The Effect of an Increase in Money Supply on the *AD* Curve

An increase in the money supply (M^s) causes the aggregate demand curve to shift to the right, from AD_0 to AD_1. This shift occurs because the increase in M^s lowers the interest rate, which increases planned investment (and thus planned aggregate expenditure). The final result is an increase in output at each possible price level.

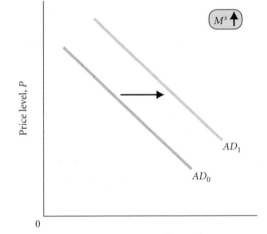

An increase in government purchases or a decrease in net taxes also increases aggregate output (income) at each possible price level even though some of the increase will be crowded out if the money supply is held constant. An increase in government purchases directly increases planned aggregate expenditure, which leads to an increase in output. A decrease in net taxes results in a rise in consumption, which increases planned aggregate expenditure, which also leads to an increase in output. As Figure 12.8 shows, an increase in government purchases or a decrease in net taxes shifts the aggregate demand curve to the right.

The same kind of reasoning applies to decreases in the quantity of money supplied, decreases in government purchases, and increases in net taxes. All of these shift the aggregate demand curve to the left.

Figure 12.9 summarizes the ways the aggregate demand curve shifts in response to changes in M^s, G, and T. To test your understanding of the *AD* curve, go through the figure piece by piece and explain the necessary steps for each of its components to create the shift in aggregate demand.

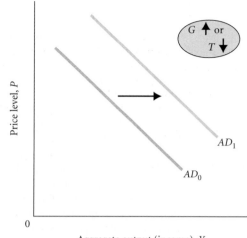

▲ **FIGURE 12.8 The Effect of an Increase in Government Purchases or a Decrease in Net Taxes on the *AD* Curve**

An increase in government purchases (G) or a decrease in net taxes (T) causes the aggregate demand curve to shift to the right, from AD_0 to AD_1. The increase in G increases planned aggregate expenditure, which leads to an increase in output at each possible price level. A decrease in T causes consumption to rise. The higher consumption then increases planned aggregate expenditure, which leads to an increase in output at each possible price level.

Expansionary monetary policy	**Contractionary monetary policy**
$M^s \uparrow \rightarrow AD$ curve shifts to the right	$M^s \downarrow \rightarrow AD$ curve shifts to the left
Expansionary fiscal policy	**Contractionary fiscal policy**
$G \uparrow \rightarrow AD$ curve shifts to the right	$G \downarrow \rightarrow AD$ curve shifts to the left
$T \downarrow \rightarrow AD$ curve shifts to the right	$T \uparrow \rightarrow AD$ curve shifts to the left

◀ **FIGURE 12.9**

Factors That Shift the Aggregate Demand Curve

Looking Ahead: Determining the Price Level

Our discussion of aggregate output (income) and the interest rate in the goods and money markets is now complete. You should have a good understanding of how the two markets work together. The *AD* curve is a useful summary of this analysis in that every point on the curve corresponds to equilibrium in both the goods and money markets for the given value of the price level. We have not yet, however, determined the price level. This is the task of the next chapter.

SUMMARY

1. The *goods market* and the *money market* do not operate independently. Events in the money market have effects on the goods market, and events in the goods market have effects on the money market.

PLANNED INVESTMENT AND THE INTEREST RATE *p. 219*

2. There is a negative relationship between planned investment and the interest rate because the interest rate affects the cost of investment projects. When the interest rate rises, planned investment decreases, and when the interest rate falls, planned investment increases.

3. For every value of the interest rate, there is a different level of planned investment spending and a different equilibrium level of output.

EQUILIBRIUM IN BOTH THE GOODS AND MONEY MARKETS *p. 222*

4. In the goods market, there is a negative relationship between the interest rate and output because there is a negative relationship between the interest rate and planned investment. In the money market, there is a positive relationship between the interest rate and output for a fixed money supply because if output increases, the interest rate must increase to achieve equilibrium in the money market.

5. Combining the goods and money markets determines the equilibrium values of both the interest rate and output.

POLICY EFFECTS IN THE GOODS AND MONEY MARKETS *p. 223*

6. An *expansionary fiscal policy* is an increase in government spending (*G*) or a reduction in net taxes (*T*) aimed at increasing aggregate output (income) (*Y*). An expansionary fiscal policy based on increases in government spending tends to lead to a *crowding-out effect*: Because increased government expenditures mean more transactions in the economy and thus an increased demand for money, the interest rate will rise. The decrease in planned investment spending that accompanies the higher interest rate will then partially offset the increase in aggregate expenditures brought about by the increase in *G*.

7. The size of the crowding-out effect, affecting the size of the government spending multiplier, depends on two things: the assumption that the Fed does not change the quantity of money supplied and the *sensitivity or insensitivity of planned investment* to changes in the interest rate.

8. An *expansionary monetary policy* is an increase in the money supply aimed at increasing aggregate output (income) (*Y*). An increase in the money supply leads to a lower interest rate, increased planned investment, increased planned aggregate expenditure, and ultimately a higher equilibrium level of aggregate output (income) (*Y*). Expansionary policies have been used to lift the economy out of recessions.

9. A *contractionary fiscal policy* is a decrease in government spending or an increase in net taxes aimed at decreasing aggregate output (income) (*Y*). A decrease in government spending or an increase in net taxes leads to a decrease in aggregate output (income) (*Y*), a decrease in the demand for money, and a decrease in the interest rate. However, the decrease in *Y* is somewhat offset by the additional planned investment resulting from the lower interest rate.

10. A *contractionary monetary policy* is a decrease in the money supply aimed at decreasing aggregate output (income) (*Y*). The higher interest rate brought about by the reduced money supply causes a decrease in planned investment spending and a lower level of equilibrium output. However, the lower equilibrium level of output brings about a decrease in the demand for money, which means the increase in the interest rate will be less than it would be if we did not take the goods market into account. Contractionary policies have been used to fight inflation.

11. The *policy mix* is the combination of monetary and fiscal policies in use at a given time. There is no rule about what constitutes the best policy mix or the best composition of output. In part, one's preference for a certain composition of output depends on one's stance concerning such issues as the proper role of government in the economy.

THE AGGREGATE DEMAND (*AD*) CURVE *p. 227*

12. *Aggregate demand* is the total demand for goods and services in the economy. The *aggregate demand (AD) curve* illustrates the negative relationship between aggregate output (income) and the price level. Each point on the *AD* curve is a point at which both the goods market and the money market are in equilibrium for a given value of the price level. The *AD* curve is *not* the sum of all the market demand curves in the economy.

13. At every point along the aggregate demand curve, the aggregate quantity demanded in the economy is exactly equal to planned aggregate expenditure for the given value of the price level.

14. An increase in the quantity of money supplied, an increase in government purchases, or a decrease in net taxes at a given price level shifts the aggregate demand curve to the right. A decrease in the quantity of money supplied, a decrease in government purchases, or an increase in net taxes shifts the aggregate demand curve to the left.

REVIEW TERMS AND CONCEPTS

aggregate demand, *p. 227*
aggregate demand (*AD*) curve, *p. 227*
contractionary fiscal policy, *p. 225*
contractionary monetary policy, *p. 226*

crowding-out effect, *p. 223*
expansionary fiscal policy, *p. 223*
expansionary monetary policy, *p. 223*
goods market, *p. 219*

interest sensitivity *or* insensitivity of planned investment, *p. 224*
money market, *p. 220*
policy mix, *p. 226*
real wealth, *or* real balance, effect, *p. 229*

PROBLEMS

Visit **www.myeconlab.com** to complete the problems marked in orange online. You will receive instant feedback on your answers, tutorial help, and access to additional practice problems.

myeconlab

1. On June 5, 2003, the European Central Bank acted to decrease the short-term interest rate in Europe by half a percentage point, to 2 percent. The bank's president at the time, Willem Duisenberg, suggested that, in the future, the bank could reduce rates further. The rate cut was made because European countries were growing very slowly or were in recession. What effect did the bank hope the action would have on the economy? Be specific. What was the hoped-for result on *C*, *I*, and *Y*?

2. [Related to the *Economics in Practice* on p. 221] In 2007, the Federal Reserve began a series of cuts in interest rates designed to stimulate investment spending by firms. At the same time, housing construction, a component of investment, was dropping sharply. Go to www.census.gov and click on "Housing and New Construction" to see what happened between 2007 and 2009. Also go to www.bea.gov and look at the current GDP release to see what happened to both residential and nonresidential fixed investment spending between 2007 and 2009. Besides the drop in interest rates, what other factors might have influenced the level of investment spending during those years? Do you think the Federal Reserve achieved its goal? Explain.

3. During the third quarter of 1997, Japanese GDP was falling at an annual rate of over 11 percent. Many blamed the big increase in Japan's taxes in the spring of 1997, which was designed to balance the budget. Explain how an increase in taxes with the economy growing slowly could precipitate a recession. Do not skip steps in your answer. If you were head of the Japanese central bank, how would you respond? What impact would your policy have on the level of investment?

4. Some economists argue that the "animal spirits" of investors are so important in determining the level of investment in the economy that interest rates do not matter at all. Suppose that this were true—that investment in no way depends on interest rates.
   a. How would Figure 12.1 be different?
   b. What would happen to the level of planned aggregate expenditures if the interest rate changed?
   c. What would be different about the relative effectiveness of monetary and fiscal policy?

5. For each of the following scenarios, tell a story and predict the effects on the equilibrium levels of aggregate output (Y) and the interest rate (r):
   a. During 2005, the Federal Reserve was tightening monetary policy in an attempt to slow the economy. Congress passed a substantial cut in the individual income tax at the same time.
   b. During the summer of 2003, Congress passed and President George W. Bush signed the third tax cut in 3 years. Many of the tax cuts took effect in 2005. Assume that the Fed holds M^s fixed.
   c. In 1993, the government raised taxes. At the same time, the Fed was pursuing an expansionary monetary policy.
   d. In 2005, conditions in Iraq led to a sharp drop in consumer confidence and a drop in consumption. Assume that the Fed holds the money supply constant.

   e. The Fed attempts to increase the money supply to stimulate the economy, but plants are operating at 65 percent of their capacities and businesses are pessimistic about the future.

6. Occasionally, the Federal Open Market Committee (FOMC) sets a policy designed to "track" the interest rate. This means that the FOMC is pursuing policies designed to keep the interest rate constant. If, in fact, the Fed were acting to counter any increases or decreases in the interest rate to keep it constant, what specific actions would you expect to see the Fed take if the following were to occur? (In answering, indicate the effects of each set of events on Y, C, S, I, M^s, M^d, and r.)
   a. An unexpected increase in investor confidence leads to a sharp increase in orders for new plants and equipment.
   b. A major New York bank fails, causing a number of worried people (not trusting even the FDIC) to withdraw a substantial amount of cash from other banks and put it in their cookie jars.

7. Paranoia, the largest country in central Antarctica, receives word of an imminent penguin attack. The news causes expectations about the future to be shaken. As a consequence, there is a sharp decline in investment spending plans.
   a. Explain in detail the effects of such an event on the economy of Paranoia assuming no response on the part of the central bank or the Treasury. (M^s, T, and G all remain constant.) Make sure you discuss the adjustments in the goods market and the money market.
   b. To counter the fall in investment, the king of Paranoia calls for a proposal to increase government spending. To finance the program, the chancellor of the exchequer has proposed three alternative options:
      (1) Finance the expenditures with an equal increase in taxes
      (2) Keep tax revenues constant and borrow the money from the public by issuing new government bonds
      (3) Keep taxes constant and finance the expenditures by printing new money

   Consider the three financing options and rank them from most expansionary to least expansionary. Explain your ranking.

8. Why might investment not respond positively to low interest rates during a recession? Why might investment not respond negatively to high interest rates during a boom?

9. The aggregate demand curve slopes downward because when the price level is lower, people can afford to buy more and aggregate demand rises. When prices rise, people can afford to buy less and aggregate demand falls. Is this a good explanation of the shape of the AD curve? Why or why not?

APPENDIX

The *IS-LM* Diagram

There is a useful way of depicting graphically the determination of aggregate output (income) and the interest rate in the goods and money markets. Two curves are involved in this diagram, the *IS* curve and the *LM* curve. In this Appendix, we will derive these two curves and use them to see how changes in government purchases (G) and the money supply (M^s) affect the equilibrium values of aggregate output (income) and the interest rate. The effects we describe here are the same as the effects we described in the main text; here we illustrate the effects graphically.

THE *IS* CURVE

We know that in the goods market there is an equilibrium level of aggregate output (income) (Y) for each value of the interest rate (r). For a given value of r, we can determine the equilibrium value of Y. The equilibrium value of Y falls when r rises and rises when r falls. There is thus a *negative* relationship between the equilibrium value of Y and r. The reason for this negative relationship is the negative relationship between planned investment and the interest rate. When the interest rate rises, planned investment (I) falls, and this decrease in *I* leads to a decrease in the equilibrium value of *Y*. The negative relationship between the equilibrium value of *Y* and *r* is shown in Figure 12A.1. This curve is called the **IS curve**.[1] Each point on the *IS* curve represents the equilibrium point in the goods market for the given interest rate.

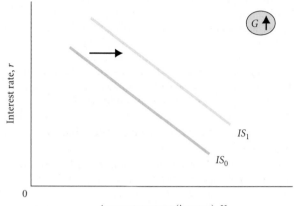

▲ **FIGURE 12A.1 The *IS* Curve**
Each point on the *IS* curve corresponds to the equilibrium point in the goods market for the given interest rate. When government spending (*G*) increases, the *IS* curve shifts to the right, from IS_0 to IS_1.

We also know from our earlier analysis of the goods market that when government purchases (*G*) increase with a constant interest rate, the equilibrium value of *Y* increases. This means the *IS* curve shifts to the right when *G* increases. With the same value of *r* and a higher value of *G*, the equilibrium value of *Y* is larger; when *G* decreases, the *IS* curve shifts to the left.

THE *LM* CURVE
In the money market, there is an equilibrium value of the interest rate (*r*) for every value of aggregate output (income) (*Y*). The equilibrium value of *r* is determined at the point at which the quantity of money demanded equals the quantity of money supplied. For a given value of *Y*, we can determine the equilibrium value of *r* in the money market. We also know from Figure 12.5 that the equilibrium value of *r* rises when *Y* rises and falls when *Y* falls—a *positive* relationship between the equilibrium value of *r* and *Y*. The reason for this positive relationship is the positive relationship between the demand for money and *Y*. When *Y* increases, the demand for money increases because more money is demanded for the increased volume of transactions in the economy. An increase in the demand for money increases the equilibrium value of *r*—thus the positive relationship between the equilibrium value of *r* and *Y*.

The positive relationship between the equilibrium value of *r* and *Y* is shown in Figure 12A.2. This curve is called the **LM curve**.[2] Each point on the *LM* curve represents equilibrium

in the money market for the given value of aggregate output (income).

We also know from our analysis of the money market that when the money supply (*M^s*) increases with a constant level of *Y*, the equilibrium value of *r* decreases. As Figure 12A.2 shows, this means that the *LM* curve shifts to the right when *M^s* increases. With the same value of *Y* and a higher value of *M^s*, the equilibrium value of *r* is lower. When *M^s* decreases, the *LM* curve shifts to the left.

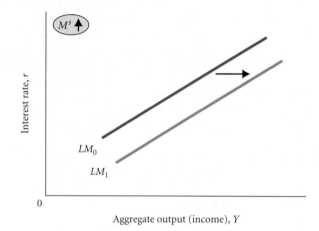

▲ **FIGURE 12A.2 The *LM* Curve**
Each point on the *LM* curve corresponds to the equilibrium point in the money market for the given value of aggregate output (income). Money supply (*M^s*) increases shift the *LM* curve to the right, from LM_0 to LM_1.

THE *IS-LM* DIAGRAM
Figure 12A.3 shows the *IS* and *LM* curves together on one graph. The point at which the two curves intersect is the point at which equilibrium exists in *both* the goods market and the money market. There is equilibrium in the goods market because the point is on the *IS* curve, and there is equilibrium in the money market because the point is on the *LM* curve.

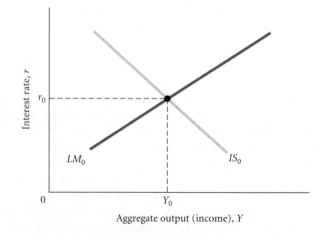

▲ **FIGURE 12A.3 The *IS-LM* Diagram**
The point at which the *IS* and *LM* curves intersect corresponds to the point at which both the goods market and the money market are in equilibrium. The equilibrium values of aggregate output and the interest rate are Y_0 and r_0.

[1] The letter *I* stands for investment, and the letter *S* stands for saving. *IS* refers to the fact that in equilibrium in the goods market, planned investment equals saving.
[2] The letter *L* stands for liquidity, a characteristic of money. The letter *M* stands for money.

We now have only two tasks left. The first is to see how the equilibrium values of Y and r are affected by changes in G—fiscal policy. This is easy. We have just seen that an increase in G shifts the IS curve to the right. Thus, an increase in G leads to higher equilibrium values of Y and r. This situation is illustrated in Figure 12A.4. Conversely, a decrease in G leads to lower equilibrium values of Y and r because the lower level of G causes the IS curve to shift to the left. (The effects are similar for changes in net taxes, T.)

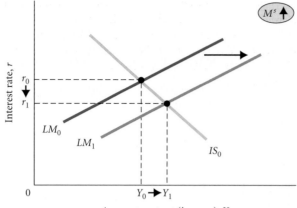

▲ **FIGURE 12A.5 An Increase in the Money Supply (M^s)**
When M^s increases, the LM curve shifts to the right. This increases the equilibrium value of Y and decreases the equilibrium value of r.

The IS-LM diagram is a useful way of seeing the effects of changes in monetary and fiscal policies on equilibrium aggregate output (income) and the interest rate through shifts in the two curves. Always keep in mind the economic theory that lies *behind* the two curves. Do not memorize what curve shifts when; be able to understand and explain *why* the curves shift. This means going back to the behavior of households and firms in the goods and money markets.

It is easy to use the IS-LM diagram to see how there can be a monetary and fiscal policy mix that leads to, say, an increase in aggregate output (income) but no increase in the interest rate. If both G and M^s increase, both curves shift to the right and the shifts can be controlled in such a way as to bring about no change in the equilibrium value of the interest rate.

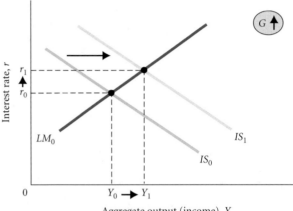

▲ **FIGURE 12A.4 An Increase in Government Purchases (G)**
When G increases, the IS curve shifts to the right. This increases the equilibrium value of both Y and r.

Our second task is to see how the equilibrium values of Y and r are affected by changes in M^s—monetary policy. This is also easy. We have just seen that an increase in M^s shifts the LM curve to the right. Thus, an increase in M^s leads to a higher equilibrium value of Y and a lower equilibrium value of r. This is illustrated in Figure 12A.5. Conversely, a decrease in M^s leads to a lower equilibrium value of Y and a higher equilibrium value of r because a decreased money supply causes the LM curve to shift to the left.

SUMMARY

An *IS curve* illustrates the negative relationship between the equilibrium value of aggregate output (income) (Y) and the interest rate in the goods market. An *LM curve* illustrates the positive relationship between the equilibrium value of the interest rate and aggregate output (income) (Y) in the money market. The point at which the IS and LM curves intersect is the point at which equilibrium exists in both the goods market and the money market.

REVIEW TERMS AND CONCEPTS

IS curve A curve illustrating the negative relationship between the equilibrium value of aggregate output (income) (Y) and the interest rate in the goods market. *p. 234*

LM curve A curve illustrating the positive relationship between the equilibrium value of the interest rate and aggregate output (income) (Y) in the money market. *p. 234*

PROBLEMS

1. Illustrate each of the following situations with *IS-LM* curves:
   a. An increase in G with the money supply held constant by the Fed
   b. An increase in G with the Fed changing M^s by enough to keep interest rates constant
   c. A decrease in G and an increase in T while the Fed expands M^s
   d. An increase in G and T while the Fed holds M^s constant during a period of inflation

Aggregate Supply and the Equilibrium Price Level

13

In the summer of 2008 both the United States and Europe were facing increases in their price levels. The president of the European Central Bank (ECB), Jean-Claude Trichet, made a number of announcements during that summer suggesting that the ECB was likely to take action to try to control inflation. Ben Bernanke, the head of the Federal Reserve Bank, who had been less hawkish on inflation, also indicated some concern with rising price levels. What causes price levels to rise and why might rising price levels be a problem for an economy? What tools do Trichet and Bernanke have to try to control inflation? These are the subjects of this chapter.

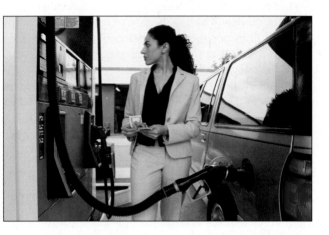

The determination of the overall price level in an economy is one of the central issues in macroeconomics. As the examples of Trichet and Bernanke in the summer of 2008 suggest, inflation—an increase in the overall price level—is one of the key concerns of macroeconomists and government policy makers. In Chapter 7, we discussed how inflation is measured and the costs of inflation, but made no mention of the *causes* of inflation. For simplicity, our analysis in Chapters 8 through 12 took the price level as fixed. This allowed us to discuss the links between the goods market and the money market without the complication of a changing price level. Having considered how the two markets work, we are ready to take up flexible prices.

We derived the aggregate demand curve in Chapter 12. The first step in this chapter is to introduce the aggregate supply curve. Given the aggregate demand and aggregate supply curves, the equilibrium price level is just the intersection of the two curves. Once the equilibrium price level is determined, we can examine how fiscal and monetary policies affect the price level.

The Aggregate Supply Curve

Aggregate supply is the total supply of goods and services in an economy. Although there is little disagreement among economists about how the aggregate demand curve is derived, there is a great deal of disagreement about how the aggregate supply curve is derived. Differences among economists regarding the shape of the aggregate supply curve is one important factor giving rise to differences in policies they suggest to deal with macroeconomic problems such as inflation and unemployment.

The Aggregate Supply Curve: A Warning

The **aggregate supply (*AS*) curve** shows the relationship between the aggregate quantity of output supplied by all the firms in an economy and the overall price level. To understand the aggregate supply curve, we need to understand something about the behavior of the individual firms that make up the economy.

237

aggregate supply   The total supply of all goods and services in an economy.

aggregate supply (AS) curve   A graph that shows the relationship between the aggregate quantity of output supplied by all firms in an economy and the overall price level.

It may seem logical to derive the aggregate supply curve by adding together the supply curves of all the individual firms in the economy. However, the logic behind the relationship between the overall price level in the economy and the level of aggregate output (income)—that is, the *AS* curve—is very different from the logic behind an individual firm's supply curve. The aggregate supply curve is *not* a market supply curve, and it is *not* the simple sum of all the individual supply curves in the economy. (Recall a similar warning for the aggregate demand curve in the last chapter.) The reason is that many firms (some would argue most firms) do not simply respond to prices determined in the market. Instead, they actually *set prices*. Only in perfectly competitive markets do firms simply react to prices determined by market forces. Firms in other kinds of industries (imperfectly competitive industries) make both output and price decisions based on their perceptions of demand and costs. Price-setting firms do not have individual supply curves because these firms are choosing both output and price at the same time. To derive an individual supply curve, we need to imagine calling out a price to a firm and having the firm tell us how much output it will supply at that price. We cannot do this if firms are also setting prices. If supply curves do not exist for imperfectly competitive firms, we certainly cannot add them together to get an aggregate supply curve!

What can we say about the relationship between aggregate output and the overall price level? Because many firms in the economy set prices as well as output, it is clear that an "aggregate supply curve" in the traditional sense of the word *supply* does not exist. What does exist is what we might call a "price/output response" curve—a curve that traces out the price decisions and output decisions of all firms in the economy under a given set of circumstances.

What might such a curve look like?

Aggregate Supply in the Short Run

Many argue that the aggregate supply curve (or the price/output response curve) has a positive slope, at least in the short run. (We will discuss the short-run/long-run distinction in more detail later in this chapter.) In addition, many argue that at very low levels of aggregate output—for example, when the economy is in a recession—the aggregate supply curve is fairly flat and that at high levels of output—for example, when the economy is experiencing a boom—it is vertical or nearly vertical. Such a curve is shown in Figure 13.1.

▶ **FIGURE 13.1**

The Short-Run Aggregate Supply Curve

In the short run, the aggregate supply curve (the price/output response curve) has a positive slope. At low levels of aggregate output, the curve is fairly flat. As the economy approaches capacity, the curve becomes nearly vertical. At capacity, the curve is vertical.

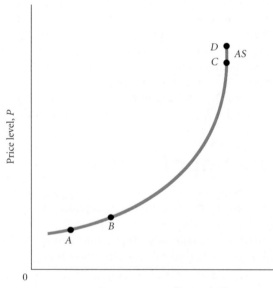

Why might the *AS* curve have a positive slope in the short run? One reason is that wages may lag prices in responding to a change in demand. Consider the case in which there is an increase in aggregate demand, and assume that firms in the economy are imperfectly competitive. The increase in aggregate demand shifts the demand curves facing individual firms out. If the firms' marginal cost curves do not also shift, then firms can increase their profits by raising prices and increasing output.[1] In other words, the response of the overall economy to the aggregate demand increase will be an increase in output and the price level—a positive slope of the short-run *AS* curve.

A key assumption in this story is that firms' marginal cost curves do not also shift. This is where wages come into the picture. A key input into the production processes of firms is labor, and labor costs are a large fraction of total costs. If wages do not respond quickly to price increases, there may be some period of time in which firms raise prices without seeing wage rates rise. In practice wages do tend to lag prices. We discuss in the next chapter various reasons that have been advanced for why wages might be "sticky" in the short run. The main point of this chapter is that if wages are sticky in the short run in the sense that wages lag prices, this is a reason for an upward-sloping short-run *AS* curve. Firms' demand curves will shift without a corresponding shift in their marginal cost curves.

We should add a word of caution at this point. It may be that some of a firm's input costs are rising even in the short run after the aggregate demand increase has taken place because some of a firm's inputs may be purchased from other firms who are raising prices. For example, one input to a Dell computer is a chip produced by Intel or AMD. The fact that some of a firm's input costs rise along with a shift in the demand for its product complicates the picture because it means that at the same time that there is an outward shift in a firm's demand curve there is a upward shift in its marginal cost curve. In deriving an upward-sloping *AS* curve, we are in effect assuming that these kinds of input costs are small relative to wage costs. So the story is that wages are a large fraction of total costs and that wage changes lag price changes. This gives us an upward-sloping short-run *AS* curve.

So far we have explained why the short-run *AS* curve might be upward sloping, but we have not explained why it may have the shape in Figure 13.1 with a flat part and then a steeper part. To do this, we need to turn to the concept of capacity utilization. Capacity utilization is a measure of how much of a firm's existing capital and labor the firm is using. When firms are at low levels of capacity utilization, increasing output can be accomplished without large cost increases. On the other hand, when firms are approaching full capacity utilization, further expansions are harder to do. It is this difference in the levels of firms' capacity utilization that gives rise to the flat and then steep parts of the short-run *AS* curve.

Let us first consider the flat segment of the short-run *AS* curve, pictured in Figure 13.1 between points *A* and *B*. Here the economy is operating at a low level of output, and thus firms are likely to have excess capacity. At this point, firms may be holding more capital and labor than they need for their current production levels. In Chapter 16, we will discuss further some of the reasons firms might hold excess capital and excess labor. It may be hard in the short run for firms to sell off their capital equipment. If there are costs of getting rid of capital once it is in place, a firm may choose to hold on to some of this capital even if the economy is in a downturn and the firm has decreased its output. In this case, the firm will not be fully utilizing its capital stock. Firms may be especially likely to behave this way if they expect that the downturn will be short and that they will need the capital in the future to produce a higher level of output. Firms may have similar reasons for holding excess labor. It may be costly, both in worker morale and administrative costs, to lay off a large number of workers. With excess labor and capital, the costs of producing an additional unit of output in response to demand increases will not rise much. The response of a firm in this position will be primarily to increase output rather than to increase its price. In moving from *A* to *B* in Figure 13.1, there is a large increase in output and only a small increase in the price level. The short-run *AS* (price/output response) curve is fairly flat at levels of output in which there is excess capacity.

If demand continues to expand, things will change. As firms move closer to capacity, their responses to demand increases change from mainly increasing output to mainly increasing prices. As demand increases firms move toward holding no excess capital and excess labor. Now firms begin to come up against the constraints imposed by their inability to quickly expand their

---

[1] This is a standard result in microeconomics. An outward demand shift for an imperfectively competitive firm with an unchanged marginal cost curve leads the firm to raise its price and its quantity produced. In the perfectly competitive case the industry output price is determined in the market, and firms take this price as given in deciding how much output to produce. If aggregate demand increases and results in a larger industry output price and if there is no increase in firms' costs, they will respond by increasing output. There will thus be an increase in both industry output prices and output, resulting in a positive sloping short-run *AS* curve.

capacity. In any short-run period, firms' output decisions are constrained by some fixed factor of production. Manufacturing firms will find it difficult to expand the physical size of their plant in the short run. Farmers are constrained in the short run by the number of acres of land on their farms. Because firms cannot easily expand their capital stock, increasing output typically involves rising marginal costs, perhaps by running a plant on double or triple shifts. At this point, increases in demand will be met by the firms mostly increasing prices rather than output. At some level of aggregate demand, it is virtually impossible for firms to expand any further, and firms will respond to any further increases in demand only by raising prices. This case is pictured in Figure 13.1 at points C and D. Moving from C to D results in no increase in aggregate output but a large increase in the price level.

Shifts of the Short-Run Aggregate Supply Curve

Given the above discussion, it is straightforward to consider what shifts the short-run AS curve: Anything that shifts a firm's marginal cost curve shifts the short-run AS curve. If wage rates change, this will shift the short-run AS curve. In fact, in deriving the long-run AS curve below, we use the fact that as wage rates increase in response to price increases this shifts the short-run AS curve back (to the left). A leftward shift of a firm's marginal cost curve with no change in demand leads the firm to raise its price and lower its output.

Another important input aside from labor in firms' production processes is energy. Many energy prices, like the price of oil, are determined in world markets. We can think of the short-run AS curve as being derived under the assumption of fixed energy prices (as well as fixed wage rates). In other words, we can treat energy like labor in deriving the short-run AS curve. If we do this, then, as with wage rates, when the price of, say, oil changes, this shifts the short-run AS curve. An increase in the price of oil shifts firms' marginal costs curves to the left and thus the short-run AS curve to the left.

Not only is oil a large component of U.S. energy use, its price undergoes large fluctuations. During the summer of 2005, the price of oil doubled from about $35 to $70 a barrel. Once it became clear that the severe hurricanes of that year would not cause a large disruption of oil supplies, the price fell back below $60. In contrast, in 1973–1974 and again in 1979, the price of oil increased substantially and remained at a higher level. In the summer of 2008, the price of oil rose to over $140 a barrel. Given that oil price changes shift the short-run AS curve, this is a lot of shifting.

Figure 13.2(a) shows a leftward shift of the short-run AS curve. This can be caused by an increase in wages rates or energy prices. Figure 13.2(b) shows a rightward shift of the short-run AS curve. This can be caused by a decrease in wage rates or energy prices. Shifts like these that are brought about by a change in costs are referred to as **cost shocks** or **supply shocks**. One of the sources of the concerns in 2008 raised by both the Federal Reserve chair and the president of the European Central Bank, described in the opening of this chapter, was the large increase in the price of oil in the first half of 2008. This was a fairly large cost shock.

Natural disasters, such as a drought or a flood, shift the AS curve to the left. For a given set of prices firms produce less because their production processes have been damaged. The resource base of the economy has been reduced.

One can also think of the AS curve shifting to the right over time due to technical progress and labor force growth. Recall that the vertical part of the short run AS curve represents the economy's maximum (capacity) output. This maximum output is determined by the economy's existing resources, like the size of its labor force and the current state of technology. The labor force grows naturally with an increase in the working-age population, but it can also increase for other reasons. Since the 1960s, for example, the percentage of women in the labor force has grown sharply. This increase in the supply of women workers has shifted the AS curve to the right. Immigration can also shift the AS curve. During the 1970s, Germany, faced with a serious labor shortage, opened its borders to large numbers of "guest workers," largely from Turkey. The United States has experienced significant immigration, legal and illegal, from Mexico, from Central and South American countries, and from Asia. (We discuss economic growth in more detail in Chapter 17.)

cost shock, *or* **supply shock** A change in costs that shifts the short-run aggregate supply (AS) curve.

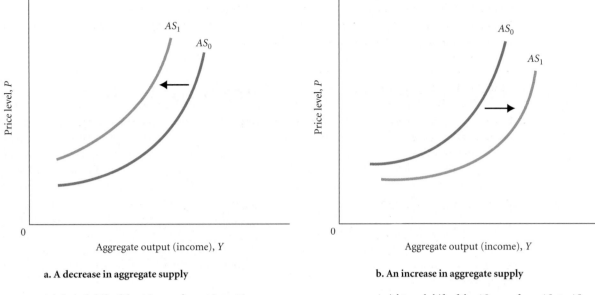

a. A decrease in aggregate supply

A leftward shift of the AS curve from AS_0 to AS_1 could be caused by an increase in costs—for example, an increase in wage rates or energy prices.

b. An increase in aggregate supply

A rightward shift of the AS curve from AS_0 to AS_1 could be caused by a decrease in costs—for example, a decrease in wage rates or energy prices.

▲ **FIGURE 13.2 Shifts of the Short-Run Aggregate Supply Curve**

The Equilibrium Price Level

The **equilibrium price level** in the economy occurs at the point at which the AD curve and the AS curve intersect, shown in Figure 13.3, where the equilibrium price level is P_0 and the equilibrium level of aggregate output (income) is Y_0.

Figure 13.3 looks simple, but it is a powerful device for analyzing a number of macroeconomic questions. Consider first what is true at the intersection of the AS and AD curves. Each point on the AD curve corresponds to equilibrium in both the goods market and the money market. Each point on the AS curve represents the price/output responses of all the firms in the economy. That means that the point at which the AS and AD curves intersect corresponds to equilibrium in the goods and money markets and to a set of price/output decisions on the part of all the firms in the economy.

equilibrium price level
The price level at which the aggregate demand and aggregate supply curves intersect.

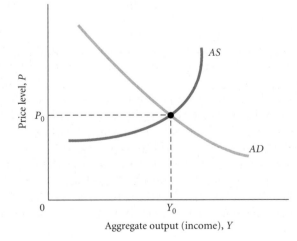

◀ **FIGURE 13.3**
The Equilibrium Price Level

At each point along the AD curve, both the money market and the goods market are in equilibrium. Each point on the AS curve represents the price/ output decisions of all the firms in the economy. P_0 and Y_0 correspond to equilibrium in the goods market and the money market and to a set of price/ output decisions on the part of all the firms in the economy.

We will use this *AS/AD* framework to analyze the effects of monetary and fiscal policy on the economy and to analyze the causes of inflation. For example, what can Trichet and Bernanke do if they are worried about inflation? To answer these kinds of questions, we need to return to the *AS* curve and discuss its shape in the long run.

The Long-Run Aggregate Supply Curve

We derived the short-run *AS* curve under the assumption that wage changes lag price changes. This does not mean, however, that, say, wages never increase after prices increases. Over time, wages adjust to higher prices. When workers negotiate with firms over their wages, they take into account what prices have been doing in the recent past. If wages fully adjust to prices in the long run, then the long-run *AS* curve will be vertical. We can see why in Figure 13.4. Initially, the economy is in equilibrium at a price level of P_0 and aggregate output of Y_0 (the point *A* at which AD_0 and AS_0 intersect). Now imagine a shift of the *AD* curve from AD_0 to AD_1. In response to this shift, both the price level and aggregate output rise in the short run, to P_1 and Y_1, respectively (the point *B* at which AD_1 and AS_0 intersect). The movement along the upward-sloping AS_0 curve as *Y* increases from Y_0 to Y_1 assumes that wages lag prices.

▶ **FIGURE 13.4**

The Long-Run Aggregate Supply Curve

When the *AD* curve shifts from AD_0 to AD_1, the equilibrium price level initially rises from P_0 to P_1 and output rises from Y_0 to Y_1. Wages respond in the longer run, shifting the *AS* curve from AS_0 to AS_1. If wages fully adjust, output will be back at Y_0. Y_0 is sometimes called *potential GDP*.

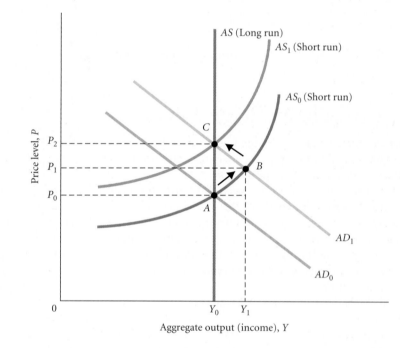

Now, as wages increase the short-run *AS* curve shifts to the left. If wages fully adjust, the *AS* curve will over time have shifted from AS_0 to AS_1 in Figure 13.4, and output will be back to Y_0 (the point C at which AD_1 and AS_1 intersect). So when wages fully adjust to prices, the long-run *AS* curve is vertical.

By looking at Figure 13.4, you can begin to see why arguments about the shape of the *AS* curve are so important in policy debates. If the long-run *AS* curve is vertical as we have drawn it, factors that shift the *AD* curve to the right—including policy actions such as increasing government spending—simply end up increasing the price level. If the short-run *AS* curve also is quite steep, even in the short run, most of the effect of any shift in the *AD* curve will be felt in an increase in the price level rather than an increase in aggregate output. If the *AS* curve, on the other hand, is flat, *AD* shifts can have a large effect on aggregate output, at least in the short run. We discuss these effects of policy in more detail later in this chapter.

ECONOMICS IN PRACTICE

The Simple "Keynesian" Aggregate Supply Curve

There is a great deal of disagreement concerning the shape of the AS curve. One view of the aggregate supply curve, the simple "Keynesian" view, holds that at any given moment, the economy has a clearly defined capacity, or maximum, output. This maximum output, denoted by Y_F, is defined by the existing labor force, the current capital stock, and the existing state of technology. If planned aggregate expenditure increases when the economy is producing *below* this maximum capacity, this view holds, inventories will be lower than planned, and firms will increase output, but the price level will not change. Firms are operating with underutilized plants (excess capacity), and there is cyclical unemployment. Expansion does not exert any upward pressure on prices. However, if planned aggregate expenditure increases when the economy is producing near or at its maximum (Y_F), inventories will be lower than planned, but firms cannot increase their output. The result will be an increase in the price level, or inflation.

This view is illustrated in the figure. In the top half of the diagram, aggregate output (income) (Y) and planned aggregate expenditure ($C + I + G \equiv AE$) are initially in equilibrium at AE_1, Y_1, and price level P_1. Now suppose a tax cut or an increase in government spending increases planned aggregate expenditure. If such an increase shifts the AE curve from AE_1 to AE_2 and the corresponding aggregate demand curve from AD_1 to AD_2, the equilibrium level of output will rise from Y_1 to Y_F. (Remember, an expansionary policy shifts the AD curve to the right.) Because we were initially producing below capacity output (Y_1 is lower than Y_F), the price level will be unaffected, remaining at P_1.

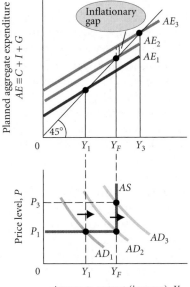

With planned aggregate expenditure of AE_1 and aggregate demand of AD_1, equilibrium output is Y_1. A shift of planned aggregate expenditure to AE_2, corresponding to a shift of the AD curve to AD_2, causes output to rise but the price level to remain at P_1. If planned aggregate expenditure and aggregate demand exceed Y_F, however, there is an inflationary gap and the price level rises to P_3.

Now consider what would happen if AE increased even further. Suppose planned aggregate expenditure shifted from AE_2 to AE_3, with a corresponding shift of AD_2 to AD_3. If the economy were producing below capacity output, the equilibrium level of output would rise to Y_3. However, the output of the economy cannot exceed the maximum output of Y_F. As inventories fall below what was planned, firms encounter a fully employed labor market and fully utilized plants. Therefore, they cannot increase their output. The result is that the aggregate supply curve becomes vertical at Y_F, and the price level is driven up to P_3.

The difference between planned aggregate expenditure and aggregate output at full capacity is sometimes referred to as an *inflationary gap*. You can see the inflationary gap in the top half of the figure. At Y_F (capacity output), planned aggregate expenditure (shown by AE_3) is greater than Y_F. The price level rises to P_3 until the aggregate quantity supplied and the aggregate quantity demanded are equal.

Despite the fact that the kinked aggregate supply curve provides some insights, most economists find it unrealistic. It does not seem likely that the whole economy suddenly runs into a capacity "wall" at a specific level of output. As output expands, some firms and industries will hit capacity before others.

Potential GDP

Recall that even the short-run *AS* curve becomes vertical at some particular level of output. The vertical portion of the short-run *AS* curve exists because there are physical limits to the amount that an economy can produce in any given time period. At the physical limit, all plants are operating around the clock, many workers are on overtime, and there is no cyclical unemployment.

Note that the vertical portions of the short-run *AS* curves in Figure 13.4 on p. 242 are to the right of Y_0. If the vertical portions of the short-run *AS* curves represent "capacity," what is the nature of Y_0, the level of output corresponding to the long-run *AS* curve? Y_0 represents the level of aggregate output that can be *sustained* in the long run without inflation. It is sometimes called **potential output** or **potential GDP**. Output can be pushed above Y_0 under a variety of circumstances, but when it is, there is upward pressure on wages. As the economy approaches short-run capacity, wage rates tend to rise as firms try to attract more people into the labor force and to induce more workers to work overtime. Rising wages shift the short-run *AS* curve to the left (in Figure 13.4 from AS_0 to AS_1) and drive output back to Y_0.

potential output, *or* **potential GDP** The level of aggregate output that can be sustained in the long run without inflation.

Short-Run Equilibrium Below Potential Output   Thus far we have argued that if the short-run aggregate supply and aggregate demand curves intersect to the right of Y_0 in Figure 13.4, wages will rise, causing the short-run *AS* curve to shift to the left and pushing aggregate output back down to Y_0. Although different economists have different opinions on how to determine whether an economy is operating at or above potential output, there is general agreement that there is a maximum level of output (below the vertical portion of the short-run aggregate supply curve) that can be sustained without inflation.

What about short-run equilibria that occur to the *left* of Y_0? If the short-run aggregate supply and aggregate demand curves intersect at a level of output below potential output, what will happen? Here again economists disagree. Those who believe the aggregate supply curve is vertical in the long run believe that when short-run equilibria exist below Y_0, output will tend to rise—just as output tends to fall when short-run equilibria exist above Y_0. The argument is that when the economy is operating below full employment with excess capacity and high unemployment, wages are likely to *fall*. A decline in wages shifts the aggregate supply curve to the *right*, causing the price level to fall and the level of aggregate output to rise back to Y_0. This automatic adjustment works only if wages fall when excess capacity and unemployment exist. We will discuss wage adjustment during periods of unemployment in detail in Chapter 14.

Monetary and Fiscal Policy Effects

We are now ready to use the *AS/AD* framework to consider the effects of monetary and fiscal policy. We will first consider the short-run effects.

Recall that the two fiscal policy variables are government purchases (G) and net taxes (T). The monetary policy variable is the quantity of money supplied (M^s). An *expansionary* policy aims at stimulating the economy through an increase in G or M^s or a decrease in T. A *contractionary* policy aims at slowing down the economy through a decrease in G or M^s or an increase in T. We saw earlier in this chapter that an expansionary policy shifts the *AD* curve to the right and that a contractionary policy shifts the *AD* curve to the left. How do these policies affect the equilibrium values of the price level (P) and the level of aggregate output (income)?

When considering the effects of a policy change, we must be careful to note where along the (short-run) *AS* curve the economy is at the time of the change. If the economy is initially on the flat portion of the *AS* curve, as shown by point A in Figure 13.5, an expansionary policy, which shifts the *AD* curve to the right, will result in a small price increase relative to the output increase: The increase in equilibrium Y (from Y_0 to Y_1) is much greater than the increase in equilibrium P (from P_0 to P_1). This is the case in which an expansionary policy works well. There is an increase in output with little increase in the price level.

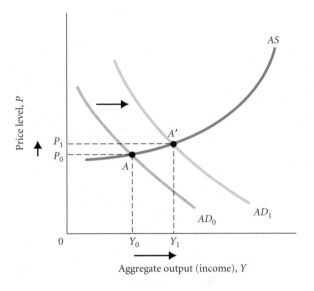

◀ **FIGURE 13.5**

A Shift of the Aggregate Demand Curve When the Economy Is on the Nearly Flat Part of the AS Curve

Aggregate demand can shift to the right for a number of reasons, including an increase in the money supply, a tax cut, or an increase in government spending. If the shift occurs when the economy is on the nearly flat portion of the AS curve, the result will be an increase in output with little increase in the price level from point A to point A'.

If the economy is initially on the steep portion of the AS curve, as shown by point B in Figure 13.6, an expansionary policy will result in a small increase in equilibrium output (from Y_0 to Y_1) and a large increase in the equilibrium price level (from P_0 to P_1). In this case, an expansionary policy does not work well. It results in a much higher price level with little increase in output. The multiplier is therefore close to zero: Output is initially close to capacity, and attempts to increase it further lead mostly to a higher price level.

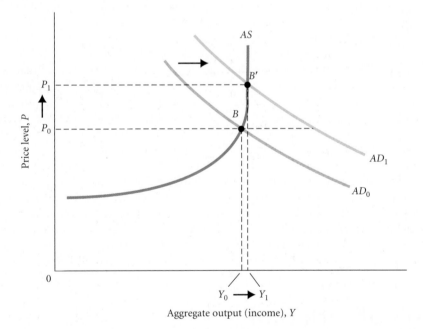

◀ **FIGURE 13.6**

A Shift of the Aggregate Demand Curve When the Economy Is Operating at or Near Maximum Capacity

If a shift of aggregate demand occurs while the economy is operating near full capacity, the result will be an increase in the price level with little increase in output from point B to point B'.

Figures 13.5 and 13.6 show that it is important to know where the economy is *before* a policy change is put into effect. The economy is producing on the nearly flat part of the AS curve when most firms are producing well below capacity. When this is the case, firms will respond to an increase in demand by increasing output much more than they increase prices. When the economy is producing on the steep part of the AS curve, firms are close to capacity and will respond to an increase in demand by increasing prices much more than they increase output.

To see what happens when the economy is on the steep part of the AS curve, consider the effects of an increase in G with no change in the money supply. What will happen is that when G is increased, there will be virtually no increase in Y. In other words, the expansionary fiscal policy will fail to stimulate the economy. To consider this, we need to go back to Chapter 12 and review what is behind the AD curve.

The first thing that happens when G increases is an unanticipated decline in firms' inventories. Because firms are very close to capacity output when the economy is on the steep part of the AS curve, they cannot increase their output very much. The result, as Figure 13.6 shows, is a substantial increase in the price level. The increase in the price level increases the demand for money, which (with a fixed money supply) leads to an increase in the interest rate, decreasing planned investment. *There is nearly complete crowding out of investment.* If firms are producing at capacity, prices and interest rates will continue to rise until the increase in G is completely matched by a decrease in planned investment and there is complete crowding out.

Long-Run Aggregate Supply and Policy Effects

We have so far been considering monetary and fiscal policy effects in the short run. It is important to realize that if the AS curve is vertical in the long run, neither monetary policy nor fiscal policy has any effect on aggregate output in the long run. Look back at Figure 13.4 on p. 242. Monetary and fiscal policy shift the AD curve. If the long-run AS curve is vertical, output always comes back to Y_0. In this case, policy affects *only* the price level in the long run and the multiplier effect of a change in government spending on aggregate output in the long run is zero. Under the same circumstances, the tax multiplier is also zero.

The conclusion that policy has no effect on aggregate output in the long run is perhaps startling. Do most economists agree that the aggregate supply curve is vertical in the long run? Most economists agree that wages tend to lag behind output prices in the short run, giving the AS curve some positive slope. Most also agree the AS curve is likely to be steeper in the long run, but how long is the long run? The longer the lag time, the greater the potential impact of monetary and fiscal policy on aggregate output. If wages follow output prices within, say, 3 to 6 months, policy has little chance to affect output. If the long run is 3 or 4 years, policy can have significant effects. A good deal of research in macroeconomics focuses on the length of time lags between wages and output prices. In a sense, the length of the long run is one of the most important open questions in macroeconomics.

Another source of disagreement centers on whether equilibria below potential output, Y_0 in Figure 13.4, are self-correcting (that is, without government intervention). Recall that those who believe in a vertical long-run AS curve believe that slack in the economy will put downward pressure on wages, causing the short-run AS curve to shift to the right and pushing aggregate output back toward Y_0. However, some argue that wages do *not* fall during slack periods and that the economy can get "stuck" at an equilibrium below potential output. In this case, monetary and fiscal policy would be necessary to restore full employment. We will return to this debate in Chapter 14.

The "new classical" economics, which we will discuss in Chapter 18, assumes that prices and wages are fully flexible and adjust very quickly to changing conditions. New classical economists believe, for example, that wage rate changes do not lag behind price changes. The new classical view is consistent with the existence of a vertical AS curve, even in the short run. At the other end of the spectrum is what is sometimes called the simple "Keynesian" view of aggregate supply. Those who hold this view believe there is a kink in the AS curve at capacity output, as we discussed in *Economics in Practice*, "The Simple 'Keynesian' Aggregate Supply Curve."

Causes of Inflation

We now turn to inflation and use the AS/AD framework to consider the causes of inflation.

Demand-Pull Inflation

demand-pull inflation
Inflation that is initiated by an increase in aggregate demand.

Inflation initiated by an increase in aggregate demand is called **demand-pull inflation**. You can see how demand-pull inflation works by looking at Figures 13.5 and 13.6. In both, the inflation begins with a shift of the aggregate demand schedule from AD_0 to AD_1, which causes the price level to increase from P_0 to P_1. (Output also increases, from Y_0 to Y_1.) If the economy is operating on the steep portion of the AS curve at the time of the increase in aggregate demand, as in Figure 13.6, most of the effect will be an increase in the price level instead of an increase in output. If the economy is operating on the flat portion of the AS curve, as in Figure 13.5, most of the effect will be an increase in output instead of an increase in the price level.

Remember, in the long run the initial increase in the price level will cause the *AS* curve to shift to the left as wages respond to the increase in output prices. If the long-run *AS* curve is vertical, as depicted in Figure 13.4, the increase in wages will shift the short-run *AS* curve (AS_0) to the left to AS_1, pushing the price level even higher, to P_2. If the long-run *AS* curve is vertical, a shift in aggregate demand from AD_0 to AD_1 will result, in the long run, in *no* increase in output and a price-level increase from P_0 to P_2.

Cost-Push, or Supply-Side, Inflation

Inflation can also be caused by an increase in costs, referred to as **cost-push**, or **supply-side, inflation**. Several times in the last three decades oil prices in world markets increased sharply. Because oil is used in virtually every line of business, costs increased.

An increase in costs (a cost shock) shifts the *AS* curve to the left, as Figure 13.7 shows. If we assume the government does not react to this shift in *AS* by changing fiscal or monetary policy, the *AD* curve will not shift. The supply shift will cause the equilibrium price level to rise (from P_0 to P_1) and the level of aggregate output to decline (from Y_0 to Y_1). Recall from Chapter 5 that **stagflation** occurs when output is falling at the same time prices are rising—in other words, when the economy is experiencing both a contraction and inflation simultaneously. Figure 13.7 shows that one possible cause of stagflation is an increase in costs.

cost-push, *or* **supply-side, inflation** Inflation caused by an increase in costs.

stagflation Occurs when output is falling at the same time that prices are rising.

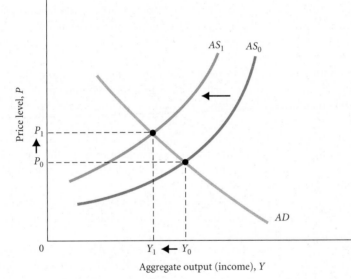

◀ **FIGURE 13.7**

Cost-Push, or Supply-Side, Inflation

An increase in costs shifts the *AS* curve to the left. By assuming the government does not react to this shift, the *AD* curve does not shift, the price level rises, and output falls.

To return to monetary and fiscal policy for a moment, note from Figure 13.7 that the government could counteract the increase in costs (the cost shock) by engaging in an expansionary policy (an increase in *G* or M^s or a decrease in *T*). This would shift the *AD* curve to the right, and the new *AD* curve would intersect the new *AS* curve at a higher level of output. The problem with this policy, however, is that the intersection of the new *AS* and *AD* curves would take place at a price even higher than P_1 in Figure 13.7. Cost shocks are thus bad news for policy makers. The only way they can counter the output loss brought about by a cost shock is by having the price level increase even more than it would without the policy action. This situation is illustrated in Figure 13.8.

Expectations and Inflation

When firms are making their price/output decisions, their *expectations* of future prices may affect their current decisions. If a firm expects that its competitors will raise their prices, in anticipation, it may raise its own price.

Consider a firm that manufactures toasters in an imperfectly competitive market. The toaster maker must decide what price to charge retail stores for its toaster. If it overestimates price and charges much more than other toaster manufacturers are charging, it will lose many customers. If

▶ **FIGURE 13.8**

Cost Shocks Are Bad News for Policy Makers

A cost shock with no change in monetary or fiscal policy would shift the aggregate supply curve from AS_0 to AS_1, lower output from Y_0 to Y_1, and raise the price level from P_0 to P_1. Monetary or fiscal policy could be changed enough to have the AD curve shift from AD_0 to AD_1. This policy would raise aggregate output Y again, but it would raise the price level further, to P_2.

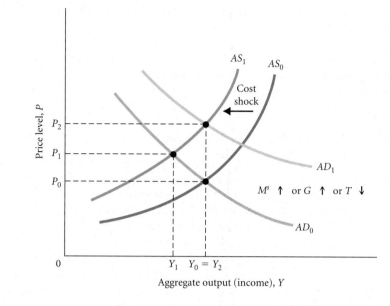

it underestimates price and charges much less than other toaster makers are charging, it will gain customers but at a considerable loss in revenue per sale. The firm's *optimum price*—the price that maximizes the firm's profits—is presumably not too far from the average of its competitors' prices. If it does not know its competitors' projected prices before it sets its own price, as is often the case, it must base its price on what it expects its competitors' prices to be.

Suppose inflation has been running at about 10 percent per year. Our firm probably expects its competitors will raise their prices about 10 percent this year, so it is likely to raise the price of its own toaster by about 10 percent. This response is how expectations can get "built into the system." If every firm expects every other firm to raise prices by 10 percent, every firm will raise prices by about 10 percent. Every firm ends up with the price increase it expected.

The fact that expectations can affect the price level is vexing. Expectations can lead to an inertia that makes it difficult to stop an inflationary spiral. If prices have been rising and if people's expectations are *adaptive*—that is, if they form their expectations on the basis of past pricing behavior—firms may continue raising prices even if demand is slowing or contracting. In terms of the *AS/AD* diagram, an increase in inflationary expectations that causes firms to increase their prices shifts the *AS* curve to the left. Remember that the *AS* curve represents the price/output responses of firms. If firms increase their prices because of a change in inflationary expectations, the result is a leftward shift of the *AS* curve.

Given the importance of expectations in inflation, the central banks of many countries survey consumers about their expectations. In Great Britain, for example, a survey of consumers by the Bank of England found a rise in expectations of inflation from 3.9 percent in February 2008 to 4.9 percent in May 2008. One of the aims of central banks is to try to keep these expectations low.

Money and Inflation

It is easy to see that an increase in the money supply can lead to an increase in the aggregate price level. As Figures 13.5 and 13.6 show, an increase in the money supply (M^s) shifts the AD curve to the right and results in a higher price level. This is simply a demand-pull inflation.

However, the supply of money may also play a role in creating inflation that persists over a long period of time, which we will call a "sustained" inflation. Consider an initial increase in government spending (G) with the money supply (M^s) unchanged. Because the money supply is unchanged, this is an increase in G that is not "accommodated" by the Fed. The increase in G shifts the AD curve to the right and results in a higher price level. This is shown in Figure 13.9 as a shift from AD_0 to AD_1. (In Figure 13.9, the economy is assumed to be operating on the vertical portion of the AS curve.)

Remember what happens when the price level increases. The higher price level causes the demand for money to increase. With an unchanged money supply and an increase in the quantity of money demanded, the interest rate will rise and the result will be a decrease in planned investment (I) spending. The new equilibrium corresponds to higher G, lower I, a higher interest rate, and a higher price level.

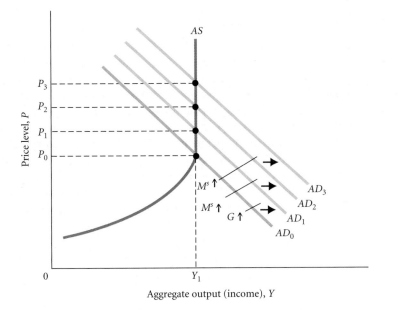

Sustained Inflation from an Initial Increase in G and Fed Accommodation

An increase in G with the money supply constant shifts the AD curve from AD_0 to AD_1. Although not shown in the figure, this leads to an increase in the interest rate and crowding out of planned investment. If the Fed tries to keep the interest rate unchanged by increasing the money supply, the AD curve will shift farther and farther to the right. The result is a sustained inflation, perhaps even hyperinflation.

Now let us take our example one step further. Suppose that the Fed is sympathetic to the expansionary fiscal policy (the increase in G we just discussed) and decides to expand the supply of money to keep the interest rate constant. As the higher price level pushes up the demand for money, the Fed expands the supply of money with the goal of keeping the interest rate unchanged, eliminating the crowding-out effect of a higher interest rate.

When the supply of money is expanded, the AD curve shifts to the right again, from AD_1 to AD_2. This shift of the AD curve, brought about by the increased money supply, pushes prices up even further. Higher prices, in turn, increase the demand for money further, which requires a further increase in the money supply and so on.

What would happen if the Fed tried to keep the interest rate constant when the economy was operating on the steep part of the AS curve? The situation could lead to a hyperinflation, a period of very rapid increases in the price level. If no more output can be coaxed out of the economy and if planned investment is not allowed to fall (because the interest rate is kept unchanged), it is not possible to increase G. As the Fed keeps pumping more and more money into the economy to keep the interest rate unchanged, the price level will keep rising.

Sustained Inflation as a Purely Monetary Phenomenon

Virtually all economists agree that an increase in the price level can be caused by anything that causes the AD curve to shift to the right or the AS curve to shift to the left. These include expansionary fiscal policy actions, monetary expansion, cost shocks, changes in expectations, and so on. It is also generally agreed that for a *sustained* inflation to occur, the Fed must accommodate it. In this sense, a sustained inflation can be thought of as a purely monetary phenomenon.

This argument, first put forth by monetarists (coming in Chapter 18), has gained wide acceptance. It is easy to show, as we just did, how expanding the money supply can continuously shift the AD curve. It is not as easy to come up with other reasons for continued shifts of the AD curve if the money supply is constant. One possibility is for the government to increase spending continuously without increasing taxes, but this process cannot continue forever. To finance spending without taxes, the government must borrow. Without any expansion of the money supply, the interest rate will rise dramatically because of the increase in the supply of government bonds. The public must be willing to buy the government bonds that are being issued to finance the spending increases. At some point, the public may be unwilling to buy any more bonds even though the interest rate is very high.[2] At this point, the government is no longer able to increase non-tax-financed spending without the Fed's cooperation. If this is true, a sustained inflation cannot exist without the Fed's cooperation.

---

[2] This means that the public's demand for money no longer depends on the interest rate. Even though the interest rate is very high, the public cannot be induced to have its real money balances fall any farther. There is a limit concerning how much the public can be induced to have its real money balances fall.

The Behavior of the Fed

We have so far in this book talked about monetary policy as consisting of changes in the money supply (M^S), which affects the interest rate (r). We saw in Chapter 10 that the Fed can change the money supply by (1) changing the required reserve ratio, (2) changing the discount rate, and (3) engaging in open market operations (buying and selling government securities). We also pointed out that the main way in which the Fed changes the money supply is by engaging in open market operations. Through these operations the Fed can achieve whatever value of the money supply it wants.

We must add two key points to the monetary policy story to make the story realistic, as we do in this section. The first point is that *in practice, the Fed controls the interest rate rather than the money supply*. The second point is that *the interest rate value that the Fed chooses depends on the state of the economy*. We will first explain these two points and then turn to a discussion of actual Fed policy from 1970 on. Figure 13.10 outlines how the Fed behaves in practice. It will be useful to keep this figure in mind in the following discussion.

▶ **FIGURE 13.10**

Fed Behavior

Controlling the Interest Rate

Controlling the Interest Rate

Figure 11.7 on page 212 in Chapter 11 shows that when the Fed increases the money supply, the interest rate falls. As the money supply curve shifts to the right, there is a movement of the equilibrium interest rate down the money demand curve. The buying and selling of government securities by the Fed thus has two effects at the same time: It changes the money supply, and it changes the interest rate. If the Fed buys securities, this purchase increases the money supply and lowers the interest rate, and if the Fed sells securities, this sale decreases the money supply and raises the interest rate. How much the interest rate changes depends on the shape of the money demand curve. The steeper the money demand curve, the larger the change in the interest rate for a given size change in government securities.

What this means is that if the Fed wants to achieve a particular value of the money supply, it must accept whatever interest rate value is implied by this choice. (Again, the interest rate value depends on the shape of the money demand curve.) Conversely, if the Fed wants to achieve a particular value of the interest rate, it must accept whatever money supply value is implied by this. If, for example, the Fed wants to lower the interest rate by one percentage point, it must keep buying government securities until the interest rate value is reached. As the Fed is buying government securities, the money supply is increasing. In short, the Fed can pick a money supply value and accept the interest rate consequences, or it can pick an interest rate value and accept the money supply consequences. The first key point is that in practice, the Fed chooses the interest rate value and accepts the money supply consequences, rather than vice versa.

Why might the Fed want to control the interest rate rather than the money supply? In practice, it is the interest rate that directly affects economic activity, for example, by affecting firms' decisions about investing. Controlling the interest rate thus gives the Fed more control over the key variable that matters to the economy. Focusing on the money supply leaves the Fed one step removed from the key processes.

The Federal Open Market Committee (FOMC) meets every 6 weeks and sets the value of the interest rate. It then instructs the Open Market Desk at the New York Federal Reserve Bank to keep buying or selling government securities until the desired interest rate value is achieved.

The FOMC announces the interest rate value at 2:15 P.M. eastern time on the day it meets. This is a key time for financial markets around the world. At 2:14 P.M., thousands of people are staring at their computer screens waiting for the word from on high. If the announcement is a surprise, it can have very large and immediate effects on bond and stock markets.

For most of the rest of this text, we will talk about monetary policy as being a change in the interest rate. Keep in mind, of course, that monetary policy also changes the money supply. We can talk about an expansionary monetary policy as one in which the money supply is increased or one in which the interest rate is lowered. We will talk about the interest rate being lowered because the interest rate is what the Fed targets in practice. However we talk about it, an expansionary monetary policy is achieved by the Fed's buying government securities.

The Fed's Response to the State of the Economy

When the FOMC meets every 6 weeks to set the value of the interest rate, it does not set the value in a vacuum. An important question in macroeconomics is what influences the interest rate decision. To answer this, we must consider the main goals of the Fed. What ultimately is the Fed trying to achieve?

The Fed's main goals are high levels of output and employment and a low rate of inflation. From the Fed's point of view, the best situation is a fully employed economy with an inflation rate near zero. The worst situation is *stagflation*—high unemployment and high inflation.

If the economy is in a low output/low inflation situation, it will be producing on the relatively flat portion of the aggregate supply (*AS*) curve (Figure 13.11). In this case, the Fed can increase output by lowering the interest rate (and thus increasing the money supply) with little effect on the price level. The expansionary monetary policy will shift the aggregate demand (*AD*) curve to the right, leading to an increase in output with little change in the price level. The Fed is likely to lower the interest rate (and thus increase the money supply) during times of low output and low inflation.

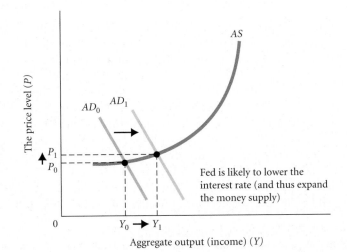

◀ **FIGURE 13.11**

The Fed's Response to Low Output/Low Inflation

During periods of low output/ low inflation, the economy is on the relatively flat portion of the *AS* curve. In this case, the Fed is likely to lower the interest rate (and thus expand the money supply). This will shift the *AD* curve to the right, from AD_0 to AD_1, and lead to an increase in output with very little increase in the price level.

ECONOMICS IN PRACTICE

Federal Reserve Behavior in 2008

The U.S. economy was in serious trouble in 2008. The problem began in the housing and mortgage markets. In 2003–2005, housing prices rose rapidly in what some called a housing "bubble." Banks issued mortgages to some people with poor credit ratings, so-called "sub-prime borrowers," and encouraged other people to take out mortgages they could not necessarily afford. There was very little regulation of these activities and investors took on huge risks. When housing prices began to fall in late 2005 and continued into 2008, the stage was set for a worldwide financial crisis.

The Federal Reserve responded to the events in 2008 in a number of ways. As we described in Chapter 10, p. 193, in March 2008 the Fed began lending to financial institutions other than commercial banks and guaranteed $30 billion of Bear Stearns' liabilities to JPMorgan. No longer was the Fed just a lender of last resort. On September 7, 2008, the Fed participated in a government takeover of the Federal National Mortgage Association (Fannie Mae) and the Federal Home Loan Mortgage Corporation (Freddie Mac), who at that point owned or guaranteed about half of the $12 trillion mortgage market in the United States. On September 17, the Fed loaned $85 billion to the American International Group (AIG) insurance company to help it avoid bankruptcy. In mid September, the Fed urged Congress to pass a $700 billion bailout bill, which was signed into law on October 3.

The Fed also rapidly lowered interest rates in 2008. On January 22, 2008, it lowered the target value of the interest rate that it directly controls, the "federal funds rate," from 4.25 percent to 3.50 percent. The Fed then lowered the rate further to 3.00 percent on January 30. On March 18, the rate was lowered to 2.25 percent, and by October 29, the rate was down to 1.00 percent.

Why did the Fed take these actions? We know from the text that the Fed is concerned about both inflation and output. Inflation was a concern in early 2008 because of rising food and commodity prices, particularly oil prices. (See the *Economics in Practice* box on p. 255.) But output was more of a concern. The fall in housing prices led to a fall in housing investment. (See the *Economics in Practice* box on p. 305.) By 2008, there was growing concern that problems in the housing market would spill into other markets and lead to a serious contraction in output. The Fed responded by lowering interest rates.

What about the other moves the Fed made in 2008? These nontraditional moves were designed to deal with the fact that many large financial institutions had bet on rising housing prices and lost. While the Fed tried in 2008 to alleviate the crisis, critics say it bears some of the blame for the crisis by its lax regulations and oversight in 2003–2005.

The opposite is true in times of high output and high inflation. In this situation, the economy is producing on the relatively steep portion of the *AS* curve (Figure 13.12), and the Fed can increase the interest rate (and thus decrease the money supply) with little effect on output. The contractionary monetary policy will shift the *AD* curve to the left, which will lead to a fall in the price level and little effect on output.[3] The Fed is likely to increase the interest rate (and thus decrease the money supply) during times of high output and high inflation. In this discussion, we see again the role of the shape of *AS* curve in determining the likely effect of government policy.

Stagflation is a more difficult problem to solve. If the Fed lowers the interest rate, output will rise, but so will the inflation rate (which is already too high). If the Fed increases the interest rate, the inflation rate will fall, but so will output (which is already too low). (You should be able to draw *AS/AD* diagrams to see why this is true.) The Fed is faced with a trade-off. In this case, the Fed's decisions depend on how it weights output relative to inflation. If it dislikes high inflation

---

[3] In practice, the price level rarely falls. What the Fed actually achieves in this case is a decrease in the *rate of inflation*—that is, in the percentage change in the price level—not a decrease in the price level itself. The discussion here is sliding over the distinction between the price level and the rate of inflation. This distinction is discussed further in the next chapter.

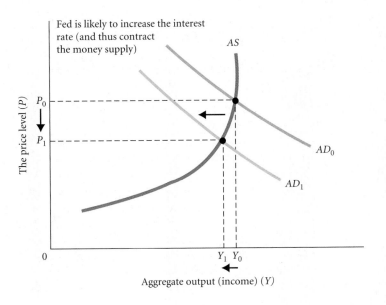

◀ **FIGURE 13.12**

The Fed's Response to High Output/High Inflation

During periods of high output/high inflation, the economy is on the relatively steep portion of the AS curve. In this case, the Fed is likely to increase the interest rate (and thus contract the money supply). This will shift the AD curve to the left, from AD_0 to AD_1, and lead to a decrease in the price level with very little decrease in output.

more than low output, it will increase the interest rate; if it dislikes low output more than high inflation, it will lower the interest rate. In practice, the Fed probably dislikes high inflation more than low output, but how the Fed behaves depends in part on the beliefs of the chair of the Fed.

The Fed is sometimes said to "lean against the wind," meaning that as the economy expands, the Fed uses open market operations to raise the interest rate gradually to try to prevent the economy from expanding too quickly. Conversely, as the economy contracts, the Fed lowers the interest rate gradually to lessen (and eventually stop) the contraction.

Fed Behavior Since 1970

Figure 13.13 plots three variables that can be used to describe Fed behavior since 1970. The interest rate is the 3-month Treasury bill rate, which moves closely with the interest rate that the Fed actually controls, which is the federal funds rate. For simplicity, we will take the 3-month Treasury bill rate to be the rate that the Fed controls and we will just call it "the interest rate." Inflation is the percentage change in the GDP deflator over the previous 4 quarters. This variable is also plotted in Figure 5.6 on p. 100. Output is the percentage deviation of real GDP from its trend. (Real GDP itself is plotted in Figure 5.4 on p. 98.) It is easier to see fluctuations in real GDP by looking at percentage deviations from its trend.

Recall from Chapter 5 that we have called four periods since 1970 "recessionary periods" and two periods "high inflation periods." These periods are highlighted in Figure 13.13. The recessionary and high inflation periods have considerable overlap in the last half of the 1970s and early 1980s. After 1981, there are no more high inflation periods and two more fairly short recessionary periods. There is thus some stagflation in the early part of the period since 1970 but not in the later part.

We know from earlier in this chapter that stagflation is bad news for policy makers. Should the Fed raise the interest rate to lessen inflation at a cost of making the output situation worse, or should it lower the interest rate to help output growth at a cost of making inflation worse? What did the Fed actually do? You can see from Figure 13.13 that the Fed generally raised the interest rate when inflation was high—even when output was low. In particular, the interest rate was very high in the 1979–1983 period even though output was low. Had the Fed not had such high interest rates in this period, the recession would likely have been less severe, but inflation would have been even worse.

After inflation got back down to about 4 percent in 1983, the Fed began lowering the interest rate, which helped output. The Fed increased the interest rate in 1988 as inflation began to pick up a little and output was strong. The Fed acted aggressively in lowering the interest rate during the 1990–1991 recession and again in the 2001 recession. The Treasury bill rate got below 1 percent in 2003. The Fed then reversed course, and the interest rate rose to nearly 5 percent in 2006.

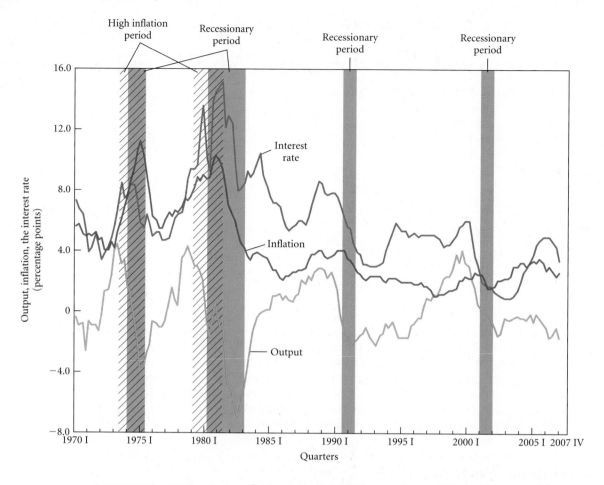

▲ FIGURE 13.13 Output, Inflation, and the Interest Rate 1970 I–2007 IV

The Fed generally had high interest rates in the two inflationary periods and low interest rates from the mid 1980s on. It aggressively lowered interest rates in the 1990 IV–1991 I and 2001 I–2001 III recessions. Output is the percentage deviation of real GDP from its trend. Inflation is the 4-quarter average of the percentage change in the GDP deflator. The interest rate is the 3-month Treasury bill rate.

The Fed then reversed course again near the end of 2007 and began lowering the interest rate in an effort to fight a recession that it expected was coming.

Fed behavior in the period since 1970 is thus fairly easy to summarize. The Fed generally had high interest rates in the 1970s and early 1980s as it fought inflation. Since 1983, inflation has been low by historical standards, and the Fed focused in this period on trying to smooth fluctuations in output.

Inflation Targeting

inflation targeting
When a monetary authority chooses its interest rate values with the aim of keeping the inflation rate within some specified band over some specified horizon.

Some monetary authorities in the world engage in what is called **inflation targeting**. If a monetary authority behaves this way, it announces a *target* value of the inflation rate, usually for a horizon of a year or more, and then it chooses its interest rate values with the aim of keeping the actual inflation rate within some specified band around the target value. For example, the target value might be 2 percent with a band of 1 to 3 percent. Then the monetary authority would try to keep the actual inflation rate between 1 and 3 percent. With a horizon of a year or more, the monetary authority would not expect to keep the inflation rate between 1 and 3 percent each month because there are a number of temporary factors that move the inflation rate around each month (such as weather) over which the monetary authority has no control. But over a year or more, the expectation would be that the inflation rate would be between 1 and 3 percent. For example, in Hungary in 2008 the central bank set a medium term inflation target of 3 percent. In the United Kingdom the chancellor of the Exchequer sets the inflation target.

ECONOMICS IN PRACTICE

Rising Food Prices Worry Central Banks Around the World

Some central banks in the world (for example, the European Central Bank (ECB)) are primarily inflation targeters, whereas others (for example, the Fed) are not. All central banks, however, even the Fed, worry about inflation. The following article shows the concern of the ECB and the Bank of China, among others, regarding possible inflationary pressures on 2008 from rising food prices. It is clear from the third paragraph that Jean-Claude Trichet, the president of the ECB, will do his best to keep inflation from getting out of hand.

Food Prices Worry Central Bankers

Wall Street Journal

BASEL, Switzerland—Central bankers from around the globe voiced concern about the risks that rising food and commodity prices present for the worldwide inflation outlook.

"On a global level, inflationary risks are significant," European Central Bank President Jean-Claude Trichet told reporters Monday, in his capacity as chairman of the global economy meeting at the Bank for International Settlements. Global policy makers gather at the BIS—often called the central bankers' central bank—every other month.

"There is no time for complacency for central banks in any respect," Mr. Trichet said, "The present level of inflation must be transitory."

The ECB is expected to keep interest rates steady at 4% when it meets on Thursday, as policy makers struggle to balance the risks of slowing growth and high inflation.

"Food prices are an issue everywhere for two reasons: First, the impact on inflation, and second, the impact on the situation of many poor people around the world," said ECB Governing Council member Erkki Liikanen of Finland.

Some policy makers said there may be little that monetary policy can do to slow runaway food prices. "It's a global problem.... But we cannot use monetary policy to manage this problem," said Slawomir Skrzypek, president of the Polish central bank.

People's Bank of China governor Zhou Xiaochuan said interest rates were one way to control price gains, but they weren't the Chinese central bank's only option: "We always say there is [the] possibility to use interest rates to go further to control the inflation in China. But whether we chose this instrument or that instrument, we still have some options."

Source: Nina Koeppen, May 6, 2008

In the discussion at the beginning of this section about the Fed's response to the state of the economy, we assumed that the Fed was concerned about both inflation and output. When output is low, other things being equal, it was argued that the Fed is likely to lower the interest rate to stimulate the economy. If at the same time inflation is high (stagflation), the Fed is faced with a trade-off, and whether it raises or lowers the interest rate depends on how it weights output relative to inflation. In the case of inflation targeting, all the weight is on inflation. So inflation targeting is a special case of Fed behavior just discussed—namely, the case in which all of the Fed's focus is on setting the interest rate to keep the inflation rate within some band over some horizon.

There has been much debate about whether inflation targeting is a good idea. The Fed under Alan Greenspan and previous chairs never engaged in inflation targeting, but the issue arose in the United States with the appointment of Ben Bernanke in 2006 as the new Fed chair. Bernanke had argued in the past in favor of inflation targeting, and people wondered whether the Fed would move in this direction under Bernanke. You can see in Figure 13.13 that the Fed began lowering the interest rate in 2007 in anticipation of a recession, which doesn't look like inflation targeting.

Looking Ahead

In Chapters 8 and 9, we discussed the concept of an equilibrium level of aggregate output and income, the idea of the multiplier, and the basics of fiscal policy. Those two chapters centered on the workings of the goods market alone.

In Chapters 10 and 11, we analyzed the money market by discussing the supply of money, the demand for money, the equilibrium interest rate, and the basics of monetary policy. In Chapter 12, we brought our analysis of the goods market together with our analysis of the money market and we derived the aggregate demand curve.

In this chapter, we introduced the aggregate supply curve. By using the aggregate supply and aggregate demand curves, we can determine the equilibrium price level in the economy and understand some causes of inflation.

We have still said little about employment, unemployment, and the functioning of the labor market in the macroeconomy. The next chapter will link everything we have done so far to this third major market arena—the labor market—and to the problem of unemployment.

SUMMARY

THE AGGREGATE SUPPLY CURVE p. 237

1. *Aggregate supply* is the total supply of goods and services in an economy. The *aggregate supply (AS) curve* shows the relationship between the aggregate quantity of output supplied by all the firms in an economy and the overall price level. The AS curve is *not* a market supply curve, and it is *not* the simple sum of all the individual supply curves in the economy. For this reason, it is helpful to think of the AS curve as a "price/output response" curve—that is, a curve that traces out the price decisions and output decisions of all the markets and firms in the economy under a given set of circumstances.

2. The shape of the short-run AS curve is a source of much controversy in macroeconomics. Many economists believe that at very low levels of aggregate output, the AS curve is fairly flat and that at high levels of aggregate output, the AS curve is vertical or nearly vertical. Thus, the AS curve slopes upward and becomes vertical when the economy reaches its capacity, or maximum, output.

3. Anything that affects an individual firm's marginal cost curve can shift the AS curve. The two main factors are wage rates and energy prices.

THE EQUILIBRIUM PRICE LEVEL p. 241

4. The *equilibrium price level* in the economy occurs at the point at which the AS and AD curves intersect. The intersection of the AS and AD curves corresponds to equilibrium in the goods and money markets *and* to a set of price/output decisions on the part of all the firms in the economy.

THE LONG-RUN AGGREGATE SUPPLY CURVE p. 242

5. If wages fully adjust to prices in the long run, then the long-run AS curve will be vertical.

6. The level of aggregate output that can be sustained in the long run without inflation is called *potential output* or *potential GDP*.

MONETARY AND FISCAL POLICY EFFECTS p. 244

7. If the economy is initially producing on the flat portion of the AS curve, an expansionary policy—which shifts the AD curve to the right—will result in a small increase in the equilibrium price level relative to the increase in equilibrium output. If the economy is initially producing on the steep portion of the AS curve, an expansionary policy results in a small increase in equilibrium output and a large increase in the equilibrium price level.

8. If the *AS* curve is vertical in the long run, neither monetary nor fiscal policy has any effect on aggregate output in the long run. For this reason, the exact length of the long run is one of the most pressing questions in macroeconomics.

CAUSES OF INFLATION *p. 246*

9. *Demand-pull inflation* is inflation initiated by an increase in aggregate demand. *Cost-push*, or *supply-side, inflation* is inflation initiated by an increase in costs like energy prices. An increase in costs may also lead to *stagflation*—the situation in which the economy is experiencing a contraction and inflation simultaneously.

10. Inflation can become "built into the system" as a result of expectations. If prices have been rising and people form their expectations on the basis of past pricing behavior, firms may continue raising prices even if demand is slowing or contracting.

11. When the price level increases, so too does the demand for money. If the economy is operating on the steep part of the *AS* curve and the Fed tries to keep the interest rate constant by increasing the supply of money, the result could be a *hyperinflation*—a period of very rapid increases in the price level.

THE BEHAVIOR OF THE FED *p. 250*

12. In practice, the Fed controls the interest rate rather than the money supply. The interest rate value that the Fed chooses depends on the state of the economy. The Fed wants high output and low inflation. The Fed is likely to decrease the interest rate during times of low output and low inflation, and is likely to increase the interest rate during times of high output and high inflation.

13. The Fed generally had high interest rates in the 1970s and early 1980s as it fought inflation. Since 1983, inflation has been low by historical standards and the Fed focused in this period on trying to smooth fluctuations in output.

14. Inflation targeting is the case where the monetary authority weights only inflation. It chooses its interest rate values with the aim of keeping the inflation rate within some specified band over some specified horizon.

REVIEW TERMS AND CONCEPTS

PROBLEMS

Visit **www.myeconlab.com** to complete the problems marked in orange online. You will receive instant feedback on your answers, tutorial help, and access to additional practice problems.

1. In Japan during the first half of 2000, the Bank of Japan kept interest rates at a near zero level in an attempt to stimulate demand. In addition, the government passed a substantial increase in government expenditure and cut taxes. Slowly, Japanese GDP began to grow with absolutely no sign of an increase in the price level. Illustrate the position of the Japanese economy with aggregate supply and demand curves. Where on the short-run *AS* curve was Japan in 2000?

2. In 2008, the price of oil rose sharply on world markets. What impact would you expect there to be on the aggregate price level and on real GDP? Illustrate your answer with aggregate demand and supply curves. What would you expect to be the effect on interest rates if the Fed held the money supply constant? Tell a complete story.

3. By using aggregate supply and demand curves to illustrate your points, discuss the impacts of the following events on the price level and on equilibrium GDP (*Y*) in the *short run*:
   a. A tax cut holding government purchases constant with the economy operating at near full capacity
   b. An increase in the money supply during a period of high unemployment and excess industrial capacity

   c. An increase in the price of oil caused by a war in the Middle East, assuming that the Fed attempts to keep interest rates constant by accommodating inflation
   d. An increase in taxes and a cut in government spending supported by a cooperative Fed acting to keep output from falling

4. During 1999 and 2000, a debate raged over whether the United States was at or above potential GDP. Some economists feared the economy was operating at a level of output above potential GDP and inflationary pressures were building. They urged the Fed to tighten monetary policy and increase interest rates to slow the economy. Others argued that a worldwide glut of cheap products was causing input prices to be lower, keeping prices from rising.

   By using aggregate supply and demand curves and other useful graphs, illustrate the following:
   a. Those pushing the Fed to act were right, and prices start to rise more rapidly in 2000. The Fed acts belatedly to slow money growth (contract the money supply), driving up interest rates and pushing the economy back to potential GDP.
   b. The worldwide glut gets worse, and the result is a *falling* price level (deflation) in the United States despite expanding aggregate demand.

5. [Related to the *Economics in Practice* on *p. 243*] The *Economics in Practice* describes the simple Keynesian aggregate supply curve as one in which there is a maximum level of output given the constraints of a fixed capital stock and a fixed supply of labor. The presumption is that increases in demand when firms are operating below capacity will result in output increases and no input price or output price changes but that at levels of output above full capacity, firms have no choice but to raise prices of demand increases. In reality, however, the short-run aggregate supply curve isn't flat and then vertical. Rather, it becomes steeper as we move from left to right on the diagram. Explain why. What circumstances might lead to an equilibrium at a very flat portion of the AS curve? at a very steep portion?

6. Using aggregate supply and aggregate demand curves to illustrate, describe the effects of the following events on the price level and on equilibrium GDP in the *long run* assuming that input prices fully adjust to output prices after some lag:
   a. An increase occurs in the money supply above potential GDP
   b. A decrease in government spending and in the money supply with GDP above potential GDP occurs
   c. Starting with the economy at potential GDP, a war in the Middle East pushes up energy prices temporarily. The Fed expands the money supply to accommodate the inflation.

7. Two separate capacity constraints are discussed in this chapter: (1) the actual physical capacity of existing plants and equipment, shown as the vertical portion of the short-run AS curve, and (2) potential GDP, leading to a vertical long-run AS curve. Explain the difference between the two. Which is greater, full-capacity GDP or potential GDP? Why?

8. In country A, all wage contracts are indexed to inflation. That is, each month wages are adjusted to reflect increases in the cost of living as reflected in changes in the price level. In country B, there are no cost-of-living adjustments to wages, but the workforce is completely unionized. Unions negotiate 3-year contracts. In which country is an expansionary monetary policy likely to have a larger effect on aggregate output? Explain your answer using aggregate supply and aggregate demand curves.

9. During 2001, the U.S. economy slipped into a recession. For the next several years, the Fed and Congress used monetary and fiscal policies in an attempt to stimulate the economy. Obtain data on interest rates (such as the prime rate or the federal funds rate). Do you see evidence of the Fed's action? When did the Fed begin its expansionary policy? Obtain data on total federal expenditures, tax receipts, and the deficit. (Try www.commerce.gov). When did fiscal policy become "expansionary"? Which policy seems to have suffered more from policy lags?

10. Describe the Fed's tendency to "lean against the wind." Do the Fed's policies tend to stabilize or destabilize the economy?

11. [Related to the *Economics in Practice* on *p. 255*] The *Economics in Practice* describes the increase in food prices around the world in 2008. Since food, in large measure, affects the real income of households, increasing prices will eventually push up wages and have an impact on the aggregate supply curve. Central banks were very worried about the prospects for inflation becoming generalized. To stop the inflation, what would the Fed be likely to do? What are the consequences for the economy? Illustrate graphically how the *AD* curve is likely to respond? Specifically, what would be the effects on employment and unemployment? How would you, as a board member, decide whether to increase or decrease the money supply?

12. [Related to the *Economics in Practice* on *p. 252*] Two of the Fed's main goals are high levels of output and employment and a low rate of inflation. During times of low output and low inflation, the Fed is likely to lower the interest rate to increase the money supply. During times of high output and high inflation, the Fed is likely to increase the interest rate to decrease the money supply. What was the state of the U.S economy in 2008? Go to www.bls.gov and click on CPI to find inflation data, and www.bea.gov to find GDP data. What were the inflation and output numbers in 2008? What was the Fed's response to the 2008 economy? Go to www.federalreserve.gov and find data on the discount rate changes made by the Fed during 2008. Did the actions of the Fed seem appropriate based on the state of the economy? What were the results of the Fed's actions?

The Labor Market In the Macroeconomy

14

In previous chapters, we stressed the three broadly defined markets in which households, firms, the government, and the rest of the world interact: (1) the *goods market*, discussed in Chapters 8 and 9; (2) the *money market*, discussed in Chapters 10 and 11; and (3) the *labor market*. In Chapter 7, we described some features of the U.S. labor market and explained how the unemployment rate is measured. Then in Chapter 13, we considered the labor market briefly

in our discussion of the aggregate supply curve. Because labor is an input, what goes on in the labor market affects the shape of the aggregate supply (*AS*) curve. If wages lag prices the *AS* curve will be upward-sloping; if wages are completely flexible and rise every time prices rise by the same percentage, the *AS* curve will be vertical.

In this chapter, we look further at the labor market's role in the macroeconomy. First, we consider the classical view, which holds that wages always adjust to clear the labor market, that is, to equate the supply of and demand for labor. We then consider why the labor market may not always clear and why unemployment may exist. Finally, we discuss the relationship between inflation and unemployment. As we go through the analysis, it is important to recall why unemployment is one of the three primary concerns of macroeconomics. Go back and reread "The Cost of Unemployment" in Chapter 7 (pp. 128–130). It is clear that unemployment imposes heavy costs on the unemployed and on society. In 2008, more than 7 million people in the United States were looking for work and did not have even a part-time job.

The Labor Market: Basic Concepts

Let us briefly review what the unemployment rate measures, which we discussed in Chapter 7. On the first Friday of every month, the Labor Department releases the results of a household survey that provides an estimate of the number of people with a job, the employed (*E*), as well as the number of people who are looking for work but cannot find a job, the unemployed (*U*). The labor force (*LF*) is the number of employed plus unemployed:

$$LF = E + U$$

The **unemployment rate** is the number of people unemployed as a percentage of the labor force:

$$\text{unemployment rate} = \frac{U}{LF}$$

To repeat, to be unemployed, a person must be out of a job and actively looking for work. When a person stops looking for work, he or she is considered *out of the labor force* and is no longer counted as unemployed.

259

unemployment rate The number of people unemployed as a percentage of the labor force.

frictional unemployment The portion of unemployment that is due to the normal working of the labor market; used to denote short-run job/skill matching problems.

structural unemployment The portion of unemployment that is due to changes in the structure of the economy that result in a significant loss of jobs in certain industries.

cyclical unemployment The increase in unemployment that occurs during recessions and depressions.

It is important to realize that even if the economy is running at or near full capacity, the unemployment rate will never be zero. The economy is dynamic. Students graduate from schools and training programs; some businesses make profits and grow, while others suffer losses and go out of business; people move in and out of the labor force and change careers. It takes time for people to find the right job and for employers to match the right worker with the jobs they have. This **frictional** and **structural unemployment** is inevitable and in many ways desirable. (Review Chapter 7 if these terms are hazy to you.)

In this chapter, we are concerned with **cyclical unemployment**, the increase in unemployment that occurs during recessions and depressions. When the economy contracts, the number of people unemployed and the unemployment rate rise. The United States has experienced several periods of high unemployment. During the Great Depression, the unemployment rate remained high for nearly a decade. In December 1982, more than 12 million people were unemployed, putting the unemployment rate at 10.8 percent.

In one sense, the reason employment falls when the economy experiences a downturn is obvious. When firms cut back on production, they need fewer workers, so people get laid off. Employment tends to fall when aggregate output falls and to rise when aggregate output rises. *Nevertheless, a decline in the demand for labor does not necessarily mean that unemployment will rise.* If markets work as we described in Chapters 3 and 4, a decline in the demand for labor will initially create an excess supply of labor. As a result, the wage rate will fall until the quantity of labor supplied again equals the quantity of labor demanded, restoring equilibrium in the labor market. At the new lower wage rate, everyone who wants a job will have one.

If the quantity of labor demanded and the quantity of labor supplied are brought into equilibrium by rising and falling wage rates, there should be no persistent unemployment above the frictional and structural amount. This was the view held by the classical economists who preceded Keynes, and it is still the view of a number of economists today. Other economists believe that wage rates adjust only slowly to decreases in the demand for labor and, as a result, economies can suffer bouts of involuntary unemployment.

The Classical View of the Labor Market

The classical view of the labor market is illustrated in Figure 14.1. Classical economists assumed that the wage rate adjusts to equate the quantity demanded with the quantity supplied, thereby implying that unemployment does not exist. To see how this adjustment might take place, we can use the supply and demand curves in Figure 14.1. Curve D_0 is the **labor demand curve**. Each point on D_0 represents the amount of labor firms want to employ at each given wage rate. Each firm's decision about how much labor to demand is part of its overall profit-maximizing decision. A firm makes a profit by selling output to households. It will hire workers if the value of its output is sufficient to justify the wage that is being paid. Thus, the amount of labor that a firm hires depends on the value of output that workers produce.

Figure 14.1 also shows a **labor supply curve**, labeled S. Each point on the labor supply curve represents the amount of labor households want to supply at each given wage rate. Each household's decision concerning how much labor to supply is part of the overall consumer choice problem of a household. Each household member looks at the market wage rate, the prices of outputs, and the value of leisure time (including the value of staying at home and working in the yard or raising children) and chooses the amount of labor to supply (if any). A household member not in the labor force has decided that his or her time is more valuable in nonmarket activities.

Those individuals who stay out of the labor force place a higher value on the use of their time than do potential employers, whose demand reflects the value that those individuals can produce in the formal job market. Consider households in less developed countries. In many such households, the alternative to working for a wage is subsistence farming. If the wage rate in the labor market is very low, many people will choose to farm for themselves. In this case, the value of what these people produce in farming must be greater than the value that society currently places on what they would produce if they worked for a wage. If this were not true, wages would rise and more people would join the labor force.

labor demand curve A graph that illustrates the amount of labor that firms want to employ at each given wage rate.

labor supply curve A graph that illustrates the amount of labor that households want to supply at each given wage rate.

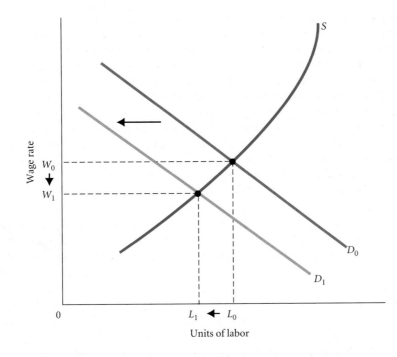

◀ FIGURE 14.1

The Classical Labor Market

Classical economists believe that the labor market always clears. If the demand for labor shifts from D_0 to D_1, the equilibrium wage will fall from W_0 to W_1. Anyone who wants a job at W_1 will have one.

In Figure 14.1 the labor market is initially in equilibrium at W_0 and L_0. Now consider what classical economists think would happen if there is a decrease in the demand for labor. The demand for labor curve shifts in from D_0 to D_1. The new demand curve intersects the labor supply curve at L_1 and W_1. There is a new equilibrium at a lower wage rate, in which fewer people are employed. Note that the fall in the demand for labor has not caused any unemployment. There are fewer people working, but all people interested in working at the wage W_1 are in fact employed.

The classical economists saw the workings of the labor market—the behavior of labor supply and labor demand—as optimal from the standpoint of both individual households and firms and from the standpoint of society. If households want more output than is currently being produced, output demand will increase, output prices will rise, the demand for labor will increase, the wage rate will rise, and more workers will be drawn into the labor force. (Some of those who preferred not to be a part of the labor force at the lower wage rate will be lured into the labor force at the higher wage rate.) At equilibrium, prices and wages reflect a trade-off between the value households place on outputs and the value of time spent in leisure and nonmarket work. At equilibrium, the people who are not working have *chosen* not to work at that market wage. There is always *full employment* in this sense. The classical economists believed that the market would achieve the optimal result if left to its own devices, and there is nothing the government can do to make things better.

The Classical Labor Market and the Aggregate Supply Curve

How does the classical view of the labor market relate to the theory of the vertical *AS* curve we covered in Chapter 13? The classical idea that wages adjust to clear the labor market is consistent with the view that wages respond quickly to price changes. Recall that the argument that the *AS* curve is vertical in the long run involves wage adjustments. If the short-run *AS* and aggregate demand (*AD*) curves intersected above potential output (Y_0 in Figure 13.4), wages would rise, shifting the *AS* curve to the left and pushing Y back down to Y_0. Similarly, if the short-run *AS* and *AD* curves intersected to the left of Y_0, unemployment and excess capacity would cause wages to fall, shifting the *AS* curve to the right and pushing Y back up to Y_0. Also remember that if the *AS* curve is vertical, monetary and fiscal policy cannot affect the level of output and employment in the economy. It therefore follows that those who believe that the wage rate adjusts quickly to clear the labor market are likely to believe that the *AS* curve is vertical (or almost vertical) and that monetary and fiscal policy have little or no effect on output and employment.

The Unemployment Rate and the Classical View

If, as the classical economists assumed, the labor market works well, how can we account for the fact that the unemployment rate at times seems high? There seem to be times when millions of people who want jobs at prevailing wage rates cannot find them. How can we reconcile this situation with the classical assumption about the labor market?

Some economists answer by arguing that the unemployment rate is not a good measure of whether the labor market is working well. We know the economy is dynamic and at any given time some industries are expanding and some are contracting. Consider, for example, a carpenter who is laid off because of a contraction in the construction industry. He had probably developed specific skills related to the construction industry—skills not necessarily useful for jobs in other industries. If he were earning $40,000 per year as a carpenter, he may be able to earn only $30,000 per year in another industry. He may eventually work his way back up to a salary of $40,000 in the new industry as he develops new skills, but this process will take time. Will this carpenter take a job at $30,000? There are at least two reasons he may not. First, he may believe that the slump in the construction industry is temporary and that he will soon get his job back. Second, he may mistakenly believe that he can earn more than $30,000 in another industry and will continue to look for a better job.

If our carpenter decides to continue looking for a job paying more than $30,000 per year, he will be considered unemployed because he is actively looking for work. This does not necessarily mean that the labor market is not working properly. The carpenter has *chosen* not to work for a wage of $30,000 per year, but if his value to any firm outside the construction industry is no more than $30,000 per year, we would not expect him to find a job paying more than $30,000. In this case, a positive unemployment rate as measured by the government does not necessarily indicate that the labor market is working poorly.

If the degree to which industries are changing in the economy fluctuates over time, there will be more people like our carpenter at some times than at others. This variation will cause the measured unemployment rate to fluctuate. Some economists argue that the measured unemployment rate may sometimes *seem* high even though the labor market is working well. The quantity of labor supplied at the current wage is equal to the quantity demanded at the current wage. The fact that there are people willing to work at a wage higher than the current wage does not mean that the labor market is not working. Whenever there is an upward-sloping supply curve in a market (as is usually the case in the labor market), the quantity supplied at a price higher than the equilibrium price is always greater than the quantity supplied at the equilibrium price.

Economists who view unemployment this way do not see it as a major problem. Yet the haunting images of the bread lines in the 1930s are still with us, and many find it difficult to believe everything was optimal when over 12 million people were looking for work at the end of 1982. There are other views of unemployment, as we will now see.

Explaining the Existence of Unemployment

If unemployment is a major macroeconomic problem—and many economists believe that it is—then we need to explore some of the reasons that have been suggested for its existence. Among these are sticky wages, efficiency wages, imperfect information, and minimum wage laws.

Each of these explanations for unemployment focuses on a particular reason that wage rates do not completely adjust when the demand for labor falls. Because wage rates do not fall as far as needed, there will be more people who wish to work at the current wage rates than there are jobs for those people. This is what one means by unemployment.

Sticky Wages

sticky wages The downward rigidity of wages as an explanation for the existence of unemployment.

One explanation for unemployment (above and beyond normal frictional and structural unemployment) is that wages are **sticky** on the downward side. That is, the equilibrium wage gets stuck at a particular level and does not fall when the demand for labor falls. This situation is illustrated in Figure 14.2, where the equilibrium wage gets stuck at W_0 (the original wage) and does not fall to W^* when demand decreases from D_0 to D_1. The result is unemployment of the amount

$L_0 - L_1$, where L_0 is the quantity of labor that households want to supply at wage rate W_0 and L_1 is the amount of labor that firms want to hire at wage rate W_0. $L_0 - L_1$ is the number of workers who would like to work at W_0 but cannot find jobs.

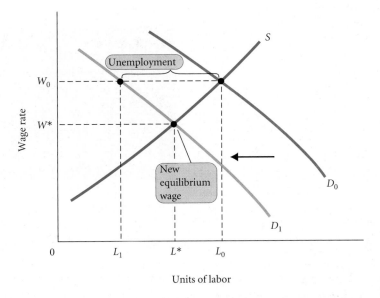

◀ **FIGURE 14.2**

Sticky Wages

If wages "stick" at W_0 instead of falling to the new equilibrium wage of W^* following a shift of demand from D_0 to D_1, the result will be unemployment equal to $L_0 - L_1$.

The sticky wage explanation of unemployment, however, begs the question. *Why* are wages sticky, if they are, and *why* do wages not fall to clear the labor market during periods of high unemployment? Many answers have been proposed, but as yet no one answer has been agreed on. This lack of consensus is one reason macroeconomics has been in a state of flux for so long. The existence of unemployment continues to be a puzzle. Although we will discuss the major theories that economists have proposed to explain why wages may not clear the labor market, we can offer no conclusions. The question is still open.

Social, or Implicit, Contracts   One explanation for downwardly sticky wages is that firms enter into **social**, or **implicit**, **contracts** with workers not to cut wages. It seems that extreme events—deep recession, deregulation, or threat of bankruptcy—are necessary for firms to cut wages. Wage cuts did occur in the Great Depression, in the airline industry following deregulation of the industry in the 1980s, and recently when some U.S. manufacturing firms found themselves in danger of bankruptcy from stiff foreign competition. These are exceptions to the general rule. For reasons that may be more sociological than economic, cutting wages seems close to being a taboo. In a recent study, Truman Bewley of Yale University surveyed hundreds of managers about why they did not reduce wage rates in downturns. The most common response was that wage cuts hurt worker morale and thus negatively affect worker productivity. Breaking the taboo and cutting wages may be costly in this sense.

social, *or* **implicit, contracts**   Unspoken agreements between workers and firms that firms will not cut wages.

A related argument, the **relative-wage explanation of unemployment**, holds that workers are concerned about their wages *relative* to the wages of other workers in other firms and industries and may be unwilling to accept wage cuts unless they know that other workers are receiving similar cuts. Because it is difficult to reassure any one group of workers that all other workers are in the same situation, workers may resist any cut in their wages. There may be an implicit understanding between firms and workers that firms will not do anything that would make their workers worse off relative to workers in other firms.

relative-wage explanation of unemployment   An explanation for sticky wages (and therefore unemployment): If workers are concerned about their wages relative to other workers in other firms and industries, they may be unwilling to accept a wage cut unless they know that all other workers are receiving similar cuts.

Explicit Contracts   Many workers—in particular unionized workers—sign 1- to 3-year employment contracts with firms. These contracts stipulate the workers' wages for each year of the contract. Wages set in this way do not fluctuate with economic conditions, either upward or downward. If the economy slows down and firms demand fewer workers, the wage will not fall. Instead, some workers will be laid off.

ECONOMICS IN PRACTICE

Graduate School Applications in Recessions

In early 2008, there were a number of indications that the U.S. economy was slowing down. For many soon-to-graduate college students, forecasting the economy became a very personal enterprise. If the economy moved into a recession, as some economists were predicting because of the subprime housing problem, the graduates' job prospects would be poor. As the following article suggests, many students found a way to partially protect themselves from the possibility of a recession:

apply to graduate school. Some observers of the economy argue that applications to take the GRE—standardized test required for graduate school admissions—increase when recessions loom. Young people may thus time when they go to graduate school based on their forecasts of the economy.

Graduate School Offers Relief During Economic Recession

Oklahoma Daily (U. Oklahoma)

(U-WIRE) NORMAN, Okla. – A shaky economy may make it difficult for students to find jobs and pay off loans after graduation, but one option for graduates is more promising: Graduate school.

Bette Scott, OU Career Services director, said during her time at Career Services, she has seen economic recession cause graduating students to become more interested in continuing their education rather than entering an uncertain job market.

"Generally, what will happen when the job market slows down is that more students will look at going on to grad school," Scott said. "During good job markets like we've been in, grad school applications are down."

A recession is a decrease in gross domestic product for two straight quarters. Though that isn't the current situation, early indicators, such as a .4 percent rise in national unemployment to 5 percent and a failing stock market, tell economists a recession could occur.

During the last recession between 2001 and 2003, graduate school applications across the nation were up, according to University of Washington researchers.

Students beginning graduate school in the natural sciences and engineering fields increased by 31 percent from before the recession in 1998.

"The high-tech economy siphoned people away from graduate school, and when the bubble burst, that temporarily turned things around," William Zumeta, a University of Washington professor who did the research, said in his published findings from 2004.

Another indicator the researchers found was the number of people who took the Graduate Record Exam increased 9 percent, suggesting more people were preparing for varied programs.

If graduate school is not an option for students, Scott said students should be prepared to look outside their comfort zone when searching for a job.

"Students will be more willing to look at jobs they haven't looked at previously," he said. "In that kind of job market, you take whatever is available."

Scott said she is not seeing employment numbers wavering despite recent reports of a looming recession flood the media.

"We are not yet seeing that in our office in terms of hiring new college graduates," he said. "As a matter of fact, we are looking at a record number of employers wanting to come to the career fair."

Still, Oklahoma's unemployment rose from 4 percent in 2006 to 4.5 percent in December 2007.

Scott said Oklahoma's geographical location helps when economic trouble hits.

"In the past, it's always been worst on the east and west coast[s] before it hits here." The office can adjust when the signs of recession are prominent on the coasts.

Scott said, though her office may not see an unemployment crunch now, the situation could be different tomorrow.

"We've seen it before change overnight," Scott said.

Kevin Bruns, American Student Loan Providers executive director, said the trend also is in the student loan market.

"The traditional pattern is going back to school during a recession," he said.

Source: Jerry Wofford, February 8, 2008

Although **explicit contracts** can explain why some wages are sticky, a deeper question must also be considered. Workers and firms surely know at the time a contract is signed that unforeseen events may cause the wages set by the contract to be too high or too low. Why do firms and workers bind themselves in this way? One explanation is that negotiating wages is costly. Negotiations between unions and firms can take a considerable amount of time—time that could be spent producing output—and it would be very costly to negotiate wages weekly or monthly. Contracts are a way of bearing these costs at no more than 1-, 2-, or 3-year intervals. There is a trade-off between the costs of locking workers and firms into contracts for long periods of time and the costs of wage negotiations. The length of contracts that minimizes negotiation costs seems to be (from what we observe in practice) between 1 and 3 years.

Some multiyear contracts adjust for unforeseen events by **cost-of-living adjustments (COLAs)** written into the contract. COLAs tie wages to changes in the cost of living: The greater the rate of inflation, the more wages are raised. COLAs thus protect workers from unexpected inflation, although many COLAs adjust wages by a smaller percentage than the percentage increase in prices.

explicit contracts
Employment contracts that stipulate workers' wages, usually for a period of 1 to 3 years.

cost-of-living adjustments (COLAs)
Contract provisions that tie wages to changes in the cost of living. The greater the inflation rate, the more wages are raised.

Efficiency Wage Theory

Another explanation for unemployment centers on the **efficiency wage theory**, which holds that the productivity of workers increases with the wage rate. If this is true, firms may have an incentive to pay wages *above* the wage at which the quantity of labor supplied is equal to the quantity of labor demanded.

The key argument of the efficiency wage theory is that by offering workers a wage in excess of the market wage, the productivity of those workers is increased. Some economists have likened the payment of this higher wage as a gift-exchange: firms pay a wage in excess of the market wage and in return workers work harder or more productively than they otherwise would. Under these circumstances, there will be people who want to work at the wage paid by firms and cannot find employment. Indeed, for the efficiency wage theory to operate, it must be the case that the wage offered by firms is above the market wage. It is the gap between the two that motivates workers who do have jobs to outdo themselves.

Empirical studies of labor markets have identified several potential benefits that firms receive from paying workers more than the market-clearing wage. Among them are lower turnover, improved morale, and reduced "shirking" of work. Even though the efficiency wage theory predicts some unemployment, the behavior it is describing is unlikely to account for much of the observed large cyclical fluctuations in unemployment over time.

efficiency wage theory
An explanation for unemployment that holds that the productivity of workers increases with the wage rate. If this is so, firms may have an incentive to pay wages above the market-clearing rate.

Imperfect Information

Thus far we have been assuming that firms know exactly what wage rates they need to set to clear the labor market. They may not choose to set their wages at this level, but at least they know what the market-clearing wage is. In practice, however, firms may not have enough information at their disposal to know what the market-clearing wage is. In this case, firms are said to have *imperfect information*. If firms have imperfect or incomplete information, they may simply set wages wrong—wages that do not clear the labor market.

If a firm sets its wages too high, more workers will want to work for that firm than the firm wants to employ, resulting in some potential workers being turned away. The result is, of course, unemployment. One objection to this explanation is that it accounts for the existence of unemployment only in the very short run. As soon as a firm sees that it has made a mistake, why would it not immediately correct its mistake and adjust its wages to the correct market-clearing level? Why would unemployment *persist*?

If the economy were simple, it should take no more than a few months for firms to correct their mistakes, but the economy is complex. Although firms may be aware of their past mistakes and may try to correct them, new events are happening all the time. Because constant change—including a constantly changing equilibrium wage level—is characteristic of the economy, firms may find it hard to adjust wages to the market-clearing level. The labor market is not like the stock market or the market for wheat, where prices are determined in organized exchanges every day. Instead, thousands of firms are setting wages and millions of workers are responding to these wages. It may take considerable time for the market-clearing wages to be determined after they have been disturbed from an equilibrium position.

Minimum Wage Laws

minimum wage laws
Laws that set a floor for wage rates—that is, a minimum hourly rate for any kind of labor.

Minimum wage laws explain at least a small fraction of unemployment. These laws set a floor for wage rates—a minimum hourly rate for any kind of labor. In 2008, the federal minimum wage was $6.55 per hour. If the market-clearing wage for some groups of workers is below this amount, this group will be unemployed. In Figure 14.2, if the minimum wage is W_0 and the market-clearing wage is W^*, the number of unemployed will be $L_0 - L_1$.

Teenagers, who have relatively little job experience, are most likely to be hurt by minimum wage laws. If some teenagers can produce only $5.90 worth of output per hour, no firm would be willing to hire them at a wage of $6.55. To do so would incur a loss of $0.65 per hour. In an unregulated market, these teenagers would be able to find work at the market-clearing wage of $5.90 per hour. If the minimum wage laws prevent the wage from falling below $6.55, these workers will not be able to find jobs and they will be unemployed. Others who may be hurt include people with very low skills and some recent immigrants.

In response to this argument against the minimum wage, Congress in 1996 established a subminimum wage for teenagers. The law allowed employers to hire teenagers at an "opportunity wage" of $4.25 for up to 90 days.

An Open Question

As we have seen, there are many explanations for why the labor market may not clear. The theories we have just set forth are not necessarily mutually exclusive, and there may be elements of truth in all of them. The aggregate labor market is very complicated, and there are no simple answers to why there is unemployment. Much current work in macroeconomics is concerned directly or indirectly with this question, and it is an exciting area of study. Which argument or arguments will win out in the end is an open question.

The Short-Run Relationship Between the Unemployment Rate and Inflation

At the Boston Fed in June 2008, Ben Bernanke, the Fed chair, gave a speech in which he referred to both the "upside risk to inflation," and the "unwelcome rise in the unemployment rate." Unemployment and inflation are the two central concerns of macroeconomics and of policy makers like Bernanke. But what is the relationship between the two? When Bernanke chooses to fight inflation, is he inevitably increasing unemployment and visa versa? We are now in a position to tackle this question.

We begin by looking at the relation between aggregate output (income) (Y) and the unemployment rate (U). For an economy to increase aggregate output, firms must hire more labor to produce that output. Thus, more output implies greater employment. An increase in employment means more people working (fewer people unemployed) and a lower unemployment rate. An increase in Y corresponds to a *decrease* in U. Thus, U and Y are *negatively* related: when Y rises, the unemployment rate falls, and when Y falls, the unemployment rate rises.

What about the relationship between aggregate output and the overall price level? The AS curve, reproduced in Figure 14.3, shows the relationship between Y and the overall price level (P). The relationship is a positive one: When P increases, Y increases, and when P decreases, Y decreases.

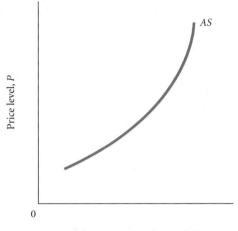

◀ FIGURE 14.3

The Aggregate Supply Curve

The AS curve shows a positive relationship between the price level (P) and aggregate output (income) (Y).

As you will recall from the last chapter, the shape of the AS curve is determined by the behavior of the firms and how they react to an increase in demand. If aggregate demand shifts to the right and the economy is operating on the nearly flat part of the AS curve—far from capacity—output will increase, but the price level will not change much. However, if the economy is operating on the steep part of the AS curve—close to capacity—an increase in demand will drive up the price level, but output will be constrained by capacity and will not increase much.

Now let us put the two pieces together and think about what will happen following an event that leads to an increase in aggregate demand. First, firms experience an unanticipated decline in inventories. They respond by increasing output (Y) and hiring workers—the unemployment rate falls. If the economy is not close to capacity, there will be little increase in the price level. If, however, aggregate demand continues to grow, the ability of the economy to increase output will eventually reach its limit. As aggregate demand shifts farther and farther to the right along the AS curve, the price level increases more and more and output begins to reach its limit. At the point at which the AS curve becomes vertical, output cannot rise any farther. If output cannot grow, the unemployment rate cannot be pushed any lower. There is a negative relationship between the unemployment rate and the price level. As the unemployment rate declines in response to the economy's moving closer and closer to capacity output, the overall price level rises more and more, as shown in Figure 14.4.

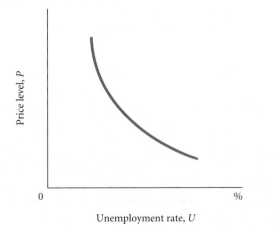

◀ FIGURE 14.4

The Relationship Between the Price Level and the Unemployment Rate

This curve shows a negative relationship between the price level (P) and the unemployment rate (U). As the unemployment rate declines in response to the economy's moving closer and closer to capacity output, the price level rises more and more.

inflation rate   The percentage change in the price level.

Phillips Curve   A curve showing the relationship between the inflation rate and the unemployment rate.

The *AS* curve shows the relationship between the price level and aggregate output and thus implicitly between the price level and the unemployment rate. In policy formulation and discussions, however, economists have focused less on the *AS* curve than on the relationship between the **inflation rate**—the percentage change in the price level—and the unemployment rate. Note that the price level and the percentage change in the price level are not the same. The curve describing the relationship between the inflation rate and the unemployment rate, which is shown in Figure 14.5, is called the **Phillips Curve**, after British economist A. W. Phillips, who first examined it using data for the United Kingdom. Fortunately, the analysis we have just done with the *AS* curve on the price level and aggregate output will enable us to see both why the Phillips Curve initially looked so appealing as an explanation of the relationship between inflation and unemployment and how more recent history has changed our views of the interpretation of the Phillips Curve.

▶ **FIGURE 14.5**

The Phillips Curve

The Phillips Curve shows the relationship between the inflation rate and the unemployment rate.

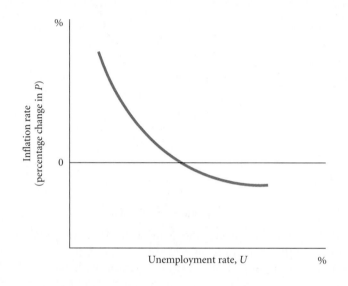

The Phillips Curve: A Historical Perspective

In the 1950s and 1960s, there was a remarkably smooth relationship between the unemployment rate and the rate of inflation, as Figure 14.6 shows for the 1960s. As you can see, the data points fit fairly closely around a downward-sloping curve; in general, the higher the unemployment rate is, the lower the rate of inflation. The Phillips Curve in Figure 14.6 shows a trade-off between inflation and unemployment. To lower the inflation rate, we must accept a higher unemployment rate, and to lower the unemployment rate, we must accept a higher rate of inflation.

▶ **FIGURE 14.6**

Unemployment and Inflation, 1960–1969

During the 1960s, there seemed to be an obvious trade-off between inflation and unemployment. Policy debates during the period revolved around this apparent trade-off.

Source: see Table 7.5

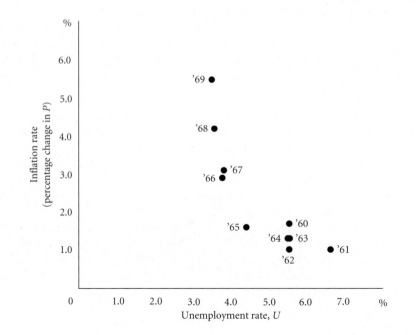

Textbooks written in the 1960s and early 1970s relied on the Phillips Curve as the main explanation of inflation. Things seemed simple—inflation appeared to respond in a fairly predictable way to changes in the unemployment rate. For this reason, policy discussions in the 1960s revolved around the Phillips Curve. The role of the policy maker, it was thought, was to choose a point on the curve. Conservatives usually argued for choosing a point with a low rate of inflation and were willing to accept a higher unemployment rate in exchange for this. Liberals usually argued for accepting more inflation to keep unemployment at a low level.

Life did not turn out to be quite so simple. The Phillips Curve broke down in the 1970s and 1980s. This change can be seen in Figure 14.7, which graphs the unemployment rate and inflation rate for the period from 1970 to 2007. The points in Figure 14.7 show no particular relationship between inflation and unemployment.

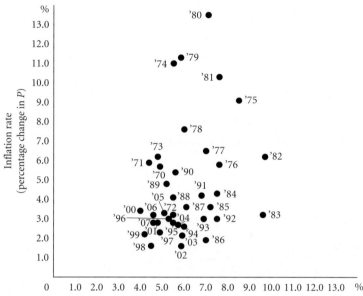

◀ **FIGURE 14.7**

Unemployment and Inflation, 1970–2007

From the 1970s on, it became clear that the relationship between unemployment and inflation was anything but simple.

Source: See Table 7.5.

Aggregate Supply and Aggregate Demand Analysis and the Phillips Curve

How can we explain the stability of the Phillips Curve in the 1950s and 1960s and the lack of stability after that? To answer, we need to return to *AS/AD* analysis.

If the *AD* curve shifts from year to year but the *AS* curve does not, the values of *P* and *Y* each year will lie along the *AS* curve [Figure 14.8(a)]. The plot of the relationship between *P* and *Y* will be upward-sloping. Correspondingly, the plot of the relationship between the unemployment rate (which decreases with increased output) and the rate of inflation will be a curve that slopes downward. In other words, we would expect to see a negative relationship between the unemployment rate and the inflation rate.

However, the relationship between the unemployment rate and the inflation rate will look different if the *AS* curve shifts from year to year but the *AD* curve does not. A leftward shift of the *AS* curve will cause an *increase* in the price level (*P*) and a *decrease* in aggregate output (*Y*) [Figure 14.8(b)]. When the *AS* curve shifts to the left, the economy experiences both inflation *and* an increase in the unemployment rate (because decreased output means increased unemployment). In other words, if the *AS* curve is shifting from year to year, we would expect to see a positive relationship between the unemployment rate and the inflation rate.

If both the *AS* and the *AD* curves are shifting simultaneously, however, there is no systematic relationship between *P* and *Y* [Figure 14.8(c)] and thus no systematic relationship between the unemployment rate and the inflation rate. One explanation for the change in the Phillips Curve between the 1960s and later periods is that both the *AS* and the *AD* curves appear to be shifting in the later periods. Why might this be?

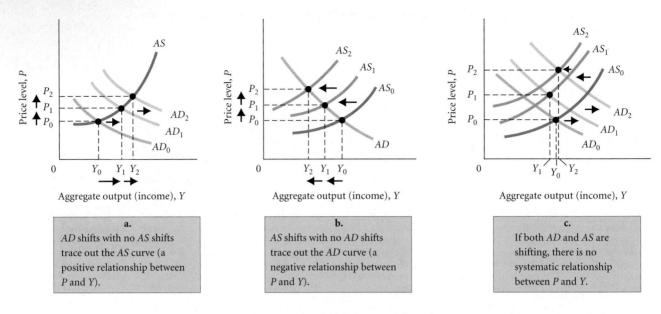

a.
AD shifts with no *AS* shifts trace out the *AS* curve (a positive relationship between *P* and *Y*).

b.
AS shifts with no *AD* shifts trace out the *AD* curve (a negative relationship between *P* and *Y*).

c.
If both *AD* and *AS* are shifting, there is no systematic relationship between *P* and *Y*.

▲ **FIGURE 14.8 Changes in the Price Level and Aggregate Output Depend on Shifts in Both Aggregate Demand and Aggregate Supply**

The Role of Import Prices   We discussed in the previous chapter that some of the main factors that causes the *AS* curve to shift are energy prices, particularly the price of oil. Since the United States imports much of its oil, the price index of U.S. imports is highly correlated with the (world) price of oil. We can thus consider that a change in the U.S. import price index, which we will call "the price of imports," shifts the *AS* curve. The price of imports is plotted in Figure 14.9 for the 1960 I–2007 IV period. As you can see, the price of imports changed very little between 1960 and 1970. There were no large shifts in the *AS* curve in the 1960s due to changes in the price of imports. There were also no other large changes in input prices in the 1960s, so overall the *AS* curve shifted very little during the decade. The main variation in the 1960s was in aggregate demand, so the shifting *AD* curve traced out points along the *AS* curve.

▲ **FIGURE 14.9 The Price of Imports, 1960 I–2007 IV**
The price of imports changed very little in the 1960s and early 1970s. It increased substantially in 1974 and again in 1979–1980. Between 1981 and 2002, the price of imports changed very little. Since 2002, it has been rising.

Figure 14.9 also shows that the price of imports increased considerably in the 1970s. This rise led to large shifts in the *AS* curve during the decade, but the *AD* curve was also shifting throughout the 1970s. With both curves shifting, the data points for *P* and *Y* were scattered all over the graph and the observed relationship between *P* and *Y* was not at all systematic.

This story about import prices and the *AS* and *AD* curves in the 1960s and 1970s carries over to the Phillips Curve. The Phillips Curve was stable in the 1960s because the primary source of variation in the economy was demand, not costs. In the 1970s, both demand *and* costs were varying so no obvious relationship between the unemployment rate and the inflation rate was apparent. To some extent, what is remarkable about the Phillips Curve is not that it was not smooth after the 1960s, but that it ever was smooth.

Expectations and the Phillips Curve

Another reason the Phillips Curve is not stable concerns expectations. We saw in Chapter 13 that if a firm expects other firms to raise their prices, the firm may raise the price of its own product. If all firms are behaving this way, prices will rise because they are expected to rise. In this sense, expectations are self-fulfilling. Similarly, if inflation is expected to be high in the future, negotiated wages are likely to be higher than if inflation is expected to be low. Wage inflation is thus affected by expectations of future price inflation. Because wages are input costs, prices rise as firms respond to the higher wage costs. Price expectations that affect wage contracts eventually affect prices themselves.

If the rate of inflation depends on expectations, the Phillips Curve will shift as expectations change. For example, if inflationary expectations increase, the result will be an increase in the rate of inflation even though the unemployment rate may not have changed. In this case, the Phillips Curve will shift to the right. If inflationary expectations decrease, the Phillips Curve will shift to the left—there will be less inflation at any given level of the unemployment rate.

It so happened that inflationary expectations were quite stable in the 1950s and 1960s. The inflation rate was moderate during most of this period, and people expected it to remain moderate. With inflationary expectations not changing very much, there were no major shifts of the Phillips Curve, a situation that helps explain its stability during the period.

Near the end of the 1960s, inflationary expectations began to increase, primarily in response to the actual increase in inflation that was occurring because of the tight economy caused by the Vietnam War. Inflationary expectations increased even further in the 1970s as a result of large oil price increases. These changing expectations led to shifts of the Phillips Curve and are another reason the curve was not stable during the 1970s.

Is There a Short-Run Trade-Off between Inflation and Unemployment?

Does the fact that the Phillips Curve broke down during the 1970s mean that there is no trade-off between inflation and unemployment in the short run? Not at all: It simply means that other things affect inflation aside from unemployment. Just as the relationship between price and quantity demanded along a standard demand curve shifts when income or other factors change, so does the relationship between unemployment and inflation change when other factors change.

In 1975, for example, inflation and unemployment were both high. As we explained earlier, this stagflation was caused partly by an increase in oil costs that shifted the aggregate supply curve to the left and partly by expectations of continued inflation that kept prices rising despite high levels of unemployment. In the summer of 2008, many observers, including Fed chair Ben Bernanke, were becoming concerned about both rising unemployment and rising inflation. In response to the 1975 situation, the Federal Reserve (Fed) pursued a contractionary monetary policy, which shifted the *AD* curve to the left and led to even higher unemployment. By 1977, the rate of inflation had dropped from over 11 percent to about 6 percent. So the rise in the unemployment rate did lead to a decrease in inflation, an outcome that reflects the trade-off. There *is* a short-run trade-off between inflation and unemployment, but other factors besides unemployment affect inflation. Policy involves more than simply choosing a point along a nice smooth curve.

The Long-Run Aggregate Supply Curve, Potential Output, and the Natural Rate of Unemployment

Recall from Chapter 13 that many economists believe the *AS* curve is vertical in the long run. This situation is illustrated in Figure 14.10. Assume that the initial equilibrium is at the intersection of AD_0 and the long-run aggregate supply curve. Now consider a shift of the aggregate demand curve from AD_0 to AD_1. If wages lag prices, aggregate output will rise from Y_0 to Y_1. (This is a movement along the short-run *AS* curve AS_0.) In the longer run, wages may catch up. For example, next year's labor contracts may make up for the fact that wage increases did not keep up with the cost of living this year. If wages catch up in the longer run, the *AS* curve will shift from AS_0 to AS_1 and drive aggregate output back to Y_0. If wages ultimately rise by exactly the same percentage as output prices, firms will produce the same level of output as they did before the increase in aggregate demand.

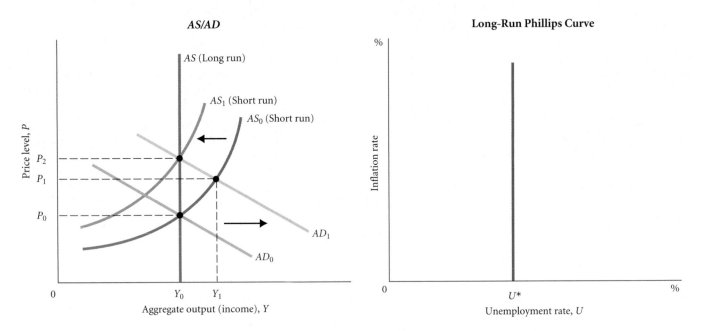

▲ **FIGURE 14.10 The Long-Run Phillips Curve: The Natural Rate of Unemployment**

If the *AS* curve is vertical in the long run, so is the Phillips Curve. In the long run, the Phillips Curve corresponds to the natural rate of unemployment—that is, the unemployment rate that is consistent with the notion of a fixed long-run output at potential output. U^* is the natural rate of unemployment.

In Chapter 13, we said that Y_0 is sometimes called *potential output*. Aggregate output can be pushed above Y_0 in the short run. When aggregate output exceeds Y_0, however, there is upward pressure on input prices and costs. The unemployment rate is already quite low, firms are beginning to encounter the limits of their plant capacities, and so on. At levels of aggregate output above Y_0, costs will rise, the *AS* curve will shift to the left, and the price level will rise. Thus, potential output is the level of aggregate output that can be sustained in the long run without inflation.

This story is directly related to the Phillips Curve. Those who believe that the *AS* curve is vertical in the long run at potential output also believe that the Phillips Curve is vertical in the long run at some natural rate of unemployment. Recall from Chapter 7 that the **natural rate of unemployment** refers to unemployment that occurs as a normal part of the functioning of the economy. It is sometimes taken as the sum of frictional unemployment and structural unemployment. The logic behind the vertical Phillips Curve is that whenever the unemployment rate is pushed below the natural rate, wages begin to rise, thus pushing up costs. This leads to a *lower* level of output, which pushes the unemployment rate back up to the natural rate. At the natural rate, the economy can be considered to be at full employment.

natural rate of unemployment The unemployment that occurs as a normal part of the functioning of the economy. Sometimes taken as the sum of frictional unemployment and structural unemployment.

The Nonaccelerating Inflation Rate of Unemployment (NAIRU)

In Figure 14.10, the long-run vertical Phillips Curve is a graph with the inflation rate on the vertical axis and the unemployment rate on the horizontal axis. The natural rate of unemployment is U^*. In the long run, according to advocates of the long-run vertical Phillips Curve, the actual unemployment rate moves to U^* because of the natural workings of the economy.

Another graph of interest is Figure 14.11, which plots the *change in* the inflation rate on the vertical axis and the unemployment rate on the horizontal axis. Many economists believe that the relationship between the change in the inflation rate and the unemployment rate is as depicted by the *PP* curve in the figure. The value of the unemployment rate where the *PP* curve crosses zero is called the *nonaccelerating inflation rate of unemployment* (**NAIRU**). If the actual unemployment rate is to the left of the NAIRU, the change in the inflation rate will be positive. As depicted in the figure, at U_1, the change in the inflation rate is 1. Conversely, if the actual unemployment rate is to the right of the NAIRU, the change in the inflation rate is negative: At U_2, the change is -1.

NAIRU The nonaccelerating inflation rate of unemployment.

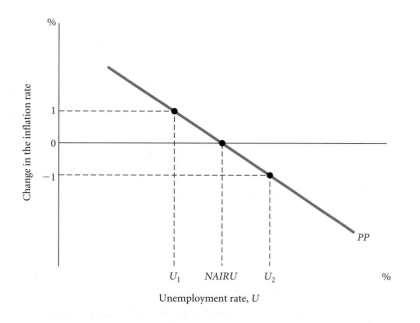

◀ **FIGURE 14.11**
The NAIRU Diagram
To the left of the NAIRU, the price level is accelerating (positive changes in the inflation rate); to the right of the NAIRU, the price level is decelerating (negative changes in the inflation rate). Only when the unemployment rate is equal to the NAIRU is the price level changing at a constant rate (no change in the inflation rate).

Consider what happens if the unemployment rate decreases from the NAIRU to U_1 and stays at U_1 for many periods. Assume also that the inflation rate at the NAIRU was 2 percent. Then in the first period the inflation rate will increase from 2 percent to 3 percent. The inflation rate does not, however, just stay at the higher 3 percent value. In the next period, the inflation rate will increase from 3 percent to 4 percent and so on. The price level will be accelerating—that is, the change in the inflation rate will be positive—when the actual unemployment rate is below the NAIRU. Conversely, the price level will be decelerating—that is, the change in the inflation rate will be negative—when the actual unemployment rate is above the NAIRU.[1]

The *PP* curve in Figure 14.11 is like the *AS* curve in Figure 14.3—the same factors that shift the *AS* curve, such as cost shocks, can also shift the *PP* curve. Figure 13.8 on p. 248 summarizes the various factors that can cause the *AS* curve to shift, and these are also relevant for the *PP* curve. A favorable shift for the *PP* curve is to the left because the *PP* curve crosses zero at a lower unemployment rate, indicating that the NAIRU is lower. Some have argued that one possible recent source of favorable shifts is increased foreign competition, which may have kept wage costs and other input costs down.

Before about 1995, proponents of the NAIRU theory argued that the value of the NAIRU in the United States was around 6 percent. By the end of 1995, the unemployment rate declined to 5.6 percent, and by 2000, the unemployment rate was down to 3.8 percent. If the NAIRU had been 6 percent, one should have seen a continuing increase in the inflation rate beginning about 1995. In fact, the 1995 to 2000 period saw slightly declining inflation. Not only did inflation not continually increase, it did not even increase once to a new, higher value and then stay there. As the unemployment rate declined during this period, proponents of the NAIRU lowered their estimates of it, more or less in line with the actual fall in the unemployment rate. This recalibration can be justified by arguing that there have been continuing favorable shifts of the *PP* curve, such

---

[1] The NAIRU is actually misnamed. It is the *price level* that is accelerating or decelerating, not the inflation rate, when the actual unemployment rate differs from the NAIRU. The inflation rate is not accelerating or decelerating, but simply changing by the same amount each period. The namers of the NAIRU forgot their physics.

as possible increased foreign competition. Critics, however, have argued that this procedure is close to making the NAIRU theory vacuous. Can the theory really be tested if the estimate of the NAIRU is changed whenever it is not consistent with the data? How trustworthy is the appeal to favorable shifts?

Macroeconomists are currently debating whether equations estimated under the NAIRU theory are good approximations. More time is needed before any definitive answers can be given.

Looking Ahead

This chapter concludes our basic analysis of how the macroeconomy works. In the preceding seven chapters, we have examined how households and firms behave in the three market arenas—the goods market, the money market, and the labor market. We have seen how aggregate output (income), the interest rate, and the price level are determined in the economy, and we have examined the relationship between two of the most important macroeconomic variables, the inflation rate and the unemployment rate. In Chapter 15, we use everything we have learned up to this point to examine a number of important policy issues.

S U M M A R Y

THE LABOR MARKET: BASIC CONCEPTS *p. 259*

1. Because the economy is dynamic, *frictional* and *structural unemployment* are inevitable and in some ways desirable. Times of *cyclical unemployment* are of concern to macroeconomic policy makers.

2. In general, employment tends to fall when aggregate output falls and rise when aggregate output rises.

THE CLASSICAL VIEW OF THE LABOR MARKET *p. 260*

3. Classical economists believe that the interaction of supply and demand in the labor market brings about equilibrium and that unemployment (beyond the frictional and structural amounts) does not exist.

4. The classical view of the labor market is consistent with the theory of a vertical aggregate supply curve.

EXPLAINING THE EXISTENCE OF UNEMPLOYMENT *p. 262*

5. Some economists argue that the unemployment rate is not an accurate indicator of whether the labor market is working properly. Unemployed people who are considered part of the labor force may be offered jobs but may be unwilling to take those jobs at the offered salaries. Some of the unemployed may have chosen not to work, but this result does not mean that the labor market has malfunctioned.

6. Those who do not subscribe to the classical view of the labor market suggest several reasons why unemployment exists. Downwardly *sticky wages* may be brought about by *social (implicit)* or *explicit contracts* not to cut wages. If the equilibrium wage rate falls but wages are prevented from falling also, the result will be unemployment.

7. *Efficiency wage theory* holds that the productivity of workers increases with the wage rate. If this is true, firms may have an incentive to pay wages above the wage at which the quantity of labor supplied is equal to the quantity of labor demanded. At all wages above the equilibrium, there will be an excess supply of labor and therefore unemployment.

8. If firms are operating with incomplete or imperfect information, they may not know what the market-clearing wage is. As a result, they may set their wages incorrectly and bring about unemployment. Because the economy is so complex, it may take considerable time for firms to correct these mistakes.

9. *Minimum wage laws*, which set a floor for wage rates, are one factor contributing to unemployment of teenagers and very low-skilled workers. If the market-clearing wage for some groups of workers is below the minimum wage, some members of this group will be unemployed.

THE SHORT-RUN RELATIONSHIP BETWEEN THE UNEMPLOYMENT RATE AND INFLATION *p. 266*

10. There is a negative relationship between the unemployment rate (U) and aggregate output (income) (Y): When Y rises, U falls. When Y falls, U rises.

11. The relationship between the unemployment rate and the price level is negative: As the unemployment rate declines and the economy moves closer to capacity, the price level rises more and more.

12. The *Phillips Curve* represents the relationship between the *inflation rate* and the *unemployment rate*. During the 1950s and 1960s, this relationship was stable and there seemed to be a predictable trade-off between inflation and unemployment. As a result of import price increases (which led to shifts in aggregate supply), the relationship between the inflation rate and the unemployment rate was erratic in the 1970s. There *is* a short-term trade-off between inflation and unemployment, but other things besides unemployment affect inflation.

THE LONG-RUN AGGREGATE SUPPLY CURVE, POTENTIAL OUTPUT, AND THE NATURAL RATE OF UNEMPLOYMENT *p. 271*

13. Those who believe that the *AS* curve is vertical in the long run also believe that the Phillips Curve is vertical in the long run at the *natural rate of unemployment*. The natural rate is generally the sum of the frictional and structural rates. If the Phillips Curve is vertical in the long run, then there is a limit to how low government policy can push the unemployment rate without setting off inflation.

14. The *NAIRU* theory says that the price level will accelerate when the unemployment rate is below the NAIRU and decelerate when the unemployment rate is above the NAIRU.

REVIEW TERMS AND CONCEPTS

cost-of-living adjustments (COLAs), *p. 265*

cyclical unemployment, *p. 260*

efficiency wage theory, *p. 265*

explicit contracts, *p. 265*

frictional unemployment, *p. 260*

inflation rate, *p. 268*

labor demand curve, *p. 260*

labor supply curve, *p. 260*

minimum wage laws, *p. 266*

NAIRU, *p. 273*

natural rate of unemployment, *p. 272*

Phillips Curve, *p. 268*

relative-wage explanation of unemployment, *p. 263*

social, *or implicit*, contracts, *p. 263*

sticky wages, *p. 262*

structural unemployment, *p. 260*

unemployment rate, *p. 260*

PROBLEMS

Visit **www.myeconlab.com** to complete the problems marked in orange online. You will receive instant feedback on your answers, tutorial help, and access to additional practice problems.

myeconlab

1. In April 2000, the U.S. unemployment rate dropped below 4 percent for the first time in 30 years. At the same time, inflation remained at a very low level by historical standards. Can you offer an explanation for what seems to be an improved trade-off between inflation and unemployment? What factors might improve the trade-off? What factors might make it worse?

2. [Related to the *Economics in Practice* on *p. 264*] The *Economics in Practice* describes the potential effects of a decline in employment on graduate school enrollment in the United States. Take time to review how the Bureau of Labor Statistics measures the unemployment rate. (See Chapter 7, pp. 123–125) As of July 2008, the total labor force was 155 million. Of that number, 146 million were classified as employed. That left about 8.8 million unemployed and an unemployment rate of 5.7 percent. Suppose next year that 60,000 students stayed in school without working rather than looking for a job but there were no other changes in the labor force or the number employed. Estimate the size of the change on unemployment and the unemployment rate.

3. Obtain monthly data on the unemployment rate and the inflation rate for the last 2 years. (This data can be found at www.bls.gov or in a recent issue of the *Survey of Current Business* or in the *Monthly Labor Review* or *Employment and Earnings*, all published by the government and available in many college libraries.)

  a. What trends do you observe? Can you explain what you see using aggregate supply and aggregate demand curves?

  b. Plot the 24 monthly rates on a graph with the unemployment rate measured on the x-axis and the inflation rate on the y-axis. Is there evidence of a trade-off between these two variables? Provide an explanation.

4. In 2008, the country of Ruba was suffering from a period of high unemployment. The new president, Clang, appointed Laurel Tiedye as his chief economist. Ms. Tiedye and her staff estimated these supply and demand curves for labor from data obtained from the secretary of labor, Robert Small:

$$Q_D = 100 - 5W$$
$$Q_S = 10W - 20$$

where Q is the quantity of labor supplied/demanded in millions of workers and W is the wage rate in slugs, the currency of Ruba.

  a. Currently, the law in Ruba says that no worker shall be paid less than 9 slugs per hour. Estimate the quantity of labor supplied, the number of unemployed, and the unemployment rate.

  b. President Clang, over the objection of Secretary Small, has recommended to the congress that the law be changed to allow the wage rate to be determined in the market. If such a law was passed and the market adjusted quickly, what would happen to total employment, the size of the labor force, and the unemployment rate? Show the results graphically.

  c. Will the Rubanese labor market adjust quickly to such a change in the law? Why or why not?

5. The following policies have at times been advocated for coping with unemployment. Briefly explain how each might work and explain which type or types of unemployment (frictional, structural, or cyclical) each policy is designed to alter.

  a. A computer list of job openings and a service that matches employees with job vacancies (sometimes called an "economic dating service")

  b. Lower minimum wage for teenagers

  c. Retraining programs for workers who need to learn new skills to find employment

  d. Public employment for people without jobs

  e. Improved information about available jobs and current wage rates

  f. The president's going on nationwide TV and attempting to convince firms and workers that the inflation rate next year will be low

6. Your boss offers you a wage increase of 10 percent. Is it possible that you are worse off with the wage increase than you were before? Explain your answer.

7. How will the following affect labor force participation rates, labor supply, and unemployment?
   a. Because the retired elderly are a larger and larger fraction of the U.S. population, Congress and the president decide to raise the Social Security tax on individuals to continue paying benefits to the elderly.
   b. A national child care program is enacted, requiring employers to provide free child care services.
   c. The U.S. government reduces restrictions on immigration into the United States.
   d. The welfare system is eliminated.
   e. The government subsidizes the purchase of new capital by firms (an investment tax credit).

8. Draw a graph to illustrate the following:
   a. A Phillips Curve based on the assumption of a vertical long-run aggregate supply curve
   b. The effect of a change in inflationary expectations on a recently stable Phillips Curve
   c. Unemployment caused by a recently enacted minimum wage law

9. Obtain data on "average hourly earnings of production workers" and the unemployment rate for your state or area over a recent 2-year period. Has unemployment increased or decreased? What has happened to wages? Does the pattern of unemployment help explain the movement of wages? Provide an explanation.

10. Suppose the inflation–unemployment relationship depicted by the Phillips Curve was stable. Do you think the U.S. trade-off and the Japanese trade-off would be identical? If not, what kinds of factors might make the trade-offs dissimilar?

Policy Timing, Deficit Targeting, and Stock Market Effects

15

The year 2008 was a national election year in the United States and by the late summer and early fall of the year most polls suggested that the state of the economy would be the central political issue in the presidential election. On almost any day of the year, the front page of most newspapers has at least one article on some macroeconomic issue. Most of the financial investment decisions made both by financial institutions and household investors are affected by the state of the macroeconomy.

In this chapter, we use the tools we have already learned to examine three key issues in macroeconomics. First, how is the use of fiscal and monetary policy influenced by the time lags we see in the economy? It is not easy to get the timing right when we try to stabilize the economy, particularly when using fiscal policy instruments. How do timing lags affect our choice of policy instruments? Second, in recent years, the United States has run large budget deficits. What happens when we try to implement policy initiatives based on targeting the size of those deficits? How does deficit targeting affect stabilization policy more broadly? Third, we look at the connection between financial markets and the macroeconomy. Next time Ben Bernanke, the Chair of the Federal Reserve, is scheduled to make a major announcement about monetary policy, log on to one of the online financial sites. Often you will see that the major stock indices react to Bernanke's announcements. Why might this be true and when exactly do we most expect to see a reaction? These are the questions we treat in this chapter.

Time Lags Regarding Monetary and Fiscal Policy

One of the objectives of monetary and fiscal policy is stabilization of the economy. Consider the two possible time paths for aggregate output (income) (Y) shown in Figure 15.1. In path B (the light blue line), the fluctuations in GDP are smaller than those in path A (the dark blue line). One aim of **stabilization policy** is to smooth out fluctuations in output to try to move the economy along a path like B instead of A. Stabilization policy is also concerned with the stability of prices. Here the goal is not to prevent the overall price level from rising at all, but instead to achieve an inflation rate that is as close as possible to a target rate of about 2 percent given the government's other goals of high and stable levels of output and employment.

Stabilization goals are not easy to achieve. The existence of various kinds of **time lags**, or delays in the response of the economy to stabilization policies, can make the economy difficult to control. Economists generally recognize three kinds of time lags: recognition lags, implementation lags, and response lags.

stabilization policy Describes both monetary and fiscal policy, the goals of which are to smooth out fluctuations in output and employment and to keep prices as stable as possible.

time lags Delays in the economy's response to stabilization policies.

▶ FIGURE 15.1

Two Possible Time Paths for GDP

Path *A* is less stable—it varies more over time—than path *B*. Other things being equal, society prefers path *B* to path *A*.

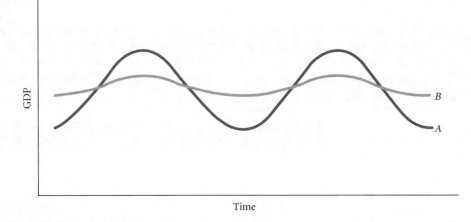

Stabilization

Figure 15.2 shows timing problems a government may face when trying to stabilize the economy. Suppose the economy reaches a peak and begins to slide into recession at point *A* (at time t_0). Policy makers do not observe the decline in GDP until it has sunk to point *B* (at time t_1). By the time they have begun to stimulate the economy (point *C*, time t_2), the recession is well advanced and the economy has almost bottomed out. When the policies finally begin to take effect (point *D*, time t_3), the economy is already on its road to recovery. The policies push the economy to point *E'*—a much greater fluctuation than point *E*, which is where the economy would have been without the stabilization policy. Sometime after point *D*, policy makers may begin to realize that the economy is expanding too quickly. By the time they have implemented contractionary policies and the policies have made their effects felt, the economy is starting to weaken. The contractionary policies therefore end up pushing GDP to point *F'* instead of point *F*.

Because of the various time lags, the expansionary policies that should have been instituted at time t_0 do not begin to have an effect until time t_3, when they are no longer needed. The light blue line in Figure 15.2 shows how the economy behaves as a result of the "stabilization" policies. The dark blue line shows the time path of GDP if the economy had been allowed to run its course and no stabilization policies had been attempted. In this case, stabilization policy makes income more erratic, not less—the policy results in a peak income of *E'* as opposed to *E* and a trough income of *F'* instead of *F*.

Critics of stabilization policy argue that the situation in Figure 15.2 is typical of the interaction between the government and the rest of the economy. This claim is not necessarily true. We need to know more about the nature of the various kinds of lags before deciding whether stabilization policy is good or bad.

▶ FIGURE 15.2

Possible Stabilization Timing Problems

Attempts to stabilize the economy can prove destabilizing because of time lags. An expansionary policy that should have begun to take effect at point *A* does not actually begin to have an impact until point *D*, when the economy is already on an upswing. Hence, the policy pushes the economy to points *E'* and *F'* (instead of points *E* and *F*). Income varies more widely than it would have if no policy had been implemented.

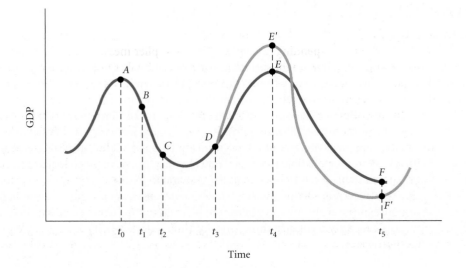

Recognition Lags

It takes time for policy makers to recognize a boom or a slump. Many important data—those from the national income and product accounts, for example—are available only quarterly. It usually takes several weeks to compile and prepare even the preliminary estimates for these figures. If the economy goes into a slump on January 1, the recession may not be detected until the data for the first quarter are available at the end of April.

Moreover, the early national income and product accounts data are only preliminary, based on an incomplete compilation of the various data sources. These estimates can, and often do, change as better data become available. This situation makes the interpretation of the initial estimates difficult, and **recognition lags** result.

recognition lag The time it takes for policy makers to recognize the existence of a boom or a slump.

Implementation Lags

The problems that lags pose for stabilization policy do not end once economists and policy makers recognize that the economy is in a boom or a slump. Even if everyone knows that the economy needs to be stimulated or reined in, it takes time to put the desired policy into effect, especially for actions that involve fiscal policy. **Implementation lags** result.

Each year Congress decides on the federal government's budget for the coming year. The tax laws and spending programs embodied in this budget are hard to change once they are in place. If it becomes clear that the economy is entering a recession and is in need of a fiscal stimulus during the middle of the year, there is a limited amount that can be done. Until Congress authorizes more spending or a cut in taxes, changes in fiscal policy are not possible.[1]

Monetary policy is less subject to the kinds of restrictions that slow down changes in fiscal policy. As we saw in Chapter 10, the Fed's main tool for controlling the supply of money or the interest rate is open market operations—buying and selling government securities. Transactions in these securities take place in a highly developed market, and if the Fed chooses, it can buy or sell a large volume of securities in a very short period of time. The implementation lag for monetary policy is generally much shorter than for fiscal policy. When the Fed wants to increase the supply of money, it goes into the open market and purchases government securities. This action instantly increases the stock of money (bank reserves held at the Fed), and an expansion of the money supply begins.

implementation lag The time it takes to put the desired policy into effect once economists and policy makers recognize that the economy is in a boom or a slump.

Response Lags

Even after a macroeconomic problem has been recognized and the appropriate policies to correct it have been implemented, there are **response lags**—lags that occur because of the operation of the economy itself. Even after the government has formulated a policy and put it into place, the economy takes time to adjust to the new conditions. Although monetary policy can be adjusted and implemented more quickly than fiscal policy, it takes longer to make its effect felt on the economy because of response lags. What is most important is the total lag between the time a problem first occurs and the time the corrective policies are felt.

response lag The time that it takes for the economy to adjust to the new conditions after a new policy is implemented; the lag that occurs because of the operation of the economy itself.

Response Lags for Fiscal Policy One way to think about the response lag in fiscal policy is through the government spending multiplier. This multiplier measures the change in GDP caused by a given change in government spending or net taxes. It takes time for the multiplier to reach its full value. The result is a lag between the time a fiscal policy action is initiated and the time the full change in GDP is realized.

The reason for the response lag in fiscal policy—the delay in the multiplier process—is simple. During the first few months after an increase in government spending or a tax cut, there is not enough time for the firms or individuals who benefit directly from the extra government spending or the tax cut to increase their own spending. Neither individuals nor firms revise their spending plans instantaneously. Until they can make those revisions, extra government spending does not stimulate extra private spending.

---

[1] Do not forget, however, about the existence of automatic stabilizers (Chapter 9). Many programs contain built-in countercyclical features that expand spending or cut tax collections automatically (without the need for congressional or executive action) during a recession.

ECONOMICS IN PRACTICE

More on Fiscal Policy in 2008

In February 2008 concern about a possible contraction in output in the United States pushed Congress to pass an economic stimulus bill. (See the *Economics in Practice* box on p. 174.) Much of this stimulus was in the form of a tax rebate, which increased disposable personal income by about $78 billion in the second quarter of 2008 and by about $15 billion in the third quarter. While this undoubtedly helped, it was not enough, even combined with an expansionary monetary policy (see the *Economic in Practice* on p. 252), to completely offset the negative effects on demand from the fall in housing investment and from the worldwide financial crisis.

The U.S. Treasury, headed by Henry Paulson, led the charge for more stimulus. On September 19, 2008, Paulson proposed a financial rescue plan. The plan essentially asked Congress for permission to use up to $700 billion to prop up shaky financial institutions. Treasury's plan was to buy risky (sometimes called "toxic") mortgage-backed securities from financial institutions so as to free up their ability to make loans. In a dramatic move on September 29, the U.S. House of Representatives defeated the $700 billion "bailout" bill by a vote of 228–205. There was concern that the bill would transfer money from middle-income tax payers on "Main Street" to fat cats on "Wall Street." The bailout bill was hurriedly modified and passed by the Senate on October 1, then passed by the House and signed by the President on October 3.

Within weeks, policy changed from buying toxic securities to having the Federal government take direct equity positions (become shareholders) in the financial institutions. Various European governments implemented similar plans for their troubled financial institutions.

There was also talk in October of further fiscal stimulus measures—perhaps tax cuts or government spending increases. One growing concern, however, was the possible size of the Federal government deficit in 2009. With no significant contraction, the deficit was projected to be about $400 billion. With a contraction, the deficit would probably rise about $200 billion because of lost tax revenue. On top of this, the bailout spending could add another $400 billion. If all this happened, the deficit would be about $1 trillion. As with the Fed, the fiscal branch of the Federal government tried in 2008 to mitigate the effects of the worldwide financial crisis, but critics also say it bears some of the blame for the crisis because of its lax regulation in 2003–2005.

Changes in government purchases are a component of aggregate expenditure. When *G* rises, aggregate expenditure increases directly; when *G* falls, aggregate expenditure decreases directly. When personal taxes are changed, however, an additional step intervenes, giving rise to another lag. Suppose a tax cut has lowered personal income taxes across the board. Each household must decide what portion of its tax cut to spend and what portion to save. This decision is the extra step. Before the tax cut gets translated into extra spending, households must take the step of increasing their spending, which usually takes some time.

With a business tax cut, there is a further complication. Firms must decide what to do with their added after-tax profits. If they pay out their added profits to households as dividends, the result is the same as with a personal tax cut. Households must decide whether to spend or to save the extra funds. Firms may also retain their added profits and use them for investment, but investment is a component of aggregate expenditure that requires planning and time.

In practice, it takes about a year for a change in taxes or in government spending to have its full effect on the economy. This response lag means that if we increase spending to counteract a recession today, the full effects will not be felt for 12 months. By that time, the state of the economy might be very different.

Response Lags for Monetary Policy   Monetary policy works by changing interest rates, which then change planned investment. Interest rates can also affect consumption spending, as we discuss further in Chapter 16. For now, it is enough to know that lower interest rates usually stimulate consumption spending and that higher interest rates decrease consumption spending.

The response of consumption and investment to interest rate changes takes time. Even if interest rates were to drop by 5 percent overnight, firms would not immediately increase their investment purchases. Firms generally make their investment plans several years in advance. If General Motors (GM) wants to respond to a decrease in interest rates by investing more, it will take time—perhaps up to a year—for the firm to come up with plans for a new factory or assembly line. While drawing up such plans, GM may spend little on new investments. The effect of the decrease in interest rates may not make itself felt for quite some time.

The response lags for monetary policy are even longer than response lags for fiscal policy. When government spending changes, there is a direct change in the sales of firms, which sell more as a result of the increased government purchases. When interest rates change, however, the sales of firms do not change until households change their consumption spending and/or firms change their investment spending. It takes time for households and firms to respond to interest rate changes. In this sense, interest rate changes are like tax-rate changes. The resulting change in firms' sales must wait for households and firms to change their purchases of goods.

Summary   Stabilization is not easily achieved. It takes time for policy makers to recognize the existence of a problem, more time for them to implement a solution, and yet more time for firms and households to respond to the stabilization policies taken. Monetary policy can be adjusted more quickly and easily than taxes or government spending, making it a useful instrument in stabilizing the economy. However, because the economy's response to monetary changes is probably slower than its response to changes in fiscal policy, tax and spending changes may also play a useful role in macroeconomic management.

To end on a positive note, the Congress and the president responded quickly to the possibility of a recession in 2008, recognized in late 2007, by passing a stimulus package in February 2008 that began to go into effect in April 2008. The main part of the package was a tax rebate of about a \$120 billion, with rebate checks starting in April. This was a very rapid fiscal policy response to an expected recession.

Fiscal Policy: Deficit Targeting

Every year from 2002 through 2008, the U.S. government ran a budget deficit. Despite the overall prosperity of the U.S. economy during most of this period, these persistent deficits worried a number of observers. In fact, during this recent period, as well as early periods of deficits, some policy makers suggested that the government focus on reducing the deficit as a central policy goal. What might the effects be on the overall economy of deficit targeting?

The deficit first emerged as a policy concern in the early 1980s, as you can see from Figure 9.6 on p. 172. In the 1980s the government was simply spending much more than it was receiving in taxes. When the deficit reached 4.7 percent of GDP in 1986, the U.S. Congress passed and President Reagan signed the **Gramm-Rudman-Hollings Act** (named for its three congressional sponsors), referred to as GRH.

GRH set a target for reducing the federal deficit by a set amount each year. As Figure 15.3 shows, the deficit was to decline by \$36 billion per year between 1987 and 1991, with a deficit of zero slated for fiscal year 1991. What was interesting about the GRH legislation was that the targets were not merely guidelines. If Congress, through its decisions about taxes and spending programs, produced a budget with a deficit larger than the targeted amount, GRH called for automatic spending cuts. The cuts were divided proportionately among most federal spending programs so that a program that made up 5 percent of total spending was to endure a cut equal to 5 percent of the total spending cut.[2]

Gramm-Rudman-Hollings Act   Passed by the U.S. Congress and signed by President Reagan in 1986, this law set out to reduce the federal deficit by \$36 billion per year, with a deficit of zero slated for 1991.

---

[2] Programs such as Social Security were exempt from cuts or were treated differently. Interest payments on the federal debt were also immune from cuts.

▶ **FIGURE 15.3**

Deficit Reduction Targets under Gramm-Rudman-Hollings

The GRH legislation, passed in 1986, set out to lower the federal deficit by $36 billion per year. If the plan had worked, a zero deficit would have been achieved by 1991.

In 1986, the U.S. Supreme Court declared part of the GRH bill unconstitutional. In effect, the Court said that Congress would have to approve the "automatic" spending cuts before they could take place. The law was changed in 1986 to meet the Supreme Court ruling and again in 1987, when new targets were established. The new targets had the deficit reaching zero in 1993 instead of 1991. The targets were revised again in 1991, when the year to achieve a zero deficit was changed from 1993 to 1996.

In practice, these targets never came close to being achieved. As time wore on, even the revised targets became completely unrealistic, and by the end of the 1980s, the GRH legislation was not taken seriously.

As Figure 9.6 on p. 172 shows, the deficit problem continued in the 1990s, and one of President Clinton's goals when he took office in 1993 was to reduce the deficit. The first step was the Omnibus Budget Reconciliation Act of 1993. The act, which barely made it through Congress, was projected to reduce the deficit in the 5 fiscal years 1994 to 1998 by $504.8 billion—$254.7 billion would come from cuts in federal spending, and $250.1 billion would come from tax increases. Most of the tax increases were levied on high-income taxpayers.

There was also some sentiment in the mid-1990s for the passage of a *balanced-budget amendment*, intended to prevent Congress from doing what it did in the 1980s. The balanced-budget amendment passed the House in early 1995, but it failed by one vote in the Senate. It turned out that the passage of the Omnibus Budget Reconciliation Act of 1993 and a robust economy were enough to lead to a balanced budget by 1998. You can see from Figure 9.6 that by 2000, there was a large budget surplus. Between 1998 and 2001, the federal government was in the process of paying off its debt and there was talk that the debt would be completely paid off. The surplus turned to deficit in 2002, however; and the federal government began again to worry about deficits. As we think about current deficits, it is thus useful to review the approach that the government considered in the late 1980s and early 1990s to cope with the deficit problem, namely the GRH legislation and the balanced-budget amendment. In addition to its policy relevance, this material is a great learning tool. If you understand the macroeconomic consequences of the GRH legislation and the balanced-budget amendment, you have come a long way toward being a macroeconomist.

The Effects of Spending Cuts on the Deficit

Suppose the terms of the balanced-budget amendment or some other deficit-reduction measure dictate that the deficit must be cut by $20 billion. By how much must government spending be cut to achieve this goal? You might be tempted to think the spending cuts should add up to the amount the deficit is to be cut—$20 billion. (This is what GRH dictated: If the deficit needed to be cut by a certain amount, automatic spending cuts were to be equal to that amount.) This approach seems reasonable. If you decrease your personal spending by $100 over a year, your personal deficit will fall by the full $100 of your spending cut.

However, the government is not an individual household. A cut in government spending shifts the AD curve to the left and results in a decrease in aggregate output (income) (Y) and a contraction in the economy. When the economy contracts, both the taxable income of households and the profits of firms fall. This effect means in turn that revenue from the personal income tax and the corporate profits tax will fall.

How do these events affect the size of the deficit? To estimate the response of the deficit to changes in government spending, we need to go through two steps. First, we must decide how much a $1 change in government spending will change GDP. That means we need to know the size of the government spending multiplier. ((Recall that the government spending multiplier measures the increase (or decrease) in GDP (Y) brought about by a $1 increase (or decrease) in government spending.)) Based on empirical evidence, a reasonable value for the government spending multiplier seems to be around 1.4 after 1 year, and this is the value we will use. A $1 billion decrease in government spending lowers GDP by about $1.4 billion after 1 year.

Next, we must see what happens to the deficit when GDP changes. We have just noted that when GDP falls—the economy contracts—taxable income and corporate profits fall, so tax revenues fall. In addition, some categories of government expenditures tend to rise when the economy contracts. For example, unemployment insurance benefits (a transfer payment) rise as the economy contracts because more people become unemployed and eligible for benefits. Both the decrease in tax revenues and the rise in government expenditures cause the deficit to increase. The deficit tends to rise when GDP falls and tends to fall when GDP rises.

The **deficit response index (DRI)** is the amount by which the deficit changes with a $1 change in GDP. Assume that the DRI is $-.22$. That is, for every $1 billion decrease in GDP, the deficit rises by $.22 billion. This number seems close to what is true in practice. We can now use the multiplier and the DRI to answer the question that began this section. Suppose government spending is reduced by $20 billion, the exact amount of the necessary deficit reduction. This will lower GDP by 1.4 × $20 billion, or $28 billion, if the value of the multiplier is 1.4. A $28 billion fall in GDP will increase the deficit by .22 × $28 billion, or $6.2 billion, if the value of the DRI is $-.22$. Because we initially cut government spending (and therefore lowered the deficit from this source) by $20 billion, the net effect of the spending cut is to lower the deficit by $20 billion − $6.2 billion = $13.8 billion.

A $20 billion government spending cut does not lower the deficit by $20 billion. To lower the deficit by $20 billion, we need to cut government spending by about $30 billion. By using 1.4 as the value of the government spending multiplier and $-.22$ as the value of the DRI, we see that a spending cut of $30 billion lowers GDP by 1.4 × $30 billion, or $42 billion. This raises the deficit by .22 × $42 billion, or $9.2 billion. The net effect on the deficit is −$30 billion (from the government spending cut) + $9.2 billion, which is −$20.8 billion (slightly larger than the necessary $20 billion reduction). This means that the spending cut must be nearly 50 percent larger than the deficit reduction we want to achieve. Congress would have had trouble achieving the deficit targets under the GRH legislation even if it had allowed GRH's automatic spending cuts to take place.

deficit response index (DRI)   The amount by which the deficit changes with a $1 change in GDP.

Monetary Policy to the Rescue?   Was Congress so poorly informed about macroeconomics that it would pass legislation that could not possibly work? In other words, are there any conditions under which it would be reasonable to assume that a spending cut needs to be only as large as the desired reduction in the deficit? If the government spending multiplier is zero, government spending cuts will not contract the economy and the cut in the deficit will be equal to the cut in government spending.

Could the government spending multiplier ever be zero? Before the GRH bill was passed, some argued that it could. The argument went as follows: If households and firms are worried about the large government deficits and hold back on consumption and investment because of these worries, the passage of GRH might make them more optimistic and induce them to consume and invest more. This increased consumption and investment would offset the effects of the decreased government spending, and the net result would be a multiplier effect of zero.

Another argument in favor of the GRH bill centered on the Fed and monetary policy. We know that an expansionary monetary policy shifts the AD curve to the right. Because a cut in government spending shifts the AD curve to the left, the Fed could respond to the spending cut enough to shift the AD curve back (to the right) to its original position, preventing any change in aggregate output (income). Some argued the Fed would behave this way after the passage of the GRH bill because it would see that Congress finally "got its house in order."

How large would the interest rate cuts have to be to offset the decrease in G completely, thus resulting in a multiplier of zero? Studies at the time of the original GRH bill showed that the decrease in the interest rate that would be necessary for a multiplier of zero—that is, for a government spending cut to have no effect on aggregate output (income)—is quite large. The Fed would have had to engage in extreme behavior with respect to interest rate changes for the multiplier to be zero. A zero multiplier can come about through renewed optimism on the part of households and firms or through very aggressive behavior on the part of the Fed, but because neither of these situations is very plausible, the multiplier is likely to be greater than zero. Thus, it is likely that to lower the deficit by a certain amount, the cut in government spending must be larger than that amount.

Economic Stability and Deficit Reduction

So lowering the deficit by a given amount is likely to require a government spending decrease larger than this amount. However, this is not the only point to learn from our analysis of deficit targeting. We will now show how deficit targeting can adversely affect the way the economy responds to a variety of stimuli.

In a world with no GRH, no balanced-budget amendment, and no similar deficit-targeting measure, the Congress and the president make decisions each year about how much to spend and how much to tax. The federal government deficit is a result of these decisions and the state of the economy. However, with GRH or the balanced-budget amendment, the size of the deficit is set in advance. Taxes and government spending must be adjusted to produce the required deficit. In this situation, the deficit is no longer a consequence of the tax and spending decisions. Instead, taxes and spending become a consequence of the deficit decision.

What difference does it make whether Congress chooses a target deficit and adjusts government spending and taxes to achieve that target or decides how much to spend and tax and lets the deficit adjust itself? The difference may be substantial. Consider a leftward shift of the *AD* curve caused by some negative demand shock. A **negative demand shock** is something that causes a negative shift in consumption or investment schedules or that leads to a decrease in U.S. exports.

We know that a leftward shift of the *AD* curve lowers aggregate output (income), which causes the government deficit to increase. In a world without deficit targeting, the increase in the deficit during contractions provides an **automatic stabilizer** for the economy. (Review Chapter 9 if this point is hazy.) The contraction-induced decrease in tax revenues and increase in transfer payments tend to reduce the fall in after-tax income and consumer spending due to the negative demand shock. Thus, the decrease in aggregate output (income) caused by the negative demand shock is lessened somewhat by the growth of the deficit [Figure 15.4(a)].

In a world with deficit targeting, the deficit is not allowed to rise. Some combination of tax increases and government spending cuts would be needed to offset what would have otherwise been an increase in the deficit. We know that increases in taxes or cuts in spending are contractionary in themselves. The contraction in the economy will therefore be larger than it would have been without deficit targeting because the initial effect of the negative demand shock is worsened by the rise in taxes or the cut in government spending required to keep the deficit from rising. As Figure 15.4(b) shows, deficit targeting acts as an **automatic destabilizer**. It requires taxes to be raised and government spending to be cut during a contraction. This reinforces, rather than counteracts, the shock that started the contraction.

---

negative demand shock Something that causes a negative shift in consumption or investment schedules or that leads to a decrease in U.S. exports.

automatic stabilizers Revenue and expenditure items in the federal budget that automatically change with the economy in such a way as to stabilize GDP.

automatic destabilizers Revenue and expenditure items in the federal budget that automatically change with the economy in such a way as to destabilize GDP.

▶ **FIGURE 15.4**

Deficit Targeting as an Automatic Destabilizer

Deficit targeting changes the way the economy responds to negative demand shocks because it does not allow the deficit to increase. The result is a smaller deficit but a larger decline in income than would have otherwise occurred.

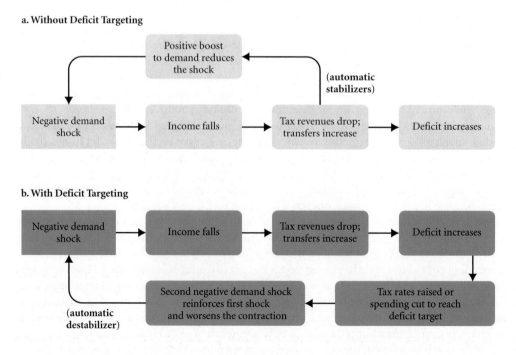

Summary

It is clear that the GRH legislation, the balanced-budget amendment, and similar deficit targeting measures have some undesirable macroeconomic consequences. Deficit targeting requires cuts in spending or increases in taxes at times when the economy is already experiencing problems. This drawback does not mean that Congress should ignore deficits when they arise. Instead, it means that locking the economy into spending cuts during periods of negative demand shocks, as deficit-targeting measures do, is not a good way to manage the economy.

The Stock Market and the Economy

Introductory macroeconomic texts written a decade ago could more or less ignore the stock market. The effects of the stock market on the macroeconomy were small enough to be put aside in introductory discussions. This changed in the 1990s. We will see that the stock market boom that began in 1995 had a large impact on the economy. The economy grew well in the last half of the 1990s, and many came to believe in the existence of a new economy or a "new age." How much of the growth in the last half of the 1990s was due to the stock market boom? Did the economy in fact enter a new age? We try to answer those questions in this section.

Stocks and Bonds

It will be useful to begin by briefly discussing the three main ways in which firms borrow or raise money to finance their investments. How do firms use financial markets in practice?

When a firm wants to make a large purchase to build a new factory or buy machines, it often cannot pay for the purchase out of its own funds. In this case, it must "finance" the investment. One way to do this is to borrow from a bank. The bank loans the money to the firm, the firms uses the money to buy the factory or machine, and the firm pays back the loan (with interest) to the bank over time.

Another possible way for a firm to borrow money is for the firm to issue a bond. If you buy a bond from a firm, you are making a loan to the firm. Bonds were discussed at the beginning of Chapter 11.

A third way for a firm to finance an investment is for it to issue additional shares of **stock**. When a firm issues new shares of stock, it does not add to its debt. Instead, it brings in additional owners of the firm, owners who agree to supply it with funds. Such owners are treated differently than bondholders, who are owed the amount they have loaned.

A share of common stock is a certificate that represents the ownership of a share of a business, almost always a corporation. For example, Lincoln Electric is a Cleveland-based company that makes welding and cutting equipment. The company has 41 million shares of common stock that are owned by tens of thousands of shareholders, some of whom are simply private individuals, some of whom are institutions such as Carleton College, and some of whom may be employees of the firm. Shareholders are entitled to a share of the company's profit. When profits are paid directly to shareholders, the payment is called a *dividend*. In a recent year, Lincoln Electric made a profit of $54 million, which was $1.31 per share, of which $0.43 was paid out to shareholders as dividends and the rest was retained for investment.

Stockholders who own stocks that increase in value earn what are called **capital gains**. **Realized capital gains** (or losses) are increases (or decreases) in the value of assets, including stocks, that households receive when they actually sell those assets. The government considers realized capital gains net of losses to be income, although their treatment under the tax code has been very complex and subject to change every few years. The total return that an owner of a share of stock receives is the sum of the dividends received and the capital gain or loss.

stock A certificate that certifies ownership of a certain portion of a firm.

capital gain An increase in the value of an asset.

realized capital gain The gain that occurs when the owner of an asset actually sells it for more than he or she paid for it.

Determining the Price of a Stock

What determines the price of a stock? If a share of stock is selling for $25, why is someone willing to pay that much for it? As we have noted, when you buy a share of stock, you own part of the firm. If a firm is making profits, it may be paying dividends to its shareholders. If it is not paying dividends but is making profits, people may expect that it will pay dividends in the future. Dividends are important in thinking about stocks because dividends are the form in which shareholders receive income from the firm. So one thing that is likely to affect the price of a stock is what people expect its future dividends will be. The larger the expected future dividends, the larger the current stock price, other things being equal.

Another important consideration in thinking about the price of a stock is the time the dividends are expected to be paid. A $2 per share dividend that is expected to be paid 4 years from now is worth less than a $2 per share dividend that is expected to be paid next year. In other words, the farther into the future the dividend is expected to be paid, the more it will be "discounted." The amount by which expected future dividends are discounted depends on the interest rate. The larger the interest rate, the more expected future dividends will be discounted. If the interest rate is 10 percent, I can invest $100 today and receive $110 a year from now. I am thus willing to pay $100 today to someone who will pay me $110 in a year. If instead, the interest rate were only 5 percent, I would be willing to pay $104.76 today to receive $110 a year from now because the alternative of $104.76 today at a 5 percent interest rate also yields $110.00 at the end of the year. I am thus willing to pay more for the promise of $110 a year from now when the interest rate is lower. In other words, I "discount" the $110 less when the interest rate is lower.

Another discount factor aside from the interest rate must be taken into account; it is the discount for risk. People prefer certain outcomes to uncertain ones for the same expected values. For example, I prefer a certain $50 over a bet in which there is a 50 percent chance I will get $100 and a 50 percent chance I will get nothing. The expected value of the bet is $50, but I prefer the certain $50 over the bet, where there is a 50 percent chance that I will end up with nothing. The same reasoning holds for future dividends. If, say, I expect dividends for both firms A and B to be $2 per share next year but firm B has a much wider range of possibilities (is riskier), I will prefer firm A. Put another way, I will "discount" firm B's expected future dividends more than firm A's because the outcome for firm B is more uncertain.

We can thus say that the price of a stock should equal the discounted value of its expected future dividends, where the discount factors depend on the interest rate and risk. If for some reason (say, a positive surprise news announcement from the firm) expected future dividends increase, this development should lead to an increase in the price of the stock. If the interest rate falls, this decrease should also lead to a stock price increase. Finally, if the perceived risk of a firm falls, this perception should increase the firm's stock price.

Some stock analysts talk about the possibility of stock market "bubbles." Given the preceding discussion, what might a bubble be? Assume that given your expectations about the future dividends of a firm and given the discount rate, you value the firm's stock at $20 per share. Is there any case in which you would pay more than $20 for a share? You can, of course, buy the stock and sell it later; you don't need to hold the stock forever. If the stock is currently selling for $25, which is above your value of $20, but you think that the stock will rise to $30 in the next few months, you might buy it now in anticipation of selling it later for a higher price. If others have similar views, the price of the stock may be driven up.

In this case, what counts is not the discounted value of expected future dividends, but rather your view of what others will pay for the stock in the future. If everyone expects that everyone else expects that the price will be driven up, the price may be driven up. One might call this outcome a bubble because the stock price depends on what people expect that other people expect and so on.

When a firm's stock price has risen rapidly, it is difficult to know whether the reason is that people have increased their expectations of the firm's future dividends or that there is a bubble. Because people's expectations of future dividends are not directly observed, it is hard to test alternative theories.

The Stock Market Since 1948

If you follow the stock market at all, you know that much attention is paid to two stock price indices: the **Dow Jones Industrial Average** and the **NASDAQ Composite**. From a macroeconomic perspective, however, these two indices cover too small a sample of firms. One would like an index that includes firms whose total market value is close to the market value of all firms in the economy. For this purpose a much better measure is the **Standard and Poor's 500** stock price index, called the **S&P 500**. This index includes most of the companies in the economy by market value.

The S&P 500 index is plotted in Figure 15.5 for 1948 I–2007 IV. What perhaps stands out most in this plot is the huge increase in the index between 1995 and 2000. Between December 31, 1994, and March 31, 2000, the S&P 500 index rose 226 percent, an annual rate of increase of 25 percent.

Dow Jones Industrial Average An index based on the stock prices of 30 actively traded large companies. The oldest and most widely followed index of stock market performance.

NASDAQ Composite An index based on the stock prices of over 5,000 companies traded on the NASDAQ Stock Market. The NASDAQ market takes its name from the National Association of Securities Dealers Automated Quotation System.

Standard and Poor's 500 (S&P 500) An index based on the stock prices of 500 of the largest firms by market value.

This is by far the largest stock market boom in U.S. history, completely dominating the boom of the 1920s. This boom added roughly $14 trillion to household wealth, about $2.5 trillion per year.

▲ **FIGURE 15.5 The S&P 500 Stock Price Index, 1948 I–2007 IV**

What caused this boom? You can see from Figure 13.13 on p. 241 that interest rates did not change much in the last half of the 1990s, so the boom cannot be explained by any large fall in interest rates. Perhaps profits rose substantially during this period, and this growth led to a large increase in expected future dividends? We know from the preceding discussion that if expected future dividends increase, stock prices should increase. Figure 15.6 plots for 1948 I–2007 IV the ratio of after-tax profits to GDP. It is clear from the figure that nothing unusual happened in the last half of the 1990s. The share of after-tax profits in GDP rose from the middle of 1995 to the middle of 1997, but then generally fell after that through 2000. Thus, there does not appear to be any surge of profits that would have led people to expect much higher future dividends.

◀ **FIGURE 15.6**
Ratio of After-Tax Profits to GDP, 1948 I–2007 IV

It could be that the perceived riskiness of stocks fell in the last half of the 1990s. This change would have led to smaller discount rates for stocks and thus, other things being equal, to higher stock prices. Although this possibility cannot be completely ruled out, there is no strong independent evidence that perceived riskiness fell.

The stock market boom is thus a puzzle, and many people speculate that it was simply a bubble. For some reason, stock prices started rising rapidly in 1995 and people expected that other people expected that prices would continue to rise. This led stock prices to rise further, thus fulfilling the expectations, which led to expectations of further increases, and so on. Bubble believers note that once stock prices started falling in 2000, they fell a great deal. It is not the case that stock prices just leveled out in 2000; they fell rapidly. People of the bubble view argue that this is simply the bubble bursting.

Remember that we are talking about the S&P 500 index, which includes most of the firms in the U.S. economy by market value. We are not just talking about a few dot-com companies. The entire stock market went up by 25 percent per year for 5 years! We will see in the next section the effects of this increase in wealth on the economy.

Stock Market Effects on the Economy

We mentioned in Chapter 8 that one of the factors that affects consumption expenditures is wealth. Other things being equal, the more wealth a family has, the more it spends. We discuss this in detail in the next chapter, but all we need for now is to note that an increase in wealth increases consumer spending. An increase in stock prices may also affect investment. If a firm is considering an investment project, one way in which it can finance the project is to issue additional shares of stock. The higher the price of the firm's stock, the more money it can get per additional share. A firm is thus likely to undertake more investment projects the higher its stock price. The cost of an investment project in terms of shares of stock is smaller the higher the price of the stock. This is the way in which a stock market boom may increase investment.

The effect of the stock market on the economy is thus fairly straightforward. If stock prices increase, the wealth of households increases, as in turn does consumer spending. Investment also increases because firms can raise more money per share to finance investment projects. As a rough rule of thumb, a $1.00 change in the value of stocks leads to about a $0.03 to $0.04 change in consumer and investor spending per year. We will use the $0.04 number in the following discussion.

The Crash of October 1987   Before considering the boom of the late 1990s, it is useful to review a crash—namely, the crash of October 1987. The value of stocks in the United States fell by about a trillion dollars between August 1987 and the end of October 1987. In one day—October 19, 1987—the value of stocks fell nearly $700 billion. If we assume that a $1.00 decrease in stock prices results in a $0.04 decrease in consumer and investor spending per year, we can see that the $1 trillion decrease in wealth in 1987 implies a $40 billion lower level of spending in 1988. The level of gross domestic product (GDP) was around $4 trillion in 1987, so a $40 billion decrease in spending is around 1.0 percent of GDP. A multiplier effect would also be at work here. A decrease in spending leads to a decrease in aggregate output (income), which leads to a further decrease in spending and so on. The total decrease in GDP would be somewhat larger than the initial decrease of $40 billion. If the multiplier is 1.4, the total decrease in GDP would be about 1.4 × $40 billion = $56 billion, or about 1.4 percent of GDP.

Although 1.4 percent of GDP is a large amount, it is not large enough to imply that a recession would result from the crash. The life-cycle theory, which we will discuss in Chapter 17, helps explain why. If households are making lifetime decisions and want to have as smooth a consumption path as possible over their lifetimes, they will respond to a decrease in wealth by cutting consumption a little each year. They will *not* decrease their consumption in the current year by the full amount of the decrease in wealth.

Why were people predicting that the economy would go into a recession, or worse, a depression, after the crash? The reasons all pertain to expectations. If households and firms had expected the economy to contract sharply after the crash, they probably would have cut back on consumption and investment much more than otherwise. (This reaction would be Keynes's animal spirits at work.) These expectations would have become self-fulfilling in the sense that the economy would have gone into a recession because of the cuts in consumption and investment brought about by lowered expectations.

However, the economy did not go into a recession in 1988. Expectations were not changed drastically following the crash. The Fed helped out by easing monetary policy right after the crash to counteract any large negative reaction. The 3-month Treasury bill rate fell from 6.4 percent to 5.8 percent between October and November 1987. In addition, the value of stocks gradually increased over time to their earlier levels. Because the initial decrease in wealth turned out to be temporary, the negative wealth effect was not nearly as large as it otherwise would have been.

The Boom of 1995–2000   We pointed out earlier that between 1995 and 2000, the value of stocks increased about $2.5 trillion per year. If we assume that a $1.00 increase in stock prices results in a $0.04 increase in consumption and investment per year and if we use a multiplier of 1.4, the added increase in spending is .04 × $2.5 trillion × 1.4, which is $140 billion per year. In 1998, GDP was around $9 trillion, and so an increase of $140 billion is 1.5 percent of GDP.

The annual growth rate of GDP from the end of 1995 to the middle of 2000 was 4.5 percent. The preceding numbers thus suggest that about 1.5 of the 4.5 percent was due to the stock market boom. In other words, had there been no boom, the growth rate would likely have been around 3.0 percent instead of 4.5 percent. Households simply spent much more than they would have had there been no huge increase in their wealth, and firms invested much more than they would have had stock prices not risen so much.

A more detailed analysis of the effects of the stock market boom on the economy is presented in Figure 15.7–15.13. This analysis uses a model of the economy[3] to see what the economy would have been like had there been no stock market boom. In each figure, the "actual" line represents the actual values of the variable over the 1995 I–2002 III period. These values reflect the stock market boom (because the boom actually took place!). The "no boom" line represents the values that the model estimates would have taken place had overall stock prices simply grown at a normal rate. In the no boom case, there was neither the huge increase in stock prices between 1995 and 2000 nor the large fall in prices from 2000 on.

The plots in the seven figures are interesting. They show that had there been no stock market boom, the U.S. economy would not have looked unusual in the last half of the 1990s. There would have been no talk of a "new economy" or a "new age." It would have been more or less business as usual. We will now discuss the figures one by one. Given what you have learned so far about macroeconomics, you should be able to understand the reasons for the various results.

Figure 15.7 shows that the personal saving rate is considerably higher in the no boom case. No longer are the values below the range of historical experience. This is the wealth effect on consumption at work. With no huge increase in wealth, households consume less.

◀ **FIGURE 15.7**
Personal Saving Rate, 1995 I–2002 III

Figure 15.8 shows that investment also is less in the no boom case. Firms invest less in plant and equipment because the cost to them in terms of extra shares issued is higher (the price per share is lower). Many people believe that investment was excessively high in the late 1990s, a phenomenon that led to the large falls in 2000 and 2001. Figure 15.8 shows that much of this would not have happened had there been no stock market boom.

[3] Ray C. Fair, *Estimating How the Macroeconomy Works* (Cambridge, MA: Harvard University Press, 2004).

▶ **FIGURE 15.8**

Investment-Output Ratio, 1995 I–2002 III

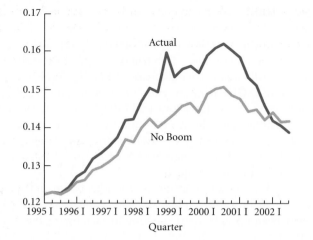

Figure 15.9 shows that the federal government surplus would not have been as high in the late 1990s and in 2000 were it not for the stock market boom. It should be clear why this is the case. In the no boom case, taxable income and profits are less, and so there is less tax revenue. Also, spending on unemployment benefits is greater because (as we will see) unemployment is higher.

▶ **FIGURE 15.9**

Ratio of Federal Government Budget Surplus to GDP, 1995 I–2002 III

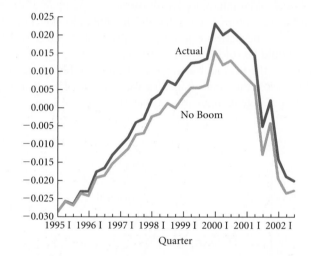

Figure 15.10 shows that real growth was higher in the last half of the 1990s than would have been the case with no boom. This figure gives a more accurate impression of the growth rate effects than the simple use of the 4 percent wealth spending response and the 1.4 multiplier on p. 288. Note from Figure 15.10 that the growth rate is higher in the no boom case in 2001 and 2002 because in the no boom case, there is no large stock market correction in these two years.

▶ **FIGURE 15.10**

Growth Rate of Real GDP, 1995 I–2002 III

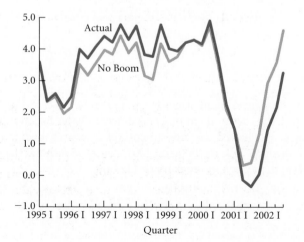

Figure 15.11 shows that the fall in the unemployment rate in the last half of the 1990s to 4 percent from 5.5 percent was due to the stock market boom. Had there been no boom, the unemployment rate would have remained at about 5.5 percent.

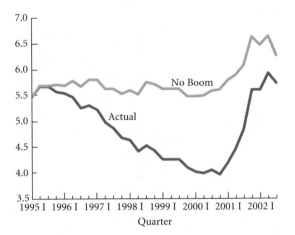

◀ FIGURE 15.11

The Unemployment Rate, 1995 I–2002 III

Figure 15.12 shows that inflation would have been lower in the no boom case. The simple reason is that output would have been lower and thus demand pressure would have been less. In either case, however, the inflation rate is not high by historical standards.

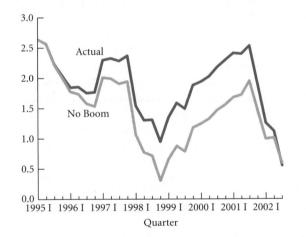

◀ FIGURE 15.12

Inflation Rate, 1995 I–2002 III

Finally, Figure 15.13 plots the 3-month Treasury bill rate. Remember from the last chapter that this rate reflects the behavior of the Fed. The Fed essentially decides each 6 weeks what it wants the rate to be and uses open market operations to achieve this value. The figure shows that the interest rate would have been lower in the last half of the 1990s had there been no boom. This should make sense from the last chapter. Without the boom, real growth would have been lower and the unemployment rate higher and the Fed would have responded with lower interest rates.

Fed Policy and the Stock Market   Figure 15.13 is useful for thinking about how Fed policy is related to the stock market. Policy questions arise from time to time as to whether the Fed should be influenced by the stock market. Should the Fed try to influence stock prices by changing interest rates? Figure 15.13 says that the Fed is in fact influenced by the stock market. The Fed kept the interest rate higher than it would have had there been no stock market boom. It should be clear why this is the case. If ultimately the Fed cares about output, unemployment, and inflation and if the stock market affects these variables, the Fed will be indirectly affected by the stock market. In other words, the Fed cares about the stock market to the extent that the stock market affects the things that it ultimately cares about—namely, output, unemployment, and inflation.

▶ **FIGURE 15.13**

3-Month Treasury Bill Rate, 1995 I–2002 III

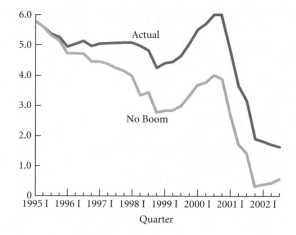

The Post-Boom Economy Figure 15.5 shows that there was a fairly large fall in stock prices between the fourth quarter of 2000 and the third quarter of 2002. In this period, the fall in household wealth from the stock market was about $7 trillion. We mentioned earlier that the stock market boom in the last half of the 1990s added about $14 trillion to household wealth, and so about half of this increase was reversed in the 2000 IV–2002 III period.

Given that the stock market boom in the last half of the 1990s led to a more expansionary economy than would otherwise have been the case, it seems likely that the stock market correction in 2000–2002 led to a less expansionary economy. This is in fact the case: The $7 trillion fall in household wealth had a negative effect on the economy. There were two quarters of negative growth in 2001, and the growth rate in 2002 was modest. The economy did not begin growing well again until the middle of 2003.

What is remarkable about the sluggish economy in 2001 and 2002 is that it came at a time of very expansionary monetary and fiscal policy. Figure 13.13 on p. 254 shows that the Fed lowered the bill rate by over 4 percentage points in this period, perhaps the most expansionary policy in its history. Figures 9.4 and 9.5 on pp. 171–172 show that fiscal policy was also very expansionary. Tax rates were lowered substantially in the Bush administration and government spending and transfer payments were increased considerably. Despite these huge expansionary policies, the economy did not do particularly well, and one of the main reasons was the fall in household wealth from the stock market decline. Had there been no stock market correction but the same monetary and fiscal policies, the economy would have grown much more rapidly in 2001 and 2002 than it in fact did.

The importance of the stock market in the economy should now be clear. It played a big role in the economic boom of the last half of the 1990s and in the economic slack of 2000–2002. This is why introductory macroeconomic texts can no longer ignore the stock market.

A final point that is interesting about the post-boom U.S. economy is the role that housing values played from 2003 through 2005. The stock market began to recover in this period, as can be seen from Figure 15.5 on p. 287, but perhaps more important, the housing market boomed. Many homeowners saw the value of their homes soar. Many responded to this rise by taking out "home equity" loans, which were available at low interest rates, and increasing their spending on consumer goods and services. Consumption was thus stimulated by this increase in housing wealth, which helped fuel the recovery. So both stock market wealth and housing wealth have important effects on the economy.

Some believed by 2005 that a housing bubble was just waiting to be burst. Would housing prices continue to increase or at least not fall? Or was the economy in for a large and rapid fall in prices, as had occurred in the stock market a few years earlier? In fact, in 2006 there began to be a large correction in housing prices, with prices falling in many parts of the country. This had serious repercussions on the mortgage market and by the end of 2007 on real output growth. So this is another example where housing wealth (in this case, the fall in housing wealth from the fall in house prices) has important effects on the economy.

ECONOMICS IN PRACTICE

Bubbles or Rational Investors?

We discussed in the text that the huge increase in U.S. stock prices in the last half of the 1990s is a puzzle. So also is the huge increase in U.S. housing prices between 2002 and 2006. Recently, many other countries also have seen large increases in asset prices. An interesting question is whether these rapid run-ups in prices are bubbles, generated by irrational consumers and investors, or are instead the result of actions of rational investors that simply turned out with hindsight to be wrong. This question is of interest to both academics and policy makers. A key policy question is whether the Fed should ignore asset prices or try to use interest rates to control them. The following article discusses some research that is currently being done on bubbles and its implications for Fed behavior.

Bernanke's Bubble Laboratory: Princeton Protégés of Fed Chief Study the Economics of Manias

Wall Street Journal

PRINCETON, N.J.—First came that tech-stock bubble. Then there were bubbles in housing and credit. Chinese stocks took off like a rocket. Now, as prices soar on every material from oil to corn, some suggest there's a bubble in commodities.

But how and why do bubbles form? Economists traditionally haven't offered much insight. From World War II till the mid-1990s, there weren't many U.S. investing manias for them to look at. The study of bubbles was left to economic historians sifting through musty records of 17th-century Dutch tulip-bulb prices and the like.

The dot-com boom began to change that. "You were seeing live, in action, the unfolding of lots of examples of valuations disconnecting from fundamentals," says Princeton economist Harrison Hong. Now, the study of financial bubbles is hot.

Its hub is Princeton, 40 miles south of Wall Street, home to a band of young scholars hired by former professor Ben Bernanke, now the nation's chief bubble watcher as Federal Reserve chairman. The group includes Mr. Hong, a Vietnam native raised in Silicon Valley; a Chinese wunderkind who started as a physicist [Wei Xiong]; and a German who'd been groomed to take over the family carpentry business [Markus Brunnermeier]. Among their conclusions:

Bubbles emerge at times when investors profoundly disagree about the significance of a big economic development, such as the birth of the Internet. Because it's so much harder to bet on prices going down than up, the bullish investors dominate.

Once they get going, financial bubbles are marked by huge increases in trading, making them easier to identify.

Manias can persist even though many smart people suspect a bubble, because no one of them has the firepower to successfully attack it. Only when skeptical investors act simultaneously—a moment impossible to predict—does the bubble pop.

As a result of all that and more, the Princeton squad argues that the Fed can and should try to restrain bubbles, rather than following former Chairman Alan Greenspan's approach: watchful waiting while prices rise and then cleaning up the mess after a bubble bursts.

If the tech-stock collapse didn't make that clear, the damage done by the housing and credit bubbles should, argues José Scheinkman, 60 years old, a theorist Mr. Bernanke recruited in 1999 from the University of Chicago. "Advanced economies are very dependent on the health of the financial system. What this bubble did was destroy the capacity of the financial system to finance the U.S. economy," Mr. Scheinkman says.

The Fed is giving the activist approach some thought. In a speech scheduled for delivery Thursday night, Fed Governor Frederic Mishkin suggested that while it was inappropriate to use the blunt instrument of interest-rate increases to prick bubbles, if too-easy credit appeared to be fueling a mania, policy makers might craft a regulatory response that could "help reduce the magnitude of the bubble."

Yet the very concept of bubbles is at odds with the view of some that market prices reflect the collective knowledge of multitudes. There are economists who dispute the existence of bubbles—arguing, for instance, that what happened to prices in the dot-com boom was a rational response to the possibility that nascent Internet firms might turn into Microsofts. But these economists' numbers are thinning.

Source: Justin Lahart, May 16, 2008

SUMMARY

TIME LAGS REGARDING MONETARY AND FISCAL POLICY *p. 277*

1. *Stabilization policy* describes both fiscal and monetary policy, the goals of which are to smooth out fluctuations in output and employment and to keep prices as stable as possible. Stabilization goals are not necessarily easy to achieve because of the existence of certain *time lags*, or delays in the response of the economy to macroeconomic policies.

2. A *recognition lag* is the time it takes for policy makers to recognize the existence of a boom or a slump. An *implementation lag* is the time it takes to put the desired policy into effect once economists and policy makers recognize that the economy is in a boom or a slump. A *response lag* is the time it takes for the economy to adjust to the new conditions after a new policy is implemented—in other words, a lag that occurs because of the operation of the economy itself. In general, monetary policy can be implemented more rapidly than fiscal policy but fiscal policy generally has a shorter response lag than monetary policy.

FISCAL POLICY: DEFICIT TARGETING *p. 281*

3. In fiscal year 1986, Congress passed and President Reagan signed the *Gramm-Rudman-Hollings Act* (*GRH*), which set out to reduce the federal deficit by \$36 billion per year, with a zero deficit slated for fiscal year 1991. If Congress passed a budget with a deficit larger than the targeted amount, the law called for automatic spending cuts. A Supreme Court ruling later overturned this provision, and the actual figures for each year never came close to the targets. Thanks to the Omnibus Budget Reconciliation Act of 1993 and a robust economy, the federal deficit had been eliminated by 1998.

4. The deficit tends to rise when GDP falls and to fall when GDP rises. The *deficit response index (DRI)* is the amount by which the deficit changes with a \$1 change in GDP.

5. For spending cuts of a certain amount to reduce the deficit by the same amount, the government spending multiplier must be zero. Before GRH was passed, some argued that a government spending multiplier of zero can be achieved through renewed optimism on the part of households or through very aggressive behavior by the Fed to decrease the interest rate. Empirical evidence has shown that both situations are not very plausible. So to lower the deficit by a certain amount, government spending cuts must be larger than that amount to lower the deficit.

6. Deficit-targeting measures that call for automatic spending cuts to eliminate or reduce the deficit may have the effect of destabilizing the economy because they prevent automatic stabilizers from working.

THE STOCK MARKET AND THE ECONOMY *p. 285*

7. A firm can finance an investment project by borrowing from banks, by issuing *bonds*, or by issuing new shares of its *stock*. People who own shares of stock own a fraction of the firm.

8. The price of a stock should equal the discounted value of its expected future dividends, where the discount factors depend on the interest rate and risk.

9. A bubble exists when the price of a stock exceeds the discounted value of its expected future dividends. In this case, what matters is what people expect that other people expect about how much the stock can be sold for in the future.

10. The largest stock market boom in U.S. history occurred between 1995 and 2000, when the S&P 500 index rose by 25 percent per year. The boom added \$14 trillion to household wealth.

11. Why there was a stock market boom in 1995–2000 appears to be a puzzle. There was nothing unusual about earnings that would predict such a boom. Many people believe that the boom was merely a bubble.

12. The boom of 1995–2000 and the large fall in stock prices after that had significant effects on millions of people's lives. Many people overspent during the boom years and were seriously affected when the boom didn't last.

13. When stock prices increase, household wealth increases, which leads to increased consumer spending. Investment also rises because firms can raise more money per share to finance investment projects. As a rough rule of thumb, a $1.00 change in the value of stocks leads to about a $0.03 to $0.04 change in consumer and investor spending per year.

14. The boom in the economy between 1995 and 2000 was fueled by the stock market boom. Estimates show that had there been no stock market boom, the economy would not have looked historically unusual in the last half of the 1990s.

15. The economy in 2001–2002 was more sluggish than it would have been had there been no stock market "correction" following the boom.

16. The boom in housing prices in 2003–2005 helped sustain the recovery, and the fall in housing prices in 2006–2007 had a serious negative impact on the economy.

REVIEW TERMS AND CONCEPTS

automatic destabilizers, *p. 284*
automatic stabilizers, *p. 284*
capital gain, *p. 285*
deficit response index (DRI), *p. 283*
Dow Jones Industrial Average, *p. 286*
Gramm-Rudman-Hollings Act, *p. 281*

implementation lag, *p. 279*
NASDAQ Composite, *p. 286*
negative demand shock, *p. 284*
realized capital gain, *p. 285*
recognition lag, *p. 279*

response lag, *p. 279*
stabilization policy, *p. 277*
Standard and Poor's 500 (S&P 500), *p. 286*
stock, *p. 285*
time lags, *p. 277*

PROBLEMS

Visit www.myeconlab.com to complete the problems marked in orange online. You will receive instant feedback on your answers, tutorial help, and access to additional practice problems.

1. In July 2003, the S&P 500 index was at 1,000.
   a. What is the S&P 500 index?
   b. Where is the S&P today?
   c. If you had invested $10,000 in July 2003 and your investments had increased in value by the same percentage as the S&P 500 index had increased, how much would you have today?
   d. Assume that the total stock market holdings of the household sector were about $12 trillion and that the entire stock market went up/down by the same percentage as the S&P. Evidence suggests that the "wealth effect" of stock market holdings on consumer spending is about 4 percent of wealth annually. How much additional or reduced spending would you expect to see as a result of the stock market moves since July 2003? Assuming a multiplier of 2 and a GDP of $10,000 billion, how much additional/less GDP would you predict for next year if all of this was true?

2. During 1997, stock markets in Asia collapsed. Hong Kong's was down nearly 30 percent, Thailand's was down 62 percent, and Malaysia's was down 60 percent. Japan and Korea experienced big drops as well. What impacts would these events have on the economies of the countries themselves? Explain your answer. In what ways would you have expected these events to influence the U.S. economy? How might the spending of Asians on American goods be affected? What about Americans who have invested in these countries?

3. Explain why the government deficit rises as the economy contracts.

4. You are given the following information about the economy in 2001 (all in billions of dollars):

Consumption function:	$C = 100 + (.8 \times Y_d)$
Taxes:	$T = -150 + (.25 \times Y)$
Investment function:	$I = 60$
Disposable income:	$Y_d = Y - T$
Government spending:	$G = 80$
Equilibrium:	$Y = C + I + G$

Hint: Deficit is $D = G - T = G - [-150 + (.25 \times Y)]$.

   a. Find equilibrium income. Show that the government budget deficit (the difference between government spending and tax revenues) is $5 billion.
   b. Congress passes the Foghorn-Leghorn (F-L) amendment, which requires that the deficit be zero this year. If the budget adopted by Congress has a deficit that is larger than zero, the deficit target must be met by cutting spending. Suppose spending is cut by $5 billion (to $75 billion). What is the new value for equilibrium GDP? What is the new deficit? Explain carefully why the deficit is not zero.
   c. What is the deficit response index, and how is it defined? Explain why the DRI must equal .25 in this example. By using this information, by how much must we cut spending to achieve a deficit of zero?
   d. Suppose the F-L amendment was not in effect and planned investment falls to $I = 55$. What is the new value of GDP? What is the new government budget deficit? What happens to GDP if the F-L amendment is in effect and spending is cut to reach the deficit target? (*Hint:* Spending must be cut by $21.666 billion to balance the budget.)

5. Some states are required to balance their budgets. Is this measure stabilizing or destabilizing? Suppose all states were committed to a balanced-budget philosophy and the economy moved into a recession. What effects would this philosophy have on the size of the federal deficit?

6. Explain why stabilization policy may be difficult to carry out. How is it possible that stabilization policies can actually be destabilizing?

7. [Related to the *Economics in Practice* on *p. 293*] The housing boom of 2000–2005 created wealth of over $10 trillion. Many claim that the spending of this new wealth prevented a serious recession in the early 2000s. If people spent 4% of that new housing wealth annually by taking out home equity loans or simply saving less, what would be the increase in annual consumption expenditures? (Be careful in counting decimal places.) What would happen to GDP growth as a result?

8. [Related to the *Economics in Practice* on *p. 280*] In February, 2008, Congress passed and President Bush signed the Economic Stimulus Act of 2008. Included in this stimulus package were tax rebate checks of up to $600 per individual ($1,200 per couple) and an additional $300 per child. The checks, with a total value of more than $100 billion, were sent to eligible recipients beginning in May, 2008. Go to www.bea.gov and click on Personal Income and Outlays. Look up the percent change in personal consumption expenditures for 2008 (Table 2.3.1). Does it appear that the tax rebate checks had a positive impact on the economy? Do you think the timing of these rebates was appropriate? Briefly explain, using the personal consumption expenditure data and the information from the text about time lags.

Household and Firm Behavior in the Macroeconomy: A Further Look*

16

In Chapters 8 through 14, we considered the interactions of households, firms, and the government in the goods, money, and labor markets. The macroeconomy is complicated, and there is much to learn about these interactions. To keep our discussions as uncomplicated as possible, so far we have assumed simple behavior of households and firms—the two basic decision-making units in the economy. We assumed that household consumption (C) depends only on income and that firms' planned investment (I) depends only on the interest rate. We did not consider that households make consumption and labor supply decisions simultaneously and that firms make investment and employment decisions simultaneously.

Now that we understand the basic interactions in the economy, we must relax these assumptions. In the first part of this chapter, we present a more realistic picture of the influences on households' consumption and labor supply decisions. In the second part, we present a more detailed and realistic picture of the influences on firms' investment and employment decisions. We then use what we have learned to analyze more macroeconomic issues.

Households: Consumption and Labor Supply Decisions

For most of our analysis so far, we have been assuming that consumption depends simply on income. While this is a useful starting point, it is far from a complete description of the consumption decision of households. We need to consider other theories of consumption to build a more realistic case.

The Life-Cycle Theory of Consumption

The main idea of the **life-cycle theory of consumption** is that people make lifetime consumption plans. By realizing that they are likely to earn more in their prime working years than they earn earlier or later, people make consumption decisions based on their expectations of lifetime income. People tend to consume less than they earn during their main working years—they *save* during those years—and people tend to consume more than they earn during their early and

---

* This chapter is somewhat more advanced, but it contains a lot of interesting information!

life-cycle theory of consumption A theory of household consumption: Households make lifetime consumption decisions based on their expectations of lifetime income.

later years—they *dissave*, or use up savings, during those years. Students in medical school generally have very low current incomes, but few live in the poverty that those incomes might predict. Instead, they borrow now and plan to pay back later when their incomes improve.

The lifetime income and consumption pattern of a representative individual is shown in Figure 16.1. As you can see, this person has a low income during the first part of her life, high income in the middle, and low income again in retirement. Her income in retirement is not zero because she has income from sources other than her own labor—Social Security payments, interest and dividends, and so on.

▶ **FIGURE 16.1**

Life-Cycle Theory of Consumption

In their early working years, people consume more than they earn. This is also true in the retirement years. In between, people save (consume less than they earn) to pay off debts from borrowing and to accumulate savings for retirement.

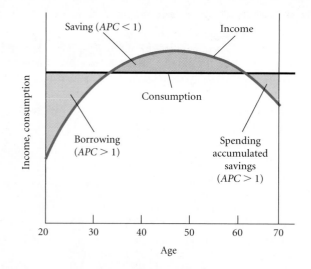

The consumption path as drawn in Figure 16.1 is constant over the person's life. This is an extreme assumption, but it illustrates the point that the path of consumption over a lifetime is likely to be more stable than the path of income. We consume an amount greater than our incomes during our early working careers. We do so by borrowing against future income by taking out a car loan, a mortgage to buy a house, or a loan to pay for college. This debt is repaid when our incomes have risen and we can afford to use some of our income to pay off past borrowing without substantially lowering our consumption. The reverse is true for our retirement years. Here, too, our incomes are low. Because we consume less than we earn during our prime working years, we can save up a "nest egg" that allows us to maintain an acceptable standard of living during retirement.

Fluctuations in wealth are also an important component of the life-cycle story. Many young households borrow in anticipation of higher income in the future. Some households actually have *negative wealth*—the value of their assets is less than the debts they owe. A household in its prime working years saves to pay off debts and to build up assets for its later years, when income typically goes down. Households whose assets are greater than the debts they owe have *positive wealth*. With its wage earners retired, a household consumes its accumulated wealth. Generally speaking, wealth starts out negative, turns positive, and then approaches zero near the end of life. Wealth, therefore, is intimately linked to the cumulative saving and dissaving behavior of households.

The key difference between the Keynesian theory of consumption and the life-cycle theory is that the life-cycle theory suggests that consumption and saving decisions are likely to be based not only on current income but also on expectations of future income. The consumption behavior of households immediately following World War II clearly supports the life-cycle story. Just after the war ended, income fell as wage earners moved out of war-related work. However, consumption spending did not fall commensurately, as Keynesian theory would predict. People expected to find jobs in other sectors eventually, and they did not adjust their consumption spending to the temporarily lower incomes they were earning in the meantime.

permanent income The average level of a person's expected future income stream.

The term **permanent income** is sometimes used to refer to the average level of a person's expected future income stream. If you expect your income will be high in the future (even though it may not be high now), your permanent income is said to be high. With this concept, we can sum up the life-cycle theory by saying that current consumption decisions are likely to be based on permanent income instead of current income.[1] This means that policy changes such as tax-rate changes are likely to have more of an effect on household behavior if they are expected to be permanent instead of temporary.

One-time tax rebates such as we saw in the United States in 2001 and 2008 provide an interesting test of the permanent income hypothesis. In both cases, the tax rebate was a one-time stimulus. In 2008, for example, the tax rebate was $300 to $600 for individual tax payers eligible for the rebate. How much would we expect this rebate to influence consumption? The simple Keynesian model that we introduced earlier in this text would just apply the marginal propensity to consume to the $600. If the marginal propensity to consume is .8, we would expect the $600 to generate $480 in incremental spending per rebate. The permanent income hypothesis instead looks at the $600 in the context of an individual's permanent income. As a fraction of one's lifetime income, $600 is a modest number, and we would thus expect individuals to increase their spending only modestly in response to the rebate. Research on the 2001 tax rebate by Matthew Shapiro and Joel Slemrod, based on surveys of consumers, suggested that most people planned to use their rebates to lower debt, rather than increase spending.

Although the life-cycle model enriches our understanding of the consumption behavior of households, the analysis is still missing something. What is missing is the other main decision of households: the labor supply decision.

The Labor Supply Decision

The size of the labor force in an economy is of obvious importance. A growing labor force is one of the ways in which national income/output can be expanded, and the larger the percentage of people who work, the higher the potential output per capita.

So far we have said little about what determines the size of the labor force. Of course, demographics are a key; the number of children born in 2008 will go a long way toward determining the potential number of 20-year-old workers in 2028. In addition, immigration, both legal and illegal, plays a role.

Behavior also plays a role. Households make decisions about whether to work and how much to work. These decisions are closely tied to consumption decisions because for most households, the bulk of their spending is financed out of wages and salaries. Households make consumption and labor supply decisions simultaneously. Consumption cannot be considered separately from labor supply because it is precisely by selling your labor that you earn income to pay for your consumption.

As we discussed in Chapter 3, the alternative to supplying your labor in exchange for a wage or a salary is leisure or other nonmarket activities. Nonmarket activities include raising a child, going to school, keeping a house, or—in a developing economy—working as a subsistence farmer. What determines the quantity of labor supplied by a household? Among the list of factors are the wage rate, prices, wealth, and nonlabor income.

The Wage Rate   A changing wage rate can affect labor supply, but whether the effect is positive or negative is ambiguous. An increase in the wage rate affects a household in two ways. First, work becomes more attractive relative to leisure and other nonmarket activities. Because every hour spent in leisure now requires giving up a higher wage, the opportunity cost of leisure is higher. As a result, you would expect that a higher wage would lead to a larger quantity of labor supplied—a larger workforce. This is called the *substitution effect of a wage rate increase*.

On the other hand, household members who work are clearly better off after a wage rate increase. By working the same number of hours as they did before, they will earn more income. If we assume that leisure is a normal good, people with higher income will spend some of it on leisure by working less. This is the *income effect of a wage rate increase*.

---

[1] The pioneering work on this topic was done by Milton Friedman, *A Theory of the Consumption Function* (Princeton, NJ: Princeton University Press, 1957). In the mid-1960s, Franco Modigliani did closely related work that included the formulation of the life-cycle theory.

When wage rates rise, the substitution effect suggests that people will work more, while the income effect suggests that they will work less. The ultimate effect depends on which separate effect is more powerful. The data suggest that the substitution effect seems to win in most cases. That is, higher wage rates usually lead to a larger labor supply and lower wage rates usually lead to a lower labor supply.

Prices   Prices also play a major role in the consumption/labor supply decision. In our discussions of the possible effects of an increase in the wage rate, we have been assuming that the prices of goods and services do not rise at the same time. If the wage rate and all other prices rise simultaneously, the story is different. To make things clear, we need to distinguish between the nominal wage rate and the real wage rate.

nominal wage rate   The wage rate in current dollars.

real wage rate   The amount the nominal wage rate can buy in terms of goods and services.

The **nominal wage rate** is the wage rate in current dollars. When we adjust the nominal wage rate for changes in the price level, we obtain the **real wage rate**. The real wage rate measures the amount that wages can buy in terms of goods and services. Workers do not care about their nominal wage—they care about the purchasing power of this wage—the real wage.

Suppose skilled workers in Indianapolis were paid a wage rate of $20 per hour in 2008. Now suppose their wage rate rose to $22 in 2009, a 10 percent increase. If the prices of goods and services were the same in 2009 as they were in 2008, the real wage rate would have increased by 10 percent. An hour of work in 2009 ($22) buys 10 percent more than an hour of work in 2008 ($20). What if the prices of all goods and services also increased by 10 percent between 2008 and 2009? The purchasing power of an hour's wages has not changed. The real wage rate has not increased at all. In 2009, $22 bought the same quantity of goods and services that $20 bought in 2008.

To measure the real wage rate, we adjust the nominal wage rate with a price index. As we saw in Chapter 7, there are several such indexes that we might use, including the consumer price index and the GDP price index.[2]

We can now apply what we have learned from the life-cycle theory to our wage/price story. Recall that the life-cycle theory says that people look ahead in making their decisions. Translated to real wage rates, this idea says that households look at expected future real wage rates as well as the current real wage rate in making their current consumption and labor supply decisions. Consider, for example, medical students who expect that their real wage rate will be higher in the future. This expectation obviously has an effect on current decisions about things like how much to buy and whether to take a part-time job.

Wealth and Nonlabor Income   Life-cycle theory says that wealth fluctuates over the life cycle. Households accumulate wealth during their working years to pay off debts accumulated when they were young and to support themselves in retirement. This role of wealth is clear, but the existence of wealth poses another question. Consider two households that are at the same stage in their life cycle and have similar expectations about future wage rates, prices, and so on. They expect to live the same length of time, and both plan to leave the same amount to their children. They differ only in their wealth. Because of a past inheritance, household 1 has more wealth than household 2. Which household is likely to have a higher consumption path for the rest of its life? Household 1 is because it has more wealth to spread out over the rest of its life. Holding everything else constant (including the stage in the life cycle), the more wealth a household has, the more it will consume both now and in the future.

Now consider a household that has a sudden unexpected increase in wealth, perhaps an inheritance from a distant relative. How will the household's consumption pattern be affected? The household will increase its consumption both now and in the future as it spends the inheritance over the course of the rest of its life.

nonlabor, *or* **nonwage, income**   Any income received from sources other than working—inheritances, interest, dividends, transfer payments, and so on.

An increase in wealth can also be looked on as an increase in nonlabor income. **Nonlabor, or nonwage, income** is income received from sources other than working—inheritances, interest, dividends, and transfer payments such as welfare payments and Social Security payments. As

[2] To calculate the real wage rate, we divide the nominal wage rate by the price index. Suppose the wage rate rose from $10 per hour in 1994 to $18 per hour in 2006 and the price level rose 50 percent during the same period. Using 1994 as the base year, the price index would be 1.00 in 1994 and 1.50 in 2006. The real wage rate is W/P, where W is the nominal wage rate and P is the price level. Using 1994 as the base year, the real wage rate is $10 in 1994 ($10.00/1.00) and $12 in 2006 ($18.00/1.50).

with wealth, an unexpected increase in nonlabor income will have a positive effect on a household's consumption.

What about the effect of an increase in wealth or nonlabor income on labor supply? We already know that an increase in income results in an increase in the consumption of normal goods, including leisure. Therefore, an unexpected increase in wealth or nonlabor income results in an increase in consumption and an increase in leisure. With leisure increasing, labor supply must fall. So an unexpected increase in wealth or nonlabor income leads to a *decrease* in labor supply. This point should be obvious. If you suddenly win a million dollars in the state lottery or make a killing in the stock market, you will probably work less in the future than you otherwise would have.

Interest Rate Effects on Consumption

Recall from the last few chapters that the interest rate affects a firm's investment decision. A higher interest rate leads to a lower level of planned investment and vice versa. This was a key link between the money market and the goods market, and it was the channel through which monetary policy had an impact on planned aggregate expenditure.

We can now expand on this link: The interest rate also affects household behavior. Consider the effect of a fall in the interest rate on consumption. A fall in the interest rate lowers the reward to saving. If the interest rate falls from 10 percent to 5 percent, you earn 5¢ instead of 10¢ per year on every dollar saved. This means that the opportunity cost of spending a dollar today (instead of saving it and consuming it plus the interest income a year from now) has fallen. You will substitute toward current consumption and away from future consumption when the interest rate falls: You consume more today and save less. A rise in the interest rate leads you to consume less today and save more. This effect is called the *substitution effect*.

There is also an *income effect* of an interest rate change on consumption. If a household has positive wealth and is earning interest on that wealth, a fall in the interest rate leads to a fall in interest income. This is a decrease in its nonlabor income, which, as we just saw, has a negative effect on consumption. For households with positive wealth, the income effect works in the opposite direction from the substitution effect. On the other hand, if a household is a debtor and is paying interest on its debt, a fall in the interest rate will lead to a fall in interest payments. The household is better off in this case and will consume more. In this case, the income and substitution effects work in the same direction. The total household sector in the United States has positive wealth, and so in the aggregate, the income and substitution effects work in the opposite direction.

On balance, the data suggest that the substitution effect dominates the income effect so that the interest rate has a negative net effect on consumption: Interest rate increases cause consumption to fall. There is also some evidence, however, that the income effect is getting larger over time. U.S. households own most of the U.S. government debt, and the size of this debt has increased dramatically in the last 25 years. This means that the change in government interest payments (and so the change in household interest income) is now larger for a given change in interest rates than before, which leads to a larger income effect than before for a given change in interest rates. On net, this tells us that interest rate increases will cause consumption to fall less as the income effect grows.

Government Effects on Consumption and Labor Supply: Taxes and Transfers

The government influences household behavior mainly through income tax rates and transfer payments. When the government raises income tax rates, after-tax real wages decrease, lowering consumption. When the government lowers income tax rates, after-tax real wages increase, raising consumption. A change in income tax rates also affects labor supply. If the substitution effect dominates, as we are generally assuming, an increase in income tax rates, which lowers after-tax wages, will lower labor supply. A decrease in income tax rates will increase labor supply.

Transfer payments are payments such as Social Security benefits, veterans' benefits, and welfare benefits. An increase in transfer payments is an increase in nonlabor income, which we have seen has a positive effect on consumption and a negative effect on labor supply. Increases in transfer payments thus increase consumption and decrease labor supply, while decreases in transfer payments decrease consumption and increase labor supply. Table 16.1 summarizes these results.

TABLE 16.1	The Effects of Government on Household Consumption and Labor Supply			
	Income Tax Rates		Transfer Payments	
	Increase	Decrease	Increase	Decrease
Effect on consumption	Negative	Positive	Positive	Negative
Effect on labor supply	Negative*	Positive*	Negative	Positive

*If the substitution effect dominates.
Note: The effects are larger if they are expected to be permanent instead of temporary.

A Possible Employment Constraint on Households

Our discussion of the labor supply decision has so far proceeded as if households were free to choose how much to work each period. If a member of a household decides to work an additional 5 hours a week at the current wage rate, we have assumed that the person *can* work 5 hours more—that work is available. If someone who has not been working decides to work at the current wage rate, we have assumed that the person *can find a job*.

There are times when these assumptions do not hold. The Great Depression, when unemployment rates reached 25 percent of the labor force, led to the birth of macroeconomics in the 1930s. Since the mid-1970s, the United States has experienced four recessions, with millions of unemployed workers unable to find work.

When there is unemployment, some households feel an additional constraint on their behavior. Some people may want to work 40 hours per week at the current wage rates but may find only part-time work. Others may not find any work at all.

How does a household respond when it is constrained from working as much as it would like? It consumes less. If your current wage rate is $10 per hour and you normally work 40 hours a week, your normal income from wages is $400 per week. If your average tax rate is 20 percent, your after-tax wage income is $320 per week. You are likely to spend much of this income during the week. If you are prevented from working, this income will not be available to you and you will have less to spend. You will spend something, of course. You may receive some form of nonlabor income, and you may have assets such as savings deposits or stocks and bonds that can be withdrawn or sold. You also may be able to borrow during your period of unemployment. Even though you will spend something during the week, you almost certainly will spend less than you would have if you had your usual income of $320 in after-tax wages.

A household constrained from working as much as it would like at the current wage rate faces a different decision from the decision facing a household that can work as much as it wants. The work decision of the former household is, in effect, forced on it. The household works as much as it can—a certain number of hours per week or perhaps none at all—but this amount is less than the household would choose to work at the current wage rate if it could find more work. The amount that a household would like to work at the current wage rate if it could find the work is called its **unconstrained supply of labor**. The amount that the household actually works in a given period at current wage rates is called its **constrained supply of labor**.

A household's constrained supply of labor is not a variable over which it has any control. The amount of labor the household supplies is imposed on it from the outside by the workings of the economy. However, the household's consumption *is* under its control. We have just seen that the less a household works—that is, the smaller the household's constrained supply of labor is—the lower its consumption. Constraints on the supply of labor are an important determinant of consumption when there is unemployment.

unconstrained supply of labor The amount a household would like to work within a given period at the current wage rate if it could find the work.

constrained supply of labor The amount a household actually works in a given period at the current wage rate.

Keynesian Theory Revisited   Recall the Keynesian theory that current income determines current consumption. We now know the consumption decision is made jointly with the labor supply decision and the two depend on the real wage rate. It is incorrect to think that consumption depends only on income, at least when there is full employment. However, if there is unemployment, Keynes is closer to being correct because income is not determined by households. When there is unemployment, the level of income (at least workers' income) depends exclusively on the employment decisions made by firms. There are unemployed workers who are willing to work at the current wage rate, and their income is in effect determined by firms' hiring decisions. This income affects current consumption, which is consistent with Keynes's theory. This is one of the reasons Keynesian theory is considered to pertain to periods of unemployment. It was, of course, precisely during such a period that the theory was developed.

A Summary of Household Behavior

This completes our discussion of household behavior in the macroeconomy. Household consumption depends on more than current income. Households determine consumption and labor supply simultaneously, and they look ahead in making their decisions.

The following factors affect household consumption and labor supply decisions:

- Current and expected future real wage rates
- Initial value of wealth
- Current and expected future nonlabor income
- Interest rates
- Current and expected future tax rates and transfer payments

If households are constrained in their labor supply decisions, income is directly determined by firms' hiring decisions. In this case, we can say (in the traditional, Keynesian way) that "income" affects consumption.

The Household Sector Since 1970

To better understand household behavior, let us examine how some of the aggregate household variables have changed over time. We will discuss the period 1970 I–2007 IV. (Remember, Roman numerals refer to quarters, that is, 1970 I means the first quarter of 1970.) Within this span, there have been four recessionary periods: 1974 I–1975 IV, 1980 II–1983 I, 1990 III–1991 I, and 2001 I–2001 III. How did the household variables behave during each period?

Consumption   Data on the total consumption of the household sector are in the national income accounts. As we saw in Table 6.2 on p. 108, personal consumption expenditures accounted for 70.3 percent of GDP in 2007. The three basic categories of consumption expenditures are services, nondurable goods, and durable goods.

Figure 16.2 plots the data for consumption expenditures on services and nondurable goods combined and for consumption expenditures on durable goods. The variables are in real terms. You can see that expenditures on services and nondurable goods are "smoother" over time than expenditures on durable goods. For example, the decrease in expenditures on services and nondurable goods was much smaller during the four recessionary periods than the decrease in expenditures on durable goods.

Why do expenditures on durables fluctuate more than expenditures on services and nondurables? When times are bad, people can postpone the purchase of durable goods, which they do. It follows that expenditures on these goods change the most. When times are tough, you do not *have* to have a new car or a new washer-dryer; you can make do with your old Chevy or Maytag until things get better. When your income falls, it is not as easy to postpone the service costs of day care or health care. Nondurables fall into an intermediate category, with some items (such as new clothes) easier to postpone than others (such as food).

▶ **FIGURE 16.2**

Consumption Expenditures, 1970 I–2007 IV

Over time, expenditures on services and nondurable goods are "smoother" than expenditures on durable goods.

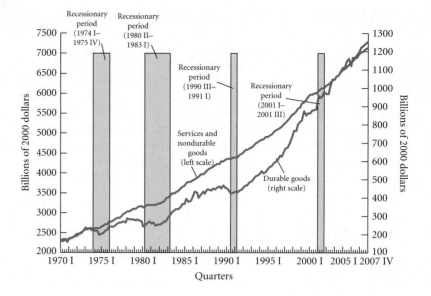

Housing Investment Another important expenditure of the household sector is housing investment (purchases of new housing), plotted in Figure 16.3. This variable fluctuates greatly, for at least two reasons. Housing investment is the most easily postponable of all household expenditures. Also, housing investment is sensitive to the general level of interest rates, and interest rates fluctuate considerably over time. When interest rates are low, housing investment is high and vice versa.

▶ **FIGURE 16.3**

Housing Investment of the Household Sector, 1970 I–2007 IV

Housing investment fell during the four recessionary periods since 1970. Like expenditures for durable goods, expenditures for housing investment are postponable.

Labor Supply As we noted in Chapters 7 and 14, a person is considered a part of the labor force when he or she is working or has been actively looking for work in the past few weeks. The ratio of the labor force to the total working-age population—those 16 and over—is the *labor force participation rate*.

It is informative to divide the labor force into three categories: males 25 to 54, females 25 to 54, and all others 16 and over. Ages 25 to 54 are sometimes called "prime" ages, presuming that a person is in the prime of working life during these ages. The participation rates for these three groups are plotted in Figure 16.4.

As the figure shows, most men of prime age are in the labor force, although the participation rate has fallen slightly since 1970—from .961 in 1970 I to .909 in 2007 IV. (A rate of .909 means that

ECONOMICS IN PRACTICE

Housing Problems Spread to the Rest of the Economy

Housing prices fell across much of the United States in 2007 and 2008. For many households, housing constitutes a large portion of their wealth. So a fall in housing prices translates into a large fall in wealth for households. The lessons of this chapter suggest—as the following article confirms—that the consequence of a housing-related wealth decrease is a cutback in other household consumption. The article describes the recent housing slowdown and its consequences for the U.S. economy, along with the attempts by the Federal Reserve (Fed) to counteract these effects with an interest rate cut.

Decline in Home Prices Accelerates: Fed's Efforts Have Only Muted Effect On Mortgage Rates

Wall Street Journal

The decline in U.S. home prices accelerated in the fourth quarter, according to two leading barometers, compounding two of the biggest threats facing the nation's economy: faltering consumer spending and tight credit markets.

The S&P/Case-Shiller national home-price index for the fourth quarter fell 8.9% from a year earlier, the largest drop in its 20 years of data. And the Office of Federal Housing Enterprise Oversight's index—which tracks only homes purchased with mortgages guaranteed by home-loan giants Fannie Mae or Freddie Mac—was down 0.3%, the first year-to-year decline in the measure's 16 years.

Lower home prices threaten the economy's growth by making consumers feel less wealthy and thus less willing to spend. They also curtail home-owners' ability to borrow against the value of their homes to finance other purchases. In addition,

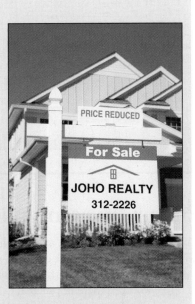

lower housing prices erode the value of banks' collateral, prompting them to tighten their lending standards, which further damps the economic growth.

A top Federal Reserve official indicated the housing slump and its broadening impact on the economy probably would keep the central bank biased in favor of more interest-rate cuts. "It appears that the correction in the housing market has further to go," Fed Vice Chairman Donald Kohn said yesterday in a speech in North Carolina. Mr. Kohn said that the downturn, after being "contained" for nearly two years, "appears to have spread to other sectors of the economy." He added that if the housing market deteriorates more than expected, "lenders might further reduce credit availability."

The housing-market slump also is taking its toll on consumer sentiment, which could lead to further pullbacks in spending, depressing the economy. The Conference Board, a New York-based business-research group, said yesterday that its index of consumer confidence fell sharply to 75.0 in February from 87.3 in January. The index is closely watched because consumer spending drives much of the U.S. economy.

"Consumer spending is going to take a hit," said Patrick Newport, an economist at Global Insight in Waltham, Mass. "The hit will be bigger the more home prices drop."

Source: Kelly Evans, Serena Ng and Ruth Simon, February 27, 2008

90.9 percent of prime-age men were in the labor force.) The participation rate for prime-age women, on the other hand, rose dramatically between 1970 and 1990—from .501 in 1970 I to .741 in 1990 I. Although economic factors account for some of this increase, a change in social attitudes and preferences probably explains much of the increase. Since 1990, the participation rate for prime-age women has changed very little. In 2007 IV, it was .755, still considerably below the .909 rate for prime-age men.

Figure 16.4 also shows the participation rate for all individuals 16 and over except prime-age men and women. This rate has some cyclical features—it tends to fall in recessions and to rise or fall less during expansions. These features reveal the operation of the *discouraged-worker effect*, discussed in Chapter 7. During recessions, some people get discouraged about ever finding a job. They stop looking and are then not considered a part of the labor force. During expansions, people become encouraged again. Once they begin looking for jobs, they are again considered a part of the labor force. Because prime-age women and men are likely to be fairly attached to the labor force, the discouraged-worker effect for them is quite small.

▶ **FIGURE 16.4**

Labor Force Participation Rates for Men 25 to 54, Women 25 to 54, and All Others 16 and Over, 1970 I–2007 IV

Since 1970, the labor force participation rate for prime-age men has been decreasing slightly. The rate for prime-age women has been increasing dramatically. The rate for all others 16 and over has been declining since 1979 and shows a tendency to fall during recessions (the discouraged-worker effect).

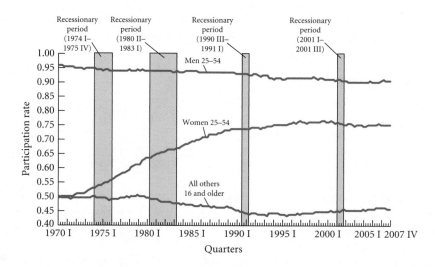

Firms: Investment and Employment Decisions

Having taken a closer look at the behavior of households in the macroeconomy, we now look more closely at the behavior of firms—the other major decision-making unit in the economy. In discussing firm behavior earlier, we assumed that planned investment depends only on the interest rate. However, there are several other determinants of planned investment. We now discuss them and the factors that affect firms' employment decisions. Once again, microeconomic theory can help us gain some insight into the working of the macroeconomy.

In a market economy, firms determine which goods and services are available to consumers today and which will be available in the future, how many workers are needed for what kinds of jobs, and how much investment will be undertaken. Stated in macroeconomic terms, the decisions of firms, taken together, determine output, labor demand, and investment.

Expectations and Animal Spirits

Time is a key factor in investment decisions. Capital has a life that typically extends over many years. A developer who decides to build an office tower is making an investment that will be around (barring earthquakes, floods, or tornadoes) for several decades. In deciding where to build a plant, a manufacturing firm is committing a large amount of resources to purchase capital that will presumably yield services over a long time. Furthermore, the decision to build a plant or to purchase large equipment must often be made years before the actual project is completed. Whereas the acquisition of a small business computer may take only a few days, the planning process for downtown developments in large U.S. cities has been known to take decades.

For these reasons, investment decisions require looking into the future and forming expectations about it. In forming their expectations, firms consider numerous factors. At a minimum, they gather information about the demand for their specific products, about what their competitors are planning, and about the macroeconomy's overall health. A firm is not likely to increase its production capacity if it does not expect to sell more of its product in the future. Hilton will not put up a new hotel if it does not expect to fill the rooms at a profitable rate. Ford will not build a new plant if it expects the economy to enter a long recession.

Forecasting the future is fraught with dangers. Many events cannot be foreseen. Investments are therefore always made with imperfect knowledge. Keynes pointed this out in 1936:

> The outstanding fact is the extreme precariousness of the basis of knowledge on which our estimates of prospective yield have to be made. Our knowledge of the factors which will govern the yield of an investment some years hence is usually very slight and often negligible. If we speak frankly, we have to admit that our basis of knowledge for estimating the yield ten years hence of a railway, a copper mine, a textile factory, the goodwill of a patent medicine, an Atlantic liner, a building in the City of London amounts to little and sometimes nothing.

Keynes concludes from this line of thought that much investment activity depends on psychology and on what he calls the **animal spirits of entrepreneurs**:

> Our decisions . . . can only be taken as a result of animal spirits. In estimating the prospects of investment, we must have regard, therefore, to nerves and hysteria and even the digestions and reactions to the weather of those upon whose spontaneous activity it largely depends.[3]

animal spirits of entrepreneurs A term coined by Keynes to describe investors' feelings.

Because expectations about the future are, as Keynes points out, subject to great uncertainty, they may change often. Thus, animal spirits help to make investment a volatile component of GDP.

The Accelerator Effect Expectations, at least in part, determine the level of planned investment spending. At any interest rate, the level of investment is likely to be higher if businesses are optimistic. If businesses are pessimistic, the level of planned investment will be lower, but what determines expectations?

One possibility, is that expectations are optimistic when aggregate output (Y) is rising and pessimistic when aggregate output is falling. At any given level of the interest rate, expectations may be more optimistic and planned investment higher when output is growing rapidly than when it is growing slowly or falling. It is easy to see why this might be so. When firms expect future prospects to be good, they may plan now to add productive capacity, and one indicator of future prospects is the current growth rate.

If this is the case in reality, the ultimate result will be an **accelerator effect**. If aggregate output (income) (Y) is rising, investment will increase even though the level of Y may be low. Higher investment spending leads to an added increase in output, further "accelerating" the growth of aggregate output. If Y is falling, expectations are dampened and investment spending will be cut even though the level of Y may be high, accelerating the decline.

accelerator effect The tendency for investment to increase when aggregate output increases and to decrease when aggregate output decreases, accelerating the growth or decline of output.

Profit Maximization

When firms decide to increase output, perhaps because of new animal spirits, they will typically need to increase their inputs. By **inputs**, we mean the goods and services that firms purchase and turn into output. Two important inputs that firms use are capital and labor. (Other inputs are energy, raw materials, and semifinished goods.) Each period firms must decide how much capital and labor to use in producing output.

At any point in time, a firm has a certain stock of capital on hand. *Stock of capital* means the factories and buildings (sometimes called "plants") that firms own, the equipment they need to do business, and their inventories of partly or wholly finished goods. Firms add to their capital stock by buying machinery and building new factories. This kind of addition to the capital stock is **plant-and-equipment investment**.

inputs The goods and services that firms purchase and turn into output.

plant-and-equipment investment Purchases by firms of additional machines, factories, or buildings within a given period.

[3] John Maynard Keynes, *The General Theory of Employment, Interest, and Money (1936)*, First Harbinger Ed. (New York: Harcourt Brace Jovanovich, 1964), pp. 149, 152.

In addition to decisions about capital investments, firms also make employment decisions. At the beginning of each period, a firm has a certain number of workers on its payroll. On the basis of its current situation and its upcoming plans, the firm must decide whether to hire additional workers, keep the same number, or reduce its workforce by laying off some employees.

To start our analysis, we assume that firms make choices about capital investment and employment levels to maximize their profits. One of the most important profit-maximizing decisions that a firm must make is how to produce its output. In most cases, a firm must choose among alternative methods of production, or technologies. Different technologies generally require different combinations of capital and labor.

Consider a factory that manufactures shirts. Shirts can be made entirely by hand, with workers cutting the pieces of fabric and sewing them together. However, shirts like those can be made on complex machines that cut and sew and produce shirts with very little human supervision. Between these two extremes are dozens of alternative technologies. Shirts can be partly hand-sewn, with the stitching done on electric sewing machines.

Firms' decisions concerning the amount of capital and labor they will use in production are closely related. If firms maximize profits, they will choose the technology that minimizes the cost of production. That is, it is logical to assume that firms will choose the technology that is most efficient.

The most efficient technology depends on the relative prices of capital and labor. A shirt factory in the Philippines that decides to increase its production faces a large supply of relatively inexpensive labor. Wage rates in the Philippines are quite low. Capital equipment must be imported and is very expensive. A shirt factory in the Philippines is likely to choose a **labor-intensive technology**—a large amount of labor relative to capital. When labor-intensive technologies are used, expansion is likely to increase the demand for labor substantially while increasing the demand for capital only modestly.

A shirt factory in Germany that decides to expand production is likely to buy a large amount of capital equipment and to hire relatively few new workers. It will probably choose a **capital-intensive technology**—a large amount of capital relative to labor. German wage rates are quite high, higher in many occupations than in the United States. Capital, however, is plentiful. Firms' decisions about labor demand and investment are likely to depend on the relative costs of labor and capital. The relative impact of an expansion of output on employment and investment demand depends on the wage rate and the cost of capital.

labor-intensive technology A production technique that uses a large amount of labor relative to capital.

capital-intensive technology A production technique that uses a large amount of capital relative to labor.

Excess Labor and Excess Capital Effects

excess labor, excess capital Labor and capital that are not needed to produce the firm's current level of output.

In practice, firms appear at times to hold what we will call **excess labor** and/or **excess capital**. A firm holds excess labor (or capital) if it can reduce the amount of labor it employs (or capital it holds) and still produce the same amount of output. Why would a firm want to employ more workers or have more capital on hand than it needs? Both labor and capital are costly—a firm has to pay wages to its workers, and it forgoes interest on funds tied up in machinery or buildings. Why would a firm want to incur costs that do not yield revenue?

To see why, suppose a firm suffers a sudden and large decrease in sales, but it expects the lower sales level to last only a few months, after which it believes sales will pick up again. In this case, the firm is likely to lower production in response to the sales change to avoid too large an increase in its stock of inventories. This decrease in production means that the firm could get rid of some workers and some machines because it needs less labor and less capital to produce the now-lower level of output.

However, things are not that simple. Decreasing its workforce and capital stock quickly can be costly for a firm. Abrupt cuts in the workforce hurt worker morale and may increase personnel administration costs, and abrupt reductions in capital stock may be disadvantageous because of the difficulty of selling used machines. These types of costs are sometimes called **adjustment costs** because they are the costs of adjusting to the new level of output. There are also adjustment costs to increasing output. For example, it is usually costly to recruit and train new workers.

adjustment costs The costs that a firm incurs when it changes its production level—for example, the administration costs of laying off employees or the training costs of hiring new workers.

Adjustment costs may be large enough that a firm chooses not to decrease its workforce and capital stock when production falls. The firm may at times choose to have more labor and capital on hand than it needs to produce its current amount of output simply because getting rid of them is more costly than keeping them. In practice, excess labor takes the form of workers not working at their normal level of activity (more coffee breaks and more idle time, for instance). Some of this excess labor may receive new training so that productivity will be higher when production picks up again.

The existence of excess labor and capital at any given moment is likely to affect future employment and investment decisions. Suppose a firm already has excess labor and capital due to a fall in its sales and production. When production picks up again, the firm will not need to hire as many new workers or acquire as much new capital as it would otherwise. The more excess capital a firm already has, the less likely it is to invest in new capital in the future. The more excess labor it has, the less likely it is to hire new workers in the future.

Inventory Investment

We now turn to a brief discussion of the inventory investment decision. **Inventory investment** is the change in the stock of inventories. Although inventory investment is another way in which a firm adds to its capital stock, the inventory investment decision is quite different from the plant-and-equipment investment decision.

inventory investment The change in the stock of inventories.

The Role of Inventories Recall the distinction between a firm's sales and its output. If a firm can hold goods in inventory, which is usually the case unless the good is perishable or unless the firm produces services, then within a given period, it can sell a quantity of goods that differs from the quantity of goods it produces during that period. When a firm sells more than it produces, its stock of inventories decreases; when it sells less than it produces, its stock of inventories increases.

Stock of inventories (end of period) = Stock of inventories (beginning of period) + Production − Sales

If a firm starts a period with 100 umbrellas in inventory, produces 15 umbrellas during the period, and sells 10 umbrellas in this same interval, it will have 105 umbrellas (100 + 15 − 10) in inventory at the end of the period. A change in the stock of inventories is actually investment because inventories are counted as part of a firm's capital stock. In our example, inventory investment during the period is a positive number, 5 umbrellas (105 − 100). When the number of goods produced is less than the number of goods sold, such as 5 produced and 10 sold, inventory investment is negative.

The Optimal Inventory Policy We can now consider firms' inventory decisions. Firms are concerned with what they are going to sell and produce in the future as well as what they are selling and producing currently. At each point in time, a firm has some idea of how much it is going to sell in the current period and in future periods. Given these expectations and its knowledge of how much of its good it already has in stock, a firm must decide how much to produce in the current period.

Inventories are costly to a firm because they take up space and they tie up funds that could be earning interest. However, if a firm's stock of inventories gets too low, the firm may have difficulty meeting the demand for its product, especially if demand increases unexpectedly. The firm may lose sales. The point between too low and too high a stock of inventory is called the **desired**, or **optimal, level of inventories**. This is the level at which the extra cost (in lost sales) from decreasing inventories by a small amount is just equal to the extra gain (in interest revenue and decreased storage costs).

desired, *or* **optimal, level of inventories** The level of inventory at which the extra cost (in lost sales) from lowering inventories by a small amount is just equal to the extra gain (in interest revenue and decreased storage costs).

A firm that had no costs other than inventory costs would always aim to produce in a period exactly the volume of goods necessary to make its stock of inventories at the end of the period equal to the desired stock. If the stock of inventory fell lower than desired, the firm would produce more than it expected to sell to bring the stock up. If the stock of inventory grew above the desired level, the firm would produce less than it expected to sell to reduce the stock.

There are other costs to running a firm besides inventory costs. In particular, large and abrupt changes in production can be very costly because it is often disruptive to change a production process geared to a certain rate of output. If production is to be increased, there may be adjustment costs for hiring more labor and increasing the capital stock. If production is to be decreased, there may be adjustment costs in laying off workers and decreasing the capital stock.

Because holding inventories and changing production levels are both costly, firms face a trade-off between them. Because of adjustment costs, a firm is likely to smooth its production path relative to its sales path. This means that a firm is likely to have its production fluctuate less than its sales, with changes in inventories to absorb the difference each period. However, because there are incentives not to stray too far from the optimal level of inventories, fluctuations in production are not eliminated completely. Production is still likely to fluctuate, just not as much as sales fluctuate.

Two other points need to be made here. First, if a firm's stock of inventories is unusually or unexpectedly high, the firm is likely to produce less in the future than it otherwise would have in order to decrease its high stock of inventories. In other words, although the stock of inventories fluctuates over time because production is smoothed relative to sales, at any point in time, inventories may be unexpectedly high or low because sales have been unexpectedly low or high. An unexpectedly high stock will have a negative effect on production in the future, and an unexpectedly low stock will have a positive effect on production in the future. An unexpected increase in inventories has a negative effect on future production, and an unexpected decrease in inventories has a positive effect on future production.

Second, firms do not know their future sales exactly. They have expectations of future sales, and these expectations may not turn out to be exactly right. This has important consequences. If sales turn out to be less than expected, inventories will be higher than expected and there will be less production in the future. Furthermore, *future* sales expectations are likely to have an important effect on *current* production. If a firm expects its sales to be high in the future, it will adjust its planned production path accordingly. Even though a firm smooths production relative to sales, over a long time, it must produce as much as it sells. If it does not, it will eventually run out of inventories. The level of a firm's planned production path depends on the level of its expected future sales path. If a firm's expectations of the level of its future sales path decrease, the firm is likely to decrease the level of its planned production path, including its actual production in the current period. Current production depends on expected future sales.

Because production is likely to depend on expectations of the future, animal spirits may play a role. If firms become more optimistic about the future, they are likely to produce more now. Keynes's view that animal spirits affect investment is also likely to pertain to output.

A Summary of Firm Behavior

The following factors affect firms' investment and employment decisions:

- Firms' expectations of future output
- Wage rate and cost of capital (the interest rate is an important component of the cost of capital)
- Amount of excess labor and excess capital on hand

The most important points to remember about the relationship among production, sales, and inventory investment are

- Inventory investment—that is, the change in the stock of inventories—equals production minus sales.
- An unexpected increase in the stock of inventories has a negative effect on future production.
- Current production depends on expected future sales.

The Firm Sector Since 1970

To close our discussion of firm behavior, we now examine some aggregate investment and employment variables for the period 1970 I–2007 IV.

Plant-and-Equipment Investment   Plant-and-equipment investment by the firm sector is plotted in Figure 16.5. Investment fared poorly in the four recessionary periods after 1970. This observation is consistent with the observation that investment depends in part on output. An examination of the plot of real GDP in Figure 5.4 in on p. 98 and the plot of investment in Figure 16.5 shows that investment generally does poorly when GDP does poorly and that investment generally does well when GDP does well.

Figure 16.5 also shows that investment fluctuates greatly. This is not surprising. The animal spirits of entrepreneurs are likely to be volatile, and if animal spirits affect investment, it follows that investment too will be volatile.

◀ **FIGURE 16.5**

Plant-and-Equipment Investment of the Firm Sector, 1970 I–2007 IV

Overall, plant-and-equipment investment declined in the four recessionary periods since 1970.

Despite the volatility of plant-and-equipment investment, however, it is still true that housing investment fluctuates more than plant-and-equipment investment (as you can see by comparing Figures 16.3 and 16.5). Plant-and-equipment investment is not the most volatile component of GDP.

Employment   Employment in the firm sector is plotted in Figure 16.6, which shows that employment fell in all four recessionary periods. This is consistent with the theory that employment depends in part on output. Otherwise, employment has grown over time in response to the growing economy. Employment in the firm sector rose from 72.7 million in 1970 I to 132.8 million in 2007 IV.

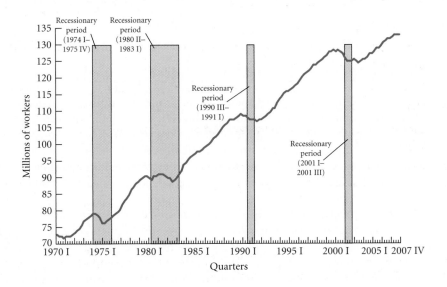

◀ **FIGURE 16.6**

Employment in the Firm Sector, 1970 I–2007 IV

Growth in employment was generally negative in the four recessions the U.S. economy has experienced since 1970.

Inventory Investment   Recall that *inventory investment* is the difference between the level of output and the level of sales. Recall also that some inventory investment is usually unplanned. This occurs when the actual level of sales is different from the expected level of sales.

Inventory investment of the firm sector is plotted in Figure 16.7. Also plotted in this figure is the ratio of the stock of inventories to the level of sales—the *inventory/sales ratio*. The figure shows that inventory investment is very volatile—more volatile than housing investment and plant-and-equipment investment. Some of this volatility is undoubtedly due to the unplanned component of inventory investment, which is likely to fluctuate greatly from one period to the next.

▶ **FIGURE 16.7**

Inventory Investment of the Firm Sector and the Inventory/Sales Ratio, 1970 I–2007 IV

The inventory/sales ratio is the ratio of the firm sector's stock of inventories to the level of sales. Inventory investment is very volatile.

When the inventory/sales ratio is high, the actual stock of inventories is likely to be larger than the desired stock. In such a case, firms have overestimated demand and produced too much relative to sales and they are likely to want to produce less in the future to draw down their stock. You can find several examples of this trend in Figure 16.7—the clearest occurred during the 1974–1975 period. At the end of 1974, the stock of inventories was very high relative to sales, an indication that firms probably had undesired inventories at the end of 1974. In 1975, firms worked off these undesired inventories by producing less than they sold. Thus, inventory investment was very low in 1975. The year 1975 is clearly a year in which output would have been higher had the stock of inventories at the beginning of the year not been so high. There was a huge fall in inventory investment in 2001.

On average, the inventory/sales ratio has been declining over time, evidence that firms are becoming more efficient in their management of inventory stocks. Firms are becoming more efficient in the sense of being able (other things equal) to hold smaller and smaller stocks of inventories relative to sales.

Productivity and the Business Cycle

productivity, *or* **labor productivity** Output per worker hour; the amount of output produced by an average worker in 1 hour.

We can now use what we have just learned about firm behavior to analyze movements in productivity. **Productivity**, sometimes called **labor productivity**, is defined as output per worker hour. If output is Y and the number of hours worked in the economy is H, productivity is Y/H. Simply stated, productivity measures how much output an average worker produces in 1 hour.

Productivity fluctuates over the business cycle, tending to rise during expansions and fall during contractions. The fact that firms at times hold excess labor explains why productivity fluctuates in the same direction as output.

Figure 16.8 shows the pattern of employment and output over time for a hypothetical economy. Employment does not fluctuate as much as output over the business cycle. It is precisely this pattern that leads to higher productivity during periods of high output and lower productivity during periods of low output. During expansions in the economy, output rises by a larger percentage than employment and the ratio of output to workers rises. During downswings, output falls faster than employment and the ratio of output to workers falls.

The existence of excess labor when the economy is in a slump means that productivity as measured by the ratio Y/H tends to fall at such times. Does this trend mean that labor is in some sense "less productive" during recessions than before? Not really: It means only that firms choose to employ more labor than they need. For this reason, some workers are in effect idle some of the time even though they are considered employed. They are not less productive in the sense of having less potential to produce output; they are merely not working part of the time that they are *counted* as working.

Productivity in the Long Run Theories of long-run economic behavior, which attempt to explain how and why economies grow over time, focus on productivity, usually measured in this case as *output per worker* or its closely related measure, *GDP per capita*. Productivity defined

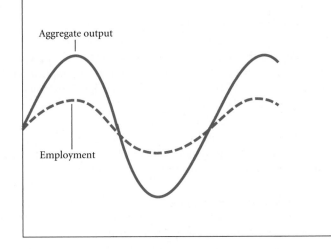

Employment and Output over the Business Cycle

In general, employment does not fluctuate as much as output over the business cycle. As a result, measured productivity (the output-to-labor ratio) tends to rise during expansionary periods and decline during contractionary periods.

this way is a key index of an economy's performance over the long run. Productivity figures can, however, be misleading when used to diagnose the health of the economy over the short run because business cycles can distort the meaning of productivity measurements. Output per worker falls in recessions because firms hold excess labor during slumps. Output per worker rises in expansions because firms put the excess labor back to work. Neither of these conditions has anything to do with the economy's long-run potential to produce output. We discuss long-run growth in the next chapter.

The Short-Run Relationship Between Output and Unemployment

We can also use what we have learned about household and firm behavior to analyze the relationship between output and unemployment. When we discussed the connections between the *AS/AD* diagram and the Phillips Curve in Chapter 14, we mentioned that output (*Y*) and the unemployment rate (*U*) are inversely related. When output rises, the unemployment rate falls, and when output falls, the unemployment rate rises. At one time, it was believed that the short-run relationship between the two variables was fairly stable. **Okun's Law** (after U.S. economist Arthur Okun, who first studied the relationship) stated that in the short run the unemployment rate decreased about 1 percentage point for every 3 percent increase in real GDP. As with the Phillips Curve, Okun's Law has not turned out to be a "law." The economy is far too complex for there to be such a simple and stable relationship between two macroeconomic variables.

Although the short-run relationship between output and the unemployment rate is not the simple relationship Okun believed, it is true that a 1 percent increase in output tends to correspond to a less than 1 percentage point decrease in the unemployment rate in the short run. In other words, there are a number of "slippages" between changes in output and changes in the unemployment rate.

The first slippage is between the change in output and the change in the number of jobs in the economy. When output increases by 1 percent, the number of jobs does not tend to rise by 1 percent in the short run. There are two reasons for this. First, a firm is likely to meet some of the increase in output by increasing the number of hours worked per job. Instead of having the labor force work 40 hours per week, the firm may pay overtime and have the labor force work 42 hours per week. Second, if a firm is holding excess labor at the time of the output increase, at least part of the increase in output can come from putting the excess labor back to work. For both reasons, the number of jobs is likely to rise by a smaller percentage than the increase in output.

The second slippage is between the change in the number of *jobs* and the change in the *number of people employed*. If you have two jobs, you are counted twice in the job data but only once in the persons-employed data. Because some people have two jobs, there are more jobs than there are people employed. When the number of jobs increases, some of the new jobs are filled by

Okun's Law The theory, put forth by Arthur Okun, that in the short run the unemployment rate decreases about 1 percentage point for every 3 percent increase in real GDP. Later research and data have shown that the relationship between output and unemployment is not as stable as Okun's "Law" predicts.

people who already have one job (instead of by people who are unemployed). This means that the increase in the number of people employed is less than the increase in the number of jobs. This is a slippage between output and the unemployment rate because the unemployment rate is calculated from data on the number of people employed, not the number of jobs.

The third slippage concerns the response of the labor force to an increase in output. Let E denote the number of people employed, let L denote the number of people in the labor force, and let u denote the unemployment rate. In these terms, the unemployment rate is

$$u = 1 - E/L$$

The unemployment rate is 1 minus the employment rate, E/L.

discouraged-worker effect The decline in the measured unemployment rate that results when people who want to work but cannot find work grow discouraged and stop looking, dropping out of the ranks of the unemployed and the labor force.

When we discussed how the unemployment rate is measured in Chapter 7, we introduced the **discouraged-worker effect**. A discouraged worker is one who would like a job but has stopped looking because the prospects seem so bleak. When output increases, job prospects begin to look better and some people who had stopped looking for work begin looking again. When they do, they are once again counted as part of the labor force. The labor force increases when output increases because discouraged workers are moving back into the labor force. This is another reason the unemployment rate does not fall as much as might be expected when output increases.

These three slippages show that the link from changes in output to changes in the unemployment rate is complicated. All three combine to make the change in the unemployment rate less than the percentage change in output in the short run. They also show that the relationship between changes in output and changes in the unemployment rate is not likely to be stable. The size of the first slippage, for example, depends on how much excess labor is being held at the time of the output increase, and the size of the third slippage depends on what else is affecting the labor force (such as changes in real wage rates) at the time of the output increase. The relationship between output and unemployment depends on the state of the economy at the time of the output change.

The Size of the Multiplier

We can finally bring together the material in this chapter and in previous chapters to consider the size of the multiplier. We mentioned in Chapter 8 that much of the analysis we would do after deriving the simple multiplier would have the effect of decreasing the size of the multiplier. We can now summarize why.

1. There are *automatic stabilizers*. We saw in the Appendix to Chapter 9 that if taxes are not a fixed amount but instead depend on income (which is surely the case in practice), the size of the multiplier is decreased. When the economy expands and income increases, the amount of taxes collected increases. The rise in taxes acts to offset some of the expansion (thus, a smaller multiplier). When the economy contracts and income decreases, the amount of taxes collected decreases. This decrease in taxes helps to lessen the contraction. Some transfer payments also respond to the state of the economy and act as automatic stabilizers, lowering the value of the multiplier. Unemployment benefits are the best example of transfer payments that increase during contractions and decrease during expansions.

2. There is the *interest rate*. We saw in Chapter 12 that if government spending increases and the money supply remains unchanged, the interest rate increases, which decreases planned investment and aggregate output (income). This *crowding out* of planned investment decreases the value of the multiplier. As we saw earlier in this chapter, increases in the interest rate also have a negative effect on consumption. Consumption is also crowded out in the same way that planned investment is, and this effect lowers the value of the multiplier even further.

3. There is the response of the *price level*. We also saw in Chapter 12 that some of the effect of an expansionary policy is to increase the price level. The multiplier is smaller because of this price response. The multiplier is particularly small when the economy is on the steep part of the AS curve, where most of the effect of an expansionary policy is to increase prices.

4. There are *excess capital* and *excess labor*. When firms are holding excess labor and capital, part of any output increase can come from putting the excess labor and capital back to work instead of increasing employment and investment. This lowers the value of the multiplier because (1) investment increases less than it would have if there were no excess capital and (2) consumption increases less than it would have if employment (and thus household income) had increased more.

5. There are *inventories*. Part of any initial increase in sales can come from drawing down inventories instead of increasing output. To the extent that firms draw down their inventories in the short run, the value of the multiplier is lower because output does not respond as quickly to demand changes.

6. There are people's *expectations* about the future. People look ahead, and they respond less to temporary changes than to permanent changes. The multiplier effects for policy changes perceived to be temporary are smaller than those for policy changes perceived to be permanent.

The Size of the Multiplier in Practice   In practice, the multiplier probably has a value of around 1.4. Its size also depends on how long ago the spending increase began. For example, in the first quarter of an increase in government spending, the multiplier is only about 1.1. If government spending rises by $1 billion, GDP will increase by about $1.1 billion during the first quarter. In the second quarter, the multiplier will rise to about 1.3. The multiplier then will rise to its peak of about 1.4 in the third or fourth quarter.

One of the main points to remember here is that if the government is contemplating a monetary or fiscal policy change, the response of the economy to the change is not likely to be large and quick. It takes time for the full effects to be felt, and in the final analysis, the effects are much smaller than the simple multiplier we discussed in Chapter 8 would lead one to believe.

A good way to review much of the material since Chapter 8 is to make sure you clearly understand how the value of the multiplier is affected by each of the additions to the simple model in Chapter 8. We have come a long way since then, and this review may help you to put all the pieces together.

S U M M A R Y

HOUSEHOLDS: CONSUMPTION AND LABOR SUPPLY DECISIONS *p. 297*

1. The *life-cycle theory of consumption* says that households make lifetime consumption decisions based on their expectations of lifetime income. Generally, households consume an amount less than their incomes during their prime working years and an amount greater than their incomes during their early working years and after they have retired.

2. Households make consumption and labor supply decisions simultaneously. Consumption cannot be considered separately from labor supply because it is precisely by selling your labor that you earn the income that makes consumption possible.

3. There is a trade-off between the goods and services that wage income will buy and leisure or other nonmarket activities. The wage rate is the key variable that determines how a household responds to this trade-off.

4. Changes in the wage rate have both an income effect and a substitution effect. The evidence suggests that the substitution effect seems to dominate for most people, which means that the aggregate labor supply responds positively to an increase in the wage rate.

5. Consumption increases when the wage rate increases.

6. The *nominal wage rate* is the wage rate in current dollars. The *real wage rate* is the amount the nominal wage can buy in terms of goods and services. Households look at expected future real wage rates as well as the current real wage rate in making their consumption and labor supply decisions.

7. Holding all else constant (including the stage in the life cycle), the more wealth a household has, the more it will consume both now and in the future.

8. An unexpected increase in *nonlabor income* (any income received from sources other than working, such as inheritances,

interest, and dividends) will have a positive effect on a household's consumption and will lead to a decrease in labor supply.

9. The interest rate also affects consumption, although the direction of the total effect depends on the relative sizes of the income and substitution effects. There is some evidence that the income effect is larger now than it used to be, making monetary policy less effective than it used to be.

10. The government influences household behavior mainly through income tax rates and transfer payments. If the substitution effect dominates, an increase in tax rates lowers after-tax income, decreases consumption, and decreases the labor supply; a decrease in tax rates raises after-tax income, increases consumption, and increases labor supply. Increases in transfer payments increase consumption and decrease labor supply; decreases in transfer payments decrease consumption and increase labor supply.

11. During times of unemployment, households' labor supply may be constrained. Households may want to work a certain number of hours at current wage rates but may not be allowed to do so by firms. In this case, the level of income (at least workers' income) depends exclusively on the employment decisions made by firms. Households consume less if they are constrained from working.

FIRMS: INVESTMENT AND EMPLOYMENT DECISIONS *p.306*

12. Expectations affect investment and employment decisions. Keynes used the term *animal spirits of entrepreneurs* to refer to investors' feelings.

13. At any level of the interest rate, expectations are likely to be more optimistic and planned investment is likely to be higher when output is growing rapidly than when it is growing slowly or falling. The result is an *accelerator effect* that can cause the economy to expand more rapidly during an expansion and contract more quickly during a recession.

14. Firms purchase *inputs* and turn them into outputs. Each period firms must decide how much capital and labor (two major inputs) to use in producing output. Firms can invest in plants and equipment or in inventory.

15. Because output can be produced using many different technologies, firms must make capital and labor decisions simultaneously. A *labor-intensive technique* uses a large amount of labor relative to capital. A *capital-intensive technique* uses a large amount of capital relative to labor. Which technology to use depends on the wage rate and the cost of capital.

16. *Excess labor and capital* are labor and capital not needed to produce a firm's current level of output. Holding excess labor and capital may be more efficient than laying off workers or selling used equipment. The more excess capital a firm has, the less likely it is to invest in new capital in the future. The more excess labor it has, the less likely it is to hire new workers in the future.

17. Holding inventories is costly to a firm because they take up space and they tie up funds that could be earning interest. Not holding inventories can cause a firm to lose sales if demand increases. The *desired*, or *optimal*, *level of inventories* is the level at which the extra cost (in lost sales) from lowering inventories by a small amount is equal to the extra gain (in interest revenue and decreased storage costs).

18. An unexpected increase in inventories has a negative effect on future production, and an unexpected decrease in inventories has a positive effect on future production.

19. The level of a firm's planned production path depends on the level of its expected future sales path. If a firm's expectations of its future sales path decrease, the firm is likely to decrease the level of its planned production path, including its actual production in the current period.

PRODUCTIVITY AND THE BUSINESS CYCLE *p. 312*

20. *Productivity*, or *labor productivity*, is output per worker hour—the amount of output produced by an average worker in 1 hour. Productivity fluctuates over the business cycle, tending to rise during expansions and fall during contractions. That workers are less productive during contractions does not mean that they have less potential to produce output; it means that excess labor exists and that workers are not working at their capacity.

THE SHORT-RUN RELATIONSHIP BETWEEN OUTPUT AND UNEMPLOYMENT *p. 313*

21. There is a negative relationship between output and unemployment: When output (Y) rises, the unemployment rate (U) falls, and when output falls, the unemployment rate rises. *Okun's Law* stated that in the short run the unemployment rate decreases about 1 percentage point for every 3 percent increase in GDP. Okun's Law is not a "law"—the economy is too complex for there to be a stable relationship between two macroeconomic variables. In general, the relationship between output and unemployment depends on the state of the economy at the time of the output change.

THE SIZE OF THE MULTIPLIER *p. 314*

22. There are several reasons why the actual value of the multiplier is smaller than the size that would be expected from the simple multiplier model: (1) Automatic stabilizers help to offset contractions or limit expansions. (2) When government spending increases, the increased interest rate crowds out planned investment and consumption spending. (3) Expansionary policies increase the price level. (4) Firms sometimes hold excess capital and excess labor. (5) Firms may meet increased demand by drawing down inventories instead of increasing output. (6) Households and firms change their behavior less when they expect changes to be temporary instead of permanent.

23. In practice, the size of the multiplier at its peak is about 1.4.

REVIEW TERMS AND CONCEPTS

accelerator effect, *p. 307*

adjustment costs, *p. 308*

animal spirits of entrepreneurs, *p. 307*

capital-intensive technology, *p. 308*

constrained supply of labor, *p. 302*

desired, *or* optimal, level of inventories, *p. 309*

discouraged-worker effect, *p. 314*

excess capital, *p. 308*

excess labor, *p. 308*

inputs, *p. 307*

inventory investment, *p. 309*

labor-intensive technology, *p. 308*

life-cycle theory of consumption, *p. 298*

nominal wage rate, *p. 300*

nonlabor, *or* nonwage, income, *p. 300*

Okun's Law, *p. 313*

permanent income, *p. 298*

plant-and-equipment investment, *p. 307*

productivity, *or* labor productivity, *p. 312*

real wage rate, *p. 300*

unconstrained supply of labor, *p. 302*

PROBLEMS

Visit **www.myeconlab.com** to complete the problems marked in orange online. You will receive instant feedback on your answers, tutorial help, and access to additional practice problems.

myeconlab

1. Between October 2004 and October 2005, real GDP in the United States increased by 3.6 percent, while nonfarm payroll jobs increased by only 1.4 percent. How is it possible for output to increase without a proportional increase in the number of workers?

2. **[Related to the *Economics in Practice* on p. 305]** Starting in 2006, home prices in the United States fell substantially. By the middle of 2008, house prices were down approximately 15 percent nationwide. Many worried that the decline in housing wealth would reduce consumption spending and slow the economy. In 2007, household holding of real estate (essentially single-family homes and condominiums) stood at about $20 trillion. In 2000, it was about $11 trillion. Go to www.federalreserve.gov and click on "Economic Research & Data," then on "Flow of Funds." Look at the most recent release and find balance sheet table B.100. What has happened to the value of household real estate holdings since 2008? Have they gone up or down? by how much? If consumption spending rises by 3 percent of any increase in real estate holdings, how much additional annual consumption would result from a $5 trillion increase in home values? What about a 15 percent decline from their level in 2007? Some argue that the effect of housing on spending is asymmetric. That is, when home values rise, spending increases; but when home values fall, spending does not fall. Provide an explanation for such an asymmetry.

3. During 2005, the Federal Reserve Bank raised interest rates in an effort to prevent an increase in the rate of inflation.
   a. What direct effects do higher interest rates have on household and firm behavior?
   b. One of the consequences of higher interest rates was that the value of existing bonds (both corporate bonds and government bonds) fell substantially. Explain why higher interest rates would decrease the value of existing fixed-rate bonds held by the public.
   c. Some economists argue that the wealth effect of higher interest rates on consumption is as important as the direct effect of higher interest rates on investment. Explain what economists mean by "wealth effects on consumption" and illustrate with *AS/AD* curves.

4. In 2005, President Bush's tax reform commission proposed and Congress enacted a decrease in taxes. One of the cuts was in the income tax rate for higher-income wage earners. Republicans claimed that raising the rewards for working (the net after-tax wage rate) would lead to more work effort and a higher labor supply. Critics of the tax cuts replied that this criticism was baseless because it "ignored the income effect of the tax cut (net wage increase)." Explain what these critics meant.

5. Graph the following two consumption functions:

$$(1)\, C = 300 + .5Y$$
$$(2)\, C = .5Y$$

   a. For each function, calculate and graph the average propensity to consume (*APC*) when income is $100, $400, and $800.
   b. For each function, what happens to the *APC* as income rises?
   c. For each function, what is the relationship between the *APC* and the marginal propensity to consume?
   d. Under the first consumption function, a family with income of $50,000 consumes a smaller proportion of its income than a family with income of $20,000; yet if we take a dollar of income away from the rich family and give it to the poor family, total consumption by the two families does not change. Explain how this is possible.

6. Throughout the late 1990s, the price of houses increased steadily around the country.
   a. What impact would you expect increases and decreases in home value to have on the consumption behavior of home owners? Explain.
   b. In what ways might events in the housing market have influenced the rest of the economy through their effects on consumption spending? Be specific.

7. Adam Smith is 45 years old. He has assets (wealth) of $20,000 and has no debts or liabilities. He knows that he will work for 20 more years and will live 5 years after that, when he will earn nothing. His salary each year for the rest of his working career is $14,000. (There are no taxes.) He wants to distribute his consumption over the rest of his life in such a way that he consumes the same amount each year. He cannot consume in total more than his current wealth plus the sum of his income for the next 20 years. Assume that the rate of interest is zero and that Smith decides not to leave any inheritance to his children.

a. How much will Adam consume this year and next year? How did you arrive at your answer?

b. Plot on a graph Adam's income, consumption, and wealth from the time he is 45 until he is 70 years old. What is the relationship between the annual increase in his wealth and his annual saving (income minus consumption)? In what

year does Adam's wealth start to decline? Why? How much wealth does he have when he dies?

c. Suppose Adam receives a tax rebate of $100 per year, so his income is $14,100 per year for the rest of his working career. By how much does his consumption increase this year and next year?

d. Now suppose Adam receives a 1-year-only tax refund of $100—his income this year is $14,100; but in all succeeding years, his income is $14,000. What happens to his consumption this year? in succeeding years?

8. Explain why a household's consumption and labor supply decisions are interdependent. What impact does this interdependence have on the way in which consumption and income are related?

9. Why do expectations play such an important role in investment demand? How, if at all, does this explain why investment is so volatile?

10. How can a firm maintain a smooth production schedule even when sales are fluctuating? What are the benefits of a smooth production schedule? What are the costs?

---

* Note: Problems marked with an asterisk are more challenging.

Long-Run Growth   17

In 1975, the per capita GDP of the sub-Saharan African nations was $1,928. By 2005, that number had fallen to $1,768. In the same period, nations in East Asia and the Pacific increased GDP per capita from $905 to $4,595. On almost any measure that one could use, the economies of most of the sub-Saharan countries have been languishing, while much of Asia has seen rapid growth. How do we explain these differences? Will China continue to grow, becoming as some have predicted, the next economic superpower? Is the very recent economic progress we observe in parts of sub-Saharan Africa likely to continue? Even the United States has seen substantial differences in growth over time. In the mid-nineteenth century, U.S. growth was over 5 percent. The

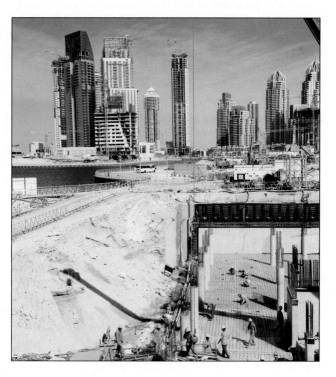

1930s, as you may recall from Chapter 5, experienced growth rates of less than 2 percent. As China and other Asian countries grow rapidly, many observers wonder whether the United States can keep up. These questions form the heart of the study of economic growth.

Recall from Chapter 1 that **economic growth** occurs when an economy experiences an increase in total output. The increase in real output that began in the Western world with the Industrial Revolution and continues today has been so sustained and so rapid that economists refer to this as the period of **modern economic growth**.

It is through economic growth that living standards improve, but growth brings change. New things are produced while others become obsolete. Some believe that growth is the fundamental objective of a society because it lifts people out of poverty and enhances the quality of their lives. Others say that economic growth erodes traditional values and leads to exploitation, environmental destruction, and corruption.

The first part of this chapter describes economic growth in some detail and identifies sources of economic growth across the world. We then turn to look more narrowly at the U.S. growth picture. After a review of the U.S. economy's growth record since the nineteenth century, we examine the role of public policy in the growth process. We conclude with a discussion of growth and the environment, returning to the world perspective.

economic growth An increase in the total output of an economy.

modern economic growth The period of rapid and sustained increase in output that began in the Western world with the Industrial Revolution.

The Growth Process: From Agriculture to Industry

The easiest way to understand the growth process and to identify its causes is to think about a simple economy. Recall from Chapter 2, Colleen and Bill washed up on a deserted island. At first, they had only a few simple tools and whatever human capital they brought with them to the island. They gathered nuts and berries and built a small cabin. Their "GDP" consisted of basic food and shelter.

Over time, things improved. The first year they cleared some land and began to cultivate a few vegetables they found growing on the island. They made some tools and dug a small reservoir to store rainwater. As their agricultural efforts became more efficient, they shifted their resources—their time—into building a larger, more comfortable home.

Colleen and Bill were accumulating capital in two forms. First, they built *physical capital*, material things used in the production of goods and services—a better house, tools, a water system, perhaps a boat to let them fish farther off shore. Second, they acquired more *human capital*—knowledge, skills, and talents. Through trial and error, they learned about the island and its soil and its climate and learned what did and did not work. Both kinds of capital made them more efficient and increased their productivity. Because it took less time to produce the food they needed to survive, they could devote more energy to producing other things or to leisure.

At any given time, Colleen and Bill faced limits on what they could produce. These limits were imposed by the existing state of their technical knowledge and the resources at their disposal. Over time, they expanded their possibilities, developed new technologies, accumulated capital, and made their labor more productive. In Chapter 2, we defined a society's *production possibility frontier* (*ppf*), which shows all possible combinations of output that can be produced given present technology and whether all available resources are fully and efficiently employed. Economic growth expands those limits and shifts society's production possibilities frontier out to the right, as Figure 17.1 shows.

▶ **FIGURE 17.1**

Economic Growth Shifts Society's Production Possibility Frontier Up and to the Right

The production possibility frontier shows all the combinations of output that can be produced if all society's scarce resources are fully and efficiently employed. Economic growth expands society's production possibilities, shifting the ppf up and to the right.

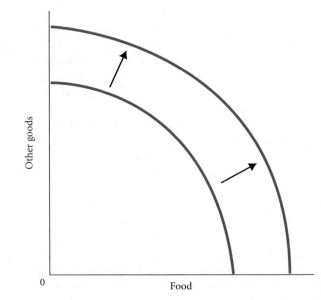

From Agriculture to Industry: The Industrial Revolution Before the Industrial Revolution in Great Britain, every society in the world was agrarian. Towns and cities existed here and there, but almost everyone lived in rural areas. People spent most of their time producing food and other basic subsistence goods. Then beginning in England around 1750, technical change and capital accumulation increased productivity significantly in two important industries: agriculture and textiles. New and more efficient methods of farming were developed. New inventions and new machinery in spinning and weaving meant that more could be produced with fewer resources. Just as new technology, capital equipment, and resulting higher productivity made it possible for Colleen and Bill to spend time working on other projects and new "products," the British turned from agricultural production to industrial production. In both cases, growth meant new products, more output, and wider choice.

Those changes meant that peasants and workers in eighteenth-century England who in the past would have continued in subsistence farming could make a better living as urban workers. A rural agrarian society was very quickly transformed into an urban industrial society.

The transition from agriculture to industry has been more recent in developing countries in Asia. One of the hallmarks of current growth in China and Vietnam, for example, has been the focus on manufacturing exports as a growth strategy. A visitor to Vietnam cannot help but be struck by the pace of industrialization.

Growth in Modern Society   Economic growth continues today in the developed world. And while the underlying process is still the same, the face is different. Just as Colleen and Bill devoted time to building a boat and designing tools, the developed economies are still creating capital to increase productivity. Just as a shovel makes it possible to dig a bigger hole, new microwave towers bring cell phone service to places that had been out of range. Scientists work on finding a cure for Alzheimer's disease using tools they couldn't have dreamed of a decade ago. Tools available on the Web make it possible for a single law clerk in a busy law office to check hundreds of documents for the opinions of potential expert witnesses in a court case in an hour, a task that took a dozen law clerks weeks to perform just a few years ago. In each case, we have become more proficient at producing what we want and need and we have freed up resources to produce new things that we want and need. For Colleen and Bill, it was a better diet; with a boat they could catch more fish in less time. Today it may be better cell phone service; a fast, inexpensive color printer; or a better medical procedure.

The basic building blocks are the same. Growth comes from a bigger workforce and more productive workers. Higher productivity comes from tools (capital), a better-educated and more highly skilled workforce (human capital), and increasingly from innovation and technical change (new techniques of production) and newly developed products and services.

Growth Patterns and the Possibility of Catch-Up   Table 17.1 provides estimates of the growth of GDP for a number of developed and developing countries. One fact that should strike you as you look at these numbers is the high rates of growth of China and India relative to those of the developed countries. Some economists argue that when poorer, less developed countries begin to develop, they typically have higher growth rates as they **catch-up** with the more developed countries. This idea is called *convergence theory* since it suggests that gaps in national incomes tend to close over time. Indeed, more than 50 years ago, the economic historian Alexander Gerschenkron coined the term *the advantages of backwardness* as a description of the phenomenon by which less developed countries could leap ahead by borrowing technology from more developed countries. This idea seems to fit the current experiences of China and India as shown in the table. On the other hand, growth rates in Africa are more modest. For a country such as Zimbabwe, growth in real GDP has been poor, resulting in a growing disadvantage relative to much of the rest of the world. Understanding why some countries appear to be converging and others are falling further behind is the subject of considerable political, economic, and social interest. We turn now to look at the sources of economic growth.

catch-up The theory stating that the growth rates of less developed countries will exceed the growth rates of developed countries, allowing the less developed countries to catch up.

TABLE 17.1   Growth of Real GDP: 1999–2007

Country	Average Growth Rates per Year, 1999–2007
United States	2.7
Japan	1.5
Germany	1.5
France	2.1
United Kingdom	2.7
China	9.6
India	7.0
Africa (continent)	4.5
Republic of South Africa (2002–2007)	3.9
Cameroon (2002–2007)	4.0
Zimbabwe (2002–2007)	1.0

Source: Economic Report of the President, 2008.

The Sources of Economic Growth

Economic growth occurs when (1) society acquires more resources or (2) society discovers ways of using available resources more efficiently. For economic growth to increase living standards, the rate of growth must exceed the rate of population increase. Economic growth is generally defined as *an increase in real GDP per capita*.

As we discuss the factors that contribute to economic growth, it will be helpful to think of an **aggregate production function**. An individual firm's production function is a mathematical representation of the relationship between the firm's inputs and its output. Output for an aggregate production function is national output, or GDP. Stated simply, GDP (output) (Y) depends on the amount of labor (L) and the amount of capital (K) available in the economy (assuming the amount of land is fixed).[1] If you think of GDP as a function of both labor and capital, you can see the following:

An increase in GDP can come about through

1. An increase in the labor supply.
2. An increase in physical or human capital.
3. An increase in productivity (the amount of product produced by each unit of capital or labor).

aggregate production function The mathematical representation of the relationship between inputs and national output, or gross domestic product.

An Increase in Labor Supply

Consider what would happen if another person joined Colleen and Bill on the island. That individual would join in the work and produce, so GDP would rise. Suppose that a person who had not been a part of the labor force were to begin to work and use time and energy to produce pottery. Real output would rise in this case also. An increase in labor supply can generate more output.

Whether output *per capita* rises when the labor supply increases is another matter. If the capital stock remains fixed while labor increases, the new labor will likely be less productive than the old labor. This effect is called *diminishing returns*, and it worried Thomas Malthus, David Ricardo, and other early economists.

Malthus and Ricardo, who lived in England during the nineteenth century, were concerned that the fixed supply of land would lead to diminishing returns. With land in strictly limited supply, the ppf could be pushed out only so far as population increased. To increase agricultural output, people would be forced to farm less productive land or to farm land more intensively. In either case, the returns to successive increases in population would diminish. Both Malthus and Ricardo predicted a gloomy future as population outstripped the land's capacity to produce. What both economists left out of their calculations was technological change and capital accumulation. New and better farming techniques have raised agricultural productivity so much that less than 3 percent of the U.S. population now provides enough food for the country's entire population.

Diminishing returns can also occur if a nation's capital stock grows more slowly than its workforce. Capital enhances workers' productivity. A person with a shovel digs a bigger hole than a person without one, and a person with a steam shovel outdoes them both. If a society's stock of plant and equipment does not grow and the technology of production does not change, additional workers will not be as productive because they do not have machines with which to work.

Table 17.2 illustrates how growth in the labor force, without a corresponding increase in the capital stock or technological change, might lead to growth of output but declining productivity and a lower standard of living. As labor increases, output rises from 300 units in period 1 to 320 in period 2, to 339 in period 3, and so forth, but **labor productivity** (output per worker hour) falls. Output per worker hour, Y/L, is a measure of labor's productivity.

The fear that new workers entering the labor force will displace existing workers and generate unemployment has been with us for a long time. New workers can come from many places. They might be immigrants, young people looking for their first jobs, or older people entering the labor force for the first time. Between 1947 and 2007, the number of women in the labor force quadrupled, jumping from 17 million to 71 million. Table 17.3 shows that in the United States since World War II, the civilian noninstitutional population (those not in jails or mental institutions) over 16 years of age increased by 127.8 percent, while the labor force grew by 157.7 percent.

labor productivity Output per worker hour; the amount of output produced by an average worker in 1 hour.

[1] All the numbers in the tables to follow were derived from the simple production function $Y = 3 \times K^{1/3} L^{2/3}$.

TABLE 17.2	Economic Growth from an Increase in Labor—More Output but Diminishing Returns and Lower Labor Productivity			
Period	Quantity of Labor L (Hours)	Quantity of Capital K (Units)	Total Output Y (Units)	Measured Labor Productivity Y/L
1	100	100	300	3.0
2	110	100	320	2.9
3	120	100	339	2.8
4	130	100	357	2.7

The U.S. economy, however, has shown a remarkable ability to expand right along with the labor force. The number of people employed jumped by 89.0 million—156.1 percent—during the same period. As long as the economy and the capital stock are expanding rapidly enough, new entrants into the labor force do not displace other workers.

TABLE 17.3	Employment, Labor Force, and Population Growth, 1947–2007			
	Civilian Noninstitutional Population Over 16 Years Old (Millions)	Civilian Labor Force		Employment (Millions)
		Number (Millions)	Percentage of Population	
1947	101.8	59.4	58.3	57.0
1960	117.3	69.6	59.3	65.8
1970	137.1	82.8	60.4	78.7
1980	167.7	106.9	63.7	99.3
1990	189.2	125.8	66.5	118.8
2000	212.6	142.6	67.1	136.9
2007	231.9	153.1	66.0	146.0
Percentage change, 1947–2007	+127.8%	+157.7%		+156.1%
Annual rate	+1.4%	+1.6%		+1.6%

Source: Economic Report of the President, 2008, Table B-35.

Increases in Physical Capital

An increase in the stock of capital can also increase output even if it is not accompanied by an increase in the labor force. Physical capital both enhances the productivity of labor and provides valuable services directly.

It is easy to see how capital provides services directly. Consider what happened on Bill and Colleen's island. In the first few years, they built a house, putting many hours of work into it that could have gone into producing other things for immediate consumption. With the house for shelter, Colleen and Bill can spend time on other things. In the same way, capital equipment produced in 1 year can add to the value of a product over many years. For example, we still derive use and value from bridges and tunnels built decades ago.

It is also easy to see how capital used in production enhances the productivity of labor. Computers enable us to do almost instantly tasks that once were impossible or might have taken years to complete. An airplane with a small crew can transport hundreds of people thousands of miles in a few hours. A bridge over a river at a critical location may save thousands of labor hours that would be spent transporting materials and people the long way around. New technology is opening up communications impossible to imagine a decade ago. The strongest growth area today for cell phones is in Africa. Technology has allowed phone services to reach geographically remote areas, increasing the productivity of villages. It is precisely this yield in the form of future valuable services that provides private and public investors with the incentive to devote resources to capital production.

Table 17.4 shows how an increase in capital without a corresponding increase in labor might increase output. Observe several things about these numbers. First, additional capital increases measured productivity; output per worker hour (Y/L) increases from 3.0 to 3.1, to 3.2, and finally to 3.3 as the quantity of capital (K) increases. Second, there are diminishing returns to capital. Increasing capital by 10 units first increases output by 10 units—from 300 in period 1 to 310 in period 2. However, the second increase of 10 units yields only 9 units of output, and the third increase yields only 8 units.

TABLE 17.4	Economic Growth from an Increase in Capital—More Output, Diminishing Returns to Added Capital, Higher Measured Labor Productivity			
Period	Quantity of Labor L (Hours)	Quantity of Capital K (Units)	Total Output Y (Units)	Measured Labor Productivity Y/L
1	100	100	300	3.0
2	100	110	310	3.1
3	100	120	319	3.2
4	100	130	327	3.3

Table 17.5 shows the values of the private nonresidential capital stock in the United States since 1960. The increase in capital stock is the difference between gross investment and depreciation. (Remember, some capital becomes obsolete and some wears out every year.) Between 1960 and 2006, the stock of equipment increased at a rate of 4.4 percent per year and the stock of structures increased at a rate of 2.4 percent per year.

TABLE 17.5	Fixed Private Nonresidential Net Capital Stock, 1960–2006 (Billions of 2000 Dollars)	
	Equipment	Structures
1960	645.7	2,273.3
1970	1,108.5	3,094.8
1980	1,910.0	4,047.7
1990	2,613.3	5,304.5
2000	4,090.5	6,301.6
2006	4,841.8	6,776.9
Percentage change, 1960–2006	+649.9%	+198.1%
Annual rate	+4.4%	+2.4%

Source: Survey of Current Business, September 2007, Table 15, p. 32 and authors' estimates.

By comparing Table 17.3 and Table 17.5, you can see that in the United States, capital has been increasing faster than labor since 1960. In all economies experiencing modern economic growth, capital expands at a more rapid rate than labor. That is, the ratio of capital to labor (K/L) increases, and this too is a source of increasing productivity.

Role of Institutions in Attracting Capital The importance of capital in a country's economic growth naturally leads one to ask the question of what determines a country's stock of capital. In the modern open economy, new capital can come from the saving of a country's residents and/or from the investments of foreigners. **Foreign direct investment** is any investment in enterprises made in a country by residents outside that country. Foreign direct investment has been quite influential in providing needed capital for growth in much of Southeast Asia. In Vietnam, for example, rapid growth has been led by foreign direct investment. Very recently, we have seen signs of Chinese foreign direct investment in parts of Africa and in other parts of Asia.

Recent work in economics has focused on the role that institutions play in creating a capital-friendly environment that encourages home savings and foreign investment. In a series of papers, LaPorta, Lopez de Silanes, Shleifer, and Vishny argue that countries with English common law origins (as opposed to French) provide the strongest protection for shareholders, less corrupt governments, and better court systems. In turn, these financial and legal institutions promote

foreign direct investment (FDI)
Investment in enterprises made in a country by residents outside that country.

growth by encouraging capital investment. Countries with poor institutions, corruption, and inadequate protection for lenders and investors struggle to attract capital. The World Bank calls countries with weak institutions *fragile countries.*

Many of the World Bank's fragile countries are in sub-Saharan Africa. Many observers believe that the relative stagnation of some of the sub-Saharan African nations comes in part from their relatively weak institutions. High costs of doing business, including corruption and investment risks associated with conflict, have made countries such as Zimbabwe less attractive to domestic and foreign capital. Ethnic and linguistic fractionalization have also played a role.

China's growth in the last several decades, however, suggests that weak institutions may not completely block growth. Beginning in 1978, the Chinese government embarked on a series of reforms that introduced private profit-making business to the economy. Growth since that period has been quite rapid, averaging 9 percent in the years since reform. This growth period was accomplished despite a relatively weak set of property rights protections and financial institutions. Stock exchanges were introduced only in 1990, and the two Chinese exchanges, the Shanghai Exchange and the ShenZhen Exchange, remain small given the size of the economy. Most of the lending is controlled by four state-owned banks. In the early 1980s, corruption continued to be a problem. While many observers now believe that better institutions will be necessary to sustain the Chinese growth miracle (and the government is clearly moving in that direction), it is clear that China's early growth spurt was accomplished despite a relatively weak set of institutions.

Increases in Human Capital

Investment in human capital is another source of economic growth. People in good health are more productive than people in poor health; people with skills are more productive than people without skills.

Consider again the sub-Saharan African nations. The World Bank estimated in 2007 that there were 72 million primary-aged school children in the world who were not in school. Of those children, 37 percent were in the fragile states of Africa. Another key problem facing this area in terms of human capital is health. Rates of HIV/AIDS infections remain very high, particularly in southern Africa. Moreover, HIV/AIDS, unlike many other diseases, affects prime-age workers. Parts of southern Africa have seen reductions in life expectancy in the last 20 years. Interesting work trying to measure the size of the effects of health issues on growth in Africa is being done by a number of economists, including Simon Johnson of the IMF and Daron Acemoglu of MIT.

Human capital can be produced in many ways. Individuals can invest in themselves by going to college or by completing vocational training programs. Firms can invest in human capital through on-the-job training. The government invests in human capital with programs to improve health and to provide schooling and job training.

Table 17.6 shows that the level of educational attainment in the United States has risen significantly since 1940. The percentage of the population with at least 4 years of college rose from under 5 percent in 1940 to 28.0 percent in 2006. In 1940, fewer than 1 person in 4 had completed high school; in 2006, 85.5 percent had.

TABLE 17.6 Years of School Completed by People Over 25 Years Old, 1940–2006

	Percentage with Less than 5 Years of School	Percentage with 4 Years of High School or More	Percentage with 4 Years of College or More
1940	13.7	24.5	4.6
1950	11.1	34.3	6.2
1960	8.3	41.1	7.7
1970	5.5	52.3	10.7
1980	3.6	66.5	16.2
1990	NA	77.6	21.3
2000	NA	84.1	25.6
2006	NA	85.5	28.0

NA = not available.

Source: Statistical Abstract of the United States, 1990, Table 215; and 2008, Table 217.

Increases in Productivity

Growth that cannot be explained by increases in the *quantity* of inputs can be explained only by an increase in the *productivity* of those inputs—each unit of input must be producing more output. The **productivity of an input** can be affected by factors including technological change, other advances in knowledge, and economies of scale.

productivity of an input The amount of output produced per unit of an input.

Technological Change   The Industrial Revolution was in part sparked by new technological developments. New techniques of spinning and weaving—the invention of the machines known as the mule and the spinning jenny, for example—were critical. The high-tech boom that swept the United States in the early 1980s was driven by the rapid development and dissemination of semiconductor technology. In India, new high-yielding seeds in the 1960s helped to create a "green revolution" in agriculture.

Technological change affects productivity in two stages. First, there is an advance in knowledge, or an **invention**. However, knowledge by itself does nothing unless it is used. When new knowledge is used to produce a new product or to produce an existing product more efficiently, there is **innovation**.

invention   An advance in knowledge.

innovation   The use of new knowledge to produce a new product or to produce an existing product more efficiently.

Technological change cannot be measured directly. Some studies have presented data on "indicators" of the rate of technical change—the number of new patents, for example—but none are satisfactory. Still, we know that technological changes that have improved productivity are all around us. Wireless technology has revolutionized the office, hybrid seeds have increased the productivity of land, and more efficient and powerful aircraft have made air travel routine and inexpensive.

Over and above invention and innovation in new products and technology, advances in other kinds of knowledge can also improve productivity. One is what we might call managerial knowledge. For example, because of the very high cost of capital during the early 1980s, firms learned to manage their inventories much better. Many were able to keep production lines and distribution lines flowing with a much lower stock of inventories. Inventories are part of a firm's capital stock, and trimming them reduces costs and raises productivity. This is an example of a *capital-saving* innovation. Many of the advances that we are used to thinking about, such as the introduction of robotics, are *labor-saving*.

In addition to managerial knowledge, improved personnel management techniques, accounting procedures, data management, and the like can also make production more efficient, reduce costs, and increase measured productivity.

Economies of Scale   *External economies of scale* are cost savings that result from increases in the size of industries. The economies that accompany growth in size may arise from a variety of causes. For example, as firms in a growing industry build plants at new locations, they may lower transport costs. There may also be some economies of scale associated with research and development (R&D) spending and job-training programs.

Other Influences on Productivity   In addition to technological change, other advances in knowledge, and economies of scale, other forces may affect productivity. During the 1970s and 1980s, the U.S. government required many firms to reduce the air and water pollution they were producing. These requirements diverted capital and labor from the production of measured output, therefore *reducing* measured productivity. Similarly, in recent years, requirements imposed by the Occupational Safety and Health Act (OSHA) have required firms to protect workers better from accidental injuries and potential health problems. These laws also divert resources from measured output.

Negative effects such as these are more a problem of *measurement* than of declining productivity. The Environmental Protection Agency (EPA) regulates air and water quality because clean air and water presumably have a value to society. The resources diverted to produce that value are not wasted. A perfect measure of output produced that is of value to society includes environmental quality and good health.

Recent experiences in the Chinese economy point to another set of influences on productivity. Working with the IMF, Zuliu Hu and Mohsin Khan have pointed to the large role of productivity gains in the 20 years following the market reforms in China. In the period after the reforms, productivity growth rates tripled, averaging almost 4 percent a year. Hu and Khan argue that the productivity gains came principally from the unleashing of profit incentives that came with the opening of business to the private sector.

Climate and geography also play a role in productivity. Daron Acemoglu of MIT, Simon Johnson of the IMF, and James Robinson of Harvard have argued that the geography and climate of Africa, by creating high mortality rates among early colonial settlers, gave rise to a colonial strategy of expropriation rather than development. In turn, the weak institutions that emerged from this colonial strategy have hampered further economic development in the area. The role of geography in growth and development remains a fascinating area in economic research.

Growth and Productivity in the United States

Modern economic growth in the United States began in the middle of the nineteenth century. After the Civil War, railroads spread across the country and the economy took off. Table 17.7 shows the growth rate of real output in the United States for selected subperiods since 1871. Between 1871 and 1909, the growth rate was very strong—5.5 percent in the 1871–1889 period and 4.0 percent in the 1889–1909 period. The growth rate slowed to 2.8 percent in the 1909–1929 period and even further to 1.6 percent in the period that includes the Great Depression, 1929–1940. The growth rate was a strong 5.6 percent in the period that includes World War II, 1940–1950. It was then 3.5 percent in the 1950s, 4.2 percent in the 1960s, and roughly 3.2 percent since then.

TABLE 17.7	Growth of Real GDP in the United States, 1871–2000		
Period	Average Growth Rate per Year	Period	Average Growth Rate per Year
1871–1889	5.5	1950–1960	3.5
1889–1909	4.0	1960–1970	4.2
1909–1929	2.8	1970–1980	3.2
1929–1940	1.6	1980–1990	3.2
1940–1950	5.6	1990–2000	3.2

Sources: Historical Statistics of the United States: Colonial Times to 1970, Tables F47–70, F98–124; U.S. Department of Commerce, Bureau of Economic Analysis.

Sources of Growth in the U.S. Economy

For many years, Edward Denison of the Brookings Institution in Washington studied the growth process in the United States and sorted out the relative importance of the various causal factors. Table 17.8 presents some of his results. Denison estimates that about half of U.S. growth in output over the entire period from 1929 to 1982 came from increases in factors of production and the other half from increases in productivity. Growth in the labor force accounted for about 20 percent of overall growth, while growth in capital stock (both human and physical) accounted for 33 percent. Of the capital stock growth figure, human capital (education and training) accounted for 19 percent of the total and physical capital accounted for 14 percent. Growth of knowledge was the most important factor contributing to increases in the productivity of inputs.

TABLE 17.8 Sources of Growth in the United States, 1929–1982				
	Percent of Growth Attributable to Each Source			
	1929–1982	1929–1948	1948–1973	1973–1979
Increases in inputs	**53**	**49**	**45**	**94**
Labor	20	26	14	47
Capital	14	3	16	29
Education (human capital)	19	20	15	18
Increases in productivity	**47**	**51**	**55**	**6**
Advances in knowledge	31	30	39	8
Other factors[a]	16	21	16	−2
Annual growth rate in real national income	2.8	2.4	3.6	2.6

[a]Economies of scale, weather, pollution abatement, worker safety and health, crime, labor disputes, and so on.

Source: Edward Denison, *Trends in American Economic Growth, 1929–1982* (Washington: Brookings Institution, 1985). Reprinted with permission of The Brookings Institution.

The relative importance of these causes of growth varied considerably over the years. Between 1929 and 1948, for example, physical capital played a much smaller role than it did in other periods. Each period included times that were atypical for one reason or another. The period between 1929 and 1948 included the dislocations and uncertainties of the Great Depression and World War II. From 1948 to 1973, the economy enjoyed a period of unusual stability and expansion.

In looking at the sources of U.S. growth since the 1970s, Professor Dale Jorgenson of Harvard University and a number of colleagues have done a similar accounting that breaks out the contributions of a specific kind of capital: information technology (IT) capital, including computers, software, and communications equipment. The results are presented in Table 17.9. The precise meaning of these numbers is quite complex, but they clearly indicate a number of trends. You can see that the portion of overall growth contributed by productivity is rising and that information technology has played a big role in recent years.

TABLE 17.9 Sources of U.S. Growth, 1995–2004		
Percent Contribution 1995–2004		
Increases in inputs		71.6
Labor	20.6	
Capital	50.7	
IT capital	22.8	
Non-IT capital	27.9	
Increases in productivity		28.4

Source: Information Technology and the American Growth Resurgence. Dale W. Jorgenson, Mun S. Ho and Kevin J. Stiroh (Cambridge, MA: MIT Press, 2005). Data update provided by the authors.

Labor Productivity: 1952 I–2007 IV

In Figure 7.2 on p. 135, we presented a plot of labor productivity for the 1952 I–2007 IV period. It is now time to return to this figure, and it is repeated as Figure 17.2. Productivity in the figure is output per worker hour. Remember that the line segments are drawn to smooth out the short-run fluctuations in productivity. We saw in the last chapter that productivity as it is measured moves with the business cycle because firms tend to hold excess labor in recessions. We are not interested in business cycles in this chapter, and the line segments are a way of ignoring business cycle effects.

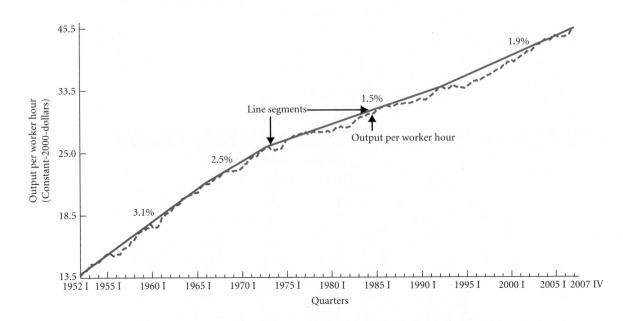

▲ FIGURE 17.2 **Output per Worker Hour (Productivity), 1952 I–2007 IV**

ECONOMICS IN PRACTICE

Improving Productivity in Health Care

In the United States, health care spending has become an increasingly large share of the GDP. For a number of people, part of their health care costs are borne by their employers. These firms thus have strong incentives to find ways to increase the productivity of health care. But productivity growth in health care has been hard to measure. In manufacturing, we often look to capital expenditures to reduce production costs. In health care, most capital investments result in an increase in the quality of care, not a reduction of its costs. New medical devices to stabilize heart rhythm, for example, have the potential to reduce mortality, but they come at a high price. Fewer investments are made that allow doctors to produce a fixed quality of care at a lower cost, a form of productivity growth familiar in the manufacturing world. As the following article suggests, firms have looked elsewhere to lower costs of health care: increasing the availability of preventive services and wellness programs such as smoking cessation and exercise. In other words, firms have looked at trying to change the production technology to lower costs.

Firms' Health Clinics Cut Costs

Wall Street Journal

In the latest attempt to motivate workers to adopt more-healthful lifestyles, American employers are offering wellness coaching to employees at on-site clinics.

While American employers may like the idea of getting out of the business of providing health care, a growing number of corporations are discovering they can save money and boost employee productivity by getting more closely involved at an earlier stage.

"On-site clinics have undergone a huge transformation," said Marne Bell, a senior consultant at Watson Wyatt. "There's much more emphasis on prevention."

Gone are the days when on-site clinics were the sole preserve of manufacturing companies that founded facilities to treat employees' work-related injuries. Some three in 10 large employers—from financial firms to hair-care companies—have on-site clinics, offering everything from primary care to travel medicine, pregnancy support and nutrition counseling. Walt Disney Co. just broke ground on a $6 million, 15,000-square-foot health-and-wellness center for employees at Walt Disney World.

Preventive services, such as health screenings and immunizations, are the most common type at the latest wave of clinics, according to a recent survey by Watson Wyatt and the National Business Group on Health. Four in 10 clinics offer pharmacy services, making it easier for those taking medications to fill their prescriptions.

Faced with escalating health-care costs, Harrah's Entertainment Inc. three years ago opened its first health-and-wellness center in Atlantic City, N.J. Since then, the casino-entertainment company has opened four more facilities, most recently in Las Vegas, where in January 2007 it opened a 7,000-square-foot clinic offering acute and primary-care services, nutritional counseling and physiotherapy. Downstairs there is a 12,000 square-foot gym.

"We recognized that there was going to come a point where we couldn't pass on the additional cost of providing health care to employees," said Jeff Shovlin, vice president of benefits at Harrah's. "We concluded that the only way to control costs was by helping employees to get and stay healthy."

Source: Victoria E. Knight, April 9, 2008

There was much talk in the late 1970s and early 1980s about the "productivity problem." Some economics textbooks published in the early 1980s had entire chapters discussing the decline in productivity that seemed to be taking place during the late 1970s. In January 1981, the Congressional Budget Office published a report, *The Productivity Problem: Alternatives for Action*.

It is clear from Figure 17.2 that there was a slowdown in productivity growth in the 1970s. The growth rate went from 3.1 percent in the 1950s and first half of the 1960s to 2.5 percent in the last half of the 1960s and early 1970s and then to 1.5 percent from the early 1970s to the 1990s. Many explanations were offered at the time for the productivity slowdown of the late 1970s and early 1980s. Some economists pointed to the low rate of saving in the United States compared with other parts of the world. Others blamed increased environmental and government regulation of U.S. business. Still others argued that the country was not spending as much on R&D as it should be. Finally, some suggested that high energy costs in the 1970s led to investment designed to save energy instead of to enhance productivity. (Later in this chapter we discuss how each of these factors influences growth.)

Many of these factors turned around in the 1980s and 1990s and yet, as you can see from Figure 17.2 on p. 328, productivity growth rose to only 1.9 percent in the 1990s and through 2007. This early discussion is now quite dated. The interesting question as we move into the second decade of the twenty-first century is whether the continued growth of the Internet and wireless devices will return productivity growth to the values observed in the 1950s and 1960s or whether the period of the 1950s and 1960s was simply an unusually good period for productivity growth.

Economic Growth and Public Policy in the United States

The decline in productivity in the 1970s that caused so much concern led to a protracted national discussion about the role of government in stimulating economic growth. This debate was spurred in part by increasing concern on the part of many Americans that the United States was not doing as well as the Asian countries.

Suggested Public Policies

Several strategies for increasing the rate of growth in the United States have been suggested, and some have been enacted into law. These strategies include policies aimed toward improving the quality of education, increasing the saving rate, stimulating investment, increasing R&D, reducing regulation, and pursuing an industrial policy.

Policies to Improve the Quality of Education   The Denison study shows that the contribution of education and training (human capital production) to growth in the United States has remained relatively constant at about 20 percent since 1929.

The quality of public education has been a concern since the 1970s. Increasingly, attention has been focused on the uneven quality of public education across the country and in particular on the large gap in educational achievement for poor children. Partly in response to perceived educational disparities, in 2001, the Bush administration passed the No Child Left Behind Act. This legislation, which increases state accountability for student performance via a system of increased testing and a wider set of federally imposed "carrots and sticks" for states and local governments, has been very controversial. There is considerable dispute about how to measure educational progress and how to create incentives to produce good outcomes. Nevertheless, there was widespread bipartisan agreement in the United States about the importance of improving education for future prosperity and growth. In the last few years, battles have also been waged in Congress over the amount of federal dollars set aside for scholarships and loans to college students. Whatever the policies of the moment, however, all federal, state, and local expenditures on education acknowledge the need to build the nation's stock of human capital.

The Taxpayer Relief Act of 1997 contained provisions that focused on education. First, the HOPE Scholarship credit allows taxpayers to claim a credit up to $1,500 for postsecondary education expenses on behalf of any family member. Other provisions included an Education Individual Retirement Account that allows savings to earn tax-free returns as long as the balance is used to pay educational expenses.

Policies to Increase the Saving Rate   The amount of capital accumulation in an economy is ultimately constrained by its rate of saving. The more saving in an economy, the more funds available for investment. Many people have argued that the tax system and the Social Security system in the United States are biased against saving. Some public finance economists favor shifting to a system of consumption taxation instead of income taxation to reduce the tax burden on saving.

Others claim the Social Security system, by providing guaranteed retirement incomes, reduces the incentive for people to save. Private pension plans make deposits to workers' accounts, the balances of which are invested in the stock market and bond market and are made available to firms for capital investment. In contrast, Social Security benefits are mostly paid out of current tax receipts. Thus, the argument goes, if Social Security substitutes for private saving, the national saving rate is reduced. Evidence on the extent to which taxes and Social Security reduce the saving rate has not been clear to date.

A provision of the 1997 Taxpayer Relief Act allowed for new "backloaded" retirement accounts [the so-called Roth Individual Retirement Accounts (IRAs)] to stimulate saving. Individuals can deposit up to $2,000 annually to specified retirement accounts that accumulate earnings without paying income tax. Withdrawals made after age 59 1/2 or for the purchase of a first home can be made tax free.

Policies to Stimulate Investment   For the growth rate to increase, saving must be used to finance new investment. In an effort to revive a slow-growing economy in 1961, President Kennedy proposed and Congress passed the *investment tax credit* (ITC). The ITC provided a tax reduction for firms that invest in new capital equipment. For most investments, the reduction took the form of a direct credit equal to 10 percent of the investment. A firm investing in a new computer system costing $100,000 would have its tax liability reduced by $10,000. The ITC was changed periodically over the years, and it was on the books until it was repealed in 1986. Many states have adopted ITCs against their state corporation taxes.

In 1982, the federal Economic Recovery Tax Act contained a number of provisions designed to encourage investment. Among them was the *Accelerated Cost Recovery System (ACRS)*, which gave firms the opportunity to reduce their taxes by using artificially rapid rates of depreciation for purposes of calculating taxable profits. Although these rules were complicated, their effect was similar to the effect of the ITC. The government effectively reduced the cost of capital to firms that undertook investment in plant or equipment.

The Bush tax plan, which became law as the Jobs and Growth Tax Relief Reconciliation Act of 2003, was an attempt to stimulate both labor supply and investment. The centerpiece of the plan was a sharp reduction in the taxation of dividends and capital gains. While long-term capital gains have long been afforded special tax treatment, dividends have essentially always been treated as ordinary income. Under the 2003 act, both are taxed at a reduced rate of 15 percent. In addition, the act generally lowered tax rates for most taxpayers. The top rate was reduced to 35 percent, effective in 2003.

In 2005, the president received the report of a federal advisory panel on tax reform. The panel report was entitled *Simple, Fair and Pro-Growth: Proposals to Fix America's Tax System*. The report contained a set of recommendations aimed directly at growth, including allowing businesses to expense all capital purchases immediately rather than depreciating them over time, reducing tax rates on interest, repealing the corporate alternative minimum tax, and reducing tax rates in general. Only time will tell which of those provisions will become law.

Policies to Increase Research and Development   In the United States, expenditures on R&D in 2006 were $340 billion. The two largest funders of research and development were industry, with a 67 percent share, and government, with a 28 percent share. High private returns on investment are clearly the stimulus for industry investments. Early work suggests that the private return on investment is quite high, on the order of 30 percent.[2] The large investment by government reflects its view about the role that research plays in long-run economic growth. As Table 17.8 shows, increases in knowledge accounted for 31 percent of total growth in the United States between 1929 and 1982. Although not shown in the table, during the years of high R&D expenditures, 1953 to 1973, the figure reached 40 percent.

---

[2] See M. Nadiri, "Contributions and Determinants of Research and Development Expenditures in the U.S. Manufacturing Industries," in *Capital Efficiency and Growth*, George M. von Furstenberg, ed. (Cambridge, MA: Ballinger Press, 1980).

ECONOMICS IN PRACTICE

Can We Really Measure Productivity Changes?

When the government publishes numbers on changes in productivity, most people consider them to be "true." Even though we don't really know much about how they are constructed, we assume they are the best measurements we can get.

Yet such data are often the source of controversy. Some have argued that the mix of products produced in the United States and the increased pace of technological change in recent years have made

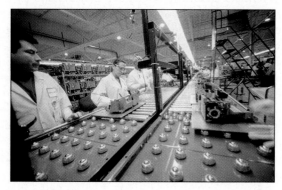

it increasingly difficult to measure productivity changes accurately. The observed productivity growth decline in recent decades may be measurement error.

These arguments make a certain amount of sense at an intuitive level. Even in agriculture, where it is relatively easy to measure productivity growth, the possibility of mismeasurement exists. The output of a soybean farm can be measured in bushels; and labor, capital, and land inputs present no serious measurement problems. So over time, as farming techniques improved and farmers acquired new and better machinery, output per acre and output per worker rose and have continued to rise. But today we have biotechnology. Genetic engineering now makes it possible to make soybeans higher in protein and more disease-resistant. Technology has improved and "output" has increased, but these increases do not show up in the data because of crude measures of output.

A similar problem exists with computers. If you simply counted the number of personal computers produced and measured the cost of the inputs used in their production, you would no doubt see some productivity advances. But computers being produced for under $1,000 in 2008 contained processors capable of performing tasks literally thousands of times faster than computers produced a decade earlier. If we were to measure computer outputs not in terms of units produced but in terms of the actual "services" they provided to users, we would find massive productivity advances. The problem is that many of the products we now use are qualitatively different from the comparable products we used only a few years ago, and the standard measures of productivity miss much of these quality changes.

The problems are greater in the service sector, where output is extremely difficult to measure. It is easy to understand the problem if you think of what information technology has done for legal services. As recently as 15 years ago, a lawyer doing research to support a legal case might spend hundreds of hours looking through old cases and public documents. Today's lawyers can log on to a computer and in seconds do a keyword search on a massive legal database. Such time- and labor-saving productivity advances are not counted in the official data.

One of the leading experts on technology and productivity estimates that we have reasonably good measures of output and productivity in only about 31 percent of the U.S. economy. Does this mean that slow productivity growth is not a problem? On this topic economists have agreed to disagree.[a]

[a]This argument was described most clearly by Professor Zvi Grilliches of Harvard in his presidential address to the American Economic Association in January 1994. The full text, entitled "Productivity, R&D, and the Data Constraint," is published in the *American Economic Review*, March 1994. The counterargument is best advanced by Professor Dale Jorgenson in *Productivity* (Harvard University Press, 1995).

Given the centrality of innovation to growth, it is interesting to look at what has been happening to research in the United States over time. A commonly used measure of inputs into research is the fraction of GDP spent. In 2007, the United States spent 2.6 percent of it GDP on R&D, down from a high of 2.9 percent in the early 1960s. Moreover, over time, the balance of research funding has shifted away from government toward industry. Since industry research tends to be more applied, some observers are concerned that the United States will lose some of its edge in technology unless more funding is provided. In 2007, the National Academies of Science argued as follows:

> Although many people assume that the United States will always be a world leader in science and technology, this may not continue to be the case inasmuch as great minds and ideas exist throughout the world. We fear the abruptness with which a lead in science and technology can be lost—and the difficulty of recovering a lead once lost, if indeed it can be recovered at all.[3]

As we suggested earlier, the theory of convergence suggests that newly developing countries can leap forward by exploiting the technology of the developed countries. Indeed, all countries benefit when a better way of doing things is discovered. Innovation and the diffusion of that innovation push the production possibility frontier outward. But there is at least some evidence that a country that leads in a discovery retains some advantage in exploiting it, at least for some time.

What evidence do we have that the United States might be losing its edge? As a share of GDP, the United States ranked seventh among OECD countries in 2006. If we look at patenting data, the evidence is more encouraging: For patents simultaneously sought in the United States, Japan, and the European Union, known as triadic patents, U.S. inventors are the leading source, having taken the lead from the EU in 1989. On the output side, then, the United States appears still to be quite strong.

Industrial Policy   In the 1980s, a number of policy makers began to call for increased government involvement in the allocation of capital across manufacturing sectors, a practice known as industrial policy. Those who favored industrial policy, including Robert Reich, the Secretary of Labor under President Clinton, argued that because governments of other nations were "targeting" industries for special subsidies and rapid investment, the United States should do likewise to avoid losing out to global competition.

There is no question that in developing countries, some targeted investment by governments is common. In 2004, for example, Taiwan, which had traditionally been a large exporter of sugar, faced declining world demand and prices. In response, the government made a conscious decision, backed by a strategic investment, to develop a world-class orchid industry for the export market. Low-interest credit was supplied to farmers to help them make the conversion, and a range of industry-specific infrastructure was created. Today Taiwan is a major player in the orchid industry.

Despite the orchids and other stories of government intervention in markets elsewhere, most economists now believe that targeted industrial policy is useful mainly in less developed countries. Dani Rodrik, an economist at Harvard's Kennedy School of Government, has argued that industrial policy is most helpful in less developed economies in which investments in strategic areas can have cascading effects across a range of economic activity. In the case of sectors of activities that are new to an economy—like orchids in Taiwan—the risks to the individual entrepreneur are very high and some government program may be useful. At the same time, many observers are sensitive to charges that many government policy programs in less developed countries are subject to strong political influences that may undermine decision making. Certainly, in the United States, most economists and policy makers at this time favor investments in education and research as ways to increase growth.

---

[3] National Academies, "Rising Above the Gathering Storm: Energizing the Employing America for a Brighter Future," National Academies Press, 2007.

Growth and the Environment and Issues of Sustainability

In 2000, the United Nations unanimously adopted the Millennium Development Goals, a set of quantifiable, time-based targets for developing countries to meet. Included in these targets, as you might expect, were measures of education, mortality, and income growth. But the UN resolution also included a set of environmental criteria. Specific criteria have been developed around clean air, clean water, and conservation management. Table 17.10 provides the 2005 ranking of a series of developing countries on the UN index.

TABLE 17.10	Environmental Scores in the World Bank Country Policy and Institutional Assessment 2005 Scores (min = 1, max = 6)
Albania	3
Angola	2.5
Bhutan	4.5
Cambodia	2.5
Cameroon	4
Gambia	3
Haiti	2.5
Madagascar	4
Mozambique	3
Papua New Guinea	1.5
Sierra Leone	2.5
Sudan	2.5
Tajikistan	2.5
Uganda	4
Vietnam	3.5
Zimbabwe	2.5

Source: World Bank, "Policies and Institutions for Environmental Sustainability."

The inclusion of environmental considerations in the development goals speaks to the importance of environmental infrastructure in the long-run growth prospects of a country. Environmental considerations also address some concerns that in the process of growth, environmental degradation will occur. Evidence on global warming has increased some of the international concerns about growth and the environment. The connections between the environment and growth are complex and remain debated among economists.

The classic work on growth and the environment was done in the mid-1990s by Gene Grossman and Alan Krueger.[4] It is well known that as countries develop, they typically generate air and water pollutants. China's recent rapid growth provides a strong example of this trend. Grossman and Krueger found, however, that as growth progresses and countries become richer, pollution tends to fall. The relationship between growth, as measured in per-capita income, and pollution is an inverted *U*. Figure 17.3 shows Grossman and Krueger's evidence on one measure of air pollution.

How do we explain the inverted *U*? Clean water and clean air are what economists call *normal goods*. That is, as people get richer, they want to consume more of these goods. You have already seen in the Keynesian model that aggregate consumption increases with income. As it happens, microeconomics finds that this relationship is true for most individual types of goods as well. Demand for clean water and clean air turns out to increase with income levels. As countries develop, their populace increasingly demands improvements on these fronts. So while increased industrialization with growth initially degrades the environment, in the long run environmental quality improves.

Grossman and Krueger found this inverted *U* in a number of countries. Economic historians remind us that in the heyday of industrialization, northern England suffered from very serious air pollution. Some of you may recall the description of air pollution in nineteenth-century English novels such as Elizabeth Gaskell's *North and South*.

---

[4] Gene Grossman and Alan Krueger, "Economic Growth and the Environment," *Quarterly Journal of Economics*, May 1995.

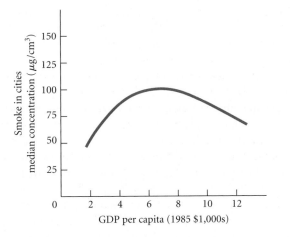

◀ **FIGURE 17.3**

The Relationship Between Per-Capita GDP and Urban Air Pollution

One measure of air pollution is smoke in cities. The relationship between smoke concentration and per-capita GDP is an inverted *U*: As countries grow wealthier, smoke increases and then declines.

Source: Gene Grossman and Alan Krueger, *QJE*, May 1995.

If environmental pollution eventually declines as growth brings rising per-capita incomes, why should we be worried? First, as Grossman and Krueger point out, the inverted *U* represents historical experience, but it is not inevitable. In particular, if public opinion moves governments and the economy at large toward technologies that reduce pollution, this requires an empowered populace and a responsive government. Here too we see the importance of institutions in growth. A second issue arises in cases in which high levels of current emissions produce irreversible outcomes. Some would argue that by the time nations such as China and Vietnam develop enough to reduce their emissions, it will be too late. Many believe that global warming is such an example.

Another important problem that has made itself known recently comes from pollution sources that move across country boundaries. Carbon emissions associated with global warming are one such by-product of increased industrialization. Other air pollution problems move across national borders as well. In the heyday of industrialization by the Soviet Union, prevailing winds blew much of the Soviet-produced pollution to Finland. Choices that countries make about levels of growth and levels of environmental control affect the well-being of other countries' populations. Nor is it easy for countries at very different levels of GDP per capita to agree on common standards of environmental control. As we suggested earlier, demand for clean air increases with income, when needs for food and shelter are better met. It should surprise no one who has studied economics that there are debates between developing countries and developed countries about optimal levels of environmental control. These debates are further complicated when we recognize the gains that consumers in developed economies reap from economic activity in the developing world. Much of the increased carbon emitted by Chinese businesses, for example, is associated with goods that are transported and traded to Europe and the United States. These consumers thus share the benefits of this air pollution through the cheaper goods they consume.

Sustainability of Resource Extraction Growth Strategies Much of Southeast Asia has fueled its growth through export-led manufacturing. For countries that have based their growth on resource extraction, there is another set of potential sustainability issues. Many of the African nations are in this category. Nigeria relies heavily on oil; South Africa and the Congo are large producers of diamonds and other gems. Extraction methods, of course, may carry environmental problems. Many people also question whether growth based on extraction is economically sustainable: What happens when the oil or minerals run out? The answer is quite complicated and depends in some measure on how the profits from the extraction process are used. Because extraction can be accomplished without a well-educated labor force, while other forms of development are more dependent on a skilled-labor base, public investment in infrastructure is especially important. To the extent that countries use the revenues from extraction to invest in infrastructure such as roads and schools and to increase the education and health of their populace, the basis for growth can be shifted over time. With weak institutions, these proceeds may be expropriated by corrupt governments or invested outside the country, and long-run sustainable growth will not result.

The question of whether the natural resource base imposes strong natural limits on growth has been debated since the time of Malthus. Earlier in this chapter we described the concerns of Thomas Malthus that population growth in England would outstrip the ability of the land to provide. In that case, technology stepped in.

In 1972, the Club of Rome, a group of "concerned citizens," contracted with a group at MIT to do a study entitled *The Limits to Growth*.[5] The book-length final report presented the results of computer simulations that assumed present growth rates of population, food, industrial output, and resource exhaustion. According to these data, sometime after the year 2000 the limits will be reached and the entire world economy will come crashing down:

> Collapse occurs because of nonrenewable resource depletion. The industrial capital stock grows to a level that requires an enormous input of resources. In the very process of that growth, it depletes a large fraction of the resource reserves available. As resource prices rise and mines are depleted, more and more capital must be used for obtaining resources, leaving less to be invested for future growth. Finally, investment cannot keep up with depreciation and the industrial base collapses, taking with it the service and agricultural systems, which have become dependent on industrial inputs (such as fertilizers, pesticides, hospital laboratories, computers, and especially energy for mechanization)....Population finally decreases when the death rate is driven upward by the lack of food and health services.[6]

This argument is similar to one offered almost 200 years ago by Thomas Malthus, mentioned earlier in this chapter.

In the early 1970s, many thought that the Club of Rome's predictions had come true. It seemed the world was starting to run up against the limits of world energy supplies. In the years since, new reserves have been found and new sources of energy have been discovered and developed. At present, issues of global warming and biodiversity are causing many people to question the process of growth. How should one trade off the obvious gains from growth in terms of the lives of those in the poorer nations against environmental goals? Recognizing the existence of these trade-offs and trying to design policies to deal with them is one of the key tasks of policy makers.

---

[5] Donella H. Meadows et al., *The Limits to Growth* (Washington, DC: Potomac Associates, 1972).
[6] Meadows et al., pp. 131–132.

SUMMARY

1. *Modern economic growth* is the period of rapid and sustained increase in real output per capita that began in the Western world with the Industrial Revolution.

THE GROWTH PROCESS: FROM AGRICULTURE TO INDUSTRY *p. 320*

2. All societies face limits imposed by the resources and technologies available to them. Economic growth expands these limits and shifts society's production possibilities frontier up and to the right.

3. There is considerable variation across the globe in growth rates. Some countries—particularly in Southeast Asia—appear to be catching up.

4. The process by which some less developed, poorer countries experience high growth and begin to catch up to more developed areas is known as convergence.

THE SOURCES OF ECONOMIC GROWTH *p. 322*

5. If growth in output outpaces growth in population and if the economic system is producing what people want, growth will increase the standard of living. Growth occurs when (1) society acquires more resources or (2) society discovers ways of using available resources more efficiently.

6. An *aggregate production function* embodies the relationship between inputs—the labor force and the stock of capital—and total national output.

7. A number of factors contribute to *economic growth*: (1) an increase in the labor supply; (2) an increase in physical capital—plant and equipment—and/or human capital—education, training, and health; (3) an increase in productivity brought about by technological change and advances in knowledge (for example, managerial skills); and/or economies of scale.

8. Changes in institutions, including property rights and legal institutions as well as the introduction of incentives, can also contribute to economic growth by attracting capital and improving productivity.

GROWTH AND PRODUCTIVITY IN THE UNITED STATES p. 327

9. Modern economic growth in the United States dates to the middle of the nineteenth century. For the last 100 years, the nation's growth in real output has averaged about 3 percent per year. Between 1929 and 1982, about half of U.S. growth in output came from increases in factors of production and half from increases in productivity.

10. There has been much concern that the rate of growth of productivity in the United States is slowing. The growth rate of *labor productivity* decreased from about 3.3 percent in the 1950s and 1960s to about 1.9 percent in the 1990s.

ECONOMIC GROWTH AND PUBLIC POLICY IN THE UNITED STATES p. 330

11. A number of public policies have been pursued with the aim of improving the growth of real output. These policies include efforts to improve the quality of education, to encourage saving, to stimulate investment, and to increase research and development. Some economists also argue for increased government involvement in the allocation of capital across manufacturing sectors, a practice known as *industrial policy*.

GROWTH AND THE ENVIRONMENT AND ISSUES OF SUSTAINABILITY p. 334

12. As countries begin to develop and industrialize, environmental problems are common. As development progresses further, however, most countries experience improvements in their environmental quality.

13. The limits placed on a country's growth by its natural resources have been debated for several hundred years. Growth strategies based on extraction of resources may pose special challenges to a country's growth.

REVIEW TERMS AND CONCEPTS

aggregate production function, *p. 322*

catch-up, *p. 321*

economic growth, *p. 319*

foreign direct investment (FDI), *p. 324*

innovation, *p. 326*

invention, *p. 326*

labor productivity, *p. 322*

modern economic growth, *p. 319*

productivity of an input, *p. 326*

PROBLEMS

Visit www.myeconlab.com to complete the problems marked in orange online. You will receive instant feedback on your answers, tutorial help, and access to additional practice problems.

1. One way that less developed countries catch up with the growth of the more developed countries is by adopting the technology of the developed countries. On average, however, developed countries are capital-rich and labor-short relative to the developing nations. Think of the kinds of technology that a typical developing country with a short supply of capital and a large marginally employed labor force would find when "shopping" for technology in a more developed country. As a hint, the Japanese have developed the field of robotics such as assembly line machines. Such machines are designed to replace expensive workers with capital (robots) in order to lower the overall cost of production. In what ways does it help a developing country to transfer and use a new technology in its country? What are the costs?

2. Tables 1, 2, and 3 present some data on three hypothetical economies. Complete the tables by figuring the measured productivity of labor and the rate of output growth. What do the data tell you about the causes of economic growth? (*Hint*: How fast are *L* and *K* growing?)

TABLE 1

PERIOD	L	K	Y	Y/L	GROWTH RATE OF OUTPUT
1	1,052	3,065	4,506		
2	1,105	3,095	4,674		
3	1,160	3,126	4,842		
4	1,218	3,157	5,019		

TABLE 2

PERIOD	L	K	Y	Y/L	GROWTH RATE OF OUTPUT
1	1,052	3,065	4,506		
2	1,062	3,371	4,683		
3	1,073	3,709	4,866		
4	1,084	4,079	5,055		

TABLE 3

PERIOD	L	K	Y	Y/L	GROWTH RATE OF OUTPUT
1	1,052	3,065	4,506		
2	1,062	3,095	4,731		
3	1,073	3,126	4,967		
4	1,084	3,157	5,216		

3. Go to a recent issue of *The Economist* magazine. In the back of each issue is a section called "economic indicators." That section lists the most recent growth data for a substantial number of countries. Which countries around the world are growing most rapidly according to the most recent data? Which countries around the world are growing more slowly? Flip through the stories in *The Economist* to see if there is any explanation for the pattern that you observe. Write a brief essay on current general economic conditions around the world.

4. In the fall of 2005, the president's tax reform commission issued a final report. The commission called for a general cut in marginal tax rates; lower tax rates on dividends, capital gains, and interest income; and, more importantly, the expensing of investment in capital equipment. These provisions were argued to be "pro-growth." In what ways would you expect each of these proposals to be favorable to economic growth?

5. In earlier chapters, you learned that aggregate expenditure ($C + I + G$) must equal aggregate output for the economy to be in equilibrium. You also saw that when consumption spending rises, $C + I + G$ increases, inventories fall, and aggregate output rises. Thus, policies that simultaneously increase consumer spending and reduce saving lead to a higher level of GDP. In this chapter, we have argued that a higher saving rate, even with lower consumption spending, is the key to long-run GDP growth. How can both arguments be correct?

6. Suppose you have just been elected to Congress and you find yourself on the Ways and Means Committee—the committee in the House that decides on tax matters. The committee is debating a bill that would make major changes in tax policy. First, the corporate tax would be lowered substantially in an effort to stimulate investment. The bill contains a 15 percent investment tax credit—firms would be able to reduce their taxes by 15 percent of the value of investment projects that they undertake. To keep revenues constant, the bill would impose a national sales tax that would raise the price of consumer goods and reduce consumption. What trade-offs do you see implied in this bill? What are the pros and cons? How would you vote?

7. [Related to the *Economics in Practice* on p. 329] Education, like health care, is another area in which it has been hard to create productivity gains that reduce costs. Collect data on the tuition rates of your own college in the last twenty years and compare that increase to the overall rate of inflation using the CPI. What do you observe? Can you suggest some productivity-enhancing measures?

8. Economists generally agree that high budget deficits today will reduce the growth rate of the economy in the future. Why? Do the reasons for the high budget deficit matter? In other words, does it matter whether the deficit is caused by lower taxes, increased defense spending, more job-training programs, and so on?

9. Why can growth lead to a more unequal distribution of income? By assuming this is true, how is it possible for the poor to benefit from economic growth?

10. [Related to the *Economics in Practice* on p. 332] For each of the following items how would you measure output? If you used a simple measure of productivity such as output per worker or output per hour of labor, what things might raise productivity in each sector?
   a. Automobiles
   b. Corn
   c. Music players
   d. Insurance
   e. Health care

Debates in Macroeconomics: Monetarism, New Classical Theory, and Supply-Side Economics

18

Throughout this book, we have noted that there are many disagreements and questions in macroeconomics. For example, economists disagree on whether the aggregate supply curve is vertical, either in the short run or in the long run. Some economists even doubt that the aggregate supply curve is a useful macroeconomic concept. There are different views on whether cyclical employment exists and, if it does, what causes it. Economists disagree about whether monetary and fiscal policies are effective at stabilizing the economy, and they support different views on the primary determinants of consumption and investment spending.

We discussed some of these disagreements in previous chapters, but only briefly. In this chapter, we discuss in more detail a number of alternative views of how the macroeconomy works.

Keynesian Economics

John Maynard Keynes's *General Theory of Employment, Interest, and Money*, published in 1936, remains one of the most important works in economics. While a great deal of the material in the previous 10 chapters is drawn from modern research that postdates Keynes, much of the material is built around a framework constructed by Keynes.

What exactly is *Keynesian economics*? In one sense, it is the foundation of all of macroeconomics. Keynes was the first to stress aggregate demand and links between the money market and the goods market. Keynes also stressed the possible problem of sticky wages. Virtually all the debates in this chapter can be understood in terms of the aggregate output/aggregate expenditure framework suggested by Keynes.

In recent years, the term *Keynesian* has been used narrowly. Keynes believed in an activist federal government. He believed that the government had a role to play in fighting inflation and unemployment, and he believed that monetary and fiscal policy should be used to manage the macroeconomy. This is why *Keynesian* is sometimes used to refer to economists who advocate active government intervention in the macroeconomy.

During the 1970s and 1980s, it became clear that managing the macroeconomy was more easily accomplished on paper than in practice. The inflation problems of the 1970s and early 1980s and the seriousness of the recessions of 1974 to 1975 and 1980 to 1982 led many economists to challenge the idea of active government intervention in the economy. Some of the challenges were simple attacks on the bureaucracy's ability to act in a timely manner. Others were theoretical assaults that claimed to show that monetary and fiscal policy could have *no effect whatsoever* on the economy, even if it were efficiently managed.

Two major schools decidedly against government intervention developed: monetarism and new classical economics.

Monetarism

The debate between "monetarist" and "Keynesian" economics is complicated because they mean different things to different people. If we consider the main monetarist message to be that "money matters," then almost all economists would agree. In the aggregate supply/aggregate demand (*AS/AD*) story, for example, an increase in the money supply shifts the *AD* curve to the right, which leads to an increase in both aggregate output (*Y*) and the price level (*P*). Monetary policy thus has an effect on output and the price level. *Monetarism*, however, is usually considered to go beyond the notion that money matters.

The Velocity of Money

velocity of money The number of times a dollar bill changes hands, on average, during a year; the ratio of nominal *GDP* to the stock of money.

To understand monetarist reasoning, you must understand the **velocity of money**. Think of velocity as the number of times a dollar bill changes hands, on average, during a year.

Suppose on January 1 you buy a new ballpoint pen with a $5 bill. The owner of the stationery store does not spend your $5 right away. She may hold it until, say, May 1, when she uses it to buy a dozen doughnuts. The doughnut store owner does not spend the $5 he receives until July 1, when he uses it (along with other cash) to buy 100 gallons of oil. The oil distributor uses the bill to buy an engagement ring for his fiancée on September 1, but the $5 bill is not used again in the remaining 3 months of the year. Because this $5 bill has changed hands four times during the year, its velocity of circulation is 4. A velocity of 4 means that the $5 bill stays with each owner for an average of 3 months, or one quarter of a year.

In practice, we use gross domestic product (GDP), instead of the total value of all transactions in the economy, to measure velocity[1] because GDP data are more readily available. The income velocity of money (*V*) is the ratio of nominal GDP to the stock of money (*M*):

$$V \equiv \frac{GDP}{M}$$

If $6 trillion worth of final goods and services is produced in a year and if the money stock is $1 trillion, then the velocity of money is $6 trillion ÷ $1 trillion, or 6.0.

We can expand this definition slightly by noting that nominal income (GDP) is equal to real output (income) (*Y*) times the overall price level (*P*):

$$GDP \equiv P \times Y$$

Through substitution:

$$V \equiv \frac{P \times Y}{M}$$

or

$$M \times V \equiv P \times Y$$

At this point, it is worth pausing to ask whether our definition has provided us with any insights into the workings of the economy. The answer is no. Because we defined *V* as the ratio of GDP to the money supply, the statement $M \times V \equiv P \times Y$ is an identity—it is true by definition. It

---

[1] Recall that GDP does not include transactions in intermediate goods (for example, flour sold to a baker to be made into bread) or in existing assets (for example, the sale of a used car). If these transactions are made using money, however, they do influence the number of times money changes hands during the course of a year. GDP is an imperfect measure of transactions to use in calculating the velocity of money.

contains no more useful information than the statement "A bachelor is an unmarried man." The definition does not, for example, say anything about what will happen to $P \times Y$ when M changes. The final value of $P \times Y$ depends on what happens to V. If V falls when M increases, the product $M \times V$ could stay the same, in which case the change in M would have had no effect on nominal income. To give monetarism some economic content, a simple version of monetarism known as the **quantity theory of money** is used.

The Quantity Theory of Money

The key assumption of the quantity theory of money is that the velocity of money is constant (or virtually constant) over time. If we let $\overline{V}$ denote the constant value of V, the equation for the quantity theory can be written as follows:

$$M \times \overline{V} = P \times Y$$

Note that the double equal sign has replaced the triple equal sign because the equation is no longer an identity. The equation is true if velocity is constant (and equal to V) but not otherwise. If the equation is true, it provides an easy way to explain nominal GDP. Given M, which can be considered a policy variable set by the Federal Reserve (Fed), nominal GDP is just $M \times \overline{V}$. In this case, the effects of monetary policy are clear. Changes in M cause equal percentage changes in nominal GDP. For example, if the money supply doubles, nominal GDP also doubles. If the money supply remains unchanged, nominal GDP remains unchanged.

The key is whether the velocity of money is really constant. Early economists believed that the velocity of money was determined largely by institutional considerations, such as how often people are paid and how the banking system clears transactions between banks. Because these factors change gradually, early economists believed velocity was essentially constant.

When there is equilibrium in the money market, then the quantity of money supplied is equal to the quantity of money demanded. That could mean that M in the quantity-theory equation equals both the quantity of money supplied and the quantity of money demanded. If the quantity-theory equation is looked on as a demand-for-money equation, it says that the demand for money depends on nominal income (GDP, or $P \times Y$), but *not* on the interest rate.[2] If the interest rate changes and nominal income does not, the equation says that the quantity of money demanded will not change. This is contrary to the theory of the demand for money in Chapter 11, which had the demand for money depending on both income and the interest rate.

Testing the Quantity Theory of Money One way to test the validity of the quantity theory of money is to look at the demand for money using recent data on the U.S. economy. The key is this: Does money demand depend on the interest rate? Most empirical work says yes. When demand-for-money equations are estimated (or "fit to the data"), the interest rate usually turns out to be a factor. The demand for money does not appear to depend only on nominal income.

Another way of testing the quantity theory is to plot velocity over time and see how it behaves. Figure 18.1 plots the velocity of money for the 1960 I–2007 IV period. The data show that velocity is far from constant. There is a long-term trend—on average, velocity has been rising during these years—but fluctuations around this trend have also occurred and some have been quite large. Velocity rose from 6.1 in 1980 III to 6.7 in 1981 III, fell to 6.3 in 1983 I, rose to 6.7 in 1984 III, and fell to 5.7 in 1986 IV. Changes of a few tenths of a point may seem small, but they are actually large. For example, the money supply in 1986 IV was $799 billion. If velocity changes by 0.3 with a money supply of this amount and if the money supply is unchanged, we have a change in nominal GDP ($P \times Y$) of $240 billion (0.3 × $799 billion), which is about 5 percent of the level of GDP in 1986.

The debate over monetarist theories is more subtle than our discussion so far indicates. First, there are many definitions of the money supply. M1 is the money supply variable used for the graph in Figure 18.1, but there may be some other measure of the money supply that would lead to a smoother plot. For example, many people shifted their funds from checking account deposits to money market accounts when the latter became available in the late 1970s. Because GDP did not change as a result of this shift while M1 decreased, velocity—the ratio of GDP to M1—must have gone up. Suppose instead we measured the supply of money by M2 (which includes both checking accounts and money market accounts). In this case, the decrease in checking deposits would be exactly offset by the rise in money market account deposits and M2 would not change.

quantity theory of money The theory based on the identity $M \times V \equiv P \times Y$ and the assumption that the velocity of money (V) is constant (or virtually constant).

---

[2] In terms of the Appendix to Chapter 12, this means that the LM curve is vertical.

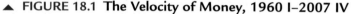

▲ **FIGURE 18.1 The Velocity of Money, 1960 I–2007 IV**

Velocity has not been constant over the period from 1960 to 2007. There is a long-term trend—velocity has been rising. There are also fluctuations, some of them quite large.

With no change in GDP and no change in M2, the velocity of money would not change. Whether or not velocity is constant may depend partly on how we measure the money supply.

Second, there may be a time lag between a change in the money supply and its effects on nominal GDP. Suppose we experience a 10 percent increase in the money supply today, but it takes 1 year for nominal GDP to increase by 10 percent. If we measured the ratio of today's money supply to today's GDP, it would seem that velocity had fallen by 10 percent. However, if we measured today's money supply against GDP 1 year from now, when the increase in the supply of money had its full effect on income, velocity would have been constant.

The debate over the quantity theory of money is primarily empirical. It is a debate that can be resolved by looking at facts about the real world and seeing whether they are in accord with the predictions of theory. Is there a measure of the money supply and a choice of the time lag between a change in the money supply and its effects on nominal GDP such that V is in effect constant? If so, the monetarist theory is a useful approach to understanding how the macroeconomy works and how changes in the money supply will cause a proportionate increase in nominal GDP. If not, some other theory is likely to be more appropriate. (We discuss the testing of alternative theories at the end of this chapter.)

Inflation as a Purely Monetary Phenomenon

So far we have talked only about nominal output ($P \times Y$). We have said nothing about how a monetarist would break down a change in nominal output (due to a money-supply change) into a change in P and a change in Y. Here again it is not possible to make a general statement about what all monetarists believe. Some may believe that all of the change occurs in P, and others may believe that at least sometimes some of the change occurs in Y. If all the change occurs in P, then there is a proportional relationship between changes in the money supply and changes in the price level. For example, a 10 percent change in M will lead to a 10 percent change in P if Y remains unchanged. In this case, inflation (an increase in P) is always a purely monetary phenomenon. The price level will not change if the money supply does not change. We call this view, that changes in M affect only P and not Y, the "strict monetarist" view.

There is considerable disagreement as to whether the strict monetarist view is a good approximation of reality. For example, the strict view is not compatible with a nonvertical AS curve in the AS/AD model in Chapter 13. In the case of a nonvertical AS curve, an increase in M, which shifts the AD curve to the right, increases both P and Y. (You may want to review why.)

Almost all economists agree, however, that *sustained* inflation—inflation that continues over many periods—is a purely monetary phenomenon. In the context of the AS/AD framework, inflation cannot continue indefinitely unless the Fed "accommodates" it by increasing the money supply. Let us review this.

Consider a continuously increasing level of government spending (G) without any corresponding increase in taxes. The increases in G keep shifting the AD curve to the right, which leads to an increasing price level (P). (You may find it useful to draw a graph now.) With a fixed money supply, the increases in P lead to a higher and higher interest rate; but there is a limit to how far this can go. Because taxes are unchanged, the government must finance the increases in G by issuing bonds; and there is a limit to how many bonds the public is willing to hold regardless of how high the interest rate goes. At the point at which the public cannot be induced to hold any more bonds, the government will be unable to borrow any more to finance its expenditures. Only if the Fed is willing to increase the money supply (buy some of the government bonds) can the government spending (with its inflationary consequences) continue. Inflation cannot continue indefinitely without increases in the money supply.

The Keynesian/Monetarist Debate

The debate between Keynesians and monetarists was perhaps the central controversy in macroeconomics in the 1960s. As we will see next, this changed in the 1970s with the rise of new classical macroeconomics. From a historical perspective, however, it is useful to review this debate.

The leading spokesman for monetarism was Milton Friedman from the University of Chicago. Most monetarists, including Friedman, blamed much of the instability in the economy on the Federal Reserve, arguing that the high inflation that the United States encountered from time to time could have been avoided if only the Fed had not expanded the money supply so rapidly. Monetarists were skeptical of the Fed's ability to "manage" the economy—to expand the money supply during bad times and contract it during good times. A common argument against such management is the one discussed in Chapter 15: Time lags may make attempts to stimulate and contract the economy counterproductive.

Friedman advocated instead a policy of steady and slow money growth—specifically, that the money supply should grow at a rate equal to the average growth of real output (income) (Y). That is, the Fed should pursue a constant policy that accommodates real growth but not inflation.

Many Keynesians, on the other hand, advocated the application of coordinated monetary and fiscal policy tools to reduce instability in the economy—to fight inflation and unemployment. However, not all Keynesians advocated an activist federal government. Some rejected the strict monetarist position that changes in money affect only the price level in favor of the view that both monetary and fiscal policies make a difference. *At the same time*, though, they believed that the best possible policy for the government to pursue was basically noninterventionist.

Most economists now agree, after the experience of the 1970s, that monetary and fiscal tools are not finely calibrated. The notion that monetary and fiscal expansions and contractions can "fine-tune" the economy is gone forever. Still, many believe that the experiences of the 1970s also show that stabilization policies can help prevent even bigger economic disasters. Had the government not cut taxes and expanded the money supply in 1975 and in 1982, they argue, the recessions of those years might have been significantly worse. The same people would also argue that had the government not resisted the inflations of 1974 to 1975 and 1979 to 1981 with tight monetary policies, the inflations probably would have become much worse.

As noted previously, the debate between Keynesians and monetarists subsided with the advent of new classical macroeconomics, to which we now turn.

New Classical Macroeconomics

The challenge to Keynesian and related theories has come from a school sometimes referred to as the new classical macroeconomics.[3] Like monetarism and Keynesianism, this term is vague. No two new classical macroeconomists think exactly alike, and no single model completely represents this school. The following discussion, however, conveys the flavor of the new classical views.

The Development of New Classical Macroeconomics

New classical macroeconomics has developed from two different although related sources. These sources are the theoretical and the empirical critiques of existing, or traditional, macroeconomics.

On the theoretical level, there has been growing dissatisfaction with the way traditional models treat expectations. Keynes himself recognized that expectations (in the form of "animal spirits")

---

[3] The term *new classical* is used because many of the assumptions and conclusions of this group of economists resemble those of the classical economists—that is, those who wrote before Keynes.

play a big part in economic behavior. The problem is that traditional models have assumed that expectations are formed in naive ways. A common assumption, for example, is that people form their expectations of future inflation by assuming present inflation will continue. If they turn out to be wrong, they adjust their expectations by some fraction of the difference between their original forecast and the actual inflation rate. Suppose you expect 10 percent inflation next year. When next year comes, the inflation rate turns out to be only 5 percent, so you have made an error of 5 percentage points. You might then predict an inflation rate for the following year of 7.5 percent, halfway between your earlier expectation (10 percent) and actual inflation last year (5 percent).

The problem with this treatment of expectations is that it is not consistent with the assumptions of microeconomics. It implies that people systematically overlook information that would allow them to make better forecasts, even though there are costs to being wrong. If, as microeconomic theory assumes, people are out to maximize their satisfaction and firms are out to maximize their profits, they should form their expectations in a smarter way. Instead of naively assuming the future will be like the past or the present, they should actively seek to forecast the future. Any other behavior is not in keeping with the microeconomic view of the forward-looking, rational people who compose households and firms.

On the empirical level, there was stagflation in the U.S. economy during the 1970s. Remember, stagflation is simultaneous high unemployment and rising prices. The Phillips Curve theory of the 1960s predicted that demand pressure pushes up prices so that when demand is weak—in times of high unemployment, for example—prices should be stable (or perhaps even falling). The new classical theories were an attempt to explain the apparent breakdown in the 1970s of the simple inflation–unemployment trade-off predicted by the Phillips Curve. Just as the Great Depression of the 1930s motivated the development of Keynesian economics, so the stagflation of the 1970s helped motivate the formulation of new classical economics.

Rational Expectations

In previous chapters, we stressed households' and firms' expectations about the future. A firm's decision to build a new plant depends on its expectations of future sales. The amount of saving a household undertakes today depends on its expectations about future interest rates, wages, and prices.

rational-expectations hypothesis The hypothesis that people know the "true model" of the economy and that they use this model to form their expectations of the future.

How are expectations formed? Do people assume that things will continue as they are at present (such as predicting rain tomorrow because it is raining today)? What information do people use to make their guesses about the future? Questions such as these have become central to current macroeconomic thinking and research. One theory, the **rational-expectations hypothesis**, offers a powerful way of thinking about expectations.

Suppose we want to forecast inflation. What does it mean to say that my expectations of inflation are "rational"? The rational-expectations hypothesis assumes that people know the "true model" that generates inflation—they know how inflation is determined in the economy—and they use this model to forecast future inflation rates. If there were no random, unpredictable events in the economy and if people knew the true model generating inflation, their forecasts of future inflation rates would be perfect. Because it is true, the model would not permit mistakes and thus the people using it would not make mistakes.

However, many events that affect the inflation rate are not predictable—they are random. By "true" model, we mean a model that is, *on average*, correct in forecasting inflation. Sometimes the random events have a positive effect on inflation, which means that the model underestimates the inflation rate, and sometimes they have a negative effect, which means that the model overestimates the inflation rate. On average, the model is correct. Therefore, rational expectations are correct on average even though their predictions are not exactly right all the time.

To see why, suppose you have to forecast how many times a fair coin will come up heads out of 100 tosses. The true model in this case is that the coin has a 50/50 chance of coming up heads on any one toss. Because the outcome of the 100 tosses is random, you cannot be sure of guessing correctly. If you know the true model—that the coin is fair—your rational expectation of the outcome of 100 tosses is 50 heads. You are not likely to be exactly right—the actual number of heads is likely to be slightly higher or slightly lower than 50—but *on average*, you will be correct.

Sometimes people are said to have rational expectations if they use "all available information" in forming their expectations. This definition is vague because it is not always clear what "all available information" means. The definition is precise if by "all available information" we mean that people know and use the true model. We cannot have more or better information than the true model!

If information can be obtained at no cost, people are not behaving rationally when they fail to use all available information. Because there are usually costs to making a wrong forecast, it is not rational to overlook information that could help improve the accuracy of a forecast as long as the costs of acquiring that information do not outweigh the benefits of improving its accuracy.

Rational Expectations and Market Clearing   If firms have rational expectations and if they set prices and wages on this basis, on average, prices and wages will be set at levels that ensure equilibrium in the goods and labor markets. When a firm has rational expectations, it knows the demand curve for its output and the supply curve of labor that it faces, except when random shocks disrupt those curves. Therefore, on average, the firm will set the market-clearing prices and wages. The firm knows the true model, and it will not set wages different from those it expects will attract the number of workers it wants. If all firms behave this way, wages will be set in such a way that the total amount of labor supplied will, on average, be equal to the total amount of labor that firms demand. In other words, on average, there will be full employment.

In Chapter 14, we argued that there might be disequilibrium in the labor market (in the form of either unemployment or excess demand for workers) because firms may make mistakes in their wage-setting behavior due to expectation errors. If, on average, firms do not make errors, on average, there will be equilibrium. When expectations are rational, disequilibrium exists only temporarily as a result of random, unpredictable shocks—obviously an important conclusion. If true, it means that disequilibrium in any market is only temporary because firms, on average, set market-clearing wages and prices.

The assumption that expectations are rational radically changes the way we can view the economy. We go from a world in which unemployment can exist for substantial periods and the multiplier can operate to a world in which (on average) all markets clear and there is full employment. In this world, there is no need for government stabilization policies. Unemployment is not a problem that governments need to worry about; if it exists at all, it is because of unpredictable shocks that, on average, amount to zero. There is no more reason for the government to try to change the outcome in the labor market than there is for it to change the outcome in the banana market. On average, prices and wages are set at market-clearing levels.

The Lucas Supply Function   The **Lucas supply function**, named after Robert E. Lucas of the University of Chicago, is an important part of a number of new classical macroeconomic theories. It yields, as we shall see, a surprising policy conclusion. The function is deceptively simple. It says that real output (Y) depends on (is a function of) the difference between the actual price level (P) and the expected price level (P^e):

$$Y = f(P - P^e)$$

The actual price level minus the expected price level ($P - P^e$) is the **price surprise**. Before considering the policy implications of this function, we should look at the theory behind it.

Lucas begins by assuming that people and firms are specialists in production but generalists in consumption. If someone you know is a manual laborer, the chances are that she sells only one thing—labor. If she is a lawyer, she sells only legal services. In contrast, people buy a large bundle of goods—ranging from gasoline to ice cream and pretzels—on a regular basis. The same is true for firms. Most companies tend to concentrate on producing a small range of products, but they typically buy a larger range of inputs—raw materials, labor, energy, and capital. According to Lucas, this divergence between buying and selling creates an asymmetry. People know more about the prices of the things they sell than they do about the prices of the things they buy.[4]

At the beginning of each period, a firm has some expectation of the average price level for that period. If the actual price level turns out to be different, there is a price surprise. Suppose the average price level is higher than expected. Because the firm learns about the actual price level slowly, some time goes by before it realizes that all prices have gone up. The firm *does* learn *quickly* that the price of its *output* has gone up. The firm perceives—incorrectly, it turns out—that its price has risen relative to other prices, and this perception leads it to produce more output.

Lucas supply function   The supply function embodies the idea that output (Y) depends on the difference between the actual price level and the expected price level.

price surprise   Actual price level minus expected price level.

---

[4] It is not entirely obvious why this should be true, and some critics of the new classical school have argued that this is unrealistic. Some have also criticized the Lucas supply function as being too simple, arguing that other things besides price surprises affect aggregate output.

ECONOMICS IN PRACTICE

How Are Expectations Formed?

A current debate among macroeconomists and policy makers is how people form expectations about the future state of the economy. Of particular interest is the formation of inflationary expectations. One possible way that inflation can be transmitted in an economy is if individuals expect there to be inflation and then, because of these expectations, demand higher wages, leading in turn to increases in inflation. In 2008, a number of central bankers began to worry about the possibility that inflationary expectations were heating up. For example, Thomas Hoenig, the president of the Federal Reserve Bank of Kansas City, said on May 6, 2008: "The bigger concern is that these price increases are beginning to generate an inflation psychology to the extent that I have not seen since the 1970s and early 1980s."

How are expectations in fact formed? Are expectations rational, as some macroeconomists believe, reflecting an accurate understanding of how the economy works? Or are they formed in simpler, more mechanical ways? A recent research paper by Ronnie Driver and Richard Windram from the Bank of England sheds some light on this issue. Since 1999, the Bank of England has done a survey four times a year of 2,000 British consumers about their views of future inflation and future interest rates. The surveys suggest that consumers tend to expect future inflation to be what they perceive past inflation to have been. Also, there are some differences between what consumers perceive past inflation to have been and the actual estimates of past inflation made by the government. In other words, consumers are more influenced by their own experience than by actual government numbers and their expectations of the future are based on their past experiences. Consumers mostly expect the future to look the way they perceive the past to have looked. Two factors that appear to be important in influencing consumer perceptions of inflation are gas prices and the attention the media pays to price increases. All this suggests that, at least for the British consumers surveyed, the formation of inflationary expectations is a less sophisticated process than some economic theorists suggest. This research also suggests that to the extent that gas prices increase and media attention to inflation increases, both of which were occurring in 2008, are important in influencing consumers' expectations, there may be an increase in inflationary expectations in 2008. Thomas Hoenig may have reason to worry.

A similar argument holds for workers. When there is a positive price surprise, workers at first believe that their "price"—their wage rate—has increased relative to other prices. Workers believe that their real wage rate has risen. We know from theory that an increase in the real wage is likely to encourage workers to work more hours.[5] The real wage has not actually risen, but it takes workers a while to figure this out. In the meantime, they supply more hours of work than they would have. This increase means that the economy produces more output when prices are unexpectedly higher than when prices are at their expected level.

This is the rationale for the Lucas supply function. Unexpected increases in the price level can fool workers and firms into thinking that relative prices have changed, causing them to alter the amount of labor or goods they choose to supply.

Policy Implications of the Lucas Supply Function   The Lucas supply function in combination with the assumption that expectations are rational implies that anticipated policy changes have no effect on real output. Consider a change in monetary policy. In general, the change will have some effect on the average price level. If the policy change is announced to the public, people will know the effect on the price level because they have rational expectations (and know the way changes in monetary policy affect the price level). This means that the change in

---

[5] This is true if we assume that the substitution effect dominates the income effect (see Chapter 17).

monetary policy affects the actual price level and the expected price level in the same way. The new price level minus the new expected price level is zero—no price surprise. In such a case, there will be no change in real output because the Lucas supply function states that real output can change from its fixed level only if there is a price surprise.

The general conclusion is that *any* announced policy change—in fiscal policy or any other policy—has no effect on real output because the policy change affects both actual and expected price levels in the same way. If people have rational expectations, known policy changes can produce no price surprises—and no increases in real output. The only way any change in government policy can affect real output is if it is kept in the dark so it is not generally known. Government policy can affect real output only if it surprises people; otherwise, it cannot. Rational-expectations theory combined with the Lucas supply function proposes a very small role for government policy in the economy.

Evaluating Rational-Expectations Theory

What are we to make of all this? It should be clear that the key question concerning the new classical macroeconomics is how realistic is the assumption of rational expectations. If it approximates the way expectations are actually formed, then it calls into question any theory that relies at least in part on expectation errors for the existence of disequilibrium. The arguments in favor of the rational-expectations assumption sound persuasive from the perspective of microeconomic theory. When expectations are not rational, there are likely to be unexploited profit opportunities—most economists believe such opportunities are rare and short-lived.

The argument *against* rational expectations is that it requires households and firms to know too much. This argument says that it is unrealistic to think that these basic decision-making units know as much as they need to know to form rational expectations. People must know the true model (or at least a good approximation of the true model) to form rational expectations, and this knowledge is a lot to expect. Even if firms and households are capable of learning the true model, it may be costly to take the time and gather the relevant information to learn it. The gain from learning the true model (or a good approximation of it) may not be worth the cost. In this sense, there may not be unexploited profit opportunities around. Gathering information and learning economic models may be too costly to bother with, given the expected gain from improving forecasts.

Although the assumption that expectations are rational seems consistent with the satisfaction-maximizing and profit-maximizing postulates of microeconomics, the rational-expectations assumption is more extreme and demanding because it requires more information on the part of households and firms. Consider a firm engaged in maximizing profits. In some way or other, it forms expectations of the relevant future variables; and given these expectations, it figures out the best thing to do from the point of view of maximizing profits. Given a set of expectations, the problem of maximizing profits may not be too hard. What may be hard is forming accurate expectations in the first place. This requires firms to know much more about the overall economy than they are likely to, so the assumption that their expectations are rational is not necessarily realistic. Firms, like the rest of us—so the argument goes—grope around in a world that is difficult to understand, trying to do their best but not always understanding enough to avoid mistakes.

In the final analysis, the issue is empirical. Does the assumption of rational expectations stand up well against empirical tests? This question is difficult to answer. Much work is currently being done to answer it. There are no conclusive results yet, but it is one of the questions that makes macroeconomics an exciting area of research.

Real Business Cycle Theory

Recent work in new classical macroeconomics has been concerned with whether the existence of business cycles can be explained under the assumptions of complete price and wage flexibility (market clearing) and rational expectations. This work is called **real business cycle theory**. As we discussed in Chapter 13, if prices and wages are completely flexible, then the *AS* curve is vertical, even in the short run. If the *AS* curve is vertical, then events or phenomena that shift the *AD* curve (such as changes in the money supply, changes in government spending, and shocks to consumer and investor behavior) have no effect on real output. Real output does fluctuate over time, so the puzzle is how the fluctuations can be explained if they are not due to policy changes or other shocks that shift the *AD* curve. Solving this puzzle is one of the main missions of real business cycle theory.

It is clear that if shifts of the *AD* curve cannot account for real output fluctuations (because the *AS* curve is vertical), then shifts of the *AS* curve must be responsible. However, the task is to come up

real business cycle theory An attempt to explain business cycle fluctuations under the assumptions of complete price and wage flexibility and rational expectations. It emphasizes shocks to technology and other shocks.

with convincing explanations as to what causes these shifts and why they persist over a number of periods. The problem is particularly difficult when it comes to the labor market. If prices and wages are completely flexible, then there is never any unemployment aside from frictional unemployment. For example, because the measured U.S. unemployment rate was 9.7 percent in 1982 and 4.2 percent in 1999, the puzzle is to explain why so many more people chose not to work in 1982 than in 1999.

Early real business cycle theorists emphasized shocks to the production technology. Suppose there is a negative shock in a given year that causes the marginal product of labor to decline. This leads to a fall in the real wage, which leads to a decrease in the quantity of labor supplied. People work less because the negative technology shock has led to a lower return from working. The opposite happens when there is a positive shock: The marginal product of labor rises, the real wage rises, and people choose to work more. This early research was not as successful as some had hoped because it required what seemed to be unrealistically large shocks to explain the observed movements in labor supply over time.

Since this initial work, economists have explored other sources of shocks to labor or capital productivity, and work is actively continuing in this area. To date, fluctuations of some variables, but not all, have been explained fairly well. Some argue that this work is doomed to failure because it is based on the unrealistic assumption of complete price and wage flexibility, whereas others hold more hope. Real business cycle theory is another example of the current state of flux in macroeconomics.

Supply-Side Economics

From our discussion of equilibrium in the goods market, beginning with the simple multiplier in Chapter 8 and continuing through Chapter 13, we have focused primarily on *demand*. Supply increases and decreases in response to changes in aggregate expenditure (which is closely linked to aggregate demand). Fiscal policy works by influencing aggregate expenditure through tax policy and government spending. Monetary policy works by influencing investment and consumption spending through increases and decreases in the interest rate. The theories we have been discussing are "demand-oriented."

The 1970s were difficult times for the U.S. economy. The United States found itself in 1974 to 1975 with stagflation—high unemployment and inflation. In the late 1970s, inflation returned to the high levels of 1974 to 1975. It seemed as if policy makers were incapable of controlling the business cycle.

As a result of these seeming failures, orthodox economics came under fire. One assault was from a group of economists who expounded *supply-side economics*. The argument of the supply-siders was simple. Basically, they said, all the attention to demand in orthodox macroeconomic theory distracted our attention from the real problem with the U.S. economy. The real problem, said supply-siders, was that high rates of taxation and heavy regulation had reduced the incentive to work, to save, and to invest. What was needed was not a demand stimulus, but better incentives to stimulate *supply*.

If we cut taxes so people take home more of their paychecks, the argument continued, they will work harder and save more. If businesses get to keep more of their profits and can get away from government regulations, they will invest more. This added labor supply and investment, or capital supply, will lead to an expansion of the supply of goods and services, which will reduce inflation and unemployment at the same time. The ultimate solution to the economy's woes, the supply-siders concluded, was on the *supply side* of the economy.

At their most extreme, supply-siders argued that the incentive effects of supply-side policies were likely to be so great that a major cut in tax rates would actually *increase* tax revenues. Even though *tax rates* would be lower, more people would be working and earning income and firms would earn more profits, so that the increases in the *tax bases* (profits, sales, and income) would then outweigh the decreases in rates, resulting in increased government revenues.

The Laffer Curve Figure 18.2 presents a key diagram of supply-side economics. The tax rate is measured on the vertical axis, and tax revenue is measured on the horizontal axis. The assumption behind this curve is that there is some tax rate beyond which the supply response is large enough to lead to a decrease in tax revenue for further increases in the tax rate. There is obviously some tax rate between zero and 100 percent at which tax revenue is at a maximum. At a tax rate of zero, work effort is high but there is no tax revenue. At a tax rate of 100, the labor supply is presumably zero because people are not allowed to keep any of their income. Somewhere between zero and 100 is the maximum-revenue rate.

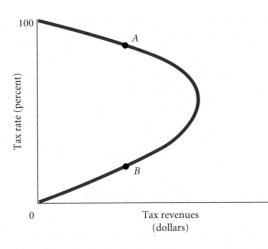

◀ FIGURE 18.2
The Laffer Curve
The Laffer curve shows that the amount of revenue the government collects is a function of the tax rate. It shows that when tax rates are very high, an increase in the tax rate could cause tax revenues to fall. Similarly, under the same circumstances, a cut in the tax rate could generate enough additional economic activity to cause revenues to rise.

The big debate in the 1980s was whether tax rates in the United States put the country on the upper or lower part of the curve in Figure 18.2. The supply-side school claimed that the United States was around *A* and that taxes should be cut. Others argued that the United States was nearer *B* and that tax cuts would lead to lower tax revenue.

The diagram in Figure 18.2 is the **Laffer curve**, named after economist Arthur Laffer, who, legend has it, first drew it on the back of a napkin at a cocktail party. The Laffer curve had some influence on the passage of the Economic Recovery Tax Act of 1981, the tax package put forward by the Reagan administration that brought with it substantial cuts in both personal and business taxes. Individual income tax rates were cut by as much as 25 percent over 3 years. Corporate taxes were cut sharply in a way designed to stimulate capital investment. The new law allowed firms to depreciate their capital at a rapid rate for tax purposes, and the bigger deductions led to taxes that were significantly lower than before.

Laffer curve   With the tax rate measured on the vertical axis and tax revenue measured on the horizontal axis, the Laffer curve shows that there is some tax rate beyond which the supply response is large enough to lead to a decrease in tax revenue for further increases in the tax rate.

Evaluating Supply-Side Economics

Supporters of supply-side economics claim that Reagan's tax policies were successful in stimulating the economy. They point to the fact that almost immediately after the tax cuts of 1981 were put into place, the economy expanded and the recession of 1980 to 1982 came to an end. In addition, inflation rates fell sharply from the high rates of 1980 and 1981. Except for 1 year, federal receipts continued to rise throughout the 1980s despite the cut in tax rates.

Critics of supply-side policies do not dispute these facts, but offer an alternative explanation of how the economy recovered. The Reagan tax cuts were enacted just as the U.S. economy was in the middle of its deepest recession since the Great Depression. The unemployment rate stood at 10.8 percent in the fourth quarter of 1982. It was the recession, critics argue, that was responsible for the reduction in inflation—not the supply-side policies. Also among the criticisms of supply-side economics is that it is unlikely a tax cut would substantially increase the supply of labor. In addition, in theory, a tax cut could even lead to a *reduction* in labor supply. Recall our discussion of income and substitution effects in Chapter 16. Although it is true that a higher after-tax wage rate provides a higher reward for each hour of work and thus more incentive to work, a tax cut also means that households receive a higher income for a given number of hours of work. Because they can earn the same amount of money working fewer hours, households might choose to work *less*. They might spend some of their added income on leisure. Research done during the 1980s suggests that tax cuts seem to increase the supply of labor somewhat but that the increases are very modest.

What about the recovery from the recession? Why did real output begin to grow rapidly in late 1982, precisely when the supply-side tax cuts were taking effect? Two reasons have been suggested. First, the supply-side tax cuts had large *demand*-side effects that stimulated the economy. Second, the Fed pumped up the money supply and drove interest rates down at the same time the tax cuts were being put into effect. The money supply expanded about 20 percent between 1981 and 1983, and interest rates succumbed. In 1981, the average 3-month U.S. Treasury bill paid 14 percent interest. In 1983, the figure had dropped to 8.6 percent.

Certainly, traditional theory suggests that a huge tax cut will lead to an increase in disposable income and, in turn, an increase in consumption spending (a component of aggregate expenditure). In addition, although an increase in planned investment (brought about by a lower interest rate) leads to added productive capacity and added supply in the long run, it also increases expenditures on capital goods (new plant and equipment investment) in the short run.

Whether the recovery from the 1981–1982 recession was the result of supply-side expansion or supply-side policies that had demand-side effects, one thing is clear: The extreme promises of the supply-siders did not materialize. President Reagan argued that because of the effect depicted in the Laffer curve, the government could maintain expenditures (and even increase defense expenditures sharply), cut tax rates, *and* balance the budget. This was not the case. Government revenues fell sharply from levels that would have been realized without the tax cuts. After 1982, the federal government ran huge deficits, with nearly $2 trillion added to the national debt between 1983 and 1992.

Testing Alternative Macroeconomic Models

You may wonder why there is so much disagreement in macroeconomics. Why can't macroeconomists test their models against one another and see which performs best?

One problem is that macroeconomic models differ in ways that are hard to standardize. If one model takes the price level to be given, or not explained within the model, and another one does not, the model with the given price level may do better in, for instance, predicting output—not because it is a better model but simply because the errors in predicting prices have not been allowed to affect the predictions of output. The model that takes prices as given has a head start, so to speak.

Another problem arises in the testing of the rational-expectations assumption. Remember, if people have rational expectations, they are using the true model to form their expectations. Therefore, to test this assumption, we need the true model. There is no way to be sure that whatever model is taken to be the true model is in fact the true one. Any test of the rational-expectations hypothesis is therefore a *joint* test (1) that expectations are formed rationally and (2) that the model being used is the true one. If the test rejects the hypothesis, it may be that the model is wrong rather than that the expectations are not rational.

Another problem for macroeconomists is the small amount of data available. Most empirical work uses data beginning about 1950, which in 2008 was about 59 years' (236 quarters) worth of data. Although this may seem like a lot of data, it is not. Macroeconomic data are fairly "smooth," which means that a typical variable does not vary much from quarter to quarter or from year to year. For example, the number of business cycles within this 59-year period is small, about eight. Testing various macroeconomic hypotheses on the basis of eight business cycle observations is not easy, and any conclusions must be interpreted with caution.

To give an example of the problem of a small number of observations, consider trying to test the hypothesis that import prices affect domestic prices. Import prices changed very little in the 1950s and 1960s. Therefore, it would have been very difficult at the end of the 1960s to estimate the effect of import prices on domestic prices. The variation in import prices was not great enough to show any effects. We cannot demonstrate that changes in import prices help explain changes in domestic prices if import prices do not change. The situation was different by the end of the 1970s because by then, import prices had varied considerably. By the end of the 1970s, there were good estimates of the import price effect, but not before. This kind of problem is encountered again and again in empirical macroeconomics. In many cases, there are not enough observations for much to be said and hence there is considerable room for disagreement.

We said in Chapter 1 that it is difficult in economics to perform controlled experiments. Economists, are for the most part, at the mercy of the historical data. If we were able to perform experiments, we could probably learn more about the economy in a shorter time. Alas, we must wait. In time, the current range of disagreements in macroeconomics should be considerably narrowed.

SUMMARY

KEYNESIAN ECONOMICS *p. 339*

1. In a broad sense, Keynesian economics is the foundation of modern macroeconomics. In a narrower sense, *Keynesian* refers to economists who advocate active government intervention in the economy.

MONETARISM *p. 340*

2. The monetarist analysis of the economy places a great deal of emphasis on the *velocity of money*, which is defined as the number of times a dollar bill changes hands, on average, during the course of a year. The velocity of money is the ratio of nominal GDP to the stock of money, or $V \equiv GDP/M \equiv (P \times Y)/M$. Alternately, $M \times V \equiv P \times Y$.

3. The *quantity theory of money* assumes that velocity is constant (or virtually constant). This implies that changes in the supply of money will lead to equal percentage changes in nominal GDP. The quantity theory of money equation is $M \times \overline{V} = P \times Y$. The equation says that demand for money does not depend on the interest rate.

4. Most economists believe that sustained inflation is a purely monetary phenomenon. Inflation cannot continue indefinitely unless the Fed "accommodates" it by expanding the money supply.

5. Most monetarists blame most of the instability in the economy on the federal government and are skeptical of the government's ability to manage the macroeconomy. They argue that the money supply should grow at a rate equal to the average growth of real output (income) (Y)—the Fed should expand the money supply to accommodate real growth but not inflation.

NEW CLASSICAL MACROECONOMICS *p. 343*

6. The *new classical macroeconomics* has developed from two different but related sources: the theoretical and the empirical critiques of traditional macroeconomics. On the theoretical level, there has been growing dissatisfaction with the way traditional models treat expectations. On the empirical level, the stagflation in the U.S. economy during the 1970s caused many people to look for alternative theories to explain the breakdown of the Phillips Curve.

7. The *rational-expectations hypothesis* assumes that people know the "true model" that generates economic variables. For example, rational expectations assumes that people know how inflation is determined in the economy and use this model to forecast future inflation rates.

8. The *Lucas supply function* assumes that real output (Y) depends on the actual price level minus the expected price level, or the *price surprise*. This function combined with the assumption that expectations are rational implies that anticipated policy changes have no effect on real output.

9. *Real business cycle theory* is an attempt to explain business cycle fluctuations under the assumptions of complete price and wage flexibility and rational expectations. It emphasizes shocks to technology and other shocks.

SUPPLY-SIDE ECONOMICS *p. 348*

10. *Supply-side economics* focuses on incentives to stimulate supply. Supply-side economists believe that if we lower taxes, workers will work harder and save more and firms will invest more and produce more. At their most extreme, supply-siders argue that incentive effects are likely to be so great that a major cut in taxes will actually increase tax revenues.

11. The *Laffer curve* shows the relationship between tax rates and tax revenues. Supply-side economists use it to argue that it is possible to generate higher revenues by cutting tax rates. This does not appear to have been the case during the Reagan administration, however, where lower tax rates decreased tax revenues significantly and contributed to the large increase in the federal debt during the 1980s.

TESTING ALTERNATIVE MACROECONOMIC MODELS *p. 350*

12. Economists disagree about which macroeconomic model is best for several reasons: (1) Macroeconomic models differ in ways that are hard to standardize; (2) when testing the rational-expectations assumption, we are never sure that whatever model is taken to be the true model is the true one; and (3) the amount of data available is fairly small.

REVIEW TERMS AND CONCEPTS

Laffer curve, *p. 349*

Lucas supply function, *p. 345*

price surprise, *p. 345*

quantity theory of money, *p. 341*

rational-expectations hypothesis, *p. 344*

real business cycle theory, *p. 347*

velocity of money, *p. 340*

$$V \equiv \frac{GDP}{M}$$

$$M \times V \equiv P \times Y$$

$$M \times \overline{V} = P \times Y$$

PROBLEMS

Visit **www.myeconlab.com** to complete the problems marked in orange online. You will receive instant feedback on your answers, tutorial help, and access to additional practice problems.

myeconlab

1. The table gives estimates of the rate of money supply growth and the rate of real GDP growth for five countries in 2000:
   a. If you were a monetarist, what would you predict about the rate of inflation across the five countries?
   b. If you were a Keynesian and assuming activist central banks, how might you interpret the same data?

	RATE OF GROWTH IN MONEY SUPPLY (M1)	RATE OF GROWTH OF REAL GDP
Australia	+ 9.3	+4.4
Britain	+ 7.6	+4.4
Canada	+18.7	+4.9
Japan	+ 9.0	+0.7
United States	+ 0.2	+5.1

2. The three diagrams in Figure 1 represent in a simplified way the predictions of the three theories presented in this chapter about the likely effects of a major tax cut.
   a. Match each of the following theories with a graph: (1) Keynesian economics, (2) supply-side economics, (3) rational expectations/monetarism. Explain the logic behind the three graphs.
   b. Which theory do you find most convincing? Explain.

3. [Related to the *Economics in Practice* on p. 346] Suppose you are thinking about where to live after you finish your degree. You discover that an apartment building near your new job has identical units—one for rent and the other for sale as a condominium. Given your salary, both are affordable and you like them. Would you buy or rent? How would you go about deciding? Would your expectations play a role? Be specific. Where do you think those expectations come from? In what ways could expectations change things in the housing market as a whole?

4. In 2000, a well-known economist was heard to say, "The problem with supply-side economics is that when you cut taxes, they have both supply and demand side effects and you cannot separate the effects." Explain this comment. Be specific and use the 1997 tax cuts or the Reagan tax cuts of 1981 as an example.

5. A cornerstone of new classical economics is the notion that expectations are "rational." What do you think will happen to the prices of single-family homes in your community over the next several years? On what do you base your expectations? Is your thinking consistent with the notion of rational expectations? Explain.

6. You are a monetarist given the following information: The money supply is $1,000. The velocity of money is 5. What is nominal income? real income? What happens to nominal income if the money supply is doubled? What happens to real income?

7. When Bill Clinton took office in January 1993, he faced two major economic problems: a large federal budget deficit and high unemployment resulting from a very slow recovery from the recession of 1990 to 1991. In his first State of the Union message, the president called for spending cuts and substantial tax increases to reduce the deficit. Most of these proposed spending cuts were in the defense budget. The following day Alan Greenspan, chair of the Federal Reserve Board of Governors, signaled his support for the president's plan. Many elements of the president's original plan were later incorporated into the deficit reduction bill passed in 1993.
   a. Some said at the time that without the Fed's support, the Clinton plan would be a disaster. Explain this argument.
   b. Supply-side economists and monetarists were very worried about the plan and the support it received from the Fed. What specific problems might a monetarist and a supply-side economist worry about?
   c. Suppose you were hired by the Federal Reserve Bank of St. Louis to report on the events of 1995 and 1996. What specific evidence would you look for to see whether the Clinton plan was effective or whether the critics were right to be skeptical?

8. In an economy with reasonably flexible prices and wages, full employment is almost always maintained. Explain why that statement is true.

9. During the 1980 presidential campaign, Ronald Reagan promised to cut taxes, increase expenditures on national defense, and balance the budget. During the New Hampshire primary of 1980, George Bush called this policy "voodoo economics." The two men were arguing about the relative merits of supply-side economics. Explain their disagreement.

*10. In a hypothetical economy, there is a simple proportional tax on wages imposed at a rate t. There are plenty of jobs around; so if people enter the labor force, they can find work. We define total government receipts from the tax as

$$T = t \times W \times L$$

where t = the tax rate, W = the gross wage rate, and L = the total supply of labor. The net wage rate is

$$W_n = (1 - t)\,W$$

The elasticity of labor supply is defined as

$$\frac{\text{Percentage of change in } L}{\text{Percentage of change in } W_n} = \frac{\Delta L / \Delta L}{\Delta W_n / W_n}$$

Suppose t was cut from .25 to .20. For such a cut to *increase* total government receipts from the tax, how elastic must the supply of labor be? (Assume a constant gross wage.) What does your answer imply about the supply-side assertion that a cut in taxes can increase tax revenues?

---

*Note: Problems marked with an asterisk are more challenging.

| I. | II. | III. |

FIGURE 1

International Trade, Comparative Advantage, and Protectionism

19

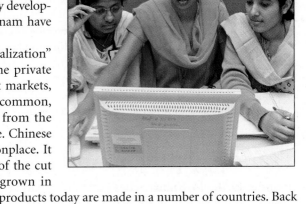

Over the last 40 years, international transactions have become increasingly important to the U.S. economy. In 1970, imports represented only about 7 percent of U.S. gross domestic product (GDP). The share is now around 17 percent. In 2007, the United States imported on average more than $195 billion worth of goods and services each month. The increased trade we observe in the United States is mirrored throughout the world. From 1980 to 2005, world trade in real terms grew more than 5 times. This trend has been especially rapid in the newly industrialized Asian economies, but many developing countries such as Malaysia and Vietnam have been increasing their openness to trade.

The "internationalization" or "globalization" of the U.S. economy has occurred in the private and public sectors, in input and output markets, and in firms and households. Once uncommon, foreign products are now everywhere, from the utensils we eat with to the cars we drive. Chinese textiles and Indian software are commonplace. It might surprise you to learn that many of the cut flowers sold in the United States are grown in Africa and South America. In fact, most products today are made in a number of countries. Back in Chapter 1, we presented an *Economics in Practice* that described the production of Apple's iPod. An iPod contains 451 parts made in countries scattered around the world including Korea, Japan, China, and the United States. The bottom of the iPod has the following information: "Assembled in China; Designed in California." Suzuki makes cars in Hungary and employs workers from Romania and Slovakia. Honda started producing Japanese motorcycles in Ohio in 1977 with 64 employees in Marysville. The company now employs over 12,000 workers who assemble Honda automobiles. Bose is based in the United States but has its electronic components assembled in Mexico.

At the same time, the United States exports billions of dollars' worth of agricultural goods, aircraft, and industrial machinery. Korea imports substantial amounts of U.S. beef. In addition,

TABLE 19.1

	Exports Minus Imports
1929	+0.4
1933	+0.1
1945	−0.8
1955	+0.5
1960	+4.2
1965	+5.6
1970	+4.0
1975	+16.0
1976	−1.6
1977	−23.1
1978	−25.4
1979	−22.5
1980	−13.1
1981	−12.5
1982	−20.0
1983	−51.7
1984	−102.7
1985	−115.2
1986	−132.7
1987	−145.2
1988	−110.4
1989	−88.2
1990	−78.0
1991	−27.5
1992	−33.2
1993	−65.0
1994	−93.6
1995	−91.4
1996	−96.2
1997	−101.6
1998	−159.9
1999	−260.5
2000	−379.5
2001	−367.0
2002	−424.4
2003	−499.4
2004	−615.4
2005	−714.6
2006	−762.0
2007	−708.0

Source: U.S. Department of Commerce, Bureau of Economic Analysis.

trade surplus The situation when a country exports more than it imports.

trade deficit The situation when a country imports more than it exports.

the United States exports and imports large quantities of services. When a Pakistani student enrolls in an American college or university, or a sick woman from Chile seeks medical attention in a U.S. hospital, or a Kenyan hires a lawyer in Miami to help him with a real estate deal, or a tourist from Indonesia eats at a restaurant in New York City, the United States is exporting a service. Similarly, when a student from the United States takes her junior year abroad in Scotland, or a tourist stays in a hotel in Singapore or gets a massage at a spa in Jamaica, the United States is importing a service.

Nor are the patterns of trade that we observe in one period set in stone. Consider the case of textiles and apparel. As recently as 2000, Mexico was the major supplier to the United States of textiles and apparel with almost 15 percent of total U.S. imports in this category. By 2006, China had overtaken Mexico's lead with 29 percent of the share of U.S. textile and apparel imports. The Dominican Republic and Honduras, which had been the fourth and fifth largest sources of U.S. imports, respectively, had been replaced by Bangladesh and Indonesia. In 2004, for the first time, India became one of the top five exporters to the United States in this category.

In addition to the fact that goods and services (outputs) flow easily across borders, so too do inputs: capital and labor. Certainly, it is very easy to buy financial assets abroad. Millions of Americans own shares in foreign stocks or have invested in bonds issued by foreign countries. At the same time, millions of foreigners have put money into the U.S. stock and bond markets.

A new phenomenon, outsourcing, is also changing the nature of the global labor market. It is now simple and very common for a customer service call to a software company from a user of its product in Bend, Oregon, to be routed to Bangalore, India, where a young, ambitious Indian man or woman provides assistance to a customer over the Internet. The Internet has in essence made it possible for labor to flow smoothly across international borders.

The inextricable connection of the U.S. economy to the economies of the rest of the world has had a profound impact on the discipline of economics and is the basis of one of its most important insights: All economies, regardless of their size, depend to some extent on other economies and are affected by events outside their borders.

To get you more acquainted with the international economy, this chapter discusses the economics of international trade. First, we describe the recent tendency of the United States to import more than it exports. Next, we explore the basic logic of trade. Why should the United States or any other country engage in international trade? Finally, we address the controversial issue of protectionism. Should a country provide certain industries with protection in the form of import quotas or tariffs, which are taxes imposed on imports? Should a country help a domestic industry compete in international markets by providing subsidies?

Trade Surpluses and Deficits

Until the 1970s, the United States generally exported more than it imported. When a country exports more than it imports, it runs a **trade surplus**. When a country imports more than it exports, it runs a **trade deficit**. Table 19.1 shows that before 1976 the United States generally ran a trade surplus. This changed in 1976, and since 1976 the United States has run a trade deficit. The deficit reached a local peak of $145.2 billion in 1987, fell to $27.5 billion in 1991, and then rose dramatically to over $700 billion by 2005.

The large trade deficits in the middle and late 1980s sparked political controversy that continues today. Foreign competition hit U.S. markets hard. Less expensive foreign goods—among them steel, textiles, and automobiles—began driving U.S. manufacturers out of business; and thousands of jobs were lost in important industries. Cities such as Pittsburgh, Youngstown, and Detroit had major unemployment problems. In more recent times, the outsourcing of software development to India has caused complaints from white-collar workers.

The natural reaction to trade-related job dislocation is to call for protection of U.S. industries. Many people want the president and Congress to impose taxes and import restrictions that would make foreign goods less available and more expensive, protecting U.S. jobs. This argument is not new. For hundreds of years, industries have petitioned governments for protection and societies have debated the pros and cons of free and open trade. For the last century and a half, the principal argument against protection has been the theory of comparative advantage, first discussed in Chapter 2.

The Economic Basis for Trade: Comparative Advantage

Perhaps the best-known debate on the issue of free trade took place in the British Parliament during the early years of the nineteenth century. At that time, the landed gentry—the landowners—controlled Parliament. For a number of years, imports and exports of grain had been subject to a set of tariffs, subsidies, and restrictions collectively called the **Corn Laws**. Designed to discourage imports of grain and to encourage exports, the Corn Laws' purpose was to keep the price of food high. The landlords' incomes, of course, depended on the prices they got for what their land produced. The Corn Laws clearly worked to the advantage of those in power.

With the Industrial Revolution, a class of wealthy industrial capitalists emerged. The industrial sector had to pay workers at least enough to live on, and a living wage depended greatly on the price of food. Tariffs on grain imports and export subsidies that kept grain and food prices high increased the wages that capitalists had to pay, cutting into their profits. The political battle raged for years. However, as time went by, the power of the landowners in the House of Lords was significantly reduced. When the conflict ended in 1848, the Corn Laws were repealed.

On the side of repeal was David Ricardo, a businessman, economist, member of Parliament, and one of the fathers of modern economics. Ricardo's principal work, *Principles of Political Economy and Taxation*, was published in 1817, two years before he entered Parliament. Ricardo's **theory of comparative advantage**, which he used to argue against the Corn Laws, claimed that trade enables countries to specialize in producing the products they produce best. According to the theory specialization and free trade will benefit all trading partners (real wages will rise), even those that may be absolutely less efficient producers. This basic argument remains at the heart of free-trade debates even today, as policy makers argue about the effects of tariffs on agricultural development in sub-Saharan Africa and the gains and losses from outsourcing software development to India.

The easiest way to understand the theory of comparative advantage is to examine a simple two-person society. Suppose Bill and Colleen, stranded on a deserted island in Chapter 2, have only two tasks to accomplish each week: gathering food to eat and cutting logs to construct a house. If Colleen could cut more logs than Bill in a day and Bill could gather more berries and fruits, specialization would clearly benefit both of them.

But suppose Bill is slow and clumsy and Colleen is better at cutting logs *and* gathering food. Ricardo's point is that it still pays for them to specialize. They can produce more in total by specializing than they can by sharing the work equally. We now turn to look at the application of the powerful idea of comparative advantage to international trade.

Corn Laws The tariffs, subsidies, and restrictions enacted by the British Parliament in the early nineteenth century to discourage imports and encourage exports of grain.

theory of comparative advantage Ricardo's theory that specialization and free trade will benefit all trading partners (real wages will rise), even those that may be absolutely less efficient producers.

Absolute Advantage versus Comparative Advantage

A country enjoys an **absolute advantage** over another country in the production of a good if it uses fewer resources to produce that good than the other country does. Suppose country A and country B produce wheat, but A's climate is more suited to wheat and its labor is more productive. Country A will produce more wheat per acre than country B and use less labor in growing it and bringing it to market. Country A enjoys an absolute advantage over country B in the production of wheat.

A country enjoys a **comparative advantage** in the production of a good if that good can be produced at lower cost *in terms of other goods*. Suppose countries C and D both produce wheat and corn and C enjoys an absolute advantage in the production of both—that is, C's climate is better than D's and fewer of C's resources are needed to produce a given quantity of both wheat and corn. Now C and D must each choose between planting land with either wheat or corn. To produce more wheat, either country must transfer land from corn production; to produce more corn, either country must transfer land from wheat production. The cost of wheat in each country can be measured in bushels of corn, and the cost of corn can be measured in bushels of wheat.

Suppose that in country C, a bushel of wheat has an opportunity cost of 2 bushels of corn. That is, to produce an additional bushel of wheat, C must give up 2 bushels of corn. At the same time, producing a bushel of wheat in country D requires the sacrifice of only 1 bushel of corn. Even though C has an *absolute* advantage in the production of both products, D enjoys a *comparative* advantage in the production of wheat because the *opportunity cost* of producing wheat is lower in D. Under these circumstances, Ricardo claims, D can benefit from trade if it specializes in the production of wheat.

absolute advantage The advantage in the production of a good enjoyed by one country over another when it uses fewer resources to produce that good than the other country does.

comparative advantage The advantage in the production of a good enjoyed by one country over another when that good can be produced at lower cost in terms of other goods than it could be in the other country.

Gains from Mutual Absolute Advantage To illustrate Ricardo's logic in more detail, suppose Australia and New Zealand each have a fixed amount of land and do not trade with the rest of the world. There are only two goods—wheat to produce bread and cotton to produce clothing. This kind of two-country/two-good world does not exist, but its operations can be generalized to many countries and many goods.

To proceed, we have to make some assumptions about the preferences of the people living in New Zealand and the people living in Australia. If the citizens of both countries walk around naked, there is no need to produce cotton, so all the land can be used to produce wheat. However, assume that people in both countries have similar preferences with respect to food and clothing: The populations of both countries use both cotton and wheat, and preferences for food and clothing are such that both countries consume equal amounts of wheat and cotton.

Finally, we assume that each country has only 100 acres of land for planting and that land yields are as given in Table 19.2. New Zealand can produce 3 times the wheat that Australia can on 1 acre of land, and Australia can produce 3 times the cotton that New Zealand can in the same space. New Zealand has an absolute advantage in the production of wheat, and Australia has an absolute advantage in the production of cotton. In cases like this, we say the two countries have *mutual absolute advantage*.

TABLE 19.2 Yield per Acre of Wheat and Cotton		
	New Zealand	Australia
Wheat	6 bushels	2 bushels
Cotton	2 bales	6 bales

If there is no trade and each country divides its land to obtain equal units of cotton and wheat production, each country produces 150 bushels of wheat and 150 bales of cotton. New Zealand puts 75 acres into cotton but only 25 acres into wheat, while Australia does the reverse (Table 19.3).

TABLE 19.3 Total Production of Wheat and Cotton Assuming No Trade, Mutual Absolute Advantage, and 100 Available Acres		
	New Zealand	Australia
Wheat	25 acres × 6 bushels/acre 150 bushels	75 acres × 2 bushels/acre 150 bushels
Cotton	75 acres × 2 bales/acre 150 bales	25 acres × 6 bales/acre 150 bales

We can organize the same information in graphic form as production possibility frontiers for each country. In Figure 19.1, which presents the positions of the two countries before trade, each country is constrained by its own resources and productivity. If Australia put all its land into cotton, it would produce 600 bales of cotton (100 acres × 6 bales/acre) and no wheat; if it put all its land into wheat, it would produce 200 bushels of wheat (100 acres × 2 bushels/acre) and no cotton. The opposite is true for New Zealand. Recall from Chapter 2 that a country's production possibility frontier represents all combinations of goods that can be produced, given the country's resources and state of technology. Each country must pick a point along its own production possibility curve.

When both countries have an absolute advantage in the production of one product, it is easy to see that specialization and trade will benefit both. Australia should produce cotton, and New Zealand should produce wheat. Transferring all land to wheat production in New Zealand yields 600 bushels, while transferring all land to cotton production in Australia yields 600 bales. An agreement to trade 300 bushels of wheat for 300 bales of cotton would double both wheat and cotton consumption in both countries. (Remember, before trade, both countries produced 150 bushels of wheat and 150 bales of cotton. After trade, each country will have 300 bushels of wheat and 300 bales of cotton to consume. Final production and trade figures are provided in Table 19.4 and Figure 19.2.) Trade enables both countries to move beyond their previous resource and productivity constraints.

The advantages of specialization and trade seem obvious when one country is technologically superior at producing one product and another country is technologically superior at producing another product. However, let us turn to the case in which one country has an absolute advantage in the production of *both* goods.

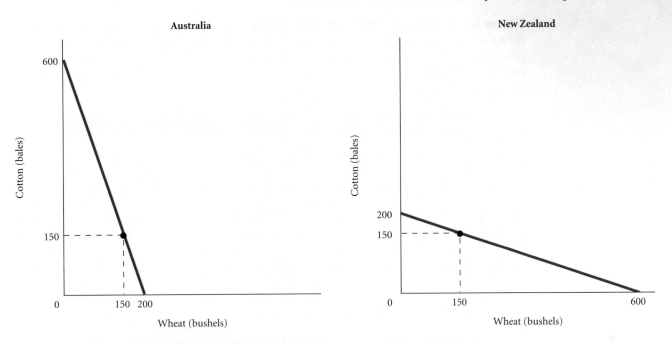

▲ **FIGURE 19.1 Production Possibility Frontiers for Australia and New Zealand Before Trade**

Without trade, countries are constrained by their own resources and productivity.

TABLE 19.4	Production and Consumption of Wheat and Cotton After Specialization				
	Production			Consumption	
	New Zealand	Australia		New Zealand	Australia
Wheat	100 acres × 6 bushels/acre 600 bushels	0 acres 0	Wheat	300 bushels	300 bushels
Cotton	0 acres 0	100 acres × 6 bales/acre 600 bales	Cotton	300 bales	300 bales

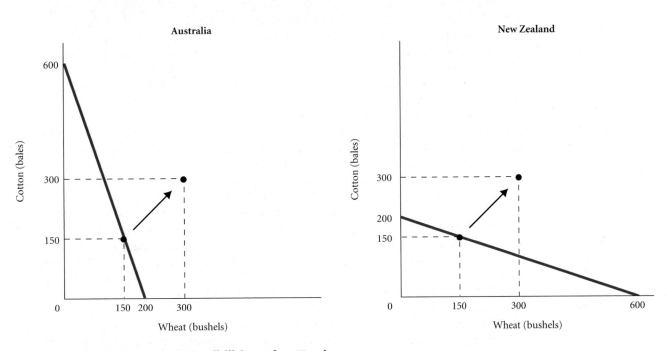

▲ **FIGURE 19.2 Expanded Possibilities After Trade**

Trade enables both countries to move beyond their own resource constraints—beyond their individual production possibility frontiers.

Gains from Comparative Advantage Table 19.5 contains different land yield figures for New Zealand and Australia. Now New Zealand has a considerable absolute advantage in the production of both cotton and wheat, with 1 acre of land yielding 6 times as much wheat and twice as much cotton as 1 acre in Australia. Ricardo would argue that *specialization and trade are still mutually beneficial.*

TABLE 19.5	Yield per Acre of Wheat and Cotton	
	New Zealand	Australia
Wheat	6 bushels	1 bushel
Cotton	6 bales	3 bales

Again, preferences imply consumption of equal units of cotton and wheat in both countries. With no trade, New Zealand would divide its 100 available acres evenly, or 50/50, between the two crops. The result would be 300 bales of cotton and 300 bushels of wheat. Australia would divide its land 75/25. Table 19.6 shows that final production in Australia would be 75 bales of cotton and 75 bushels of wheat. (Remember, we are assuming that in each country, people consume equal amounts of cotton and wheat.) Again, before any trade takes place, each country is constrained by its own domestic production possibility curve.

TABLE 19.6	Total Production of Wheat and Cotton Assuming No Trade and 100 Available Acres	
	New Zealand	Australia
Wheat	50 acres × 6 bushels/acre 300 bushels	75 acres × 1 bushel/acre 75 bushels
Cotton	50 acres × 6 bales/acre 300 bales	25 acres × 3 bales/acre 75 bales

Imagine we are at a meeting of trade representatives of both countries. As a special adviser, David Ricardo is asked to demonstrate that trade can benefit both countries. He divides his demonstration into three stages, which you can follow in Table 19.7.

TABLE 19.7	Realizing a Gain from Trade When One Country Has a Double Absolute Advantage					

	STAGE 1			STAGE 2	
	New Zealand	Australia		New Zealand	Australia
Wheat	50 acres × 6 bushels/acre 300 bushels	0 acres 0	Wheat	75 acres × 6 bushels/acre 450 bushels	0 acres 0
Cotton	50 acres × 6 bales/acre 300 bales	100 acres × 3 bales/acre 300 bales	Cotton	25 acres × 6 bales/acre 150 bales	100 acres × 3 bales/acre 300 bales

	STAGE 3	
	New Zealand	Australia
Wheat	100 bushels (trade) ⟶	
	350 bushels	100 bushels
	(after trade)	
Cotton	200 bales (trade) ⟵	
	350 bales	100 bales
	(after trade)	

In stage 1, Australia transfers all its land into cotton production. It will have no wheat and 300 bales of cotton. New Zealand cannot completely specialize in wheat because it needs 300 bales of cotton and will not be able to get enough cotton from Australia. The reason is that we are assuming that each country wants to consume equal amounts of cotton and wheat.

In stage 2, New Zealand transfers 25 acres out of cotton and into wheat. Now New Zealand has 25 acres in cotton that produce 150 bales and 75 acres in wheat that produce 450 bushels.

Finally, the two countries trade. We assume that New Zealand ships 100 bushels of wheat to Australia in exchange for 200 bales of cotton. After the trade, New Zealand has 350 bales of cotton and 350 bushels of wheat; Australia has 100 bales of cotton and 100 bushels of wheat. Both countries are better off than they were before the trade (Table 19.6), and both have moved beyond their own production possibility frontiers.

Why Does Ricardo's Plan Work?   To understand why Ricardo's scheme works, let us return to the definition of comparative advantage.

The real cost of producing cotton is the wheat that must be sacrificed to produce it. *When we think of cost this way, it is less costly to produce cotton in Australia than to produce it in New Zealand, even though an acre of land produces more cotton in New Zealand.* Consider the "cost" of 3 bales of cotton in the two countries. In terms of opportunity cost, 3 bales of cotton in New Zealand cost 3 bushels of wheat; in Australia, 3 bales of cotton cost only 1 bushel of wheat. Because 3 bales are produced by 1 acre of Australian land, to get 3 bales, an Australian must transfer 1 acre of land from wheat to cotton production. Because an acre of land produces a bushel of wheat, losing 1 acre to cotton implies the loss of 1 bushel of wheat. *Australia has a comparative advantage in cotton production* because its opportunity cost, in terms of wheat, is lower than New Zealand's. This is illustrated in Figure 19.3.

New Zealand has a comparative advantage in wheat production

Australia has a comparative advantage in cotton production

◀ **FIGURE 19.3**
Comparative Advantage Means Lower Opportunity Cost
The real cost of cotton is the wheat sacrificed to obtain it. The cost of 3 bales of cotton in New Zealand is 3 bushels of wheat (a half acre of land must be transferred from wheat to cotton—refer to Table 19.5). However, the cost of 3 bales of cotton in Australia is only 1 bushel of wheat. Australia has a comparative advantage over New Zealand in cotton production, and New Zealand has a comparative advantage over Australia in wheat production.

Conversely, New Zealand has a comparative advantage in wheat production. A unit of wheat in New Zealand costs 1 unit of cotton, while a unit of wheat in Australia costs 3 units of cotton. When countries specialize in producing goods in which they have a comparative advantage, they maximize their combined output and allocate their resources more efficiently.

Terms of Trade

Ricardo might suggest a number of options for exchanging wheat and cotton to the trading partners. The one we just examined benefited both partners; in percentage terms, Australia made out slightly better. Other deals might have been more advantageous to New Zealand.

The ratio at which a country can trade domestic products for imported products is the **terms of trade**. The terms of trade determine how the gains from trade are distributed among trading partners. In the case just considered, the agreed-to terms of trade were 1 bushel of wheat for 2 bales of cotton. Such terms of trade benefit New Zealand, which can get 2 bales of cotton for each bushel of wheat. If it were to transfer its own land from wheat to cotton, it would get only 1 bale of cotton. The same terms of trade benefit Australia, which can get 1 bushel of wheat for 2 bales of cotton. A direct transfer of its own land would force it to give up 3 bales of cotton for 1 bushel of wheat.

If the terms of trade changed to 3 bales of cotton for every bushel of wheat, only New Zealand would benefit. At those terms of trade, *all* the gains from trade would flow to New Zealand. Such terms do not benefit Australia at all because the opportunity cost of producing wheat domestically

terms of trade   The ratio at which a country can trade domestic products for imported products.

is *exactly the same* as the trade cost: A bushel of wheat costs 3 bales of cotton. If the terms of trade went the other way—1 bale of cotton for each bushel of wheat—only Australia would benefit. New Zealand gains nothing because it can already substitute cotton for wheat at that ratio. To get a bushel of wheat domestically, however, Australia must give up 3 bales of cotton, and one-for-one terms of trade would make wheat much less costly for Australia.

Both parties must have something to gain for trade to take place. In this case, you can see that both Australia and New Zealand will gain when the terms of trade are set between 1:1 and 3:1, cotton to wheat.

Exchange Rates

The examples used thus far have shown that trade can result in gains to both parties. When trade is free—unimpeded by government-instituted barriers—patterns of trade and trade flows result from the independent decisions of thousands of importers and exporters and millions of private households and firms.

Private households decide whether to buy Toyotas or Chevrolets, and private firms decide whether to buy machine tools made in the United States or machine tools made in Taiwan, raw steel produced in Germany or raw steel produced in Pittsburgh.

But how does this trade actually come about? Before a citizen of one country can buy a product made in another country or sold by someone in another country, a currency swap must take place. Consider Shane, who buys a Toyota from a dealer in Boston. He pays in dollars, but the Japanese workers who made the car receive their salaries in yen. Somewhere between the buyer of the car and the producer, a currency exchange must be made. The regional distributor probably takes payment in dollars and converts them into yen before remitting the proceeds to Japan.

To buy a foreign-produced good, a consumer, in effect, has to buy foreign currency. The price of Shane's Toyota in dollars depends on the price of the car stated in yen and the dollar price of yen. You probably know the ins and outs of currency exchange very well if you have ever traveled in another country.

In May 2008, the British pound was worth $1.97. Now suppose you are in London having dinner. On the menu is a nice bottle of wine for 15 pounds. How can you figure out whether you want to buy it? You know what dollars will buy in the United States, so you have to convert the price into dollars. Each pound will cost you $1.97, so 15 pounds will cost you $1.97 × 15 = $29.55.

exchange rate The ratio at which two currencies are traded. The price of one currency in terms of another.

The attractiveness of foreign goods to U.S. buyers and of U.S. goods to foreign buyers depends in part on the **exchange rate**, the ratio at which two currencies are traded. If the price of pounds were to fall to $1.20, that same bottle of wine would cost $18.

To understand the patterns of trade that result from the actions of hundreds of thousands of independent buyers and sellers—households and firms—we must know something about the factors that determine exchange rates. Exchange rate determination is very complicated. Here, however, we can demonstrate two things. First, for any pair of countries, there is a range of exchange rates that can lead automatically to both countries' realizing the gains from specialization and comparative advantage. Second, within that range, the exchange rate will determine which country gains the most from trade. In short, exchange rates determine the terms of trade.

Trade and Exchange Rates in a Two-Country/Two-Good World   Consider first a simple two-country/two-good model. Suppose both the United States and Brazil produce only two goods—raw timber and rolled steel. Table 19.8 gives the current prices of both goods as domestic buyers see them. In Brazil, timber is priced at 3 reals (R) per foot and steel is priced at 4 R per meter. In the United States, timber costs $1 per foot and steel costs $2 per meter.

TABLE 19.8	Domestic Prices of Timber (per Foot) and Rolled Steel (per Meter) in the United States and Brazil	
	United States	**Brazil**
Timber	$1	3 Reals
Rolled steel	$2	4 Reals

Suppose U.S. and Brazilian buyers have the option of buying at home or importing to meet their needs. The options they choose will depend on the exchange rate. For the time being, we will ignore transportation costs between countries and assume that Brazilian and U.S. products are of equal quality.

Let us start with the assumption that the exchange rate is $1 = 1 R. From the standpoint of U.S. buyers, neither Brazilian steel nor Brazilian timber is competitive at this exchange rate. A dollar buys a foot of timber in the United States, but if converted into a real, it will buy only one-third of a foot. The price of Brazilian timber to an American is $3 because it will take $3 to buy the necessary 3 R. Similarly, $2 buys a meter of rolled steel in the United States, but the same $2 buys only half a meter of Brazilian steel. The price of Brazilian steel to an American is $4, twice the price of domestically produced steel.

At this exchange rate, however, Brazilians find that U.S.-produced steel and timber are less expensive than steel and timber produced in Brazil. Timber at home—Brazil—costs 3 R, but 3 R buys $3, which buys 3 times as much timber in the United States. Similarly, steel costs 4 R at home, but 4 R buys $4, which buys twice as much U.S.-made steel. At an exchange rate of $1 = 1 R, Brazil will import steel and timber and the United States will import nothing.

However, now suppose the exchange rate is 1 R = $0.25. This means that 1 dollar buys 4 R. At this exchange rate, the Brazilians buy timber and steel at home and the Americans import both goods. At this exchange rate, Americans must pay a dollar for a foot of U.S. timber, but the same amount of timber can be had in Brazil for the equivalent of $0.75. (Because 1 R costs $0.25, 3 R can be purchased for $0.75.) Similarly, steel that costs $2 per meter in the United States costs an American half as much in Brazil because $2 buys 8 R, which buys 2 meters of Brazilian steel. At the same time, Brazilians are not interested in importing because both goods are cheaper when purchased from a Brazilian producer. In this case, the United States imports both goods and Brazil imports nothing.

So far we can see that at exchange rates of $1 = 1 R and $1 = 4 R, we get trade flowing in only one direction. Let us now try an exchange rate of $1 = 2 R, or 1 R = $0.50. First, Brazilians will buy timber in the United States. Brazilian timber costs 3 R per foot, but 3 R buys $1.50, which is enough to buy 1.5 feet of U.S. timber. Buyers in the United States will find Brazilian timber too expensive, but Brazil will import timber from the United States. At this same exchange rate, however, both Brazilian and U.S. buyers will be indifferent between Brazilian and U.S. steel. To U.S. buyers, domestically produced steel costs $2. Because $2 buys 4 R, a meter of imported Brazilian steel also costs $2. Brazilian buyers also find that steel costs 4 R, whether domestically produced or imported. Thus, there is likely to be no trade in steel.

What happens if the exchange rate changes so that $1 buys 2.1 R? While U.S. timber is still cheaper to both Brazilians and Americans, Brazilian steel begins to look good to U.S. buyers. Steel produced in the United States costs $2 per meter, but $2 buys 4.2 R, which buys more than a meter of steel in Brazil. When $1 buys more than 2 R, trade begins to flow in both directions: Brazil will import timber, and the United States will import steel.

If you examine Table 19.9 carefully, you will see that trade flows in both directions as long as the exchange rate settles between $1 = 2 R and $1 = 3 R. Stated the other way around, trade will flow in both directions if the price of a real is between $0.33 and $0.50.

TABLE 19.9	Trade Flows Determined by Exchange Rates	
Exchange Rate	Price of Real	Result
$1 = 1 R	$ 1.00	Brazil imports timber and steel.
$1 = 2 R	.50	Brazil imports timber.
$1 = 2.1 R	.48	Brazil imports timber; United States imports steel.
$1 = 2.9 R	.34	Brazil imports timber; United States imports steel.
$1 = 3 R	.33	United States imports steel.
$1 = 4 R	.25	United States imports timber and steel.

Exchange Rates and Comparative Advantage   If the foreign exchange market drives the exchange rate to anywhere between 2 and 3 R per dollar, the countries will automatically adjust and comparative advantage will be realized. At these exchange rates, U.S. buyers begin buying all their steel in Brazil. The U.S. steel industry finds itself in trouble. Plants close, and U.S. workers begin to lobby for tariff protection against Brazilian steel. At the same time, the U.S. timber industry does well, fueled by strong export demand from Brazil. The timber-producing sector expands. Resources, including capital and labor, are attracted into timber production.

The opposite occurs in Brazil. The Brazilian timber industry suffers losses as export demand dries up and Brazilians turn to cheaper U.S. imports. In Brazil, lumber companies turn to the government and ask for protection from cheap U.S. timber. However, steel producers in Brazil are happy. They are not only supplying 100 percent of the domestically demanded steel but also selling to U.S. buyers. The steel industry expands, and the timber industry contracts. Resources, including labor, flow into steel.

With this expansion-and-contraction scenario in mind, let us look again at our original definition of comparative advantage. If we assume that prices reflect resource use and resources can be transferred from sector to sector, we can calculate the opportunity cost of steel/timber in both countries. In the United States, the production of a meter of rolled steel consumes twice the resources that the production of a foot of timber consumes. Assuming that resources can be transferred, the opportunity cost of a meter of steel is 2 feet of timber (Table 19.8). In Brazil, a meter of steel uses resources costing 4 R, while a unit of timber costs 3 R. To produce a meter of steel means the sacrifice of only four-thirds (or one and one-third) feet of timber. Because the opportunity cost of a meter of steel (in terms of timber) is lower in Brazil, we say that Brazil has a comparative advantage in steel production.

Conversely, consider the opportunity cost of timber in the two countries. Increasing timber production in the United States requires the sacrifice of half a meter of steel for every foot of timber—producing a meter of steel uses $2 worth of resources, while producing a foot of timber requires only $1 worth of resources. Nevertheless, each foot of timber production in Brazil requires the sacrifice of three-fourths of a meter of steel. Because the opportunity cost of timber is lower in the United States, the United States has a comparative advantage in the production of timber. If exchange rates end up in the right ranges, the free market will drive each country to shift resources into those sectors in which it enjoys a comparative advantage. Only those products in which a country has a comparative advantage will be competitive in world markets.

The Sources of Comparative Advantage

Specialization and trade can benefit all trading partners, even those that may be inefficient producers in an absolute sense. If markets are competitive and if foreign exchange markets are linked to goods-and-services exchange, countries will specialize in producing products in which they have a comparative advantage.

factor endowments   The quantity and quality of labor, land, and natural resources of a country.

So far, we have said nothing about the sources of comparative advantage. What determines whether a country has a comparative advantage in heavy manufacturing or in agriculture? What explains the actual trade flows observed around the world? Various theories and empirical work on international trade have provided some answers. Most economists look to **factor endowments**—the quantity and quality of labor, land, and natural resources of a country—as the principal sources of comparative advantage. Factor endowments seem to explain a significant portion of actual world trade patterns.

Heckscher-Ohlin theorem   A theory that explains the existence of a country's comparative advantage by its factor endowments: A country has a comparative advantage in the production of a product if that country is relatively well endowed with inputs used intensively in the production of that product.

The Heckscher-Ohlin Theorem

Eli Heckscher and Bertil Ohlin, two Swedish economists who wrote in the first half of the twentieth century, expanded and elaborated on Ricardo's theory of comparative advantage. The **Heckscher-Ohlin theorem** ties the theory of comparative advantage to factor endowments. It assumes that products can be produced using differing proportions of inputs and that inputs are mobile between sectors in each economy but that factors are not mobile *between* economies. According to this theorem, a country has a comparative advantage in the production of a product if that country is relatively well endowed with inputs used intensively in the production of that product.

This idea is simple. A country with a great deal of good fertile land is likely to have a comparative advantage in agriculture. A country with a large amount of accumulated capital is likely to have a comparative advantage in heavy manufacturing. A country well-endowed with human capital is likely to have a comparative advantage in highly technical goods.

Other Explanations for Observed Trade Flows

Comparative advantage is not the only reason countries trade. It does not explain why many countries import and export the same kinds of goods. The United States, for example, exports and imports automobiles.

Just as industries within a country differentiate their products to capture a domestic market, they also differentiate their products to please the wide variety of tastes that exists worldwide. The Japanese automobile industry, for example, began producing small, fuel-efficient cars long before U.S. automobile makers did. In doing so, the Japanese auto industry developed expertise in creating products that attracted a devoted following and considerable brand loyalty. BMWs, made mostly in Germany, and Volvos, made mostly in Sweden, also have their champions in many countries. Just as product differentiation is a natural response to diverse preferences within an economy, it is also a natural response to diverse preferences across economies.

This idea is not inconsistent with the theory of comparative advantage. If the Japanese developed skills and knowledge that gave them an edge in the production of fuel-efficient cars, that knowledge can be thought of as a very specific kind of capital that is not currently available to other producers. The Volvo company invested in a form of intangible capital called *goodwill*. That goodwill, which may come from establishing a reputation for safety and quality over the years, is one source of the comparative advantage that keeps Volvos selling on the international market. Some economists distinguish between gains from *acquired comparative advantages* and gains from *natural comparative advantages*.

Another explanation for international trade is that some economies of scale may be available when firms are producing for a world market that would not be available when they are producing for a more limited domestic market. But because the evidence suggests that economies of scale are exhausted at a relatively small size in most industries, it seems unlikely that they constitute a compelling explanation of world trade patterns.

Trade Barriers: Tariffs, Export Subsidies, and Quotas

Trade barriers—also called *obstacles to trade*—take many forms. The three most common are tariffs, export subsidies, and quotas. All are forms of **protection** shielding some sector of the economy from foreign competition.

A **tariff** is a tax on imports. The average tariff on imports into the United States is less than 5 percent. Certain protected items have much higher tariffs. For example, in 2008, tariffs were 61 percent on rubber footware and 35 percent for canned tuna.

Export subsidies—government payments made to domestic firms to encourage exports—can also act as a barrier to trade. One of the provisions of the Corn Laws that stimulated Ricardo's musings was an export subsidy automatically paid to farmers by the British government when the price of grain fell below a specified level. The subsidy served to keep domestic prices high, but it flooded the world market with cheap subsidized grain. Foreign farmers who were not subsidized were driven out of the international marketplace by the artificially low prices.

Farm subsidies remain a part of the international trade landscape today. Many countries continue to appease their farmers by heavily subsidizing exports of agricultural products. The political power of the farm lobby in many countries has had an important effect on recent international trade negotiations aimed at reducing trade barriers. The prevalence of farm subsidies in the developed world has become a major rallying point for less developed countries as they strive to compete in the global marketplace. Many African nations, in particular, have a comparative advantage in agricultural land. In producing agricultural goods for export to the world marketplace, however, they must compete with food produced on heavily subsidized farms in

protection The practice of shielding a sector of the economy from foreign competition.

tariff A tax on imports.

export subsidies Government payments made to domestic firms to encourage exports.

Europe and the United States. Countries such as France have particularly high farm subsidies, which, it argues, helps preserve the rural heritage of France. One side effect of these subsidies, however, is to make it more difficult for some of the poorer nations in the world to compete. Some have argued that if developed nations eliminated their farm subsidies, this would have a much larger effect on the economies of some African nations than is currently achieved by charitable aid programs.

dumping A firm's or an industry's sale of products on the world market at prices below its own cost of production.

Closely related to subsidies is **dumping**. Dumping occurs when a firm or industry sells its products on the world market at prices lower than its cost of production. Charges of dumping are often brought by a domestic producer that believes itself to be subject to unfair competition. In the United States, claims of dumping are brought before the International Trade Commission. In 2007, for example, a small manufacturer of thermal paper charged China and Germany with dumping. In 2006, the European Union brought a dumping charge against Chinese shoes. Determining whether dumping has actually occurred can be difficult. Domestic producers argue that foreign firms will dump their product in the United States, drive out American competitors, and then raise prices, thus harming consumers. Foreign exporters, on the other hand, claim that their prices are low simply because their costs are low and that no dumping has occurred. Figuring out the costs for German thermal paper or Chinese shoes is not easy. In the case of the Chinese shoe claim, for example, the Chinese government pointed out that shoes are a very labor-intensive product and that given China's low wages, it should not be a surprise that it is able to produce shoes very cheaply. In other words, the Chinese claim that shoes are an example of the theory of comparative advantage at work rather than predatory dumping.

quota A limit on the quantity of imports.

A **quota** is a limit on the quantity of imports. Quotas can be mandatory or voluntary, and they may be legislated or negotiated with foreign governments. The best-known voluntary quota, or "voluntary restraint," was negotiated with the Japanese government in 1981. Japan agreed to reduce its automobile exports to the United States by 7.7 percent, from the 1980 level of 1.82 million units to 1.68 million units. Many quotas limit trade around the world today. Perhaps the best-known recent case is the textile quota imposed in August 2005 by the European Union on imports of textiles from China. Because China had exceeded quotas that had been agreed to earlier in the year, the EU blocked the entry of Chinese-produced textiles into Europe; as a result, more than 100 million garments piled up in European ports.

U.S. Trade Policies, GATT, and the WTO

Smoot-Hawley tariff The U.S. tariff law of the 1930s, which set the highest tariffs in U.S. history (60 percent). It set off an international trade war and caused the decline in trade that is often considered one of the causes of the worldwide depression of the 1930s.

The United States has been a high-tariff nation, with average tariffs of over 50 percent, for much of its history. The highest were in effect during the Great Depression following the **Smoot-Hawley tariff**, which pushed the average tariff rate to 60 percent in 1930. The Smoot-Hawley tariff set off an international trade war when U.S. trading partners retaliated with tariffs of their own. Many economists say the decline in trade that followed was one of the causes of the worldwide depression of the 1930s.[1]

General Agreement on Tariffs and Trade (GATT) An international agreement signed by the United States and 22 other countries in 1947 to promote the liberalization of foreign trade.

In 1947, the United States, with 22 other nations, agreed to reduce barriers to trade. It also established an organization to promote liberalization of foreign trade. This **General Agreement on Tariffs and Trade (GATT)**, at first considered to be an interim arrangement, continues today and has been quite effective. The most recent round of world trade talks sponsored by GATT, the Uruguay Round, began in Uruguay in 1986. It was initialed by 116 countries on December 15, 1993, and was formally approved by the U.S. Congress after much debate following the election in 1994. The Final Act of the Uruguay Round of negotiations is the most comprehensive and complex multilateral trade agreement in history.

World Trade Organization (WTO) A negotiating forum dealing with rules of trade across nations.

In 1995, as part of GATT, the **World Trade Organization (WTO)** was established. The WTO is a negotiating forum designed to deal with rules of trade across nations. It helps facilitate freer trade across countries, negotiate trade disputes that arise, and broker trade agreements.

Doha Development Agenda An initiative of the World Trade Organization focused on issues of trade and development.

While the WTO was founded to promote free trade, its member countries clearly have different incentives as they confront trade cases. In recent years, differences between developed and developing countries have come to the fore. In 2001, at a WTO meeting in Doha, Qatar, the WTO launched a new initiative, the **Doha Development Agenda**, to deal with some of the issues that intersect the areas of trade and development. In 2007, the Doha Development Agenda continued to struggle over

---

[1] See especially Charles Kindleberger, *The World in Depression 1929–1939* (London: Allen Lane, 1973).

the issue of agriculture and farm subsidies that were described earlier in this chapter. The less developed countries, with sub-Saharan Africa taking the lead, seek to eliminate all farm subsidies currently paid by the United States and the European Union (EU). The EU has, for its part, tried to push the less developed countries toward better environmental policies as part of a broader free trade package.

The movement in the United States has been away from tariffs and quotas and toward freer trade. The Reciprocal Trade Agreements Act of 1934 authorized the president to negotiate trade agreements on behalf of the United States. As part of trade negotiations, the president can confer *most-favored-nation status* on individual trading partners. Imports from countries with most-favored-nation status are taxed at the lowest negotiated tariff rates. In addition, in recent years, several successful rounds of tariff-reduction negotiations have reduced trade barriers to their lowest levels ever.

Despite this general trend toward freer trade, most American presidents in the last 50 years have made exceptions to protect one economic sector or another. Eisenhower and Kennedy restricted imports of Japanese textiles; Johnson restricted meat imports to protect Texas beef producers; Nixon restricted steel imports; Reagan restricted automobiles from Japan. In early 2002, President George W. Bush imposed a 30 percent tariff on steel imported from the EU. In 2003, the WTO ruled that these tariffs were unfair and allowed the EU to slap retaliatory tariffs on U.S. products. Shortly thereafter, the steel tariffs were rolled back, at least on EU steel. At present, the United States has high tariffs on sugar-based ethanol, an energy source competitive with corn-based ethanol.

Economic Integration

Economic integration occurs when two or more nations join to form a free-trade zone. In 1991, the European Community (EC, or the Common Market) began forming the largest free-trade zone in the world. The economic integration process began that December, when the 12 original members (the United Kingdom, Belgium, France, Germany, Italy, the Netherlands, Luxembourg, Denmark, Greece, Ireland, Spain, and Portugal) signed the Maastricht Treaty. The treaty called for the end of border controls, a common currency, an end to all tariffs, and the coordination of monetary and political affairs. The **European Union (EU)**, as the EC is now called, has 27 members and 3 applicants (for a list, see the Summary, p. 373). On January 1, 1993, all tariffs and trade barriers were dropped among the member countries. Border checkpoints were closed in early 1995. Citizens can now travel among member countries without passports.

The United States is not a part of the EU. However, in 1988, the United States (under President Reagan) and Canada (under Prime Minister Mulroney) signed the **U.S.-Canadian Free Trade Agreement**, which removed all barriers to trade, including tariffs and quotas, between the two countries in 1998.

During the last days of the George H. W. Bush administration in 1992, the United States, Mexico, and Canada signed the **North American Free Trade Agreement (NAFTA)**, with the three countries agreeing to establish all of North America as a free-trade zone. The agreement eliminated all tariffs over a 10- to 15-year period and removed restrictions on most investments. During the presidential campaign of 1992, NAFTA was hotly debated. Both Bill Clinton and George Bush supported the agreement. Industrial labor unions that might be affected by increased imports from Mexico (such as those in the automobile industry) opposed the agreement, while industries whose exports to Mexico might increase as a result of the agreement—for example, the machine tool industry—supported it. Another concern was that Mexican companies were not subject to the same environmental regulations as U.S. firms, so U.S. firms might move to Mexico for this reason.

NAFTA was ratified by the U.S. Congress in late 1993 and went into effect on the first day of 1994. The U.S. Department of Commerce estimated that as a result of NAFTA, trade between the United States and Mexico increased by nearly $16 billion in 1994. In addition, exports from the United States to Mexico outpaced imports from Mexico during 1994. In 1995, however, the agreement fell under the shadow of a dramatic collapse of the value of the peso. U.S. exports to Mexico dropped sharply, and the United States shifted from a trade surplus to a large trade deficit with Mexico. Aside from a handful of tariffs, however, all of NAFTA's commitments were fully implemented by 2003, and an 8-year report signed by all three countries declared the pact a success. The report concludes, "Eight years of expanded trade, increased employment and investment, and enhanced opportunity for the citizens of all three countries have demonstrated that NAFTA works and will continue to work." In 2007, trade among the NAFTA nations reached $930 billion.

economic integration
Occurs when two or more nations join to form a free-trade zone.

European Union (EU)
The European trading bloc composed of 27 countries.

U.S.-Canadian Free Trade Agreement An agreement in which the United States and Canada agreed to eliminate all barriers to trade between the two countries by 1998.

North American Free Trade Agreement (NAFTA) An agreement signed by the United States, Mexico, and Canada in which the three countries agreed to establish all North America as a free-trade zone.

ECONOMICS IN PRACTICE

Trade Barriers Take a Hit in 2008

Sometimes trade barriers rise and fall as a consequence of changes in the international economy. In 2008, the combination of a diminished supply and a rising demand pushed agricultural prices up dramatically worldwide. The arguments posed by the agricultural lobby to maintain trade barriers was offset by the need for an affordable food supply, and tariff barriers fell. The following article describes what happened.

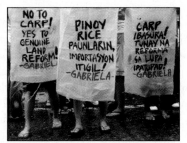

High Food Prices Stir Movement on Tarriffs

The Wall Street Journal

BRUSSELS—The world's scramble for affordable food is tearing at the patchwork of agricultural tariffs that governments have long used to control trade—and offering a glimmer of hope to those trying to kick-start a stalled global trade deal.

Some countries are slashing import duties to attract staples like wheat, rice and cooking oil. Europe, traditionally the world's most outspoken advocate of protected food markets, recently removed cereal-import duties for the first time. Others—notable China—are raising export duties to keep domestic markets well stocked.

So far, the situation hasn't forced a rethinking of subsidies that farmers in the developed world receive. But some say that is an inevitable consequence of higher global food prices. "The market situation now means there's less pressure on farmers," says Peter Mandelson, the European Union's trade commissioner.

Manipulating tariffs to meet market demands isn't new. In the early 1970s, the Soviet Union suffered from shortages of soybeans, wheat and other crops. Western powers set stiff export tariffs or quotas to stop Moscow from buying up too much production. After World War II, weakened European powers protected their battered farm sector with import tariffs and subsidies.

If food prices fall sharply, the global shift on tariffs could reverse. The U.N. and other agencies forecast that prices will remain high, although this year better weather is expected to boost production in Europe and Australia.

"Trade and trade policy are adjusting to a simple fact," says Michael Mann, the EU's agricultural spokesman. "We used to have too much food, and now we have too little."

Source: John W. Miller, February 12, 2008. —Lauren Etter in Chicago contributed to this article.

Free Trade or Protection?

One of the great economic debates of all time revolves around the free-trade-versus-protection controversy. We briefly summarize the arguments in favor of each.

The Case for Free Trade

In one sense, the theory of comparative advantage *is* the case for free trade. Trade has potential benefits for all nations. A good is not imported unless its net price to buyers is below the net price of the domestically produced alternative. When the Brazilians in our earlier example found U.S. timber less expensive than their own, they bought it, yet they continued to pay the same price for homemade steel. Americans bought less expensive Brazilian steel, but they continued to buy domestic timber at the same lower price. Under these conditions, *both Americans and Brazilians ended up paying less and consuming more.*

At the same time, resources (including labor) move out of steel production and into timber production in the United States. In Brazil, resources (including labor) move out of timber production and into steel production. The resources in both countries are used more efficiently. Tariffs, export subsidies, and quotas, which interfere with the free movement of goods and services around the world, reduce or eliminate the gains of comparative advantage.

We can use supply and demand curves to illustrate this. Suppose Figure 19.4 shows domestic supply and demand for textiles. In the absence of trade, the market clears at a price of $4.20. At equilibrium, 450 million yards of textiles are produced and consumed.

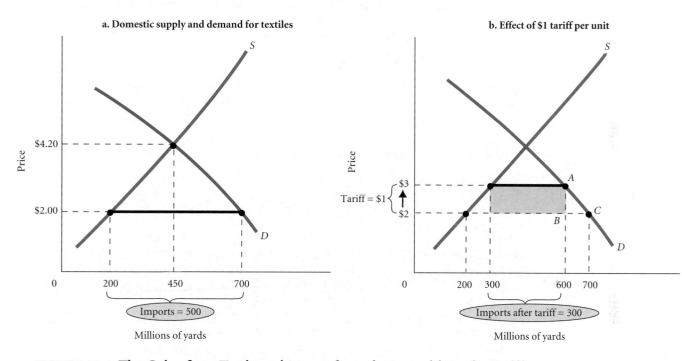

a. Domestic supply and demand for textiles

b. Effect of $1 tariff per unit

▲ **FIGURE 19.4 The Gains from Trade and Losses from the Imposition of a Tariff**
A tariff of $1 increases the market price facing consumers from $2 per yard to $3 per yard. The government collects revenues equal to the gray shaded area in **b**. The loss of efficiency has two components. First, consumers must pay a higher price for goods that could be produced at lower cost. Second, marginal producers are drawn into textiles and away from other goods, resulting in inefficient domestic production. The triangle labeled ABC in **b** is the dead weight loss or excess burden resulting from the tariff.

Assume now that textiles are available at a world price of $2. This is the price in dollars that Americans must pay for textiles from foreign sources. If we assume that an unlimited quantity of textiles is available at $2 and there is no difference in quality between domestic and foreign textiles, no domestic producer will be able to charge more than $2. In the absence of trade barriers, the world price sets the price in the United States. As the price in the United States falls from $4.20 to $2.00, the quantity demanded by consumers increases from 450 million yards to 700 million yards, but the quantity supplied by domestic producers drops from 450 million yards to 200 million yards. The difference, 500 million yards, is the quantity of textiles imported.

The argument for free trade is that each country should specialize in producing the goods and services in which it enjoys a comparative advantage. If foreign producers can produce textiles at a much lower price than domestic producers, they have a comparative advantage. As the world price of textiles falls to $2, domestic (U.S.) quantity supplied drops and resources are transferred to other sectors. These other sectors, which may be export industries or domestic industries, are not shown in Figure 19.4a. It is clear that the allocation of resources is more efficient at a price of $2. Why should the United States use domestic resources to produce what foreign producers can produce at a lower cost? U.S. resources should move into the production of the things it produces best.

Now consider what happens to the domestic price of textiles when a trade barrier is imposed. Figure 19.4b shows the effect of a set tariff of $1 per yard imposed on imported textiles. The tariff raises the domestic price of textiles to $2 + $1 = $3. The result is that some of the gains from trade are lost. First, consumers are forced to pay a higher price for the same good. The quantity of textiles demanded drops from 700 million yards under free trade to 600 million yards because some consumers are not willing to pay the higher price. Notice in Figure 19.4b the triangle labeled ABC. This is the deadweight loss or excess burden resulting from the tariff. Absent the tariff, these 100 added units of textiles would have generated benefits in excess of the $2 that each one cost.

At the same time, the higher price of textiles draws some marginal domestic producers who could not make a profit at $2 into textile production. (Recall that domestic producers do not pay a tariff.) As the price rises to $3, the quantity supplied by producers rises from 200 million yards to 300 million yards. The result is a decrease in imports from 500 million yards to 300 million yards.

Finally, the imposition of the tariff means that the government collects revenue equal to the shaded area in Figure 19.4b. This shaded area is equal to the tariff rate per unit ($1) times the number of units imported after the tariff is in place (300 million yards). Thus, receipts from the tariff are $300 million.

What is the final result of the tariff? Domestic producers receiving revenues of only $2 per unit before the tariff was imposed now receive a higher price and earn higher profits. However, these higher profits are achieved at a loss of efficiency. Trade barriers prevent a nation from reaping the benefits of specialization, push it to adopt relatively inefficient production techniques, and force consumers to pay higher prices for protected products than they would otherwise pay.

The Case for Protection

A case can also be made in favor of tariffs and quotas. Over the course of U.S. history, protectionist arguments have been made so many times by so many industries before so many congressional committees that it seems all pleas for protection share the same themes. We describe the most frequently heard pleas next.

Protection Saves Jobs The main argument for protection is that foreign competition costs Americans their jobs. When Americans buy imported Toyotas, U.S. produced cars go unsold. Layoffs in the domestic auto industry follow. When Americans buy Chinese textiles, American workers may lose their jobs. When Americans buy shoes or textiles from Korea or Taiwan, the millworkers in Maine and Massachusetts, as well as in South Carolina and Georgia, lose their jobs.

It is true that when we buy goods from foreign producers, domestic producers suffer. However, there is no reason to believe that the workers laid off in the contracting sectors will not ultimately be reemployed in expanding sectors. Foreign competition in textiles, for example, has meant the loss of U.S. jobs in that industry. Thousands of textile workers in New England lost their jobs as the textile mills closed over the last 40 years. Nevertheless, with the expansion of high-tech industries, the unemployment rate in Massachusetts fell to one of the lowest in the country in the mid-1980s, and New Hampshire, Vermont, and Maine also boomed. By the 1990s, New England had suffered another severe downturn, due partly to high-technology hardware manufacturing that had moved abroad. But by the late 1990s, its economy was booming again, this time on the back of what was called a "New Industrial Revolution": the rise of Internet-based business.

The adjustment is far from costless. The knowledge that some other industry, perhaps in some other part of the country, may be expanding is of little comfort to the person whose skills become obsolete or whose pension benefits are lost when his or her company abruptly closes a plant or goes bankrupt. The social and personal problems brought about by industry-specific unemployment, obsolete skills, and bankruptcy as a result of foreign competition are significant.

These problems can be addressed in two ways. We can ban imports and give up the gains from free trade, acknowledging that we are willing to pay premium prices to save domestic jobs in industries that can produce more efficiently abroad; or we can aid the victims of free trade in a constructive way, helping to retrain them for jobs with a future. In some instances, programs to relocate people in expanding regions may be in order. Some programs deal directly with the transition without forgoing the gains from trade.

ECONOMICS IN PRACTICE

A Petition

While most economists argue in favor of free trade, it is important to recognize that some groups are likely to lose from freer trade. Arguments by the losing groups against trade have been around for hundreds of years. In the following article, you will find an essay by a French satirist of the nineteenth century, Frederic Bastiat, complaining about the unfair competition that the sun provides to candle makers. You see that the author proposes a quota, as opposed to a tariff, on the sun.

From the Manufacturers of Candles, Tapers, Lanterns, Sticks, Street Lamps, Snuffers, and Extinguishers, and from Producers of Tallow, Oil, Resin, Alcohol, and Generally of Everything Connected with Lighting.

To the Honourable Members of the Chamber of Deputies.

Gentlemen:

You are on the right track. You reject abstract theories and [have] little regard for abundance and low prices. You concern yourselves mainly with the fate of the producer. You wish to free him from foreign competition, that is, to reserve the *domestic market* for *domestic industry*.

We come to offer you a wonderful opportunity for your—what shall we call it? Your theory? No, nothing is more deceptive than theory. Your doctrine? Your system? Your principle? But you dislike doctrines, you have a horror of systems, as for principles, you deny that there are any in political economy; therefore we shall call it your practice— your practice without theory and without principle.

Screening out the sun would increase the demand for candles. Should candlemakers be protected from unfair competition?

We are suffering from the ruinous competition of a rival who apparently works under conditions so far superior to our own for the production of light that he is *flooding* the *domestic market* with it at an incredibly low price; for the moment he appears, our sales cease, all the consumers turn to him, and a branch of French industry whose ramifications are innumerable is all at once reduced to complete stagnation. This rival, which is none other than the sun, is waging war on us so mercilessly we suspect he is being stirred up against us by perfidious Albion (excellent diplomacy nowadays!), particularly because he has for that haughty island a respect that he does not show for us. [A reference to Britain's reputation as a foggy island.]

We ask you to be so good as to pass a law requiring the closing of all windows, dormers, skylights, inside and outside shutters, curtains, casements, bull's-eyes, deadlights, and blinds—in short, all openings, holes, chinks, and fissures through which the light of the sun is wont to enter houses, to the detriment of the fair industries with which, we are proud to say, we have endowed the country, a country that cannot, without betraying ingratitude, abandon us today to so unequal a combat.

Source: Frederic Bastiat (1801 to 1850), New Australian. Reprinted by permission.

Some Countries Engage in Unfair Trade Practices   Attempts by U.S. firms to monopolize an industry are illegal under the Sherman and Clayton acts. If a strong company decides to drive the competition out of the market by setting prices below cost, it would be aggressively prosecuted by the Antitrust Division of the Justice Department. However, the argument goes, if we will not allow a U.S. firm to engage in predatory pricing or monopolize an industry or a market, can we stand by and let a German firm or a Japanese firm do so in the name of free trade? This is a legitimate argument and one that has gained significant favor in recent years. How should we respond when a large international company or a country behaves strategically against a domestic firm or industry? Free trade may be the best solution when everybody plays by the rules, but sometimes we have to fight back. The WTO is the vehicle currently used to negotiate disputes of this sort.

Cheap Foreign Labor Makes Competition Unfair   Let us say that a particular country gained its "comparative advantage" in textiles by paying its workers low wages. How can U.S. textile companies compete with companies that pay wages that are less than a quarter of what U.S. companies pay? Questions like this are often asked by those concerned with competition from China and India.

First, remember that wages in a competitive economy reflect productivity: a high ratio of output to units of labor. Workers in the United States earn higher wages because they are more productive. The United States has more capital per worker; that is, the average worker works with better machinery and equipment and its workers are better trained. Second, trade flows not according to *absolute* advantage, but according to *comparative* advantage: All countries benefit, even if one country is more efficient at producing everything.

Protection Safeguards National Security   Beyond saving jobs, certain sectors of the economy may appeal for protection for other reasons. The steel industry has argued for years with some success that it is vital to national defense. In the event of a war, the United States would not want to depend on foreign countries for a product as vital as steel. Even if we acknowledge another country's comparative advantage, we may want to protect our own resources.

Virtually no industry has ever asked for protection without invoking the national defense argument. Testimony that was once given on behalf of the scissors and shears industry argued that "in the event of a national emergency and imports cutoff, the United States would be without a source of scissors and shears, basic tools for many industries and trades essential to our national defense." The question lies not in the merit of the argument, but in just how seriously it can be taken if *every* industry uses it.

Protection Discourages Dependency   Closely related to the national defense argument is the claim that countries, particularly small or developing countries, may come to rely too heavily on one or more trading partners for many items. If a small country comes to rely on a major power for food or energy or some important raw material in which the large nation has a comparative advantage, it may be difficult for the smaller nation to remain politically neutral. Some critics of free trade argue that larger countries, such as the United States, Russia, and China have consciously engaged in trade with smaller countries to create these kinds of dependencies.

Therefore, should small, independent countries consciously avoid trading relationships that might lead to political dependence? This objective may involve developing domestic industries in areas where a country has a comparative disadvantage. To do so would mean protecting that industry from international competition.

Environmental Concerns   In recent years, concern about the environment has led some people to question advantages of free trade. Some environmental groups, for example, argue that the WTO's free trade policies may harm the environment. The central argument is that poor countries will become havens for polluting industries that will operate their steel and auto factories with few environmental controls.

These issues are quite complex, and there is much dispute among economists about the interaction between free trade and the environment. One relatively recent study of sulphur dioxide, for example, found that in the long run, free trade reduces pollution, largely by increasing the income of countries; richer countries typically choose policies to improve the environment.[2] Thus, while free trade and increased development initially may cause pollution levels to rise, in the long run, prosperity is a benefit to the environment. Many also argue that there are complex trade-offs to be made between pollution control and problems such as malnutrition and health for poor countries. The United States and Europe both traded off faster economic growth and income against cleaner air and water at earlier times in their development. Some argue that it is unfair for the developed countries to impose their preferences on other countries facing more difficult trade-offs.

Nevertheless, the concern with global climate change has stimulated new thinking in this area. A recent study by the Tyndall Centre for Climate Change Research in Britain found that in 2004, 23 percent of the greenhouse gas emissions produced by China were created in the production of exports. In other words, these emissions come not as a result of goods that China's population is enjoying as its income rises, but as a consequence of the consumption of the United States and Europe, where most of these goods are going. In a world in which the effects of carbon emissions are global and all countries are not willing to sign binding global agreements to control emissions, trade with China may be a way for developed nations to avoid their commitments to pollution reduction. Some have argued that penalties could be imposed on high-polluting products produced in countries that have not signed international climate control treaties as a way to ensure that the prices of goods imported this way reflect the harm that those products cause the Earth.[3] Implementing these policies is, however, likely to be very complex, and some have argued that it is a mistake to bundle trade and environmental issues. As with other areas covered in this book, there is still disagreement among economists as to the right answer.

Protection Safeguards Infant Industries Young industries in a given country may have a difficult time competing with established industries in other countries. In a dynamic world, a protected **infant industry** might mature into a strong industry worldwide because of an acquired, but real, comparative advantage. If such an industry is undercut and driven out of world markets at the beginning of its life, that comparative advantage might never develop.

infant industry A young industry that may need temporary protection from competition from the established industries of other countries to develop an acquired comparative advantage.

Yet efforts to protect infant industries can backfire. In July 1991, the U.S. government imposed a 62.67 percent tariff on imports of active-matrix liquid crystal display screens (also referred to as "flat-panel displays" used primarily for laptop computers) from Japan. The Commerce Department and the International Trade Commission agreed that Japanese producers were selling their screens in the U.S. market at a price below cost and that this dumping threatened the survival of domestic laptop screen producers. The tariff was meant to protect the infant U.S. industry until it could compete head-on with the Japanese.

Unfortunately for U.S. producers of laptop computers and for consumers who purchase them, the tariff had an unintended (although predictable) effect on the industry. Because U.S. laptop screens were generally recognized to be of lower quality than their Japanese counterparts, imposition of the tariff left U.S. computer manufacturers with three options: (1) They could use the screens available from U.S. producers and watch sales of their final product decline in the face of *higher-quality* competition from abroad, (2) they could pay the tariff for the higher-quality screens and watch sales of their final product decline in the face of *lower-priced* competition from abroad, or (3) they could do what was most profitable for them to do—move their production facilities abroad to avoid the tariff completely. The last option is what Apple and IBM did. In the end, not only were the laptop industry and its consumers hurt by the imposition of the tariff (due to higher costs of production and to higher laptop computer prices), but the U.S. screen industry was hurt as well (due to its loss of buyers for its product) by a policy specifically designed to help it.

---

[2] Werner Antweiler, Brian Copeland, and M. Scott Taylor, "Is Free Trade Good for the Environment?" *AER*, September, 2001.
[3] Judith Chevalier, "A Carbon Cap That Starts in Washington," *New York Times*, December 16, 2007.

The case for free trade has been made across the world as increasing numbers of countries have joined the world marketplace. Figure 19.5 traces the path of tariffs across the world from 1980–2005. The lines show an index of trade openness, calculated as 100 minus the tariff rate. (So higher numbers mean lower tariffs.) We see rapid reductions in the last 25 years across the world, most notably in countries in the emerging and developing markets.

▶ **FIGURE 19.5 Trade Openness Across the World (Index is 100 minus the average effective tariff rate in the region.)**

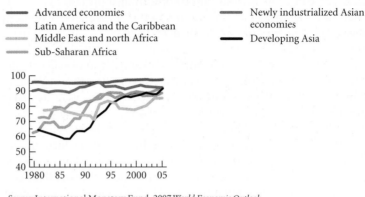

Changes in Openness to Trade Over Time across the World

— Advanced economies
— Latin America and the Caribbean
— Middle East and north Africa
— Sub-Saharan Africa

— Newly industrialized Asian economies
— Developing Asia

Source: International Monetary Fund, *2007 World Economic Outlook.*
Trade openness is measured as 100 minus the average effective tariff rate in the region.

Source: International Monetary Fund, 2007 *World Economic Outlook.*
Trade openness is measured as 100 minus the average effective tariff rate in the region.

An Economic Consensus

You now know something about how international trade fits into the structure of the economy.

Critical to our study of international economics is the debate between free traders and protectionists. On one side is the theory of comparative advantage, formalized by David Ricardo in the early part of the nineteenth century. According to this view, all countries benefit from specialization and trade. The gains from trade are real, and they can be large; free international trade raises real incomes and improves the standard of living.

On the other side are the protectionists, who point to the loss of jobs and argue for the protection of workers from foreign competition. Although foreign competition can cause job loss in specific sectors, it is unlikely to cause net job loss in an economy and workers will, over time, be absorbed into expanding sectors. Foreign trade and full employment can be pursued simultaneously. Although economists disagree about many things, the vast majority of them favor free trade.

S U M M A R Y

1. All economies, regardless of their size, depend to some extent on other economies and are affected by events outside their borders.

TRADE SURPLUSES AND DEFICITS p. 354

2. Until the 1970s, the United States generally exported more than it imported—it ran a *trade surplus*. In the mid-1970s, the United States began to import more merchandise than it exported—a *trade deficit*.

THE ECONOMIC BASIS FOR TRADE: COMPARATIVE ADVANTAGE p. 355

3. The *theory of comparative advantage*, dating to David Ricardo in the nineteenth century, holds that specialization

and free trade will benefit all trading partners, even those that may be absolutely less efficient producers.

4. A country enjoys an *absolute advantage* over another country in the production of a product if it uses fewer resources to produce that product than the other country does. A country has a *comparative advantage* in the production of a product if that product can be produced at a lower cost in terms of other goods.

5. Trade enables countries to move beyond their previous resource and productivity constraints. When countries specialize in producing those goods in which they have a comparative advantage, they maximize their combined output and allocate their resources more efficiently.

6. When trade is free, patterns of trade and trade flows result from the independent decisions of thousands of importers and exporters and millions of private households and firms.

7. The relative attractiveness of foreign goods to U.S. buyers and of U.S. goods to foreign buyers depends in part on *exchange rates*, the ratios at which two currencies are traded for each other.

8. For any pair of countries, there is a range of exchange rates that will lead automatically to both countries realizing the gains from specialization and comparative advantage. Within that range, the exchange rate will determine which country gains the most from trade. This leads us to conclude that exchange rates determine the terms of trade.

9. If exchange rates end up in the right range (that is, in a range that facilitates the flow of goods between nations), the free market will drive each country to shift resources into those sectors in which it enjoys a comparative advantage. Only those products in which a country has a comparative advantage will be competitive in world markets.

THE SOURCES OF COMPARATIVE ADVANTAGE *p. 362*

10. The *Heckscher-Ohlin theorem* looks to relative *factor endowments* to explain comparative advantage and trade flows. According to the theorem, a country has a comparative advantage in the production of a product if that country is relatively well endowed with the inputs that are used intensively in the production of that product.

11. A relatively short list of inputs—natural resources, knowledge capital, physical capital, land, and skilled and unskilled labor—explains a surprisingly large portion of world trade patterns. However, the simple version of the theory of comparative advantage cannot explain why many countries import and export the same goods.

12. Some theories argue that comparative advantage can be acquired. Just as industries within a country differentiate their products to capture a domestic market, they also differentiate their products to please the wide variety of tastes that exists worldwide. This theory is consistent with the theory of comparative advantage.

TRADE BARRIERS: TARIFFS, EXPORT SUBSIDIES, AND QUOTAS *p. 363*

13. Trade barriers take many forms. The three most common are *tariffs, export subsidies*, and *quotas*. All are forms of *protection* through which some sector of the economy is shielded from foreign competition.

14. Although the United States has historically been a high-tariff nation, the general movement is now away from tariffs and quotas. The *General Agreement on Tariffs and Trade (GATT)*, signed by the United States and 22 other countries in 1947, continues in effect today; its purpose is to reduce barriers to world trade and keep them down. Also important are the *U.S.-Canadian Free Trade Agreement*, signed in 1988, and the *North American Free Trade Agreement*, signed by the United States, Mexico, and Canada in the last days of the George H. W. Bush administration in 1992, taking effect in 1994.

15. The World Trade Organization (WTO) was set up by GATT to act as a negotiating forum for trade disputes across countries.

16. The *European Union (EU)* is a free-trade bloc composed of 27 nations: Austria, Belgium, Bulgaria, Cyprus, the Czech Republic, Denmark, Estonia, Finland, France, Germany, Greece, Hungary, Ireland, Italy, Latvia, Lithuania, Luxembourg, Malta, the Netherlands, Poland, Portugal, Romania, Slovakia, Slovenia, Spain, Sweden, and the United Kingdom. Three others have applied for membership: Croatia, the Republic of Macedonia, and Turkey. Many economists believe that the advantages of free trade within the bloc, a reunited Germany, and the ability to work well as a bloc will make the EU the most powerful player in the international marketplace in the coming decades.

FREE TRADE OR PROTECTION? *p. 366*

17. In one sense, the theory of comparative advantage is the case for free trade. Trade barriers prevent a nation from reaping the benefits of specialization, push it to adopt relatively inefficient production techniques, and force consumers to pay higher prices for protected products than they would otherwise pay.

18. The case for protection rests on a number of propositions, one of which is that foreign competition results in a loss of domestic jobs, but there is no reason to believe that the workers laid off in the contracting sectors will not be ultimately reemployed in other expanding sectors. This adjustment process is far from costless, however.

19. Other arguments for protection hold that cheap foreign labor makes competition unfair; that some countries engage in unfair trade practices; that free trade might harm the environment; and that protection safeguards the national security, discourages dependency, and shields *infant industries*. Despite these arguments, most economists favor free trade.

REVIEW TERMS AND CONCEPTS

absolute advantage, *p. 355*

comparative advantage, *p. 355*

Corn Laws, *p. 355*

Doha Development Agenda, *p. 364*

dumping, *p. 364*

economic integration, *p. 365*

European Union (EU), *p. 365*

exchange rate, *p. 360*

export subsidies, *p. 363*

factor endowments, *p. 362*

General Agreement on Tariffs and Trade (GATT), *p. 364*

Heckscher-Ohlin theorem, *p. 362*

infant industry, *p. 371*

North American Free Trade Agreement (NAFTA), *p. 365*

protection, *p. 363*

quota, *p. 364*

Smoot-Hawley tariff, *p. 364*

tariff, *p. 363*

terms of trade, *p. 359*

theory of comparative advantage, *p. 355*

trade deficit, *p. 354*

trade surplus, *p. 354*

U.S.-Canadian Free Trade Agreement, *p. 365*

World Trade Organization (WTO), *p. 364*

PROBLEMS

Visit www.myeconlab.com to complete the problems marked in orange online. You will receive instant feedback on your answers, tutorial help, and access to additional practice problems.

1. Suppose Germany and France each produce only two goods, guns and butter. Both are produced using labor alone. Assuming both countries are at full employment, you are given the following information:

Germany: 10 units of labor required to produce 1 gun
          5 units of labor required to produce 1 pound of butter
          Total labor force: 1,000,000 units
France: 15 units of labor required to produce 1 gun
          10 units of labor required to produce 1 pound of butter
          Total labor force: 750,000 units

a. Draw the production possibility frontiers for each country in the absence of trade.
b. If transportation costs are ignored and trade is allowed, will France and Germany engage in trade? Explain.
c. If a trade agreement was negotiated, at what rate (number of guns per unit of butter) would they agree to exchange?

2. The United States and Russia each produce only bearskin caps and wheat. Domestic prices are given in the following table:

	RUSSIA	UNITED STATES	
Bearskin caps	10 Ru	$ 7	Per hat
Wheat	15 Ru	$10	Per bushel

On April 1, the Zurich exchange listed an exchange rate of $1 = 1 Ru.
a. Which country has an absolute advantage in the production of bearskin caps? wheat?
b. Which country has a comparative advantage in the production of bearskin caps? wheat?
c. If the United States and Russia were the only two countries engaging in trade, what adjustments would you predict assuming exchange rates are freely determined by the laws of supply and demand?

3. The following table shows imports and exports of goods during the first half of 2005 for the United States:

| | JAN.–JUNE 2005 (BILLIONS OF DOLLARS) ||
	EXPORTS	IMPORTS
Total	439.0	795.1
Airplanes	15.5	6.1
Clothing	2.1	35.8
Crude oil	.3	81.6
Vehicles	35.4	95.1
Agricultural goods	30.6	29.8

What, if anything, can you conclude about the comparative advantage that the United States has relative to its trading partners in the production of goods? What stories can you tell about the wide disparities in clothing and airplanes?

4. The following table gives recent figures for yield per acre in Illinois and Kansas:

	WHEAT	SOYBEANS
Illinois	48	39
Kansas	40	24

Source: U.S. Dept. of Agriculture, *Crop Production.*

a. If we assume that farmers in Illinois and Kansas use the same amount of labor, capital, and fertilizer, which state has an absolute advantage in wheat production? soybean production?
b. If we transfer land out of wheat into soybeans, how many bushels of wheat do we give up in Illinois per additional bushel of soybeans produced? in Kansas?
c. Which state has a comparative advantage in wheat production? in soybean production?
d. The following table gives the distribution of land planted for each state in millions of acres in the same year.

	TOTAL ACRES UNDER TILL	WHEAT	SOYBEANS
Illinois	22.9	1.9	9.1
		(8.3%)	(39.7%)
Kansas	20.7	11.8	1.9
		(57.0%)	(9.2%)

Are these data consistent with your answer to part c? Explain.

5. You can think of the United States as a set of 50 separate economies with no trade barriers. In such an open environment, each state specializes in the products that it produces best.
a. What product or products does your state specialize in?
b. Can you identify the source of the comparative advantage that lies behind the production of one or more of these products (for example, a natural resource, plentiful cheap labor, or a skilled labor force)?
c. Do you think that the theory of comparative advantage and the Heckscher-Ohlin theorem help to explain why your state specializes the way that it does? Explain your answer.

6. Australia and the United States produce white and red wines. Current domestic prices for each wine are given in the following table:

	AUSTRALIA	UNITED STATES
White wine	5 AU$	10 US$
Red wine	10 AU$	15 US$

Suppose the exchange rate is 1 AU$ = 1 US$.
a. If the price ratios within each country reflect resource use, which country has a comparative advantage in the production of red wine? white wine?

b. Assume that there are no other trading partners and that the only motive for holding foreign currency is to buy foreign goods. Will the current exchange rate lead to trade flows in both directions between the two countries? Explain.

c. What adjustments might you expect in the exchange rate? Be specific.

d. What would you predict about trade flows between Australia and the United States after the exchange rate has adjusted?

7. Some empirical trade economists have noted that for many products, countries are both importers and exporters. For example, the United States both imports and exports shirts. How do you explain this?

8. [Related to the *Economics in Practice* on *p. 366*] Review the *Economics in Practice* on p. 366. Given the fact that food prices rose in world markets during 2008, many countries reduced tariffs and other trade barriers to food. Why did this happen? Who benefits when food prices rise, and who is hurt? Who is likely to be in favor of cutting tariffs on food, and who might be in favor of maintaining those tariffs? Go to newspaper archives such as nytimes.com and online.wsj.com to see if there is evidence to support your answer.

9. [Related to the *Economics in Practice* on *p. 369*] When a president presents a trade agreement for ratification to Congress, many domestic industries fight the ratification. In 2005, the United States was negotiating the Central America-Dominican Republic Free Trade Agreement (CAFTA-DR). Write a brief essay on the U.S. political opposition to CAFTA-DR in 2004 and 2005. What industries in the United States opposed the trade agreement? Is it fair to compare the arguments of these industries to the arguments posed by the candle makers?

Open-Economy Macroeconomics: The Balance of Payments and Exchange Rates

20

The economies of the world have become increasingly interdependent over the last four decades. No economy operates in a vacuum, and economic events in one country can have significant repercussions on the economies of other countries.

International trade is a major part of today's world economy. U.S. imports now account for about 15 percent of U.S. gross domestic product (GDP), and billions of dollars flow through the international capital market each day. In Chapter 19, we explored the main reasons why there is international exchange. Countries trade with one another to obtain goods and services they cannot produce themselves or to take advantage of the fact that other countries can produce goods and services at a lower cost than they can. You can see the various connections between the domestic economy and the rest of the world in the circular flow diagram in Figure 5.3 on p. 93. Foreign countries supply goods and services to the United States, and the United States supplies goods and services to the rest of the world.

From a macroeconomic point of view, the main difference between an international transaction and a domestic transaction concerns currency exchange. When people in countries with different currencies buy from and sell to each other, an exchange of currencies must also take place. Brazilian coffee exporters cannot spend U.S. dollars in Brazil—they need Brazilian reals. A U.S. wheat exporter cannot use Brazilian reals to buy a tractor from a U.S. company or to pay the rent on warehouse facilities. Somehow international exchange must be managed in a way that allows both partners in the transaction to wind up with their own currency.

As you know from Chapter 19, the direction of trade between two countries depends on **exchange rates**—the price of one country's currency in terms of the other country's currency. If the Japanese yen were very expensive (making the dollar cheap), both Japanese and Americans would buy from U.S. producers. If the yen were very cheap (making the U.S. dollar expensive), both Japanese and Americans would buy from Japanese producers. Within a certain range of exchange rates, trade flows in both directions, each country specializes in producing the goods in which it enjoys a comparative advantage, and trade is mutually beneficial.

Because exchange rates are a factor in determining the flow of international trade, the way they are determined is very important. Since 1900, the world monetary system has been changed several times by international agreements and events. In the early part of the twentieth century, nearly all currencies were backed by gold. Their values were fixed in terms of a specific number of ounces of gold, which determined their values in international trading—exchange rates.

exchange rate The price of one country's currency in terms of another country's currency; the ratio at which two currencies are traded for each other.

In 1944, with the international monetary system in chaos as the end of World War II drew near, a large group of experts unofficially representing 44 countries met in Bretton Woods, New Hampshire, and drew up a number of agreements. One of those agreements established a system of essentially fixed exchange rates under which each country agreed to intervene by buying and selling currencies in the foreign exchange market when necessary to maintain the agreed-to value of its currency.

In 1971, most countries, including the United States, gave up trying to fix exchange rates formally and began allowing them to be determined essentially by supply and demand. For example, without government intervention in the marketplace, the price of British pounds in dollars is determined by the interaction of those who want to exchange dollars for pounds (those who "demand" pounds) and those who want to exchange pounds for dollars (those who "supply" pounds). If the quantity of pounds demanded exceeds the quantity of pounds supplied, the price of pounds will rise, just as the price of peanuts or paper clips would rise under similar circumstances. A more detailed discussion of the various monetary systems that have been in place since 1900 is provided in the Appendix to this chapter.

In this chapter, we explore in more detail what has come to be called *open-economy macroeconomics*. First, we discuss the *balance of payments*—the record of a nation's transactions with the rest of the world. We then go on to consider how the analysis changes when we allow for the international exchange of goods, services, and capital.

The Balance of Payments

We sometimes lump all foreign currencies—euros, Swiss francs, Japanese yen, Brazilian reals, and so forth—together as "foreign exchange." **Foreign exchange** is simply all currencies other than the domestic currency of a given country (in the case of the United States, the U.S. dollar). U.S. demand for foreign exchange arises because its citizens want to buy things whose prices are quoted in other currencies, such as Australian jewelry, vacations in Mexico, and bonds or stocks issued by Sony Corporation of Japan. Whenever U.S. citizens make these purchases, they first buy the foreign currencies and then make the purchases.

Where does the *supply* of foreign exchange come from? The answer is simple: The United States (actually U.S. citizens or firms) earns foreign exchange when it sells products, services, or assets to another country. Just as Mexico earns foreign exchange when U.S. tourists visit Cancún, the United States earns foreign exchange (in this case, Mexican pesos) when Mexican tourists come to the United States to visit Disney World. Similarly, Saudi Arabian purchases of stock in General Motors and Colombian purchases of real estate in Miami increase the U.S. supply of foreign exchange.

The record of a country's transactions in goods, services, and assets with the rest of the world is its **balance of payments**. The balance of payments is also the record of a country's sources (supply) and uses (demand) of foreign exchange.[1]

The Current Account

The balance of payments is divided into two major accounts, the *current account* and the *capital account*. These are shown in Table 20.1, which provides data on the U.S. balance of payments for 2007. We begin with the current account.

The first item in the current account is U.S. trade in goods. This category includes exports of computer chips, potato chips, and CDs of U.S. musicians and imports of Scotch whiskey, Chinese toys, and Mexican oil. U.S. exports *earn* foreign exchange for the United States and are a credit (+) item on the current account. U.S. imports *use up* foreign exchange and are a debit (−) item. In 2007, the United States imported $815.4 billion more in goods than it exported.

Next in the current account is services. Like most other countries, the United States buys services from and sells services to other countries. For example, a U.S. firm shipping wheat to

foreign exchange All currencies other than the domestic currency of a given country.

balance of payments The record of a country's transactions in goods, services, and assets with the rest of the world; also the record of a country's sources (supply) and uses (demand) of foreign exchange.

---

[1] Bear in mind the distinction between the balance of payments and a balance sheet. A *balance sheet* for a firm or a country measures that entity's stock of assets and liabilities at a moment in time. The *balance of payments*, by contrast, measures *flows*, usually over a period of a month, a quarter, or a year. Despite its name, the balance of payments is *not* a balance sheet.

England might purchase insurance from a British insurance company. A Dutch flower grower may fly flowers to the United States aboard an American airliner. In the first case, the United States is importing services and therefore using up foreign exchange; in the second case, it is selling services to foreigners and earning foreign exchange. In 2007, the United States exported $106.9 billion more in services than it imported.

TABLE 20.1   United States Balance of Payments, 2007

All transactions that bring foreign exchange into the United States are credited (+) to the current account; all transactions that cause the United States to lose foreign exchange are debited (−) to the current account

Current Account	Billions of dollars
Goods exports	1,149.2
Goods imports	−1,964.6
(1) Net export of goods	−815.4
Exports of services	479.2
Imports of services	−372.3
(2) Net export of services	106.9
Income received on investments	782.2
Income payments on investments	−707.9
(3) Net investment income	74.3
(4) Net transfer payments	−104.4
(5) Balance on current account (1 + 2 + 3 + 4)	−738.6
Capital Account	
(6) Change in private U.S. assets abroad (increase is −)	−1,183.3
(7) Change in foreign private assets in the United States	1,451.0
(8) Change in U.S. government assets abroad (increase is −)	−23.0
(9) Change in foreign government assets in the United States	412.7
(10) Balance on capital account (6 + 7 + 8 + 9)	657.4
(11) Net capital account transactions	−2.2
(12) Statistical discrepancy	83.6
(13) Balance of payments (5 + 10 + 11 + 12)	0

Source: U.S. Department of Commerce, Survey of Current Business, April 2008.

The difference between a country's exports of goods and services and its imports of goods and services is its **balance of trade**. When exports of goods and services are less than imports of goods and services, a country has a **trade deficit**. The U.S. trade deficit in 2007 was huge: $708.5 billion (that is, $815.4 billion less $106.9 billion).

The third item in the current account concerns investment income. U.S. citizens hold foreign assets (stocks, bonds, and real assets such as buildings and factories). Dividends, interest, rent, and profits paid to U.S. asset holders are a source of foreign exchange. Conversely, when foreigners earn dividends, interest, and profits on assets held in the United States, foreign exchange is used up. In 2007, investment income received from foreigners exceeded investment income paid to foreigners by $74.3 billion.

The fourth item in Table 20.1 is net transfer payments. Transfer payments from the United States to foreigners are another use of foreign exchange. Some of these transfer payments are from private U.S. citizens, and some are from the U.S. government. You may send a check to a relief agency in Africa. Many immigrants in the United States send remittances to their countries of origin to help support extended families. Conversely, some foreigners make transfer payments to the United States. *Net* refers to the difference between payments from the United States to foreigners and payments from foreigners to the United States.

If we add net exports of goods, net export of services, net investment income, and net transfer payments, we get the **balance on current account**. The balance on current account shows how much a nation has spent on foreign goods, services, investment income payments, and

balance of trade   A country's exports of goods and services minus its imports of goods and services.

trade deficit   Occurs when a country's exports of goods and services are less than its imports of goods and services.

balance on current account   Net exports of goods plus net exports of services plus net investment income plus net transfer payments.

transfers relative to how much it has earned from other countries. When the balance is negative, which it was for the United States in 2007, a nation has spent more on foreign goods and services (plus investment income and transfers paid) than it has earned through the sales of its goods and services to the rest of the world (plus investment income and transfers received). If a nation has spent more on foreign goods, services, investment income payments, and transfers than it has earned, its net wealth position vis-à-vis the rest of the world must decrease. By *net*, we mean a nation's assets abroad minus its liabilities to the rest of the world. The capital account of the balance of payments records the changes in these assets and liabilities. We now turn to the capital account.

The Capital Account

For each transaction recorded in the current account, there is an offsetting transaction recorded in the capital account. Consider the purchase of a Japanese car by a U.S. citizen. Say that the yen/dollar exchange rate is 100 yen to a dollar and that the yen price of the car is 2.0 million yen, which is $20,000. The U.S. citizen (probably an automobile dealer) takes $20,000, buys 2.0 million yen, and then buys the car. In this case, U.S. imports are increased by $20,000 in the current account and foreign assets in the United States (in this case, Japanese holdings of dollars) are increased by $20,000 in the capital account. The net wealth position of the United States vis-à-vis the rest of the world has decreased by $20,000. The key point to realize is that an increase in U.S. imports results in an increase in foreign assets in the United States. The United States must "pay" for the imports, and whatever it pays with (in this example, U.S. dollars) is an increase in foreign assets in the United States. Conversely, an increase in U.S. exports results in an increase in U.S. assets abroad because foreigners must pay for the U.S. exports.

balance on capital account In the United States, the sum of the following (measured in a given period): the change in private U.S. assets abroad, the change in foreign private assets in the United States, the change in U.S. government assets abroad, and the change in foreign government assets in the United States.

Table 20.1 shows that U.S. assets abroad are divided into private holdings (line 6) and U.S. government holdings (line 8). Similarly, foreign assets in the United States are divided into foreign private (line 7) and foreign government (line 9). The sum of lines 6, 7, 8, and 9 is the **balance on capital account** (line 10). The next item is called net capital account transactions (line 11). It is quite small in value and includes things such as U.S. government debt forgiveness. These kinds of transactions affect the capital account but not the current account. Ignoring this item, if there were no errors of measurement in the data collection, the balance on capital account would equal the negative of the balance on current account because, as mentioned previously, for each transaction in the current account, there is an offsetting transaction in the capital account. Another way of looking at the balance on capital account is that it is the change in the net wealth position of the country vis-à-vis the rest of the world. When the balance on capital account is positive, this means that the change in foreign assets in the country is greater than the change in the country's assets abroad, which is a decrease in the net wealth position of the country.

Table 20.1 shows that in 2007, the U.S. balance on current account was −$738.6 billion, which means that the United States spent considerably more than it made vis-à-vis the rest of the world. If the balance on current account is measured correctly, the net wealth position of the United States vis-à-vis the rest of the world should have decreased by $738.6 billion in 2007 plus the $2.2 billion in line 11 of $740.8 billion. The balance on capital account (line 10) is in fact $657.4 billion; so the error of measurement, called the statistical discrepancy, is $83.6 billion (line 12) in 2007. The balance of payments (line 13) is the sum of the balance on current account, the balance on capital account, net capital account transactions, and the statistical discrepancy. By construction, it is always zero.

It is important to note from Table 20.1 that even though the net wealth position of the United States decreased in 2007, the change in U.S. assets abroad increased considerably ($1,183.3 billion private plus $23.0 billion government). How can this be? Because there was an even larger increase in foreign assets in the United States ($1,451.0 billion private plus $412.7 billion government). It is the *net* change (that is, the change in foreign assets in the United States minus the change in U.S. assets abroad) that is equal to the negative of the balance on current account (aside from the statistical discrepancy), not the change in just U.S. assets abroad. Much of the increase of $412.7 billion in foreign government assets was the accumulation of dollars by Japan and China.

Many transactions get recorded in the capital account that do not pertain to the current account. Consider a purchase of a U.K. security by a U.S. resident. This is done by the U.S.

resident's selling dollars for pounds and using the pounds to buy the U.K. security. After this transaction, U.S. assets abroad have increased (the United States now holds more U.K. securities) and foreign assets in the United States have increased (foreigners now hold more dollars). The purchase of the U.K. security is recorded as a minus item in line 6 in Table 20.1, and the increase in foreign holdings of dollars is recorded as a plus item in line 7. These two balance out. This happens whenever there is a switch of one kind of asset for another vis-à-vis the rest of the world. In recent years, a number of business people from the oil-rich Middle East purchased apartments in U.S. cities like New York and San Francisco. These real estate investments increased foreign assets in the United States (real estate) and increased U.S. assets abroad (foreign currency from the Middle East).

The United States as a Debtor Nation

If a country has a positive net wealth position vis-à-vis the rest of the world, it can be said to be a creditor nation. Conversely, if it has a negative net wealth position, it can be said to be a debtor nation. Remember that a country's net wealth position increases if it has a positive current account balance and decreases if it has a negative current account balance. It is important to realize that the *only* way a country's net wealth position can change is if its current account balance is nonzero. Simply switching one form of asset for another, such as trading real estate for foreign currency, is not a change in a country's net wealth position. Another way of putting this is that a country's net wealth position is the sum of all its past current account balances.

Prior to the mid-1970s, the United States had generally run current account surpluses, and thus its net wealth position was positive. It was a creditor nation. This began to turn around in the mid-1970s, and by the mid-1980s, the United States was running large current account deficits. Sometime during this period, the United States changed from having a positive net wealth position vis-à-vis the rest of the world to having a negative position. In other words, the United States changed from a creditor nation to a debtor nation. The current account deficits persisted into the 1990s, and the United States is now the largest debtor nation in the world. In 2006, foreign assets in the United States totaled $16.3 trillion and U.S. assets abroad totaled $13.8 trillion.[2] The U.S. net wealth position was thus −$2.5 trillion. This large negative position reflects the fact that the United States spent much more in the 1980s, 1990s, and 2000s on foreign goods and services (plus investment income and transfers paid) than it earned through the sales of its goods and services to the rest of the world (plus investment income and transfers received).

Equilibrium Output (Income) in an Open Economy

Everything we have said so far has been descriptive. Now we turn to analysis. How are all these trade and capital flows determined? What impacts do they have on the economies of the countries involved? To simplify our discussion, we will assume that exchange rates are fixed. We will relax this assumption later.

The International Sector and Planned Aggregate Expenditure

Our earlier descriptions of the multiplier took into account the consumption behavior of households (C), the planned investment behavior of firms (I), and the spending of the government (G). We defined the sum of those three components as planned aggregate expenditure (AE).

To analyze the international sector, we must include the goods and services a country exports to the rest of the world as well as what it imports. If we call our exports of goods and services EX, it should be clear that EX is a component of total output and income. A U.S. razor sold to a buyer

---

[2] U.S. Department of Commerce, *Survey of Current Business*, April 2008, Table F.1.

in Mexico is as much a part of U.S. production as a similar razor sold in Pittsburgh. Exports simply represent demand for domestic products not by domestic households and firms and the government, but by the rest of the world.

What about imports (*IM*)? Remember, imports are *not a part of domestic output* (*Y*). By definition, imports are not produced by the country that is importing them. Remember also, when we look at households' total consumption spending, firms' total investment spending, and total government spending, imports are included. Therefore, to calculate domestic output correctly, we must subtract the parts of consumption, investment, and government spending that constitute imports. The definition of planned aggregate expenditure becomes:

> Planned aggregate expenditure in an open economy:
>
> $$AE \equiv C + I + G + EX - IM$$

net exports of goods and services (*EX* − *IM*) The difference between a country's total exports and total imports.

The last two terms (*EX* − *IM*) together are the country's **net exports of goods and services**.

Determining the Level of Imports   What determines the level of imports and exports in a country? For now, we assume that the level of imports is a function of income (*Y*). The rationale is simple: When U.S. income increases, U.S. citizens buy more of everything, including U.S. cars and peanut butter, Japanese TV sets, and Korean steel and DVD players. When income rises, imports tend to go up. Algebraically,

$$IM = mY$$

where *Y* is income and *m* is some positive number. (*m* is assumed to be less than 1; otherwise, a $1 increase in income generates an increase in imports of more than $1, which is unrealistic.) Recall from Chapter 8 that the marginal propensity to consume (*MPC*) measures the change in consumption that results from a $1 change in income. Similarly, the **marginal propensity to import**, abbreviated as *MPM* or *m*, is the change in imports caused by a $1 change in income. If *m* = .2, or 20 percent, and income is $1,000, then imports, *IM*, are equal to .2 × $1,000 = $200. If income rises by $100 to $1,100, the change in imports will equal *m* × (the change in income) = .2 × $100 = $20.

marginal propensity to import (*MPM*) The change in imports caused by a $1 change in income.

For now we will assume that exports (*EX*) are given (that is, they are not affected, even indirectly, by the state of the economy.) This assumption is relaxed later in this chapter.

Solving for Equilibrium   Given the assumption about how imports are determined, we can solve for equilibrium income. This procedure is illustrated in Figure 20.1. Starting from the consumption function (blue line) in Figure 20.1(a), we gradually build up the components of planned aggregate expenditure (red line). Assuming for simplicity that planned investment, government purchases, and exports are all constant and do not depend on income, we move easily from the blue line to the red line by adding the fixed amounts of *I*, *G*, and *EX* to consumption at every level of income. In this example, we take *I* + *G* + *EX* to equal 80.

C + *I* + *G* + *EX*, however, includes spending on imports, which are not part of domestic production. To get spending on domestically produced goods, we must subtract the amount that is imported at each level of income. In Figure 20.1(b), we assume *m* = .25, which is the assumption that 25 percent of total income is spent on goods and services produced in foreign countries. Imports under this assumption are a constant fraction of total income; therefore, at higher levels of income, a larger amount is spent on foreign goods and services. For example, at *Y* = 200, *IM* = .25 *Y*, or 50. Similarly, at *Y* = 400, *IM* = .25 *Y*, or 100. Figure 20.1(b) shows the planned *domestic* aggregate expenditure curve.

Equilibrium is reached when planned domestic aggregate expenditure equals domestic aggregate output (income). This is true at only one level of aggregate output, *Y** = 200, in Figure 20.1(b). If *Y* were below *Y**, planned expenditure would exceed output, inventories would be lower than planned, and output would rise. At levels above *Y**, output would exceed planned expenditure, inventories would be larger than planned, and output would fall.

The Open-Economy Multiplier   All of this has implications for the size of the multiplier. Recall the multiplier, introduced in Chapter 8, and consider a sustained rise in government purchases (*G*). Initially, the increase in *G* will cause planned aggregate expenditure to be greater

▲ **FIGURE 20.1 Determining Equilibrium Output in an Open Economy**
In **a.**, planned investment spending (*I*), government spending (*G*), and total exports (*EX*) are added to consumption (*C*) to arrive at planned aggregate expenditure. However, *C* + *I* + *G* + *EX* includes spending on imports. In **b.**, the amount imported at every level of income is subtracted from planned aggregate expenditure. Equilibrium output occurs at *Y** = 200, the point at which planned domestic aggregate expenditure crosses the 45-degree line.

than aggregate output. Domestic firms will find their inventories to be lower than planned and thus will increase their output, but added output means more income. More workers are hired, and profits are higher. Some of the added income is saved, and some is spent. The added consumption spending leads to a second round of inventories being lower than planned and raising output. Equilibrium output rises by a multiple of the initial increase in government purchases. This is the multiplier.

In Chapters 8 and 9, we showed that the simple multiplier equals $1/(1 - MPC)$, or $(1/MPS)$. That is, a sustained increase in government purchases equal to ΔG will lead to an increase in aggregate output (income) of $\Delta G\,[1/(1 - MPC)]$. If the *MPC* were .75 and government purchases rose by $10 billion, equilibrium income would rise by $4 \times \$10$ billion, or $40 billion. The multiplier is $[1/(1 - .75)] = [1/.25] = 4.0$.

In an open economy, some of the increase in income brought about by the increase in *G* is spent on imports instead of domestically produced goods and services. The part of income spent on imports does not increase domestic income (*Y*) because imports are produced by foreigners. To compute the multiplier, we need to know how much of the increased income is used to increase domestic consumption. (We are assuming all imports are consumption goods. In practice, some imports are investment goods and some are goods purchased by the government.) In other words, we need to know the marginal propensity to consume *domestic* goods. Domestic consumption is $C - IM$. So the marginal propensity to consume domestic goods is the marginal propensity to consume all goods (the *MPC*) minus the marginal propensity to import (the *MPM*). The marginal propensity to consume domestic goods is (*MPC* − *MPM*). Consequently,

$$\text{open-economy multipler} = \frac{1}{1 - (MPC - MPM)}$$

If the *MPC* is .75 and the *MPM* is .25, then the multiplier is 1/.5, or 2.0. This multiplier is smaller than the multiplier in which imports are not taken into account, which is 1/.25, or 4.0. The effect of a sustained increase in government spending (or investment) on income—that is, the multiplier—is smaller in an open economy than in a closed economy. The reason: When government spending (or investment) increases and income and consumption rise, some of the extra consumption spending that results is on foreign products and not on domestically produced goods and services.

Imports and Exports and the Trade Feedback Effect

For simplicity, we have so far assumed that the level of imports depends only on income and that the level of exports is fixed. In reality, the amount of spending on imports depends on factors other than income and exports are not fixed. We will now consider the more realistic picture.

The Determinants of Imports   The same factors that affect households' consumption behavior and firms' investment behavior are likely to affect the demand for imports because some imported goods are consumption goods and some are investment goods. For example, anything that increases consumption spending is likely to increase the demand for imports. We saw in Chapters 8 and 11 that factors such as the after-tax real wage, after-tax nonlabor income, and interest rates affect consumption spending; thus, they should also affect spending on imports. Similarly, anything that increases investment spending is likely to increase the demand for imports. A decrease in interest rates, for example, should encourage spending on both domestically produced goods and foreign-produced goods.

There is one additional consideration in determining spending on imports: the *relative prices* of domestically produced and foreign-produced goods. If the prices of foreign goods fall relative to the prices of domestic goods, people will consume more foreign goods relative to domestic goods. When Japanese cars are inexpensive relative to U.S. cars, consumption of Japanese cars should be high and vice versa.

The Determinants of Exports   We now relax our assumption that exports are fixed. The demand for U.S. exports by other countries is identical to their demand for imports from the United States. Germany imports goods, some of which are U.S.-produced. France, Spain, and so on do the same. Total expenditure on imports in Germany is a function of the factors we just discussed except that the variables are German variables instead of U.S. variables. This is true for all other countries as well. The demand for U.S. exports depends on economic activity in the rest of the world—rest-of-the-world real wages, wealth, nonlabor income, interest rates, and so forth—as well as on the prices of U.S. goods relative to the price of rest-of-the-world goods. When foreign output increases, U.S. exports tend to increase. U.S. exports also tend to increase when U.S. prices fall relative to those in the rest of the world.

trade feedback effect
The tendency for an increase in the economic activity of one country to lead to a worldwide increase in economic activity, which then feeds back to that country.

The Trade Feedback Effect   We can now combine what we know about the demand for imports and the demand for exports to discuss the **trade feedback effect**. Suppose the United States finds its exports increasing, perhaps because the world suddenly decides it prefers U.S. computers to other computers. Rising exports will lead to an increase in U.S. output (income), which leads to an increase in U.S. imports. Here is where the trade feedback begins. Because U.S. imports are somebody else's exports, the extra import demand from the United States raises the exports of the rest of the world. When other countries' exports to the United States go up, their output and incomes also rise, in turn leading to an increase in the demand for imports from the rest of the world. Some of the extra imports demanded by the rest of the world come from the United States, so U.S. exports increase. The increase in U.S. exports stimulates U.S. economic activity even more, triggering a further increase in the U.S. demand for imports and so on. An increase in U.S. imports increases other countries' exports, which stimulates those countries' economies and increases their imports, which increases U.S. exports, which stimulates the U.S. economy and increases its imports, and so on. This is the trade feedback effect. In other words, an increase in U.S. economic activity leads to a worldwide increase in economic activity, which then "feeds back" to the United States.

Import and Export Prices and the Price Feedback Effect

We have talked about the price of imports, but we have not yet discussed the factors that influence import prices. The consideration of import prices is complicated because more than one currency is involved. When we talk about "the price of imports," do we mean the price in dollars, in yen, in U.K. pounds, in Mexican pesos, and so on? Because the exports of one country are the imports of another, the same question holds for the price of exports. When Mexico exports auto parts to the United States, Mexican manufacturers are interested in the price of auto parts in terms of pesos because pesos are what they use for transactions in Mexico. U.S. consumers are interested in the price of auto parts in dollars because dollars are what they use for transactions in the United States. The link between the two prices is the dollar/peso exchange rate.

Suppose Mexico is experiencing inflation and the price of radiators in pesos rises from 1,000 pesos to 1,200 pesos per radiator. If the dollar/peso exchange rate remains unchanged at, say, $0.10 per peso, Mexico's export price for radiators in terms of dollars will also rise, from $100 to $120 per radiator. Because Mexico's exports to the United States are, by definition, U.S. imports from Mexico, an increase in the dollar prices of Mexican exports to the United States means an increase in the prices of U.S. imports from Mexico. Therefore, when Mexico's export prices rise with no change in the dollar/peso exchange rate, U.S. import prices rise. Export prices of other countries affect U.S. import prices.

A country's export prices tend to move fairly closely with the general price level in that country. If Mexico is experiencing a general increase in prices, this change likely will be reflected in price increases of all domestically produced goods, both exportable and nonexportable. The general rate of inflation abroad is likely to affect U.S. import prices. If the inflation rate abroad is high, U.S. import prices are likely to rise.

The Price Feedback Effect We have just seen that when a country experiences an increase in domestic prices, the prices of its exports will increase. It is also true that when the prices of a country's *imports* increase, the prices of domestic goods may increase in response. There are at least two ways this effect can occur.

First, an increase in the prices of imported inputs will shift a country's aggregate supply curve to the left. In Chapter 13, we discussed the macroeconomy's response to a cost shock. Recall that a leftward shift in the aggregate supply curve due to a cost increase causes aggregate output to fall and prices to rise (stagflation).

Second, if import prices rise relative to domestic prices, households will tend to substitute domestically produced goods and services for imports. This is equivalent to a rightward shift of the aggregate demand curve. If the domestic economy is operating on the upward-sloping part of the aggregate supply curve, the overall domestic price level will rise in response to an increase in aggregate demand. Perfectly competitive firms will see market-determined prices rise, and imperfectly competitive firms will experience an increase in the demand for their products. Studies have shown, for example, that the price of automobiles produced in the United States moves closely with the price of imported cars.

Still, this is not the end of the story. Suppose a country—say, Mexico—experiences an increase in its domestic price level. This will increase the price of its exports to Canada (and to all other countries). The increase in the price of Canadian imports from Mexico will lead to an increase in domestic prices in Canada. Canada also exports to Mexico. The increase in Canadian prices causes an increase in the price of Canadian exports to Mexico, which then further increases the Mexican price level.

This is called the **price feedback effect**, in the sense that inflation is "exportable." An increase in the price level in one country can drive up prices in other countries, which in turn further increases the price level in the first country. Through export and import prices, a domestic price increase can "feed back" on itself.

It is important to realize that the discussion so far has been based on the assumption of fixed exchange rates. Life is more complicated under flexible exchange rates, to which we now turn.

The Open Economy with Flexible Exchange Rates

To a large extent, the fixed exchange rates set by the Bretton Woods agreements served as international monetary arrangements until 1971. Then in 1971, the United States and most other countries decided to abandon the fixed exchange rate system in favor of **floating**, or **market-determined, exchange rates**. Although governments still intervene to ensure that exchange rate movements are "orderly," exchange rates today are largely determined by the unregulated forces of supply and demand.

price feedback effect The process by which a domestic price increase in one country can "feed back" on itself through export and import prices. An increase in the price level in one country can drive up prices in other countries. This in turn further increases the price level in the first country.

floating, *or* **market-determined, exchange rates** Exchange rates that are determined by the unregulated forces of supply and demand.

Understanding how an economy interacts with the rest of the world when exchange rates are not fixed is not as simple as when we assume fixed exchange rates. Exchange rates determine the price of imported goods relative to domestic goods and can have significant effects on the level of imports and exports. Consider a 20 percent drop in the value of the dollar against the British pound. Dollars buy fewer pounds, and pounds buy more dollars. Both British residents, who now get more dollars for pounds, and U.S. residents, who get fewer pounds for dollars, find that U.S. goods and services are more attractive. Exchange rate movements have important impacts on imports, exports, and the movement of capital between countries.

The Market for Foreign Exchange

What determines exchange rates under a floating rate system? To explore this question, we assume that there are just two countries, the United States and Great Britain. It is easier to understand a world with only two countries, and most of the points we will make can be generalized to a world with many trading partners.

The Supply of and Demand for Pounds Governments, private citizens, banks, and corporations exchange pounds for dollars and dollars for pounds every day. In our two-country case, those who *demand* pounds are holders of dollars seeking to exchange them for pounds. Those who *supply* pounds are holders of pounds seeking to exchange them for dollars. It is important not to confuse the supply of dollars (or pounds) on the foreign exchange market with the U.S. (or British) money supply. The latter is the sum of all the money currently in circulation. The supply of dollars on the foreign exchange market is the number of dollars that holders seek to exchange for pounds in a given time period. The demand for and supply of dollars on foreign exchange markets determine *exchange* rates; the demand for money balances, and the total domestic money supply determine the *interest* rate.

The common reason for exchanging dollars for pounds is to buy something produced in Great Britain. U.S. importers who purchase Jaguar automobiles or Scotch whiskey must pay with pounds. U.S. citizens traveling in Great Britain who want to ride the train, stay in a hotel, or eat at a restaurant must acquire pounds for dollars to do so. If a U.S. corporation builds a plant in Great Britain, it must pay for that plant in pounds.

At the same time, some people may want to buy British stocks or bonds. Implicitly, when U.S. citizens buy a bond issued by the British government or by a British corporation, they are making a loan, but the transaction requires a currency exchange. The British bond seller must ultimately be paid in pounds.

On the supply side of the market, the situation is reversed. Here we find people—usually British citizens—holding pounds they want to use to buy dollars. Again, the common reason is to buy things produced in the United States. If a British importer decides to import golf carts made in Georgia, the producer must be paid in dollars. British tourists visiting New York may ride in cabs, eat in restaurants, and tour Ellis Island. Doing those things requires dollars. When a British firm builds an office complex in Los Angeles, it must pay the contractor in dollars.

In addition to buyers and sellers who exchange money to engage in transactions, some people and institutions hold currency balances for speculative reasons. If you think that the U.S. dollar is going to decline in value relative to the pound, you may want to hold some of your wealth in the form of pounds. Table 20.2 summarizes some of the major categories of private foreign exchange demanders and suppliers in the two-country case of the United States and Great Britain.

Figure 20.2 shows the demand curve for pounds in the foreign exchange market. When the price of pounds (the exchange rate) is lower, it takes fewer dollars to buy British goods and services, to build a plant in Liverpool, to travel to London, and so on. Lower net prices (in dollars) should increase the demand for British-made products and encourage investment and travel in Great Britain. If prices (in pounds) in Britain do not change, an increase in the quantity of British goods and services demanded by foreigners will increase the quantity of pounds demanded. The demand-for-pounds curve in the foreign exchange market has a negative slope.

Figure 20.3 shows a supply curve for pounds in the foreign exchange market. At a higher exchange rate, each pound buys more dollars, making the price of U.S.-produced goods and services lower to the British. The British are more apt to buy U.S.-made goods when the price of

TABLE 20.2   Some Buyers and Sellers in International Exchange Markets: United States and Great Britain

The Demand for Pounds (Supply of Dollars)

1. Firms, households, or governments that import British goods into the United States or want to buy British-made goods and services
2. U.S. citizens traveling in Great Britain
3. Holders of dollars who want to buy British stocks, bonds, or other financial instruments
4. U.S. companies that want to invest in Great Britain
5. Speculators who anticipate a decline in the value of the dollar relative to the pound

The Supply of Pounds (Demand for Dollars)

1. Firms, households, or governments that import U.S. goods into Great Britain or want to buy U.S.-made goods and services
2. British citizens traveling in the United States
3. Holders of pounds who want to buy stocks, bonds, or other financial instruments in the United States
4. British companies that want to invest in the United States
5. Speculators who anticipate a rise in the value of the dollar relative to the pound

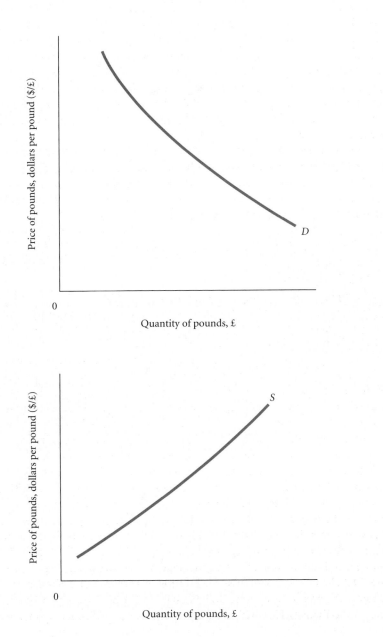

◀ **FIGURE 20.2 The Demand for Pounds in the Foreign Exchange Market**

When the price of pounds falls, British-made goods and services appear less expensive to U.S. buyers. If British prices are constant, U.S. buyers will buy more British goods and services and the quantity of pounds demanded will rise.

◀ **FIGURE 20.3 The Supply of Pounds in the Foreign Exchange Market**

When the price of pounds rises, the British can obtain more dollars for each pound. This means that U.S.-made goods and services appear less expensive to British buyers. Thus, the quantity of pounds supplied is likely to rise with the exchange rate.

pounds is high (the value of the dollar is low). An increase in British demand for U.S. goods and services is likely to increase the quantity of pounds supplied. The curve representing the supply of pounds in the foreign exchange market has a positive slope.

The Equilibrium Exchange Rate When exchange rates are allowed to float, they are determined the same way other prices are determined: The equilibrium exchange rate occurs at the point at which the quantity demanded of a foreign currency equals the quantity of that currency supplied. This is illustrated in Figure 20.4. An excess demand for pounds (quantity demanded in excess of quantity supplied) will cause the price of pounds to rise—the pound will **appreciate** relative to the dollar. An excess supply of pounds will cause the price of pounds to fall—the pound will **depreciate** relative to the dollar.[3]

appreciation of a currency The rise in value of one currency relative to another.

depreciation of a currency The fall in value of one currency relative to another.

▶ **FIGURE 20.4**

The Equilibrium Exchange Rate

When exchange rates are allowed to float, they are determined by the forces of supply and demand. An excess demand for pounds will cause the pound to appreciate against the dollar. An excess supply of pounds will lead to a depreciating pound.

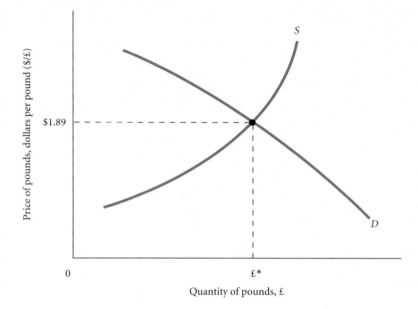

Factors that Affect Exchange Rates

We now know enough to discuss the factors likely to influence exchange rates. Anything that changes the behavior of the people in Table 20.2 can cause demand and supply curves to shift and the exchange rate to adjust accordingly.

Purchasing Power Parity: The Law of One Price If the costs of transporting goods between two countries are small, we would expect the price of the same good in both countries to be roughly the same. The price of basketballs should be roughly the same in Canada and the United States, for example.

It is not hard to see why. If the price of basketballs is cheaper in Canada, it will pay for someone to buy balls in Canada at a low price and sell them in the United States at a higher price. This decreases the supply and pushes up the price in Canada and increases the supply and pushes down the price in the United States. This process should continue as long as the price differential, and therefore the profit opportunity, persists. For a good with trivial transportation costs, we would expect this **law of one price** to hold. The price of a good should be the same regardless of where we buy it.

law of one price If the costs of transportation are small, the price of the same good in different countries should be roughly the same.

---

[3] Although Figure 20.3 shows the supply-of-pounds curve in the foreign exchange market with a positive slope, under certain circumstances the curve may bend back. Suppose the price of a pound rises from $1.50 to $2.00. Consider a British importer who buys 10 Chevrolets each month at $15,000 each, including transportation costs. When a pound exchanges for $1.50, he will supply 100,000 pounds per month to the foreign exchange market—100,000 pounds brings $150,000, enough to buy 10 cars. Now suppose the cheaper dollar causes him to buy 12 cars. Twelve cars will cost a total of $180,000; but at $2 = 1 pound, he will spend only 90,000 pounds per month. The supply of pounds on the market falls when the price of pounds rises. The reason for this seeming paradox is simple. The number of pounds a British importer needs to buy U.S. goods depends on both the quantity of goods he buys and the price of those goods in pounds. If demand for imports is inelastic so that the percentage decrease in price resulting from the depreciated currency is greater than the percentage increase in the quantity of imports demanded, importers will spend fewer pounds and the quantity of pounds supplied in the foreign exchange market will fall. The supply of pounds will slope upward as long as the demand for U.S. imports is elastic.

If the law of one price held for all goods and if each country consumed the same market basket of goods, the exchange rate between the two currencies would be determined simply by the relative price levels in the two countries. If the price of a basketball were $10 in the United States and $12 in Canada, the U.S.–Canada exchange rate would have to be $1 U.S. per $1.20 Canadian. If the rate were instead one-to-one, it would pay people to buy the balls in the United States and sell them in Canada. This would increase the demand for U.S. dollars in Canada, thereby driving up their price in terms of Canadian dollars to $1 U.S. per $1.2 Canadian, at which point no one could make a profit shipping basketballs across international lines and the process would cease.[4]

The theory that exchange rates will adjust so that the price of similar goods in different countries is the same is known as the **purchasing-power-parity theory**. According to this theory, if it takes 10 times as many Mexican pesos to buy a pound of salt in Mexico as it takes U.S. dollars to buy a pound of salt in the United States, the equilibrium exchange rate should be 10 pesos per dollar.

In practice, transportation costs for many goods are quite large and the law of one price does not hold for these goods. (Haircuts are often cited as a good example. The transportation costs for a U.S. resident to get a British haircut are indeed large unless that person is an airline pilot.) Also, many products that are potential substitutes for each other are not precisely identical. For instance, a Rolls Royce and a Honda are both cars, but there is no reason to expect the exchange rate between the British pound and the yen to be set so that the prices of the two are equalized. In addition, countries consume different market baskets of goods, so we would not expect the aggregate price levels to follow the law of one price. Nevertheless, a high rate of inflation in one country relative to another puts pressure on the exchange rate between the two countries, and there is a general tendency for the currencies of relatively high-inflation countries to depreciate.

Figure 20.5 shows the adjustment likely to occur following an increase in the U.S. price level relative to the price level in Great Britain. This change in relative prices will affect citizens of both countries. Higher prices in the United States make imports relatively less expensive. U.S. citizens are likely to increase their spending on imports from Britain, shifting the demand for pounds to the right, from D_0 to D_1. At the same time, the British see U.S. goods getting more expensive and reduce their demand for exports from the United States. Consequently, the supply of pounds shifts to the left, from S_0 to S_1. The result is an increase in the price of pounds. Before the change in relative prices, 1 pound sold for $1.89; after the change, 1 pound costs $2.25. The pound appreciates, and the dollar depreciates.

purchasing-power-parity theory   A theory of international exchange holding that exchange rates are set so that the price of similar goods in different countries is the same.

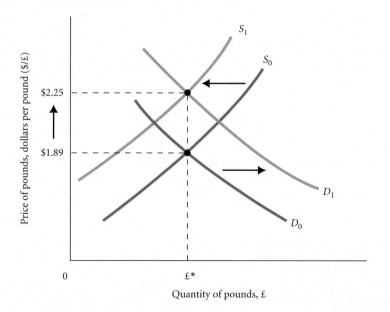

◀ **FIGURE 20.5**
Exchange Rates Respond to Changes in Relative Prices

The higher price level in the United States makes imports relatively less expensive. U.S. citizens are likely to increase their spending on imports from Britain, shifting the demand for pounds to the right, from D_0 to D_1. At the same time, the British see U.S. goods getting more expensive and reduce their demand for exports from the United States. The supply of pounds shifts to the left, from S_0 to S_1. The result is an increase in the price of pounds. The pound appreciates, and the dollar is worth less.

---

[4] Of course, if the rate were $1 U.S. to $2 Canadian, it would pay people to buy basketballs in Canada (at $12 Canadian, which is $6 U.S.) and sell them in the United States. This would weaken demand for the U.S. dollar, and its price would fall from $2 Canadian until it reached $1.20 Canadian.

Relative Interest Rates Another factor that influences a country's exchange rate is the level of its interest rate relative to other countries' interest rates. If the interest rate is 6 percent in the United States and 8 percent in Great Britain, people with money to lend have an incentive to buy British securities instead of U.S. securities. Although it is sometimes difficult for individuals in one country to buy securities in another country, it is easy for international banks and investment companies to do so. If the interest rate is lower in the United States than in Britain, there will be a movement of funds out of U.S. securities into British securities as banks and firms move their funds to the higher-yielding securities.

How does a U.S. bank buy British securities? It takes its dollars, buys British pounds, and uses the pounds to buy the British securities. The bank's purchase of pounds drives up the price of pounds in the foreign exchange market. The increased demand for pounds increases the price of the pound (and decreases the price of the dollar). A high interest rate in Britain relative to the interest rate in the United States tends to depreciate the dollar.

Figure 20.6 shows the effect of rising interest rates in the United States on the dollar–pound exchange rate. Higher interest rates in the United States attract British investors. To buy U.S. securities, the British need dollars. The supply of pounds (the demand for dollars) shifts to the right, from S_0 to S_1. The same relative interest rates affect the portfolio choices of U.S. banks, firms, and households. With higher interest rates at home, there is less incentive for U.S. residents to buy British securities. The demand for pounds drops at the same time the supply increases and the demand curve shifts to the left, from D_0 to D_1. The net result is a depreciating pound and an appreciating dollar. The price of pounds falls from $1.89 to $1.25.

▶ **FIGURE 20.6**

Exchange Rates Respond to Changes in Relative Interest Rates

If U.S. interest rates rise relative to British interest rates, British citizens holding pounds may be attracted into the U.S. securities market. To buy bonds in the United States, British buyers must exchange pounds for dollars. The supply of pounds shifts to the right, from S_0 to S_1. However, U.S. citizens are less likely to be interested in British securities because interest rates are higher at home. The demand for pounds shifts to the left, from D_0 to D_1. The result is a depreciated pound and a stronger dollar.

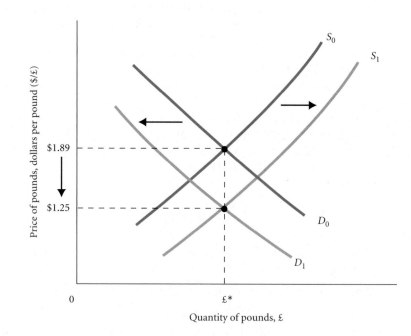

The Effects of Exchange Rates on the Economy

We are now ready to discuss some of the implications of floating exchange rates. Recall, when exchange rates are fixed, households spend some of their incomes on imports and the multiplier is smaller than it would be otherwise. Imports are a "leakage" from the circular flow, much like taxes and saving. Exports, in contrast, are an "injection" into the circular flow; they represent spending on U.S.-produced goods and services from abroad and can stimulate output.

The world is far more complicated when exchange rates are allowed to float. First, the level of imports and exports depends on exchange rates as well as on income and other factors. When events cause exchange rates to adjust, the levels of imports and exports will change. Changes in exports and imports can, in turn, affect the level of real GDP and the price level. Further, exchange rates themselves also adjust to changes in the economy. Suppose the government decides to stimulate the economy with an expansionary monetary policy. This will affect interest rates, which may affect exchange rates.

Exchange Rate Effects on Imports, Exports, and Real GDP   As we already know, when a country's currency depreciates (falls in value), its import prices rise and its export prices (in foreign currencies) fall. When the U.S. dollar is cheap, U.S. products are more competitive with products produced in the rest of the world and foreign-made goods look expensive to U.S. citizens.

A depreciation of a country's currency can serve as a stimulus to the economy. Suppose the U.S. dollar falls in value, as it did sharply between 1985 and 1988. If foreign buyers increase their spending on U.S. goods, and domestic buyers substitute U.S.-made goods for imports, aggregate expenditure on domestic output will rise, inventories will fall, and real GDP (Y) will increase. A depreciation of a country's currency is likely to increase its GDP.[5]

Exchange Rates and the Balance of Trade: The J Curve   Because a depreciating currency tends to increase exports and decrease imports, you might think that it also will reduce a country's trade deficit. In fact, the effect of a depreciation on the balance of trade is ambiguous.

Many economists believe that when a currency starts to depreciate, the balance of trade is likely to worsen for the first few quarters (perhaps three to six). After that, the balance of trade may improve. This effect is graphed in Figure 20.7. The curve in this figure resembles the letter *J*, and the movement in the balance of trade that it describes is sometimes called the **J-curve effect**. The point of the *J* shape is that the balance of trade gets worse before it gets better following a currency depreciation.

J-curve effect   Following a currency depreciation, a country's balance of trade may get worse before it gets better. The graph showing this effect is shaped like the letter *J*, hence the name J-curve effect.

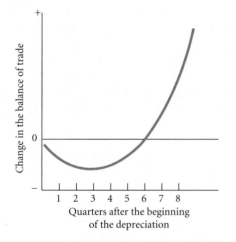

◀ **FIGURE 20.7 The Effect of a Depreciation on the Balance of Trade (the J Curve)**

Initially, a depreciation of a country's currency may worsen its balance of trade. The negative effect on the price of imports may initially dominate the positive effects of an increase in exports and a decrease in imports.

How does the J curve come about? Recall that the balance of trade is equal to export revenue minus import costs, including exports and imports of services:

$$\text{balance of trade} = \text{dollar price of exports} \times \text{quantity of exports}$$
$$- \text{dollar price of imports} \times \text{quantity of imports}$$

A currency depreciation affects the items on the right side of this equation as follows: First, the quantity of exports increases and the quantity of imports decreases; both have a *positive* effect on the balance of trade (lowering the trade deficit or raising the trade surplus). Second, the dollar price of exports is not likely to change very much, at least not initially. The dollar price of exports changes when the U.S. price level changes, but the initial effect of a depreciation on the domestic price level is not likely to be large. Third, the dollar price of imports increases. Imports into the United States are more expensive because $1 U.S. buys fewer yen, euros, and so on, than before. An increase in the dollar price of imports has a *negative* effect on the balance of trade.

---

[5] For this reason, some countries are tempted at times to intervene in foreign exchange markets, depreciate their currencies, and stimulate their economies. If all countries attempted to lower the value of their currencies simultaneously, there would be no gain in income for any of them. Although the exchange rate system at the time was different, such a situation actually occurred during the early years of the Great Depression. Many countries practiced so-called *beggar-thy-neighbor* policies of competitive devaluations in a desperate attempt to maintain export sales and employment.

An example to clarify this last point follows: The dollar price of a Japanese car that costs 1,200,000 yen rises from $10,000 to $12,000 when the exchange rate moves from 120 yen per dollar to 100 yen per dollar. After the currency depreciation, the United States ends up spending more (in dollars) for the Japanese car than it did before. Of course, the United States will end up buying fewer Japanese cars than it did before. Does the number of cars drop enough so that the quantity effect is bigger than the price effect or vice versa? Does the value of imports increase or decrease?

The net effect of a depreciation on the balance of trade could go either way. The depreciation stimulates exports and cuts back imports, but it also increases the dollar price of imports. It seems that the negative effect dominates initially. The impact of a depreciation on the price of imports is generally felt quickly, while it takes time for export and import quantities to respond to price changes. In the short run, the value of imports increases more than the value of exports, so the balance of trade worsens. The initial effect is likely to be negative; but after exports and imports have had time to respond, the net effect turns positive. The more elastic the demand for exports and imports, the larger the eventual improvement in the balance of trade.

Exchange Rates and Prices The depreciation of a country's currency tends to increase its price level. There are two reasons for this effect. First, when a country's currency is less expensive, its products are more competitive on world markets, so exports rise. In addition, domestic buyers tend to substitute domestic products for the now-more-expensive imports. This means that planned aggregate expenditure on domestically produced goods and services rises and that the aggregate demand curve shifts to the right. The result is a higher price level, a higher output, or both. (You may want to draw an *AS/AD* diagram to verify this outcome.) If the economy is close to capacity, the result is likely to be higher prices. Second, a depreciation makes imported inputs more expensive. If costs increase, the aggregate supply curve shifts to the left. If aggregate demand remains unchanged, the result is an increase in the price level.

Monetary Policy with Flexible Exchange Rates Let us now put everything in this chapter together and consider what happens when monetary policy is used first to stimulate the economy and then to contract the economy.

Suppose the economy is below full employment and the Federal Reserve (Fed) decides to expand the money supply. The volume of reserves in the system is expanded, perhaps through open market purchases of U.S. government securities by the Fed. The result is a decrease in the interest rate. The lower interest rate stimulates planned investment spending and consumption spending.

This added spending causes inventories to be lower than planned and aggregate output (income) (Y) to rise, but there are two additional effects: (1) The lower interest rate has an impact in the foreign exchange market. A lower interest rate means a lower demand for U.S. securities by foreigners, so the demand for dollars drops. (2) U.S. investment managers will be more likely to buy foreign securities (which are now paying relatively higher interest rates), so the supply of dollars rises. Both events push down the value of the dollar.

A cheaper dollar is a good thing if the goal of the monetary expansion is to stimulate the domestic economy because a cheaper dollar means more U.S. exports and fewer imports. If consumers substitute U.S.-made goods for imports, both the added exports and the decrease in imports mean more spending on domestic products, so the multiplier actually increases.

Now suppose inflation is a problem and the Fed wants to slow it down with tight money. Here again, floating exchange rates help. Tight monetary policy works through a higher interest rate. A higher interest rate lowers investment and consumption spending, reducing aggregate expenditure, reducing output, and lowering the price level. The higher interest rate also attracts foreign buyers into U.S. financial markets, driving up the value of the dollar, which reduces the price of imports. The reduction in the price of imports causes a shift of the aggregate supply curve to the right, which helps fight inflation.

Fiscal Policy with Flexible Exchange Rates The openness of the economy and flexible exchange rates do not always work to the advantage of policy makers. Consider a policy of cutting taxes to stimulate the economy. Suppose Congress enacts a major tax cut designed to raise output. Spending by households rises, but not all this added spending is on domestic products—some leaks out of the U.S. economy, reducing the multiplier.

ECONOMICS IN PRACTICE

Exchange Rates in 2008

There were large changes in exchange rates in 2008. The figures below graph the euro/dollar and yen/dollar exchanges rates between January and October 2008.

The euro/dollar figure shows that the dollar was low until the middle of 2008. On April 22, the exchange rate was 0.625, which means that one dollars buys 0.625 euros (or one euro buys $1/0.625 = 1.60$ dollars). Remember from the text that when a currency is cheap, there may be concern in the country about inflation. This was in fact the case in the United States in the summer of 2008. Some thought that the cheap dollar would lead to a rise in inflation because of the rise in import prices (European imports were expensive because the euro was expensive relative to the dollar). Then in August the value of the dollar began to rise, and by the end of October it was up to about 0.8 euros. This is a 28 percent increase from the low value on April 22.

Why the large increase in the value of the dollar? We know from the text that relative interest rates can affect exchange rates, and this effect is relevant in explaining the increase in the dollar. By the end of the summer of 2008 it became apparent that Europe was also having economic troubles and that the European Central Bank was likely to lower interest rates to stimulate demand. The lower European interest rate relative to the U.S. rate led to an appreciation of the dollar relative to the euro.

The interesting feature about the yen/dollar figure is the large depreciation of the dollar relative to the yen beginning in September 2008. Again, the relative interest rate effect plays a role. The interest rate in Japan in 2008 was close to zero. With interest rates higher abroad than in Japan, people borrowed yen in Japan, used the yen to buy dollars, euros, pounds, and other currencies, which they used to buy higher yielding securities in the other currencies. (This activity is called the "carry trade.") This investment activity, other things being equal, has a positive effect on the yen/dollar exchange rate because of the increased yen demand for dollars. In the fall of 2008 interest rates in the United States and Europe fell, which made the carry trade less profitable. As the carry trade shrunk, there was an increased dollar demand for yen (as people tried to move out of dollars back into yen). The yen appreciated (dollar depreciated). So again, a major reason for the appreciation of the yen in the fall of 2008 was the relative interest rate effect.

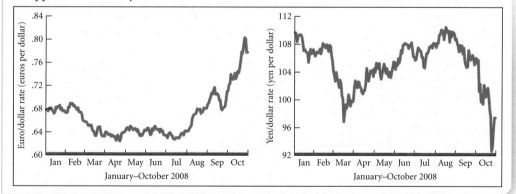

As income rises, so does the demand for money (M^d)—not the demand for dollars in the foreign exchange market, but the amount of money people want to hold for transactions. Unless the Fed is fully accommodating, the interest rate will rise. A higher interest rate tends to attract foreign demand for U.S. securities. This rise in demand tends to drive the price of the dollar up, which further blunts the effectiveness of the tax cut. If the value of the dollar rises, U.S. exports are less competitive in world markets and the quantity of exports will decline. Similarly, a strong dollar makes imported goods look cheaper and U.S. citizens spend more on foreign goods and less on U.S. goods, an effect that again reduces the multiplier.

There is another caveat to the multiplier story of Chapters 8 and 9. Without a fully accommodating Fed, three factors work to reduce the multiplier: (1) A higher interest rate from the increase in money demand may crowd out private investment and consumption; (2) some of the increase in income from the expansion will be spent on imports; and (3) a higher interest rate may cause the dollar to appreciate, discouraging exports and further encouraging imports.

Monetary Policy with Fixed Exchange Rates   Although most major countries in the world today have a flexible exchange rate (counting for this purpose the euro zone countries as one country), it is interesting to ask what role monetary policy can play when a country has a fixed exchange rate. The answer is, no role. In order for a country to keep its exchange rate fixed to, say, the U.S. dollar, its interest rate cannot change relative to the U.S. interest rate. If the monetary authority of the country lowered the interest rate because it wanted to stimulate the economy, the country's currency would depreciate (assuming the U.S. interest rate did not change). People would want to sell the country's currency and buy dollars and invest in U.S. securities because the country's interest rate would have fallen relative to the U.S. interest rate. In other words, the monetary authority cannot change its interest rate relative to the U.S. interest rate without having its exchange rate change. The monetary authority is at the mercy of the United States, and it has no independent way of changing its interest rate if it wants to keep its exchange rate fixed to the dollar.

This restriction means that when the various European countries moved in 1999 to a common currency, the euro, each of the countries gave up its monetary policy. There is now only one monetary policy for all the euro zone countries, and it is decided by the European Central Bank (ECB).

The one case in which a country can change its interest rate and keep its exchange rate fixed is if it imposes capital controls. Imposing capital controls means that the country limits or prevents people from buying or selling its currency in the foreign exchange markets. A citizen of the country may be prevented, for example, from using the country's currency to buy dollars. The problem with capital controls is that they are hard to enforce, especially for large countries and for long periods of time.

An Interdependent World Economy

The increasing interdependence of countries in the world economy has made the problems facing policy makers more difficult. We used to be able to think of the United States as a relatively self-sufficient region. Forty years ago economic events outside U.S. borders had relatively little effect on its economy. This situation is no longer true. The events of the past four decades have taught us that the performance of the U.S. economy is heavily dependent on events outside U.S. borders.

This chapter and the previous chapter have provided only the bare bones of open-economy macroeconomics. If you continue your study of economics, more will be added to the basic story we have presented. The next chapter concludes with a discussion of the problems of developing countries.

SUMMARY

1. The main difference between an international transaction and a domestic transaction concerns currency exchange: When people in different countries buy from and sell to each other, an exchange of currencies must also take place.

2. The *exchange rate* is the price of one country's currency in terms of another country's currency.

THE BALANCE OF PAYMENTS *p. 378*

3. *Foreign exchange* is all currencies other than the domestic currency of a given country. The record of a nation's transactions in goods, services, and assets with the rest of the world is its *balance of payments*. The balance of payments is also the record of a country's sources (supply) and uses (demand) of foreign exchange.

EQUILIBRIUM OUTPUT (INCOME) IN AN OPEN ECONOMY *p. 381*

4. In an open economy, some income is spent on foreign produced goods instead of domestically produced goods. To measure planned domestic aggregate expenditure in an open economy, we add total exports but subtract total imports: $C + I + G + EX - IM$. The open economy is in equilibrium when domestic aggregate output (income) (Y) equals planned domestic aggregate expenditure.

5. In an open economy, the multiplier equals $1/[1 - (MPC - MPM)]$, where MPC is the marginal propensity to consume and MPM is the marginal propensity to import. The *marginal propensity to import* is the change in imports caused by a $1 change in income.

6. In addition to income, other factors that affect the level of imports are the after-tax real wage rate, after-tax nonlabor income, interest rates, and relative prices of domestically-produced and foreign-produced goods. The demand for exports is determined by economic activity in the rest of the world and by relative prices.

7. An increase in U.S. economic activity leads to a worldwide increase in economic activity, which then "feeds back" to the United States. An increase in U.S. imports increases other countries' exports, which stimulates economies and increases their imports, which increases U.S. exports, which stimulates the U.S. economy and increases its imports, and so on. This is the *trade feedback effect*.

8. Export prices of other countries affect U.S. import prices. The general rate of inflation abroad is likely to affect U.S. import prices. If the inflation rate abroad is high, U.S. import prices are likely to rise.

9. Because one country's exports are another country's imports, an increase in export prices increases other countries' import prices. An increase in other countries' import prices leads to an increase in their domestic prices—and their export prices. In short, export prices affect import prices and vice versa. This *price feedback effect* shows that inflation is "exportable"; an increase in the price level in one country can drive up prices in other countries, making inflation in the first country worse.

THE OPEN ECONOMY WITH FLEXIBLE EXCHANGE RATES *p. 385*

10. The equilibrium exchange rate occurs when the quantity demanded of a foreign currency in the foreign exchange market equals the quantity of that currency supplied in the foreign exchange market.

11. *Depreciation of a currency occurs* when a nation's currency falls in value relative to another country's currency. *Appreciation of a currency* occurs when a nation's currency rises in value relative to another country's currency.

12. According to the *law of one price*, if the costs of transportation are small, the price of the same good in different countries should be roughly the same. The theory that exchange rates are set so that the price of similar goods in different countries

is the same is known as the *purchasing-power-parity* theory. In practice, transportation costs are significant for many goods, and the law of one price does not hold for these goods.

13. A high rate of inflation in one country relative to another country puts pressure on the exchange rate between the two countries. There is a general tendency for the currencies of relatively high-inflation countries to depreciate.

14. A depreciation of the dollar tends to increase U.S. GDP by making U.S. exports cheaper (hence, more competitive abroad) and by making U.S. imports more expensive (encouraging consumers to switch to domestically produced goods and services).

15. The effect of a depreciation of a nation's currency on its balance of trade is unclear. In the short run, a currency depreciation may increase the balance-of-trade deficit because it raises the price of imports. Although this price increase causes a decrease in the quantity of imports demanded, the impact of a depreciation on the price of imports is generally felt quickly, but it takes time for export and import quantities to respond to price changes. The initial effect is likely to be negative; but after exports and imports have had time to respond, the net effect turns positive. The tendency for the balance-of-trade deficit to widen and then to decrease as the result of a currency depreciation is known as the *J-curve effect*.

16. The depreciation of a country's currency tends to raise its price level for two reasons. First, a currency depreciation increases planned aggregate expenditure, an effect that shifts the aggregate demand curve to the right. If the economy is close to capacity, the result is likely to be higher prices. Second, a depreciation makes imported inputs more expensive. If costs increase, the aggregate supply curve shifts to the left. If aggregate demand remains unchanged, the result is an increase in the price level.

17. When exchange rates are flexible, a U.S. expansionary monetary policy decreases the interest rate and stimulates planned investment and consumption spending. The lower interest rate leads to a lower demand for U.S. securities by foreigners and a higher demand for foreign securities by U.S. investment-fund managers. As a result, the dollar depreciates. A U.S. contractionary monetary policy appreciates the dollar.

18. Flexible exchange rates do not always work to the advantage of policy makers. An expansionary fiscal policy can appreciate the dollar and work to reduce the multiplier.

REVIEW TERMS AND CONCEPTS

appreciation of a currency, *p. 388*

balance of payments, *p. 378*

balance of trade, *p. 379*

balance on capital account, *p. 380*

balance on current account, *p. 379*

depreciation of a currency, *p. 388*

exchange rate, *p. 377*

floating, *or* market-determined, exchange rates, *p. 385*

foreign exchange, *p. 378*

J-curve effect, *p. 391*

law of one price, *p. 388*

marginal propensity to import (*MPM*), *p. 382*

net exports of goods and services (*EX − IM*), *p. 382*

price feedback effect, *p. 385*

purchasing-power-parity theory, *p. 389*

trade deficit, *p. 379*

trade feedback effect, *p. 384*

Planned aggregate expenditure in an open economy:

$$AE \equiv C + I + G + EX - IM$$

Open-economy multiplier =

$$\frac{1}{1 - (MPC - MPM)}$$

PROBLEMS

Visit **www.myeconlab.com** to complete the problems marked in orange online. You will receive instant feedback on your answers, tutorial help, and access to additional practice problems.

1. In June 2008, the euro was trading at $1.50. Check the Web or any daily newspaper to see what the "price" of a euro is today. What explanations can you give for the change? Make sure you check what has happened to interest rates and economic growth.

2. Suppose the following graph shows what prevailed on the foreign exchange market in 2008 with floating exchange rates.
   a. Name three phenomena that might shift the demand curve to the right.
   b. Which, if any, of these three phenomena might cause a simultaneous shift of the supply curve to the left?
   c. What effects might each of the three phenomena have on the balance of trade if the exchange rate floats?

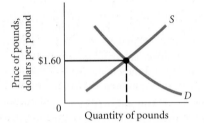

3. Obtain a recent issue of *The Economist*. Turn to the section entitled "Financial Indicators." Look at the table entitled "Trade, exchange rates and budgets." Which country had the largest trade deficit over the last year and during the last month? Which country had the largest trade surplus over the last year and during the last month? How does the current account deficit/surplus compare to the overall trade balance? How can you explain the difference?

4. The exchange rate between the U.S. dollar and the Japanese yen is floating freely—both governments do not intervene in the market for each currency. Suppose a large trade deficit with Japan prompts the United States to impose quotas on certain Japanese products imported into the United States and, as a result, the quantity of these imports falls.
   a. The decrease in spending on Japanese products increases spending on U.S.-made goods. Why? What effect will this have on U.S. output and employment and on Japanese output and employment?
   b. What happens to U.S. imports from Japan when U.S. output (or income) rises? If the quotas initially reduce imports from Japan by $25 billion, why is the final reduction in imports likely to be less than $25 billion?
   c. Suppose the quotas do succeed in reducing imports from Japan by $15 billion. What will happen to the demand for yen? Why?
   d. What will happen to the dollar–yen exchange rate? Why? (*Hint:* There is an excess supply of yen, or an excess demand for dollars.) What effects will the change in the value of each currency have on employment and output in the United States? What about the balance of trade? (Ignore complications such as the J curve.)
   e. Considering the macroeconomic effects of a quota on Japanese imports, could a quota reduce employment and output in the United States? have no effect at all? Explain.

5. What effect will each of the following events have on the current account balance and the exchange rate if the exchange rate is fixed? if the exchange rate is floating?

   a. The U.S. government cuts taxes and income rises.
   b. The U.S. inflation rate increases, and prices in the United States rise faster than those in countries with which the United States trades.
   c. The United States adopts an expansionary monetary policy. Interest rates fall (and are now lower than those in other countries) and income rises.
   d. The textile companies' "Buy American" campaign is successful, and U.S. consumers switch from purchasing imported products to buying products made in the United States.

6. You are given the following model that describes the economy of Hypothetica.
   (1) Consumption function: $C = 100 + .8Y_d$
   (2) Planned investment: $I = 38$
   (3) Government spending: $G = 75$
   (4) Exports: $EX = 25$
   (5) Imports: $IM = .05\,Y_d$
   (6) Disposable income: $Y_d \equiv Y - T$
   (7) Taxes: $T = 40$
   (8) Planned aggregate expenditure:
   $$AE \equiv C + I + G + EX - IM$$
   (9) Definition of equilibrium income: $Y = AE$
   a. What is equilibrium income in Hypothetica? What is the government deficit? What is the current account balance?
   b. If government spending is increased to $G = 80$, what happens to equilibrium income? Explain using the government spending multiplier. What happens to imports?
   c. Now suppose the amount of imports is limited to $IM = 40$ by a quota on imports. If government spending is again increased from 75 to 80, what happens to equilibrium income? Explain why the same increase in G has a bigger effect on income in the second case. What is it about the presence of imports that changes the value of the multiplier?
   d. If exports are fixed at $EX = 25$, what must income be to ensure a current account balance of zero? (*Hint:* Imports depend on income, so what must income be for imports to be equal to exports?) By how much must we cut government spending to balance the current account? (*Hint:* Use your answer to the first part of this question to determine how much of a decrease in income is needed. Then use the multiplier to calculate the decrease in G needed to reduce income by that amount.)

7. [Related to the *Economics in Practice* on p. 393] Go to www.federalreserve.gov and under Statistical Releases, click on Foreign Exchange rates. Click on Historical Data to find the exchange rates between the U.S. dollar and the euro, the Canadian dollar, the Japanese yen and the Chinese yuan at the beginning of 2008 and at the end of 2008. Did the U.S. dollar appreciate or depreciate against these currencies during 2008? Go to www.census.gov and find the value of U.S. exports, imports and the U.S trade balance at the beginning of 2008 and at the end of 2008. Did these values increase or decrease during 2008? Explain how the changes in the exchange rates may have had an impact on the changes in U.S. exports, imports and the trade balance.

APPENDIX

WORLD MONETARY SYSTEMS SINCE 1900

Since the beginning of the twentieth century, the world has operated under a number of different monetary systems. This Appendix provides a brief history of each and a description of how they worked.

THE GOLD STANDARD

The gold standard was the major system of exchange rate determination before 1914. All currencies were priced in terms of gold—an ounce of gold was worth so much in each currency. When all currencies exchanged at fixed ratios to gold, exchange rates could be determined easily. For instance, 1 ounce of gold was worth $20 U.S.; that same ounce of gold exchanged for £4 (British pounds). Because $20 and £4 were each worth 1 ounce of gold, the exchange rate between dollars and pounds was $20/£4, or $5 to £1.

For the gold standard to be effective, it had to be backed up by the country's willingness to buy and sell gold at the determined price. As long as countries maintain their currencies at a fixed value in terms of gold *and* as long as each country is willing to buy and sell gold, exchange rates are fixed. If at the given exchange rate the number of U.S. citizens who want to buy things produced in Great Britain is equal to the number of British citizens who want to buy things produced in the United States, the currencies of the two countries will simply be exchanged. What if U.S. citizens suddenly decide they want to drink imported Scotch instead of domestic bourbon? If the British do not have an increased desire for U.S. goods, they will still accept U.S. dollars because those dollars can be redeemed in gold. This gold can then be immediately turned into pounds.

As long as a country's overall balance of payments remained in balance, no gold would enter or leave the country and the economy would be in equilibrium. If U.S. citizens bought more from the British than the British bought from the United States, however, the U.S. balance of payments would be in deficit and the U.S. stock of gold would begin to fall. Conversely, Britain would start to accumulate gold because it would be exporting more than it spent on imports.

Under the gold standard, gold was a big determinant of the money supply.[1] An inflow of gold into a country caused that country's money supply to expand, and an outflow of gold caused that country's money supply to contract. If gold were flowing from the United States to Great Britain, the British money supply would expand and the U.S. money supply would contract.

Now recall from earlier chapters the impacts of a change in the money supply. An expanded money supply in Britain will lower British interest rates and stimulate aggregate demand. As a result, aggregate output (income) and the price level in Britain will increase. Higher British prices will discourage U.S. citizens from buying British goods. At the same time, British citizens will have more income and will face relatively lower import prices, causing them to import more from the States.

On the other side of the Atlantic, U.S. citizens will face a contracting domestic money supply. This will cause higher interest rates, declining aggregate demand, lower prices, and falling output (income). The effect will be lower demand in the United States for British goods. Thus, changes in relative prices and incomes that resulted from the inflow and outflow of gold would automatically bring trade back into balance.

PROBLEMS WITH THE GOLD STANDARD

Two major problems were associated with the gold standard. First, the gold standard implied that a country had little control over its money supply. The reason, as we have just seen, is that the money stock increased when the overall balance of payments was in surplus (gold inflow) and decreased when the overall balance was in deficit (gold outflow). A country that was experiencing a balance-of-payments deficit could correct the problem only by the painful process of allowing its money supply to contract. This contraction brought on a slump in economic activity, a slump that would eventually restore balance-of-payments equilibrium, but only after reductions in income and employment. Countries could (and often did) act to protect their gold reserves, and this precautionary step prevented the adjustment mechanism from correcting the deficit.

Making the money supply depend on the amount of gold available had another disadvantage. When major new gold fields were discovered (as in California in 1849 and South Africa in 1886), the world's supply of gold (and therefore of money) increased. The price level rose and income increased. When no new gold was discovered, the supply of money remained unchanged and prices and income tended to fall.

When President Reagan took office in 1981, he established a commission to consider returning the nation to the gold standard. The final commission report recommended against such a move. An important part of the reasoning behind this recommendation was that the gold standard puts enormous economic power in the hands of gold-producing nations.

FIXED EXCHANGE RATES AND THE BRETTON WOODS SYSTEM

As World War II drew to a close, a group of economists from the United States and Europe met to formulate a new set of rules for exchange rate determination that they hoped would avoid the difficulties of the gold standard. The rules they designed became known as the *Bretton Woods system*, after the town in New Hampshire where the delegates met. The Bretton Woods system was based on two (not necessarily compatible) premises. First, countries were to maintain fixed exchange rates

---

[1] In the days when currencies were tied to gold, changes in the amount of gold influenced the supply of money in two ways. A change in the quantity of gold coins in circulation had a direct effect on the supply of money; indirectly, gold served as a backing for paper currency. A decrease in the central bank's gold holdings meant a decline in the amount of paper money that could be supported.

with one another. Instead of pegging their currencies directly to gold, however, currencies were fixed in terms of the U.S. dollar, which was fixed in value at $35 per ounce of gold. The British pound, for instance, was fixed at roughly $2.40, so that an ounce of gold was worth approximately £14.6. As we shall see, the pure system of fixed exchange rates would work in a manner very similar to the pre-1914 gold standard.

The second aspect of the Bretton Woods system added a new wrinkle to the operation of the international economy. Countries experiencing a "fundamental disequilibrium" in their balance of payments were allowed to change their exchange rates. (The term *fundamental disequilibrium* was necessarily vague, but it came to be interpreted as a large and persistent current account deficit.) Exchange rates were not really fixed under the Bretton Woods system; they were, as someone remarked, only "fixed until further notice."

The point of allowing countries with serious current account problems to alter the value of their currency was to avoid the harsh recessions that the operation of the gold standard would have produced under these circumstances. However, the experience of the European economies in the years between World War I and World War II suggested that it might not be a good idea to give countries complete freedom to change their exchange rates whenever they wanted.

During the Great Depression, many countries undertook so-called competitive devaluations to protect domestic output and employment. That is, countries would try to encourage exports—a source of output growth and employment—by attempting to set as low an exchange rate as possible, thereby making their exports competitive with foreign-produced goods. Unfortunately, such policies had a built-in flaw. A devaluation of the pound against the French franc might help encourage British exports to France; but if those additional British exports cut into French output and employment, France would likely respond by devaluing the franc against the pound, a move that, of course, would undo the effects of the pound's initial devaluation.

To solve this exchange rate rivalry, the Bretton Woods agreement created the International Monetary Fund (IMF). Its job was to assist countries experiencing temporary current account problems.[2] It was also supposed to certify that a "fundamental disequilibrium" existed before a country was allowed to change its exchange rate. The IMF was like an international economic traffic cop whose job was to ensure that all countries were playing the game according to the agreed-to rules and to provide emergency assistance where needed.

"Pure" Fixed Exchange Rates

Under a pure fixed exchange rate system, governments set a particular *fixed* rate at which their currencies will exchange for one another and then commit themselves to maintaining that rate. A true fixed exchange rate system is like the gold standard

[2] The idea was that the IMF would make short-term loans to a country with a current account deficit. The loans would enable the country to correct the current account problem gradually, without bringing on a deep recession, running out of foreign exchange reserves, or devaluing the currency.

in that exchange rates are supposed to stay the same forever. Because currencies are no longer backed by gold, they have no fixed, or standard, value relative to one another. There is, therefore, no automatic mechanism to keep exchange rates aligned with each other, as with the gold standard.

The result is that under a pure fixed exchange rate system, governments must at times intervene in the foreign exchange market to keep currencies aligned at their established values. Economists define government intervention in the foreign exchange market as the buying or selling of foreign exchange for the purpose of manipulating the exchange rate. What kind of intervention is likely to occur under a fixed exchange rate system, and how does it work?

We can see how intervention works by looking at Figure 20A.1. Initially, the market for Australian dollars is in equilibrium. At the fixed exchange rate of 0.96, the supply of dollars is exactly equal to the demand for dollars. No government intervention is necessary to maintain the exchange rate at this level. Now suppose Australian wines are found to be contaminated with antifreeze and U.S. citizens switch to California wines. This substitution away from the Australian product shifts the U.S. demand curve for Australian dollars to the left: The United States demands fewer Australian dollars at every exchange rate (cost of an Australian dollar) because it is purchasing less from Australia than it did before.

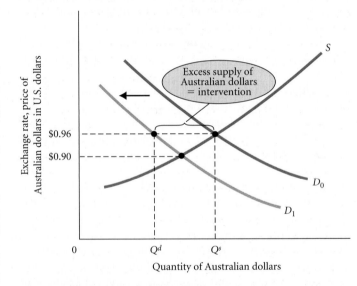

▲ **FIGURE 20A.1 Government Intervention in the Foreign Exchange Market**

If the price of Australian dollars were set in a completely unfettered market, one Australian dollar would cost 0.96 U.S. dollars when demand is D_0 and 0.90 when demand is D_1. If the government has committed to keeping the value at 0.96, it must buy up the excess supply of Australian dollars ($Q^s - Q^d$).

If the price of Australian dollars were set in a completely unfettered market, the shift in the demand curve would lead to a fall in the price of Australian dollars, just the way the price of wheat would fall if there was an excess supply of wheat. Remember, the Australian and U.S. governments have committed themselves to maintaining the rate at 0.96. To do so, either the U.S. government or the Australian government (or both) must buy up the excess supply of Australian dollars to keep its price from falling. In essence, the fixed exchange rate policy commits governments to making up any difference between the supply of a currency and the demand so as to keep the price of the currency (exchange rate) at the desired level. The government promises to act as the supplier (or demander) of last resort, who will ensure that the amount of foreign exchange demanded by the private sector will equal the supply at the fixed price.

PROBLEMS WITH THE BRETTON WOODS SYSTEM

As it developed after the end of World War II, the system of more-or-less fixed exchange rates had some flaws that led to its abandonment in 1971.

First, there was a basic asymmetry built into the rules of international finance. Countries experiencing large and persistent current account deficits—what the Bretton Woods agreements termed "fundamental disequilibria"—were obliged to devalue their currencies and/or take measures to cut their deficits by contracting their economies. Both of these alternatives were unpleasant because devaluation meant rising prices and contraction meant rising unemployment. However, a country with a current account deficit had no choice because it was losing stock of foreign exchange reserves. When its stock of foreign currencies became exhausted, it had to change its exchange rate because further intervention (selling off some of its foreign exchange reserves) became impossible.

Countries experiencing current account surpluses were in a different position because they were gaining foreign exchange reserves. Although these countries were supposed to stimulate their economies and/or revalue their currencies to restore balance to their current account, they were not obliged to do so. They could easily maintain their fixed exchange rate by buying up any excess supply of foreign exchange with their own currency, of which they had plentiful supply.

In practice, this meant that some countries—especially Germany and Japan—tended to run large and chronic current account surpluses and were under no compulsion to take steps to correct the problem. The U.S. economy, stimulated by expenditures on the Vietnam War, experienced a large and prolonged current account deficit (capital outflow) in the 1960s, which was the counterpart of these surpluses. The United States was, however, in a unique position under the Bretton Woods system. The value of gold was fixed in terms of the U.S. dollar at $35 per ounce of gold. Other countries fixed their exchange rates in terms of U.S. dollars (and therefore only indirectly in terms of gold). Consequently, the United States could never accomplish anything by devaluing its currency in terms of gold. If the dollar was devalued from $35 to

$40 per ounce of gold, the yen, pegged at 200 yen per dollar, would move in parallel with the dollar (from 7,000 yen per ounce of gold to 8,000 yen per ounce), with the dollar–yen exchange rate unaffected. To correct its current account deficits vis-à-vis Japan and Germany, it would be necessary for those two countries to adjust their currencies' exchange rates with the dollar. These countries were reluctant to do so for a variety of reasons. As a result, the U.S. current account was chronically in deficit throughout the late 1960s.

A second flaw in the Bretton Woods system was that it permitted devaluations only when a country had a "chronic" current account deficit and was in danger of running out of foreign exchange reserves. This meant that devaluations could often be predicted quite far in advance, and they usually had to be rather large if they were to correct any serious current account problem. The situation made it tempting for speculators to "attack" the currencies of countries with current account deficits.

Problems such as these eventually led the United States to abandon the Bretton Woods rules in 1971. The U.S. government refused to continue pegging the value of the dollar in terms of gold. Thus, the prices of all currencies were free to find their own levels.

The alternative to fixed exchange rates is a system that allows exchange rates to move freely or flexibly in response to market forces. Two types of flexible exchange rate systems are usually distinguished. In a *freely floating system*, governments do not intervene at all in the foreign exchange market.[3] They do not buy or sell currencies with the aim of manipulating the rates. In a *managed floating system*, governments intervene if markets are becoming "disorderly"—fluctuating more than a government believes is desirable. Governments may also intervene if they think a currency is increasing or decreasing too much in value even though the day-to-day fluctuations may be small.

Since the demise of the Bretton Woods system in 1971, the world's exchange rate system can be described as "managed floating." One of the important features of this system has been times of large fluctuations in exchange rates. For example, the yen–dollar rate went from 347 in 1971 to 210 in 1978, to 125 in 1988, and to 80 in 1995. Those are very large changes, changes that have important effects on the international economy, some of which we have covered in this text.

---

[3] However, governments may from time to time buy or sell foreign exchange for their own needs (instead of influencing the exchange rate). For example, the U.S. government might need British pounds to buy land for a U.S. embassy building in London. For our purposes, we ignore this behavior because it is not "intervention" in the strict sense of the word.

SUMMARY

1. The gold standard was the major system of exchange rate determination before 1914. All currencies were priced in terms of gold. Difficulties with the gold standard led to the Bretton Woods agreement following World War II. Under this system, countries maintained fixed exchange rates with one another and fixed the value of their currencies in terms of the U.S. dollar. Countries experiencing a "fundamental disequilibrium" in their current accounts were permitted to change their exchange rates.

2. The Bretton Woods system was abandoned in 1971. Since then, the world's exchange rate system has been one of managed floating rates. Under this system, governments intervene if foreign exchange markets are fluctuating more than the government thinks desirable.

PROBLEMS

1. The currency of Atlantis is the wimp. In 2008, Atlantis developed a balance-of-payments deficit with the United States as a result of an unanticipated decrease in exports; U.S. citizens cut back on the purchase of Atlantean goods. Assume Atlantis is operating under a system of fixed exchange rates.

   a. How does the drop in exports affect the market for wimps? Identify the deficit graphically.

   b. How must the government of Atlantis act (in the short run) to maintain the value of the wimp?

   c. If originally Atlantis had been operating at full employment (potential GDP), what impact would those events have had on its economy? Explain your answer.

   d. The chief economist of Atlantis suggests an expansionary monetary policy to restore full employment; the secretary of commerce suggests a tax cut (expansionary fiscal policy). Given the fixed exchange rate system, describe the effects of these two policy options on Atlantis's current account.

   e. How would your answers to **a**, **b**, and **c** change if the two countries operated under a floating rate system?

Economic Growth in Developing and Transitional Economies

21

Our primary focus in this text has been on countries with modern industrialized economies that rely heavily on markets to allocate resources, but what about the economic problems facing countries such as Somalia and Haiti? Can we apply the same economic principles that we have been studying to these less developed nations?

Yes. All economic analysis deals with the problem of making choices under conditions of scarcity, and the problem of satisfying people's wants and needs is as real for Somalia and Haiti as it is for the United States, Germany, and Japan. The universality of scarcity is what makes economic analysis relevant to all nations, regardless of their level of material well-being or ruling political ideology.

The basic tools of supply and demand, theories about consumers and firms, and theories about the structure of markets all contribute to an understanding of the economic problems confronting the world's developing nations. However, these nations often face economic problems quite different from those that richer, more developed countries face. In developing nations, an economist may have to worry about chronic food shortages, explosive population growth, and hyperinflations that reach triple, and even quadruple, digits. The United States and other industrialized economies rarely encounter such difficulties.

The instruments of economic management also vary from nation to nation. The United States has well-developed financial market institutions and a strong central bank (the Federal Reserve) through which the government can control the macroeconomy to some extent. Even limited intervention is impossible in some of the developing countries. In the United States, tax laws can be changed to stimulate saving, to encourage particular kinds of investments, or to redistribute income. In most developing countries, there are neither meaningful personal income taxes nor effective tax policies.

Even though economic problems and the policy instruments available to tackle them vary across nations, economic thinking about these problems can be transferred easily from one setting to another. In this chapter, we discuss several of the economic problems specific to developing nations in an attempt to capture some of the insights that economic analysis can offer.

Life in the Developing Nations: Population and Poverty

In 2008, the population of the world reached over 6.6 billion people. Most of the world's more than 200 nations belong to the developing world, in which about three-fourths of the world's population lives.

In the early 1960s, the nations of the world could be assigned rather easily to categories: The *developed countries* included most of Europe, North America, Japan, Australia, and New Zealand; the *developing countries* included the rest of the world. The developing nations were often referred to as the *Third World* to distinguish them from the Western industrialized nations (the *First World*) and the former Socialist bloc of Eastern European nations (the *Second World*).

In 2008, the world did not divide easily into three neat parts. Rapid economic progress brought some developing nations closer to developed economies. Countries such as Argentina and Chile, still considered to be "developing," are often referred to as middle-income or newly industrialized countries. Other countries, such as those in much of sub-Saharan Africa and some in South Asia, have stagnated and fallen so far behind the economic advances of the rest of the world that the term *Fourth World* has been used to describe them. China and India, while usually labeled developing countries, are fast becoming economic superpowers. It is not clear yet where some of the republics of the former Soviet Union and other formerly Communist countries of Eastern Europe will end up. Production fell sharply in many of them in the early transition stage to a market economy. For example, between 1990 and 1997, real gross domestic product (GDP) fell about 40 percent in the transition economies and over 50 percent in Russia and Central Asia. Post-2000, however, the Russian economy began growing more rapidly, in part fueled by rising energy prices, and by 2008, parts of the Russian economy were thriving.

Although the countries of the developing world exhibit considerable diversity in both their standards of living and their particular experiences of growth, marked differences continue to separate them from the developed nations. The developed countries have a higher average level of material well-being (the amount of food, clothing, shelter, and other commodities consumed by the average person). Comparisons of gross national income (GNI) are often used as a crude index of the level of material well-being across nations. GNI is a new measure of a nation's income, computed using a more accurate way of converting purchasing power into dollars. See Table 21.1, where GNI per-capita in the industrial market economies significantly exceeds GNI of both the low- and middle-income developing economies.

Other characteristics of economic development include improvements in basic health and education. The degree of political and economic freedom enjoyed by individual citizens might also be part of what it means to be a developed nation. Some of these criteria are easy to quantify. Table 21.1 presents data for different types of economies according to some of the more easily measured indexes of development. As you can see, the industrial market economies enjoy higher standards of living according to whatever indicator of development is chosen.

TABLE 21.1 Indicators of Economic Development

Country Group	Population, 2006	Gross National Income per Capita, 2006 (dollars)	Literacy Rate (percent over 15 years of age)	Infant Mortality, 2006 (deaths before age 5 per 1,000 births)	Internet Users per 1,000 people, 2005
Low-income	2.4 billion	650	60.8	114	44
Lower middle-income	2.3 billion	1,778	88.9	39.8	86
Upper middle-income	810 million	5,913	93.1	29.9	194
High-income	1.0 billion	36,487	98.7	6.9	523

Source: World Bank, www.worldbank.org.

Behind these statistics lies the reality of the very difficult life facing the people of the developing world. For most people, meager incomes provide only the basic necessities. Most meals are the same, consisting of the region's food staple—rice, wheat, or corn. Shelter is primitive. Many people share a small room, usually with an earthen floor and no sanitary facilities. The great majority of the population lives in rural areas where agricultural work is hard and extremely time-consuming. Productivity (output produced per worker) is low because household plots are small and only the crudest of farm implements are available. Low productivity means farm output per person is barely sufficient to feed a farmer's own family, with nothing left to sell to others. School-age children may receive some formal education, but illiteracy remains chronic for young and old. Infant mortality runs 20 times higher than in the United States. Although parasitic infections are common and debilitating, there is only one physician per 5,000 people. In addition, many developing nations are engaged in civil and external warfare.

Life in the developing nations is a continual struggle against the circumstances of poverty, and prospects for dramatic improvements in living standards for most people are dim. As with all generalizations, there are exceptions. Some nations are better off than others, and in any given nation an elite group always lives in considerable luxury. India is on the World Bank's list of low-income countries, yet Mumbai, a state capital, is one of the top 10 centers of commerce in the world, home to Bollywood, the world's largest film industry.

Poverty—not affluence—dominates the developing world. Recent studies suggest that 40 percent of the population of the developing nations has an annual income insufficient to provide for adequate nutrition. While the developed nations account for only about one-quarter of the world's population, they are estimated to consume three-quarters of the world's output. This leaves the developing countries with about three-fourths of the world's people but only one-fourth of the world's income. The simple result is that most of our planet's population is poor.

In the United States in 2005, the poorest one-fifth (bottom 20 percent) of the families received 3.4 percent of total income; the richest one-fifth received 50 percent. Inequality in the world distribution of income is much greater. When we look at the world population, the poorest one-fifth of the families earns about .5 percent and the richest one-fifth earns 79 percent of total world income.

Economic Development: Sources and Strategies

Economists have been trying to understand economic growth and development since Adam Smith and David Ricardo in the eighteenth and nineteenth centuries, but the study of development economics as it applies to the developing nations has a much shorter history. The geopolitical struggles that followed World War II brought increased attention to the developing nations and their economic problems. During this period, the new field of development economics asked simply: Why are some nations poor and others rich? If economists could understand the barriers to economic growth that prevent nations from developing and the prerequisites that would help them to develop, economists could prescribe strategies for achieving economic advancement.

The Sources of Economic Development

Although a general theory of economic development applicable to all nations has not emerged and probably never will, some basic factors that limit a poor nation's economic growth have been suggested. These include insufficient capital formation, a shortage of human resources and entrepreneurial ability, a lack of social overhead capital, and constraints imposed by dependency on the already developed nations.

Capital Formation   One explanation for low levels of output in developing nations is insufficient quantities of necessary inputs. Developing nations have diverse resource endowments—Congo, for instance, is abundant in natural resources, while Bangladesh is resource-poor. Almost all developing nations have a scarcity of physical capital relative to other resources, especially labor. The small stock of physical capital (factories, machinery, farm equipment, and other productive capital) constrains labor's productivity and holds back national output.

vicious-circle-of-poverty hypothesis   Suggests that poverty is self-perpetuating because poor nations are unable to save and invest enough to accumulate the capital stock that would help them grow.

Nevertheless, citing capital shortages as the cause of low productivity does not explain much. We need to know why capital is in such short supply in developing countries. There are many explanations. One, the **vicious-circle-of-poverty hypothesis**, suggests that a poor nation must consume most of its income just to maintain its already low standard of living. Consuming most of national income implies limited saving, and this implies low levels of investment. Without investment, the capital stock does not grow, the income remains low, and the vicious circle is complete. Poverty becomes self-perpetuating.

The difficulty with the vicious-circle argument is that if it were true, no nation would ever develop. For example, Japanese GDP per capita in 1900 was well below that of many of today's developing nations. The vicious-circle argument fails to recognize that every nation has some surplus above consumption needs that is available for investment. Often this surplus is most visible in the conspicuous consumption habits of the nation's richest families. Poverty alone cannot explain capital shortages, and poverty is not necessarily self-perpetuating.

capital flight   The tendency for both human capital and financial capital to leave developing countries in search of higher expected rates of return elsewhere with less risk.

In a developing economy, scarcity of capital may have more to do with a lack of incentives for citizens to save and invest productively than with any absolute scarcity of income available for capital accumulation. Many of the rich in developing countries invest their savings in Europe or in the United States instead of in their own country, which may have a riskier political climate. Savings transferred to the United States do not lead to physical capital growth in the developing countries. The term **capital flight** refers to the fact that both human capital and financial capital (domestic savings) leave developing countries in search of higher expected rates of return elsewhere or returns with less risk. In addition, government policies in the developing nations—including price ceilings, import controls, and even outright appropriation of private property—tend to discourage investment. There has been increased attention to the role that financial institutions, including accounting systems and property right rules, play in encouraging domestic capital formation.

Whatever the causes of capital shortages, it is clear that the absence of productive capital prevents income from rising in any economy. The availability of capital is a necessary, but not a *sufficient*, condition for economic growth. The landscape of the developing countries is littered with idle factories and abandoned machinery. Other ingredients are required to achieve economic progress.

Human Resources and Entrepreneurial Ability   Capital is not the only factor of production required to produce output. Labor is equally important. First of all, to be productive, the workforce must be healthy. Disease today is the leading threat to development in much of the world. The most devastating health problem in the world today is the HIV/AIDS pandemic. In 2005 alone, 3.1 million people died of AIDS and 4.9 million were newly infected with HIV. At the end of 2005, more than 40 million people were infected with the virus. In total, more than 25 million have died. AIDS is the leading cause of death in sub-Saharan Africa, where the disease threatens to reverse the developmental achievements of the last 50 years. Beyond AIDS, health and nutrition are essential to workforce development. Programs in nutrition and health can be seen as investments in human capital that lead to increased productivity and higher incomes.

But health is not the only issue. Look back at Table 21.1 You will notice that low-income countries lag behind high-income countries not only in infant health but also in literacy rates. To be productive, the workforce must be educated and trained. The more familiar forms of human capital investment, including formal education and on-the-job training, are essential. Basic literacy as well as specialized training in farm management, for example, can yield high returns to both the individual worker and the economy. Education has grown to become the largest category of government expenditure in many developing nations, in part because of the belief that human resources are the ultimate determinant of economic advance.

Nevertheless, in many developing countries, many children, especially girls, receive only a few years of formal education.

Just as financial capital seeks the highest and safest return, so does human capital. Thousands of students from developing countries, many of whom were supported by their governments, graduate every year from U.S. colleges and universities as engineers, doctors, scientists, economists, and other professionals. After graduation, these people face a difficult choice: to remain in the United States and earn a high salary or to return home and accept a job at a much lower salary. Many remain in the United States. This **brain drain** siphons off many of the most talented minds from developing countries. Recently, economists have begun studying *remittances*, compensation sent back from recent immigrants to their families in less developed countries. While measurement is difficult, estimates of these remittances are approximately $100 billion per year. Remittances fund housing and education for families left behind, but they also can provide investment capital for small businesses. In 2007, it appeared that remittances from illegal immigrants in the United States to Mexico, which had been growing by 20 percent per year, were beginning to fall with tightening of enforcement of immigration rules.

Innovative entrepreneurs who are willing to take risks are an essential human resource in any economy. In a developing nation, new techniques of production rarely need to be invented because they usually can be adapted from the technology already developed by the technologically advanced nations. However, entrepreneurs who are willing and able to organize and carry out economic activity appear to be in short supply. Family and political ties often seem to be more important than ability when it comes to securing positions of authority. Whatever the explanation, development cannot proceed without human resources capable of initiating and managing economic activity

> **brain drain** The tendency for talented people from developing countries to become educated in a developed country and remain there after graduation.

Social Overhead Capital Anyone who has spent time in a developing nation knows how difficult it can be to send a letter, make a local phone call, or travel within the country. Add to this problems with water supplies, frequent electrical power outages—in the few areas where electricity is available—and often ineffective mosquito and pest control, and you soon realize how deficient even the simplest, most basic government-provided goods and services can be.

In any economy, developing or otherwise, the government has considerable opportunity and responsibility for involvement where conditions encourage natural monopoly (as in the utilities industries) and where public goods (such as roads and pest control) must be provided. In a developing economy, the government must put emphasis on creating a basic infrastructure—roads, power generation, and irrigation systems. There are often good reasons why such projects, referred to as **social overhead capital**, cannot successfully be undertaken by the private sector. First, many of these projects operate with economies of scale, which means they can be efficient only if they are very large. In that case, they may be too large for any private company or group of companies to carry out.

Second, many socially useful projects cannot be undertaken by the private sector because there is no way for private agents to capture enough of the returns to make such projects profitable. This so-called *free-rider problem* is common in the economics of the developed world. Consider national defense: All people in a country benefit from national defense, whether they have paid for it or not. Anyone who attempted to go into the private business of providing national defense would go broke. Why should I buy any national defense if your purchase of defense will also protect me? Why should you buy any if my purchase will also protect you? The governments of developing countries can do important and useful things to encourage development, but many of their efforts must be concentrated in areas that the private sector would never touch. If government action in these realms is not forthcoming, economic development may be curtailed by a lack of social overhead capital. Considerable economic work has been done recently on the role that inefficient government bureaucracies play in retarding economic development. Many less developed countries in sub-Saharan Africa, Asia, and Latin America have only a small fraction of GDP raised in tax revenues and invested by the government. Levels of corruption also matter and vary a great deal by country, as the *Economics in Practice* on p. 406 suggests.

> **social overhead capital** Basic infrastructure projects such as roads, power generation, and irrigation systems.

ECONOMICS IN PRACTICE

Corruption

Many people have argued that one barrier to economic development in a number of countries is the level of corruption and inefficiency in the government. Measuring levels of corruption and inefficiency can be difficult. Some researchers have tried surveys and experiments. Ray Fisman[1] had a more unusual way to measure the way in which political connections interfere with the workings of the market in Indonesia.

From 1967 to 1998, Indonesia was ruled by President Suharto. While Suharto ruled, his children and longtime allies were affiliated with a number of Indonesian companies. Fisman had the clever idea of looking at what happened to the stock market prices of those firms connected to the Suharto clan relative to unaffiliated firms when Suharto unexpectedly fell ill. Fisman found a large and significant reduction in the value of those affiliated firms on rumors of illness. What does this tell us? A firm's stock price reflects investors' views of what earnings the firm can expect to have. In the case of firms connected to Suharto, the decline in their stock prices tells us that a large part of the reason investors think that those firms are doing well is because of the family connection rather than the firm's inherent efficiency. One reason corruption is bad for an economy is that it often leads to the wrong firms, the less efficient firms, producing the goods and services in the society.

The following chart shows the World Bank's rating of corruption levels in a number of countries around the world. The countries are ranked from those with the strongest controls on corruption—Germany and France—to those with the lowest controls—Pakistan and Nigeria. Indonesia, as you can see, is near the bottom of the list.

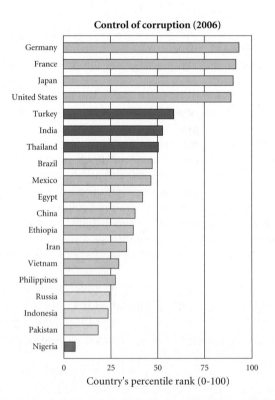

Control of corruption (2006)

Country's percentile rank (0-100)

Source: D. Kaufmann, A. Kraay, and M. Mastruzzi, 2007: Governance Matters VI: Governance Indicators for 1996–2006.
Note: The governance indicators presented here aggregate the views on the quality of governance provided by a large number of enterprise, citizen, and expert survey respondents in industrial and developing countries. These data are gathered from a number of survey institutes, think tanks, nongovernmental organizations, and international organizations. The aggregate indicators do not reflect the official views of the World Bank, its executive directors, or the countries they represent.

[1] Raymond Fisman, "Estimating the Value of Political Connections," *The American Economic Review,* September 2001.

Strategies for Economic Development

Just as no single theory appears to explain lack of economic advancement, no one development strategy will likely succeed in all nations. Many alternative development strategies have been proposed over the past years. Although these strategies have been very different, they all recognize that a developing economy faces basic trade-offs. An insufficient amount of both human and physical resources dictates that choices must be made, including those between agriculture and industry, exports and import substitution, and central planning and free markets.

Agriculture or Industry?   Most Third World countries began to gain political independence just after World War II. The tradition of promoting industrialization as the solution to the problems of the developing world dates from this time. The early 5-year development plans of India called for promoting manufacturing; the current government in Ethiopia (an extremely poor country) has similar intentions.

Industry has several apparent attractions over agriculture. First, if it is true that capital shortages constrain economic growth, the building of factories will be an obvious step toward increasing a nation's stock of capital. Second, and perhaps most important, one of the primary characteristics of more developed economies is their structural transition away from agriculture toward manufacturing and modern services. As Table 21.2 shows, agriculture's share in GDP declines substantially as per-capita incomes increase. The share of services increases correspondingly, especially in the early phases of economic development.

TABLE 21.2   The Structure of Production in Selected Developed and Developing Economies, 2003

Country	Per-Capita Gross National Income (GNI)	Percentage of Gross Domestic Product		
		Agriculture	Industry	Services
Tanzania	$ 375	45	17	37
Bangladesh	480	20	28	52
China	2,010	12	47	41
Colombia	2,740	12	34	54
Thailand	2,990	10	46	44
Brazil	4,730	5	31	64
Korea (Rep.)	17,690	2	23	75
Japan	38,410	2	30	68
United States	44,970	2	23	75

Source: World Bank, World Development Indicators, 2008; Sectoral numbers for U.S. and Japan are for 2003.

Many economies have pursued industry at the expense of agriculture. In many countries, however, industrialization has been unsuccessful or disappointing—that is, it has not brought the benefits that were expected. Experience suggests that simply trying to replicate the structure of developed economies does not in itself guarantee, or even promote, successful development.

Since the early 1970s, the agricultural sector has received considerably more attention. Agricultural development strategies have had numerous benefits. Although some agricultural projects (such as the building of major dams and irrigation networks) are very capital-intensive, many others (such as services to help teach better farming techniques and small-scale fertilizer programs) have low capital and import requirements. Programs such as these can affect large numbers of households, and because the benefits of these programs are directed at rural areas, they are most likely to help a country's poorest families.

Experience over the last three decades suggests that some balance between these approaches leads to the best outcome—that is, it is important and effective to pay attention to both industry and agriculture. The Chinese have referred to this dual approach to development as "walking on two legs."

Exports or Import Substitution?
As developing nations expand their industrial activities, they must decide what type of trade strategy to pursue, usually one of two alternatives: import substitution or export promotion.

import substitution An industrial trade strategy that favors developing local industries that can manufacture goods to replace imports.

Import substitution is an industrial trade strategy to develop local industries that can manufacture goods to replace imports. For example, if fertilizer is imported, import substitution calls for a domestic fertilizer industry to produce replacements for fertilizer imports. This strategy gained prominence throughout South America in the 1950s. At that time, most developing nations exported agricultural and mineral products, goods that faced uncertain and often unstable international markets. Under these conditions, the call for import substitution policies was understandable. Special government actions, including tariff and quota protection and subsidized imports of machinery, were set up to encourage new domestic industries. Multinational corporations were also invited into many countries to begin domestic operations.

Most economists believe that import substitution strategies have failed almost everywhere they have been tried. With domestic industries sheltered from international competition by high tariffs (often as high as 200 percent), major economic inefficiencies were created. For example, Peru has a population of approximately 29 million, only a tiny fraction of whom can afford to buy an automobile. Yet at one time, the country had five or six different automobile manufacturers, each of which produced only a few thousand cars per year. Because there are substantial economies of scale in automobile production, the cost per car was much higher than it needed to be, and valuable resources that could have been devoted to another, more productive, activity were squandered producing cars.

Furthermore, policies designed to promote import substitution often encouraged capital-intensive production methods, which limited the creation of jobs and hurt export activities. A country such as Peru could not export automobiles because it could produce them only at a cost far greater than their price on the world market. Worse still, import substitution policies encouraged the use of expensive domestic products, such as tractors and fertilizer, instead of lower-cost imports. These policies taxed the sectors that might have successfully competed in world markets. To the extent that the Peruvian sugar industry had to rely on domestically produced, high-cost fertilizer, for example, its ability to compete in international markets was reduced because its production costs were artificially raised.

export promotion A trade policy designed to encourage exports.

As an alternative to import substitution, some nations have pursued strategies of export promotion. **Export promotion** is the policy of encouraging exports. As an industrial market economy, Japan was a striking example to the developing world of the economic success that exports can provide. Japan had an average annual per-capita real GDP growth rate of roughly 6 percent per year from 1960–1990. This achievement was, in part, based on industrial production oriented toward foreign consumers.

Several countries in the developing world have attempted to emulate Japan's success. Starting around 1970, Hong Kong, Singapore, Korea, and Taiwan (the "four little dragons" between the two "big dragons," China and Japan) began to pursue export promotion of manufactured goods. Today their growth rates have surpassed Japan's. Other nations, including Brazil, Colombia, and Turkey, have also had some success at pursuing an outward-looking trade policy.

Government support of export promotion has often taken the form of maintaining an exchange rate favorable enough to permit exports to compete with products manufactured in developed economies. For example, many people believe Japan kept the value of the yen artificially low during the 1970s. Because "cheap" yen means inexpensive Japanese goods, in the United States, sales of Japanese goods (especially automobiles) increased dramatically. Governments also have provided subsidies to export industries.

A big issue for countries growing or trying to grow by selling exports on world markets is free trade. In 2003, the United States and Europe were accused of protecting their own agricultural producers with large subsidies that allowed domestic farmers a big advantage selling on world markets. African nations in particular have pushed for reductions in tariffs imposed on their agricultural goods by Europe and the United States, arguing that these tariffs substantially reduce Africa's ability to compete in the world marketplace.

Central Planning or the Market? As part of its strategy for achieving economic development, a nation must decide how its economy will be directed. Its basic choices lie between a market-oriented economic system and a centrally planned one.

In the 1950s and into the 1960s, development strategies that called for national planning commanded wide support. The rapid economic growth of the Soviet Union, a centrally planned economy, provided an example of how fast a less developed agrarian nation could be transformed into a modern industrial power. (The often appalling costs of this strategy—severe discipline, gross violation of human rights, and environmental damage—were less widely known.) In addition, the underdevelopment of many commodity and asset markets in the developing world led many experts to believe that market forces could not direct an economy reliably and that major government intervention was therefore necessary. Even the United States, with its commitment to free enterprise in the marketplace, supported early central planning efforts in many developing nations.

Today, planning takes many forms in the developing nations. In some countries, central planning has replaced market-based outcomes with direct, administratively determined controls over economic variables such as prices, output, and employment. In other countries, national planning amounts to little more than the formulation of general 5- or 10-year goals as rough blueprints for a nation's economic future.

The economic appeal of planning lies theoretically in its ability to channel savings into productive investment and to coordinate economic activities that private actors in the economy might not otherwise undertake. The reality of central planning, however, is that it is a technically difficult, highly politicized nightmare to administer. Given the scarcity of human resources and the unstable political environment in many developing nations, planning itself—let alone the execution of the plan—becomes a formidable task.

The failure of many central planning efforts has brought increasing calls for less government intervention and more market orientation in developing economies. The elimination of price controls, privatization of state-run enterprises, and reductions in import restraints are examples of market-oriented reforms recommended by such international agencies as the **International Monetary Fund (IMF)**, whose primary goals are to stabilize international exchange rates and to lend money to countries that have problems financing their international transactions, and the **World Bank**, which lends money to a country for projects that promote economic development.

Members' contributions to both organizations are determined by the size of their economies. Only 20 percent of the World Bank's funding comes from contributions; 80 percent comes from retained earnings and investments in capital markets. Increasingly, the developing world is recognizing the value of market forces in determining the allocation of scarce resources. Nonetheless, government still has a major role to play. In the decades ahead, the governments of developing nations will need to determine those situations where planning is superior to the market and those where the market is superior to planning.

Microfinance: A New Idea In the mid 1970s, Muhammad Yunus, a young Bangladeshi economist created the Grameen Bank in Bangladesh. Yunus, who trained at Vanderbilt University and was a former professor at Middle Tennessee State University, used this bank as a vehicle to introduce microfinance to the developing world. In 2006, Yunus received a Nobel Peace Prize for his work. Microfinance is the practice of lending very small amounts of money, with no collateral, and accepting very small savings deposits.[2] It is aimed at introducing entrepreneurs in the poorest parts of the developing world to the capital market. By 2002, more than 2,500 institutions were making these small loans, serving over 60 million people. Two-thirds of borrowers were living below the poverty line in their own countries, the poorest of the poor.

Yunus, while teaching economics in Bangladesh, began lending his own money to poor households with entrepreneurial ambitions. He found that with even very small amounts of money, villagers could start simple businesses: bamboo weaving or hair dressing. Traditional banks found these borrowers unprofitable: The amounts were too small, and it was too expensive

International Monetary Fund (IMF) An international agency whose primary goals are to stabilize international exchange rates and to lend money to countries that have problems financing their international transactions.

World Bank An international agency that lends money to individual countries for projects that promote economic development.

[2] An excellent discussion of microfinance is contained in Beatriz Armendariz de Aghion and Jonathan Morduch, *The Economics of Microfinance,* (MIT Press, 2005.)

to figure out which of the potential borrowers was a good risk. With a borrower having no collateral, information about his or her character was key but was hard for a big bank to discover. Local villagers, however, typically knew a great deal about one another's characters. This insight formed the basis for Yunus's microfinance enterprise. Within a village, people who are interested in borrowing money to start businesses are asked to join lending groups of five people. Loans are then made to two of the potential borrowers, later to a second two, and finally to the last. As long as everyone is repaying their loans, the next group receives theirs. But if the first borrowers fail to pay, all members of the group are denied subsequent loans. What does this do? It makes community pressure a substitute for collateral. Moreover, once the peer lending mechanism is understood, villagers have incentives to join only with other reliable borrowers. The mechanism of peer lending is a way to avoid the problems of imperfect information described in an earlier chapter.

The Grameen model grew rapidly. By 2002, Grameen was lending to two million members. Thirty countries and thirty U.S. states have microfinance lending copied from the Grameen model. Relative to traditional bank loans, microfinance loans are much smaller, repayment begins very quickly, and the vast majority of the loans are made to women (who, in many cases, have been underserved by mainstream banks). A growing set of evidence shows that providing opportunities for poor women has stronger spillovers in terms of improving the welfare of children than does comparable opportunities for men. While the field of microfinance has changed considerably since Yunus's introduction and some people question how big a role it will ultimately play in spurring major development and economic growth, it has changed many people's views about the possibilities of entrepreneurship for the poor of the world.

Growth versus Development: The Policy Cycle

Until now, we have used *growth* and *development* as if they meant the same thing, but this may not always be the case. You can easily imagine instances in which a country has achieved higher levels of income (growth) with little or no benefit accruing to most of its citizens (development). Thus, the question is whether economic growth necessarily brings about economic development.

In the past, most development strategies were aimed at increasing the growth rate of income per capita. Many still are, based on the theory that benefits of economic growth will "trickle down" to all members of society. If this theory is correct, growth should promote development.

By the early 1970s, the relationship between growth and development was being questioned more and more. A study by the World Bank in 1974 concluded the following:

> It is now clear that more than a decade of rapid growth in underdeveloped countries has been of little or no benefit to perhaps a third of their population.... Paradoxically, while growth policies have succeeded beyond the expectations of the first development decade, the very idea of aggregate growth as a social objective has increasingly been called into question.

The World Bank study indicated that increases in GDP per capita did not guarantee significant improvements in development indicators such as nutrition, health, and education. Although GDP per capita did rise, its benefits trickled down to a small minority of the population. This very limited success prompted new development strategies that would directly address the problems of poverty. Such new strategies favored agriculture over industry, called for domestic redistribution of income and wealth (especially land), and encouraged programs to satisfy such basic needs as food and shelter.

In the late 1970s and early 1980s, the international macroeconomic crises of high oil prices, worldwide recession, and Third World debt forced attention away from programs designed to eliminate poverty directly. Then, during the 1980s and 1990s, the policy focus turned 180 degrees. The World Bank and the United States began demanding "structural adjustment" in the developing countries as a prerequisite for sending aid to them. **Structural adjustment** programs entail reducing the size of the public sector through privatization and/or expenditure reductions, substantially cutting budget deficits, reining in inflation, and encouraging private saving and investment with tax reforms. These pro-market demands were an attempt to stimulate growth; distributional consequences took a back seat.

structural adjustment
A series of programs in developing nations designed to: (1) reduce the size of their public sectors through privatization and/or expenditure reductions, (2) decrease their budget deficits, (3) control inflation, and (4) encourage private saving and investment through tax reform.

ECONOMICS IN PRACTICE

Cell Phones Increase Profits for Fishermen in India

Kerala is a poor state in a region of India. The fishing industry is a major part of the local economy, employing more than one million people and serving as the main source of protein for the population. Every day fishing boats go out; and when they return, the captain of the ship needs to decide where to take the fish to sell. There is much uncertainty in this decision: How much fish will they catch; what other boats will come to a particular location; how many buyers will there be at a location? Moreover, fuel costs are high and timing is difficult, so that once a boat comes ashore, it does not pay for the fishermen to search for a better marketplace. In a recent study of this area, Robert Jensen[1] found on a Tuesday morning in November 1997, 11 fishermen in Badagara were dumping their load of fish because they faced no buyers at the dock. However, unbeknownst to them, 15 kilometers away, 27 buyers were leaving their marketplace empty-handed, with unsatisfied demand for fish.

Beginning in 1997 and continuing for the next several years, mobile phone service was introduced to this region of India. By 2001, the majority of the fishing fleet had mobile phones, which they use to call various vendors ashore to confirm where the buyers are. What was the result? Once the phones were introduced, waste, which had averaged 5 to 8 percent of the total catch, was virtually eliminated. Moreover, just as we would have predicted from the simple laws of supply and demand, the prices of fish across the various villages along the fishing market route were closer to each other than they were before. Jensen found that with less waste fishermen's profits rose on average by 8 percent, while the average price of fish fell by 4 percent.

In fact, cell phones are improving the way markets in less developed countries work by providing price and quantity information so that both producers and consumers can make better economic decisions.

[1] Robert Jensen, "The Digital Provide: Information Technology, Market Performance, and Welfare in the South Indian Fisheries Sector," *The Quarterly Journal of Economics,* August 2007.

Two Examples of Development: China and India

China and India provide two interesting examples of rapidly developing economies. While low per-capita incomes still mean that both countries are typically labeled developing as opposed to developed countries, many expect that to change in the near future. In the 25-year period from 1978 to 2003, China grew, on average, 8 percent per year, a rate faster than any other country in the world. While India's surge has been more recent, in the last 5 years, it too has seen annual growth rates in the 8 to 9 percent range. Many commentators expect India and China to dominate the world economy in the twenty-first century.

How did these two rather different countries engineer their development? Consider institutions: India is a democratic country, has a history of the rule of law, and has an English-speaking heritage—all factors typically thought to provide a development advantage. China is still an authoritarian country politically, and property rights are still not well established—both characteristics that were once thought to hinder growth. Both China and India have embraced free market economics, with China taking the lead as India has worked to remove some of its historical regulatory apparatus.

What about social capital? Both India and China remain densely populated. While China is the most populous country in the world, India, with a smaller land mass, is the world's most densely populated country. Nevertheless, as is true in most developing nations, birth rates in both countries have fallen. Literacy rates and life expectancy in China are quite high, in part a legacy from an earlier period. India, on the other hand, has a literacy rate that is less than that of

China's and a lower life expectancy. In terms of human capital, China appears to have the edge, at least for now.

What about the growth strategies used by the two countries? China has adopted a pragmatic, gradual approach to development, sharply in contrast to that adopted some years ago in Poland. China's approach has been called *moshi guohe*, or "Crossing the river by feeling for stepping stones." In terms of sector, most of China's growth has been fueled by manufacturing. The focus on manufacturing is one reason that China's energy consumption and environmental issues have increased so rapidly in the last decade. In India, services have led growth, particularly in the software industry. In sum, it is clear that there is no single recipe for development.

Issues in Economic Development

Every developing nation has a cultural, political, and economic history all its own and therefore confronts a unique set of problems. Still, it is possible to discuss common economic issues that each nation must face in its own particular way. These issues include rapid population growth and how to manage it.

Population Growth

The populations of the developing nations are estimated to be growing at about 1.7 percent per year. (Compare this with a population growth rate of only .5 percent per year in the industrial market economies.) If the Third World's population growth rate remains at 1.7 percent, within 41 years its population will double from the 1990 level of 4.1 billion to over 8 billion by the year 2031. On the other hand, it will take the industrialized nations 139 years to double their populations. What is so immediately alarming about these numbers is that given the developing nations' current economic problems, it is hard to imagine how they can possibly absorb so many more people in such a relatively short period.

Concern over world population growth is not new. The Reverend Thomas Malthus (who became England's first professor of political economy) expressed his fears about the population increases he observed 200 years ago. Malthus believed that populations grow geometrically at a constant growth rate—thus the absolute size of the increase each year gets larger and larger—but that food supplies grow more slowly because of the diminishing marginal productivity of land.[3] These two phenomena led Malthus to predict the increasing impoverishment of the world's people unless population growth could be slowed.

Malthus's fears for Europe and America proved unfounded. He did not anticipate the technological changes that revolutionized agricultural productivity and the eventual decrease in population growth rates in Europe and North America. Nevertheless, Malthus's prediction may have been right, only premature. Do the circumstances in the developing world now fit his predictions? Although some contemporary observers believe that the Malthusian view is correct and the earth's population will eventually grow to a level that the world's resources cannot support, others say technological change and demographic transitions (to slower population growth rates) will permit further increases in global welfare.

The Consequences of Rapid Population Growth   We know far less about the economic consequences of rapid population growth than you might expect. Conventional wisdom warns of dire economic consequences from the developing nations' "population explosion," but these predictions are difficult to substantiate with the available evidence. The rapid economic growth of the United States, for example, was accompanied by relatively rapid population growth by historical standards. Any slowing of population growth has not been necessary for the economic progress achieved by many of the newly industrialized countries. Nonetheless, population expansion in many of today's poorest nations is of a magnitude unprecedented in world history,

---

[3] The law of diminishing marginal productivity says that with a fixed amount of a resource (land), additions of more and more of a variable resource (labor) will produce smaller and smaller gains in output.

as Figure 21.1 clearly shows. From the year 1 A.D. until the mid-1600s, populations grew slowly, at rates of only about .04 percent per year. Since then, and especially since 1950, rates have skyrocketed. Today populations are growing at rates of 1.5 percent to 4.0 percent per year throughout the developing world.

Because growth rates like these never occurred before the twentieth century, no one knows what impact they will have on future economic development. However, a basic economic concern is that such rapid population growth may limit investment and restrain increases in labor productivity and income. Rapid population growth changes the age composition of a population, generating many dependent children relative to the number of productive working adults. Such a situation may diminish saving rates, and hence investment, as the immediate consumption needs of the young take priority over saving for the future.

Even if low saving rates are not a necessary consequence of rapid population growth, as some authorities contend, other economic problems remain. The ability to improve human capital through a broad range of programs, from infant nutrition to formal secondary education, may be severely limited if the population explosion continues. Such programs are most often the responsibility of the state, and governments that are already weak cannot be expected to improve their

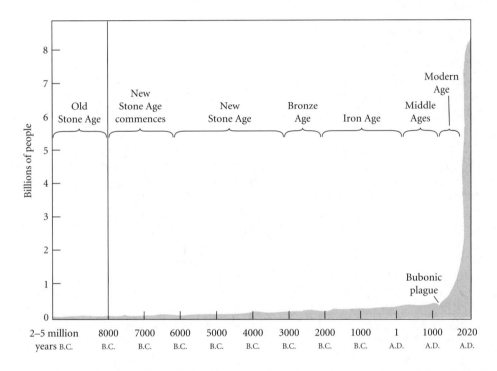

◀ FIGURE 21.1
The Growth of World Population, Projected to A.D. 2020
For thousands of years, population grew slowly. From A.D. 1 until the mid-1600s, population grew at about .04 percent per year. Since the Industrial Revolution, population growth has occurred at an unprecedented rate.

services under the burden of population pressures that rapidly increase demands for all kinds of public goods and services.

For example, Uganda's 2008 population growth rate—3.6 percent—is one of the highest in the world. Its 2003 population of 25.8 million had grown by 5 million people by 2007. This is a daunting prospect, and it is hard to imagine how in so little time, Uganda, with per-capita GNP of $300, will be able to provide its population with the physical and human capital needed to maintain, let alone improve, already low standards of living.

Causes of Rapid Population Growth

Population growth is determined by the relationship between births and deaths—that is, between **fertility rates** and **mortality rates**. The **natural rate of population increase** is defined as the difference between the birth rate and the death rate. If the birth rate is 4 percent, for example, and the death rate is 3 percent, the population is growing at a rate of 1 percent per year.

Historically, low rates of population growth were maintained because of high mortality rates despite high levels of fertility. That is, families had many children, but average life expectancies were low and many children (and adults) died young. In Europe and North America, improvements in nutrition, in public health programs (especially those concerned with drinking water

fertility rate   The birth rate. Equal to (the number of births per year divided by the population) × 100.

mortality rate   The death rate. Equal to (the number of deaths per year divided by the population) × 100.

natural rate of population increase   The difference between the birth rate and the death rate.

and sanitation services), and in medical practices have led to a drop in the mortality rate and hence to more rapid population growth. Eventually, fertility rates also fell, returning population growth to a low and stable rate.

Public health programs and improved nutrition over the past 30 years also have brought about precipitous declines in mortality rates in the developing nations. However, fertility rates have not declined as quickly, and the result has been high natural rates of population growth. Reduced population growth depends to some extent on decreased birth rates, but attempts to lower fertility rates must take into account how different cultures feel and behave with regard to fertility.

Family planning and modern forms of birth control are important mechanisms for decreasing fertility, but by themselves have had rather limited success in most countries where they have been tried. If family-planning strategies are to be successful, they must make sense to the people who are supposed to benefit from them. The planners of such strategies must understand why families in developing nations have so many children.

To a great extent, in developing countries, people want large families because they believe they need them. Economists have attempted to understand fertility patterns in the developing countries by focusing on the determinants of the demand for children. In agrarian societies, children are sources of farm labor and they may make significant contributions to household income. In societies without public old-age-support or social security programs, children may also provide a source of income for parents who are too old to support themselves. With the high value of children enhanced by high rates of infant mortality, it is no wonder that families try to have many children to ensure that a sufficient number will survive into adulthood.

Cultural and religious values also affect the number of children families want to have, but the economic incentives to have large families are extremely powerful. Only when the relationship between the costs and benefits of having children changes will fertility rates decline. The expansion of employment opportunities for women in an economy increases the opportunity costs of childrearing (by giving women a more highly valued alternative to raising children) and often leads to lower birth rates. Government incentives for smaller families, such as subsidized education for families with fewer than three children, can have a similar effect. In general, rising incomes appear to decrease fertility rates, indicating that economic development itself reduces population growth rates.

Economic theories of population growth suggest that fertility decisions made by poor families should not be viewed as uninformed and uncontrolled. An individual family may find that having many children is a rational strategy for economic survival given the conditions in which it finds itself. This does not mean, however, that having many children is a net benefit to society as a whole. When a family decides to have a large number of children, it imposes costs on the rest of society; the children must be educated, their health provided for, and so on. In other words, what makes sense for an individual household may create negative effects for the nation as a whole. Any nation that wants to slow its rate of population growth will probably find it necessary to have in place economic incentives for fewer children as well as family-planning programs.

The Transition to a Market Economy

In the last several decades, a number of countries have made the transition from a planned economy to a market economy. Russia and the formerly Communist countries of Eastern Europe led the way in this transition beginning in the late-1980s. For a number of these countries, the early transition period was difficult, and there has been considerable debate about the optimal speed of transitions and ways to manage the social upheaval that often comes with economic reform.

For example, between 1992 and 2002, while per-capita income grew by 51 percent in Poland, it shrank by 63 percent in the Ukraine. Countries of the former USSR seem to have had a particularly difficult transition to market economies. Economists have attributed differences in ease of transition to reform strategies (slow versus fast), resource endowments of the country, and differences in institutions.

In more recent years, China and Vietnam have joined the collection of transition economies, coming to rely less on central planning for economic decisions and more on the market. India too is sometimes thought to be a transition economy, as it has in the last decade dismantled much of its government ownership and elaborate rules governing market transactions.

Six Basic Requirements for Successful Transition

Economists generally agree on six basic requirements for a successful transition to a market-based system: (1) macroeconomic stabilization, (2) deregulation of prices and liberalization of trade, (3) privatization of state-owned enterprises and development of new private industry, (4) establishment of market-supporting institutions such as property and contract laws and accounting systems, (5) a social safety net to deal with unemployment and poverty, and (6) external assistance. We now discuss each component.

Macroeconomic Stabilization   Many countries in transition have had a problem with inflation, but nowhere has it been worse than in Russia. As economic conditions worsened, the government found itself with serious budget problems. As revenue flows slowed and expenditure commitments increased, large budget deficits resulted. At the same time, each of the new republics established its own central bank. Each central bank began issuing "ruble credits" to keep important enterprises afloat and to pay the government's bills. The issuance of these credits, which were generally accepted as a means of payment throughout the country, led to a dramatic expansion of the money supply.

Almost from the beginning, the expanded money supply meant too much money was chasing too few goods. This was made worse by government-controlled prices set substantially below market-clearing levels. The combination of monetary expansion and price control was deadly. Government-run shops that sold goods at controlled prices were empty. People waited in line for days and often became violent when their efforts to buy goods at low official prices were thwarted. At the same time, suppliers found that they could charge much higher prices for their products on the black market—which grew bigger by the day, further exacerbating the shortage of goods at government shops. Over time, the ruble became worth less and less as black market prices continued to rise more rapidly. Russia found itself with near hyperinflation in 1992. To achieve a properly functioning market system, prices must be stabilized. To do so, the government must find a way to move toward a balanced budget and to bring the supply of money under control. China and India, in contrast to Russia and Eastern European states, initially suffered only modest inflation as they decontrolled their prices, though more recently inflation appears to be increasing in China.

Deregulation of Prices and Liberalization of Trade   To move successfully from central planning to a market system, individual prices must be deregulated. A system of freely moving prices forms the backbone of a market system. When people want more of a good than is currently being produced, its price will rise. This higher price increases producers' profits and provides an incentive for existing firms to expand production and for new firms to enter the industry. Conversely, if an industry is producing a good for which there is no market or a good that people no longer want in the same quantity, the result will be excess supply and the price of that good will fall. This outcome reduces profits or creates losses, providing an incentive for some existing firms to cut back on production and for others to go out of business. In short, an unregulated price mechanism ensures an efficient allocation of resources across industries. Until prices are deregulated, this mechanism cannot function. In practice, transition economies have moved at varying speeds in decontrolling prices. Vietnam, for example, decontrolled prices very quickly in moving to a market economy, as did Poland. China, on the other hand, took a slower path in freeing prices from state control.

Trade barriers must also be removed. Reform-minded countries must be able to import capital, technology, and ideas. In addition, it makes no sense to continue to subsidize industries that cannot be competitive on world markets. If it is cheaper to buy steel from an efficient West German steel mill than to produce it in a subsidized antiquated Russian mill, the Russian mill should be modernized or shut down. Ultimately, as the theory of comparative advantage suggests, liberalized trade will push each country to produce the products it produces best.

Deregulating prices and eliminating subsidies can bring serious political problems. Many products in Russia and the rest of the socialist world were priced below market-clearing levels for equity reasons. Housing, food, and clothing were considered by many to be entitlements. Making them more expensive, at least relative to their prices in previous times, is not likely to be popular. In 2008, rising rice prices in Southeast Asia caused considerable unrest in Vietnam, Thailand, and

Cambodia. In addition, forcing inefficient firms to operate without subsidies will lead many of them to go out of business, and jobs will be lost. So while price deregulation and trade liberalization are necessary, they are very difficult politically.

Privatization One problem with a system of central ownership is a lack of accountability. Under a system of private ownership, owners reap the rewards of their successes and suffer the consequences of their failures. Private ownership provides a strong incentive for efficient operation, innovation, and hard work that is lacking when ownership is centralized and profits are distributed to the people.

tragedy of commons
The idea that collective ownership may not provide the proper private incentives for efficiency because individuals do not bear the full costs of their own decisions but do enjoy the full benefits.

The classic story to illustrate this point is called the **tragedy of commons**, which is the idea that collective ownership may not provide the proper private incentives for efficiency because individuals do not bear the full costs of their own decisions but do enjoy the full benefits. Suppose an agricultural community has 10,000 acres of grazing land. If the land was held in common so that all farmers had unlimited rights to graze their animals, each farmer would have an incentive to overgraze. He or she would reap the full benefits from grazing additional calves while the costs of grazing the calves would be borne collectively. The system provides no incentive to manage the land efficiently. Similarly, if the efficiency and benefits of your hard work and managerial skills accrue to others or to the state, what incentive do you have to work hard or to be efficient?

One solution to the tragedy of commons attempted in eighteenth-century Britain was to divide up the land into private holdings. Today, many economists argue, the solution to the incentive problem encountered in state-owned enterprises is to privatize them and let the owners compete.

In addition to increasing accountability, privatization means creating a climate in which new enterprises can flourish. If there is market demand for a product not currently being produced, individual entrepreneurs should be free to set up a business and make a profit. During the last months of the Soviet Union's existence, private enterprises such as taxi services, car repair services, restaurants, and even hotels began to spring up all over the country.

Like deregulation of prices, privatization is difficult politically. Privatization means that many protected enterprises will go out of business because they cannot compete at world prices, resulting in a loss of jobs, at least temporarily.

Market-Supporting Institutions Between 1991 and 1997, U.S. firms raced to Eastern Europe in search of markets and investment opportunities and immediately became aware of a major obstacle. The institutions that make the market function relatively smoothly in the United States did not exist in Eastern Europe. For example, the capital market, which channels private saving into productive capital investment in developed capitalist economies, is made up of hundreds of different institutions. The banking system, venture capital funds, the stock market, the bond market, commodity exchanges, brokerage houses, investment banks, and so on, have developed in the United States over hundreds of years, and they could not be replicated overnight in the formerly Communist world.

Similar problems exist in the Chinese economy. While the Chinese equity market has grown rapidly in the last decade, that growth has been accompanied by problems with weak governance and lack of transparency. These issues discourage investments by western firms.

Many market-supporting institutions are so basic that Americans take them for granted. The institution of private property, for example, is a set of rights that must be protected by laws that the government must be willing to enforce. Suppose the French hotel chain Novotel decides to build a new hotel in Moscow or Beijing. Novotel must first acquire land. Then it will construct a building based on the expectation of renting rooms to customers. These investments are made with the expectation that the owner has a right to use them and a right to the profits that they produce. For such investments to be undertaken, these rights must be guaranteed by a set of property laws. This is equally true for large business firms and for local entrepreneurs who want to start their own enterprises. China's ambiguous property rights laws may also be problematic. While farmers can own their own homes, for example, all rural land is collectively owned by villages. Farmers have the right to manage farmland, but not own it. As a result, transfer of land is difficult.

Similarly, the law must provide for the enforcement of contracts. In the United States, a huge body of law determines what happens if you break a formal promise made in good faith. Businesses exist on promises to produce and promises to pay. Without recourse to the law when a contract is breached, contracts will not be entered into, goods will not be manufactured, and services will not be provided.

Protection of intellectual property rights is also an important feature of developed market economies. When an artist puts out a record, the artist and his or her studio are entitled to reap revenues from it. When Apple developed the iPod, it too earned the right to collect revenue for its patent ownership. Many less developed countries lack laws and enforcement mechanisms to protect intellectual property of foreign investments and their own current and future investors. The lack of protection discourages trade and home-grown invention. For example, in late 2007, China, in recognition of some of these issues, began drafting a new set of laws for intellectual property protection.

Another seemingly simple matter that turns out to be quite complex is the establishment of a set of accounting principles. In the United States, the rules of the accounting game are embodied in a set of generally accepted accounting principles (GAAP) that carry the force of law. Companies are required to keep track of their receipts, expenditures, and liabilities so that their performance can be observed and evaluated by shareholders, taxing authorities, and others who have an interest in the company. If you have taken a course in accounting, you know how detailed these rules have become. Imagine trying to do business in a country operating under hundreds of different sets of rules. That is what happened in Russia during its transition.

Another institution is insurance. Whenever a venture undertakes a high-risk activity, it buys insurance to protect itself. Several years ago Amnesty International (a nonprofit organization that works to protect civil liberties around the world) sponsored a worldwide concert tour with a number of well-known rock bands and performers. The most difficult part of organizing the tour was obtaining insurance for the artists and their equipment when they played in the then-Communist countries of Eastern Europe.

Social Safety Net   In a centrally planned socialist economy, the labor market does not function freely. Everyone who wants a job is guaranteed one somewhere. The number of jobs is determined by a central plan to match the number of workers. There is essentially no unemployment. This, it has been argued, is one of the great advantages of a planned system. In addition, a central planning system provides basic housing, food, and clothing at very affordable levels for all. With no unemployment and necessities available at very low prices, there is no need for unemployment insurance, welfare, or other social programs.

Transition to a free labor market and liberalization of prices means that some workers will end up unemployed and that everyone will pay higher prices for necessities. Indeed, during the early phases of the transition process, unemployment will be high. Inefficient state-owned enterprises will go out of business; some sectors will contract while others expand. As more and more people experience unemployment, popular support for reform is likely to drop unless some sort of social safety net is erected to ease the transition. This social safety net might include unemployment insurance, aid for the poor, and food and housing assistance. The experiences of the developed world have shown that such programs are expensive.

External Assistance   Very few believe that the transition to a market system can be achieved without outside support and some outside financing. Knowledge of and experience with capitalist institutions that exist in the United States, Western Europe, and Japan are of vital interest to the Eastern European nations. The basic skills of accounting, management, and enterprise development can be taught to developing nations; many say it is in everyone's best interest to do so.

There is little agreement about the extent of *financial* support that should be given, however. In the case of Russia, the United States pushed for a worldwide effort to provide billions of dollars in aid, to stabilize its macroeconomy, and to buy desperately needed goods from abroad. For China, no such aid was thought to be necessary.

Shock Therapy or Gradualism?   Although economists generally agreed on what the former socialist economies needed to do, they debated the sequence and timing of specific reforms.

The popular press described the debate as one between those who believe in "shock therapy" (sometimes called the Big Bang approach) and those who prefer a more gradual approach. Advocates of **shock therapy** believe that the economies in transition should proceed immediately on all fronts. They should stop printing money, deregulate prices and liberalize trade, privatize, develop market institutions, build a social safety net, and acquire external aid—all as quickly as possible. The pain will be severe, the argument goes, but in the end, it will be forgotten as the transition raises living standards. Advocates of a *gradualist* approach believe the best course is to build up market institutions first, gradually decontrol prices, and privatize only the most efficient government enterprises first.

Those who favor moving quickly point to the apparent success of Poland, which moved rapidly through the first phases of reform. Russia's experience during the first years of its transition demonstrated that, at least in that country, change must, to some extent, be gradual. In theory, stabilization and price liberalization can be achieved instantaneously. To enjoy the benefits of liberalization, a good deal of privatization must have taken place—and that takes time. One analyst has said that privatization means "selling assets with no value to people with no money." Some estimates suggest that half of Russian state-owned enterprises were incapable of making a profit at world prices. Simply cutting them loose would create chaos. In a sense, Russia had no choice but to move slowly.

shock therapy The approach to transition from socialism to market capitalism that advocates rapid deregulation of prices, liberalization of trade, and privatization.

S U M M A R Y

1. The economic problems facing the developing countries are often quite different from those confronting industrialized nations. The policy options available to governments may also differ. Nonetheless, the tools of economic analysis are as useful in understanding the economies of less developed countries as in understanding the U.S. economy.

LIFE IN THE DEVELOPING NATIONS: POPULATION AND POVERTY *p. 402*

2. The central reality of life in the developing countries is poverty. Although there is considerable diversity across the developing nations, most of the people in most developing countries are extremely poor by U.S. standards.

ECONOMIC DEVELOPMENT: SOURCES AND STRATEGIES *p. 403*

3. Almost all developing nations have a scarcity of physical capital relative to other resources, especially labor. The *vicious-circle-of-poverty hypothesis* says that poor countries cannot escape from poverty because they cannot afford to postpone consumption—that is, to save—to make investments. In its crude form, the hypothesis is wrong inasmuch as some prosperous countries were at one time poorer than many developing countries are today. However, it is often difficult to mobilize saving efficiently in many developing nations.

4. Human capital—the stock of education and skills embodied in the workforce—plays a vital role in economic development.

5. Developing countries are often burdened by inadequate *social overhead capital*, ranging from poor public health and sanitation facilities to inadequate roads, telephones, and court systems. Such social overhead capital is often expensive to provide, and many governments are not in a position to undertake many useful projects because they are too costly.

6. Inefficient and corrupt bureaucracies also play a role in retarding economic development in places.

Because developed economies are characterized by a large share of output and employment in the industrial sector, many developing countries seem to believe that development and industrialization are synonymous. In many cases, developing countries have pursued industry at the expense of agriculture, with mixed results. Recent evidence suggests that some balance between industry and agriculture leads to the best outcome.

8. *Import-substitution* policies, a trade strategy that favors developing local industries that can manufacture goods to replace imports, were once very common in developing nations. In general, such policies have not succeeded as well as those promoting open, export-oriented economies.

9. The failure of many central planning efforts has brought increasing calls for less government intervention and more market orientation in developing economies.

10. Microfinance—lending small amounts to poor borrowers using peer lending groups—has become an important new tool in encouraging entrepreneurship in developing countries.

11. China and India have followed quite different paths in recent development.

ISSUES IN ECONOMIC DEVELOPMENT *p. 412*

12. Rapid population growth is characteristic of many developing countries. Large families can be economically rational because parents need support in their old age or because children offer an important source of labor. However, having many children does not mean a net benefit to society as a whole. Rapid population growth can put a strain on already overburdened public services such as education and health.

THE TRANSITION TO A MARKET ECONOMY *p. 414*

13. Economists generally agree on six requirements for a successful transition from socialism to a market-based system: (1) macroeconomic stabilization, (2) deregulation of prices and liberalization of trade, (3) privatization, (4) establishment of market-supporting institutions, (5) a social safety net, and (6) external assistance.

14. Much debate exists about the sequence and timing of specific reforms. The idea of *shock therapy* is to proceed immediately on all six fronts, including rapid deregulation of prices and privatization. The *gradualist* approach is to build up market institutions first, gradually decontrol prices, and privatize only the most efficient government enterprises first.

REVIEW TERMS AND CONCEPTS

brain drain, *p. 405*
capital flight, *p. 404*
export promotion, *p. 408*
fertility rate, *p. 413*
import substitution, *p. 408*

International Monetary Fund (IMF), *p. 409*
mortality rate, *p. 413*
natural rate of population increase, *p. 413*
shock therapy, *p. 418*
social overhead capital, *p. 405*

structural adjustment, *p. 410*
tragedy of commons, *p. 416*
vicious-circle-of-poverty hypothesis, *p. 404*
World Bank, *p. 409*

PROBLEMS

Visit **www.myeconlab.com** to complete the problems marked in orange online. You will receive instant feedback on your answers, tutorial help, and access to additional practice problems.

1. The biggest problem facing developing countries across the globe in 2006 was disease. The HIV/AIDS pandemic had infected more than 40 million worldwide and up to 40 percent of the adult populations of some African countries, such as Botswana. Describe the effects of HIV/AIDS on the economies of these countries. Make sure you discuss the sources of economic growth and the use of scarce resources.

2. For a developing country to grow, it needs capital. The major source of capital in most countries is domestic saving, but the goal of stimulating domestic saving usually is in conflict with government policies aimed at reducing inequality in the distribution of income. Comment on this trade-off between equity and growth. How would you go about resolving the issue if you were the president of a small, poor country?

3. The GDP of any country can be divided into two kinds of goods: capital goods and consumption goods. The proportion of national output devoted to capital goods determines, to some extent, the nation's growth rate.
   a. Explain how capital accumulation leads to economic growth.
   b. Briefly describe how a market economy determines how much investment will be undertaken each period.
   c. Consumption versus investment is a more painful conflict to resolve for developing countries. Comment on that statement.
   d. If you were the benevolent dictator of a developing country, what plans would you implement to increase per capita GDP?

4. The World Bank and the International Monetary Fund were scheduled to formally cancel the debts of 18 very poor countries in 2006, and the African Development Bank was committed to taking the same action during its 2006 annual meeting. Go online and find out whether these debts were indeed canceled. How much debt was forgiven during that year in each of the countries involved? What are the expected benefits to those countries?

5. Poor countries are trapped in a vicious circle of poverty. For output to grow, they must accumulate capital. To accumulate capital, they must save (consume less than they produce). Because they are poor, they have little or no extra output available for savings—it must all go to feed and clothe the present generation. Thus they are doomed to stay poor forever. Comment on each step in that argument.

6. Famines are acts of God resulting from bad weather or other natural disasters. There is nothing we can do about them except to send food relief after they occur. Explain why that position is inaccurate. Concentrate on agricultural pricing policies and distributional issues.

7. In China, rural property is owned collectively by the village while being managed under long-term contracts by individual farmers. Why might this be a problem in terms of optimal land managment, use, and allocation?

8. How does peer lending used in microfinance help to solve the problem of adverse selection?

9. [Related to the *Economics in Practice* on *p. 411*] Find another example of the use of cell phones as a way to improve market functioning in a developing economy.

10. [Related to the *Economics in Practice* on *p. 406*] Corruption in a government is often accompanied by inefficiency in the economy. Why should this be true?

11. The distribution of income in a capitalist economy is likely to be more unequal than it is in a socialist economy. Why is this so? Is there a tension between the goal of limiting inequality and the goal of motivating risk taking and hard work? Explain your answer in detail.

Glossary

absolute advantage A producer has an absolute advantage over another in the production of a good or service if he or she can produce that product using fewer resources. *p. 29 p. 355*

accelerator effect The tendency for investment to increase when aggregate output increases and to decrease when aggregate output decreases, accelerating the growth or decline of output. *p. 307*

actual investment The actual amount of investment that takes place; it includes items such as unplanned changes in inventories. *p. 146*

adjustment costs The costs that a firm incurs when it changes its production level—for example, the administration costs of laying off employees or the training costs of hiring new workers. *p. 308*

aggregate behavior The behavior of all households and firms together. *p. 89*

aggregate demand The total demand for goods and services in the economy. *p. 227*

aggregate demand (*AD*) curve A curve that shows the negative relationship between aggregate output (income) and the price level. Each point on the AD curve is a point at which both the goods market and the money market are in equilibrium. *p. 227*

aggregate income The total income received by all factors of production in a given period. *p. 141*

aggregate output The total quantity of goods and services produced in an economy in a given period. *p. 90 p. 141*

aggregate output (income) (*Y*) A combined term used to remind you of the exact equality between aggregate output and aggregate income. *p. 141*

aggregate production function The mathematical representation of the relationship between inputs and national output, or gross domestic product. *p. 322*

aggregate saving (*S*) The part of aggregate income that is not consumed. *p. 143*

aggregate supply The total supply of all goods and services in an economy. *p. 238*

aggregate supply (*AS*) curve A graph that shows the relationship between the aggregate quantity of output supplied by all firms in an economy and the overall price level. *p. 238*

animal spirits of entrepreneurs A term coined by Keynes to describe investors' feelings. *p. 307*

appreciation of a currency The rise in value of one currency relative to another. *p. 388*

automatic destabilizers Revenue and expenditure items in the federal budget that automatically change with the economy in such a way as to destabilize GDP. *p. 284*

automatic stabilizers Revenue and expenditure items in the federal budget that automatically change with the state of the economy in such a way as to stabilize GDP. *p. 175 p. 284*

balance of payments The record of a country's transactions in goods, services, and assets with the rest of the world; also the record of a country's sources (supply) and uses (demand) of foreign exchange. *p. 378*

balance of trade A country's exports of goods and services minus its imports of goods and services. *p. 379*

balance on capital account In the United States, the sum of the following (measured in a given period): the change in private U.S. assets

abroad, the change in foreign private assets in the United States, the change in U.S. government assets abroad, and the change in foreign government assets in the United States. *p. 380*

balance on current account Net exports of goods plus net exports of services plus net investment income plus net transfer payments. *p. 379*

balanced-budget multiplier The ratio of change in the equilibrium level of output to a change in government spending where the change in government spending is balanced by a change in taxes so as not to create any deficit. The balanced-budget multiplier is equal to 1: The change in *Y* resulting from the change in *G* and the equal change in *T* are exactly the same size as the initial change in *G* or *T*. *p. 168*

barter The direct exchange of goods and services for other goods and services. *p. 182*

base year The year chosen for the weights in a fixed-weight procedure. *p. 115*

black market A market in which illegal trading takes place at market-determined prices. *p. 77*

brain drain The tendency for talented people from developing countries to become educated in a developed country and remain there after graduation. *p. 405*

budget deficit The difference between what a government spends and what it collects in taxes in a given period: *G–T*. *p. 161*

business cycle The cycle of short-term ups and downs in the economy. *p. 90*

capital Things that are produced and then used in the production of other goods and services. *p. 25*

capital flight The tendency for both human capital and financial capital to leave developing countries in search of higher expected rates of return elsewhere with less risk. *p. 404*

capital gain An increase in the value of an asset. *p. 285*

capital market The input/factor market in which households supply their savings, for interest or for claims to future profits, to firms that demand funds to buy capital goods. *p. 47*

capital-intensive technology A production technique that uses a large amount of capital relative to labor. *p. 308*

Cartesian coordinate system A common method of graphing two variables that makes use of two perpendicular lines against which the variables are plotted. *p. 19 p. 22*

catch-up The theory stating that the growth rates of less developed countries will exceed the growth rates of developed countries, allowing the less developed countries to catch up. *p. 321*

***ceteris paribus*, *or* all else equal** A device used to analyze the relationship between two variables while the values of other variables are held unchanged. *p. 12*

change in business inventories The amount by which firms' inventories change during a period. Inventories are the goods that firms produce now but intend to sell later. *p. 109*

circular flow A diagram showing the income received and payments made by each sector of the economy. *p. 93*

command economy An economy in which a central government either directly or indirectly sets output targets, incomes, and prices. *p. 39*

commodity monies Items used as money that also have intrinsic value in some other use. *p. 184*

comparative advantage A producer has a comparative advantage over another in the production of a good or service if he or she can produce that product at a lower *opportunity cost*. *p. 29 p. 355*

compensation of employees Includes wages, salaries, and various supplements—employer contributions to social insurance and pension funds, for example—paid to households by firms and by the government. *p. 111*

complements, complementary goods Goods that "go together"; a decrease in the price of one results in an increase in demand for the other and vice versa. *p. 52*

constrained supply of labor The amount a household actually works in a given period at the current wage rate. *p. 302*

consumer goods Goods produced for present consumption. *p. 32*

consumer price index (CPI) A price index computed each month by the Bureau of Labor Statistics using a bundle that is meant to represent the "market basket" purchased monthly by the typical urban consumer. *p. 130*

consumer sovereignty The idea that consumers ultimately dictate what will be produced (or not produced) by choosing what to purchase (and what not to purchase). *p. 39*

consumer surplus The difference between the maximum amount a person is willing to pay for a good and its current market price. *p. 82*

consumption function The relationship between consumption and income. *p. 142*

contraction, recession, *or* slump The period in the business cycle from a peak down to a trough during which output and employment fall. *p. 90*

contractionary fiscal policy A decrease in government spending or an increase in net taxes aimed at decreasing aggregate output (income) (*Y*). *p. 225*

contractionary monetary policy A decrease in the money supply aimed at decreasing aggregate output (income) (*Y*). *p. 226*

Corn Laws The tariffs, subsidies, and restrictions enacted by the British Parliament in the early nineteenth century to discourage imports and encourage exports of grain. *p. 355*

corporate bonds Promissory notes issued by firms when they borrow money. *p. 95*

corporate profits The income of corporations. *p. 111*

cost shock, *or* supply shock A change in costs that shifts the short-run aggregate supply (*AS*) curve. *p. 240*

cost-of-living adjustments (COLAs) Contract provisions that tie wages to changes in the cost of living. The greater the inflation rate, the more wages are raised. *p. 265*

cost-push, *or* supply-side, inflation Inflation caused by an increase in costs. *p. 247*

crowding-out effect The tendency for increases in government spending to cause reductions in private investment spending. *p. 223*

currency debasement The decrease in the value of money that occurs when its supply is increased rapidly. *p. 184*

current dollars The current prices that we pay for goods and services. *p. 114*

cyclical deficit The deficit that occurs because of a downturn in the business cycle. *p. 175*

cyclical unemployment The increase in unemployment that occurs during recessions and depressions. *p. 129 p. 260*

deadweight loss The total loss of producer and consumer surplus from underproduction or overproduction. *p. 84*

deficit response index (DRI) The amount by which the deficit changes with a $1 change in GDP. *p. 283*

deflation A decrease in the overall price level. *p. 92*

demand curve A graph illustrating how much of a given product a household would be willing to buy at different prices. *p. 49*

demand schedule A table showing how much of a given product a household would be willing to buy at different prices. *p. 49*

demand-pull inflation Inflation that is initiated by an increase in aggregate demand. *p. 246*

depreciation The amount by which an asset's value falls in a given period. *p. 110*

depreciation of a currency The fall in value of one currency relative to another. *p. 388*

depression A prolonged and deep recession. *p. 90*

descriptive economics The compilation of data that describe phenomena and facts. *p. 10*

desired, or optimal, level of inventories The level of inventory at which the extra cost (in lost sales) from lowering inventories by a small amount is just equal to the extra gain (in interest revenue and decreased storage costs). *p. 309*

discount rate The interest rate that banks pay to the Fed to borrow from it. *p. 196*

discouraged-worker effect The decline in the measured unemployment rate that results when people who want to work but cannot find jobs grow discouraged and stop looking, thus dropping out of the ranks of the unemployed and the labor force. *p. 127 p. 314*

discretionary fiscal policy Changes in taxes or spending that are the result of deliberate changes in government policy. *p. 160*

disposable personal income or after-tax income Personal income minus personal income taxes. The amount that households have to spend or save. *p. 114*

disposable, or after-tax, income (Y_d) Total income minus net taxes: $Y - T$. *p. 160*

dividends The portion of a firm's profits that the firm pays out each period to its shareholders. *p. 95*

Doha Development Agenda An initiative of the World Trade Organization focused on issues of trade and development. *p. 364*

Dow Jones Industrial Average An index based on the stock prices of 30 actively traded large companies. The oldest and most widely followed index of stock market performance. *p. 286*

dumping A firm's or an industry's sale of products on the world market at prices below its own cost of production. *p. 364*

durable goods Goods that last a relatively long time, such as cars and household appliances. *p. 108*

easy monetary policy Fed policies that expand the money supply and thus lower interest rates in an effort to stimulate the economy. *p. 213*

economic growth An increase in the total output of an economy. It occurs when a society acquires new resources or when it learns to produce more using existing resources. *p. 15 p. 36 p. 319*

economic integration Occurs when two or more nations join to form a free-trade zone. *p. 365*

economic theory A statement or set of related statements about cause and effect, action and reaction. *p. 10*

economics The study of how individuals and societies choose to use the scarce resources that nature and previous generations have provided. *p. 2*

efficiency In economics, allocative efficiency. An efficient economy is one that produces what people want at the least possible cost. *p. 14*

efficiency wage theory An explanation for unemployment that holds that the productivity of workers increases with the wage rate. If this is so, firms may have an incentive to pay wages above the market-clearing rate. *p. 265*

efficient market A market in which profit opportunities are eliminated almost instantaneously. *p. 3*

empirical economics The collection and use of data to test economic theories. *p. 13*

employed Any person 16 years old or older (1) who works for pay, either for someone else or in his or her own business for 1 or more hours per week, (2) who works without pay for 15 or more hours per week in a family enterprise, or (3) who has a job but has been temporarily absent with or without pay. *p. 124*

entrepreneur A person who organizes, manages, and assumes the risks of a firm, taking a new idea or a new product and turning it into a successful business. *p. 46*

equilibrium The condition that exists when quantity supplied and quantity demanded are equal. At equilibrium, there is no tendency for price to change. In the macroeconomic goods market, equilibrium occurs when planned aggregate expenditure is equal to aggregate output. *p. 62 p. 147*

equilibrium price level The price level at which the aggregate demand and aggregate supply curves intersect. *p. 241*

equity Fairness. *p. 14*

European Union (EU) The European trading bloc composed of 27 countries. *p. 365*

excess demand or shortage The condition that exists when quantity demanded exceeds quantity supplied at the current price. *p. 62*

excess labor, excess capital Labor and capital that are not needed to produce the firm's current level of output. *p. 308*

excess reserves The difference between a bank's actual reserves and its required reserves. *p. 189*

excess supply or surplus The condition that exists when quantity supplied exceeds quantity demanded at the current price. *p. 63*

exchange rate The ratio at which two currencies are traded. The price of one country's currency in terms of another country's currency. *p. 360 p. 377*

exogenous variable A variable that is assumed not to depend on the state of the economy—that is, it does not change when the economy changes. *p. 151*

expansion or boom The period in the business cycle from a trough up to a peak during which output and employment grow. *p. 90*

expansionary fiscal policy An increase in government spending or a reduction in net taxes aimed at increasing aggregate output (income) (Y). *p. 223*

expansionary monetary policy An increase in the money supply aimed at increasing aggregate output (income) (Y). *p. 223*

expenditure approach A method of computing GDP that measures the total amount spent on all final goods and services during a given period. *p. 107*

explicit contracts Employment contracts that stipulate workers' wages, usually for a period of 1 to 3 years. *p. 265*

export promotion A trade policy designed to encourage exports. *p. 408*

export subsidies Government payments made to domestic firms to encourage exports. *p. 363*

factor endowments The quantity and quality of labor, land, and natural resources of a country. *p. 362*

factors of production (or factors) The inputs into the process of production. Another term for resources. *p. 25*

factors of production The inputs into the production process. Land, labor, and capital are the three key factors of production. *p. 47*

fallacy of composition The erroneous belief that what is true for a part is necessarily true for the whole. *p. 13*

favored customers Those who receive special treatment from dealers during situations of excess demand. *p. 76*

federal budget The budget of the federal government. *p. 169*

federal debt The total amount owed by the federal government. *p. 172*

Federal Open Market Committee (FOMC) A group composed of the seven members of the Fed's Board of Governors, the president of the New York Federal Reserve Bank, and four of the other 11 district bank presidents on a rotating basis; it sets goals concerning the money supply and interest rates and directs the operation of the Open Market Desk in New York. *p. 192*

Federal Reserve Bank (the Fed) The central bank of the United States. *p. 188*

federal surplus (+) or deficit (–) Federal government receipts minus expenditures. *p. 170*

fertility rate The birth rate. Equal to (the number of births per year divided by the population) × 100. *p. 413*

fiat, or token, money Items designated as money that are intrinsically worthless. *p. 184*

final goods and services Goods and services produced for final use. *p. 106*

financial intermediaries Banks and other institutions that act as a link between those who have money to lend and those who want to borrow money. *p. 186*

fine-tuning The phrase used by Walter Heller to refer to the government's role in regulating inflation and unemployment. *p. 96*

firm An organization that transforms resources (inputs) into products (outputs). Firms are the primary producing units in a market economy. *p. 46*

fiscal drag The negative effect on the economy that occurs when average tax rates increase because taxpayers have moved into higher income brackets during an expansion. *p. 175*

fiscal policy Government policies concerning taxes and spending. *p. 95 p. 160*

fixed-weight procedure A procedure that uses weights from a given base year. *p. 115*

floating, or market-determined, exchange rates Exchange rates that are determined by the unregulated forces of supply and demand. *p. 385*

foreign direct investment (FDI) Investment in enterprises made in a country by residents outside that country. *p. 324*

foreign exchange All currencies other than the domestic currency of a given country. *p. 378*

free enterprise The freedom of individuals to start and operate private businesses in search of profits. *p. 40*

frictional unemployment The portion of unemployment that is due to the normal working of the labor market; used to denote short-run job/skill matching problems. *p. 129 p. 260*

full-employment budget What the federal budget would be if the economy were producing at the full-employment level of output. *p. 175*

General Agreement on Tariffs and Trade (GATT) An international agreement signed by the United States and 22 other countries in 1947 to promote the liberalization of foreign trade. *p. 364*

goods market The market in which goods and services are exchanged and in which the equilibrium level of aggregate output is determined. *p. 219*

government consumption and gross investment (G) Expenditures by federal, state, and local governments for final goods and services. *p. 110*

government spending multiplier The ratio of the change in the equilibrium level of output to a change in government spending. *p. 165*

Gramm-Rudman-Hollings Act Passed by the U.S. Congress and signed by President Reagan in 1986, this law set out to reduce the federal deficit by $36 billion per year, with a deficit of zero slated for 1991. *p. 281*

graph A two-dimensional representation of a set of numbers, or data. *p. 18 p. 22*

Great Depression The period of severe economic contraction and high unemployment that began in 1929 and continued throughout the 1930s. *p. 95*

gross domestic product (GDP) The total market value of all final goods and services produced within a given period by factors of production located within a country. *p. 105*

gross investment The total value of all newly produced capital goods (plant, equipment, housing, and inventory) produced in a given period. *p. 110*

gross national income (GNI) GNP converted into dollars using an average of currency exchange rates over several years adjusted for rates of inflation. *p. 118*

gross national product (GNP) The total market value of all final goods and services produced within a given period by factors of production owned by a country's citizens, regardless of where the output is produced. *p. 107*

gross private domestic investment (I) Total investment in capital—that is, the purchase of new housing, plants, equipment, and inventory by the private (or nongovernment) sector. *p. 109*

Heckscher-Ohlin theorem A theory that explains the existence of a country's comparative advantage by its factor endowments: A country has a comparative advantage in the production of a product if that country is relatively well endowed with inputs used intensively in the production of that product. *p. 362*

households The consuming units in an economy. *p. 46*

hyperinflation A period of very rapid increases in the overall price level. *p. 92*

identity Something that is always true. *p. 143*

implementation lag The time it takes to put the desired policy into effect once economists and policy makers recognize that the economy is in a boom or a slump. *p. 279*

import substitution An industrial trade strategy that favors developing local industries that can manufacture goods to replace imports. *p. 408*

income The sum of all a household's wages, salaries, profits, interest payments, rents, and other forms of earnings in a given period of time. It is a flow measure. *p. 51*

income approach A method of computing GDP that measures the income—wages, rents, interest, and profits—received by all factors of production in producing final goods and services. *p. 107*

indirect taxes minus subsidies Taxes such as sales taxes, customs duties, and license fees less subsidies that the government pays for which it receives no goods or services in return. *p. 111*

Industrial Revolution The period in England during the late eighteenth and early nineteenth centuries in which new manufacturing technologies and improved transportation gave rise to the modern factory system and a massive movement of the population from the countryside to the cities. *p. 4*

infant industry A young industry that may need temporary protection from competition from the established industries of other countries to develop an acquired comparative advantage. *p. 371*

inferior goods Goods for which demand tends to fall when income rises. *p. 52*

inflation An increase in the overall price level. *p. 92*

inflation rate The percentage change in the price level. *p. 268*

inflation targeting When a monetary authority chooses its interest rate values with the aim of keeping the inflation rate within some specified band over some specified horizon. *p. 254*

innovation The use of new knowledge to produce a new product or to produce an existing product more efficiently. *p. 326*

input *or* factor markets The markets in which the resources used to produce goods and services are exchanged. *p. 46*

inputs The goods and services that firms purchase and turn into output. *p. 307*

inputs *or* resources Anything provided by nature or previous generations that can be used directly or indirectly to satisfy human wants. *p. 26*

interest sensitivity *or* insensitivity of planned investment The responsiveness of planned investment spending to changes in the interest rate. *Interest sensitivity* means that planned investment spending changes a great deal in response to changes in the interest rate; *interest insensitivity* means little or no change in planned investment as a result of changes in the interest rate. *p. 224*

intermediate goods Goods that are produced by one firm for use in further processing by another firm. *p. 106*

International Monetary Fund (IMF) An international agency whose primary goals are to stabilize international exchange rates and to lend money to countries that have problems financing their international transactions. *p. 409*

invention An advance in knowledge. *p. 326*

inventory investment The change in the stock of inventories. *p. 309*

investment The process of using resources to produce new capital. *p. 32*

IS curve A curve illustrating the negative relationship between the equilibrium value of aggregate output (income) (*Y*) and the interest rate in the goods market. *p. 234 p. 235*

interest The fee that borrowers pay to lenders for the use of their funds. *p. 203*

J-curve effect Following a currency depreciation, a country's balance of trade may get worse before it gets better. The graph showing this effect is shaped like the letter *J*, hence the name J-curve effect. *p. 391*

labor demand curve A graph that illustrates the amount of labor that firms want to employ at each given wage rate. *p. 260*

labor force The number of people employed plus the number of unemployed. *p. 124*

labor force participation rate The ratio of the labor force to the total population 16 years old or older. *p. 124*

labor market The input/factor market in which households supply work for wages to firms that demand labor. *p. 47*

labor productivity Output per worker hour; the amount of output produced by an average worker in 1 hour. *p. 322*

labor supply curve A graph that illustrates the amount of labor that households want to supply at each given wage rate. *p. 260*

labor-intensive technology A production technique that uses a large amount of labor relative to capital. *p. 308*

Laffer curve With the tax rate measured on the vertical axis and tax revenue measured on the horizontal axis, the Laffer curve shows that there is some tax rate beyond which the supply response is large enough to lead to a decrease in tax revenue for further increases in the tax rate. *p. 349*

laissez-faire economy Literally from the French: "allow [them] to do." An economy in which individual people and firms pursue their own self-interest without any central direction or regulation. *p. 39*

land market The input/factor market in which households supply land or other real property in exchange for rent. *p. 47*

law of demand The negative relationship between price and quantity demanded: As price rises, quantity demanded decreases; as price falls, quantity demanded increases. *p. 49*

law of one price If the costs of transportation are small, the price of the same good in different countries should be roughly the same. *p. 388*

law of supply The positive relationship between price and quantity of a good supplied: An increase in market price will lead to an increase in quantity supplied, and a decrease in market price will lead to a decrease in quantity supplied. *p. 57*

legal tender Money that a government has required to be accepted in settlement of debts. *p. 184*

lender of last resort One of the functions of the Fed: It provides funds to troubled banks that cannot find any other sources of funds. *p. 193*

life-cycle theory of consumption A theory of household consumption: Households make lifetime consumption decisions based on their expectations of lifetime income. *p. 298*

liquidity property of money The property of money that makes it a good medium of exchange as well as a store of value: It is portable and readily accepted and thus easily exchanged for goods. *p. 182*

LM curve A curve illustrating the positive relationship between the equilibrium value of the interest rate and aggregate output (income) (*Y*) in the money market. *p. 234 p. 235*

Lucas supply function The supply function embodies the idea that output (*Y*) depends on the difference between the actual price level and the expected price level. *p. 345*

M1, *or* transactions money Money that can be directly used for transactions. *p. 185*

M2, *or* broad money M1 plus savings accounts, money market accounts, and other near monies. *p. 185*

macroeconomics The branch of economics that examines the economic behavior of aggregates—income, employment, output, and so on—on a national scale. *p. 8 p. 89*

marginal propensity to consume (*MPC*) That fraction of a change in income that is consumed, or spent. *p. 143*

marginal propensity to import (*MPM*) The change in imports caused by a $1 change in income. *p. 382*

marginal propensity to save (*MPS*) That fraction of a change in income that is saved. *p. 143*

marginal rate of transformation (*MRT*) The slope of the production possibility frontier (ppf). *p. 35*

marginalism The process of analyzing the additional or incremental costs or benefits arising from a choice or decision. *p. 2*

market The institution through which buyers and sellers interact and engage in exchange. *p. 39*

market demand The sum of all the quantities of a good or service demanded per period by all the households buying in the market for that good or service. *p. 55*

market supply The sum of all that is supplied each period by all producers of a single product. *p. 61*

medium of exchange, *or* means of payment What sellers generally accept and buyers generally use to pay for goods and services. *p. 182*

microeconomics The branch of economics that examines the functioning of individual industries and the behavior of individual decision-making units—that is, firms and households. *p. 8 p. 89*

minimum wage A price floor set for the price of labor. *p. 79*

minimum wage laws Laws that set a floor for wage rates—that is, a minimum hourly rate for any kind of labor. *p. 266*

model A formal statement of a theory, usually a mathematical statement of a presumed relationship between two or more variables. *p. 11*

modern economic growth The period of rapid and sustained increase in real output per capita that began in the Western World with the Industrial Revolution. *p. 319*

monetary policy The behavior of the Federal Reserve concerning the nation's money supply. *p. 160*

monetary policy The tools used by the Federal Reserve to control the quantity of money, which in turn affects interest rates. *p. 95*

money market The market in which financial instruments are exchanged and in which the equilibrium level of the interest rate is determined. *p. 220*

money multiplier The multiple by which deposits can increase for every dollar increase in reserves; equal to 1 divided by the required reserve ratio. *p. 191*

moral suasion The pressure that in the past the Fed exerted on member banks to discourage them from borrowing heavily from the Fed. *p. 197*

mortality rate The death rate. Equal to (the number of deaths per year divided by the population) × 100. *p. 413*

movement along a demand curve The change in quantity demanded brought about by a change in price. *p. 54*

movement along a supply curve The change in quantity supplied brought about by a change in price. *p. 59*

multiplier The ratio of the change in the equilibrium level of output to a change in some exogenous variable. *p. 151*

NAIRU The nonaccelerating inflation rate of unemployment. *p. 273*

NASDAQ Composite An index based on the stock prices of over 5,000 companies traded on the NASDAQ Stock Market. The NASDAQ market takes its name from the National Association of Securities Dealers Automated Quotation System. *p. 286*

national income The total income earned by the factors of production owned by a country's citizens. *p. 111*

national income and product accounts Data collected and published by the government describing the various components of national income and output in the economy. *p. 105*

natural rate of population increase The difference between the birth rate and the death rate. *p. 413*

natural rate of unemployment The unemployment that occurs as a normal part of the functioning of the economy. Sometimes taken as the sum of frictional unemployment and structural unemployment. *p. 129 p. 272*

near monies Close substitutes for transactions money, such as savings accounts and money market accounts. *p. 185*

negative demand shock Something that causes a negative shift in consumption or investment schedules or that leads to a decrease in U.S. exports. *p. 284*

negative relationship A relationship between two variables, *X* and *Y*, in which a decrease in *X* is associated with an increase in *Y* and an increase in *X* is associated with a decrease in *Y*. *p. 19 p. 22*

net business transfer payments Net transfer payments by businesses to others. *p. 111*

net exports (*EX − IM*) The difference between exports (sales to foreigners of U.S.-produced goods and services) and imports (U.S. purchases of goods and services from abroad). The figure can be positive or negative. *p. 111*

net exports of goods and services (*EX − IM*) The difference between a country's total exports and total imports. *p. 382*

net interest The interest paid by business. *p. 111*

net investment Gross investment minus depreciation. *p. 110*

net national product (NNP) Gross national product minus depreciation; a nation's total product minus what is required to maintain the value of its capital stock. *p. 112*

net taxes (*T*) Taxes paid by firms and households to the government minus transfer payments made to households by the government. *p. 160*

nominal GDP Gross domestic product measured in current dollars. *p. 114*

nominal wage rate The wage rate in current dollars. *p. 300*

nondurable goods Goods that are used up fairly quickly, such as food and clothing. *p. 108*

nonlabor, *or* nonwage, income Any income received from sources other than working—inheritances, interest, dividends, transfer payments, and so on. *p. 300*

nonresidential investment Expenditures by firms for machines, tools, plants, and so on. *p. 109*

nonsynchronization of income and spending The mismatch between the timing of money inflow to the household and the timing of money outflow for household expenses. *p. 205*

normal goods Goods for which demand goes up when income is higher and for which demand goes down when income is lower. *p. 51*

normative economics An approach to economics that analyzes outcomes of economic behavior, evaluates them as good or bad, and may prescribe courses of action. Also called *policy economics*. *p. 10*

North American Free Trade Agreement (NAFTA) An agreement signed by the United States, Mexico, and Canada in which the three countries agreed to establish all North America as a free-trade zone. *p. 365*

not in the labor force A person who is not looking for work because he or she does not want a job or has given up looking. *p. 124*

Ockham's razor The principle that irrelevant detail should be cut away. *p. 11*

Okun's Law The theory, put forth by Arthur Okun, that in the short run the unemployment rate decreases about 1 percentage point for every 3 percent increase in real GDP. Later research and data have shown that the relationship between output and unemployment is not as stable as Okun's "Law" predicts. *p. 313*

Open Market Desk The office in the New York Federal Reserve Bank from which government securities are bought and sold by the Fed. *p. 192*

open market operations The purchase and sale by the Fed of government securities in the open market; a tool used to expand or contract the amount of reserves in the system and thus the money supply. *p. 197*

opportunity cost The best alternative that we forgo, or give up, when we make a choice or a decision. *p. 2 p. 27*

origin On a Cartesian coordinate system, the point at which the horizontal and vertical axes intersect. *p. 19 p. 22*

output growth The growth rate of the output of the entire economy. *p. 134*

outputs Goods and services of value to households. *p. 26*

per-capita output growth The growth rate of output per person in the economy. *p. 134*

perfect substitutes Identical products. *p. 52*

permanent income The average level of a person's expected future income stream. *p. 298*

personal consumption expenditures (*C*) Expenditures by consumers on goods and services. *p. 108*

personal income The total income of households. *p. 112*

personal saving The amount of disposable income that is left after total personal spending in a given period. *p. 114*

personal saving rate The percentage of disposable personal income that is saved. If the personal saving rate is low, households are spending a large amount relative to their incomes; if it is high, households are spending cautiously. *p. 114*

Phillips Curve A curve showing the relationship between the inflation rate and the unemployment rate. *p. 268*

planned aggregate expenditure (*AE*) The total amount the economy plans to spend in a given period. Equal to consumption plus planned investment: $AE \equiv C + I$. *p. 148*

planned investment (*I*) Those additions to capital stock and inventory that are planned by firms. *p. 146*

plant-and-equipment investment Purchases by firms of additional machines, factories, or buildings within a given period. *p. 307*

policy mix The combination of monetary and fiscal policies in use at a given time. *p. 226*

positive economics An approach to economics that seeks to understand behavior and the operation of systems without making judgments. It describes what exists and how it works. *p. 10*

positive relationship A relationship between two variables, *X* and *Y*, in which a decrease in *X* is associated with a decrease in *Y*, and an increase in *X* is associated with an increase in *Y*. *p. 19 p. 22*

post hoc, ergo propter hoc Literally, "after this (in time), therefore because of this." A common error made in thinking about causation: If Event A happens before Event B, it is not necessarily true that A caused B. *p. 12*

potential output, *or* potential GDP The level of aggregate output that can be sustained in the long run without inflation. *p. 244*

price ceiling A maximum price that sellers may charge for a good, usually set by government. *p. 75*

price feedback effect The process by which a domestic price increase in one country can "feed back" on itself through export and import prices. An increase in the price level in one country can drive up prices in other countries. This in turn further increases the price level in the first country. *p. 385*

price floor A minimum price below which exchange is not permitted. *p. 79*

price rationing The process by which the market system allocates goods and services to consumers when quantity demanded exceeds quantity supplied. *p. 73*

price surprise Actual price level minus expected price level. *p. 345*

privately held federal debt The privately held (non-government-owned) debt of the U.S. government. *p. 173*

producer price indexes (PPIs) Measures of prices that producers receive for products at all stages in the production process. *p. 131*

producer surplus The difference between the current market price and the full cost of production for the firm. *p. 83*

product *or* output markets The markets in which goods and services are exchanged. *p. 46*

production The process that transforms scarce resources into useful goods and services. *p. 25*

production possibility frontier (ppf) A graph that shows all the combinations of goods and services that can be produced if all of society's resources are used efficiently. *p. 32*

productivity growth The growth rate of output per worker. *p. 134*

productivity of an input The amount of output produced per unit of an input. *p. 326*

productivity, *or* labor productivity Output per worker hour; the amount of output produced by an average worker in 1 hour. *p. 312*

profit The difference between revenues and costs. *p. 57*

proprietors' income The income of unincorporated businesses. *p. 111*

protection The practice of shielding a sector of the economy from foreign competition. *p. 363*

purchasing-power-parity theory A theory of international exchange holding that exchange rates are set so that the price of similar goods in different countries is the same. *p. 389*

quantity demanded The amount (number of units) of a product that a household would buy in a given period if it could buy all it wanted at the current market price. *p. 48*

quantity supplied The amount of a particular product that a firm would be willing and able to offer for sale at a particular price during a given time period. *p. 57*

quantity theory of money The theory based on the identity $M \times V \equiv P \times Y$ and the assumption that the velocity of money (V) is constant (or virtually constant). *p. 341*

queuing Waiting in line as a means of distributing goods and services: a nonprice rationing mechanism. *p. 76*

quota A limit on the quantity of imports. *p. 364*

ration coupons Tickets or coupons that entitle individuals to purchase a certain amount of a given product per month. *p. 76*

rational-expectations hypothesis The hypothesis that people know the "true model" of the economy and that they use this model to form their expectations of the future. *p. 344*

real business cycle theory An attempt to explain business cycle fluctuations under the assumptions of complete price and wage flexibility and rational expectations. It emphasizes shocks to technology and other shocks. *p. 347*

real interest rate The difference between the interest rate on a loan and the inflation rate. *p. 133*

real wage rate The amount the nominal wage rate can buy in terms of goods and services. *p. 300*

real wealth, *or* real balance, effect The change in consumption brought about by a change in real wealth that results from a change in the price level. *p. 229*

realized capital gain The gain that occurs when the owner of an asset actually sells it for more than he or she paid for it. *p. 285*

recession A period during which aggregate output declines. Conventionally, a period in which aggregate output declines for two consecutive quarters. *p. 90*

recognition lag The time it takes for policy makers to recognize the existence of a boom or a slump. *p. 279*

relative-wage explanation of unemployment An explanation for sticky wages (and therefore unemployment): If workers are concerned about their wages relative to other workers in other firms and industries, they may be unwilling to accept a wage cut unless they know that all other workers are receiving similar cuts. *p. 263*

rental income The income received by property owners in the form of rent. *p. 111*

required reserve ratio The percentage of its total deposits that a bank must keep as reserves at the Federal Reserve. *p. 188*

reserves The deposits that a bank has at the Federal Reserve bank plus its cash on hand. *p. 188*

residential investment Expenditures by households and firms on new houses and apartment buildings. *p. 109*

response lag The time that it takes for the economy to adjust to the new conditions after a new policy is implemented; the lag that occurs because of the operation of the economy itself. *p. 279*

run on a bank Occurs when many of those who have claims on a bank (deposits) present them at the same time. *p. 187*

scarce Limited. *p. 2*

services The things we buy that do not involve the production of physical things, such as legal and medical services and education. *p. 108*

shares of stock Financial instruments that give to the holder a share in the firm's ownership and therefore the right to share in the firm's profits. *p. 95*

shift of a demand curve The change that takes place in a demand curve corresponding to a new relationship between quantity demanded of a good and price of that good. The shift is brought about by a change in the original conditions. *p. 53*

shift of a supply curve The change that takes place in a supply curve corresponding to a new relationship between quantity supplied of a good and the price of that good. The shift is brought about by a change in the original conditions. *p. 59*

shock therapy The approach to transition from socialism to market capitalism that advocates rapid deregulation of prices, liberalization of trade, and privatization. *p. 418*

slope A measurement that indicates whether the relationship between variables is positive or negative and how much of a response there is in *Y* (the variable on the vertical axis) when *X* (the variable on the horizontal axis) changes. *p. 20 p. 22*

Smoot-Hawley tariff The U.S. tariff law of the 1930s, which set the highest tariffs in U.S. history (60 percent). It set off an international trade war and caused the decline in trade that is often considered one of the causes of the worldwide depression of the 1930s. *p. 364*

social overhead capital Basic infrastructure projects such as roads, power generation, and irrigation systems. *p. 405*

social, *or* implicit, contracts Unspoken agreements between workers and firms that firms will not cut wages. *p. 263*

speculation motive One reason for holding bonds instead of money: Because the market price of interest-bearing bonds is inversely related to the interest rate, investors may want to hold bonds when interest rates are high with the hope of selling them when interest rates fall. *p. 208*

stability A condition in which national output is growing steadily, with low inflation and full employment of resources. *p. 15*

stabilization policy Describes both monetary and fiscal policy, the goals of which are to smooth out fluctuations in output and employment and to keep prices as stable as possible. *p. 277*

stagflation A situation of both high inflation and high unemployment. Occurs when output is falling at the same time that prices are rising. *p. 96 p. 247*

Standard and Poor's 500 (S&P 500) An index based on the stock prices of 500 of the largest firms by market value. *p. 286*

statistical discrepancy Data measurement error. *p. 112*

sticky prices Prices that do not always adjust rapidly to maintain equality between quantity supplied and quantity demanded. *p. 89*

sticky wages The downward rigidity of wages as an explanation for the existence of unemployment. *p. 262*

stock A certificate that certifies ownership of a certain portion of a firm. *p. 285*

store of value An asset that can be used to transport purchasing power from one time period to another. *p. 182*

structural adjustment A series of programs in developing nations designed to: (1) reduce the size of their public sectors through privatization and/or expenditure reductions, (2) decrease their budget deficits, (3) control inflation, and (4) encourage private saving and investment through tax reform. *p. 410*

structural deficit The deficit that remains at full employment. *p. 175*

structural unemployment The portion of unemployment that is due to changes in the structure of the economy that result in a significant loss of jobs in certain industries. *p. 129 p. 260*

substitutes Goods that can serve as replacements for one another; when the price of one increases, demand for the other increases. *p. 52*

sunk costs Costs that cannot be avoided because they have already been incurred. *p. 3*

supply curve A graph illustrating how much of a product a firm will sell at different prices. *p. 57*

supply schedule A table showing how much of a product firms will sell at alternative prices. *p. 57*

surplus of government enterprises Income of government enterprises. *p. 111*

tariff A tax on imports. *p. 363*

tax multiplier The ratio of change in the equilibrium level of output to a change in taxes. *p. 167*

terms of trade The ratio at which a country can trade domestic products for imported products. *p. 359*

theory of comparative advantage Ricardo's theory that specialization and free trade will benefit all trading parties, even those that may be "absolutely" more efficient producers. *p. 27 p. 355*

tight monetary policy Fed policies that contract the money supply and thus raise interest rates in an effort to restrain the economy. *p. 213*

time lags Delays in the economy's response to stabilization policies. *p. 277*

time series graph A graph illustrating how a variable changes over time. *p. 18 p. 22*

trade deficit Occurs when a country's exports of goods and services are less than its imports of goods and services in a given period. *p. 354 p. 379*

trade feedback effect The tendency for an increase in the economic activity of one country to lead to a worldwide increase in economic activity, which then feeds back to that country. *p. 384*

trade surplus The situation when a country exports more than it imports. *p. 354*

tragedy of commons The idea that collective ownership may not provide the proper private incentives for efficiency because individuals do not bear the full costs of their own decisions but do enjoy the full benefits. *p. 416*

transaction motive The main reason that people hold money—to buy things. *p. 205*

transfer payments Cash payments made by the government to people who do not supply goods, services, or labor in exchange for these payments. They include Social Security benefits, veterans' benefits, and welfare payments. *p. 93*

Treasury bonds, notes, *and* bills Promissory notes issued by the federal government when it borrows money. *p. 95*

U.S.-Canadian Free Trade Agreement An agreement in which the United States and Canada agreed to eliminate all barriers to trade between the two countries by 1998. *p. 365*

unconstrained supply of labor The amount a household would like to work within a given period at the current wage rate if it could find the work. *p. 302*

underground economy The part of the economy in which transactions take place and in which income is generated that is unreported and therefore not counted in GDP. *p. 118*

unemployed A person 16 years old or older who is not working, is available for work, and has made specific efforts to find work during the previous 4 weeks. *p. 124*

unemployment rate The percentage of the labor force that is unemployed. That is, the ratio of the number of people unemployed to the total number of people in the labor force. *p. 91 p. 124 p. 260*

unit of account A standard unit that provides a consistent way of quoting prices. *p. 182*

value added The difference between the value of goods as they leave a stage of production and the cost of the goods as they entered that stage. *p. 106*

variable A measure that can change from time to time or from observation to observation. *p. 11*

velocity of money The number of times a dollar bill changes hands, on average, during a year; the ratio of nominal GDP to the stock of money. *p. 340*

vicious-circle-of-poverty hypothesis Suggests that poverty is self-perpetuating because poor nations are unable to save and invest enough to accumulate the capital stock that would help them grow. *p. 404*

wealth *or* net worth The total value of what a household owns minus what it owes. It is a stock measure. *p. 51*

weight The importance attached to an item within a group of items. *p. 114*

World Bank An international agency that lends money to individual countries for projects that promote economic development. *p. 409*

World Trade Organization (WTO) A negotiating forum dealing with rules of trade across nations. *p. 364*

X-axis On a Cartesian coordinate system, the horizontal line against which a variable is plotted. *p. 19 p. 22*

X-intercept The point at which a graph intersects the X-axis. *p. 19 p. 22*

Y-axis On a Cartesian coordinate system, the vertical line against which a variable is plotted. *p. 19 p. 22*

Y-intercept The point at which a graph intersects the Y-axis. *p. 19 p. 22*

Index

Photo Credits

10855